THE ARCHAEOLOGY OF CYPRUS

Situated amidst the archaeologies of the Near East, Europe and Africa, the archaeology and culture of Cyprus are central to an understanding of the ancient Mediterranean world. This book treats the archaeology of Cyprus from the first-known human presence during the Late Epipalaeolithic (ca. 11,000 BC) through the end of the Bronze Age (ca. 1000 BC). A. Bernard Knapp examines the archaeological and documentary records of prehistoric Cyprus within their regional context, paying special attention to the Levant and the Aegean. The appendix (compiled by Sturt W. Manning) analyses all published radiocarbon dates from the island, providing for the first time a comprehensive chronological framework for all of Cypriot prehistory. Focusing on key themes such as (1) identity, insularity and connectivity, and (2) society, community and polity throughout, this book provides a remarkably up-to-date and integrated synthesis of human activity on the Mediterranean's third-largest island.

A. Bernard Knapp is Emeritus Professor of Mediterranean Archaeology in the Department of Archaeology at the University of Glasgow and Honorary Research Fellow at the Cyprus American Archaeological Research Institute. He co-edits the *Journal of Mediterranean Archaeology* with John F. Cherry and Peter van Dommelen and is the general editor of the series *Monographs in Mediterranean Archaeology*. He is the author and editor of several books including, most recently, *Material Connections in the Ancient Mediterranean: Mobility, Materiality, and Mediterranean Identities* (co-edited with Peter van Dommelen) and *Prehistoric and Protohistoric Cyprus: Identity, Insularity, and Connectivity* (author).

CAMBRIDGE WORLD ARCHAEOLOGY

The *Cambridge World Archaeology* series is addressed to students and professional archaeologists, and to academics in related disciplines. Most volumes present a survey of the archaeology of a region of the world, providing an up-to-date account of research and integrating recent findings with new concerns of interpretation. While the focus is on a specific region, broader cultural trends are discussed and the implications of regional findings for cross-cultural interpretations considered. The authors also bring anthropological and historical expertise to bear on archaeological problems and show how both new data and changing intellectual trends in archaeology shape inferences about the past. More recently, the series has expanded to include thematic volumes.

THE ARCHAEOLOGY OF CYPRUS

From Earliest Prehistory through the Bronze Age

A. BERNARD KNAPP

Emeritus Professor of Mediterranean Archaeology,
University of Glasgow

CAMBRIDGE
UNIVERSITY PRESS

CAMBRIDGE UNIVERSITY PRESS
Cambridge, New York, Melbourne, Madrid, Cape Town,
Singapore, São Paulo, Delhi, Mexico City

Cambridge University Press
32 Avenue of the Americas, New York, NY 10013-2473, USA

www.cambridge.org
Information on this title: www.cambridge.org/9780521723473

First published 2013

Printed in the United States of America

A catalog record for this publication is available from the British Library.

Library of Congress Cataloging in Publication data
Knapp, Arthur Bernard.
    The archaeology of Cyprus : from earliest prehistory through the Bronze
    Age / A. Bernard Knapp.
       p.   cm. – (Cambridge world archaeology)
    Includes bibliographical references and index.
    ISBN 978-0-521-89782-2 (hardback) – ISBN 978-0-521-72347-3 (paperback)
    1. Antiquities, Prehistoric – Cyprus.   2. Excavations (Archaeology) – Cyprus.
    3. Cyprus – Antiquities.   I. Title.
    GN855.C93K57   2012
    939'.37–dc23   2012002705

ISBN 978-0-521-89782-2 Hardback
ISBN 978-0-521-72347-3 Paperback

Additional resources for this publication at www.cambridge.org/9780521723473

For Stella, συνέχια και παντού

CONTENTS

LIST OF ILLUSTRATIONS AND TABLES

ILLUSTRATIONS

TABLES

PREFACE AND ACKNOWLEDGEMENTS

Over the past 30 years, the archaeology of Cyprus has developed and changed in such a way that its earlier practitioners would barely recognise it. In that time, archaeologists working on Cyprus have produced an extraordinary amount of new information stemming both from fieldwork (excavations, survey projects) and from new research on various classes of material culture. Beyond two earlier studies (Bolger 2003; Steel 2004a) published nearly a decade ago, however, none of this new work and information has been integrated into a comprehensive, theoretically informed presentation of Cyprus's prehistoric and protohistoric past. Most archaeologists working throughout Europe, the Near East and the Mediterranean, and especially those who work on Cyprus, have recognised the need for an up-to-date synthesis of all the materials, new and old, that form the basis for a prehistory of the island. Sturt W. Manning's Appendix provides a real bonus: the analysis of more than 300 available radiocarbon dates offers a comprehensive chronological framework for all of Cypriot prehistory, from the Late Epipalaeolithic to the end of the Late Bronze Age.

I began work on this monograph whilst still a full-time member of the academic staff in the Department of Archaeology, University of Glasgow. I wish to thank my colleagues and departmental staff at Glasgow for their support and the consideration (and relief from teaching) I was given as Research Professor (2006–2009). The bulk of the research and final writing of this book took place since I retired (September 2009) and was released from normal teaching and administrative demands. Much of this work was conducted in the library of the Cyprus American Archaeological Research Institute (CAARI) in Nicosia, and I am particularly grateful to Tom Davis (former director of CAARI), Evi Karyda (CAARI librarian) and Vathoulla Moustoukki (CAARI's administrator), all of whom facilitated my work in every way possible. CAARI's extensive library holdings (and online database) ensured that little time was wasted tracking down even the most obscure references I needed.

At Cambridge, I wish to thank Beatrice Rehl, the Sponsoring Editor, for all her support and help from beginning to end of this project. Sincere thanks

also to Luane Hutchinson, by far the best copy editor I have ever worked with. I am also grateful to Norm Yoffee, the CWA series editor, for inciting me to take on this project, and for encouraging me throughout.

The complexity and breadth of the materials and topics covered herein presented real challenges to me, especially those chapters on the earlier prehistory of Cyprus (Late Epipalaeolithic–Chalcolithic). I am therefore indebted to all the individuals listed below, in alphabetical order, for their comments on earlier drafts of various sections, and/or for copies of unpublished or forthcoming papers, including PhD theses. I relied constantly on the comments provided by all of these scholars, but the opinions expressed and the interpretations presented here remain my own, and my own responsibility.

Albert Ammerman (Colgate University): Late Epipalaeolithic

Sophia Antoniadou (Athens): PhD thesis (University of Edinburgh, 2004)

Seth Button (University of Michigan): Late Aceramic Neolithic

Jo Clarke (University of East Anglia): Ceramic Neolithic

Paul Croft (Lemba Archaeological Project, Cyprus): Bioarchaeology (faunal, floral)

Nikos Efstratiou (Aristotle University of Thessaloniki): Vretsia *Roudias* site (Late Epipalaeolithic)

Steven Falconer (Arizona State University, Tempe): Politiko *Troullia* (PreBA)

Nathan Harper (University of Nevada, Las Vegas): Late Aceramic Neolithic, Bronze Age mortuary data

Paula Louise Jones (University of Wales, Cardiff): Early and Late Aceramic Neolithic

Sturt W. Manning (Cornell University): Chronology and dating; Early Aceramic Neolithic; Appendix on 14C dates

Joseph Maran (Heidelberg University): Late Cypriot material in Tiryns

Carole McCartney (University of Cyprus): Cypro-PPNA; Early Aceramic Neolithic–Chalcolithic chipped stone

James D. Muhly (American School of Classical Studies, Athens): Protohistoric Bronze Age generally

Jay Noller (Oregon State University, Corvallis): Geology and geomorphology

Edgar Peltenburg (University of Edinburgh): Early–Middle Chalcolithic, Protohistoric Bronze Age

Curtis Runnels (Boston University): Palaeolithic

Anthony Russell: PhD thesis (University of Glasgow, 2011): Central Mediterranean

Alan Simmons (University of Nevada, Las Vegas): Late Epipalaeolithic, Early Aceramic Neolithic *Ais Giorkis*

Louise Steel (University of Wales, Trinity Saint David): Protohistoric Bronze Age overall

Stuart Swiny (State University of New York, Albany): Prehistoric Bronze
   Age Sotira *Kaminoudhia*

Jennifer Webb (La Trobe University, Melbourne): Late Chalcolithic,
   Prehistoric Bronze Age period overall

I must single out for thanks both Sturt Manning and Jennifer Webb. Webb's
careful reading of the entire manuscript helped me to eliminate repetition,
resolve contradictions and generally to improve the quality and consistency of
the writing and arguments throughout. Manning's Appendix adds an unprecedented temporal component to the study of Cypriot prehistory, and provides
the most comprehensive, up-to-date set of radiocarbon dates and analyses available for the island; his feedback on the discussion of chronological issues within
the volume has improved its coherence greatly. In addition to the Appendix,
Manning has prepared some Supporting Online Material (SOM henceforth),
which provides details and additional materials to support the Appendix. For
those who wish to check all the relevant data used to prepare the Appendix
and to establish the radiocarbon dates used in this volume, the SOM is essential, and should be consulted in conjunction with the Appendix. The SOM
may be accessed at: www.cambridge.org/9780521723473.

Special thanks also goes to Edgar Peltenburg (Edinburgh), who not only
commented on several sections but also provided numerous illustrations of
Neolithic and Chalcolithic sites. Thanks, too, to Luke Sollars (Glasgow) for
producing several maps and other illustrations, and to Michael Given (Glasgow)
for the ProBA 'social model' (Figure 95). Staff members at various museums
were most helpful in providing illustrations for this work: Medelhavsmuseet,
Stockholm, Sweden (Kristian Göransson); Ashmolean Museum, Oxford (Anja
Ulbrich, Amy Taylor); Cyprus Museum, Nicosia (Euthymios Shaftacolas). I also
wish to thank the following individuals for providing me with other images to
illustrate the volume:

Celia J. Bergoffen (New York): Alalakh Base-ring krater

Jo Clarke (University of East Anglia): Ceramic Neolithic material; Kalavasos
   Kokkinoyia

Lindy Crewe (Manchester University, UK): Souskiou *Laona*, spindle whorls

Steven Falconer and Patricia Fall (Arizona State University, Tempe): Politiko
   Troullia

Kevin Fisher (University of Arkansas, Fayetteville): *Ayios Dhimitrios*, Enkomi
   building plans

David Frankel, Jenny Webb and Rudy Frank (La Trobe University,
   Melbourne): Marki *Alonia*, Politiko *Kokkinorotsos*, Deneia, north-coast
   cemeteries, Karmi, Enkomi

Jean Guilaine (Collège de France, Paris): Parekklisha *Shillourokambos*
   enclosures

Sophocles Hadjisavvas (Nicosia, Cyprus): Alassa site plan, seal impression

Mara Horowitz (Columbia University): Phlamoudhi *Vounari*

Paula Louise Jones (University of Wales, Cardiff): *Shillourokambos* drawings

Priscilla Keswani (Independent Scholar): Enkomi tomb plans

Alain Le Brun and Odile Daune-Le Brun (CNRS, France): Khirokitia *Vouni*

Sturt W. Manning (Cornell University): All radiocarbon related figures

Carole McCartney (University of Cyprus) and Sturt Manning (Cornell University): Ayia Varvara *Asprokremmos*

Jay Noller (Oregon State University, Corvallis): Akrotiri Peninsula

Edgar Peltenburg (University of Edinburgh): Various Neolithic and Chalcolithic sites

Alan Simmons (University of Nevada, Las Vegas): Akrotiri *Aetokremnos*, *Ais Giorkis*

Joanna S. Smith (Princeton University): Phlamoudhi *Melissa*, *Vounari*

Alison South and Ian Todd (CAARI): Kalavasos *Tenta*, *Ayious*, *Ayios Dhimitrios*

Louise Steel (University of Wales, Trinity Saint David): Material culture, various periods

Thomas Strasser (Providence College, Rhode Island) and Nicholas Thompson: Plakias, Crete, Greece.

Stuart Swiny (State University of New York, Albany): Sotira *Kaminoudhia*

Sturt Manning also wishes to thank the Oxford Radiocarbon Laboratory, in particular Thomas Higham and Christopher Bronk Ramsey, for their collaboration and advice. Further thanks go to Christopher Bronk Ramsey for examining earlier versions of the OxCal dating models used in the Appendix and for suggesting improvements – as always he was most generous with his time and expertise.

CHAPTER I

INTRODUCTION

Cyprus has long held a strategic position in the protracted prehistory and history of the Mediterranean world, and during that time had major cultural and economic impacts throughout the region. Over the past three decades, an extraordinary amount of information stemming from new archaeological fieldwork (excavations and surveys) on the island, and from new research on individual classes of material (including single artefacts), has been published. And yet, with two recent exceptions (Bolger 2003; Steel 2004a) that follow very different research agendas, nobody has attempted to integrate all this new work and information into a comprehensive, theoretically informed presentation of Cyprus's prehistoric and protohistoric past.

In the extant archaeological literature on Cyprus, there is a tendency to see the island's political, economic and even artistic developments as the result of invasions, migrations, colonisation, diffusion or other external factors, whether Near Eastern or Aegean (or both) in origin. Steeped in culture history, such an approach to the long-term history of Cyprus is not only inadequate but also tends to render the indigenous inhabitants of Cyprus mute and invisible, all this at a time when multivocality and a local (vs. global) perspective invigorate and structure both historical and social scientific practice.

This book situates Cypriot archaeology in its wider context by examining various issues that confront archaeologists working elsewhere in the Old World (Europe, the Mediterranean, the ancient Near East) or indeed throughout the world. In presenting this new study of Cypriot prehistory and protohistory, at times I refer to but fully reformulate some of my own, earlier work on the Cypriot Chalcolithic and Bronze Ages (e.g. Knapp 1990a; 1993a; 1994; 2001; 2003; 2006; 2008). I also consider critically how new information on both earlier (Late Epipalaeolithic to Chalcolithic) and later (earliest Iron Age) periods may be assessed in a thematic and integrated manner, in particular with respect to the following, interrelated issues: seafaring and the earliest visits of people to the island; migration, colonisation and hybridisation; insularity, mobility and connectivity; distance and the exotic; gender and social identity; social complexity; community and polity; production and consumption. I examine how factors such as spatial organisation, subsistence regimes, monumental architecture, gendered representations, mortuary practices, ritual and feasting, production and exchange, and the adoption of a written script (Cypro-Minoan, from the late Middle Bronze Age onward) impacted on island society and island identity.

Throughout this work, I focus on issues of materiality, and attempt to show how people used material 'things' consciously to fashion an insular identity (or identities) and to establish distinctive, island-specific, social, economic and political practices. By drawing out some of the tensions between different ways of thinking about insularity and connectivity, mobility, migrations and hybridisation, community and polity, gender and island identities, I seek to place some key theoretical concepts on a firmer archaeological footing. Thus I engage certain interpretative approaches in archaeology in order to illuminate various social, material and ideological aspects of Cyprus's past, and where relevant I attempt to integrate such approaches through the comparative analysis of material data and documentary records.

Amongst various questions that frame and guide the writing are the following:

- How did the people of ancient Cyprus fashion their world and establish their identities?
- How do shared social practices imprinted in Cypriot material culture – ranging from chipped stone industries to monumental architecture – contribute to expressing identity?
- What kind of material and social factors are involved in intercultural contacts?
- How did mobility and 'connectivities' between Cyprus and overseas polities – changing noticeably through time – impact on the development of more complex social systems?
- How do we integrate research stemming from site excavations or landscape studies into a broader view of social interactions on ancient Cyprus?
- How can we best consider the nature and diversity of the Cypriot islandscape, and in turn examine how island communities form, interrelate and endure?
- How can archaeologists integrate historical evidence in their attempts to (re)construct mobility and migrations, materiality and identity?

To begin, it is necessary to establish some basic environmental and climatic parameters, features that form the backdrop to the suite of Cypriot sociocultural, economic and material developments discussed at length in this study.

Figure 1. View southeast from Hala Sultan Tekke *Vyzakia* to the Larnaca Salt Lake, possibly the site's harbour during the Late Bronze Age. Photograph by A. Bernard Knapp.

ENVIRONMENT, LANDSCAPE AND CLIMATE

With a territorial extent of 9,251 km², Cyprus is the third largest Mediterranean island, after Sicily and Sardinia. Isolated in the Mediterranean's northeast corner, Cyprus is situated some 70 km south of Turkey, 95 km west of Syria and 400 km north of Egypt. The Aegean world, starting at the Dodecanese island of Rhodes, lies nearly 500 km west. Several natural harbours indent Cyprus's coastline, while some of the island's best known Late Bronze Age sites (Enkomi, Maroni, Kition, Hala Sultan Tekke) (Figure 1) may have had inner harbours accessible by navigable river mouths or embayments that have since dried up or been silted in (Nicolaou 1976; Gifford 1985; Collombier 1988; Morhange et al. 2000).

In geological terms, Cyprus's orogenesis is complex, and most research treating it has focused on the formation of the ophiolite complex in the Troodos mountains, the island's main structural and topographic feature (Constantinou 1982: 13–15; Robertson 2000; Mart and Ryan 2002) (see below, Figure 2). The ultrabasic core of the Troodos is ringed by gabbros and an extensive diabase, with an encircling pillow lava series, seldom more than 5–7 km wide. The Troodos ophiolite complex is important in cultural and social terms as well because the massive copper sulphide deposits – whose ores have formed at least one major prop of Cyprus's economy over the past 4,000 years – are embedded in its pillow lavas.

Gass (1968) proposed that the Troodos massif was originally formed on a mid-Tethyan oceanic ridge and subsequently was exposed when the Afro-Arabian plate thrust beneath the European plate; in such a scenario, the present-day Troodos would represent the heavily eroded remnants of this volcanic activity. More recent geological research indicates that the ophiolite developed as part of an early island arc development in a subduction zone (Rautenschlein 1987) rather than in a spreading mid-oceanic ridge (Robertson and Woodcock

Figure 2. Cyprus satellite image. Source: *NASA, TheVisible Earth – http://visiblee-arth.nasa.gov/*

1980; Moores et al. 1984; King et al. 1997: 17–20). In this scenario, the forma-
tion of the Troodos is closely linked to a destructive collision between the
Afro-Arabian macro-plate and the Turkish micro-plate in the eastern
Mediterranean basin (Held 1989a: 69).

At least as important for archaeological purposes is that ongoing geological and geophysical research has demonstrated conclusively that no land
bridge existed between Cyprus and the Asiatic mainland at any point after the
Miocene epoch (Stanley Price 1979a: 1–5: Held 1989a: 66–69; Robertson et
al. 1995). The Miocene ended some five million years ago, not long after the
Messinian Salinity Crisis, when the Mediterranean Sea evaporated and became
partly or completely dry (Hsü 1972). Once the salt water of the (current)
Atlantic Ocean had again breached the Straits of Gibraltar after the Messinian
Event, and the Mediterranean Sea was formed more or less as we know it,
Cyprus was never connected to any mainland. Both the Adana Trough, which
separates Cyprus from Anatolia, and the Latakia Basin, which separates it from
the Levant, range down to 1,500 m in depth (Swiny 1988: 1–2, fig. 1; Mart and
Ryan 2002: 120). Taken together, these factors demonstrate that, at least since
the Pliocene, Cyprus has been an island (Held 1989a: 67–69, 71, fig. 4).

Internally, Cyprus's main physiographic features are the Kyrenia (or
Pentedaktylos) mountain range in the north, and the Troodos mountains that
extend over much of the southern and southwestern parts of the island (Figure
2). Separating the two is the central lowland plain (Christodoulou 1959: 12),

commonly known as the *Mesaoria* ('between the mountains'), whose western reaches are also referred to as the Morphou Plain. The geomorphology of these central lowlands is quite simple: it varies in elevation – from sea level to 230 m – and in make-up, with alluvial deposits, silt and a central limestone plateau, topped in its eastern sectors with a hardpan calcrete (*kafkalla*), the last covered locally by thin layers of terra rossa soils. Rainfall and perennial springs ensure that the coastal strip north of the Kyrenia range, at no point more than 5 km wide, remains relatively green and fertile. To the east of this range lies the Karpass, a long, finger-like peninsula beginning at the northern end of Famagusta Bay and pointing towards the Bay of Iskenderun in modern-day Turkey.

Through the Kyrenia range, three main passes (Panagra, Kyrenia and Lefkoniko) lead southward to a series of still-barren hillocks that form a back-drop to the predominantly alluvial *Mesaoria*, important today for agricultural and especially grain production. To the south and west of the central lowlands, the peaks of the Troodos massif rise anywhere from 700 to 2,000 m, domi-nating the landscape and restricting travel throughout the region. In the far southwest, the Paphos region is defined in some places by its narrow coastal strip, in others by outliers of the Troodos that plunge directly into the sea. In the southeast, the region around modern-day Larnaca forms part of Cyprus's southern chalk plateaus: here, a few deeply incised river valleys cut through low, gentle slopes that descend gradually to the seashore, with its raised coastal beaches or, in a few places, narrow coastal plains (Stanley Price 1979a: 5–7).

The development of soils on Cyprus's somewhat rough and rocky terrain is constrained by the island's lithology, its sharp relief and a rainfall pattern that varies from about 300 mm per annum in the lowland plains to 1,100 mm per annum in the highest reaches of the Troodos. The rough topography tends to produce soils that are thin, full of small stones and pale brown in colour, excepting the reddish Quaternary sediments that blanket some slopes and val-ley floors. Studies of the Quaternary record have demonstrated a progressive weathering of soils from recent to ancient surface sediments, noted consistently among stony slopes, valley alluvia and pediment fanglomerates (concretions of individual rocks) (Gomez 1987; Poole and Robertson 1998; Devillers 2004). Today, soil cover has almost completely disappeared from limestone bedrock on the island, leaving hill slopes barren of both soil and vegetation (King et al. 1997: 49). Soils form a dynamic – albeit very vulnerable – aspect of the land-scape, part of a *chaine opératoire* that links land cover, surface water and people in a complex process that silently underpins the daily life, yearly seasons and *la longue durée* of agricultural and industrial production alike.

In their review of fieldwork related to Cyprus's complex surface sedimen-tary record, Butzer and Harris (2007) suggest that there were cyclic alter-nations between periods of soil stability and soil formation, and other eras of soil instability, when slope erosion and sediment mobilisation accelerated. Considering their suggestion in the light of fluvial activity, however, presents

another possibility. The pronounced gradient of rivers whose valleys cut deep
into the steep slopes of the Kyrenia and Troodos ranges alike has resulted in
considerable erosion; significant deposits of vegetal soils and stony detritus are
spread across wide lowland flood plains within which the rivers tend to meander. The slow, steady erosion caused by perennial streams is rare on Cyprus
compared to the rampant erosion that occurs in river torrents following sudden downpours: one striking case was the destructive, late-autumn floods of
the Pedhaios River in 1567, 1859 and 1888 (Butzer and Harris 2007), or the 192
mm of rain that fell in four hours and inundated the Larnaca region during the
autumn of 1981 (King et al. 1997: 7).

Despite the seasonal or episodic nature of stream flow, Holocene river courses
on Cyprus seem to have remained fairly constant, and other geomorphological
work (discussed in Stanley Price 1979a: 7–9) indicates that riverine-induced
erosion and deposition were not necessarily cyclic, but often concurrent.
Cyprus has an arid to semi-arid landscape dominated throughout human
occupation by flashy discharge, that is, episodic downpours and short-duration
high-stream flows leading to a broad range of contrasting sediment and land-
form features (Devillers 2004). Alluvial deposition, shore-side sedimentation
and/or sand-blown dune formation gradually filled in the Morphou (west)
and Famagusta (east) bays at either end of the *Mesaoria*, as well as the Akrotiri
and Larnaca salt lakes, respectively in the south and the southeast of the island
(Gifford 1985; Morhange et al. 2000).

Although the relationship between (alternating or concurrent) erosional
and depositional sequences and Holocene climate remains problematic, our
concern here is with climatic effects on the inhabitants and landscape of prehistoric and early historic Cyprus (Wasse 2007: 47–50). Because Cyprus is situated at an extreme point within the nearly landlocked Mediterranean basin,
and is protected from low-pressure extremes by the mountainous regions of
southern and southwestern Turkey, its climate is notably affected by continental influences (Stanley Price 1979a: 9). Moreover, the global climatic shifts
of the past 25,000 years (Rossignol-Strick 1995; 1999; Robinson et al. 2006)
must always have had some impact on Cyprus; increasingly, it is acknowledged
that much of the archaeological record of Cyprus was laid down within the
context of dynamic and recurrent environmental and climatic change (Wasse
2007: 48).

For example, following the Last Glacial Maximum (ca. 25,000–18,000 Cal
BP), the combination of higher rainfall and warming temperatures during the
Bølling-Allerød interstadial (ca. 15,000–13,000 Cal BP) probably resulted in
the development from open woodland to full forest conditions on Cyprus.
With the onset of the Younger Dryas episode (ca. 12,800–11,600 Cal BP),
precipitation lessened, the mean annual temperature became markedly lower
and woodlands therefore must have contracted alongside any bodies of water
that may have emerged on the island during the climatic amelioration of the

preceding Bølling-Allerød. Bromage et al. (2002), in fact, attribute the extinction of pygmy hippopotamus on Cyprus around the Pleistocene–Holocene boundary to the desiccation of small pools on which these animals may have depended (discussed further in Chapter 3). Thus it seems clear that quite dramatic climatic and environmental conditions existed on the island at the very time that people began to exploit its faunal, floral, aquatic and other resources (discussed below in *Coastal Adaptations, Climate and Seafaring*). But this does not mean that sociocultural developments or change necessarily can be imputed to climatic change.

For example, despite minor fluctuations throughout the eastern Mediterranean, today's climate is thought to be more or less comparable to, if somewhat drier than, that of the earliest Holocene (Butzer 1975; 2005: 1774; various papers in Bintliff and Van Zeist 1982). It is likely that the more humid phase of the early Holocene (ca. 10,000–8000/7000 Cal BP, following the Younger Dryas episode) had begun to break down by about 8000 Cal BP, perhaps as part of the so-called 8200 Cal BP 'cold event' (e.g. Staubwasser and Weiss 2006: 378–379; Weninger et al. 2006). This event brought on a process of aridification that became well established by about 6000 Cal BP, leading to the pattern of prolonged summer drought and irregular winter rain so typical of the Mediterranean today. Although this process of aridification and a concomitant reduction in woodlands seems clear in a range of evidence from the eastern Mediterranean generally (e.g. Frumkin et al. 2001; Casana and Wilkinson 2005: 33), it is not always straightforward to distinguish between climatic and human-induced impacts on the palaeoenvironmental record. In any case, we should no longer be trying to link directly severe or abrupt changes in climate with differing episodes of social complexity or collapse (Brooks 2006). As Maher et al. (2011: 2–3) suggest, 'the correlations between archaeological phenomena and palaeoclimatic events should be treated as probability statements'. In particular, they argue that the 8200 Cal BP cold event cannot have caused the abandonment of PPNB sites in the southern Levant, as it occurred almost a full millennium too late (Maher et al. 2011: 17–18).

One crucial climatic factor for anyone living on Cyprus is that all the island's freshwater sources (including springs in the Kyrenia range) stem from autumn or winter rainfall and from winter snows in the Troodos. As already implied by reference to flooding and sudden downpours, fluctuations in rainfall can be extreme, and most rain falls during storms from late October through March. Nowadays at least, the island's major rivers are active in winter but become mere rivulets during the summer. Recent records from Cyprus show extreme annual variation in rainfall, such that it is always unreliable and often inadequate in lowland areas. As a result, rainfall has a very limited impact on Cyprus's hydrological regime, which is further exacerbated by high evaporation rates (up to 87% of total precipitation – Stanley Price 1979a: 11). Although little is known with certainty about the configuration or extent of standing bodies of water during the earlier Holocene, lacustrine resources are limited and in any case would have had restricted usage because of their high salinity and propensity for infestation by malarial mosquitoes.

Riverine streamflow in low rainfall areas like Cyprus is also affected by the nature of local geology, forest cover and ecological variables such as xerophytic or mesophytic vegetation. This vegetation cover also acts as a check on soil erosion in a country wracked by heavy winter rains and erratic summer storms. In today's hot and dry lowlands, garrigue species (grass, rock, dwarf-shrub steppes) and xerophytic weeds dominate the vegetation, but are supplemented by broadleaf cactus and juniper maquis, as well as carob, olive and date palm. The hilly flanks surrounding the Kyrenia and Troodos mountains also support garrigue and maquis, along with carob, fig, almond and pistachio trees. Along the Kyrenia range grow isolated stands of cedar and cypress, while in the southern and southwestern hill slopes of the Troodos, grapevines and fruit orchards dot the landscape. Deciduous hardwood trees can only be found today in zones above 1,200 m in the Troodos, where they are heavily outflanked by conifers or evergreens: pine, cedar, wild cypress and evergreen Cyprian oak. During the 18th century, the Troodos were described as being heavily wooded with black pine, arbutus and live oak, while the valleys were carpeted with maple, poplar, willow, alder and plane trees (Cobham 1908: 329–331, Butzer and Harris 2007: 1938).

Myres (1914: xxvii) long ago divided the prehistoric landscape of Cyprus into lowland marsh, intermediate parkland and upland coniferous forest, while Holmboe (1914: 1–3; Merrillees 1978: 6) isolated three vertical phytogeographic zones (lowland, hill, mountain), to which must be added at least a fourth, alpine zone (only above 1,600 m on Mt. Olympus in the Troodos). Meikle (1977: 4–8) divided the Late Holocene vegetation of Cyprus into eight phytogeographic regions, similar to the Evergreen Oak Belt Formation found in the coastal regions of southern Anatolia and the northern Levant, but with most of the Troodos ecozone forming part of the Sub-Humid Belt Formation; this formation is also found in the Lebanon and Anti-Lebanon mountains and in the lower reaches of the Amanus and Taurus mountains (Held 1989a: 107). The climax vegetation of the early Holocene is thought to have consisted of Mediterranean evergreen sclerophyllous forest, dominated by oaks, juniper and cypress (Jones et al. 1958: 24; Stanley Price 1979a: 13). In the more arid parts of the island, however, such as the middle parts of the *Mesaoria* and in the east and south, maquis is more likely to have been the climax vegetation (Adams and Simmons 1996a: 19–20, 22–23). *Pinus Brutia* (Aleppo pine) has been identified already in the Early Aceramic Neolithic (EAN) archaeological record (Thiébault 2003), and was certainly widespread by the Bronze Age; it was the most common species identified in charcoal samples from the archaeometallurgical site of Politiko *Phorades* (M. Ntinou, in Knapp et al., n.d.).

Although the 8200 Cal BP 'event' may have resulted in aridification, including a reduction in the extent of forest cover, it is widely assumed that human activities led to the progressive deforestation of Cyprus after its early Holocene climax state: from secondary forest to maquis, garrigue and finally batha (Meiggs 1982: 134–137, 397–399; Held 1989a: 107). This assumption is largely based upon the present-day situation, reinforced by classical authors such as Strabo (*Geographia* 685), who stated that the *Mesaoria* was at one time heavily forested; if true, and as already noted, this is likely to have been dense maquis rather than true forest (Stanley Price 1979a: 13–14). To be sure, human settlement, plant cultivation and stock grazing have contributed much to the present-day severely eroded landscape (Miksicek 1988: 470). Moreover, although the process of deforestation at times may have been offset by natural afforestation, a slow and uneven process (excepting the endemic Aleppo Pine, or *Pinus Brutia Ten* – Meikle 1977), historical accounts of the Venetian and Ottoman periods, at least, indicate there was no obvious degree of deforestation on the island at that time (Butzer and Harris 2007: 1938–1939; cf. Christodoulou 1959: 227, who argues for several phases of deforestation).

Fauna and Flora

Recent zooarchaeological and palaeobotanical studies shed further light on Cyprus's early Holocene environment. Turning first to the faunal record, remains of some of the dwarf elephant and pygmy hippopotamus that evolved on Cyprus during the Pleistocene (Davis 1985) were recovered from a controversial archaeological site – Akrotiri *Aetokremnos* – whose excavator and zooarchaeologist believe these mini-megafauna were hunted to extinction nearly 12,000 years ago (Simmons 1999). Other archaeologists and faunal specialists are less sanguine about such an interpretation (e.g. Bunimovitz and Barkai 1996; Binford 2000; Grayson 2000; Davis 2003: 258–259; Ammerman and Noller 2005). I consider this issue further below (*Late Epipalaeolithic: The Earliest Visitors*), but whatever the fate of these two species may have been, their demise left Cyprus with no mammalian herbivore larger than the mouse (Croft 2002: 172; Cucchi et al. 2002).

Subsequently, after about 10,500 years ago during the Early Aceramic Neolithic (EAN – for the chronological periods, see below Table 2; Appendix, Table A2), the first permanent settlers of the island brought with them the following animals: fallow deer (*Dama mesopotamica*), cattle, sheep, goat and pig (unless it arrived earlier –Vigne et al. 2009), along with fox, the domestic dog and at least one, possibly domesticated cat (*Felis silvestris*, the wild cat from which domestic cats descended –Vigne et al. 2004). The larger fauna all appear in the earliest phase of occupation at Parekklisha *Shillourokambos*, an EAN I site near the south-central coast of Cyprus (Vigne 2001; Vigne et al. 2003; 2009). From EAN I levels at Kissonerga *Mylouthkia* on the southwest coast, a deep well shaft (Well 116) has produced an important microfaunal assemblage and scant remains of caprine and pig, while another (Well 133), dated almost 1,000 years later (EAN 3), contained the complete carcases of 23 caprines – 9 sheep and 14 goats – as well as some deer and pig (Croft 2003a: 271–274; Peltenburg 2003a).

Croft (2002: 174–175) hinted that the pig and cattle introduced to Cyprus were somewhat smaller than their wild variants, that the caprines became smaller in size once they had arrived on Cyprus, and consequently that the cattle, pig, goat and sheep introduced to Cyprus were domesticated from the outset. Horwitz et al. (2004: 43–44) maintained that with the possible exception of pigs, all other animals found in the earliest Neolithic assemblages on Cyprus conform in size and shape to their wild variants. In their view, it was only later, during subsequent 'colonising events', that domesticated variants of sheep, goat and possibly pig were introduced, while cattle slowly went out of use. Vigne (2001: 56–57) originally suggested that, at *Shillourokambos*, only the pig was domesticated, while cattle, sheep and goat were seen to be 'pre-domesticates'.

More detailed analyses of all the faunal remains from *Shillourokambos* have vindicated some of Croft's hints. Vigne et al. (2003: 248–251) abandoned the term 'pre-domestic' and argued that, by the second phase ('B') of occupation at *Shillourokambos* (here, EAN 1), deer and goat were feral, pigs were both domestic and feral, and cattle and sheep were domesticated. Their argument for feral populations is complex, based on an assumption that people brought domesticated (or at least herded) pig, goat and deer to the island at a time after the Akrotiri phase (ending about 9000 Cal BC) but before the EAN (beginning about 8500 Cal BC) (Conolly et al. 2011: 542). More recently, however, Vigne et al. (2009) have demonstrated the presence of two small-sized pigs at *Aetokremnos* around 9500 Cal BC. They argue that these pigs were introduced to Cyprus from the Near East more than 1,000 years before the earliest known morphological changes attributable to domestication in that region (e.g. at PPNA Cayönü and Nevali Çori in eastern Anatolia; Ervynck et al. 2001; Peters et al. 2005; Conolly et al. 2011: 542–543). The dominance of pig in the faunal record at PPNA Ayia Varvara *Asprokremmos* (ca. 9100–8500 Cal BC, discussed further in Chapter 3) and in the earliest EAN phases at Parekklisha *Shillourokambos* (ca. 8300 Cal BC –Vigne et al. 2003: 240–245, table 1) indicate that pig continued to be a major food resource in the coming millennia.

The value and utility of morphological markers – including size reduction – for determining the 'domestic' status of fauna increasingly has come under scrutiny (e.g. Redding 2005; Vigne et al. 2005). Some would now argue that the reduction in body size, once seen as a marker of initial domestication in animals, instead should be attributed to differences in the culling strategies of herders (i.e. where the faunal record is dominated by bones of smaller females slaughtered after their prime reproductive years) versus the killing strategies of hunters (i.e. where the faunal record reveals a focus on large, adult, usually male animals to maximise returns) (Zeder 2008: 11,597).

On balance, and based on several other axes of the faunal record (e.g. mortality and slaughtering profiles, age and sex ratios, metric characteristics), it is difficult to imagine how people so well organised as Cyprus's new settlers would have come to a new habitat they intended to make their own without ensured and dependable food resources. Domesticated, or at least herdable animals, and cultivated if not domesticated plants would therefore seem to be essential. From a social perspective, then, and acknowledging the rationality and intentionality – what Cherry (1981: 42) termed *purposive* behaviour – of these would-be islanders in establishing a home away from home, it seems evident that they travelled primarily with animals that they could manage, at least some of which (cattle, sheep, goat, pig) may have been domesticated, or nearly so.

The appearance of such domesticated or herdable animals on Cyprus (excepting fallow deer, almost certainly introduced to stock the island as a free-ranging animal that could be hunted), at a date as early as or earlier than domesticates appear in the Levant and Anatolia (late 9th millennium Cal BC – Legge 1996; Peters et al. 1999; 2005; Vigne et al. 2003: 250–252; Vigne et al. 2009; Conolly et al. 2011: 543), has major implications for understanding the emergence of an agropastoral lifestyle in the eastern Mediterranean. I consider this issue in more detail below. The fact that Cyprus's earliest settlers brought these specific animals with them also suggests that each of them had a special status, whether economic, symbolic or more personal (Vigne 2001: 56; Masseti 2006).

Because tending cattle proved to be unsuitable in the early Holocene environment of Cyprus, their early use at two separate, coastal or near-coastal sites (Akanthou *Arkosyko* and *Shillourokambos*, both EAN 1 in date) and one upland site (Kritou Marottou *Ais Giorkis*, EAN 2 to Late Aceramic Neolithic [LAN] in date) lasted little more than 1,000 years (Simmons 1998: 237–238; Şevketoğlu 2000: 77; Croft 2003a: 274–275). To these well-known examples must be added the single, exceptional cattle metapodial fragment from Khirokitia's Ceramic Neolithic (Davis 2003: 263–264, fig. 7). If sites like *Ais Giorkis* and *Shillourokambos* were special-purpose locales rather than permanently settled villages (Simmons 2003a: 69), cattle may have been herded and kept elsewhere, depending upon the season of the year or availability of pastureland. All currently available evidence suggests that cattle disappeared altogether from the Cypriot archaeological record after the LAN, and were reintroduced as a domestic species only during the Bronze Age, nearly 4,000 years later (cf. Croft 1991). Why was this the case?

Davis (2003) suggested that cattle on Cyprus may have had some kind of bovine disease or else that tending and maintaining these large animals proved too onerous, especially in terms of feeding and foraging needs. Horwitz et al. (2004: 39) felt that the lack of fresh stock from the mainland might have made it difficult to replenish and maintain the original herds of cattle. Perhaps there were ecological reasons that selected against keeping cattle in the more developed villages of the LAN, as opposed to the smaller, quite diverse sites of the EAN (Simmons 2009: 6). In considering why cattle were dumped from the dietary regime of the island's early settlers, it must be pointed out that because of their size and long maturation rate, domesticated cattle would have required the greatest investment of energy for the longest delayed returns (Wasse 2007: 61). Cattle husbandry, in other words, may have been too inefficient in the insular context, at the same time that deer continued to be a comparatively easy economic option. From a social perspective, we might also speculate that cattle never attained, or sustained, the ideological or iconographic status it held in nearby Anatolian or Levantine societies (Stanley Price 1977a: 84; Ronen 1995: 185–186).

It is also useful here to consider the wider zooarchaeological record of the surrounding regions. In a recent study using organic residue analysis on 255 sherds of vessels that most likely served for food preparation, Evershed et al. (2008) demonstrated that a series of sites in northwestern Anatolia contained clear evidence for the extensive processing of dairy products, or at least much more so than in any other part of Anatolia, the Levant and southeastern Europe. In comparing the available faunal records from these areas, the proportion of cattle bones was considerably higher in northwest Anatolia than anywhere else. The authors concluded that the importance of milk from cattle, and indeed of processed milk (i.e. as cheese, curd, ghee) in northwestern Anatolia, must reflect higher rainfall and greener pastures, and that early farming practices developed differently in different areas, at least partly in response to climatic and environmental conditions. Indeed, Wasse (2007: 55) suggests that aridification in the southern Levant during the Late Neolithic may have led to the selective breeding of goats for drought resistance and milk production (see also Vigne and Helmer 2007: fig. 10). In the case of Cyprus, although today's climate may be somewhat drier than it was in the early Holocene (Butzer 2005: 1774), it has never been a high rainfall setting (except sporadically), nor does it have adequate grazing grounds for a ruminant like cattle, with its high-feed demands.

Because deer continued to be the key staple in the islander's diet, and remained pre-eminent in the faunal record in terms of both weight and numbers, Jones (2008) has questioned whether LAN communities should be viewed as maintaining a fully sedentary, farming way of life (discussed further below, *Late Aceramic Neolithic: Insularity, Settlement and Subsistence*). Although the use of both deer and pig declined somewhat in LAN levels at Khirokitia (Davis 2003: 262–263, fig. 6), deer hunting as a subsistence activity lasted throughout the Neolithic and Chalcolithic periods, at times amounting to as much as 70% of the faunal remains on certain sites (Croft 2002: 174; Webb et al. 2009: 221–224).

In general, however, pig and deer seem to have contributed more or less equally to the food base, with sheep and goat seldom amounting to more than 25% of the total faunal remains at any given site. Based on various adjustments to the faunal evidence from Chalcolithic Kissonerga *Mylouthkia* and *Mosphilia*, for example, Croft (2003c: 235–237) showed that deer always accounted for more than 50% of the meat supply (except at Late Chalcolithic *Mosphilia*, where it stood at 45%), and that pig also gained in importance through time while caprine use declined (never much above 8%). In Croft's view, the slowly declining importance of deer hunting (less so at *Mosphilia*) and an increasing reliance on pig may reflect the subsistence needs of village communities whose population was rising. All this suggests that the people of early prehistoric Cyprus productively exploited domesticated animals and successfully managed game as part of an insular, agropastoral strategy concerned with availability, if not sustainability.

Animal use and exploitation changed significantly during the Prehistoric Bronze Age (PreBA), that is, after ca. 2400 Cal BC. Overall, the available subsistence evidence points to a decline in the exploitation of deer, a return to the use of cattle, the introduction of screw-horned goats (Croft 1996: 218) and a change in the way that people integrated animals into their ideology (Keswani 1994). The faunal records from PreBA 1–2 Marki *Alonia* and Sotira *Kaminoudhia*, and from PreBA 2 Alambra *Mouttes*, show that caprines were now a crucial food source (up to 61% at Alambra *Mouttes*), followed by cattle (up to 32% at Sotira *Kaminoudhia*), deer (15–20% at all sites) and pig (from 3% at Marki *Alonia* to 12% at Sotira *Kaminoudhia*) (Reese 1996a; Croft 2003b: 439–440; 2006: 277–281). Donkey, fox, dog and cat round out the PreBA faunal record.

Taking bone weight rather than bone frequency as the criterion for interpretation, Croft (2003b: 440 table 11.2, 446; 2006: 279–280, table 9.1) points out that cattle and deer bones alike are much heavier than those of caprines. On the basis of bone weight, cattle formed the mainstay of the economy at both Marki *Alonia* and Sotira *Kaminoudhia* throughout the PreBA. In this regard, deer also came to exceed the importance of sheep and goat during the course of this period. Croft (2003b: 446–447), however, cautions that a 'carnivorous' assessment of the relative values of the animals most significant to the subsistence economy tends to overestimate the value of deer and pig, compared to cattle, sheep and goat, all of which yield crucial secondary products, in particular milk. The evident rise in importance of cattle, sheep and goat in the PreBA agro-pastoral economy, along with less frequent use of pig and deer, surely must be linked to all the other changes – cultural, social, environmental – that took place in Cypriot society during the PreBA. These were, notably, the 'secondary products revolution' (use of cattle with the plough) and the emergence of copper production (use of donkeys for transport), each of which is discussed in detail elsewhere in this volume (Chapter 6).

Based on the currently available bioarchaeological record, the general pattern of animal use and exploitation on Cyprus during the 4th–2nd millennia BC is as follows:

(1) gradual replacement of pig and deer by cattle;

(2) caprine-dominated assemblages in almost all Bronze Age faunal samples; and

(3) an *apparent* increase in the proportion of goats relative to sheep (Croft 1988: 452; 1989).

If accurately interpreted, there was a decreased reliance on hunting (fallow deer) and an increased emphasis on stock rearing (Croft 1985: 295–296). These patterns reflect ecological as well as cultural or behavioural factors. The use of pig instead of cattle in some contexts, for example, may reveal dietary preference as well as environmental and technological developments (forest clearance with bronze tools) that came in train with new farming techniques in a more open environment. If there was indeed an increase in the number of goats versus sheep, we may be witnessing a case of human pressure on the environment, resulting in maquis vegetation better suited to goats, as well as the goat's propensity to move into ecological niches vacated by a diminishing deer population (Croft 1989). At the same time, cattle would have become increasingly important – both as draught animals and a steady source of meat – in the Bronze Age agro-pastoral economy.

By the Protohistoric Bronze Age (ProBA), beginning ca. 1750/1700 Cal BC, the concentration of people in Cyprus's new town centres required more intensified animal exploitation. The faunal record of excavations at several ProBA sites (Hala Sultan Tekke *Vyzakia*, Kouklia *Palaipaphos*, Episkopi *Phaneromeni*, Phlamoudhi *Melissa* and *Vounari*, Athienou *Bamboulari tis Koukounninas*, Maroni and Kalavasos *Ayios Dhimitrios*) demonstrates that animal exploitation focused on goat and sheep (Knapp 1994: 283–287; Reese 1996a: 476–481). Although the remains of cattle continued to appear at sites such as Sinda, Hala Sultan Tekke and Kouklia, ovicaprines consistently outnumber them fourfold (Croft 1989; Macheridis, in Fischer 2011: 93–94). This statistic is less dramatic at Episkopi *Phaneromeni* where the percentages of cattle (31%) and caprine (32%) remains are virtually equal (Swiny 1989: 23).

Deer continued to be hunted while equids (horse, donkey) were used as draft animals. In both domestic and ceremonial contexts, few remains of pig are found, the exception being Maa *Palaeokastro* (about 10%), which also shows a higher frequency (about 20%) of fallow deer (Croft 1988: 454, table 1). The faunal component at Hala Sultan Tekke includes about 4% deer (Macheridis, in Fischer 2011: 93), more the norm for this period. The high incidence of deer (about 22%) found in a well (TE III) at Kouklia seems to be a special case, and may indicate the dietary preferences of a social élite (Halstead 1977: 261, 271). In the faunal sample from Maa, the unusually high proportion of deer and nearly equal representation of cattle and caprines (about 30%) may suggest more limited landscape clearance in southwest Cyprus than elsewhere (Miksicek 1988: 470), as well as ecological diversity and the ways that people adapted to it (Croft 1988: 453). Both archaeological evidence (Schwartz 1973: 218) and the musings of a classical author indicate that deer were hunted well into the 1st millennium BC: Aelian (*De Natura Animalium* 11.7) refers to the 'multitude' of deer and the popularity of hunting them, as well as their tendency to seek refuge in the temple of Apollo at Kourion (Stanley Price and Frankel n.d.).

In addition to the crucial role they played in the subsistence economy, animals would also have been consumed as part of feasting, rituals and mortuary practices. In other words, we need to keep in mind the possible ceremonial and symbolic significance of sheep, goat and cattle. During the ProBA, we lack evidence for the kind of large animal sacrifices associated with ritual feasting that took place during the PreBA, or Late Chalcolithic (Keswani 1994: 259; Webb and Frankel 2010: 195–198); nonetheless faunal remains do indicate that feasting continued to play some role in ProBA mortuary rituals. For example, sheep, goat and deer were recovered from various contexts at *Toumba tou Skourou* along with ash and charcoal (Vermeule and Wolsky 1990: 169, 245). Moreover, notable faunal components have been found in 'sanctuary' areas at Enkomi, Kition and Myrtou *Pigadhes* (Webb 1999: 44–53). In and around the well-known 'horns of consecration' from *Pigadhes*, for example, the antlers of at least 41 fallow deer were recovered, perhaps the remnants of ceremonial activities that included feasting (Zeuner in Du Plat Taylor 1957: 97–101; Webb 1999: 47, 53, 250–252). If ever we are to understand how all these differing faunal configurations reflect either élite or other dietary preferences, or how diverse ideologies affected feasting for the living or provisioning for the dead, we need a thorough and detailed contextual analysis of faunal evidence from the ProBA. Nonetheless it seems clear that the urban-oriented economy of this era necessitated system(s) of production and social reproduction that were flexible enough to feed and support all the specialists who formed key components of that economy.

In discussing the archaeobotanical evidence, terminology is crucial. Here, I follow Nesbitt (2002: 115) in defining 'cultivation' as the sowing and harvesting of wild plants, and 'domestication' as the repeated sowing and harvesting of the same (domesticated) cereals (see also Wasse 2007: 51–52). As is the case with animal domestication, much recent work recognises plant domestication as an extended process, a prolonged period of time when people would have manipulated morphologically wild but possibly cultivated plants that, in some cases, ultimately resulted in the development of 'domesticated', morphologically altered crops (Nesbitt 2002; Willcox 2002; Peters et al. 2005; Weiss et al. 2006). Fuller et al. (2010) discuss two alternative hypotheses about pathways to domestication: (1) gradual evolution with low selection pressure and (2) 'metastable equilibrium' that prolonged the persistence of 'semi-domesticated' crops. In their view, crop domestication included several distinct but entangled processes, some of which had inevitable consequences for interactions between people and proto-cultigens.

Considering this proposition with respect to Cyprus is suggestive. Recent finds of cereal grains (einkorn and emmer wheat, hulled barley) in EAN 1 levels at Kissonerga *Mylouthkia*, and of (*pisé* impressions of) wild barley, einkorn and emmer wheat at contemporary Parekklisha *Shillourokambos*, underscore the likelihood that cultivated if not domesticated plants, and domesticated animals, were brought to Cyprus by the island's earliest settlers from somewhere in the eastern Mediterranean (Willcox 2000; 2003; Murray 2003: 63–65; Colledge 2004: 53–55). In the nearly contemporary PPNA Levant (9700–8500 Cal BC) (Kuijt and Goring Morris 2002: 386, table 1; Bar-Yosef 2001: 131, fig. 1, 140), moreover, it is argued that the first domesticated crops appeared soon after initial experiments with cultivation had occurred. These domesticates, however, only become common in Levantine (and Anatolian) sites during the following early PPNB era (8500–8100 Cal BC) (Kuijt and Goring Morris 2002: 386, table 1; Nesbitt 2002: 121–124; Colledge 2004: 50).

Emmer wheat, barley and einkorn wheat, in that order of importance, form part of what Zohary (1996: 143–144) defined as the 'founder crops' of southwest Asian agriculture, along with lentil, pea, chickpea, bitter vetch and flax. Lentil and vetch, at least, were also recovered from EAN Kissonerga *Mylouthkia*, along with grass pea, fig, grape and pistachio (Murray in Peltenburg et al. 2001b: 72, table 4). Although the wild progenitor of domestic barley is held to be an endemic species on Cyprus (Meikle 1985: 1834), the wild relatives of emmer and einkorn wheat are not, at least according to the evidence of early botanical surveys carried out on the island (refs. and discussion by Murray, in Peltenburg et al. 2001b: 71; see also Willcox 2003: 234–235).

At this stage, the impressions in *pisé* of wild barley and einkorn/emmer wheat from *Shillourokambos* (Willcox 2000) do not add much to the more abundant evidence from *Mylouthkia*. Both sources of data nonetheless suggest that the agricultural practices so well known from the Late Aceramic Neolithic (beginning ca. 7000/6800 Cal BC) may already have been established on Cyprus well over a millennium earlier. Moreover, if Zohary (1996: 155–156) is correct in arguing that the development of grain agriculture in southwest Asia stemmed from a single (or at most a few) domestication event(s) (cf. Willcox 1999; Nesbitt 2002: 123), then the earliest permanent settlers of Cyprus must have brought domesticated forms of emmer and einkorn wheat and hulled barley with them.

Hansen's (2001) analysis of Late Aceramic Neolithic plant remains from Cape Andreas *Kastros*, Khirokitia *Vouni*, Kalavasos *Tenta* and Kholetria *Ortos* led her to conclude that, because all these species are also found in contemporary sites throughout Turkey and the Levant, no particular point of origin for the earliest settlers could be posited on the basis of floral data alone. Willcox (2003: 236), by contrast, argues pointedly that southeast Anatolia is the only area that reveals both palaeobotanical and DNA evidence for the same combination of cereals that make up the composite EAN sample from Cyprus. It must be countered, however, that just as Davis (2003: 260–261; following Zeuner 1958) has shown how the *Dama Mesopotamica* found in the earliest EAN 1 levels on Cyprus must have derived from a population inhabiting an area that extended from southeast Anatolia through the upper Euphrates region to the southern Levant, it is equally possible, indeed probable, that the palaeobotanical remains did too (Zeder 2009: 29–33). As presented in full detail in Chapter 3 (*Early Aceramic Neolithic: The First Settlers*), the full corpus of material evidence points to a (northern) Levantine source for Cyprus's earliest permanent settlers, a source that need not exclude southeast Anatolia.

Hansen (1991) also summarised prehistoric plant usage throughout the early prehistoric (Neolithic–Late Chalcolithic) and Bronze Age periods. From Aceramic Neolithic levels at Khirokitia, Kalavasos *Tenta*, Cape Andreas *Kastros* and Dhali *Agridhi*, the domesticated cereals included einkorn and emmer wheat, and hulled barley. Legumes such as lentil, peas, horse bean and vetch supplemented these cereal plants, as did olive and flax, and (wild) fruits such as fig, pistachio, plum, pear and grape, the last found only at Dhali *Agridhi* (Hansen 1991: 233–234; Murray 2003: 69, table 7.5). Breadwheat first appears on the island during the Ceramic Neolithic (only at Ayios Epiktitos *Vrysi*) and continues to be found in the Chalcolithic, along with six-row hulled barley (Lemba *Lakkous*) (Hansen 1991: 234). The charred plant remains from three pits at Chalcolithic Kissonerga *Mylouthkia* were dominated by hulled barley, emmer and einkorn wheat, while the pulses were mainly lentils, with very small numbers of chickpea, pea and bitter vetch (Colledge 2003: 239–240, table 21.1). At the same time, the people of Chalcolithic Cyprus continued to exploit wild plants such as olive, flax, fig, grape and pistachio.

Most of the plants used during earlier prehistoric periods are also found at several Bronze Age sites (Knapp 1994: 283–287; Adams and Simmons 1996b: 225–226). The body of palaeobotanical evidence from the Prehistoric Bronze Age (PreBA), previously quite limited, has now been supplemented by the work of Adams and Simmons (1996) on the remains from Marki *Alonia*, and by that of Hansen (2003) at Sotira *Kaminoudhia*. The plants used or exploited during the PreBA remain much the same as before, and in fact demonstrate that the same species were exploited continuously throughout the Mediterranean, from the Neolithic period through the classical era (Hansen 1988). At PreBA Marki *Alonia* and Sotira *Kaminoudhia*, these include emmer wheat and barley for cereals; lentil, chickpea and pea for the pulses; and fig, almond, pistachio, grape, pear (one example) and olive for the fruits. The remains of both the grape and olive are too limited or fragmentary to determine if they were still of the wild varieties.

From the subsequent Protohistoric Bronze Age (ProBA), six sites have produced palaeobotanical remains: Episkopi *Phaneromeni*, Enkomi, Kalopsidha,
Apliki *Karamallos*, Kalavasos *Ayios Dhimitrios* and Hala Sultan Tekke *Vyzakia*.
These remains include cereals (breadwheat, emmer, naked and hulled barley),
pulses (especially lentils) and olives, all of which were domesticated. A variety
of fruits (grape, fig, pomegranate, citrus) and nuts (almonds, hazel, pistachio)
were frequently exploited (Knapp 1994: 283–286, with full refs.). Again it is
evident that virtually all of these grains, pulses and fruits (excepting hazel,
pomegranate and citrus) had been exploited during earlier periods on Cyprus.
The *Pistacia terebinthus* recovered from the Uluburun wreck deposit, in some
quantity, could well have been used for its resin (Haldane 1990); the pistachio
found at Hala Sultan Tekke and Kalopsidha (Helbaek 1966; Hjelmqvist 1979:
112–113) may have served a similar purpose.

Nothing in the palaeobotanical record of ProBA Cyprus reveals anything
unexpected in an agro-pastoral economy. Cereals and pulses provided one type
of staple in the diet, while caprines and cattle provided both meat and secondary products (traction, milk, wool). Fallow deer and, in some cases, pig offered
supplementary protein, although in one case (Kouklia) it may have served to
feed an economically privileged class. In addition to cattle, equids (horses, donkeys) would also have been used as draught animals.

Supplementary evidence related to ProBA plant production and consumption comes from survey work at agricultural villages like Analiondas *Paleoklichia*
and Aredhiou *Vouppes*, both littered with *pithos* (storage jar) sherds and groundstone implements (Webb and Frankel 1994; Knapp 2003: 572–573; Steel and
Janes 2005: 234–237; Steel and McCartney 2008). Episkopi *Phaneromeni* is also
awash with querns, rubbing stones, pounders and grinders (Swiny 1986a: 5–10,
21–24). At Maroni *Vournes*, an olive-oil press from the Ashlar Building was
situated in context with burnt faunal remains and olive pips (Cadogan 1987:
83–84), several large *pithoi* and stands for others. Two walls at the rear of the
Ashlar Building had built-in stone drains designed to move liquids (olive oil?)
from the inside out. Excavations at neighbouring Kalavasos *Ayios Dhimitrios*
produced a large, stone tank used for olive-oil processing, in Building XI
(South 1992: 135–139), and another, similar tank in Building X (South 1997:
154). Building X housed an impressive hall containing some 50 massive, terracotta *pithoi* that could have held up to 50,000 kg of olive oil (Keswani 1992).
At Alassa *Paleotaverna*, a spacious storage area in the massive ashlar Building II
(Hadjisavvas 2003: 31–32, figs. 3 and 4; 2009: 130) held at least 16 enormous
pithoi and stone bases for others, as well as a storage cellar containing four more
pithoi on stone bases. Building III to the east also contained large numbers of
pithos fragments, a long narrow room reminiscent of storage magazines, and an
olive-oil (or grape-crushing?) press (Steel 2003–04: 96–97). Olive oil production is also attested by facilities at Myrtou *Pigadhes*, Episkopi *Bamboula*, Kition,
Enkomi, Apliki and Hala Sultan Tekke (Hadjisavvas 1992: 21–25).

Having presented a picture of Cyprus's landscape, environment and climate on the basis of the evidence currently available, and with an overview in hand of the plants and animals that formed the insular subsistence basis for the people of prehistoric and protohistoric Cyprus, I turn now to consider in detail the chronological framework, archaeological background and interpretative contexts that bracket and guide the remainder of this book.

CHAPTER 2

CHRONOLOGY, CURRENT RESEARCH AND INTERPRETATIVE CONTEXT

BACKGROUND

Archaeological fieldwork on Cyprus has been underway since the 1860s. Its earliest practitioners, however, most notoriously Luigi Palma di Cesnola (1877) and his brother Alexander Palma di Cesnola (1882), were often diplomats or soldiers who had developed an abiding taste for the antiquarian, and the profits that came from selling them. Another well-known antiquarian, the Scot Robert Hamilton Lang, was a businessman who in 1863 became the manager of the Imperial Ottoman Bank in Larnaca. Amongst his multiple outside interests and through his contacts with foreign consuls on the island (including Luigi Palma di Cesnola), Lang developed a genuine interest in the Cypriot past and collected antiquities rapaciously. In 1870 he bequeathed his substantial collection to the Glasgow Art Gallery and Museum (now the Kelvingrove Museum and Art Gallery), where it remains to this day, largely under wraps. Men such as these left Cypriot archaeology with a decidedly chequered pedigree (Goring 1988), and in the process helped to fill museum coffers in London, Glasgow, Cambridge, Stockholm, Paris and New York (to name a few) with vast amounts of Cypriot pottery, sculptures, metalwork and other minor arts, almost exclusively from tombs.

When in 1878 Cyprus came under British administrative control, a full ban was imposed on 'unauthorised' excavation, marking the close of what Myres called 'the mythical age of Cypriot archaeology' (Myres and Ohnefalsch-Richter 1899: vi–vii). Within a decade, the British High Commissioner had resolved to provide permits only to archaeologists associated with accredited public or scientific bodies. These included mainly British institutions, such as the British School at Athens, the Society for the Promotion of Hellenic Studies and Cambridge University, which together formed the Cyprus Exploration Fund that supported work at Paphos, Marion and Salamis (1887–1889). The British Museum also organised expeditions to excavate the necropolis at Enkomi (1896), and several other tombs at Kourion (1895) and Maroni (1897)

Figure 3. 771 boxes of antiquities excavated by the Swedish Cyprus Expedition, on docks at Famagusta awaiting shipment to Stockholm, March 1931. Courtesy of the Medelhavsmuseet, Stockholm, Sweden.

(Murray et al. 1900). Although these projects produced meagre scientific results, they provided yet another harvest of Cypriot gold, bronze and ivory objects, as well as Mycenaean pottery, for the British Museum (Karageorghis 1987: 4).

After the unrestrained plunderings of the 19th century, early 20th-century fieldwork and research gave way to a more stable and 'scientific' approach (Myres and Ohnefalsch-Richter 1899; Myres 1914). Even then, however, the 12,000 or so finds culled by the Swedish Cyprus Expedition (SCE) from its work all over the island between 1927 and 1931 – packed in 771 boxes seen in Figure 3 standing on the docks at Famagusta ready for shipment to Stockholm (Karageorghis et al. 2003: 23; Houby-Nielsen and Sleg 2005: 14–15, fig. 5) – underscore the scale on which the antiquities of Cyprus continued to leave the island.

The fieldwork and research of the SCE under Einar Gjerstad set a pattern for the culture-historical approach, established the existence of the Neolithic period, set up a working relative chronology for the Bronze Age and helped to illustrate the mortuary richness of the Iron Age (Gjerstad 1926; Gjerstad et al. 1934). Moreover, the work of the SCE helped to situate the archaeology of Cyprus within its Mediterranean (especially Aegean) and Near Eastern context. Gjerstad's Swedish colleagues, Sjöqvist (1940) and Furumark (1944), produced key works on the island's history and material culture, especially

its pottery. Both scholars used detailed typological, chronological and dis-
tributional analyses of Mycenaean or Mycenaean-style pottery in Cyprus to
elaborate on historical relations between the Aegean, the Levant and Cyprus.
Furumark went on to begin excavations at the Late Bronze Age site of Sinda
(Furumark 1965; Furumark and Adelman 2003). Ultimately, the cloak of the
SCE passed to Paul Åström, who continued to publish the pottery-based volumes of the SCE (e.g. Åström 1972; Åström and Åström 1972) and who eventually undertook excavations at the Bronze Age sites of Kalopsidha (Åström
1966) and Hala Sultan Tekke (Åström et al. 1976). With Professor Åström's passing (4 October 2008), Peter M. Fischer became the director of the SCE and is
continuing Åström's excavations at Hala Sultan Tekke *Vyzakia* (Fischer 2011).

In 1935, the (British) government of Cyprus established the Antiquities Law
and created the Cypriot Department of Antiquities, thereafter responsible for
all archaeological activity – excavations, sites, monuments and museums –
throughout the island. The first Director of Antiquities was A. H. S. ('Peter')
Megaw, a Dubliner trained at Cambridge who specialised in the Byzantine
and Medieval periods; he held the post from 1936 to 1960. The Curator of the
Cyprus Museum from 1931 to 1960 was a native Cypriote, Porphyrios Dikaios,
whose best-known work concentrated on the Neolithic and Bronze Ages; he
served as Director of the Cyprus Museum from 1960 to 1963.

The 'scientific' approach to fieldwork embraced by the SCE was adopted in
excavations undertaken by the French at Enkomi (under Claude Schaeffer –
1936; 1952); the Australians at Vounous (under James Stewart – Stewart
and Stewart 1950; Stewart 1962); the British at Myrtou *Pigadhes* and Apliki
Karamallos (under Joan Du Plat Taylor – 1952; 1957) and at Palaipaphos (under
Terence Mitford – Mitford and Iliffe 1951); the Americans at Kourion (under
George McFadden – 1946; Benson 1972); and the French at Paphos (under Jean
Bérard and Jean Deshayes – Deshayes 1963). Dikaios led major excavations
at Aceramic Neolithic Khirokitia *Vouni* (1953a), Ceramic Neolithic Sotira
Teppes (1961), Chalcolithic Erimi *Pamboules* (1936), Early Bronze Age Vounous
Bellapais (1940) and Late Bronze Age Enkomi *Ayios Iakovos* (1969–1971). Most
of the foreign expeditions (except Schaeffer's) conducted their work in cemeteries, not least because the 1935 Antiquities Law granted them a 50% share of
the finds, thus enabling expedition directors to fulfil obligations to the museums and other institutions that supported them (Karageorghis 1987: 7).

Beginning in 1952, the Department of Antiquities, under Megaw's director-
ship, embarked on a major programme of excavations at the Graeco-Roman
and early Christian site of Salamis. The excavations were overseen by two new
Assistant Curators of Antiquities, both Cypriotes: Andreas Dikigoropoulos
and Vassos Karageorghis. Karageorghis uncovered the theatre, gymnasium and
several other public buildings, partly restoring them, and in so doing made
Salamis one of the island's best-known archaeological sites (Karageorghis
1969; 1999a). Later excavations (begun in 1962) by Karageorghis in the Iron

Age necropolis of Salamis – with its famous 'royal' tombs – uncovered some of the finest known examples of Cypriot art, and ultimately led to the publication of four massive volumes on this cemetery. Karageorghis became the Director of the Department of Antiquities in 1963, a post he held until his retirement in 1989. During this time, he directed major excavations at Kition, Maa *Palaeokastro*, Pyla *Kokkinokremos*, Palaipaphos *Skales*, Gastria *Alaas* and several others. Following the 1950s, fieldwork by other Cypriote archaeologists has made multiple and impressive contributions to the field, far too numerous to mention here, but we will encounter them frequently throughout this volume.

As Director of the Department of Antiquities, Karageorghis opened up fieldwork on the island during the late 1960s and early 1970s to a number of foreign missions: American teams at Idalion (Stager et al. 1974; Stager and Walker 1989), Morphou *Toumba tou Skourou* (Vermeule and Wolsky 1990) and Phlamoudhi (Al-Radi 1983; Smith 2008a). There were French missions at Enkomi (Schaeffer 1971) and Salamis, the latter working alongside Karageorghis (*Salamine de Chypre* – 16 volumes thus far with various authors); a German team at Tamassos (Buchholz and Untiedt 1996) and a German–Swiss mission at Palaipaphos (Maier and Karageorghis 1984); an Italian team at Ayia Irini near Morphou (Pecorella 1977); an Israeli project at Athienou (Dothan and Ben-Tor 1983); and a Swedish mission at Hala Sultan Tekke (e.g. Åström et al. 1989; 2001; Fischer 2011). By the 1970s, the multidisciplinary approach of British and French prehistorians had added a 'processual' dimension to the archaeology of Cyprus (e.g. Le Brun 1981; Peltenburg 1982; Peltenburg et al. 1985; Todd 1987). Combined with a rigorously developed survey methodology (e.g. Stanley Price 1979a; Todd 2004), these new excavations increasingly brought the prehistoric archaeology of Cyprus to the attention of archaeologists working elsewhere in the Mediterranean and, indeed, around the world.

Before the initiation of regionally oriented projects on Cyprus, survey methodology was extensive and non-systematic in approach, and oriented to the site. Catling's pioneering fieldwork on the Cyprus Survey (1955–1959), for example, resulted in a long list of Bronze Age settlements still widely used in studying the settlement patterns of that era (Catling 1962). The nature of Catling's fieldwork nonetheless left many gaps in the island-wide record, making it difficult to address the kinds of diachronic, problem-oriented questions pursued by recent, more intensive survey projects. The work of the Archaeological Survey branch of the Cypriot Department of Antiquities, established in 1960, has of necessity concentrated on rescue operations rather than on actual field survey. Once Catling's fieldwork ended, therefore, systematic survey became the responsibility of foreign expeditions, but typically was restricted to examining areas surrounding site excavations (Stanley Price 1979a: 53–54).

In contrast, Merrillees (1973) and Swiny (1981) concerned themselves with the location and function of (Bronze Age) sites in the landscape, and with

TABLE 1. *Recent (post-1980) excavation sites on Cyprus and main publications*

Akrotiri *Aetokremnos*	Simmons (1999)
Paraklessia *Shillourokambos*	Guilaine et al. (2011)
Kissonerga *Mylouthkia*	Peltenburg et al. (2003)
Kritou Marottou *Ais Girokis*	Simmons (2003b; 2005; 2010)
Kissonerga *Mosphilia*	Peltenburg et al. (1998)
Kalavasos *Ayious*	Todd and Croft (2004)
Marki *Alonia*	Frankel and Webb (1996; 2006a)
Sotira *Kaminoudhia*	Swiny et al. (2003)
Pyla *Kokkinokremmos*	Karageorghis and Demas (1984)
Kition	Karageorghis and Demas (1985); Karageorghis (2005)
Maa *Palaekastro*	Karageorghis and Demas (1988)
Maroni *Tsaroukkas*	Manning (1998a); Manning et al. (2002)
Alassa *Pano Mandilares, Paleotaverna*	Hadjisavvas (1989; 1996; 2003)
Kalavasos *Ayios Dhimitrios*	South (1996; 1997); South et al. (1989)
Erimi *Laonin tou Porakou*	Bombardieri et al. (2009); Bombardieri (2010b)
Erimi *Pitharka*	Vassiliou and Stylianou (2004)

their development or abandonment. Such concerns served as a harbinger of new trends in regional survey archaeology, both extensive and intensive, and of fieldwork on a much broader spatial and temporal scope than that of earlier projects (papers in Iacovou 2004 provide an overview). Now commonplace on Cyprus (e.g. Given et al. 2002; Caraher et al. 2005), these projects followed closely the methodology of innovative survey work conducted in the Aegean region throughout the 1980s (e.g. Cherry et al. 1991; Jameson et al. 1994).

Following the 1974 seizure of the northern part of Cyprus by the Turkish army, all archaeological activity in the occupied zone came to an abrupt halt. Some projects were relocated to the southern part of Cyprus (e.g. Lemba Archaeological Project – Peltenburg 1985; new work at Khirokitia *Vouni* – Le Brun 1989a), while new excavations commenced at several sites: (Early) Aceramic Neolithic Kalavasos *Tenta* (Todd 2005); several Bronze Age sites, including Alambra *Mouttes* (Coleman et al. 1996), Kalavasos *Ayios Dhimitrios* (South et al. 1989; South 1997), Episkopi *Phaneromeni* (Swiny 1986a) and Maroni *Vournes* (Cadogan 1996); and Iron Age Amathus (Aupert and Hellman 1984; Hermary 1999). Since the 1980s, the number of new excavations and survey projects has increased to the point where it is possible to mention only those that have reached some level of interim or final publication, or else are so crucial for the interpretations presented in this volume that they must be listed (see Table 1, in order of chronological period).

During the 1980s, several culture-historical overviews encapsulated the then-current state of Cypriot archaeology during different periods (e.g. Merrillees 1978; Karageorghis 1982; Peltenburg 1982a; Le Brun et al. 1987). These works were supplemented in the 1990s by further attempts to present updated perspectives on Cypriot prehistory and protohistory (e.g. Held 1992a; Knapp et al. 1994; Papadopoulos 1997 – esp. chapters by Peltenburg and Swiny). More recently, two other volumes have presented comprehensive surveys of the archaeology of prehistoric and protohistoric Cyprus, each in a very distinctive way. Steel (2004a) provides a reasonably up-to-date, theoretically informed overview of Cypriot prehistory, from earliest settlement to the end of the Bronze Age. Bolger (2003) offers a more original contribution to the study of prehistoric Cyprus. She considers the role and pattern of gender relations in prehistoric Cyprus from the Neolithic to the end of the Bronze Age, and looks provocatively at a wide range of data to consider how gendered identities were instituted, realigned and reconstituted over this long period of time. Anyone who seeks a better understanding of the crucial role that gender plays in understanding the Cypriot past will find this work valuable.

THE CHRONOLOGICAL FRAMEWORK

In Mediterranean archaeology generally, and particularly in the Aegean and the east, Thompsen's Three Age system (Rodden 1981) remains the time scheme of choice. In a still-unsurpassed study of the chronological terminology and models employed in Cypriot prehistory, Stanley Price (1979b: 1–4) showed that the early, informal use of the Three Age system (his 'stadial' model) became conflated with a 'phasal' model based primarily on pottery seriation. Characterised by various type-sites (e.g. Khirokitia, Sotira, Erimi), each phase took on chronological significance and was given the status of a temporal period. Thus the Khirokitia Culture came to stand for the Aceramic Neolithic, the Sotira Culture for the Ceramic Neolithic, and the Erimi Culture for the Chalcolithic.

Working with Bronze Age data, Stewart (1962: 208, 210–211) and Catling (1973: 165–166) had realised the practical difficulties of trying to shoehorn all the material into a tripartite scheme. The use of arbitrary criteria to distinguish traditional periods in Cypriot prehistory and protohistory also has created chronological gaps between some of these periods, typically explained by assuming abandonment of the island and/or the introduction of new migrants, invaders or colonists. Moreover, 'transitional eras' are evoked to explain development or change within what is essentially a cultural continuum. Consequently discontinuities in material culture at times become masked or disregarded, or archaeological data are reclassified in the attempt to make them conform to presumed historical events (Kling 1989a: 68–79). The use of these traditional chronological divisions and subdivisions fosters a unilinear approach – increasingly contradicted in most areas of world archaeology – that assumes most material culture was uniform throughout the island, and thus sees depopulation or abandonment whenever a material time marker is absent from a certain region (e.g. Peltenburg 1982a: 99).

None of this is to deny the usefulness of cultural-evolutionary terms (e.g. Neolithic, Chalcolithic, Bronze Age) in establishing sequential periods, or the value of refining relative temporal divisions within those periods (e.g. Early, Middle and Late Cypriot Bronze Age). On Cyprus, all of this has been worked out assiduously over the past century on materials from multiple sites island-wide. Their continued use nevertheless tends to determine how archaeologists understand cultural continuity or change. Spatially or even site-defined material assemblages have been given 'phasal' terms, and their conflation with chronological terms consequently prejudges their chronological position relative to other phases.

The obvious way around this dilemma was to establish an independently based timescale, and thus to avoid the cultural and evolutionary assumptions noted above. Such a timescale would also overcome the stepwise logic transfers inherent in extending and placing any such intra-island relative system against the proto-historically dated cultures of the ancient Western Asia or Egypt. For Cypriot prehistory, the obvious route is via a radiocarbon chronology. This would yield a consistent and common temporal dimension, and so would help to refine the spatial issues (e.g. diverse material assemblages appearing at the same time in different areas of the island) and to resolve some of the terminological confusion. Ultimately it would enable archaeologists working on Cyprus to investigate changes in the material record without resorting to spuriously time-bound definitions (Stanley Price 1979b: 8–9). Earlier discussion of these problems (Held 1989a: 17–21; Knapp 1990a: 148–149; Coleman 1992: 279–288) called for a temporal framework based on calibrated radiocarbon dating as opposed to one using more subjective criteria – primarily stylistic developments in pottery – to fabricate temporal units.

More recently, Manning's work on a range of data from various projects of differing time periods on Cyprus has gone some way towards establishing the chronological schema used in this volume (Table 2; Appendix, Table A2) (e.g. Manning and Swiny 1994; Manning 2001; Manning et al. 2001; Manning and Kuniholm 2007; Manning et al. 2010a). The terminology used in this study for different periods (with traditional phases or cultures also indicated) still leans on the tripartite system so heavily favoured on Cyprus. Nonetheless, my own periodisation seeks to standardise and simplify the use of unwieldy terms (such as Cypro-Early/Middle/Late Pre-Pottery Neolithic B) and at the same time eschews the use of terms such as 'pre-Neolithic' to define a body of material used by fisher-foragers or hunter-gatherers (from sites such as Akrotiri *Aetokremnos*) that – anywhere else in the eastern Mediterranean – would immediately be defined as Late Epipalaeolithic. This is especially the case since material, social and technological developments in the Levantine Late Epipalaeolithic increasingly must take into account what was happening concurrently on Cyprus (Bar-Yosef 2001; Peltenburg 2004b; Watkins 2005; Vigne et al. 2009; Conolly et al. 2011).

The two main divisions of the Bronze Age – Prehistoric Bronze Age (PreBA) and Protohistoric Bronze Age (ProBA) – embrace a wide range of material

TABLE 2. *Chronological schema: Prehistoric and Protohistoric Cyprus (plus Levantine Final Natufian–Pottery Neolithic)*

Periods	Phase/Culture	Dates Cal BC
Late Epipalaeolithic	Akrotiri phase	11,000–9000
Initial Aceramic Neolithic	Cypro-PPNA	9000–8500/8400
Early Aceramic Neolithic (EAN)		8500/8400–6800
	EAN 1 (Cypro-EPPNB)	8500/8400–7900
	EAN 2 (Cypro-MPPNB)	7900–7600
	EAN 3 (Cypro-LPPNB)	7600–7000/6800
Late Aceramic Neolithic (LAN)	Khirokitia	7000/6800–5200
Ceramic Neolithic	Sotira	5200/5000–4500/4000
Chalcolithic	Erimi	4000/3900–2500/2400
	Early Chalcolithic	3900–3600/3400
	Middle Chalcolithic	3600/3400–2700
	Late Chalcolithic	2700–2500/2400
Prehistoric Bronze Age (PreBA)	(Philia–Early/Middle Cypriot)	2400–1700
PreBA 1	Philia 'Phase'	2400/2350–2250
PreBA 1	Early Cypriot I–II	2250–2000
PreBA 2	Early Cypriot III–Middle Cypriot I–II	2000–1750/1700
Protohistoric Bronze Age (ProBA)	(Middle Cypriot III–Late Cypriot IIIA)	
ProBA	(MC III–LC III)	1750/1700–1050
ProBA 1	Middle Cypriot III–Late Cypriot I	1700–1450
ProBA 2	Late Cypriot IIA–IIC early	1450–1300
ProBA 3	Late Cypriot IIC late–IIIA	1300–1125/1100
Early Iron Age	Late Cypriot IIIB	1125/1100–1050 BC
Early Iron Age	Cypro-Geometric I	1050–1000 BC

The Levantine (Cal BC) dates used in this volume follow Kuijt and Goring Morris (2002: 386, table 1):

    Final Natufian   10,500–10,000
    PPNA   9700–8500
    Early PPNB   8500–8100
    Middle PPNB   8100–7250
    Late PPNB   7250–6700
    Final PPNB   6600–6250
    Pottery Neolithic   6250–5800

indicators that call into question the traditional phasing (Early, Middle, Late Cypriot). These phases are based almost entirely on pottery typologies which, in order to accommodate observed reality, in turn end up becoming increasingly unwieldly and problematic as further subdivisions and transitional horizons are defined to try to account for the subtleties observed: e.g. 'LC IIA1' (Crewe 2007a: 213, table 2) or LC IA1-LC IA2 (Manning 2007: 117–118). It would be better to separate the timescale from the material culture, and relate these two different spheres as independent entities, each based on its own criteria.

To the extent possible, the absolute ages used in this study (see Appendix, Tables A1A–A1B, A2) are based on calibrated radiocarbon dates analysed with the IntCal09 ¹⁴C calibration curve (Reimer et al. 2009). Summary details of the analyses are given in the Appendix and full details are available online in the SOM at www.cambridge.org/9780521723473, which will be required reading for anyone who wishes to see the raw data and full information available from the analyses and models run for this study. Recent work has demonstrated that radiocarbon ages for Aegean and east Mediterranean samples may be estimated reliably within very small margins from the standard northern hemisphere record for most periods (Manning et al. 2010b). Other work has shown that careful and appropriate analysis finds an extremely good concordance between calibrated radiocarbon dates and the historical chronology of Egypt (Bronk Ramsey et al. 2010). This has only resulted, however, after some decades with many of the scholars involved expressing concern and making suggestions to the contrary (e.g. Hood 1978; Bietak 2003).

Bronze Age dates also conform closely to Manning's (1999; Bronk Ramsey et al. 2004; 2009) reappraisal and integrated analysis of archaeological, scientific, radiocarbon and dendrochronological data from or related to the Cycladic island of Thera. The high-precision recalibrated dates available for PreBA 2 Cyprus – even if derived from long-lived timbers – tally well with Manning's redating, and indicate that the ProBA 1 period (Middle Cypriot III–Late Cypriot I in conventional terms) began around 1750/1700 Cal BC, well in line with the high traditional chronology proposed for the Cypriot Middle–Late Bronze Ages (Merrillees 1977; 1992b). This same body of hard-won and carefully coordinated data seriously undermines the possibility of using any ultra-low chronology for the eastern Mediterranean or Cyprus (e.g. Åström 1987; 2001; Bietak 2003). More detailed discussion and presentation of the fullest available corpus of radiocarbon dates for prehistoric and early historic Cyprus are presented in the Appendix by Sturt W. Manning: *A New Radiocarbon Chronology for Prehistoric and Protohistoric Cyprus, ca. 11,000–1050 Cal BC.*

THE ARCHAEOLOGY OF CYPRUS IN CONTEXT

Until the 1980s, most archaeologists working on Cyprus had been trained primarily in the fields of Aegean, Levantine or Anatolian archaeology, even if Cyprus formed the core of their archaeological fieldwork and research. The island's often striking material culture – architecture, pottery, statuary and fine arts – was widely regarded as provincial and inferior, especially when compared with Greek art (Karageorghis et al. 1999: x). The same circumstances still lead most scholars to view Cyprus as a bridge or 'crossroads' between east and west (e.g. Karageorghis 1986; 2002a). In turn, cultural development and change are often seen to result from migrations, foreign invasion or else the 'revitalisation' and 'stimulation' from foreign sectors that Catling (1979) thought so crucial for reversing the 'cultural stagnation' that he read into the island's material culture of the early 2nd millennium BC (Middle Cypriot period). The end result is that social, cultural and economic development and change inevitably have become linked to external forces based in scholarly preconceptions that expect to encounter Aegean or Near Eastern cultural influences.

The material culture of Cyprus differs markedly, and during most periods of time, from that of all surrounding regions. Apart from the inevitable migrations that brought Cyprus's earliest settlers to the island at the outset of the Early Aceramic Neolithic, there is limited evidence for foreign contacts until the Bronze Age (Peltenburg et al. 1998: 256–259; cf. Clarke 2007a). Even then, the nature of such contacts remains contentious. I return time and again in this study to consider how and to what extent this perceived isolation was linked to Cyprus's insularity. Although an internal perspective thus is crucial for presenting the prehistory of Cyprus, we can only understand indigenous developments on the island by examining its material record within the wider contexts of the Aegean and eastern Mediterranean worlds.

The continuing use of the culture-historical paradigm in Cypriot archaeology has had further consequences (Antoniadou 2004: chapter 1). With an emphasis on the form, find-spot and chronological setting of artefacts, especially pottery, one overriding goal of archaeology in Cyprus has been to document and explain the historical development of different cultures through considerations of 'style'. Artefact styles are seen to denote historical relationships, while the artefacts themselves are often correlated with different cultures or ethnic groups. Although the aim is to examine developments within and differences between cultures, the end product often can be a thick, historical description of change. Such detailed descriptions are then placed into a broader regional or interregional comparative framework, accommodating particularistic interpretations based on cultural interconnections or on concepts such as migration, colonisation or acculturation. For example, the common occurrence of Late Helladic ('Mycenaean') pottery in final Late Bronze Age contexts is typically regarded as evidence for the migration to, if not the colonisation of Cyprus by an Aegean ethnic group or groups.

The culture-historical paradigm was developed in unusually volatile historical and political circumstances: 35 years under British rule (1925–1960), followed by 14 years of Cypriot independence (1960–1974), and topped off by the Turkish occupation of the northern part of the island (since 1974). During this time, Cypriot identity and its relationship to Cyprus's past were constantly being scrutinised and manipulated, often with respect to the political standards of the (modern) periods involved and the social or political background of each particular archaeologist. Take Casson (1938: v) for example: 'Cyprus is the only British possession which serves to illustrate the history and activities of the Greeks.... I prefer to see the history and the art of Cypriots as those of Oriental Greeks rather than of Hellenised Orientals'. This may seem an extreme example, yet it reveals not only Casson's personal view but also the deeply ingrained tradition of British archaeologists trained in the classics. Their negative attitude towards the Ottoman Empire, and then Turkey, nurtured a long-standing philhellenic bias that has had a tremendous impact on the structure of Cypriot archaeological research (Given 1998), and remains embedded in the archaeology of Cyprus to this day.

This negative view of the culture-historical approach must be offset with the knowledge that a widespread concern for the detailed description, classification and chronological ordering of the Cypriot archaeological record, together with a well-established, at times compulsory tradition of publishing final site reports (cf. Hadjisavvas and Karageorghis 2000), have resulted in a relatively complete (by Mediterranean or Near Eastern standards) publication record of Cypriot sites, and of the island's diverse and eclectic material culture. Several other comparative studies – from Sjöqvist (1940) to Clarke (2005) – are devoted to analysing and interpreting social, cultural and economic relations between Cyprus and the surrounding regions. So, whilst the culture-historical bias remains prominent in Cypriot archaeology, as noted elsewhere it is '... no more so than elsewhere in world archaeology, and no less than is essential for a viable programme of archaeological study and research' (Knapp and Antoniadou 1998: 31).

Politics, Archaeology and Heritage

The politics of Cypriot archaeology must be understood in the context of historical and cultural developments within Europe, the Middle East and the Mediterranean itself over the past two centuries (Meskell 1998a). During this time, as new nation states emerged throughout the region (MacConnell 1989: 107), archaeology slowly developed as an independent discipline. In most countries but to differing degrees, one of its primary aims was to legitimise each nation's independent existence (Diaz-Andreu 1995: 54). In the case of Cyprus, however, independence lay far in the future (1960). Cyprus came under direct British administration in 1878, and in 1883 the British government founded the Cyprus Museum to house its share of finds from excavations. Along with Cyprus's recognition as a Crown Colony in 1925 came a change in the nature of archaeological fieldwork. The Swedish Cyprus Expedition (1927–1931), for example, brought a new (culture-historical) direction to Cypriot archaeology; the island's antiquities, however, continued to be shipped off to foreign museums. As a result, the British colonial authorities finally enacted an Antiquities Law (1935) and established the Cypriot Department of Antiquities. Cypriot archaeology took on a definitive international character between 1935 and 1960, when Cyprus finally gained its independence. Colonial attitudes, however, guaranteed that foreign archaeologists still directed most excavations (note the entries in Åström 1971), despite the active and dedicated role that native Cypriote archaeologists played, and continue to play, in the fieldwork of their island.

Porphyrios Dikaios became the first Cypriote Director of the Department of Antiquities in 1960, following Cyprus's independence. Upon his retirement in 1963, Vassos Karageorghis became Director, and in 1964 the Antiquities Law changed forever the practice of allowing the island's heritage to be removed en masse: 'All antiquities which the holder of a licence … may discover throughout the duration of the excavations shall vest in the Cyprus Museum without any payment whatsoever' (Karageorghis 1985a: 7). While the tremendous effort of Karageorghis over the next decade brought knowledge of and participation in Cypriot archaeology to the international level, the 1974 Turkish invasion and occupation of approximately one-third of the island had a very different, inevitably negative impact on archaeological research (Knapp and Antoniadou 1998).

Archaeological fieldwork in the occupied northern part of the island ended abruptly in July 1974. Archaeological sites became inaccessible, and many Byzantine and later monuments were destroyed, while their icons began to flow into the illicit trade in antiquities. With the notable exception of Turkish Cypriotes, no other archaeologists have any legal status under international law to conduct fieldwork in the occupied northern part of the island. One of these exceptions is Müge Şevketoğlu, who has directed excavation, survey and heritage projects in the north under the aegis of the Department of Antiquities and Museums, Turkish Republic of Northern Cyprus (e.g. Şevketoğlu 2000). Şevketoğlu lectured for many years in the Department of Archaeology and Art History at the Eastern Mediterranean University in Famagusta. She also directs excavations at Akanthou, an Early Aceramic Neolithic site along the northern coast (most recently Şevketoğlu 2008, discussed further in Chapter 3, *Early Aceramic Neolithic: The First Settlers*). For the past 37 years, all other fieldwork and survey carried out on Cyprus have been concentrated in the southern part of the island, a politically imposed reality that has resulted in an archaeological bias (Knapp 1994: 434) affecting any attempt at interpretation, including the present work.

Beyond such biases in archaeological interpretation, this situation reflects a contested cultural reality and a social geography of difference. The cultural heritage of Cyprus is overburdened with popular memory and torn by the struggle of living in a sharply divided political space. The practice of archaeology and the research that stems from it are inevitably constrained by political forces that demand a nationalistic perspective. If there is ever to be any hope of promoting cooperation and establishing workable relations among the island's divided ethnic groups, the cultural heritage of each community must be safeguarded and preserved. In the wider Mediterranean world, the presentation of archaeological sites as cultural attractions (e.g. Hamilakis 2003; Skeates 2005) provides each nation with the opportunity to transcend its colonial past. As heritage constructs, sites such as Emporia in Spain, Pompeii in Italy, Delphi in Greece or Knossos on Crete exert a major influence not just on popular meanings but also on any official sanctions imposed on these meanings. On Cyprus, the situation involves a rather different, cultural translation of a far more distant colonial past (van Dommelen 1997: 306).

> For a nation like the Republic of Cyprus, with its obvious political attachment to images of Greek antiquity, the extensive excavation and presentation of classical cities like Paphos, Kition, and Ammathus [*sic*] are clearly linked to a modern, national self-consciousness. (Silberman 1995: 259)

Those places that do not become part of the national heritage, however, or are denied a role in that heritage because they are inaccessible (i.e. in occupied territory), may take on powerful political roles and come to symbolise struggles over cultural identity. Thus the national heritage has the potential to imbue certain places with symbolic value and to transform them into spaces where local or national identity is defined or contested, where the social order is reproduced or challenged (Jacobs 1996: 35). The heritage enterprise is largely a political process where places such as classical temples or well-preserved towns have become embedded in the nationalistic point of view.

Other places, however, such as Moslem shrines or Turkish cemeteries, are ignored or even desecrated, at least in part because they represent a threat to nationalistic images. There is one very important exception to this situation, namely, the mosque of Umm Haram (Muhammad's 'wet-nurse'), or Hala Sultan Tekke on the outskirts of Larnaca (Figure 4). This compound serves as the main Muslim pilgrimage site on Cyprus and is said to be the third most important holy place of Islam. It is also a listed Ancient Monument with the Cypriot Department of Antiquities. Through funding provided by the United States and the United Nations Development Program (UNDP), the United Nations Office for Project Services (UNOPS) has over the past few years sponsored extensive restoration works at Hala Sultan Tekke as part of a twin project aimed at saving the Tekke and the Greek Orthodox monastery of Apostolos Andreas in the Turkish-occupied area of Cyprus. Both are regarded as key cultural heritage sites in the two different sectors of the country.

In the current, postcolonial mood on Cyprus, the politics that emerge from reconstructing or re-imaging places serve to formulate a local identity through which notions of culture, class or community are established (Jacobs 1996: 2; Papadakis 1998; 2005). In turn, the politics of place and identity become framed within power structures built up around broader geohistorical, colonial residues and postcolonial opportunities. Postcolonial politics necessarily involve places where individual people or international polities express their

Figure 4. The mosque of Hala Sultan Tekke
(Umm Haram), near Larnaca, Cyprus.
Photograph by A. Bernard Knapp.

sense of self and their concept of 'home' – whether native or recently adopted, whether an archaeological site, a village, a region or a nation. On Cyprus, the processes through which the imperial British and the colonial Cypriotes became defined and articulated formed a crucial part of the cultural dimensions of colonialism and postcolonialism.

On Cyprus, the politics of a postcolonial archaeology are both multiple and ambiguous. The division is drawn sharply on the land itself at the 'Green Line' separating north and south, Turkish Cypriotes (as well as forcibly introduced Turkish settlers) and Greek Cypriotes, the Turkish Republic of Northern Cyprus and the Republic of Cyprus. The contrasting ideologies and identities are precisely defined. Although colonial attitudes and policies no longer dictate the orientation of Cypriot archaeology, archaeological practice now forms an important means of cultural representation and political expression. It is unlikely that the archaeology of Cyprus will ever again function outside of its contemporary political and social context (if ever it did). As long as the social identity of Cypriotes remains intricately interlinked to ethnicity and politics, and as long as politics both local and global (the European Union in this case) dictate how some 850,000 people (2006 estimate) live and survive in both regions of the island, the cultural heritage of Cyprus will continue to be formed and reformed according to changing, and opposing, nationalistic trends.

AN INTERPRETATIVE FRAMEWORK

There are many ways that archaeologists, art historians, anthropologists and ancient historians might view and analyse the complex, extensive material

record of Cyprus. In what follows, I discuss some of the interpretative constructs that help to frame the materiality and structure the arguments I present and develop throughout this book. As already noted in the Introduction,
several other theoretical as well as practical issues – seafaring, migration and
colonisation, hybridisation practices, mobility and connectivity, gender and
gendered representations, monumentality, mortuary practices, ritual and ideology – also help to elucidate the meanings of things that typify the material
culture of ancient Cyprus. Most of these theoretical parameters are by now
commonplace in the archaeological literature, and in any case I have discussed
most of them in detail elsewhere (most recently, Knapp 2008: 13–65; 2009a;
2009b; 2010; Knapp and van Dommelen 2008; van Dommelen and Knapp
2010). Time and again I turn to such issues and ideas in order to move beyond
description and classification, and in the attempt to present a social archaeology of prehistoric and protohistoric Cyprus.

Insularity, Identity and Islandscapes

Islands connote insularity, and islandscapes are integral to the study of islands
and islanders everywhere. Island archaeology today forms a well-recognised
subfield of the archaeological discipline. Its origins lie in a series of studies
carried out in the 1970s and 1980s (e.g. Evans 1977; Cherry 1981; Kirch 1986;
Terrell 1986; Keegan and Diamond 1987), inspired by the work of Vayda and
Rappaport (1963) and largely based on biogeographic factors such as dispersal,
adaptation or extinction; isolation and insularity; and size, distance and configuration (Cherry 2004). Rainbird (2004: 1–2, 63; 2007: 33–35) argues that viewing islands in isolation, as 'laboratories', is too restrictive and that the narrow
use of a biogeographic approach is environmentally deterministic (similarly
Terrell et al. 1997). Engaging with biogeographic concepts in the study of
human beings may pose certain problems (Broodbank 2000: 26–32), because
island living involves cultural factors that often outweigh biogeographic prin-
ciples. Nonetheless, the study of islands and insularity would be all the poorer
without the judicious consideration of multiple constraints and possibilities,
including those stemming from biology and the environment.

   To set the basics for presenting an archaeology of Cyprus, we must first ask
what is an island, and how exactly should we understand insularity and islandscapes? Islands may be defined prosaically as land masses smaller than a con-
tinent, entirely surrounded by water (Fitzpatrick 2004: 6), or more spiritedly:
'islands are what they are because they are living spaces (habitats) surrounded
by radical shifts in habitat' (Terrell 1999: 240). Insularity has been described as
'the quality of being isolated as a result of living on islands, or of being somewhat detached in outlook and experience' (Knapp 2008: 18). Yet insularity can
be understood from several different perspectives, and people may adopt it or
adapt to it in several different ways. Insular living, for example, sometimes only

takes place seasonally (Finlayson 2004: 18) or temporarily, as is now thought to be the case for Cyprus's earliest, pre-Neolithic visitors (Ammerman and Noller 2005; Ammerman 2010: 86–88). The concept of an islandscape, finally, incorporates both the physical properties of islands (size, location, configuration, topography) and the 'sufficiently generous' conditions that enabled people to define their surroundings in ways that were meaningful to them (Broodbank 2000: 21).

Islands elicit notions of remoteness, not least because of the journeys it takes to reach them, or the sensation of being in a separate community once there (Renfrew 2004: 275). One need only think of Easter Island or Pitcairn in the Pacific, or of Madeira in the Atlantic, to get a sense of this remoteness, of separate worlds. Not only are islands typically regarded as remote, they are also frequently portrayed as sleepy backwaters, where people of like mind live at a slower pace, closer to the natural order of things (McKechnie 2002: 128). The sea that separates an island from the nearest mainland can be seen as an immense threshold, a bridge or a barrier between what is near and familiar, or what is distant and exotic (Helms 1988: 24–25). Some island societies exhibit what might appear to us as 'strange' or even extreme cultural developments and material expressions, for example the so-called megalithic temples of Malta (Grima 2001; Robb 2001): this is what Parker Pearson (2004: 129) terms the 'Easter Island syndrome'. Strangeness, however, is a relative and subjective term (Rainbird 2004: 4), and what is strange or exotic to a mainlander or even a sailor may be perfectly normal to an islander. Seascapes and islandscapes, moreover, are knowable places, and social attitudes to the sea and to voyaging condition the extent to which islanders are isolated from or connected to the other islands, mainlands and peoples that surround them.

Here we confront a fundamental paradox in island archaeology, what Renfrew (2004: 276) terms the 'polarity … between isolation ("islands as laboratories") and interaction ("islands as reticulate networks")'. The island of Cyprus, as we shall see, reveals these polarities to extremes at different times in its prehistory and early history. Even though islands serve as essentialising metaphors for isolation and singularity, throughout prehistory as well as in historical times they have been exposed repeatedly to wider networks of mobility, interaction and exchange. People often seek out 'exotic' resources or raw materials unique to or readily accessible on certain islands (e.g. copper on Cyprus or Sardinia; iron on Elba; obsidian on Melos or Lipari; marble on Paros or Naxos). Such places not only serve as crucial intersections where seafarers meet and communicate, where long-distance trade is carried out or where island alliances form and develop (Parker Pearson 2004: 129), they also act as places for escape, banishment or even idyllic contemplation.

Horden and Purcell (2000: 76) speak of islands – literal or otherwise, Mediterranean or Pacific – as being 'in the swim' of things. Islands, after all, are surrounded by the sea with its cornucopia of exploitable resources – from salt and other minerals, to shell valuables, to seaweed and fish. Rainbird (2007: 45) goes so far as to make the sea the focal point of island archaeology. If we adopt an islander's perspective, then we must engage not only with dry land (whether wild or inhabited, mountainous or coastal), but also with the seacoast, beaches and harbours, mooring points and the sea itself. The avowedly social focus of island archaeology today, and of this book too, is concerned with the ways that islanders consciously fashion, develop and change their world, including their material world; how they establish, modify and change their identities by inter-acting with other islanders and non-islanders (Fitzpatrick 2004; Rainbird 2004; 2007). We must take care, however, that in seeking to adopt what Rainbird terms an 'archaeology of the sea' – that is, an internal, insular perspective that engages with the lives of mariners and their communities and seeks to temper the notion of isolation – we do not lose sight of the ways that external ideas, ideologies and technologies could affect these islanders' thoughts, actions and well-being. The very survival of some islanders depends on their seafaring abil-ities, on making use of the sea as a highway of communication and intercon-nections with others (Anderson 2004: 263–267; Anderson et al. 2010). During its very earliest prehistory, Cyprus seems to have been visited repeatedly by seafaring foragers, people who relied on their ability to exploit the resources of the sea and its coasts for their very livelihood (Knapp 2010).

Another important point to bear in mind is that on an island the size of Cyprus, with its extensive mountainous areas, there would always have been people who were likely unaware they were 'islanders'. Mountain dwellers not only lived in – and off of – upland resources, they would also have identified with the mountains at least in part as a barrier to the outside world (Braudel 1972: 25–53; McNeill 1992). Upland plains, valleys, forests and other insular pockets impacted on people's lives and identities as much if not more than the fact that they lived on an island. On Cyprus, there have probably always been more people we would describe as farmers, shepherds or hunters rather than as fisherman, or as 'islanders' in the sense of those who dwelt on small islands in the Cyclades or Dodecanese. The mountains, in other words, historically have played at least as crucial a role as the sea in creating Cypriot island identities.

The concept of an 'islandscape' (Broodbank 2000: 22–23) embraces not just the physical diversity of islands (mountains, coasts, plains), but also the diverse ways that islanders perceive both land and sea. Islandscapes may be social-ised symbolically through 'place-myths' to give islanders a sense of belonging (Erdogu 2003), or they may be socialised ritually to transform the open sea into a knowable and manageable space (McNiven and Feldman 2003: 189). An island constitutes one crucial point on a spectrum from which island dwellers construct their world, but it is the sea – with all its manifold impacts on island-ers and island life – that anchors the concept of the islandscape. While main-landers or mountain dwellers typically view the sea as an open, uniform body of water between landfalls, sailors often see it in terms of surface conditions, inshore or offshore currents and wind patterns that facilitate or hinder voy-aging (D'Arcy 1997: 75). For those who live on smaller islands, the concept of the sea revolves around marine and other resources, and their capacity or willingness to exploit them.

For most of human history, the sea served as the only link between island communities and the wider social world, a route of communications where people, products and ideas moved in every direction and in all manner of nautical vessels, from logboats and reed floats to oared vessels and sailing ships (Irwin 1992: 204; Horden and Purcell 2000: 224–230; Ward 2010). To under-stand long-term trends and variations in voyaging, shipping and commerce (Broodbank 2010), we have to engage with diverse perspectives and confront unexplored possibilities: (1) the accessibility of island dwellers to wider systems of production and trade; (2) the social aspirations of merchants, traders and raiders alongside those of migrants or colonists; (3) the technology and use of boats; (4) knowledge of the sea and how to navigate as well as exploit it; and (5) the social impact of distance and the exotic. During the course of Cyprus's prehistory, and particularly during the 3rd and 2nd millennia BC, we shall witness, in both material and documentary things, many of these perspectives and possibilities. On land and at sea, all these factors, whether spatial or social, combine to create islandscapes (Broodbank 2000: 33), even if they do not quite measure up to a phenomenology of 'being in the island world' (Hamilton and Whitehouse 2006).

Social Landscapes

Mediterranean archaeologists have analysed several distinctive types of land-scape – from rural and urban to civic and sacred (Knapp 1997: 21–27). Johnston (1998) suggests that all variations of archaeological landscapes may be classi-fied as either cultural or cognitive (ideational). Tilley (1994: 37) maintains that the 'unstable' concept of landscape falls between these two extremes, while Bender (1998: 8–9) adds more subliminal dimensions – multiple, contested and embodied – to the landscape domain. For many archaeologists today, the notion of a landscape entails diverse social and symbolic elements while phys-ical landscapes are seen to play a dynamic, integral role in human subsistence, and the human experience.

The everyday life of people – their routines and habits, their beliefs and morals – is what constitutes social landscapes. The human factors that give meaning to a landscape and are instrumental in its construction are not pas-sive backdrops for people's practices or performances. Moreover, the dynamic tension that exists between the 'natural' and the social world (Richards 1996: 314) cannot be differentiated into 'real' and 'perceived' landscapes. For anyone who dwells in a space that we term the landscape, these two concepts are indi-visible (Tuan 1977). People perceive the 'real' physical landscape through social and cognitive filters, and the environment becomes manifest as landscape only when people order, experience or transform space as a living place (Knapp and Ashmore 1999: 20–21). The industrial landscapes of Bronze Age Cyprus (Knapp 1999a; Given and Knapp 2003: 301–305), for example, from smelting sites and slag heaps in the foothills and mountains to the final production quarters in the island's coastal ports (Knapp 2003; Knapp and Kassinidou 2008), offer striking witnesses to the ways that the land transforms people, just as people transform their landscape.

The landscapes of prehistory were constructed and experienced by people's ideas and understandings of their world (Bender et al. 1997: 150; David and Thomas 2008). Archaeologists frequently distinguish between the 'constructed' (or built) landscape and the 'conceptualised' (or natural) landscape. The concept of a social ('ideational', 'cognitive') landscape, however, encompasses both of these realms, as well as the range of meaning archaeologists attribute to landscapes. It thus corresponds to Johnston's (1998) notion of the inherent, where landscapes are imbricated in people's lives, practices and actions. Social landscapes, in other words, are intimately associated with 'landscapes of the mind' (Knapp and Ashmore 1999: 12–13), which may involve a mental image of something (imaginative aspect) or else convey some spiritual value or ideal (emotional aspect). Social landscapes may recount or recall oral or mythic histories, keep track of genealogies, even elicit personal emotions or moral messages. They embrace sacred, symbolic, ideational and other meanings associated with and embodied in landscapes.

Most archaeologists working on Cyprus assume, implicitly or explicitly, that social power and authority were embedded in the construction or elaboration of monumental structures in urban centres (Knapp 2009b). Notions of ideology and authority extending from the Chalcolithic through the Late Cypriot periods, for example, revolve around everything from building models (Peltenburg 1994) to monumental structures typically seen as temples or the Cypriot equivalent of Aegean or Near Eastern palaces (Fisher 2006; 2009). Indeed, there is good reason to support such interpretations of the social landscape (Knapp 2008: 206–211), but in so doing we should not ignore the social and symbolic value of special places in rural or mountainous settings, or elsewhere in the non-built landscape. Natural features such as forests and mountains, caves, rivers and streams are also laden with social meaning and embedded in social practices and experience (Taçon 1999). I have argued elsewhere (Knapp 1996a) that the social landscape of prehistoric Cyprus, at least during the Bronze Age, was closely linked to mineral resources (especially copper), to the industrial activities associated with their exploitation and production, and to the élites who sought control over the consumption and distribution of these resources.

The way that people's social identity is bound up with their landscape is not confined to a single moment in time. Rather it is expressed and contained

Figure 5. Modern spoil heap of *Kokkinopezoula* near Mitsero. Photograph by A. Bernard Knapp.

within memory, through history and in the continuities and changes that people perceive. Most of the older people who live in the modern Cypriot village of Mitsero, for example, remember clearly their recent mining past, and are cognisant of the labour and travails of an older population of mineworkers. Indeed, any resident of the village, or even those passing by it, would find it difficult to overlook the modern spoil heaps and ancient slag heaps on the edge of the village (Figure 5). The mining and production of metals has always had profound social implications that not only restructured or altered people's lives but also made indelible impacts on the natural landscape. In the increasingly interconnected world that made up the eastern Mediterranean from the early 3rd millennium BC onward (Webb et al. 2006; Peltenburg 2007a; Broodbank 2009: 692–701), the interplay of socio-economic forces with landscape and resource diversity configured the mechanisms of shipping and commerce, promoted the emergence and divergence of political regimes, shaped sociopolitical ideologies, helped to implement the spread of religious doctrines and directly impacted on the ever-changing face of the landscape.

Archaeologists face a major challenge in attempting to reconstruct prehistoric or historical landscapes. In this study, the landscape is regarded as both cultural and cognitive: it plays an active role in the formation, maintenance and reconfiguration of place. As people create or modify places in the landscape, they may also refine or even redefine their identity. The articulation between (individual or collective) identity and landscape can help us to understand better the social dynamics through which people maintained or changed their livelihoods, adjusted their social relations to new technologies and practices or reoriented themselves to new and different aspects of village or town life. People use their landscapes for everything from producing food to expressing formal design to making social statements. The material record they leave behind – industrial or habitational features, the tools and artefacts of daily practices, utilitarian or prestige goods – bears witness to the social relations that developed in their community or polity, and provides clues to their social identity.

Identity, Community and Polity

Social identity has been defined as the knowledge, value and significance attached to membership in a social group (Hall 1997: 30). Although identity is often (mis-)used as a synonym for ethnicity, the former embraces a much broader category within which there are more specific elements: age, sexuality, class and gender as well as ethnicity. An islander's identity, like anyone else's, is fluid and contingent upon specific situations, something that may be embraced or rejected along with what one wishes to say about one's self, or how one wishes to be seen by others. The identities of islanders are fashioned and developed locally, and thus are intimately linked to a particular 'sense of place' (Feld and Basso 1996), typically at the level of the community. Communities, which form the social counterpart of physical settlements, then become places of memory, especially as identities are imagined or created anew (Mills 2004: 11). But identity does not simply develop as a by-product of belonging to a community, nor do social groups or individuals ever 'possess' identity. Rather communities express what Gupta and Ferguson (1997: 13) term a 'categorical identity', based on various types of exclusion, difference and constructs of the other.

In the social sciences, a community was originally seen as a natural territorial unit of human organisation, populated by people who share residence or space, and who bear a collective consciousness, knowledge and experiences. Such a community was regarded as a fundamental, internally coherent and externally bounded social institution, in which all social, cultural and biological reproduction occurred (e.g. Steward 1950; Redfield 1955; Arensberg 1954). Nowadays, communities are viewed as dynamic and historically contingent, even imagined entities (Anderson 1991; Isbell 2000). Of necessity, the members of any individual community will be involved in diverse social relations that structure and define the community's nature, its economic base and its political discourses – whether within or beyond the community (e.g. Urban 1996; Low 2000; Ashmore 2003).

Like social scientists, most archaeologists working with the concept of community today do not assume any degree of solidarity or homogeneity within a community. Instead, they examine the wider social configuration as well as the individual people who make up the community (e.g. various papers in Canuto and Yaeger 2000; Meskell 2002a). The imagined community of miners and metalworkers at the ProBA site of Politko *Phorades* on Cyprus, for example, cannot have been self-sufficient: rather they formed part of a wider, regional community, and were either reliant upon or, more likely, part of an agricultural community nearby that fulfilled other, social and subsistence needs (Knapp 2003). Communities, then, are social constructs, not necessarily tied to any specific place; they provide an important source of identity for their inhabitants (Yaeger 2000: 124).

The term polity (from Greek πολιτεία) originally referred to those classical Greek city-states whose political process involved an assembly of (adult male) citizens that formed small communities of kinship, or cult or locality. Today it refers generally to the political organisation of any social group or community, and archaeologists tend to use it when referring to any and every sociopolitical grouping, but usually at a level above the community. Thus it might refer to a political or cultural faction, a specific region or territory with a coherent political organisation, a state or even an empire. Islands might constitute a single polity (e.g. Cyprus in the Late Bronze Age) or there may be several polities within a single island (e.g. the different 'palatial' centres on Minoan Crete).

When it comes to establishing island identities, what we might see as the logical ordering of distance, or difference, comes face-to-face with other experiences and currents of imagination (McKechnie 2002: 128). On contemporary Cyprus, for example, there are people who regard themselves not just as Greeks (mainlanders) but as Greek, Turkish or Maronite Cypriotes (islanders); as enforced settlers or soldiers from Turkey (mainlanders); as villagers or urban dwellers, or both (islanders); and, finally, as foreign residents, be they expatriate mainlanders (e.g. Europeans and Lebanese) or servile islanders (e.g. Sri Lankans and Filipinos). Given the myriad Greek, Roman, Byzantine, Islamic, Venetian, Genoese, Ottoman and other conquerors or settlers who have came and gone over the past 2,500 years, it seems futile to attempt to isolate a single, contemporary Cypriot identity.

In the same vein, we might consider contemporary Cypriot cuisine. Although the current political and cultural milieux on the island might lead us to expect similarities with Greek cooking, the Cypriot menu is modelled more closely on the culinary traditions of Turkey, Lebanon and Egypt, whence came lemons, aubergines and rice, or spices such as coriander, cumin and chillis – all now traditional staples of most Mediterranean diets (Abulafia 2003). Here we have a case in which a specific (Cypriot) cuisine, one aspect of an islander's identity, has been adopted over time by people who are well aware of others' foodstuffs, but who have chosen only these features that suit them, their social circumstances or their environmental niche (Broodbank 2000: 20).

From these modern examples, we can understand that identity may be marked – at least in part – through *difference*. The concept of difference, more-over, is crucial in creating distinctive settings for human action, and distinctive human actions are those that we may be able to perceive in the archaeological record. To take some archaeological examples, consider first the (likely domes-ticated) cattle that arrived on Cyprus during the 10th millennium Cal BC along with its earliest permanent settlers (discussed in Chapter 1). Cattle were no longer kept after the Aceramic Neolithic and, unlike mainland sites, were largely replaced by deer as a staple in the island's diet (Croft 2002). They were only reintroduced to Cyprus as a domestic species nearly 5,000 years later, dur-ing the Bronze Age (Croft 1991). During the same Aceramic Neolithic period, the production of pottery as practised in the Levantine or Anatolian Neolithic was never taken up concurrently on Cyprus, where the islanders instead used stone bowls or (presumably) woven baskets for similar purposes (Stanley Price 1977a). Clarke (2003; 2007: 100–105), to take a final example, maintains that the variable styles of decorated pottery used during the Ceramic Neolithic on Cyprus demarcate regional differences if not distinctive regional identities.

In the chapters that follow, I draw upon several of these theoretical issues and interpretative themes to present the archaeology and early history of Cyprus, from its first-known exploitation in the Late Epipalaeolithic through the end of the Bronze Age. Invoking these ideas, I examine the archaeological and documentary records of or related to Cyprus, analysing them in chrono-logical sequence but eschewing a traditional cultural history. At all times, the material and documentary witnesses to Cyprus's past are discussed in their regional context, in particular with respect to the contemporary Levant and Aegean. Using historical documents to re-present the material sequence from the Middle Bronze through the end of the Late Bronze Age, this study also provides an integrated archaeological and sociohistorical synthesis of human presence and human activity on the Mediterranean's third largest island.

CHAPTER 3

EARLY PREHISTORIC CYPRUS 1: PALAEOLITHIC–EARLY ACERAMIC NEOLITHIC

THE CONTESTED PALAEOLITHIC

In an early review of fieldwork on prehistoric Cyprus, including his own, Schaeffer (1936: 1) commented that 'le paléolithique de Chypre est encore *terra incognita*'. Nearly half a century later, in what became a standard reference work on the archaeology of Cyprus, Karageorghis (1982: 16) dismissed the Palaeolithic in one sentence: 'Attempts to identify flints in the Kyrenia district near the north coast as Palaeolithic have failed'. Karageorghis was referring to two studies, only one of which was concerned with the Kyrenia region. Stockton (1968), in a casual search for 'Stone Age remains' at three locations east and west of Kyrenia village, identified a series of tools and waste flakes – scrapers, knives, backed flake tools, thumbnail scrapers and some possible microliths – as possibly belonging to the 'early Upper Palaeolithic'. The other work Karageorghis cited was by Vita-Finzi (1973), who mentions and illustrates five artefacts found (a) on a fossil beach near the mouth of the 'Moronou River' (probably the Potamos tou Ayiou Mina), east of Zygi, on the south central coast of Cyprus, and (b) within a red clayey silt into which the river is incised. The material was dated very tentatively by its (relative) geological context to the Middle Palaeolithic.

At least two further claims have been made for possible Palaeolithic evidence from the island. First are some reputed Middle Palaeolithic chipped stone assemblages found during survey work, eroding from gravels in the Khrysokou River drainage on the Akamas peninsula in northwest Cyprus (Adovasio et al. 1975; 1978). Here, at the site of Androlikou *Ayios Mamas*, the authors mentioned but never illustrated 62 tools of possible Middle or Upper Palaeolithic date: scrapers, notched pieces, burins, gravers, retouched pieces, a drill, a knife and a projectile point. The second case involves possible Upper Palaeolithic chipped stone implements from a survey and small-scale excavations at the site of Ayia Anna *Perivolia*, in the Tremithos Valley in southeast Cyprus (Baudou and Englemark 1983; Baudou et al. 1985). From the excavations, the authors mention 35 tools: 11 scrapers, 6 knives, 5 borers, 4 gravers and 9 tanged blades.

None of these claims gained much support in subsequent literature. Watkins (1973: 48–49), at least, perceptively pointed out that '…the absence of a palaeolithic in Cyprus might be more than coincidentally linked with the absence of interest in the period among archaeologists working on the island' (a point to which I return below). Stanley Price (1977a: 69) took exception to Watkins's observation, maintaining that it was an 'injustice' to earlier scholars (like Schaeffer 1936) and to the systematic survey work that had been carried out in various caves and rockshelters. He also asserted that the 'flints' reported by both Stockton (Kyrenia area) and Vita-Finzi (Zygi-Maroni area) were not exclusively characteristic of Palaeolithic (or 'Mesolithic') industries, and that none of the findspots were indisputably of Pleistocene date. In their re-surveys of the Androlikou (=Neokhorio) *Ayios Mamas* site in northwest Cyprus, neither Stanley Price (1979a: 140) nor Peltenburg (1979b: 78) identified anything specifically Palaeolithic; Stanley Price, however, recorded numerous Ceramic Neolithic sherds (54 of Red Lustrous, 2 of Red-on-White wares). Fox (1987: 19–20) reiterated that claims for the pre-Neolithic in the Khrysokou River drainage were regarded as suspect, whilst Todd (1987: 186) listed Ayia Anna *Perivolia* (Tremithos River Valley) as an excavated aceramic Neolithic site.

Held (1989b: 7) pointed out that the failure of systematic field survey projects to identify diagnostic pre-Neolithic artefacts, and the absence of culturally antecedent basal layers at excavated aceramic settlement sites, combined to make a persuasive *argumentum ex silentio*. In another, related study, Held (1990: 21) suggested that the chipped stone artefacts found by Stockton were most likely recent *dhoukani* flake-blades; that Vita-Finzi's four flakes and one bifacial core, if not 'geofacts', had no morphological attributes to set them apart from other local, early prehistoric chipped stone assemblages; and that the chipped stone implements assigned to the Upper Palaeolithic by the Tremithos Valley Project could be refuted on typological grounds. This left only the presumed geomorphological correlation of the lowest excavated, chert-bearing levels at Ayia Anna *Perivolia* with Vita-Finzi's (1969) (Palaeolithic) 'Older Fill'. Moreover, in Held's view, the abundant groundstone implements and manufacturing debris recorded at Androlikou *Ayios Mamas* by Adovasio et al. (1975: 360–361) should have cautioned them against assigning a Palaeolithic date based solely on the morphological and functional attributes of the site's chipped stone industry. Cherry (1990: 151–152), finally, echoing the critique of Stanley Price, noted that these 'poorly substantiated claims … rest wholly on the morphological characteristics of lithic artefacts which are either isolated surface finds, or which come from contexts whose date and geological setting require further careful documentation'.

None of the new intensive survey projects working on Cyprus in the 1980s and early 1990s located any pre-Neolithic sites, and thus Herscher (1995: 261), in her review of ongoing archaeological fieldwork on the island, could confidently state that there was still no evidence for a phase that could unequivocally be termed palaeolithic. Work at Akrotiri *Aetokremnos*, however, had definitively established the presence of a 'pre-Neolithic' phase (see the following section); its excavator, Alan Simmons (1999: 21–27), took on the arduous task of evaluating each claim for a palaeolithic presence in some detail. In Simmons's view, Stockton's (1968) interpretation of more than 100 chipped stone artefacts from the Kyrenia region, based on surface finds with little or no context, was marred by his illustrations and the fact that so much of the material seems undiagnostic, or might be naturally fractured cobbles, and perhaps were not even found in situ. Simmons also regarded the artefacts illustrated by Vita-Finzi (1973) and drawn by Eric Higgs as undiagnostic and completely atypical of known Middle Palaeolithic implements. Despite the more careful technological and typological comparisons made by Adovasio et al. (1975; 1978) in the Khrysokou River drainage, Simmons (1999: 22) still regarded the arguments as 'less than compelling', not least because none of the artefacts was illustrated, the representativeness of the assemblages was questionable, and the materials also included a large number of (Neolithic?) groundstone implements, as well as Ceramic Neolithic pottery (also Held 1990: 21 n.10). As to the sites recorded or excavated in the Tremithos Valley Survey (Baudou and Engelmark 1983; Baudou et al. 1985), Simmons found them 'suspect' on several counts: the chipped stone typology and the identification of tool types; the geomorphological comparisons; the viability of the stratigraphic excavations (some trenches were excavated with a tractor); the analytical reasoning behind assigning Ayia Anna *Perivolia* to the Upper Palaeolithic and defining it as a typical hunter-gatherer dwelling site.

For the sake of completeness, two palaeontological sites – with pygmy hippopotamus remains – are also worth mentioning in this context (Simmons 1999: 24–25). The first is Akanthou *Arkhangelos Mikhail*, a collapsed cave or rockshelter along the north coast near the Early Aceramic Neolithic site of Akanthou *Arkosyko* (Reese 1995: 86–89, 130–131). In addition to the abundant pygmy hippo remains, pygmy elephant remains were also present in the cave, and at least one of the bones was burnt. Some 10 possible chipped stone artefacts (now lost and unavailable for analysis) were found in the cave, and another dozen were collected above the cave. The three dates available for the site (two by Amino Acid Racemisation, one by Electron Spin Resonance) range between 15,000 and 6000 BP (Simmons 1999: 213–214, table 8.6). Like everything else about this site, these dates present only tantalising clues to its function, chronological setting and possible cultural associations. The other site is Xylophagou *Spilia tis Englezous*, near Cape Pyla in southeastern Cyprus, another cave containing pygmy hippopotamus bones and some *Monodonta* shell (a sea snail commonly called the 'toothed top shell') (Reese 1995: 138–139; Held 1992b: 34–35). Possible cultural materials include some charcoal, burnt bone and two pieces of chert, but the single radiocarbon date available (OxA 3562, 6650±95 BP) inspires little confidence in a pre-Neolithic date (note that this date was not included in analyses in the Appendix).

As Simmons (1999: 24–25) observed, any archaeological evidence for a palaeolithic presence on the island of Cyprus would necessarily be ephemeral and of low visibility. To find such evidence requires systematic and focused survey, as well as the presence of specialists trained to recognise and date crude lithic scatters that represent the most transient of human activities. Even then, it is difficult to work on sites containing fossil or sub-fossil materials, and to distinguish between natural and cultural patterns, or the types of bone fragmentation that may signal human usage. Few prehistorians have such expertise, or even the experience of working with the relevant types of data and sites (Cherry 1990: 202–203). As other recent work on possible pre-Neolithic sites on Cyprus has shown, however, by working at the right time of year (winter, for visibility), focusing on the types of landscapes or soils or formations that have never been examined but may harbour cultural materials, and above all taking with a grain of salt received wisdom about the possible presence, or absence, or existence of certain types of sites or cultural periods, it is indeed possible to revolutionise the way one thinks about archaeological sites and periods (e.g. Ammerman et al. 2006; Ammerman 2010: 86–88; see next section).

An even more significant tale stems from very recent work in the Plakias region of southwestern Crete, which has identified both Mesolithic and (Lower) Palaeolithic artefacts in association with geological contexts (paleosols, i.e. buried soils) that provide approximate ages for the finds (Strasser et al. 2010; 2011). As the archaeologists in the Plakias Survey project emphasise, previous research on pre-Neolithic periods in Crete had proved inconclusive, not least because of ambiguous data sets and 'the lack of scholarly training of archaeologists to recognize Palaeolithic or Mesolithic remains' (Strasser et al. 2010: 148). Moreover, because recent work on other Aegean islands and Cyprus had revealed evidence of human presence during the Mesolithic (Late Epipalaeolithic on Cyprus; see next section), it stood to reason that Crete too ought to reveal such evidence. Because of its size, however, the main problem was where to look for pre-Neolithic remains.

Adapting a site-location model developed in Greece to identify areas or habitats preferred by Mesolithic foragers that might also preserve the associated artefacts (Runnels et al. 2005), they chose the coastal area around Plakias with features such as caves, rockshelters and nearby coastal wetlands (Figure 6), and they used specialists experienced in identifying Mesolithic assemblages from the mainland (Strasser et al. 2010: 151). Only three years along from the inception of this project, when no pre-Neolithic presence was accepted for Crete, it has now been shown, reasonably if not definitively, that seafaring fisherforagers were exploiting the coastal resources of Crete some 10,000 years ago.

Figure 6. View of
Mesolithic cave site,
Ammoudi 3, south coast
of Crete. View from the
south. Courtesy of Thomas
Strasser and the Plakias
Survey Project. Photograph
by Nicholas Thompson.

Another unexpected and controversial result is the likelihood of a Palaeolithic presence on Crete. If confirmed, this would indicate that Palaeolithic people in the Mediterranean took to the sea at least 130,000 years ago, if not earlier; this dating is based on the association of Palaeolithic cores, flakes, scrapers and other tools with paleosols that can be dated to the late Middle or early Late Pleistocene (Strasser et al. 2011).

By the same token, and for all the same reasons, perhaps we should be less sceptical that at least some people may have visited Cyprus during the Palaeolithic. Of course, this remains an open question, and nothing thus far published provides any definitive evidence for a Palaeolithic presence on Cyprus. In the future, however, it might be worthwhile for archaeologists with direct expertise in identifying palaeolithic material, as well as geologists or geomorphologists experienced in Pleistocene studies, to revisit and re-examine carefully all the locations mentioned above, including the palaeontological sites. Of course, until archaeologists are able legally to visit and publish material from the northern, occupied area of Cyprus, we shall only have an incomplete picture. Although no site-location model comparable to the one for Greece exists for the island of Cyprus, one could readily be built by applying the lessons learnt in the Aegean. Above all, we need to get past the conventional wisdom that assumes the Mediterranean islands were unsuitable habitats for (Palaeolithic) hunter-gatherers, if not foragers and fishers. Finally, we shouldn't overlook the role of serendipity: the current, earliest known and well-excavated site on Cyprus, Akrotiri *Aetokremnos*, located on a British Royal Air Force base, was discovered in 1961 by an 11-year-old schoolboy whose father worked at the base. Never an impressive site, at least in the view of most Cypriot archaeologists, the excavation of *Aetokremnos* only began 26 years later, in 1987. Its final publication (Simmons 1999) established beyond any doubt that people were present and active on the island during the Late Epipalaeolithic, a period I now turn to examine in some detail.

LATE EPIPALAEOLITHIC: THE EARLIEST VISITORS

> It is not unexpected that the first permanently inhabited settlements on islands were preceded by earlier, archaeologically invisible, visitations for the purpose of short-term exploitation of island resources and, synchronously, obtaining information about the nature and structure of the landscape (Colledge and Conolly 2007: 53).

The past two decades of fieldwork and research have produced revolutionary insights into the earliest stages of Cypriot prehistory (Knapp 2010). Detailed published evidence from Akrotiri *Aetokremnos*, with its broad chronological resolution, reveals the presence of people exploiting pygmy hippos or their remains during the 'pre-Neolithic' era (Simmons 1999; Simmons 2004a; Simmons and Mandel 2007). In addition, new survey work and preliminary excavations at Nissi Beach (Ayia Napa) and Akamas *Aspros* suggest that seafaring fisher-foragers were exploiting marine and coastal resources from this earliest stage until well into the aceramic Neolithic period (Ammerman 2010; Ammerman and Noller 2005; Ammerman et al. 2006; 2007; 2008). Meanwhile, recent excavations at Ayia Varvara *Asprokremmos* (north central Troodos foothills), Parreklishia *Shillourokambos* and Ayios Tychonas *Klimonas* (near Limassol) and Kissonerga *Mylouthkia* (north of Paphos) have completely altered our understanding of the earliest known settlers on Cyprus (Figure 7).

These developments have resolved a long-standing debate in the earliest prehistory of Cyprus, demonstrating that the Late Aceramic Neolithic (LAN, or Khirokitia culture) did not arrive fully formed on Cyprus (Stanley Price 1977a). Instead we can now demonstrate the existence of an earlier, formative era, with several different stages (the 'antecedent hypothesis' – Dikaios 1962: 193; Watkins 1973; McCartney et al. 2006: 40). Current archaeological evidence, however, does not (yet) support the notion of any permanent habitation on the island before ca. 9100–8600 Cal BC, most likely on current evidence around 8900–8700 Cal BC, that is, during the Initial or Early Aceramic Neolithic (Manning et al. 2010a; also Watkins 2004; McCartney 2007) (Table 3). The recently published radiocarbon dates from Ayios Tychonas *Klimonas* (Vigne et al. 2011a: 13–14, table 3) are analysed and discussed in the SOM to Appendix 1. Discussions of both the material and social developments related to Levantine or Anatolian Late Epipalaeolithic foragers, fishers and hunter-gatherers must now engage the new evidence from Cyprus, especially as it concerns the seafaring capabilities of such people (Broodbank 2006: 208–213; Watkins 2005; 2008; Ammerman 2010: 81–83).

One further issue that must be resolved concerns the terminology that Cypriot prehistorians have used to categorise all this new evidence. Bar-Yosef

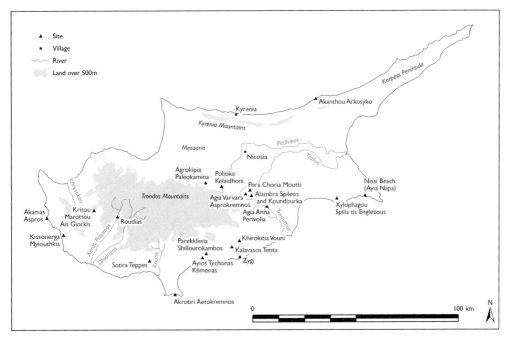

Figure 7. Map of Late Epipalaeolithic–Early Aceramic Neolithic sites mentioned in the text. Drawn by Luke Sollars.

(2001: 130) situated these new Cypriot developments specifically within their Levantine chronological and socio-economic context: 'The first visitors evidenced in the prehistory of Cyprus were late Epi-Paleolithic [sic] foragers'. Here, I follow Bar-Yosef in referring to this period not as 'pre-Neolithic' but as Late Epipalaeolithic (see also Held 1989b: 8–9), a term that has been applied to similar phenomena elsewhere in the Mediterranean. In the east Mediterranean, the term 'Mesolithic', widely used in Europe to refer to the start of the Holocene epoch (Scarre 2005: 182), could not be used because Garrod (1957) had already applied it to a Levantine, terminal Pleistocene, semi-sedentary, hunting and foraging group, the Natufians. Thus the term Epipalaeolithic came into being: it is used here instead of adding the equilavent 'pre-Neolithic' to an already overburdened Victorian terminology (Sherratt 2007: 2–3) that confounds comparative analyses in this part of the world. In any case, this terminological debate only distracts us further from understanding how these early visitors to Cyprus moved around, survived and settled – or not, all issues to which the discussion now turns.

Seafaring and Exploitation

The high antiquity of maritime crossings in the Mediterranean Sea increasingly forms a topic of research, first succinctly formulated by Marcus (2002a: 404–405) and recently synthesised by Broodbank (2006: 201–204; see also Costa et al. 2003). Whilst solid evidence for maritime ventures to the (Pleistocene)

Mediterranean islands continues to be scant (cf. Bednarik 2003: 46–47), recent survey work by the Plakias Mesolithic Survey on the south coast of Crete has not only identified chipped stone assemblages of Mesolithic type, but also what the survey team define as Lower Palaeolithic tools, flakes, cores and debitage made of massive quartz, particularly in the region around the Preveli gorge (Strasser et al. 2010; 2011). The region between Plakias and the Preveli gorge, and farther east around Ayios Pavlos, has environmental characteristics very similar to site locations preferred by Mesolithic foragers on the Greek mainland (Runnels 2009), namely caves and rock shelters at the mouths of river gorges near the early Holocene coastline. The survey thus far has identified 28 findspots or sites associated with caves and rockshelters and collected some 2,100 lithic artefacts attributable to either Mesolithic (20 sites) or (Lower) Palaeolithic industries. The Mesolithic assemblages, defined as microlithic, are made from small pebbles of quartz and red and black chert; they are similar to those from Franchthi Cave (see below) and other sites on the mainland.

Elsewhere in the Aegean, Middle Palaeolithic stone tools from the islands of Kephallonia, Zakynthos (Kourtessi-Phillipaki 1999: 284–286) and Melos (Chelidonio 2001) represent the only possible strains of evidence (Broodbank 2006: 204–205). Middle and Upper Palaeolithic evidence is reported from the Sporades (Sampson 1998: 18–20; Efstratiou 1985: 5–6, 56–59), the Ionian islands (e.g. Dousougli 1999; Kourtessi-Phillipaki 1999) and Agios Eustratios in the northern Aegean (Laskaris et al. 2011: 2475). For the Upper Palaeolithic, the site of Fontana Nuova in Sicily (Chilardi et al. 1996) provides the only other evidence for Mediterranean maritime activity before about 16,500 Cal BC, the time of the still disputed evidence from Corbeddu cave in Sardinia (human phalanx found stratified beneath a thick stratum of *Megaloceros* deer bones – Sondaar et al. 1995). Upper Palaeolithic chipped stone tools have also been found at the site of Santa Maria is Acquas in Sardinia (Mussi and Melis 2002), dated geologically to about 25,000–18,000 Cal BP.

From his detailed survey of pre-Holocene sites in the Mediterranean, Broodbank (2006: 207–208) concluded that any early human presence in Sicily or Sardinia may only have lasted until climatic conditions allowed these people to return to the mainland (if they didn't die out). More generally, but writing before the discoveries in the region around Plakias on Crete, he felt that there was currently very limited evidence for any kind of maritime activity in the Mediterranean before the end of the Pleistocene. Such limited and tentative attempts at *seagoing* (occasional forays into the sea), however, rapidly developed into a more adept and practiced form of *seafaring* during the 11th millennium Cal BC (Broodbank 2006: 200), when Cyprus begins to play a specific role in this story.

Beyond Cyprus, the best example is still Franchthi cave in the Greek Argolid, where obsidian was brought from the Cycladic island of Melos (Perlès 1987:

142–145); it is now reported that Melos obsidian may have been exploited as early as the 10th millennium Cal BC (Laskaris et al. 2011). A wealth of evidence demonstrates a 'Mesolithic' (9th–8th millennia Cal BC) presence at Cyclops Cave on Youra in the Sporades and at Maroulas on Kythnos: fish and shellfish, bone fishhooks, domesticated pig and ovicaprine, round/elliptical stone structures (Sampson et al. 2002; Trantalidou 2003; Sampson 2006; 2008). In addition to the 'Mesolithic' midden site at Sidari on Corfu (Sordinas 2003), preliminary excavations at Ouriakos on Lemnos have produced what are described as Late Epipalaeolithic chipped stone tools (Laskaris et al. 2011: 2475; see also http://www.stonepages.com/news/ – 29 June 2009). From 'Mesolithic' (late 9th–early 8th millennia Cal BC) sites such as Bonifacio-Monte Leone in southernmost Corsica (Vigne and Desse-Berset 1995) and others in northern Sardinia, there is evidence for the presence of 'trapper-fishers' who had seafaring capabilities, exploited coastal resources (fish, shellfish, small game and the endemic *Prolagus Sardus*), and stayed for short periods in small coastal sites (Vigne 1996: 118; Costa et al. 2003).

Thus there is solid and accumulating evidence from the Late Pleistocene–Early Holocene Mediterranean demonstrating that for at least two millennia before the advent of farming, seafaring fishers and foragers plied the coasts and islands of the Mediterranean. The significance of these sites is crucial for understanding the activities of the earliest people who visited Cyprus. Beyond the still tenuous but growing corpus of evidence cited from the Aegean, Corsica and Sardinia, the fully published results of excavations at Akrotiri *Aetokremnos* on Cyprus provide the best witness for human activity on a Mediterranean island in the 11th millennium Cal BC (Simmons 1999; Simmons and Mandel 2007). Moreover, new survey work and limited excavations at the sites of Nissi Beach (near Ayia Napa) and Akamas *Aspros* have produced similar types of microlithic, flake-based chipped stone materials not unlike those found at *Aetokremnos* (Ammerman 2010: 86–88; McCartney, in Ammerman et al. 2006: 11–17), and with some similarities to chipped stone assemblages from two inland sites in the northern Troodos, Agrokipia *Paleokamina* and Ayia Varvara *Asprokremnos* (Given and Knapp 2003: 183–186; McCartney et al. 2006: 51–54; McCartney 2007).

The coastal sites of *Aetokremnos*, and possibly Nissi Beach and Akamas *Aspros*, thus should be seen as places where seafaring fisher-foragers made brief seasonal visits to Cyprus, over several millennia, to exploit faunal and marine resources such as pygmy hippos and elephants, shellfish, avifauna, perhaps salt (Simmons 1999; Ammerman et al. 2008) and quite possibly sea turtles (McCartney et al. 2010: 134–135, fig. 13.2). Nonetheless it is necessary to ask what lay behind these visits, and to consider the validity of the suggestions that have been made (e.g. Simmons and Mandel 2007; Ammerman 2010). Thus we need to focus more closely on all these sites, and attempt to contextualise them within the environmental conditions of the Late Pleistocene and Early

Holocene, in particular the Younger Dryas climatic episode (Roberts 1998: 71–76; Rosen 2007: 45, 49, 67–69; Abbo et al. 2010).

The Coastal Sites

AKROTIRI *AETOKREMNOS*

The site of *Aetokremnos* ('eagle's cliff') is located in southernmost Cyprus on the Akrotiri Peninsula, once an island joined to the mainland by a sandbar (Simmons 1999: 329). Situated on a precipitous cliff some 40 m above the sea (Figure 8), *Aetokremnos* was excavated almost entirely (50 m²) between 1987–1990 (the remainder was excavated in June 2009). The entire deposit at this small, collapsed rock shelter was sealed after use by massive rock debris; when the overhang caved in, the stratification was secured. The approximately 1-m-depth of intact archaeological deposits contained four major strata (Figure 9).

Stratum 1, at the top, formed a mixed context, whilst Stratum 3 represented only a sterile layer of windblown sand and limestone. Thus most attention has fallen on the other two strata: Stratum 2 contained the bulk of the chipped stone artefacts and other cultural debris (only 12% in Stratum 4, at the bottom). Moreover, 9 of 11 archaeological features identified at *Aetokremnos* derive from Stratum 2; the two in Stratum 4 are concentrations of burned pygmy hippopotamus bones. Human use of the site is inferred primarily from these midden deposits. Simmons (2004a: 7) recently defended the stratigraphic integrity of the site, arguing that there is no evidence for mixing or natural displacements between Strata 2 and 4.

Cultural materials retrieved from the site include the formal chipped stone tool assemblage (1,021 in number), dominated by 36 distinctive 'thumbnail' scrapers (Simmons 1999: 126, table 6.1). All the raw materials used were available locally, and point to an expedient technology. Other finds include ground stone pebbles (14), fragmentary cobbles (64) and four complete cobbles showing faint signs of use wear (Swiny, in Simmons 1999: 146–149). There was one piece of worked bone (from a pygmy hippo incisor), six worked picrolite objects and a fragmentary, pierced and incised calcarenite disk (Reese, in Simmons 1999: 149–151). The immense number of marine shells recovered includes some 100 shell beads worked from *dentalium*, *Conus mediterraneus* and *Columbella rustica* or dove shell (Reese, in Simmons 1999: 188–191).

Twenty-seven radiocarbon determinations were made on bone, sediment, shell and charcoal; one new charcoal sample from Level 2 has been dated to 10,185 Cal BC (Simmons and Mandel 2007: 479; the 68.2% calibrated range for this date [OxA-15989] is 10,108–9877 Cal BC, using IntCal09 – see Appendix). In this study, by contrast, only dates on charcoal samples and some very recently measured suid bone were used (see Appendix, point 2 under Methodology). Taking all the radiocarbon dates into account, the excavators interpreted the results to show a relatively short-term 'occupation' or a series

Figure 8. View of Akrotiri *Aetokremnos*, situated on a precipitous cliff some 40 m above the Mediterranean Sea on the south coast (Akrotiri Peninsula) of Cyprus. Courtesy of Alan Simmons.

Figure 9. Akrotiri *Aetokremnos*: intact archaeological deposits showing four major strata identified (numbered 1–4, from top to bottom). Note that 'Site E', indicated on chalkboard, was the designation first given to *Aetokremnos*. Courtesy of Alan Simmons.

of seasonal visits during the 10th millennium Cal BC, centred round 9825 Cal BC with a range of 10,005–9702 Cal BC at one standard deviation (Simmons 1999: 193–215). The time difference between the four strata at the site appears to be so small it cannot be determined in radiocarbon years (Simmons 2004a: 5). Yet the charcoal data ($n = 9$) and suid bone data ($n = 2$) reanalysed here (see Appendix, Model 1) yield a potential chronological span at *Aetokremnos* of 1,818–2,584 calendar years at 68.2% probability (mean value 2,236 years), suggesting a rather longer period of human activities, whether sporadic or more regular.

Ammerman et al. (2007: 18–19, fig. 9) had already called into question the reliability of some of these radiocarbon dates, and recalculated eight charcoal samples from Stratum 2 (using Bronk Ramsey et al. 2006). Overall the calibrated ages span a period from about 12,000–9200 Cal BC (large error values are associated with four samples – Simmons 1999: 196–197, table 8.1). Four AMS-based determinations, however, with smaller error measurements, provided a date range between ca. 10,900–10,100 Cal BC. Eight of nine radiocarbon determinations on charcoal from *Aetokremnos* fall within the period of the Younger Dryas (ca. 10,800–9600 Cal BC), about the time that some Levantine hunter-gatherer-foragers are thought to have become more mobile (e.g. Bar-Yosef 2001: 140; Watkins 2004: 25–29; cf. Maher et al. 2011: 16–17), whilst others first began to cultivate staple foods (Bar-Yosef 2007: 22).

Of some 222,000 bones retrieved at *Aetokremnos*, most came from two endemic mammal species: pygmy hippopotamus (*Phanourios minutus*, minimum 505 individuals, 95% of the faunal remains) and pygmy elephant (*Elephas Cypriotis*, three individuals). The remainder included a wide range of avian, marine and other mammal resources: crabs, sea urchins, limpets, topshell (nearly 70,000 marine invertebrates); one gray mullet vertebra; dove, goose, grebe, shag, teal (73 avifauna); burnt eggshell and land snails; turtle, snake, pig (not deer) and a genet. On the basis of anatomical and morphometrical analyses, four phalanges originally attributed to Mesopotamian fallow deer (*Dama mesopotamica*) have now been shown to belong to pig (Vigne et al. 2009). Thus no deer but at least two young (aged 18–24 months), small-sized pigs were present at *Aetokremnos* ca. 9500 Cal BC. These suids were most likely introduced to Cyprus from the Levantine mainland, and the authors attribute their small size to insular isolation, perhaps the result of the pig's capacity to fill an ecological niche left by the vanishing pygmy hippos (Vigne et al. 2009: 16136).

Eighty-eight percent of the pygmy hippo remains came from Stratum 4 (the lowest), whilst most other faunal evidence came from Stratum 2. The disparity between the two levels provoked scepticism over the excavators' interpretation of *Aetokremnos*, specifically the association of the pygmy hippopotamus bones with the cultural remains (Bunimovitz and Barkai 1996; Binford 2000; Grayson 2000). Furthermore, because the taphonomic analysis of 16,000 pygmy hippo bones revealed no cutmarks or evidence for fresh bone breakage, Olsen (in

Simmons 1999: 230–237) concluded that these bones represented a natural accumulation in Stratum 4 at the bottom of the shelter. Thus human occupation at the site would have come only later, in Stratum 2, leading to the mixing of the earlier pygmy hippo material and later artefacts, as well as to the burnt bone. Mithen (2003: 97–100) revisited these arguments a few years later, and expressed further scepticism over Simmons's arguments for the extinction of the pygmy hippos at *Aetokremnos*.

In the most detailed critique, Bunimovitz and Barkai (1996: 92–93) argued that the archaeological and palaeontological data from *Aetokremnos* represent two temporally discrete episodes, the earlier (Stratum 4) a natural die-off of Pleistocene megafauna, the later (Stratum 2) a sporadic occupation by early Holocene hunter-gatherers who might have used the (burnt) bone in the shelter. Alternatively, they suggested that any perceived intermingling between Strata 2 and 4 could have resulted entirely from post-depositional, taphonomic processes. Simmons and his team responded in detail to every point raised by Bunimovitz and Barkai (Simmons 1996a; Reese 1996b), while Strasser (1996) defended the integrity of the deposits and supported the possibility that highly skilled human hunters could have overhunted these susceptible megafauna. Vigne (1996), however, suggested that Cyprus's endemic megafauna were most likely extinct by the time the first humans arrived on the island, and that these early visitors to *Aetokremnos* probably subsisted on fishing, trapping and cropping, like their contemporaries on Corsica.

Ammerman and Noller (2005) recently reassessed the environmental setting of *Aetokremnos* and raised further questions about the site's dating. They point out that sea level was some 70 m lower about 12,000 years ago, and maintain that the site was situated near the top of a tall cliff at the end of a one-km-wide coastal plain (also Strasser 1996: 113), with dune fields actively forming right in front of the site (Ammerman and Noller 2005: 538–539, fig. 1) (Figure 10). The peninsula's current bathymetry, they argue, points to the existence of a submerged landscape, sloping moderately to a depth of some 150 m at 5 km from the present-day coastline. As the presence of coastal sand dunes would have constrained any tree growth, Ammerman and Noller (2005: 536, 540) follow others in arguing that the mass of hippo bones from Stratum 4 represents a natural bone midden exploited for fuel by foragers at a later time, when wood became scarce during the Younger Dryas (Watkins 2005: 203, fig. 6d). Having conceded that a human presence is more likely in Stratum 2 than in Stratum 4, they questioned the reliability of the radiocarbon results carried out on bone samples from *Aetokremnos* and called for a new series of radiocarbon dates to facilitate comparison of the age of hippo bones from Strata 2 and 4, and of bird bones from Stratum 2.

In response, Simmons and Mandel (2007) defended their interpretation of *Aetokremnos* as a pygmy hippo processing site, and contested the suggestion that a massive sand ramp extended from the sea to the top of the cliff where

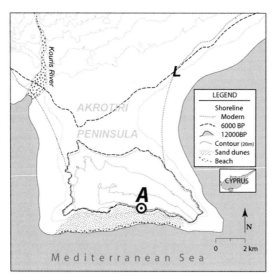

Figure 10. Akrotiri Peninsula plan showing the shoreline at the present time, at 6000 BP and at 12,000 BP. Aetokremnos is located at A; the modern-day Limassol harbour at L. Topographic contour lines are shown at 20-m intervals for the reconstructed 12,000 BP landscape without Holocene deposits and landforms. The proposed, actively forming dune fields on the coastal plain in front of the site are highlighted. Image by Jay Noller. Courtesy of Jay Noller and Albert Ammerman.

Aetokremnos is situated. Taking up the dating challenge, they carried out further 14C analyses on the pygmy hippo (11), elephant (2) and bird (9) bones from all strata, but the results were limited to one further date on charcoal (10,185 Cal BC, as already noted), so these bones of contention continue. Even so, the radiocarbon results reaffirm a Late Epipalaeolithic date for *Aetokremnos* and place it firmly within the 11th through the earlier 10th millennium Cal BC (see Appendix, under Cypriot Chronology/Late Epipalaeolithic). The site therefore lies within the broad temporal framework of some crucial environmental changes that took place at the end of the last ice age.

Most scholars who have re-examined the *Aetokremnos* evidence agree on the site's chronological placement and cultural significance, but contest the interpretation of the Stratum 4 bone bed. Nobody doubts a human presence in Stratum 2, but they question whether people actually lived there, or simply made short-term or seasonal visits to the site (Cherry 1990: 198–199). In contrast, the excavators find it '...hard to believe that a locality in which over 500 pygmy hippos were butchered, as we argue, was not occupied' (Simmons and Mandel 2007: 477). They regard *Aetokremnos* as a specialised activity site, where people not only consumed pygmy hippos but also made use of their secondary products (Simmons 1999: 310–311, 318). This debate seems irresolvable, and other points are far more enlightening.

For example, if one were to accept that pygmy hippos were killed and/ or processed, and their meat consumed or preserved at the site, then in terms of diet, the people of *Aetokremnos* shifted from reliance on pygmy hippos in Stratum 4 to avifaunal and marine resources in Stratum 2. This might indicate a change in economic strategy as the number of surviving pygmy hippos fell below people's subsistence needs. If the people who used or occupied this site remained there for any length of time, they would almost certainly have adopted a hunting strategy to suit local conditions rather than decimating what appears to have been their one vital wild food resource. There are also two other factors to consider: (1) these endemic fauna lived in evergreen forest that contained a limited and unbalanced terrestrial fauna (Boekschoten and Sondaar 1972: 333); and (2) there was a low level of marine biodiversity in the nutrient-poor waters that surrounded Cyprus (Knapp et al. 1994: 491). Both these factors would have presented a significant challenge to hunter-gatherers, and to some extent even to mobile foragers; it may be that an agricultural mode of life was a prerequisite to living year in and year out on Cyprus. Even Simmons (1999: 318, 322–323; 2004a: 9) seems to agree that *Aetokremnos* was not occupied over a long period of time, and that those who lived there ultimately returned to their mainland point(s) of origin.

The excavated fauna and archaeological features of *Aetokremnos*, along with a coherent series of radiocarbon dates, indicate that it was a specialised activity site – somehow involving pygmy hippos – visited periodically by Late Epipalaeolithic fisher-foragers and hunters from the Levantine coast. Preliminary analyses of chipped stone material from Nissi Beach, Akamas *Aspros* and *Alimman* (McCartney in Ammerman et al. 2006: 11–17; 2007: 13–15; 2008: 15–27) also allow one to make a tentative case that these were all places where fisher-foragers made short-term, seasonal visits from the Levantine mainland to exploit resources such as fish, sea turtles, salt, shellfish and avifauna. At the same time, they provide evidence for very early seafaring in the eastern Mediterranean (Ammerman 2010). Although excavations are ongoing at Nissi Beach and Akamas *Aspros*, there are as yet no dates to demonstrate any contemporaneity of these sites with *Aetokremnos* (Ammerman et al. 2008; see the next section). Before turning to more detailed discussion of the aeolianite sites at Nissi Beach and in the Akamas peninsula, I consider the faunal evidence from *Aetokremnos* in the context of faunal extinctions on Mediterranean islands.

Cyprus is an 'oceanic' island (Held 1989b: 11–15) with a very limited number of species and a high degree of endemism (i.e. species native only to this island). Even under optimal conditions, the expanse of water surrounding Cyprus kept out many east Mediterranean species. Sea-level change (−120/130 m) during the Last Glacial Maximum (ca. 25,000–18,000 Cal BP) may have reduced the distance between Cyprus and the Levantine mainland to as little as 40 km, but the island remained remote even during such sea-level regressions.

Only two large terrestrial mammals, elephant and hippopotamus, made it to the island. Over a period of tens of thousands of years on Cyprus (Sondaar and van der Geer 2000: 68 suggest a minimum of 1.8 million years), these two mammal species became entirely separated from their respective parent gene pools and evolved into dwarfed forms (*Elephas cypriotes*, *Phanourios minutus*) (Boekschoten and Sondaar 1972).

The (controversial) bone dates from *Aetokremnos* suggest that not long after humans first arrived on the island, these endemics became extinct. Elsewhere in the Mediterranean, the only purported evidence for any temporal overlap between an island endemics and humans – *Myotragus balearicus* on Mallorca – has now been discounted (Ramis et al. 2002); people probably coexisted with *Myotragus* for no longer than 200 years (Bover and Alcover 2003; Alcover 2008). Beyond Mallorca and *Aetokremnos*, the only other, highly disputed evidence in the Mediterranean for some association between the arrival of humans and the extinction of Pleistocene fauna revolves around the demise of two mammalian endemics (*Megaloceros cazioti*; *Cynotherium sardus*) on early Holocene Corsica and/or Sardinia (Cherry 1992: 31; Sondaar and van der Geer 2000: 69–70; Costa et al. 2003: 6).

Given the wider Mediterranean picture, the proposed association at *Aetokremnos* between human cultural artefacts and the remains of at least 505 pygmy hippos, as well as 3 dwarf elephants, was bound to generate controversy. Most endemic dwarf species on islands were naïve because they evolved in an ecological context devoid of large terrestrial mammals, especially humans. Easy to hunt, disadvantaged by interbreeding in small isolated populations and subject to climatic or environmental changes that would have altered their chances of survival, such animals were highly susceptible to the presence of people.

In the case of *Aetokremnos*, Cherry (1990: 195) observed that '…man has here been discovered, as it were, holding a smoking gun'. Yet Cherry also emphasised that even if people were the catalyst in the demise of these dwarf endemics, we still must consider if they were also affected by the introduction *with humans* of new animal species competing with them for food and territory, or if their demise was an indirect consequence of wider modification of the landscape through both climate change and human interference. Indeed, the deteriorating climate at the end of the last glaciation and during the Younger Dryas event may have forced these endemics to compete with humans and other animals for increasingly scarce resources (Wasse 2007: 56). The colder and dryer weather of the Younger Dryas during the 11th millennium Cal BC may well have compromised some of the resources on which pygmy hippos or elephants had come to depend during their long evolution on the island (Bromage et al. 2002: 423–425). At the very least, all such developments would have made pygmy hippos more vulnerable to extinction.

As we have seen, several archaeologists remain sceptical about the association between humans and the endemic fauna at *Aetokremnos* (cf. Sondaar and van der Geer 2000). Indeed, the archaeological sample at *Aetokremnos* is limited to one, approximately 50 m² excavated area, whilst the erratic evidence related to the evolution of Pleistocene fauna – together with a suite of possible ecological, climatic and biogeographic constraints – makes it difficult to distinguish between the proximate (likely) and the ultimate (real) cause of these proposed extinctions. If the people from *Aetokremnos* caused the extinction of hippos on Cyprus, they had to do so over the entire island, and there is no evidence for any human presence at 32 other sites around the island (19 in caves, 11 at open-air sites, 2 in rock shelters like *Aetokremnos*) where pygmy hippo remains have been found (Hadjisterkotis and Reese 2008).

At *Aetokremnos*, however, excavations uncovered not just pygmy hippos and dwarf elephants, but other, impoverished fauna (e.g. genet, mouse, great bustard, dove, goose, grebe) embedded in a human-made context. This factor makes it harder to deny some cause-and-effect relationship: people arrived, and within the 1,000 or so years indicated by the radiocarbon dates, two endemic fauna became extinct. In other words, even taking into account climatic factors and environmental change, the evidence of endemic fauna elsewhere in Cyprus, or the possibility of competition with introduced species, the liklihood of human overkill must be considered seriously at *Aetokremnos*. Even Ammerman and Noller (2005: 540), who argue that Stratum 4 at *Aetokremnos* was a natural bone midden, observe that '…there is a much better chance that pygmy hippos were hunted by the human beings who contributed to the formation of stratum 2'.

The presence of human beings on islands with animals that previously lacked predators almost certainly had disastrous results. Even in the case of Corsica–Sardinia, where we find some indicators of overlap between the arrival of people and the extinction of the insular endemic fauna, the zooarchaeologist involved concluded '…the far-reaching effects of people upon island ecosystems are the ultimate cause of most animal extinctions' (Vigne 1987: 167 and fig. 1). By slaughtering such animals, people decimated an abundant food resource and thus jeopardised their own chances of survival in an island habitat (Schüle 1993: 406). On most Mediterranean islands, it was only when people brought cultivated plants and domesticated animals with them that they managed to establish themselves more permanently. On Cyprus, however, it is possible that another scenario was unfolding in the Late Epipalaeolithic, one that had little to do with the permanent settlement of the island during the following Early Aceramic Neolithic period.

NISSI BEACH AND THE AKAMAS PENINSULA

Akrotiri *Aetokremnos* is currently the only securely dated Late Epipalaeolithic site on Cyprus. It is likely, however, that the contemporary coastal landscape

included other sites. Some possibilities came to light as recently as 2004: (a)
Nissi Beach, just west of Agia Napa on the southeast coast; (b) *Aspros* on the
Akamas peninsula along the central west coast; and (c) *Alimman*, a small satellite
site of *Aspros* (200 m to its north). Four brief seasons of survey, trial excavations
and underwater exploration have been conducted at these sites (Ammerman
et al. 2006; 2007; 2008; 2011).

All three sites are situated on aeolianite formations, fossilised sand dunes
found along most shores of the eastern Mediterraean, but none so prominent
as on Cyprus (Ammerman et al. 2006: 5 mention several other aeolianite sites
on the island). Because the sea level was some 70 m lower at the Pleistocene–
Holocene transition, these sites would have been farther from the shore than
they are today (Ammerman et al. 2007: 7). At least part of the *Aspros* site, however, lies underwater (Ammerman et al. 2008: 4–9; 2011: 264–267). Since both
sites lie adjacent to sandy beaches where a small river or drainage reaches the
coast, they could have provided suitable landing spots, as well as seasonal campsites for fishers or foragers (Ammerman et al. 2006: 17–18; cf. Simmons and
Mandel 2007: 480). Both Nissi Beach and *Aspros* stand in elevated positions,
in a hard, dry landscape with little vegetation and limited terrestrial resources.
The soils around both sites have low agricultural or woodland potential and
would have had little to offer to farmers or hunters.

At Nissi Beach, the area of the site with the highest artefact density, some
30–40 m from the current coastline, has pockets of reddish-brown soil between
30–40 cm deep (Ammerman et al. 2007: 5–6). Beneath a very thin top layer (A
horizon), all the chipped stone and ground stone artefacts were recovered at
depths of up to 25 cm in the B-horizon soils. The soil profile of Akamas *Aspros*
is quite similar, with a reddish-brown B horizon some 20 cm thick. During trial
excavations at both Nissi Beach and *Aspros* in 2007 and 2008, these reddish soils
divulged chipped stone artefacts, hand stones, seashells and avifaunal remains.

McCartney (in Ammerman et al. 2006: 11–17) maintains that the chipped
stone assemblages recovered from initial fieldwork at these new sites are related,
and are not at all unlike those from Stratum 2 at Akrotiri *Aetokremnos*. Even
so, the various raw materials used, the technologies practiced and the relative
frequency of tool types reveal differences among all these early sites. For example, more blades and bladelets were produced at *Aetokremnos* than at either
Nissi Beach or *Aspros*, while the excavations at *Aspros* revealed none of the
grey translucent beach pebbles (Lefkara chert) used to produce flake scrapers
at *Aetokremnos*. The predominant material worked at Nissi Beach was Lefkara
chert, although the assemblages include jasper and chalcedony. The people
who visited *Aspros*, however, employed a wider variety of materials, including other variants of chert available in the *Aspros* riverbed. Finally, it is worth
noting that the number of tools currently found at Nissi Beach (316) and
Akamas *Aspros* (288) is much larger than the total count of formal tools from
Aetokremnos (128) (Ammerman et al. 2008: 25–26, and table 8).

Crucially, however, all these assemblages reveal a broadly homogeneous, microlithic and flake-based tradition of stone tool production, even if some small blades and bladelets have been found (McCartney, in Ammerman et al. 2008: 24–26). This microlithic, flake-based tradition differs markedly from later, blade-oriented traditions that typify sites of the Early Aceramic Neolithic (EAN). Based on the production of flakes and small blades/bladelets, this early technological practice is also seen at *Aetokremnos* and other small sites on the Akrotiri Peninsula, where diminutive scrapers were produced from beach pebbles while geometrics were rendered on higher quality cherts (Simmons 1999: 137–138, figs. 6.3–6.4; 252–253, figs. 10.4–10.5). The most common formal tools found at *Aspros* and Nissi Beach thus far are scrapers and geometrics (truncations and backed pieces – McCartney, in Ammerman et al. 2006: 13–14, figs. 8–9). Notable among these tools are 'thumbnail' scrapers, very similar to those found at *Aetokremnos* (Simmons 1999: 245–246, figs. 10–12). In terms of relative dating, the 2008 excavations at Nissi Beach produced a small chunk of obsidian and three long blades, among other new tool types. None of these had appeared in earlier surface survey or excavation and, interestingly, such material found elsewhere is typically thought to be a signpost of the Neolithic.

With respect to absolute dating, two marine shells (*Patella caerulea* Linnaeus) excavated at Nissi Beach in 2007 produced AMS dates that, with approximate marine reservoir correction, fall in the 8th millennium Cal BC (ca. 7592–7551 and 7586–7547 Cal BC, respectively at 68.2% probability: see Appendix and SOM cited there). These dates are much later than the period (Late Epipalaeolithic) proposed by the excavator for the surface materials at Nissi Beach and the Akamas sites; they correspond to a (Levantine) Pre-Pottery Neolithic B (PPNB) date range (EAN 2–3 on Cyprus – see Table 2, above, p. 27), which accords well with the presence of obsidian and the three long blades. To explain this phenomenon, Ammerman et al. (2008: 15) suggest that the materials *excavated* at Nissi Beach represent an example of 'stratigraphic inversion', that is, the in situ sub-surface remains have a younger age than the chipped stone collected from the site's surface, which would have been deposited by the action of one or more storms or tsunamis (on tsunamis in the Holocene Mediterranean, see Pareschi et al. 2007; on Cypriot tsunamis, see Whelan and Kelletat 2002; Noller et al. 2005). Such an interpretation is strengthened by the presence at Nissi Beach, just beyond the excavated area, of several large tsunami blocks (on this phenomenon, see Stewart and Morhange 2009: 400–401) (Figure 11), and by the scattered presence all over the site's surface of small pieces of dark-coloured 'beach rock'. Indeed, this redeposited beach rock largely obscures the hundreds of pieces of chipped stone tools and debris, and thus has helped to preserve them. Put another way, the excavator contends that the materials collected on Nissi Beach's surface are not in their primary context, but instead come from a submerged area in front (south) of

Figure 11. View southeast over Nissi Beach, with several large tsunami blocks immediately next to the excavated area. Photograph by Stella Demesticha.

the excavated part of the site; some action of the sea subsequently redeposited the material on the site's surface.

This interpretation gains some credibility from underwater reconnaisance conducted at the Akamas *Aspros* site in the summer of 2007. At depths of 6–15 m below current sea level and at distances of 50–200 m off the current coast, divers recovered 38 pieces of chipped stone (10 tools, predominantly made on flakes) and 2 possible ground stone tools (Ammerman et al. 2008: 18–19, table 3; 2011: 265–266). Thus the material if not the actual spatial distribution of *Aspros* extended across some 300 m, from the eastern part of the lithic scatter on land to the findspots of the chipped stone material underwater, in the west. If one accepts that most artefacts found at Nissi Beach came from submerged areas in front of the site, it may also have been of greater spatial extent than what is evident on the surface today. In terms of where this trajectory of research stands today, all these coastal lithic assemblages – with their functionally limited toolkits – seem perfectly consonant with temporary campsites repeatedly visited by fisher-foragers over a long but still indeterminate period of time.

Future excavations at both Nissi Beach and Akamas *Aspros* should help to refine these sequences and to verify or reject such an interpretation. For the present, one of the most important conclusions to be derived from all these excavations – *Aetokremnos*, Nissi Beach, Akamas *Aspros* – is that for at least two

Figure 12. Vretsia *Roudias* site location in the upper levels of the Xeros Potamos valley, Cyprus. Courtesy of Nikos Efstratiou.

millennia before the advent of farming and for some two millennia thereafter, seafaring fisher-foragers held onto a coastal way of life, adapting to the sea and exploiting marine and other resources available along Cyprus's shores.

The Inland Sites

The same likelihood of repeated visits to what may have been a seasonal camp or chipped stone quarrying site has recently been documented in an unexpected area, in the uplands of the southwestern Troodos. The site of Vretsia *Roudias* (near the medieval bridge of the same name) is situtated on a small plateau on the cliffs of Agios Ioannis, a remnant river terrace of the upper levels of the Xeros Potamos (Figure 12); today the site lies about 80 m above the modern riverbed. Surface survey and two preliminary seasons of excavation indicate cultural material is spread over nearly 0.5 ha at *Roudias*, virtually covering the small plateau on which it is situated (Efstratiou et al. 2010). The chipped stone artefacts found at the site stem from both stratigraphic excavations in the remnants of a reddish paleosol (buried soil) some 40 cm thick, as well as from the overlying colluvium (loose sediment) that may have been formed from the reworking of this reddish paleosol. The lithic assemblage of some 4,000 artefacts points clearly to the Late Epipalaeolithic nature of the site, although surface finds also suggest a more ephemeral, Late Aceramic Neolithic (LAN, Khirokitia phase) occupation. Whilst the lithic specialist is confident that the (very fragmentary) nature of the samples thus far examined is comparable to material from Akrotiri *Aetokremnos* (McCartney, in Efstratiou et al. 2010), no radiocarbon dates are yet available.

The tool assemblage at Vretsia *Roudias* is marked by the frequent, indeed dominant occurrence of marginal retouched flakes, blades and bladelets, and unretouched utilised implements. The most common tools are notched and denticulated flakes, with lesser amounts of truncations, backed tools and scrapers. More rare are glossed tools, burins, perforators and *pièces esquillées*. The presence of microlithic tools, including the diminutive thumbnail scrapers so common at *Aetokremnos* and with other parallels in the Akamas *Aspros* and Nissi Beach assemblages, strongly suggest that the main assemblage at *Roudias* belongs to a Late Epipalaeolithic industry. The assemblage also shows similarities to Late Epipalaeolithic lithic industries from the Near East (a small number of geometrics including two lunates, a larger crescent and rectilinear pieces). In contrast to this mainly excavated assemblage, the surface collections (especially the grab samples) contain a mixture of Late Epipalaeolithic and certain diagnostic elements of LAN material. As the LAN material derives almost exclusively from the surface, the two industries at the site are separated by the excavators with considerable confidence. The chipped stone samples from *Roudias* are dominated by Lefkara translucent cherts, with lesser amounts of Lefkara basal chert, and a few examples of chalcedony, jasper and 'Moni' chert, all perhaps brought to the site from elsewhere on the island. There is thus far no obsidian in any of the lithic samples collected at the Vretsia *Roudias* site.

The opening up of areas beyond the coast to Cyprus's earliest known visitors, and indeed their archaeological visibility and prominence, are also apparent in the work of another new field project – Elaborating Early Neolithic Cyprus (EENC). The EENC project is conducting survey and excavation (at Ayia Varvara *Asprokremmos*) in landscapes that, like Vretsia *Roudias*, are quite different from those that would have suited early fisher-foragers or farmers (McCartney et al. 2007: 30–36; 2008; Manning et al. 2010a). In an area around the base of the pillow lavas in the northeastern Troodos, foragers and hunters would have had access to a broad spectrum of lowland–upland fauna and flora, as well as high-quality chert sources, basal rocks for use as grinding tools and a good water supply (McCartney et al. 2006; 2007). At sites such as Agrokipia *Paleokamina* and Politiko *Kelaïdhoni* (Given and Knapp 2003: 182–186) and Ayia Varvara *Asprokremmos* (McCartney 2005: 6–7; 2007; McCartney et al. 2006: 51–54; 2007), the EENC project has distinguished between (1) flake-based assemblages – such as those at *Paleokamina* or Pera Chorio *Moutti* – showing parallels with the coastal, Late Epipalaeolithic sites;

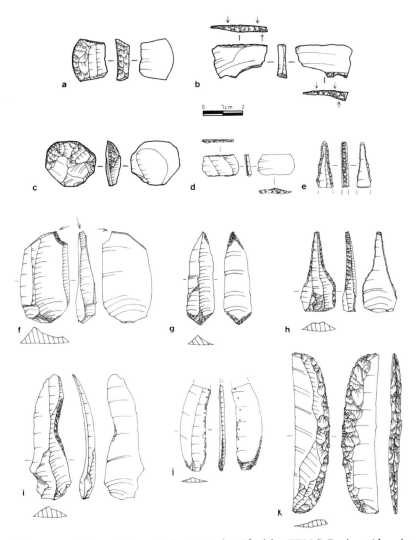

Figure 13. Chipped stone industries identified by EENC Project (drawing by Carole McCartney): (1) flake-based assemblages (Pera Chorio *Moutti*; Agrokipia *Palaeokamina*) showing some parallels with the coastal, Late Epipalaeolithic sites, and (2) blade-based assemblages (Ayia Vavara *Asprokremmos*). Courtesy of Carole McCartney. (a) Pera Chorio *Moutti* – thumbnail scraper; (b) Pera Chorio *Moutti* – double truncation; (c) Agrokipia *Palaeokamina* – thumbnail scraper; (d) Agrokipia *Palaeokamina* – double truncation; (e) Agrokipia *Palaeokamina* – perforator; (f) Ayia Vavara *Asprokremmos* – burin; (g) Ayia Vavara *Asprokremmos* – projectile point; (h) Ayia Vavara *Asprokremmos* – perforator; (i) Ayia Vavara *Asprokremmos* – notched blade; (j) Ayia Vavara *Asprokremmos* – glossed element; (k) Ayia Vavara *Asprokremmos* – backed blade.

and (2) blade-based assemblages – such as those at *Asprokremmos* and Alambra *Kourdourka* – (McCartney et al. 2006: 58), which are Neolithic traditions but with a core technology and tools quite different from those of the later, EAN sites (McCartney et al. 2007: 29) (Figure 13).

On the one hand, some aspects of the chipped stone technology and tool types identified by the EENC project among the flake-based assemblages show similarities with those used at *Aetokremnos*, Nissi Beach and Akamas *Aspros*. In particular, sites such as *Paleokamina*, *Kelaïdhoni* and *Asprokremmos* show evidence of a microlithic chipped stone industry that produced diminutive scrapers and geometrics dominated by double truncations. These elements are thus broadly reminiscent of *Aetokremnos'* chipped stone assemblage (McCartney et al. 2006). On the other hand, the production of prismatic blades at *Asprokremmos*, *Koundourka* and *Kelaïdhoni* is quite distinct, and in these assemblages one finds a suite of blade-based tool types – including arrowheads, burins, scrapers, notches glossed segments and retouched pieces – that belong to Neolithic traditions (McCartney et al. 2006; 2007: 33–35, 37, fig. 4). The presence of a few microliths and specific features of the blade core technology at *Asprokremmos*, in particular, can be seen in the chipped stone assemblage from Kalavasos *Tenta* period 5 (EAN 1) (McCartney and Todd 2005; McCartney 2003; 2007). Yet McCartney feels that these traits of *Tenta* period 5 are more in line with the assemblage at *Aetokremnos* than with other EAN assemblages. This clearly evolved Neolithic *Tenta* industry certainly cannot be equated with that of *Aetokremnos*, but the persistence of such traits into the EAN may hint at some level of cultural continuity beginning in the Late Epipalaeolithic and persisting into the Neolithic era (see Table 3, above). One primary goal of the EENC is to investigate the extent of such continuity.

Asprokremmos has but a single chip of obsidian, an imported material typically seen as a time marker for the EAN period. It is most distinctive for its arrowheads (see Figure 13g above), and the blade-based technology used there is similar to that of PPNA assemblages in southeastern Anatolia and the northern Levant (McCartney 2005: 14–15; 2008; McCartney et al. 2006: 51–54, figs. 6–7; 2007; 2008). At the same time, this technology is very distinct from those of EAN Cyprus.

Excavations at *Asprokremmos* have now uncovered a total of 150 m² and revealed three phases of early Neolithic activity across the site. Several excavated trenches divulged large artefact dumps, a complex sequence of midden deposits, a couple of arc-shaped 'channel' constructions (Features 163, 262), a small stone feature (context 260), a well-defined stake hole (context 338) and what appears to be the remains of a simple, hollow shelter (Feature 300) with a single posthole (McCartney et al. 2009: 3–8, figs. 1–2). Burnt deposits in Feature 300 may indicate the remains of some sort of industrial activity or, more likely, destruction by fire. The nature of the construction and the character of the finds (a partly cobbled floor [?], several groundstone artefacts) suggest that this was a small, (semi-)circular, semi-subterranean shelter similar to Levantine PPNA structures. If so, Feature 300 would represent the

Figure 14. Ayia Vavara *Asprokremmos*, one of two decorated (incised) 'shaft straighteners' found at the site. Courtesy of Carole McCartney and Sturt W. Manning.

earliest 'residential' feature known from Neolithic Cyprus (McCartney et al. 2009: 6). At the present stage of excavation, Ayia Varvara *Asprokremmos* seems to represent a well laid-out formal camp, with substantial evidence for residential and/or industrial activities: numerous faunal remains (especially pig, but also bird bone and freshwater crab), chipped stone refuse, groundstone implements and vessels, evidence of red and yellow ochre processing, a small clay figurine, shaft-straightners for arrows (Figure 14), and more personal ornaments (picrolite pendants and 'thimbles', dentalium beads). The site is discussed more fully below (*Ayia Varvara Asprokremmos: Beyond the PPNA 'Hiatus'*).

Overall the evidence marshalled by the EENC project points to an early Neolithic landscape of inland sites situated adjacent to riverine corridors (McCartney et al. 2006: 51). McCartney (2005: 15–16; 2007) suggests that the *Paleokamina* and *Kelaïdhoni* chipped stone assemblages may reflect temporary activity sites used by foragers, while the *Asprokremmos* material may point to a semi-permanent camp (McCartney et al. 2007; 2009: 7–8). Although it remains unclear how closely related the inland lithic assemblages are to those of the coastal sites discussed above, McCartney has emphasised the clear distinction between lithic production practices in all these sites and the *chaine opératoire* that characterises blade tool manufacture and use at the later, EAN sites of Parekklesia *Shillourokambos* (naviform) and Kissonerga *Mylouthkia* (bidirectional naviform-related blade core reduction). Such differences might be understood as either spatial (coastal vs. inland) or chronological. If the differences prove to be chronological, sites such as *Asprokremmos* would fall within a Cypriot sequence equivalent to the Levantine PPNA.

Several charcoal samples from *Asprokremmos* have now produced six radiocarbon dates that lie, individually, between ca. 9141–8569 Cal BC at 95.4% probability (Manning et al. 2010a: 698–702; see Table 2 and Appendix). This group can probably be placed more tightly between about 8803±49–8728±37 Cal BC (taking the μ±σ for the start and end boundaries for this phase in the Appendix, Model 1); if a possible, likely maximum old-wood allowance of 50±50 years is allowed for, this might suggest real dates for human presence in contexts thus far dated at the site between about, or before, 8753±79–8678±62 Cal BC. This new evidence from *Asprokremmos* suggests that the differences seen in the chipped stone repertoires of the coastal and inland sites noted are indeed chronological in nature. These dates are equivalent to a very early Neolithic phase on Cyprus, contemporary with the Levantine late PPNA– early PPNB; they speak directly to a previously unattested human presence on the island, up to 1,000 years later than *Aetokremnos*, but earlier than EAN *Mylouthkia* and *Shillourokambos*.

Finally, recently initiated excavations at the open-air site of Ayios Tychonas *Klimonas*, some 3 km inland from the sea (near Amathus on the south central coast), also demonstrates a PPNA presence on Cyprus (see further below, p. 69, 84). Excavations over an area of some 700 m² in 2011, conducted by a French Archaeological Mission, uncovered the remains of a partly subterranean circular building some 10 m in diameter (Vigne et al. 2011a). The lithic material recovered is characterised by a unidirectional blade debitage and a toolset comprising small arrowheads, burins, end-scrapers and notches, corresponding generally to PPNA assemblages in the Levant and more specficially to those already recorded at Ayia Varvara *Asprokremmos* (Vigne et al. 2011a: 9–10, figs. 6–7, table 1). There is some evidence of a bone industry (polished bone needle, two polished blades and a cylinder), as well as three picrolite beads and some shell pendants and beads. Also quite similar to finds from Ayia Varvara *Asprokremmos*, the main faunal component (93%) amongst nearly 1,000 specimens is described as an endemic 'small Cypriot wild boar' (*Sus Scrofa* spp.), reportedly like those recently identified at Akrotiri *Aetokremnos* (Vigne et al. 2009). Also present were remnants of domestic dog (*Canis Familiaris*), unknown species of birds, a freshwater tortoise and eight molluscs (Vigne et al. 2011a: 10–12, figs. 9–19, table 2). Thirteen radiocarbon dates from suid bone and tooth enamel, plus one charcoal sample, indicate a date range between 9155–8615 Cal BC, at 2σ (Vigne et al. 2011a: 13–14, table 3), fully corresponding to the dates from Ayia Varvara *Asprokremmos* and placing *Klimonas* firmly within Cyprus's PPNA phase.

Whilst the excavators suggest that *Klimonas* may represent a small, sedentary settlement, at this stage the remains are still limited, and so similar to those at *Asprokremmos* that *Klimonas* too may represent no more than a semi-permanent camp. As the authors note, here and elsewhere, the faunal remains indicate that the people who used this small site subsisted on local resources, and in particular on a small 'endemic' suid that may have been introduced to the island during the Late Glacial era, presumably by other humans (Vigne et al. 2011a: 15; Vigne et al. 2011b: S258, S260). The faunal remains of both *Klimonas* and *Asprokremmos* represent what appears to be a highly unusual case in Mediterranean and Near Eastern archaeology, one in which a human group seems to have subsisted mainly on one species of animal. Thus Cyprus seems to have embarked on its own, unique process of Neolithisation, something that becomes increasingly apparent in the subsequent, Early Aceramic Neolithic period. Even if the island struck out on its own cultural trajectory, however, it continued to maintain some level of contact with the Levantine mainland.

Given the relentless pace of change in the study of the Late Epipalaeolithic/ Mesolithic throughout the Mediterranean (e.g. Broodbank 2006; 2009; Ammerman 2010; Knapp 2010), all discussion and current interpretations remain open-ended. At the time of writing, for example, it is still not possible to argue that Cyprus was continuously occupied between the Late Epipalaeolithic 'Akrotiri phase' (11th–10th millennia Cal BC) and the earliest Aceramic Neolithic (early to mid-9th millennium Cal BC). In any case, it may be useful to decouple the issue of Cyprus's first permanent settlement from questions related to earlier seafaring visits along the island's coasts and the likelihood of semi-permanent camps inland. As Ammerman (2010: 89) observed with respect to early seafaring and a coastal way of life: '…we are now beginning to realize that the early foragers who were making seasonal trips to Cyprus were not heading toward the Neolithic but away from it (in terms of their life style and interests)'.

Coastal Adaptations, Climate and Seafaring

Archaeologists have only recently come to realise the key role that coasts and shorelines have played as zones that attracted mobile human groups, provided marine resources, promoted social contacts and stimulated population growth (Bailey 2004; Bailey and Milner 2002/3: 129; Bailey and Parkington 1988). The fossilisation of terms such as 'hunter-gatherer', fisher or forager shows that neither archaeologists nor ethnographers have understood adequately the roles played by a variety of marine or aquatic resources in prehistoric societies (Pálsson 1988). Nor have they perceived fully the diverse ways and the different degrees to which foragers or early cultivators embraced a sedentary way of life (e.g. Edwards 1989; Milner 2005). Sherratt (2007: 6), by contrast, attempted to define 'foragers' more specifically, noting that such a lifestyle might involve a range of locally available resources – wild cereals in some areas; fish, shellfish or avifauna in others – within a spectrum of hunting, gathering or fishing groups.

The material markers of fisher-foragers (e.g. boats, fish hooks, harpoons) are virtually absent from the pre-Holocene archaeological record. In this case, the

absence of evidence has to be related directly to the fact that late glacial shorelines are tens if not hundreds of metres beyond present-day coasts (Lambeck
and Chappell 2001; Bailey and Milner 2002/3: 132–135). The seafaring capabilities developed by early seafaring fishers and foragers enabled them to tap
new marine resources more expeditiously, to explore new landscapes and seascapes, and to make use of hospitable and accessible coastal sites – whether on
islands or mainlands. Gamble (2003: 232–233) believes that this type of seafaring began deep in human prehistory, because it offered attractive options for
exploration and subsistence, rather than just a response to environmental or
climatic crises. Broodbank (2006: 208), by contrast, feels that a more intensified orientation to the sea (i.e. seafaring) arose during the climatic downturn
of the Late Pleistocene and constituted '…the origin point of the seaborne
networks that gradually started to criss-cross sub-basins and archipelagos, thus
by degrees bringing trans-Mediterranean societies into being'. Whatever the
case may have been, the fact remains that both the Aegean islands and Cyprus
were highly intervisible from land or by sea (McCartney et al. 2010: 132–133,
fig. 13.1), and any maritime activity in the eastern Mediterranean inevitably
involved knowledge of Cyprus.

Le Brun (2001: 116–117) – concerned primarily with the later, Late
Aceramic Neolithic period on Cyprus – emphasised that, in order to reach the
island, some people had to have nourished a long-term intimacy with maritime exploration and the sea, gained a working knowledge of waves and currents and mastered the craft of building boats. Vigne and Cucchi (2005: 188),
attempting to explain the marine transport (in boats propelled by wind and
sail) of five ungulate and three carnivore animal species from the Levantine
mainland to Cyprus during the Neolithic, argued that people were not only
capable of reaching the island during the Late Epipalaeolithic, but that climatic
conditions favourable to navigation must have facilitated their journey. What
were these climatic conditions?

To gain a fuller understanding of what might have brought seafaring fisher-
foragers to Cyprus at this time, and of the landscapes and seascapes they
encountered, it is instructive to consider both matters within the context of
the Younger Dryas climatic cycle. The cold and dry Younger Dryas event (ca.
10,800–9600 Cal BC) is widely seen as one of the most dramatic environmental shifts of the Late Pleistocene (Wasse 2007: 45–46; Stutz et al. 2009). Despite
some concerns or criticisms (e.g. Baruch and Bottema 1991; Watkins 2008:
148–149), Aegean and Near Eastern palynological records generally reveal
good evidence for the Younger Dryas (e.g. Sanlaville 1997: 250–254; Geraga
et al. 2005), and it is difficult to deny that it had some impact in the eastern
Mediterranean (Moore and Hillman 1992; Bottema 1995). Yet we need to bear
in mind the problems in trying to link severe changes in climate to specific
cultural-chronological episodes (Brooks 2006; Maher et al. 2011).

The Younger Dryas was marked everywhere by arid conditions and an increase in plants (*Chenopodiaceae*) associated with saline soils (Rossignol-Strick 1995). The preceding Bølling–Allerød interstadial was marked by a warmer and wetter climate, while the succeeding Holocene was very wet with mild winters (Rossignol-Strick 1999). Despite some disagreement over its severity, Robinson et al. (2006: 1535–1537, and fig. 15C) maintain that the Younger Dryas was a cold and extremely arid period, perhaps the most arid of the Late Pleistocene. Roberts (1998: 76) notes that ecologically sensitive areas near climatic limits, for example the limits of tree growth in the northern Levant, would have been susceptible to even minor temperature changes or moisture variations. On Cyprus, conditions must have mirrored those taking place in the northern Levant, where forests were replaced by dry, steppe-like vegetation (Wasse 2007: 45; Rosen 2007: 69). Such conditions (in the Levant) are argued to have had two main results: (1) the appearance of droughts and significant changes in the plant and animal resources upon which Late Epipalaeolithic people depended (Rosen 2007: 104–105); and (2) population dispersals and increased mobility among Late Natufian groups (Goring-Morris and Belfer-Cohen 1997; Kuijt and Goodale 2009: 403–406; Stutz et al. 2009: 302–304). Maher et al. (2011: 16–17), it should be noted, have cautioned that the Late Natufian may have begun a few hundred years earlier than the onset of the Younger Dryas (about 12,900 Cal BP in their view); if correct, that climatic event cannot be held accountable for some of the demographic movements that have been associated with it.

Using radiocarbon data and the climatic inferences derived from them, Manning et al. (2010a: 699–704, fig. 10) suggest that the earliest human presence on Cyprus (at Akrotiri *Aetokremnos*) corresponds to the time of the cool and arid Younger Dryas climate episode (see also McCartney et al. 2010: 137). With the following, warmer and wetter climatic regime came a time of higher potential for both hunting and farming activities, making Cyprus more attractive and sustainable to increasingly permanent human populations during the Initial Aceramic Neolithic (Cypro-PPNA) and EAN 1 periods. Such a scenario would help to explain why the earliest human exploitation of Cyprus – begun in the more challenging times of the Younger Dryas (i.e. Late Epipalaeolithic) – developed into permanent occupation during the warmer periods (EAN) that followed. Ammerman (2010: 88) presents a more complex scenario, suggesting that the Younger Dryas episode may have prompted two different adaptations in the eastern Mediterranean: (1) intensification of the available flora and fauna – the pathway leading to agriculture, and (2) 'extensification' – the pathway leading to seafaring and foraging.

At this time, however, neither scenario can be verifired: we don't know whether increased seafaring predated the Younger Dryas, or whether the halt in rising sea levels associated with it (Lambeck and Chappell 2001) might have motivated these new fishers and foragers even further. There is no evidence for the means of transport or any other proxy measures (e.g. the remains of domesticated animals and cultivated plants, obsidian) that might enable us to estimate the size of the boats or the number of journeys involved (Vigne and Cucchi 2005). We can suggest, nonetheless, that early seafaring and coastal adaptations would have offered to foragers environments that were buffered from the oscillations of the Younger Dryas, thus providing subsistence advantages that enabled them to adapt more quickly to a changing world, at least more so than they could have done by intensively cultivating cereals and domesticating animals.

The people who came to *Aetokremnos* or other coastal sites left behind clear evidence of their presence, most likely during repeated visits at times of the year favourable to sailing. Excavations at *Aetokremnos* produced a diverse range of marine resources: 70,000 marine invertebrates, including crabs, sea urchins, limpets and topshell. Along with evidence of Melian obsidian found in Lithic Phase VI (11th millennium Cal BP) at Franchthi cave in the Argolid (Perlès 1987: 142–145; Renfrew and Aspinall 1990), and the new finds from sites on several other islands in the Mediterranean (discussed in the introduction to this chapter), the remains from *Aetokremnos* and the new Akamas and Nissi Beach sites (whether Late Epipalaeolithic or EAN or both in date) are indicative of coastal explorations and maritime ventures carried out on a seasonal basis to exploit resources as varied as obsidian (Franchthi only), salt (for dietary purposes, preservation, animal management), sea plants, shellfish and seashells, fish, sea turtles, seals and various avifauna (dove, goose, grebe, shag and teal at *Aetokremnos*) (Ammerman et al. 2008: 28–29, fig. 10; McCartney et al. 2010: 134–135, fig. 13.2).

These examples conform well with Sherratt's (2007: 4–6) 'forager climax', with its networks of interaction extending from the Aegean through the Anatolian plateau to the hilly flanks of the Amanus, Taurus and Zagros mountain ranges. In turn, they also would have formed part of Barker's (2005: 47–49, fig. 3.2) 'foraging seascapes', in which early Holocene fishers and foragers began to make purposeful sea ventures with substantial knowledge of Mediterranean winds, tides and currents. Broodbank (2006: 210) has summarised the essence of these changes very well:

> In different ways both the attested exploits [mainland to Cyprus and back; Argolid to Melos and back] therefore represent risky, dangerous journeys, requiring greater skill at manoeuvring craft in different conditions and over a longer duration, predictive and navigational knowledge of currents and winds, and more extensive mental maps of land- and seamarks. … Put another way, it represents a change in attitude towards the sea, from simply a local provider of resources to a vector for travel.

Because many of these maritime ventures took place during the Younger Dryas climatic episode, with its cooler, arid conditions and more stable sea level, it would seem that Late Epipalaelothic hunters and foragers broadened their spatial horizons during an era of increased pressures on the faunal, floral and mineral resources to which they had become accustomed, and on which they may have been reliant.

If we turn to consider the origin(s) of these new maritime ventures and the earliest visitors to Late Epipalaeolithic Cyprus, two possibilities emerge. Because of similarities in chipped stone assemblages (backed bladelets, microliths, thumbnail scrapers) from the region around Öküzini Cave in Anatolia's Antalya province (14,500–11,000 BC), Bar-Yosef (2001: 136–137, fig. 3) suggested that the fisher-foragers who came to *Aetokremnos* could have originated there (see also Simmons 1999: 320). From the Levantine mainland, evidence for a return by some semi-sedentary people to a more mobile way of life in order to procure diminishing resources during the Late Natufian period (Goring-Morris and Belfer-Cohen 1997; Bar-Yosef 2001: 140; cf. Maher et al. 2011: 16–17) could point to another source area (Broodbank 2006: 211). McCartney's comprehensive analysis of multiple chipped stone assemblages, however, suggests that we cannot trace the origin of those who visited Late Epipalaeolithic Cyprus to any source area on the mainland; nor should their movements be linked to a single 'colonisation' event (McCartney et al. 2007: 27, 29). Instead this very early evidence from Cyprus likely represents a mix of traits assimilated by a mobile population whose way of life was based at least in part on seafaring (Ammerman et al. 2008: 27). In any case, it is impossible at this stage to provide definitive answers when we have barely formulated the questions.

The Late Epipalaeolithic in the eastern Mediterranean was a time of stark contrast and change compared with what preceded it: the climate became colder and dryer, certain plant resources disappeared, some animal populations declined or became extinct, and some human populations may have become more mobile. Along with all these changes, the social dynamics of the people involved must have been transformed. Those who came to Akrotiri *Aetokremnos* may well have encountered the last remnants of two endemic fauna, or else exploited their bones for fuel. Those who came, now or later, on seasonal visits to Nissi Beach, the Akamas peninsula, the uplands of the western Troodos or the foothills of the east central Troodos supplemented their diets by fishing or exploiting other marine resources, and perhaps by hunting birds, practices echoed in the avifauna and marine invertebrates found in Stratum 2 at *Aetokremnos* (Simmons 1999: 170–191, 322–323; Ammerman et al. 2006: 18). However one views the origins of these early visitors to Cyprus, the material and climatic evidence associated with their maritime ventures points to a time of unprecedented demand upon a dwindling set of resources. By the onset of the Early Aceramic Neolithic, the earliest, still-growing evidence for seafaring, foraging and early farming in the eastern Mediterranean suggests that however people may have perceived the risks of insular living – including on Cyprus a restricted and unbalanced terrestrial food base and uncertain if not marginal pelagic resources, such risks must have outweighed the benefits of remaining where they were.

EARLY ACERAMIC NEOLITHIC: FIRST SETTLERS

Over the past two decades, new excavations and survey have pushed back the date for the earliest Neolithic occupation of Cyprus by at least 2,000 years, from ca. 7000/6800 Cal BC to as early as 9000 Cal BC. Moreover, new evidence on Cyprus for cultivated if not domesticated cereals and pulses (see Chapter 1, *Flora and Fauna*) is scarcely later than their earliest attestation in the Levant or Anatolia (Nesbitt 2002: 122). For example, despite ongoing controversy over the date of the earliest cereal cultivation in the Near East (Nesbitt 2002; Willcox 2002; 2007: 32–33; Willcox et al. 2009), nobody would dispute a date early in the PPNB period (ca. 8500–8100 Cal BC) (Colledge et al. 2004). Currently, only one PPNA example (Cafer Höyük, 9250–8700 Cal BC – Colledge and Conolly 2007: 67, table 4.5) is earlier than the evidence of cultivated, and likely domesticated einkorn, emmer and hulled barley found at Kissonerga *Mylouthkia* (Colledge 2004; Colledge and Conolly 2007: 53–60) (for the location of all these sites, see Figure 15, below).

With respect to animals, recall that nearly half the faunal remains recovered thus far from Ayia Varvara *Asprokremmos* are from pigs that somehow had to be brought to Cyprus; this site is now dated in absolute terms to ca. 9000–8500 Cal BC (Manning et al. 2010a: 698–702, figs. 8–9). The earliest unit at *Mylouthkia* (IA) contained only a few pig and ovicaprid bones. At Paraklessia *Shillourokambos*, however, there is abundant evidence for domesticated (or 'managed') pig (and reputedly 'feral' pig – Vigne et al. 2003: 241–243), goat, sheep and cattle that are as early as any domesticates known from the Levant or Anatolia (Conolly et al. 2011: 543). The first attested 'domesticated' pigs, sheep and goat in the Near East, for example, come from Çayönü and Nevali Çori in southeastern Anatolia, and are dated ca. 8300–8100 Cal BC (Peters et al. 1999; 2005; Hongo and Meadow 2000), largely contemporaneous with the evidence from *Shillourokambos* (Vigne and Buitenhuis 1999; Vigne et al. 2000: 100).

Following on from all the new developments associated with the Late Epipalaeolithic, the basic contours of the Cypriot Aceramic Neolithic must now be redrawn entirely, with Cyprus taking its place amongst the emerging agropastoral traditions of the Levant and Anatolia (Kuijt 2004; Simmons 2004b). Practices associated with seafaring – developed initially as a mobile, diversification response by complex fishers, foragers and hunters during the Younger Dryas – became more established in the early Neolithic. Such practices would have facilitated closer communications and connections between the various sub-basins of the Mediterranean (Broodbank 2006: 217), a phenomenon repeated in the communication webs that characterised the early Holocene 'forager complex' (Sherratt 2007: 4–5) in the Levantine Corridor and the region around the upper courses of the Balikh and Khabur rivers.

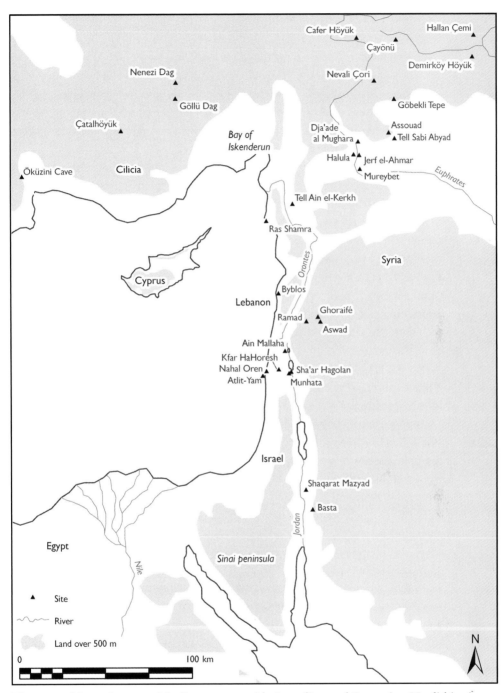

Figure 15. Map of eastern Mediterranean, with Anatolian and Levantine Neolithic sites mentioned in the text. Drawn by Luke Sollars.

The close cultural links between the earliest Neolithic archaeological evidence on Cyprus and the Pre-Pottery Neolithic (PPNA, PPNB) cultures in the Levant and Anatolia have led some of the archaeologists most closely involved to classify the material evidence as the 'Cypro–PPNB *facies*' of the mainland PPNB – in tandem with the use of the term 'Taurus *facies*' for the PPNB in southeast Anatolia (Cauvin and Cauvin 1993). Thus the period is now widely referred to as the Cypro-PPNB, with early, middle and late phases (Cypro-EPPNB, Cypro-MPPNB, Cypro-LPPNB – Peltenburg et al. 2001a: 37–38; 2001b: 65). McCartney (2004: 108, table 9.1; 2007: table 1a) has referred to these three phases as Early Cypriot Aceramic (Neolithic), Middle Cypriot Aceramic and Late Cypriot Aceramic (noted as an 'alternate system' by Peltenburg et al. 2003: 87, table 11.3).

Both Watkins (2004: 29–31) and Le Brun (2004: 10) were quite critical of the 'Cypro-PPNB' terminology, and Watkins (2008) challenged the entire concept of a PPNB 'interaction sphere', arguing that major regional differences in material culure throughout the region undermine the possibility of any cultural coherence. Croft (2003a: 270), equally concerned about the use of 'PPNB' in the Cypriot context, terms the period 'pre-Khirokitian Neolithic'. The use of the PPNB terminology exemplifies well the tendency to view material developments on Cyprus through the lenses of Near Eastern, Anatolian or Aegean archaeology, masking the unique, always different indigenous traditions of the island. In this work, therefore, the period overall is termed more simply Early Aceramic Neolithic (EAN) and divisions within it as EAN 1 (=Cypro-EPPNB), EAN 2 (=Cypro-MPPNB) and EAN 3 (=Cypro-LPPNB) (see Table 2, above, p. 27, with approximate dates). The earliest, currently attested human presence on the island during the Neolithic (McCartney et al. 2009; Manning et al. 2010a) accordingly might better be termed the Initial Aceramic Neolithic, but here, for the most part, I have adopted 'Cypro-PPNA', because the connections of this phase with preceding and subsequent periods have yet to be firmly established.

Migration and Permanent Settlement

Until the 1990s, the material culture of the Neolithic defied comparison with any mainland variant; thus it was assumed that Cyprus's Aceramic Neolithic culture was not just later than those on the mainland but independent (or a retarded variant) of them. Several sites excavated over the last 15 years, however, have radically changed this picture of the Cypriot Neolithic. Amongst some of the key issues that now challenge our understanding of this era of island settlement and development are (1) the relationship of Cyprus's EAN culture with the PPNA/B cultures of the Levant and Anatolia, and (2) the relevance of submerged sites on the Levantine coastal shelf, and of the 'Mediterranean Fishing Village' (Galili et al. 2002; 2004), for contemplating the origins of the earliest sedentary villagers on Cyprus.

Sherratt (2007: 7) maintains that the 'climatic forcing-mechanism' of the Younger Dryas (ca. 10,800–9600 Cal BC) was only one part of a complex conjunction of conditions that led Levantine foragers and hunters to experiment with the cultivation and storage of plant food resources (see also Garrard 1999; Watkins 2008; Zeder 2009: 45–48). The resulting droughts, deterioration in woodlands and steppe and reduction in food resources (Bottema 1995: 890; Bar-Yosef 2001: 140; Rosen 2007: 104–105) led to social responses – more mobile, changing lifeways; adjustment to new plant and animal regimes – that would have been strongly felt, no matter how intangible they might be in the material record. Some people were on the move, whether by land or at sea, and dispersed to previously unsettled areas (such as Cyprus) or to regions less affected by the cooler, drier climate (such as the Mediterranean coastal plain). Others, reacting to reduced food supplies (Goring-Morris and Belfer-Cohen 1997) or just optimising their resources (McCorriston and Hole 1991), began systematically to cultivate cereals. Both factors help to provide a more holistic understanding of EAN Cyprus.

The early Holocene era (ca. 11,500–7000 Cal BP), when a settled, Neolithic way of life became pre-eminent amongst the people of the Levant and western Asia, was an extremely wet phase (Robinson et al. 2006: 1535–1536, fig. 15d). By its end (about 7000–6000 years ago), along some 600 km of the eastern Mediterranean littoral, from the Bay of Iskenderun in the north to the Sinai peninsula in the south, parts of the coastal plain – ranging from 2–40 km in width – had been lost to rising sea levels. The inundation of this coast affected hunters, fishers, foragers and would-be farmers in different ways, reducing their territory, destroying their habitats and limiting their access to marine resources (Bar-Yosef 2001: 133; Petit Marie 2004: 18–19; Stewart and Morhange 2009: 401–402). The origins, motivations and movements of the people who came to Cyprus and settled must be viewed within this environmental and climatic context.

In considering their origins, however, we are immediately confronted with a paradox: on the Syrian coast nearest Cyprus, we find no evidence of occupation by agriculturalists before the late PPNB, at Ras Shamra level VC (de Contenson 1992: 197–199; Cauvin 2000: 154–155, 161), some 1,000 years after the earliest settled communities appeared on Cyprus (for all these Levantine or Anatolian sites, see Figure 15). The only possible exception is the inland site of Tell Ain el-Kerkh in the Rouj basin (Tsuneki et al. 2006; Arimura 2007). The further paradox is that the closest material and economic parallels for the Cypriot EAN culture seem to come from various PPNA/B sites in the so-called Levantine Corridor, some 200 km inland (Peltenburg et al. 2001a: 38, fig. 2, 58; see also Stordeur 2003a; Peltenburg 2004a: 3–4). It has also been suggested that close structural similarities exist between some buildings at Kalavasos *Tenta* (Period 2) and those from inland PPNA Jerf el-Ahmar in Syria and Göbekli Tepe in Anatolia (Peltenburg et al. 2001a: 41–42, fig. 4; Beile-Bohn et al. 1998: 48, fig. 20; Stordeur 2003a: 355–360).

There are also close similarities between the lithic *chaines opératoires* seen at several Cypriot sites and those from several inland Levantine PPNB sites, whether in the south (e.g. Aswad, Ramad, Ghoraifé) or in the north (e.g. Dja'ade el Mughara, Mureybet, Assouad), as well as in eastern Anatolia (e.g. Cafer Höyük, Demirköy Höyük) (McCarthy, in Peltenburg et al. 2001a: 49–53, fig. 9). Other Anatolian imports (obsidian) or material parallels (chipped stone) with the Cypriot EAN sites have been noted (Cauvin 1991; Bar-Yosef 2003: 76–77), but the only Anatolian sites – beyond those in the distant southeast – contemporary with the EAN 1 on Cyprus (ca. 8500–8000 Cal BC) are on the central plateau (Özdoğan 2004; Baird 2005). All other sites currently known are either too early or too late to be of relevance (cf. Peltenburg 2004b: xvii, for possible earlier sites on the Cilician plain).

In any case, it is unlikely that people who lived so far inland, whether in central Anatolia or in the Levantine Corridor, would have had the maritime knowledge or expertise necessary to reach an island and establish permanent bases there. Extrapolating from the slightly later, PPNC evidence from the submerged coastal site of Atlit-Yam in Israel (Galili et al. 2002; 2004), however, we can speculate that *some* early PPNB agriculturalists did live along the Cilician or Levantine costal plains, had undertaken exploratory forays overseas and thus were aware of Cyprus's potential for permanent settlement. We still need to explain, however, why we find no evidence for coastal agropastoralists before about 7000 Cal BC.

During the Late Glacial Maximum, the Mediterranean Sea fell to a point some 120 m below present-day levels. Subsequently, the most notable rise occurred between about 17,000–11,000 BP (Shackleton et al. 1984; Lambeck and Purcell 2005: 1985–1987, fig. 14). Sea level had risen to about 40–50 m lower than the present day by the 11th millennium BC (Lambeck and Chappell 2001: 683; Broodbank 2006: 209), and by the 8th millennium BC had risen to only 7 m lower than present (Cherry 1990: 192–193). Not until about 6,000 years ago did the sea reach modern levels (van Andel 1989: 736; Lambeck and Chappell 2001: 683; Pirazzoli 2005: 1996–1999). Most shorelines, coastal sites, activity areas or maritime features that existed before that time are thus by definition now submerged (Flemming 1998), and some are several kilometres from present-day coasts (Bailey and Milner 2002/3: 132–133).

The eastern Mediterranean shoreline thus was at least 15–25 m lower during the PPN than it is today. With the warmer and wetter climate of the early Holocene, the coastal plains had become rich and fertile, offering desirable habitats for foragers and farmers alike (Sherratt 2007: 4–5). However, anyone living permanently or even periodically in settlements along a coastal plain that increasingly was subject to flooding and inundation would have suffered acute social and environmental stress (Stewart and Morhange 2009: 402). In the end, they lost not only their land and homes but also the marine, plant and animal resources that provided their subsistence. In such a situation, the appeal (or 'pull', in migratory terms) of an uninhabited island like Cyprus, surely well known (through earlier visits) to any coastal dwellers in the region, would

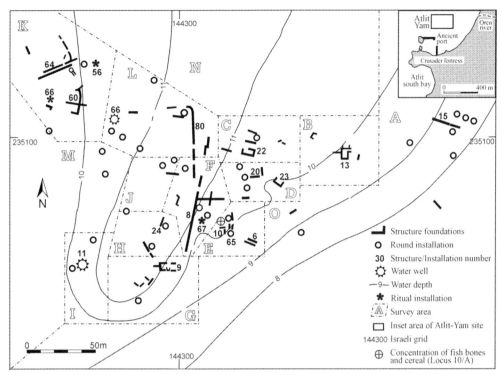

Figure 16. Atlit-Yam: Final PPNB (=PPNC) underwater site, showing distribution of installations and features. Courtesy of Ehud Galili, Israel Antiquities Authority. (Originally published in *Journal of Mediterranean Archaeology* 15 [2002] 176, fig. 6.)

have been strong. Even if ecosystemic stress served as a catalyst for the initial settlement of Cyprus, the incentive of coastal dwellers (fisher-foragers or farmers) to travel to the island already existed, as we now understand from work at *Aetokremnos* (and possibly at Nissi Beach and Akamas *Aspros*).

Whereas *Aetokremnos*, Nissi Beach and *Aspros* are suggestive of submerged sites on the coastal plain of Cyprus, the only current evidence for such sites along the south Anatolian or north Levantine coasts is either too early or too late to be relevant (cf. Peltenburg 2004b: xvii). The southern Levantine coast comes into play because of the submerged site of Atlit-Yam, dated to the final PPNB/PPNC, late 8th–early 7th millennium Cal BC (Figure 16) (Galili and Nir 1993; Galili et al. 2002). Atlit-Yam today is some 200–400 m offshore, and lies at a depth of 8–12 m beneath the sea. Extending over an area of some 40,000 m², it contains everything from structural foundations and stone-built water wells, to floral and faunal remains (wild and domestic ovicaprids, pig, cattle and dog) and marine fish, to human burials (Galili et al. 2005). Atlit-Yam has been characterised as an archetypal Mediterranean Fishing Village (MFV) whose inhabitants survived not just on agricultural production but also on the intensive exploitation of marine resources.

In discussing the wider ramifications of the MFV, Galili et al. (2002: 187–190; 2004: 94–97) make two debatable points. First, they argue that such fishing villages emerged only during the late PPNB (ca. 7000 Cal BC) in response to deforestation, overgrazing or related factors, and they discount the likelihood of similar human responses to the upheavals wrought by rising sea levels in earlier PPN times. They are sceptical that earlier Levantine coastal sites existed because intensive land and underwater surveys have failed to recover them. Their observation, however, pertains only to the southern Levant, as few coastal or underwater surveys have been undertaken elsewhere. Moreover, some coastal sites in Lebanon dated to the PPN (Tell aux Scies, Dik el-Mahdi) may well fit the MFV model (Cauvin 1968: 219–229; Peltenburg 2004b: xvii). Second, they maintain that Cyprus's EAN 1 sites are not true MFVs as they lack adequate evidence for marine resource exploitation. They could not have known when writing, however, that more recent fieldwork on the island would soon uncover Late Epipalaeolithic and EAN sites exploited by fisher-foragers, at least some parts of which may have been situated on a now submerged coastal plain.

Sites that conform to the MFV model must have emerged, developed and changed at different times, for different reasons (similarly McCartney, in Clarke 2007a: 88–89). 'Environmental degradation', as Galili et al. (2004: 95) define it, is not limited to the actions of farmers and herders. It seems much more likely that the MFV would have emerged at suitable harbour-type locations along the east Mediterranean seaboard during the environmental and social crises associated with rising sea levels in the late Pleistocene–early Holocene. Moreover, and following from that, we must assume that most Late Epipalaeolithic or early Neolithic MFVs situated along these coasts will only be found on what are today submerged coastal plains, at various depths beneath the sea and at various distances from the current eastern Mediterranean shoreline (similarly, Rollefson 2004).

When we are able to present a fuller tale of the earliest Neolithic in the Mediterranean, these submerged coastal sites will be crucial in its telling. Simmons (1999: 321–322) already observed that '…those responsible for *Aetokremnos* were a conservative group of early Levantine Neolithic peoples' who rejected an agropastoral lifestyle for hunting and gathering in a new, insular setting. We can now see that Late Epipalaeolithic sites such as *Aetokremnos* (and perhaps Nissi Beach and Akamas *Aspros*) were indeed moving away from what is typically regarded as a Neolithic (i.e. farming) way of life, or that treated farming as only one component along a resource spectrum that supported a foraging lifestyle (Sherratt 2007: 6). It is also important to emphasise once again that none of these sites reveals any direct material affinities with the best-known sites of the Early Aceramic Neolithic.

We cannot yet demonstrate the existence of any Levantine PPN fishing village that might have served as the origin of the earliest settlers of Cyprus

(Peltenburg et al. 2001a: 59; Peltenburg et al. 2003: 97). Nonetheless, the earliest settled villages on Cyprus shared many and diverse material connections with various sites in the PPNA–PPNB Levant – themselves revealing much variability in everything from their chipped stone repertoires to their mortuary traditions (McCartney 2004: 104–105; Watkins 2008). Thus we may conclude, tentatively, that the new and now permanent settlers of EAN 1 Cyprus came from somewhere along the 500–600 km of the Levantine coast (Broodbank 2006: 216; Sherratt 2007: 11). Wherever they came from, their arrival on Cyprus represents what is probably the earliest successful overseas migration of farmers in the Mediterranean, a journey that entailed the transport of both domesticated and wild fauna as well as seed crops (Peltenburg et al. 2001a: 55–60; Peltenburg et al. 2003: 98–99; Peltenburg 2004a: 4–5; Sherratt 2007: 11).

Because sophisticated excavations employing modern approaches and techniques have revealed founder crops and managed or early domesticated animals on Cyprus's most prominent EAN 1 sites at a time equivalent to or only slightly later than they first appear in the Levantine Corridor and southeastern Anatolia, we must reassess long-cherished notions about the Levant's primacy in matters of Neolithic subsistence and mobility, including the very nature, extent and relevance of exploitation and exchange in PPN 'interaction spheres' (Bar-Yosef and Belfer-Cohen 1989; cf. Kuijt 2004; Sherratt 2007; Watkins 2008). From a more radical perspective, one could even argue that the Neolithic 'revolution' in ancient western Asia lasted more than 10,000 years, and that its various components were 'rolled out' in various ways and at different times throughout a vast area extending from Iran in the east to Cyprus and the Aegean world in the west (Zeder 2009: 45).

Broodbank (2006: 216) observed that Cyprus's earliest settlement likely reflects a fusion of two competing ideologies: (1) the ethos of seafaring fisher-foragers (who continued to exploit Cyprus's coast during PPNB times – Ammerman et al. 2008: 15); and (2) the 'expansionist' outlook of stressed coastal dwellers in search of new lands to settle, new places to live. Thus in his view, the earliest permanent settlement of Cyprus was not part of an inevitable maritime expansion into the Mediterranean, but was conditioned from the outset by challenging environmental circumstances that propelled people with a working knowledge of the sea to explore and exploit the unknown. Whether seafaring on an intensive scale emerged as a human-induced response to climatic or social crises (Broodbank 2006: 217), or as an intentional, 'heroic tradition' driven by the ideology of discovery and subsistence (Gamble 2003: 232–233), a new maritime tradition and seafaring lifestyle now facilitated human movement throughout the Mediterranean, the 'extensification' process noted by Ammerman (2010: 88). At the same time, this new tradition played a critical role in transporting the people, plants and animals involved in the origins and 'intensification' of agriculture.

Adaptations, Agriculture and Social Change

All the new evidence for complex foragers and early agriculturalists on Cyprus – discussed here and in the following sections – demonstrates that Cyprus was closely involved in the social, economic and material developments previously associated exclusively with the late PPNA–early PPNB Levant, between about 9000–8000 Cal BC (see also McCartney 2010 and Table 2, above, p. 27). A tentative sequence of developments is provided in Table 3 (based on Peltenburg et al. 2003: 99, table 11.6; Peltenburg 2004a: 5–6, fig. 2, but with different dates, periodisation and practices). How well does this scenario stand up to closer examination? To answer that question, we must first look in some detail at the various sites involved.

The published results of three recent excavations have completely altered previous views on the origins and developments of the earliest Neolithic on Cyprus. These sites are Parreklishia *Shillourokambos* (northeast of Limassol, 5 km from the current coastline), Kissonerga *Mylouthkia* (north of Paphos, about 100 m from the current shoreline) and Ayia Varvara *Asprokremmos* (Troodos foothills, north central Cyprus) (see Figure 7, above, for site locations). Although future work at the last site may alter current views on its purpose, the shallow occupation deposits, the ephemeral nature of the structural features, and the lack of burials or identifiable midden deposits suggest that *Asprokremmos* may only have been occupied seasonally or periodically. By contrast, the agropastoral economies evident at the EAN 1 sites of *Shillourokambos* and *Mylouthkia*, as well as those at Kalavasos *Tenta*, Kritou Marottou *Ais Giorkis* and Akanthou *Arkosyko*, are amongst the earliest in ancient western Asia, and must represent aspects of the initial, permanent settlement of the island (Peltenburg et al. 2000; 2001a). Although these new people and their sedentary way of life spread rapidly, economic and cultural adaptations were more gradual, perhaps the result of prolonged but slowly diminishing contacts with the mainland. By the end of the Early Aceramic Neolithic, around 7000/6800 Cal BC, the chipped stone industry had changed, cattle had disappeared from the archaeological record, and deer – along with pig – had become the major components of the subsistence diet. The Late Aceramic Neolithic (LAN, or Khirokitia Culture), after a long phase of insular development that engaged the island's earliest agropastoralists (Peltenburg et al. 2000: 852), finally emerged as something quite distinctive from that which preceded it.

AYIA VARVARA *ASPROKREMMOS*: BEYOND THE PPNA 'HIATUS'

> It is a fact of human nature that people tend to see what they have an expectation of seeing. People tend not to see things with which they are unfamiliar; things that are not already part of the vocabulary of their visual memory are easily missed. (Watkins 2004: 32)

It is all too natural to assume (1) that we have yet to find adequate archaeological indicators of what would surely prove to be somewhat ephemeral sites

TABLE 3. *Periods, dates, sites and socio-economic practices: Late Epipalaeolithic–Late Aceramic Noelithic*

Period and sites (with approximate dates Cal BC)	Socio-economic practices
Late Epipalaeolithic (ca. 11,000–9000 Cal BC): *Aetokremnos* (Nissi Beach, Akamas *Aspros*??)	Seafaring; fisher-forager exploration
Initial Aceramic Neolithic (Cypro-PPNA) (ca. 9000–8500 Cal BC) *Asprokremnos, Klimonas* (*Palaeokamina, Keläidhoni*??)	Seafaring; exploration; game-stocking
Early Aceramic Neolithic – EAN (Cypro-PPNB): *Shillourokambos, Mylouthkia, Tenta, Ais Giorkis*	
EAN 1 (Cypro-EPPNB) (ca. 8500–7900 Cal BC)	Seafaring; cultivators; early farmers
EAN 2 (Cypro-MPPNB) (ca. 7900–7600 Cal BC)	Seafaring; consolidation of farming economy
EAN 3 (Cypro-LPPNB) (ca. 7600–7000/6800 Cal BC)	Seafaring; insular adaptation of farming
Late Aceramic Neolithic (ca. 7000/6800–5200 Cal BC)	Development and floruit of 'Neolithic'

to fill the temporal gap between Late Epipalaolithic *Aetokremnos* and the EAN 1 sites at *Shillourokambos* and *Mylouthkia*, and (2) that future fieldwork will remedy the situation. Following on from earlier suggestions about a phase antecedent to the EAN on Cyprus (Peltenburg 2004a: 4–5; Watkins 2004; McCartney 2005: 16; 2009: 267; McCartney et. al. 2007), Guilaine and Briois (2006: 161–162) posited the case for what they term the 'PPNA hiatus' on Cyprus. In their view, either we assume that (a) groups of people from the neighbouring mainland made periodic visits, possibly of long-term duration, to the island, or else we accept that (b), in this case, the absence of evidence actually indicates that no humans were present on Cyprus during the (unknown number of) years that separate the Late Epipalaolithic from the EAN.

Reconsideration of a range of both circumstantial and hard evidence from field survey, previous excavations and newer excavations in fact already fill this gap. For example, two radiocarbon determinations on shell (corrected) from Akrotiri *Vounarouthkia ton Lamnion* East ('Site 23') (Simmons 1999: 254–258) give an average date of 9027–8678 Cal BC, too early for EAN 1 and possibly contemporary with the Levantine PPNA. This site had a very low density of artefactual material, the most significant of which was the chipped stone (41 pieces in all, of which 8 were tools). Amongst the tools was a single projectile point that Swiny (1988: 5: 10–11) linked to Byblos points of the Levantine PPNB (cf. Simmons 1999: 256). Test excavations produced little else: marine shell (266 fragments), a single ovicaprid bone, a possible quern, and a few potsherds from later periods.

More relevant is some evidence from Parreklishia *Shillourokambos* (see following section). From its earliest levels (Early Phase A), Vigne et al. (2003) maintain that there are two distinct populations of pigs: one managed and one feral. Given that pigs are not endemic to Cyprus, it stands to reason that any 'wild' (feral) population must have been introduced prior to the occupation of *Shillourokambos*; might they represent remnants of the enigmatic suids found at *Aetokremnos* (Simmons 1999: 166–167, 321; Vigne et al. 2009)?

The excavator of *Shillourokambos* has also identified two distinct architectural sub-phases in the site's earliest level: (1) an earlier one represented by posts dug into the underlying *havara*, and (2) a later one that includes elements described as stockaded enclosures (Guilaine and Brios 2006: 162). The structures suggested by this 'palimpsest' of the earlier subsurface features are either 'sub-circular' (a dwelling?) or 'sub-horizontal rows' (animal enclosures?) (Guilaine and Brios 2006: 163, fig. 2; Guilaine et al. 2011: 143–151, figs. 1–2; 649–652). Such features recall Levantine PPNA patterns (e.g. at Ain Mallaha, Mureybet, Hallan Çemi, Çayönü) rather than the rectangular traditions of early PPNB dwellings. Could these early structures at *Shillourokambos* represent the 'heritage' of an earlier group of people, contemporaneous with the Levantine PPNA and familiar with its building tradition?

Guilaine and Brios (2006: 162; Guilaine et al. 2011: 664–667) also point to the use of a translucent Lefkara chert that characterises the earliest phases at *Shillourkambos*, now also identified amongst (surface) survey finds at two localities in the same area – Ayios Tychonas *Klimonas* and *Throumbovounos* I (see Brios et al. 2005: 42–47, 52–55). The chipped stone industries at these sites are reputedly unknown elsewhere on Cyprus, and are said to be comparable to certain lithic industries in the northern Levantine PPNA or early PPNB. They include the debitage of unidirectional small blades on conical or prismatic cores and many burins (*Throumbovounos* I), as well as early forms of a bidirectional core technology associated with projectile points having a short tang (*Klimonas*). Some of these features, however, notably the use of a unidirectional core technology and burins – along with some scrapers that have close parallels in the late PPNA in Syria (Coqueugniot 2003: 377–378; 2004: 296–297) – are also well attested and extensively documented at one excavated site that may be related to a human presence on Cyprus at this time, Ayia Varvara *Asprokremmos* (McCartney 2011: 191–192; Manning et al. 2010a: 697–698).

Most discussions of a human presence on Cyprus during a time period equivalent to the PPNA in the Levant have revolved around chipped stone tool assemblages and their related *chaines opératoires*. The lithic assemblage from *Asprokremmos* has been mentioned several times before, with respect to (1) its arrowheads and predominantly unidirectional, blade-based technology which, together with the presence of microlithic elements and bifacially retouched blades, show parallels with Late Epipalaeolithic and particularly with late PPNA assemblages of the northern Levant; and (2) its distinctiveness from the assemblages found at EAN sites such as *Mylouthkia* and *Shillourokambos*. All these factors tend to support the view that *Asprokremmos* was contemporary with the Levantine late PPNA to early PPNB, and that the site may have served as a camp for (mobile?) Neolithic groups present on Cyprus before the advent of the EAN 1 farming communities (McCartney 2003: 145–146; 2007;

McCartney et al. 2007; 2008; 2009). Beyond the lithic evidence, other aspects of material culture increasingly point in the same direction, while new radio-carbon evidence from *Asprokremmos* now confirms the dating (Manning et al. 2010a; and see above pp. 73–74).

Situated on a small saddle between two low hills in central Cyprus, *Asprokremmos* is bounded on the west by the Yialias River and is strategically located in a resource zone with abundant local cherts (for its location, see Figure 7 above). It enjoys easy access to the forests of the Troodos Mountains and even today the Yialias River holds water the year round. Its position at the junction between the open plain (*Mesaoria*) and the forested mountains would have been ideally suited to foragers, while its situation on a riverine terrace with easy access to a secure source of water might be seen as more typical of early village societies (McCartney 2011: 187). As noted previously, three stratigraphic phases within a single period of Neolithic occupation have been distinguished in separate areas of the 150 m² excavated at the site. Six charcoal samples from one trench have been radiocarbon dated to ca. 9000–8500 Cal BC (late PPNA in the Levant), and there is evidence of one, semi-subterranean hollow shelter. Thus far, however, there is nothing as complex as similar features seen in the earliest phase at *Shillourokambos* (Guilaine and Briois 2006: 164–166, figs. 2–4; Guilaine et al. 2011: 153–155, figs. 1–4) or *Tenta* (Todd 2003: 39–40, and fig. 5).

The abundant groundstone found at *Asprokremmos* (McCartney et. al. 2006: 45–47, and fig. 3a–d) suggests that its inhabitants exploited a variety of plant resources (still non-existant at the site despite systematic flotation). Many of the ground stone tools were used for grinding red and yellow ochre. Amongst several calcareous groundstone vessels recovered were some undecorated flat-based trays, as well as some shallow globular bowl fragments. More interesting, and thus far unique on Cyprus, is a small fragment of a well-made globular bowl with traces of parallel lines painted on its exterior surface in red ochre. Other notable finds from *Asprokremmos* include a fragmentary baked-clay fig-urine (the earliest known on Cyprus), ornaments made of exotic dentalium and other shells but also of local picrolite, one bone point and two decorated (incised) 'shaft straighteners' (McCartney et al. 2008: 73–75, fig. 3a–c; Manning et al. 2010a: figs. 4–6; see Figure 14 above). Both the economic and the symbolic aspects of these artefacts must be taken into account. The shaft straighteners, for example, well known from north Syrian sites (e.g. Stordeur 2003b) and presumably used for arrows or similar projectiles, intuitively may be regarded as evidence for hunting. These examples, however, are incised and thus not dissimilar to 'grooved stones' from Levantine Late Epipalaeolithic–PPNB sites. Along with the baked-clay figurine, which finds an echo in an example from PPNA levels at Gilgal in the southern Levant (Noy 1994: 518), they may have formed part of a system of symbolic (feminine?) representation (Cauvin 2000: 48–49, fig. 20.2–6; Watkins 2008: 159), which would therefore now include the island of Cyprus.

Nearly half the mammalian faunal material thus far identified at *Asprokremmos* belongs to pig; some bird and freshwater crab remains have also been recorded. Interestingly, in considering possible links between Cyprus and its mainland counterparts, this dominance of pig in the faunal assemblage is also seen at the Syrian site of Tell Ain el-Kerkh (Tsuneki et al. 2006: 57, 66), already mentioned as a possible early PPNB site near the Syrian coast opposite Cyprus. Wasse (2007: 57) suggests that the small number of pigs attested at Late Epipalaeolithic Akrotiri *Aetokremnos* may signal the earliest presence of a sizeable population of pigs on the island that may have originated in the now-submerged Syro-Cilician plain; in time it became feralised throughout the ecological niche left by the extinct pygmy hippos (see also Vigne et al. 2009). The reputed presence of a feral pig population at *Shillourokambos* (Early Phase A and at *Klimonas*) should also be recalled in this context (Guilaine and Briois 2006: 171; Vigne et al. 2011a), and both factors may be related to the apparent dependence on pig at *Asprokremmos* (McCartney 2011: 192). Indeed, if a feral pig population became established on the island at some point after the Late Epipalaeolithic, the people from *Asprokremmos* and other contemporary sites may have exploited a much less impoverished environment than is typically assumed (McCartney et al. 2010: 135). Whilst on a broader basis the whole issue of wild, feral, managed or domesticated pigs is a thorny one (see Rosenberg et al. 1998; Albarella et al. 2006; Vigne et al. 2009; Conolly et al. 2011: 540), at *Asprokremmos* it forms one more piece of evidence in a larger puzzle.

More than 800 kg of chipped stone have been recovered at *Asprokremmos*, mainly from a 'dumping' area (McCartney et al. 2008: 70). The most striking component of this assemblage is the group of more than 100 complete and fragmentary arrowheads produced on prismatic unidirectional blades (McCartney et. al. 2008: 71–73, fig. 2a–d) (see Figure 13g above); these points outstrip the total number of all such tools found in EAN assemblages combined. There are two main types of arrowheads, both manufactured with a bifacial retouch: one has a short lozenge-shaped tang while the other is formed by a convex basal truncation (McCartney 2011: 189, fig. 3). Other tool types include a wide range of burins (the dominant type), notched blades and finely retouched blades, scrapers (especially end scrapers), perforators and truncations (used as hafting devices) (McCartney et al. 2006: 53, fig. 7). Amongst the microlithic tools are a small number of geometrics that, together with some bifacially retouched blades, recall Late Epipalaeolithic tool types (Manning et al. 2010a: 697–698). By contrast, glossed tools, backed pieces and denticulates are somewhat rare.

The variability seen in the raw materials used to produce the chipped stone is clearly related to the density of chert in the area (see McCartney et. al. 2006; 2007; 2009). To the north, east and south of the site, diverse chert sources are situated along the boundary of the Pillow Lava fringe of the Troodos and in the Lefkara chert-bearing chalks. High-quality tranclucent Lefkara cherts dominate the *Asprokremmos* assemblage, but less fine, opaque and granular types were similarly exploited. Only one small chip of obsidian, found during a preliminary surface survey (McCartney 1998: 85), ever reached this inland site. The choice of raw materials selected for use seems to have changed through time, from an earlier, significant proportion of lower quality, granular, blue-grey Lefkara-translucent chert to a later predominance of higher quality, red-brown translucent cherts (McCartney 2011: 188). The people at *Asprokremmos* clearly were engaged in the intensive extraction and exploitation of a wide range of raw materials as well as their transformation into chipped stone or groundstone tools, artefacts and implements.

The material culture as well as the radiocarbon dates from Ayia Varvara *Asprokremmos* confirm a phase on Cyprus contemporary with the Levantine late PPNA–early PPNB (Manning et al. 2010a: 699). This phase is clearly distinct from the subsequent EAN and shows links to the middle Euphrates as well as western Syria (e.g. the use of unidirectional blade/bladelet cores, small lozenge points and small ovular points, well-made scrapers, glossed segments with convex basal truncations), southeast Anatolia (stone vessels; dominance of pig in the faunal assemblage – also in north Syria), and the central and southern Levant (parallels in some of the convex ovular points; the small baked-clay figurine) (McCartney 2011: 192). Above all, the arrowheads represent a breakthrough in establishing material and possibly symbolic links to the arrowhead complex of the Levantine Corridor, whilst the shaft straighteners do the same but link more specifically to the mid-Euphrates area. Such a wide range of parallels implies that the people and culture of Cyprus's earliest Neolithic evolved not in isolation but through 'imbedded interactions' with the mainland, from the Euphrates region to the southern Levant. Such interactions are evident in the continuous appearance of new lithic features and perhaps in repeated attempts to restock the island with domesticated or managed fauna (Horwitz et al. 2004: 38; Peltenburg 2004a: 6, fig. 2).

For those who remain sceptical about a PPNA-equivalent phase on Cyprus, and like the diversity of all these parallels, such differences from EAN material culture may imply similar developments along distinct but intersecting paths. With a consistent series of radiocarbon dates, however, both *Asprokremmos* and Ayios Tychonas *Klimonas* can now be seen as representing the closure of the PPNA 'hiatus' on Cyprus. Alternatively, the discontinuities that currently exist in the archaeological record (between the Late Epipalaeolithic and Initial Aceramic Neolithic/Cypro-PPNA, and between the latter and the EAN) could be regarded as evidence for the regular return visits of seafaring foragers to the Levantine homeland (McCartney 2010: 188). Further excavations at *Asprokremmos* and *Klimonas* should serve to strengthen the more circumstantial evidence from other sites (discussed above). For now, however, we can turn our attention to the undisputed evidence for the EAN 1–3 periods attested in at least five different sites.

PARREKLISHIA *SHILLOUROKAMBOS*

Indisputably one of the earliest Neolithic sites on Cyprus, *Shillourokambos* (for location, see Figure 7 above) has been assigned four chronological phases, between ca. 8400–7000/6900 Cal BC, based on its radiocarbon dates and six different lithic production phases (Briois 2003; Guilaine 2003a: 4–12; Guilaine and Briois 2006: 173–174; see also Appendix, under Cypriot Chronology/Early Aceramic Neolithic). The different phases of settlement occupy adjacent spaces extending for about 2 ha along an interfluve, although the excavators believe the actual inhabited area did not exceed 1 ha. Of the 4,000 m² excavated at the site, some 2,600 m² belong to the early stages (Guilaine and Briois 2006: 159; Guilaine et al. 2011: 38). Amongst the distinctive features of this Early Phase A (ca. 8400–7900 Cal BC) at *Shillourokambos*, as defined by (wooden) postholes, are some roughly circular dwellings and a few long, narrow enclosures with irregularly shaped postholes along their bases (Guilaine and Briois 2006: 163, fig. 2; Guilaine et al. 2011: 143–151). Shortly afterward, these enclosures seem to have been remodelled (trenches cut into the *havara*) into curvilinear and trapezoidal enclosures (Figure 17a, b), which may have served as livestock pens or domestic activity areas (Guilaine and Briois 2006: 164–165, figs. 3–4; Guilaine et al. 2011: 153–160, figs. 1–4). A series of deep, circular wells with largely standardised, 1-m apertures were used from the time the site was established right through the Middle Phase (ca. 7200 Cal BC).

During Early Phase B (ca. 7900–7600 Cal BC), the inhabitants of *Shillourokambos* began to build circular dwellings made of *pisé* (wattle and daub) and/or stones. In Sector I, a 250-m² expanse of densely packed cobbles was uncovered, which may represent dwelling foundations. Although rich in faunal remains, chipped stone and fragmentary stone vessels, only a few wall stumps remained, associated with fragments of red or white plaster. One circular building (Structure 268), some 3 m in diameter and with stone foundations laid on flat ground, had thick walls enclosing a very limited internal space; it was completely surrounded by a regular line of pebbles (Guilaine and Briois 2006: 166, 167, fig. 6). This building calls to mind the virtually contemporary (ca. 7900–7500 Cal BC), circular (3–4 m in diameter) stone structures recently uncovered at Kritou Marottou *Ais Giorkis*, particularly Features 1 and 17, which were capped by a flat pavement of small stone cobbles (Simmons 2005: 25; discussed below, p. 110). This emphasis on circular structures continued to develop throughout the EAN, and became the defining feature of all LAN architecture.

To the Middle Phase (ca. 7600–7200 Cal BC) at *Shillourokambos* belongs a large, 6 × 6 m pit or disused well (Structure 23) that contained several thousand pieces of opaque chert (perhaps a knapping area), below which was a thick deposit of faunal remains and more chert (Guilaine et al. 2011: 335–399). The contracted skeleton of an aged adult male, 2 other distinct burials, and the crania of 20 other individuals, including infants, lay in somewhat complex

Figure 17a. Parreklishia *Shillourokambos* (Early Phase A): postholes, stake holes and enclosure trench. Courtesy of Jean Guilaine.

Figure 17b. Parreklishia *Shillourokambos* (Early Phase A): curved enclosure trenches, with postholes and pits. Courtesy of Jean Guilaine.

stratigraphic contours within this pit. The excavators believe these are the earliest-known human burials in Cyprus (but note the secondary burial of a neonate in earlier Well 116 at Kissonerga *Mylouthkia* – Peltenburg et al. 2003: 88, fig. 11.3, 90), with individual and collective interments attested in one and the same place (Crubézy et al. 2003: 297–303, figs. 1–3, 310–311). Of four individual skeletons from *Shillourokambos* tested, all were infected with at least two parasites transmitted through food (Harter-Lailhegue et al. 2005; Harper and Fox 2008: 5). Another rubbish pit (*Sondage* 2) was rich in chipped stone and bone material. Together, these two Middle Phase deposits contain some 4,500 identifiable animals bones (Vigne et al. 2003: 240, table 1; Guilaine et al. 2011: 399–428, 444–453).

In the Late Phase (ca. 7200–7000 Cal BC), excavations have uncovered stone courses for a large circular building (external diameter of 7.2. m) with walls more than 1 m thick. Later reoccupation seems to have occurred during the Ceramic Neolithic period (Sotira Culture), and was characterised by a series of silos cutting through earlier levels and containing stones for grinding grain, river pebbles, chipped stone implements including sickle blades, and Combed Ware pottery.

The earliest phases at *Shillourokambos* also reveal the use of vari-coloured, vitreous, translucent chert for making projectile points, blades/bladelets and sickle elements, in large part from bidirectional naviform cores. There are also several bladelets made from Anatolian obsidian. Some groundstone pounders, querns and rubbing stones were found in the fill of the wells or pits, but the chipped stone debris from intense knapping activities is overwhelming: Well 117 produced more than 39,000 waste flakes and Well 2 some 12,000 flakes (Guilaine and Briois 2006: 167 and n.3; Guilaine et al. 2011: 238–241, 279–282, 663–664). The basic toolkit of the early phases at *Shillourokambos* consists mainly of sickle blades with parallel gloss on unretouched blades (Guilaine and Briois 2006: 170 and n.4), a common albeit regionally variable feature of the chipped stone assemblages from *Mylouthkia* IA, *Tenta* and Politiko *Kelaïdhoni* (McCartney 2004: 115). After Early Phase B, knappers began to use a more opaque chert and a more simplified core-reduction technique, whilst there was a notable increase in the number of small blades used for the shaping of diverse projectile points, including Byblos and Amuq points (Guilaine and Briois 2006: 169–170, fig. 8; Guilaine et al. 2011: 682–687, figs. 16–17). A new type of sickle with crescent shape and exhibiting oblique gloss also appeared at this time, pointing to their use in harvesting cereals. By Early Phase C, the chipped stone industry began to change, and the toolkit included mainly burins made on thick flakes, notched pieces, end scrapers on thin flakes and borers on thick blades. Glossed sickle blades are still well represented but show some diversification from earlier types. By the Middle Phase, knappers were using a more simplified bidirectional core technology, and producing projectile and bipolar blades, amongst other tool types (Briois 2003: 127–131, fig. 5).

The *chaîne opératoire* associated with several hundred thousand pieces of chipped stone – in particular the bipolar knapping and projectile points (resembling Amuq and Byblos points), as well as lunate segments with oblique sickle sheen, using a naviform core reduction technology – appears to be closely related to that of the Early–Middle PPNB Levant (Guilaine and Briois 2006: 167–170, figs. 7–8). Such a link is also indicated by grooved stones with geometric motifs (net sinkers for fishing?), a feline head made of serpentine (Early Phase A) and a small lime plaster figurine (Early Phase B) (see further below).

The obsidian recovered, primarily from Early Phases A and B, is Cappadocian in origin (from Göllü Dag) and makes up about 2% of the total amount of chipped stone (Briois 2003: 121–123, fig. 1; Briois et al. 1997: 101, tables 1–2, 105–111; Guilaine and Briois 2006: 170–171; Guilaine et al. 2011: 707–719, 721–723). Although it is debatable whether the more than 500 small obsidian pieces found at *Shillourokambos* were imported as finished products or in the form of raw materials that were worked on the island (Briois et al. 1997: 104–105), McCartney (2004: 112) suggested that these pieces, nearly all bladelets produced by the pressure technique, could have come to the island together in one small bag. This is not unexpected if we assume that, during the earliest stages of settlement, there was more contact between the homeland of the settlers and their new island habitat, or that the exchange system involved was working more frequently. During the middle and later phases at *Shillourokambos*, there is very little obsidian, naviform cores are no longer used (opposed platform cores take their place – McCartney 1999), and a local, fine-grained opaque chert was employed to produce more robust blades and harvesting knives (projectile points are no longer present). All these features may point to reduced contacts with source areas, and are more in keeping with the kinds of materials found in sites of the Final Aceramic Neolithic on Cyprus.

The rich faunal record of *Shillourokambos* (more than 6,700 identified remains – Vigne et al. 2003: 240, table 1) reveals no native endemic fauna, and very few seashells, fish, bird or small mammal remains. In contrast to the Late Epipalaeolithic, fishing, foraging and trapping appear to have had little importance in the EAN subsistence economy at *Shillourokambos* (but recall the small grooved stones that may have been used as net sinkers for fishing, and note the existence of a bone fishhook and thousands of limpet shells from Well 116 at Kissonerga *Mylouthkia*, for which see discussion of that site). Instead, we find the typical Neolithic constellation of deer, pig (the predominant species), sheep and goat, as well as fox, dog and one cat, plus the earliest-known cattle bones on the island (Vigne et al. 2000; 2003; 2004; Guilaine et al. 2011: 919–1073).

On the basis of a range of morphometric and mortality data, as well as frequency distributions, analysed at different times with increasing amounts of data, Vigne et al. have veered back and forth in interpreting the domestic status of these animals. At first, they posited that pig, sheep/goat and cattle were technically pre-domesticated, 'objects of "appropriation" for husbandry' (Vigne et al. 2000: 83). In the same article, however, they concluded that pig, sheep and goat should be considered domesticates, while the quantitative data for cattle were too limited to make such a determination (Vigne et al. 2000: 99–100). Deer, on the other hand, were certainly wild, and hunted at different times with different strategies (Croft 2002; see also Vigne et al. 2000: 89–90).

More recently, Vigne et al. (2003: 248–251) suggested (1) that the goat and one type of pig from *Shillourokambos* were feral (the other type of pig being a 'managed domestic'); (2) that sheep were husbanded and likely domesticated; and (3) that cattle were bred (i.e. domesticated). Horwitz et al. (2004: 43–44), it may be recalled, maintain that all fauna from the earliest Neolithic assemblages on Cyprus have the size and shape of wild animals ('ethnotramps'). Pigs were already present at Late Epipalaeolithic *Aetokremnos* (Reese 1996b: 109; Simmons 1999: 164; Vigne et al. 2009), and form the main component of the faunal assemblage thus far recovered from (Cypro-PPNA) *Asprokremmos* (McCartney 2011: 187) and Ayios Tychonas *Klimonas* (Vigne et al. 2011a). Given this complex array of 'unstable' faunal evidence from *Shillourokambos* – none of which had local antecedents on Cyprus and all of which had counterparts in the PPNB Levant, at the very least we can say that most of these animals had been introduced by people coming from the Levant (with pig, evidently, introduced much earlier). Whether that introduction took place in a carefully coordinated move (the Noah's Ark model), or occurred over a long period of time with 'pioneer colonizers' (Perlès 2001: 62) stocking wild game for food resources, remains a matter of debate.

The plant remains from *Shillourokambos* include impressions in *pisé* of wild barley (*Hordeum spontaneum*) and (likely) wild wheat in the earliest phase at the site, and charred remains of the same species in later phases (Willcox 2000; Colledge and Conolly 2007: 57–59, and table 4.1). Further archaeobotanical remains were recovered in 2004 from Well 431 at *Shillourokambos* (Guilaine and Briois 2006: 171; Guilaine et al. 2011: 302, 599–605). Although the wild ancestor of domestic barley is endemic to Cyprus (Meikle 1985: 1834), the wild relatives of emmer and einkorn wheat have never been recorded (Colledge 2004: 54). More importantly, impressions of domestic hulled barley grains (*Hordeum sativum*) have been recovered from the latest phase at *Shillourokambos* (Willcox 2000: 131–132, tab. 3). The limited range and types of cereal taxa found at *Shillourokambos* result from the poor preservation conditions at the site (Willcox 2003: 234), which left the only evidence of plant remains in the form of impressions in *pisé*. As we shall see, two wells and one structure at Kissonerga *Mylouthkia* produced cereal-rich assemblages containing not only

Figure 18. Parreklishia *Shillourokambos* Early Phase A (EAN 1), human–feline carved head, 9.4 cm tall. After Guilaine 2003b: 331, fig. 1a. Drawn by Simon Griffith. Courtesy of Paula Jones.

the three founder crops (einkorn and emmer wheat, hulled barley) but also a range of legumes, fruits and oil plants, much more representative of the crop complex that would continue to characterise Cyprus's subsistence economy throughout the Aceramic Neolithic and beyond.

Other notable finds from *Shillourokambos* ('Early Phase B') include a range of limestone cooking and serving vessels (bowls, cups, mortars, plates), as well as thick-walled, shallow basins ranging from 20–35 cm in diameter (Manen 2003: 194–195, figs. 4–5; Guilaine et al. 2011: 769–787). Several of the stone vessels have harder, volcanic stone counterparts in the LAN (Khirokitian) repertoire (e.g. Dikaios 1962: 14–38, figs. 5–17). One large carved basin (70–80 cm in diameter) made from local serpentine rock and decorated with a ribbed pattern, surely had more than a conventional, domestic function (Guilaine et al. 2000: 79). More striking yet are two objects that came from the fill of abandoned wells, already noted above: the backward-tilting head of a feline-like figure made of serpentine (Well 66, Early Phase A) (Figure 18) and a similarly inclined anthropomorphic lime plaster figurine standing 5.5 cm high (Well 117, Early Phase B). Whereas the only features seen on the latter are two depressions for eyes (Guilaine 2003b: 331, fig. 1b), the former reveals smooth, carved facial features: eyebrows, eyes and nose modelled in low relief, with full cheeks but no mouth. A faint ridge beneath the nose looks like a moustache or whiskers; this cat-like appearance is further heightened by a pair of small, upright ears (Guilaine et al. 1999: 6, figs. 4–6; Guilaine and Briois 2001: 51, fig. 9). Although Guilaine (2003b: 330) wonders if this might be some sort of mask with feline traits, the roughly shaped (unfinished?) neck of this figure also suggested that the head may have been intended to protrude from a wall, like the plastered bulls' heads from the later, Anatolian Neolithic site of Çatalhöyük (Guilaine et al. 1999: 9; Hodder 2006: 157, colour pl. 17; cf. also the painted and plastered leopard reliefs on p. 153, colour pls. 9–10).

The discovery at *Shillourokambos* (Middle–Recent Phase) of what seems to have been the intentional burial of an entire, ostensibly tame cat in a small pit,

Figure 19. Parreklishia *Shillourokambos* Middle–Recent Phase (EAN 2–3), plan of cat and human burials. Redrawn by Paula Jones 2008, after Vigne et al. 2004: 259, fig. 1. Courtesy of Paula Jones.

only 40 cm away from a human burial (Vigne et al. 2004: 259, fig. 1; see Figure 19), may be of more than passing interest here (at least four other cat bones have been recovered from *Shillourokambos* – Vigne et al. 2003: 241). In purely functional and more general terms, as Vigne et al. (2004) observe, during the early stages of agriculture when grain was first stored as surplus, field mice would have been attracted to it; in turn, cats would have been introduced in order to control the proliferation of mice. It is worth adding here that remains of the domestic mouse (*Mus musculus*) and those of another species (perhaps the recently identified endemic *Mus Cypriacus* – Cucchi et al. 2006) were recovered in two deep wells at Kissonerga *Mylouthkia* (Cucchi et al. 2002: 236–238). Although, alternatively, cats may have introduced themselves to human communities as part of securing their own commensal niche, there are no known endemic felids on Cyprus (Boekschoten and Sondaar 1972: 333–336). The genet, attested at Akrotiri, is likely endemic but despite it superficial cat-like appearance, is only distantly related to cats. Very limited quantities of cat remains have been identified at Aceramic Neolithic sites in general (Croft 2003d: 53, with refs.).

If we take into account how animals might have been involved within a community's social relations (e.g. as pets, wealth, icons – Frame 2002), it seems likely that the eight-month-old *Shillourokambos* cat must have come ashore along with one or more of Cyprus's early settlers. The skeletons of both the cat and the human at *Shillourokambos* were in a good state of preservation. The person involved had been interred with goods such as polished stones and greenstone axes, ochre and chipped stone tools; nearby was a small pit holding 24 marine shells. The burial nearby (but with no demonstrated stratigraphic or contextual relationship) of an entire cat only eight months old, with no signs of butchering, suggests that it may have been killed intentionally for burial with this person, whose community status was marked by the materials buried with him. If, as seems inescapable, this cat had been introduced from the Levant (like most other fauna reported from the site), we may ponder its relationship to the *Shillourokambos* feline head, and the possible symbolic relevance of both to the carved feline heads found in PPNA levels at Jerf el-Ahmar (Syria) and at PPNB Nevali Çori (eastern Anatolia), and to the full-bodied lion carved on a monumental stele from Göbekli Tepe on the upper Balikh River (all illustrated in Stordeur 2003a: 367, fig. 7).

Amongst other unique objects the excavator regards as somehow symbolic or ideological in nature are (1) a small statuette of a quadruped (indeterminate species) and an anthropomorphic phallus (both Middle Phase) (Guilaine 2003b: 330–332, fig. 1c–d); (2) some grooved pebbles, stones or miniature cups of serpentine and picrolite, and an imaginatively described, picrolite, female micro-statuette (Guilaine 2003b: 333–339, fig. 2a–e; note that similar engraved pebbles are found in the LAN sites of Khirokotia *Vouni* and Kholetris *Ortos*, discussed under those sites); and (3) several other mini-stone ornaments and some partial animal representations (mouse, wild boar), mostly of picrolite. Stordeur (2003a: 363–365, figs. 5–6) points to very broad similarities between the female micro-statuette and phallus from *Shillourokambos* and other examples from (PPNA) Mureybet and Jerf el Ahmar, and (PPNB) Dja'de el Mughara (Syria). The intricate decorations on the picrolite objects emphasise local handicraft work using this 'noble stone' (Guilaine 2003b: 340; Guilaine and Briois 2006: 172). Citing other miniature picrolite cups from Akanthou *Arkosyko* (Şevketoğlu 2002: 100, and fig. 1; 2006: 130, fig. 2), as well as the quantity of obsidian found there in both field survey and trial trenches, Peltenburg et al. (2001a: 42) suggest that picrolite, which had to be obtained from the far southern or central parts of the island, may have served as an item of exchange for the imported obsidian.

Simply labelling objects as symbolic does not get us very far in trying to understand their meanings for those who lived during the earliest Neolithic of Cyprus. The fact that the people who settled at *Shillourokambos* managed to transport some of the wild or potentially domesticated deer, pig, goat, sheep and cattle found there indicates they had an established maritime tradition, and some level of economic, social or symbolic relationships with these animals. Faunal as well as lithic evidence from *Shillourokambos* points to a significant change through time in the overall subsistence strategy. Before the end of the 8th millennium Cal BC (EAN 3), cattle ceased to exist on the island (some sites in the interior, such as *Ais Giorkis*, continued to herd cattle rather later than was the case at *Shillourokambos*), deer were less selectively hunted, and improvements in pig husbandry (lower average culling age) meant that this animal now became a key food source. Changes in the knapping technology occurred about the same time (from naviform core reduction technology to opposed platform cores), while projectile points also disappeared and the use of translucent cherts was replaced by opaque cherts (Vigne et al. 2000: 95). Beyond their symbolic value, the wide variety of remains from *Shillourokambos* tells us a great deal about the earliest stages of sedentary life on early Neolithic Cyprus. Excavated materials from another site on the southwestern coast of the island shed further light on this phenomenon.

KISSONERGA *MYLOUTHKIA*

The second site that has helped to provide a fuller understanding of early Neolithic people on Cyprus is Kissonerga *Mylouthkia* (for location, see Figure 7 above). This severely eroded, near-coastal site is situated between spring-fed slopes to its south and alluvial deposits cut by three minor rivers to its north, that is, at a topographic and resource boundary (Peltenburg 2003a: 16–18, fig. 1). In terms of chronology, a small but consistent series of AMS radiocarbon dates from mainly short-lived carbonised seeds place the Period 1, Phase A and B occupation at *Mylouthkia* between about 8517–6836 Cal BC (see Appendix, Model 1; Peltenburg 2003a: 15–16, table 1). The exavators have divided the site's EAN cultural sequence into two phases based on these dates, which come from two separate loci, Well 116 (Period IA) and Well 133 (Period IB). The site was also occupied during the Early and Middle Chalcolithic period, from/after ca. 3589±79 Cal BC to/before ca. 3347±121 Cal BC (citing the $\mu\pm\sigma$ from Appendix Model 1, and allowing for an approximate, likely maximum 50±50 years old-wood correction). It also has material associated with a later period spanning everything from the Late Bronze Age to the medieval era (Peltenburg et al. 2003: xxxv–xxxvi).

The EAN component at *Mylouthkia* comprises discrete concentrations of features spread over an area of some 400 m² (Peltenburg et al. 2001b: 65–66). Excavations were carried out in three wells (110, 116, 133), three pits (337, 338, 345) and one semi-subterranean structure (Unit 340) (Croft in Peltenburg et al. 2003: 3–9; Peltenburg 2003a). Three further wells (2030, 2070, 2100) in a nearby locality (*Skourotos*) have similar fills and upper dimensions, and may also belong to the EAN temporal horizon. Although several animal bones (deer, ovicaprine, pig) and some chipped stone material were recovered from the irregularly shaped, 5-m-deep Well 110, the bulk of the evidence published from *Mylouthkia* derives from Wells 116 and 133 (Peltenburg et al. 2003: 88, fig. 11.3).

These two features were similar in shape, consisting of deep, vertical, cylindrical shafts some 90 cm wide, cut down into the soft *havara* limestone (Figure 20). Several small cavities carved into the edges of the shaft served as toe- and

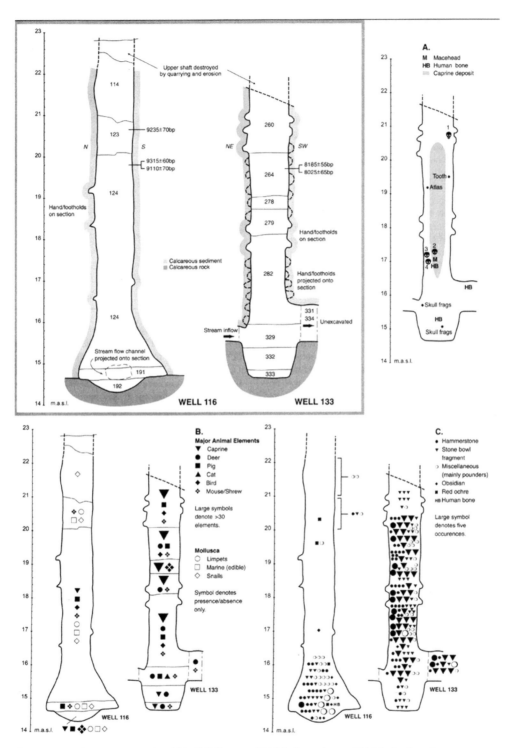

Figure 20. Kissonerga *Mylouthkia*, Wells 116 (EAN 1) and 133 (EAN 3), showing the sequence of deposits and the diverse stone, faunal, shell, bone, human and other, miscellaneous remains. Courtesy of Edgar Peltenburg.

hand-holds for climbing in and out. Both wells were designed to tap underground water from small stream channels that flowed across an essentially horizontal stratum of underlying, hard calcareous rock. Into this underlying stratum, a basin was cut at the bottom of each well, below stream level, to allow water to accumulate for collection. Within these basins, abundant microfaunal remains were found in silt deposits that presumably formed when the wells were in use. Successive use deposits above these basins (five in Well 116 and nine in Well 133) contained a wide variety of fills – including most of the cultural materials as well as the carbonised seeds from which the AMS dates were obtained – that accumulated after the wells went out of use (Peltenburg et al. 2001b: 66).

Well 116, the earlier of the two, belongs to the EAN 1 period. Reaching a preserved (minimum) depth of 8.5 m, this well had a sequence of five deposits containing a few faunal remains, molluscs, fish bones, carbonised seeds, chipped stone and groundstone tools, obsidian, red ochre and human bone (Peltenburg et al. 2003: 88, fig. 11.3; Peltenburg 2003a: 24–26). The dated grain seeds came from the top 2–3 m of the well. Unlike later Well 133, this one contained very limited amounts of human bone (one individual), and only a handful of pig and goat teeth and bones. By contrast, there were thousands of limpet shells (2,285 analysed) which, along with a few crab claws and dozens of fish bones scattered throughout the fill deposits, are thought to have been consumed at the site (Croft 2003d: 50). Microfaunal remains, mostly from the basal fill, included mice, shrews (two bones), frogs, toads, lizards and snakes, much the same as in Well 133.

Well 133 belongs to the EAN 3 period and, in contrast to Well 116, had a notable concentration of what were originally entire, unbutchered ovicaprine carcasses, as well as other bones from deer, pig, goat, sheep, pigeon, fish, owl (*Athene noctua*) and cat (Croft 2003d: 51–53; Peltenburg 2003a: 26–30). The partly disarticulated remains of one child, one adolescent and three adult humans were found scattered discontinuously throughout the shaft fill.

Of 745 groundstone artefacts recovered at EAN *Mylouthkia*, virtually all came from the wells (Jackson, in Peltenburg et al. 2003: 35–40); most were produced from soft, calcareous rocks, such as chalk or limestone (in contrast to the typical use of igneous rocks at LAN sites). Well 133 yielded 449 fragments of limestone vessels and crude hammerstones, but food processing equipment such as querns, rubbers, mortars and pestles were absent, and cutting tools rare (in contrast to the groundstone repertoire at LAN sites). The abundance and condition of stone vessel fragments in both wells (especially Well 133), and chipped stone evidence consistent with stoneworking from Well 116, have been interpreted as possible residues from stone vessel manufacture in the vicinity of the wells. Despite the 1,000-year chronological gap between the two wells, there is little morphological difference between the materials and artefact classes recovered from both of them (Jackson, in Peltenburg et al.

Figure 21. Kissonerga *Mylouthkia* groundstone macehead from Well 133 (EAN 3), made from a variegated pinkish fan conglomerate, and deposited near two human skulls. Courtesy of Edgar Peltenburg.

2003: 40). The most striking groundstone artefact is a macehead, finely crafted out of a variegated pinkish fan conglomerate and found deposited near two human skulls in Well 133 (Jackson, in Peltenburg et al. 2003: 37–38, fig. 46.9, pl. 7.4) (Figure 21). Beyond comparisons cited with maceheads found at sites in Anatolia and the Jordan Valley, the significance of this macehead surely lies in the fact that is it the earliest known example of the various red, pink or orange stone maceheads (and even calacaeous stone maceheads painted red) that appear in the LAN sites such as Cape Andreas *Kastros* and Khirokitia *Vouni* (Astruc 1994: 253–254, fig. 102.2–5, pl. 28.18; Peltenburg et al. 2001b: 74, both with further refs.).

The extremely limited use of igneous rock at *Mylouthkia* is also reflected in the chipped stone remains, amongst which there are few of the kinds of cutting tools or flaked tool scrapers commonly made from such material. The number of chipped stone artefacts recovered from the wells and other features at *Mylouthkia* is limited, totalling 836 and including 40 tools or tool fragments (and 21 pieces of obsidian) from Period IA, and 120 tools or tool fragments (and 1 piece of obsidian) from Period IB (McCartney 2003: 135–140). While the Period IA sample is dominated by the use of high-quality, red- or yellow-ish-brown translucent chert, the Period IB sample is more varied and includes some translucent chert but is dominated by the use of lower quality Lefkara cherts. The chipped stone found in Well 116 at *Mylouthkia* IA exhibits a blade-based industry with tools manufactured mainly from bidirectional cores. Three arrowhead tangs from Well 116 are similar to the Byblos points so characteristic of the Levantine Early PPNB (Gopher 1994: 36–39, fig. 4.7: 17–18). Other (often glossed) tool types from *Mylouthkia* IA – blades, *pièces esquillées*, burins – indicate a mixture of influences equally characteristic of the same Levantine time frame (McCartney, in Peltenburg et al. 2001b: 78–80).

Nearly one millennium later, during *Mylouthkia* Period IB (EAN 3), the use of unidirectional cores overtakes that of bidirectional ones, while the tools used – steeply backed blades, retouched flakes and blades, *pièces esquillées*, denticulates and notches – are more like those belonging to classic assemblages of the LAN/Khirokitia Culture (McCartney 2004: 81–82). At the same time, the use of opaque (Lefkara) chert and the greater number of flake tools correspond to changes seen during the EAN 3 period at *Shillourokambos* and *Tenta* (McCartney, in Peltenburg et al. 2003: 18–19). Typical agricultural tools, such as glossed sickle blades, are rare in the somewhat restricted assemblage from *Mylouthkia* IB. The rarity if not disappearance of arrowheads from both *Mylouthkia* and *Shillourokambos* should be seen (1) in the context of contemporary (EAN 3) changes in animal husbandry, when deer became less selectively hunted, and pig evidently became the food of choice; and (2) in terms of their possible potential as highly charged symbolic items related to social status. By the EAN 3 and on into the LAN, the arrowhead form on Cyprus was transformed into tanged blades, which served less as projectiles than as knives or daggers, and may have served in some ceremonial or symbolic capacity, like the earlier arrowheads (McCartney 2004: 114).

Although the *chaîne opératoire* that characterises the changes in the chipped stone samples from both *Mylouthkia* IA and IB also finds counterpoints in Levantine PPNB assemblages, there is little evidence on Cyprus for the kind of incipient specialisation seen at some of the large, Late PPNB/PPNC sites in the southern Levant. Instead, those who were producing blades on Cyprus focused on the kind of tools required by small scale farming communities. In terms of the chipped stone repertoire, Cypriot assemblages seem to have developed as an insular, but surely not an isolated variant of the so-called (Late) PPNB interaction sphere (McCartney, in Peltenburg et al. 2003: 19).

The 22 obsidian pieces collected from EAN contexts at *Mylouthkia* (21 from Wells 113 and 116, Period IA) represent mainly heavily reworked waste material – chips, shatter fragments, bladelet and narrow blade segments (McCartney, in Peltenburg et al. 2003: 19–21). Of five pieces that conform to known tool types, four are *pièces esquillées*, the other a large retouched blade. Laserablation ICP-MS analysis has identified the obsidian as originating from the Cappadocian Gollü Dağ source in central Anatolia (Gratuze, in Peltenburg et al. 2003: 30–34), much the same pattern seen for obsidian finds in the PPNB southern Levant. The relatively high proportions of obsidian, the only nonlocal raw material used in the chipped stone assemblages from both *Mylouthkia* (IA, 12%) and *Shillourokambos* (Early Phases A, B, 2%), and the similarity of the artefact types represented at both sites (narrow blade and bladelet segments with some retouch, *pièces esquillées*, lots of small-sized debris) suggest that, at least in the earlier stages of the EAN, obsidian was not necessarily regarded as an exotic material, even if it increasingly became so by the LAN, in tandem with its usage in the Levant (Cauvin 1991: 166–174; McCartney, in Peltenburg et al. 2003: 21).

Amongst 12 archaeobotanical samples taken from the wells and other deposits (five from Period IA, seven from Period IB) were the charred remains of cultivated, and likely domesticated einkorn and emmer wheat and hulled barley, as well as legumes (lentil, green pea, vetch), flax, pistachio, fig and grape, wood charcoal and many weed taxa (Murray, in Peltenburg et al. 2001b: 70–72, table 4; Murray 2003). These samples are thought to indicate cereal processing wastes and – along with the wood charcoal and fruit/nut remains – were likely preserved when burnt as fuel, and then dumped into the wells and pits. Because there was some question about the domesticated status of the barley grains based on morphological assessment alone, Colledge (2004: 53–54, figs. 5.1, 5.3) carried out metrical analyses on both the barley and wheat grains, comparing them with wild and domestic grains from various Levantine Neolithic sites – 10 sites for barley, 14 sites for wheat (see also Willcox 2004). In both cases, the *Mylouthkia* grains fell within the size range bracketing domesticated cereals. The evidence for cultivated wild or domesticated cereals and pulses at *Mylouthkia*, as already noted, is only marginally later than their earliest attestation in PPNA/B Anatolian and Levantine sites (Colledge 2004: 50; Colledge and Conolly 2007: 64, 67, table 4.5; Willcox et al. 2008).

The faunal record, discussed in several publications by the team that excavated *Mylouthkia* as well as by others (e.g. Peltenburg et al. 2001b: 66–68; Croft 2003a; 2003d; Horwitz et al. 2004), reveals a complete contrast between the two periods. Only a few pieces of ovicaprine and pig bones are present in Well 116 (EAN 1). Well 133 (EAN 3), however, yielded a major deposit of at least 23 whole, unburnt ovicaprine carcasses, comprising 8 immature and 1 mature sheep, along with 12 immature and 2 mature goats. Because some disarticulated human bones were scattered sporadically throughout these carcasses, Croft (2003a: 272) speculated that this deposit might bear witness to animal sacrifice and ritual deposition rather than the disposal of dead, unwanted carcasses. There are also small quantities of what may have represented the remains of food consumed by people at or near the well: fallow deer, pig, sheep, goat, pigeon and fish bones (one crab claw). By contrast, the partial remains of an owl and a cat may simply have fallen into the well, along with the microfaunal remains: mice, frogs, toads, shrews and reptiles, found in both the early and later wells. The mice remains included two species, *Mus musculus* (domestic) and *Mus Cypriacus*, the recently identified endemic (Cucchi et al. 2002; 2006).

The disarticulated human bones found in Well 133 come from one child, one late adolescent and three adults. Two possibly distinct concentrations of these human bones towards the top and bottom of the well (see profile of Well 133 in Peltenburg et al. 2003: 88 fig. 11.3A – Figure 20 above) led the excavators to suggest that they may represent two separate depositional episodes. They reason that (1) overall, the infilling of these wells was the direct result of human agency, including the selection of body parts to be interred, and that (2) specifically, a macehead found some 30 cm from one of the human skulls was likely an intentional grave good (Peltenburg 2003a: 27–28). The male found in fill 260 of this well consisted of only partially burnt skull remains. It should be noted here that the practice of skull caching, also seen at *Shillourokambos* (one example), was not uncommon in the Levantine PPN (Kuijt 2000a), and is also seen in the aceramic and later Neolithic periods of both Anatolia and Greece (Talalay 2004).

Artefactual, floral and faunal evidence combined strongly suggests that during the late 9th millennium Cal BC and again about 1,000 years afterwards, there was a permanent agricultural settlement associated with the wells and pits of *Mylouthkia*. The inhabitants of this site were engaged in diverse economic activities (cultivating crops, exploiting animal and marine resources, securing fresh water resources, obtaining obsidian from afar, producing groundstone tools) and social practices (mortuary, ritual, subsistence, exchange). From their presumed Levantine homeland, the earliest settlers at *Mylouthkia* and *Shillourokambos* brought with them various material and conceptual practices: engraved pebbles, incised stones, chipped stone traditions, plants and animals, the use of maceheads, building plans, figurative artwork and skull treatment (Peltenburg et al. 2003: 95, table 11.5). The remains from these two sites have changed forever the way we view the earliest Neolithic on Cyprus, and the role and place of the island in all the fundamental changes that were taking place contemporaneously in the Levant and Anatolia. Indeed, the many striking changes documented at *Mylouthkia* and *Shillourokambos* (the use of cattle, obsidian, the chipped stone repertoire, etc.) have led to changes in the way other sites were previously interpreted, and to newer surveys and excavations focused on the island's earliest Neolithic record.

The Wider Early Aceramic Neolithic Landscape

In order to complete the story of Cyprus's EAN as it may be told today, it is necessary to discuss briefly a few further sites. Only two of these sites, Kalavasos *Tenta* and Kritou Marottou *Ais Giorkis*, have been excavated and published to any extent. Others, like Akanthou *Arkosyko*, have yet to reveal their full potential for a better understanding of the EAN. Still others have been treated only as one aspect of much larger projects, for example Politiko *Kelaïdhoni* and Agrokipia *Paleokamina*, discussed briefly at various points above.

Figure 22. Kalavasos *Tenta*, view of the Neolithic site in the Vasilikos Valley, with parts of the outer stone wall of the settlement visible (left of the central pole of the striking modern covering). View to the northeast. Photograph by A. Bernard Knapp.

KALAVASOS *TENTA*

Lying in the south central part of the island some 3 km from the coast, the site of Kalavasos *Tenta* is situated atop a small natural hill in the lower catchment of the Vasilikos River valley, some 3 km from the sea (Figure 22). Because it gives directly onto the main east–west passage through the area, and at the same time offers easy access to the resources of the Troodos to the north and the sea to the south, its strategic location is evident (Todd 2003: 35; 2005: 379). Although the surface scatter of Neolithic material was spread over about 2.5 ha, the attested EAN remains at *Tenta* extend over only 0.25–0.30 ha. Todd (1998: 36 and fig. 57; 2005: 378–379) estimates that there may have been 40–45 structures at *Tenta*. The site was surrounded by an outer stone wall and a ditch cut into the *havara* bedrock (Todd 1987: fig. 57; 1998: 34, fig. 16, 38, 61, fig. 38). In time, the community at *Tenta* spread beyond these liminal features. At least four other Aceramic Neolithic sites are known in and around *Tenta* or the nearby village at Kalavasos (Todd 2001: 97).

Whilst stratigraphically separate architectural levels were identified in three different areas at *Tenta*, it was always difficult to determine how the levels in each area related to one another. Nevertheless, the stratigraphic relationships defined in the different areas enabled the excavator to establish a chronological framework of five periods, four of which are now associated with the Early Aceramic Neolithic (Todd 1987: 173–178; 2005: 379).

Period 5, the earliest, is represented by a series of 45 stake/postholes found on the west side of the top of the site, and by others (plus some pits or hearths) along its lower south slope. The intricately analysed chipped stone tool assemblage (McCartney in Todd 2005: 177–207, 211–227), and at least three radiocarbon dates (P-2972, 2976, 2785 – Todd 2001: 100, table 1; see Appendix and SOM), which indicate 1σ calibrated ranges (with no modeling) spanning the years 8608–7336 Cal BC, suggest that Period 5 was contemporary with the EAN 1–2 phases at *Shillourokambos* and *Mylouthkia* (Todd 2005: 382). Some of the chipped stone tools (blades, Byblos- and Amuq-type points) and the naviform core technology have clear parallels in the Levantine Early–Middle PPNB. The postholes, like those at *Shillourokambos* and *Asprokremmos*, probably indicate the use of ephemeral wooden structures, or possibly a wooden palisade surrounding the earliest habitations at the site. The extent of this earliest phase at *Tenta* is uncertain, but the excavator believes that much of this top-of-site area – where circular stone and mudbrick buildings still stand – may have been covered by impermanent structures (Todd 2003: 38, fig. 3, 40, fig. 5; Todd 2005: 378). The other series of stake/postholes and pits/hearths excavated on the lower southern slope were cut into the natural limestone *havara*, and from a pit in this area came the earliest of the radiocarbon dates (P-2972 – 9240±130 Cal BC).

The complex stratigraphy of *Tenta* makes it difficult to determine the temporal extent of occupation represented by the Period 5 remains. Some of the earliest lithic remains come from the 'top-of-site' deposits. In the earliest publication of the site, the excavator left open the possibility that some of the impressive, stone-built circular structures (e.g. the Structure 14 complex) crowning the site's summit and assigned to *Tenta*'s Period 2, the best known at the site, may have been earlier than the Late Aceramic Neolithic, as they were first dated (Todd 1987: 177–178; 2001: 103–104). Indeed, this level has now been redated to the EAN 3 period (McCartney and Todd 2005: 177–186, 211–214). Peltenburg et al. (2001a: 41–42; Peltenburg 2004b: xiv; 2004c: 73) had already argued on the basis of the three top-of-site radiocarbon dates (one mid-8th, two early 7th millennium Cal BC) that all the imposing circular stone structures associated with Period 2 actually belong to the EAN 2–3 (*Mylouthkia* IB and *Shillourokambos* Middle Phase), with possible extension into the earliest part of the LAN. Todd's (2003: 43) and McCartney's re-reading of the chipped stone evidence now fully supports this redating (further discussion below). The Period 5 material should be associated with the Levantine Early–Middle PPNB (equivalent to EAN 1–2); the Period 4 material with Levantine Late PPNB (equivalent to EAN 2–3); and the Period 2 material with the Levantine Final PPNB (equivalent to latest part of EAN 3). Any chipped stone materials from *Tenta* of LAN (Khirokitia) type postdate Period 2.

The redating of Period 2 at *Tenta* has major consequences, as it provides a clear and coherent settlement plan of the EAN, one that was established on the island by the early 8th millennium Cal BC, and had precursors in stone at

Figure 23. Kalavasos *Tenta*, Structure 14 (EAN 3), with its surrounding radial cells placed against the exterior wall; it may have served as a storage area for surplus grain production. Photograph by A. Bernard Knapp.

Shillourokambos (Guilaine 2003a: 7) and perhaps in timber at *Tenta* (the postholes) and *Mylouthkia* (Unit 340 – Peltenburg et al. 2003: 8–9; Peltenburg 2004c: 73). With the redating of Period 2 to EAN 3, the prominent location and elaborate layout of *Tenta*'s Structure 14, with its surrounding radial cells placed against the exterior wall (Todd 1987: fig. 20) (Figure 23), may be linked materially to the large, centralised PPNA structure at Jerf el-Ahmar (Syria) in the Levantine Corridor; it may also be linked functionally as a storage area for surplus grain production, and socially as indicative of 'controlling authorities' (Peltenburg et al. 2001a: 41–42).

The main raw material in use for chipped stone production at *Tenta* was a coarse, dense Lefkara translucent chert (44% of tool sample), as opposed to the high-quality Lefkara basal chert used earlier (5% of tool sample) (McCartney 2003: 144). Blades represent the preferred blank for the production of tools, and opposed platform cores were increasingly adopted for their production (McCartney 2003: 143). Flake production, by contrast, was based on the use of single platform cores.

McCartney's detailed analysis of *Tenta*'s EAN 1–2 chipped stone – nearly 3,600 pieces from securely dated contexts – paints a more complex picture (McCartney and Todd 2005: 214–221, 233, table 23). She maintains that some of *Tenta*'s Period 5 lithic types reveal enough similarities with the chipped stone from Akrotiri *Aetokremnos* to suggest a bridge linking the Late Epipalaeolithic and the EAN. Somewhat boldly, she suggests that groups of foragers were present on the island, perhaps experimenting with the cultivation of wild grains and 'predomestic husbandry' (McCartney and Todd 2005: 220). Such groups, she argues, are identifiable in a hybridised chipped stone tradition that also shows some links to lithic practices on the (PPNA) Levantine mainland, even if it conforms in other ways to particular insular qualities.

Two key conclusions are drawn from these analyses (McCartney and Todd 2005: 219–221): (1) the EAN inhabitants of *Tenta* were descendants either of people whose presence on the island is attested at *Aetokremnos* ('early colonisers'), or of 'later Early Neolithic immigrants', that is, people who arrived during the Levantine PPNA era; and (2) the EAN 1 evidence from *Mylouthkia* (IA), and *Shillourokambos* (early Phase A/B) cannot represent a single colonisation event but instead must be seen as part of a longer, more gradual process ultimately stemming from the earliest seafaring visits to the island. All this ties into McCartney's view, now confirmed in part by radiocarbon dating, that the distinctive chipped stone assemblages from *Paleokamina*, *Kelaïdhoni* and *Asprokremmos* – in comparison to those found at the EAN sites of *Shillourokambos* and *Mylouthkia* – belong to an era equivalent to the Levantine PPNA and must be included in any discussion of Cyprus's earliest permanent settlement (McCartney 2003: 145–146; 2007; McCartney et al. 2007).

The accelerated pace of change in the study of Cyprus's EAN period, like that of the Late Epipalaeolithic, means that current interpretations are bound to change, especially since the evidence from *Asprokremmos*, as well as that from *Ais Giorkis* and *Arkosyko* (discussed below), has yet to be fully published. Based on the current material record, it is uncertain if Cyprus was continuously occupied between the Late Epipalaeolithic and the Early Aceramic Neolithic periods, an unknown span of radiocarbon years here estimated to be no more than 600 (see Appendix, under Cypriot Chronology/ Late Epipalaeolithic).

The intricate study of *Tenta*'s Period 4–2 chipped stone is also linked to the construction, on the top of the site, of a series of large mudbrick and stone structures that underlie Building 14 (S36, S17). The plastered floors of Structures 36 and 17 at *Tenta* were painted red (Todd 1987: 45; 1998: 41–42, fig. 22). One pier from Structure 11 at *Tenta* (Figure 24) was decorated with a now-famous wall painting depicting the upper torso of two human figures in red pigment, depicted side-by-side with arms upraised (Todd 1987: fig. 39; 1998: 64–65, figs. 41–42) (Figure 25). McCartney and Todd (2005: 223–224) maintain that the earliest in this sequence of buildings belongs to Period 4 and represents a direct, conservative and insular reaction to the new people who had recently arrived at *Mylouthkia* and *Shillourokambos*.

However one regards this reassessment of *Tenta*'s EAN 1–3 chipped stone material, it now seems clear that the sequence of this site's somewhat unique architectural elements must be regarded as earlier than the Late Aceramic Neolithic (LAN), forerunners of the traditions so well known at Khirokitia *Vouni*, Cape Andreas *Kastros* and elsewhere. In addition, the groundstone vessels from *Tenta*, not nearly as well worked or refined as those seen at Khirokitia, may better be understood as earlier in the island's groundstone industry tradition

Figure 24. Kalavasos *Tenta*, Structure 11 (EAN 3), one pier of which is decorated with a wall painting depicting two human figures (Figure 25). Photograph by A. Bernard Knapp.

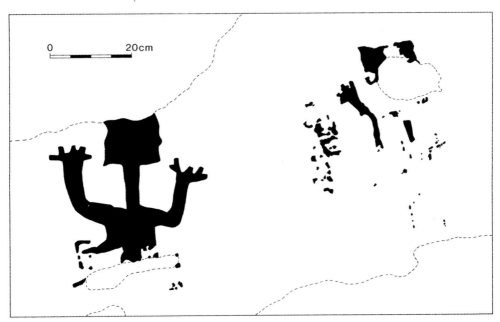

Figure 25. Kalavasos *Tenta*, pier from Structure 11 at *Tenta* decorated with wall painting showing the upper torso of two human figures in red pigment. After Todd 1987: fig. 39. Courtesy of Alison South and the Cyprus Museum, Nicosia.

(Todd 2003: 43). The obsidian found at *Tenta*, while limited in amount and mainly from Periods 4–2 (Todd 2005: 264, 380), or EAN 3, may also point to an earlier date, given the significant fall-off in the occurrence of this material through time as noted at both *Mylouthkia* and *Shillourokambos* (Briois et al. 1997; 110–111; Peltenburg et al. 2001a: 42, 52–53; McCartney in Peltenburg et al. 2003: 20–21).

The Anatolian Çiftlik source of the few obsidian pieces found at *Tenta* (Gomez et al. 1995) would seem to confirm that external contacts continued apace during the EAN. Whether or not the wall painting with two human figures also points to external contacts (e.g. as somehow related to the painted and plaster relief figures from Çatalhöyük) remains an open question. Peltenburg (2004c: 76–77, figs. 7.5–7.6) sees this painting, and more notably the pillar on which it was executed, as part of a north Syrian, southeast Anatolian ideological tradition, notably the high relief representations of people and animals on pillars at Göbekli Tepe and Nevali Çori in southeastern Anatolia. Other human representations are very rare at *Tenta*: only two fragmentary figurines were recorded (Todd 2005: 312).

In terms of subsistence, the amount of deer consumed at *Tenta* declined through time (from ca. 56% to 42%), alongside a rise in the number of pig and ovicaprine remains (Croft 2005: 348, table 106). Sheep and goat constitute nearly 30% of all mammalian bones identified at *Tenta* (Croft 2005: 342), but their contribution to the overall supply of meat at the site never rose above 9% (Todd 1998: 53; Croft 2005: 358). The use of pig increased during the time the site was occupied, from about 30% to 43% of the preserved faunal record (Croft 2005: 358, table 115). The inhabitants of *Tenta* thus seem to have had a diverse animal diet that revolved largely around hunted (or managed) deer and domesticated pig, whilst domesticated sheep and goat made a supplementary contribution to the daily fare. The domesticated plants recovered from *Tenta* overall include einkorn and emmer wheat, hulled barley and pulses (lentil, pea, horse bean, vetch); the only fruits represented are fig, pistachio and wild pear (Hansen 2001: 121–123, table 1). Whereas wild grasses (*Gramineae*) are well represented at *Tenta*, wild cereals are not. And whilst there are *pisé* impressions of wild barley and (perhaps) wild wheat in the earliest phase at *Shillourokambos* (and some charred remains of the same species in later phases), the floral evidence at *Mylouthkia* suggests that the wild grains were cultivated. Overall, then, it would seem that those who first established themselves in these EAN sites on Cyprus brought (mainly) domesticated plants with them.

KRITOU MAROTTOU *AIS GIORKIS*

Located about 20 km inland from the coast, the site of Kritou Marottou *Ais Giorkis* is situated in the uplands of the Esouzas River Valley in the island's southwest (Simmons 2008: 26–27; 2010). Most other sites of the EAN

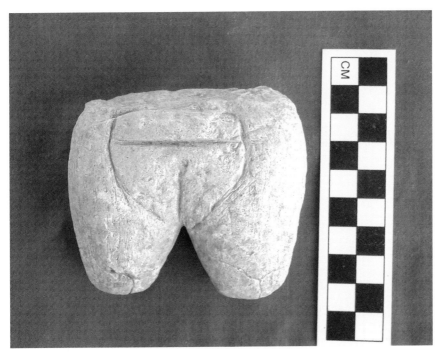

Figure 26. Kritou Marottou *Ais Giorkis*, fragmentary limestone figurine showing the pelvic region of a female figure. Courtesy of Alan Simmons.

(*Mylouthkia, Shillourokambos, Tenta*) or the LAN (Khirokitia *Vouni*, Cape
Andreas *Kastros*) have a coastal or near-coastal (~5 km) location. By contrast, *Ais Giorkis* stands at an elevation of some 460 m in the Troodos foothills
(*Asprokremmos, Paleokamina* and *Kelaïdhoni* all lie in the northern foothills of
the Troodos, at lower elevations). Based on a series of 19 (relevant) radiocarbon
dates (Simmons 2010: table 1), occupation at this site seems to have occurred
primarily between about 7700–6850 Cal BC (EAN 2 period – see Appendix,
under Early Aceramic Neolithic, and caption to Figure 6). Four dates also fall
into the LAN (Simmons 2003b: 3–4, table 1; Simmons 2010: table 1), a time
period not reflected in the artefacts, especially the chipped stone, which all
indicate an EAN 2 typology and technology.

Eight seasons of excavation (1997, 2002–2008) and one limited survey season
(2009) at *Ais Giorkis* have uncovered nearly 300 m² of the site, in four distinctive strata, and produced an array of evidence – chipped stone and groundstone,
obsidian, abundant faunal remains, large circular stone and plaster structures,
and various specialised ornaments and pendants (e.g. picrolite, one carnelian
bead) – suggestive of a small village with a mixed hunting-herding and farming economy (Simmons 2005: 27–28). One of the more striking objects found
at *Ais Giorkis* was the lower part of a limestone female figurine (Figure 26).

One of the most unique aspects of the site thus far is the presence of large,
oval stone structures, with crushed chalk (not true lime plaster) used to cover

Figure 27. Kritou Marottou *Ais Girokis* Feature 17: a large oval stone structure, covered with crushed chalk and capped by a flat pavement of uniformly sized small cobbles. Courtesy of Alan Simmons.

them (Simmons 2008: 27; 2010) (Figure 27). Feature 1, for example, is some 4 m in diameter and is capped by a flat pavement of uniformly sized small cobbles; its intact vertical sides (0.5 m high) are similarly finished (Simmons 2005: 25). The interior core is rubble and consists of large undressed stones; sectioning revealed no subterranean parts, but a small cache of blades was found near the base of the structure (Simmons 2010). It seems clear that Feature 1 rests on and is covered by contemporary, Early Aceramic Neolithic materials. According to the excavator, Feature 1 might have served as a tower, the foundation for a dwelling or an open platform for community performances. Structure 268 at *Shillourokambos*, with its thick walls and stone foundations on flat ground, is of similar construction, and of equally uncertain function (Guilaine and Briois 2006: 166, 167, fig. 6).

Since Feature 1 was recorded and published, three other, similar structures (platforms) ranging between 2–5 m in diameter have been exposed, as well as several pits and a large ditch-like feature whose purpose (possible site boundary?) is unclear. One pit in particular, Feature 4, seems to have been complex and multi-functional. Some 3 m in diameter and over 1 m deep, it contains two small, possible postholes and thus may once have served as some sort of structure. The large amount of chipped stone concentrated in Feature 4 (more than 10,500 pieces) led the excavator to suggest it may also have served as a 'reduction station' (Simmons 2010). At the same time, this pit (Feature 4) also contained well-preserved paleobotanical materials, flotation of which revealed the presence of domesticated cereals and pulses: einkorn (the majority) and barley, pistachio and lentil; some seeds (short-lived samples – Beta-213415, 256039, 256040 and 256041) date within an overall 1σ range of 7578–7480 Cal BC (Simmons 2005: 27; 2010; see also Appendix and SOM). At least four other pits were cut into Feature 4, one of which held a partial infant burial (Harper and Fox 2008: 4).

Amongst a harvest of nearly 200,000 pieces of chipped stone, mainly produced from Lefkara cherts (both translucent and basal) (Stewart 2004: 125–126), there are approximately 11,000 tools and more than 23,000 blades or bladelets (Simmons 2005: 25–26, table 1; 2010: table 2). Twenty-six per cent of the total (nearly 50,000 pieces) consists of debris or shatter, and indicates that chipped stone reduction was a major activity at *Ais Giorkis*. Based on a blade-like technology, the tools are dominated by retouched blades and flakes, notches, burins and scrapers. The occurrence of 16 rudimentary projectile points (at least some of which are quite similar to the typical, Levantine PPNB Byblos point) is worthy of note, inasmuch as similar points have now been recovered from the early phases at both *Mylouthkia* (Well 116) and *Shillourokambos* (Early Phases A, B). A few naviform or sub-naviform cores are also present. Equally noteworthy is the recovery of 42 obsidian bladelets, one of which was a burin (Simmons 2005: 25–26; 2010). Another obsidian bladelet, collected by the Canadian Palaipaphos Survey Project that originally located *Ais Giorkis* (Fox 1987: 20–22), was long ago sourced to Anatolia's Çiftlik region, also the origin of *Tenta's* obsidian. The presence of an imported material like obsidian at a somewhat remote highland site is notable in itself; it becomes even more so if obsidian, at least in some quantity as is the case here, can be taken as a material signal of the EAN period.

Whilst the groundstone artefacts thus far recovered are not at all atypical for a settlement site (mainly grinding implements such as handstones and pestles, and some vessels), there are also several fragments of larger, more elaborate vessels (platters or bowls), as well as a few fragments of a plate-like picrolite vessel (Simmons 2010: table 5). Mention must be also be made of another, quite rare object for the EAN, a pinkish 'vaiselle blanche' (whiteware) vessel made of limestone/plaster and found adjacent to the remains of the partial infant burial already noted (Simmons 2005: 27, table 4; 2010: fig. 4).

The extensive, well-preserved faunal record at *Ais Giorkis* is dominated by deer and pig but includes more than 250 identifiable cattle bones (Simmons 2003: 4; 2010: table 6). Cattle are yet another signpost to the EAN period, given their nearly exclusive presence in EAN 1 levels at *Shillourokambos* and Akanthou *Arkosyko* (Şevketoğlu 2000: 77; 2006: 125); only a single bone of cattle, a metapodial fragment, is known from the LAN, at Khirokitia (Davis 2003: 263–264, fig. 7). Cattle, however, seem to have been poorly suited to the early Holocene landscape of Cyprus, or else the people who exploited them realised that more appropriate sources of protein were available on the island. Although *Ais Giorkis* cannot be assigned to the EAN on the evidence of the faunal record alone, the combination of cattle bones, obsidian and projectile points similar in style to Levantine PPNB types is highly suggestive (but note that there are very few of the 'naviform' core types documented at other EAN sites). Moreover, the bulk of the radiocarbon dates now confirm an EAN date, including one from a cattle bone (CAMS 94861, which yields an overall 1σ age range of 7455–7307 Cal BC: see Appendix and SOM).

The evidence from *Ais Giorkis* demonstrates that cattle were exploited on Cyprus for at least 1,000 years (Simmons 1998: 237–238; Croft 2003a: 274–275). It may be that people from the western hill country persisted longer in the tradition of cattle husbandry than their counterparts along the north and south coasts (Croft 2003a: 274), but it remains to be seen whether sites such as *Ais Giorkis* and *Shillourokambos* were specialised pastoral ('ranching') occupations, when the cattle component of the extant faunal record is so limited. Simmons (2009) and Ronen (1995: 184–186) have made tentative cases for the possible ritual use of cattle, both on the Levantine mainland and in Cyprus. But most cattle bones at *Ais Giorkis*, at least, co-occur with other faunal elements rather than in feasting or otherwise notable contexts, and there is simply not enough evidence, contextual or otherwise, to argue for the ritual use of cattle (Simmons 2009: 6–7). In any case, the current faunal record from *Ais Giorkis* – about 53% deer, 28% pig, 16% ovicaprines, slightly under 2% cattle, plus small numbers of fox, cat, dog, bird and fish – suggests that the inhabitants of this site, if it was permanently occupied, enjoyed a diverse animal diet that revolved largely around hunted (or managed) deer, but also included domesticated sheep/goat, pig and cattle (Simmons 2003: 3–5, tables 2–3; 2010: table 6).

AKANTHOU *ARKOSYKO*

Located on the northern coast of Cyprus, Akanthou *Arkosyko* may have been up to 4 ha in extent (Şevketoğlu 2008: 68). The site lies atop a 10–15-m-high marine terrace with limestone cliffs on the seaward side, a small pebble beach and narrow strip of soil immediately below the cliff (a possible landing place), as well as another sheltered bay to the east (Şevketoğlu 2006: 122–123). A small spring at the west end of the beach immediately north of the site, and cultivable soils all along the tops of the cliff to the south, could have formed the basis for a reasonably well-protected, agriculturally oriented dwelling spot. Although known only from surveys and limited excavation (an 'evaluation trench' measuring 15 × 24 m – Şevketoğlu 2008: 65–66), the site of *Arkosyko* has assumed some importance because of the substantial quantities of obsidian and cattle bones discovered there (Şevketoğlu 2002: 103, 105; 2006: 124–125; 2008: 67–69; Frame 2002: 235–236).

In an earlier survey of the site, Stanley Price (1979a: 119) recorded stone vessel fragments and stone implements, bone fragments (sheep, pig, fallow deer), a perforated shell, abundant chipped stone, and four obsidian tools. Şevketoğlu (2000: 124–137; 2002) carried out more focused survey in 1996 and 1999, followed by two seasons of excavation in 2000 and 2001. Preliminary site reports indicate there are five broad phases of Neolithic activity at the site (Şevketoğlu 2008: 66). Various features, artefacts and faunal/marine remains are listed, some of which are quite significant for understanding the function and date of the site. Several pieces of finely painted red, black or brown plaster with moulded edges indicate that the walls of buildings were decorated with unknown designs (Şevketoğlu 2008: 66). Beyond several pits (one sub-rectangular, plaster-lined and perhaps used to produce lime plaster) and postholes, the structural features mentioned comprise six 'dwellings' of sub-rectangular or rounded shapes, some 5–6 m in diameter. These buildings were made of mudbrick on stone and mudbrick foundations, all with plaster floors (Şevketoğlu 2006: 123–124; 2008: 66–67). Their contents include shallow plastered bins or pits, hearths and ovens variously filled with chert pebbles, a grinding stone, and a complete fallow deer antler. One stone-lined circular structure with a grinding stone placed in its centre has been compared to a similar feature at *Shillourokambos* (Şevketoğlu 2002: 103–104 and pl. 1).

Amongst the artefacts recovered from the site overall were a white stone pendant incised with what seems to be a female genital area (Şevketoğlu 2002: 104 pl. 2); other fragmentary black and orange (carnelian?) stone pendants; green, white and black stone beads and shell beads (bivalves, cowrie, dentalium); and some worked bone (fish-hooks, needle, awls, a long pin and a small spatula). Nearly 500 groundstone vessels were tabulated, including flat querns and bowls, most of which were quite fragmentary and all of which were made of sandstone or limestone, unlike the igneous groundstone industry of the following, LAN period (Şevketoğlu 2002: 100–105, and figs. 1–3; 2006: 125, 134, fig. 17). The presence of picrolite objects is notable because there are no local sources. Amongst the picrolite artefacts are beads, tokens, 'chisels' and miniature cups or 'thimbles', all of which were decorated with hatched lines (Şevketoğlu 2002: 100, fig. 1; 2006: 125, 134, fig. 16). Comparable thimbles have been found at *Ais Giorkis* (Fox 1987: 21 and ill. 2.5; Simmons 2003a: 66) and *Shillourkambos* (Guilaine 2003b: 334, fig. 2c, 336).

Notably, the excavator reports more than 5,000 pieces of obsidian (Şevketoğlu 2008: 67), including complete tools (bidirectional blade industry) and debitage, which exceeds by a factor of 10 the total amount of obsidian published from all other EAN sites combined. Chemical analysis of 10 obsidian samples indicate two central Anatolian sources: east Göllü Dağ (nine pieces) and Nenezi Dağ (one piece). The lack of cores suggests that the blades and bladelets might have been imported as tools. Not only does this

quantity of obsidian point to an EAN date (comparable to the situation at
Mylouthkia, Shillourokambos, Tenta and *Ais Giorkis*), it has also led to the suggestion that Akanthou may have served as a gateway community, funnelling
central Anatolian obsidian into Cyprus, possibly in exchange for picrolite
from central or southern Cyprus (Peltenburg et al. 2001a: 42; Peltenburg 2004:
xiv; Şevketoğlu 2008: 68).

In addition to well-preserved fish vertebrae (hake, dogfish, shark, tunny) and
marine turtles, the animal bones from Akanthou *Arkosyko* include the usual
EAN lineup of sheep, goat, pig, deer and cattle, as well as cat, fox, dog and turtle (Şevketoğlu 2002: 105; 2006: 125; 2008: 66). Şevketoğlu (2008: 66) recently
reported that several fragments of human bone were found, but with no clear
evidence of formal burials. Frame's (2002) detailed discussion of the mammal
bones is limited to those found in specific contexts (e.g. pits, plastered bins, fill
of floors) and processed during the 2002 field season. The species identified
include, in order of frequency, ovicaprids, fallow deer, pig, dog, fox and cattle.
Although the two cattle bones recorded were found in the topsoil level, Frame
(2002: 235) states that '…a small number of cattle bones are scattered throughout the site, including the lowest levels so far excavated'. The species of cattle
has yet to be determined, but the bones are '…unusually small with some
atypical features, and [are] definitely not modern' (Şevketoğlu 2000: 77). Given
the small size of the cattle bones found at *Shillourkambos* (Vigne et al. 2003:
248), this suggestion seems plausible. Sheep and goat account for nearly 50%
of the animal bones reported, with sheep three and a half times as common as
goat. Fallow deer comprise nearly 37%, pig nearly 13% and dogs a notable 9%
of the currently reported faunal remains. The age and element (specific bone
components) distribution of the bones suggest that the deer were hunted (and
perhaps butchered away from the habitational area) and the pigs domesticated (Frame 2002: 236–237, and table 2). The large percentage of canine bones
implies that they may have had a special importance for the people who dwelt
at Akanthou, perhaps as hunting or herding breeds. The bones of all four main
species – sheep, goat, deer, pig – were found mixed throughout the excavated
deposits and so may have been discarded in similar ways.

The significance of Akanthou *Arkosyko* and its likely role in the EAN culture
of Cyprus remains to be determined. Not least, the chronology of the site needs
to be placed on a firmer footing through radiocarbon dating, now supported
by one published radiocarbon date on carbonised seeds found near a hearth
excavated in 2003: OxA-13996 (8820±38 BP), which at 95.4% confidence level
is (overall range) 8010–7740 Cal BC (Higham et al. 2007: S34) (see Appendix
and SOM, Tables S2–S4). The actual counts of cattle, deer, sheep and pig need
to be confirmed through additional analyses and preferably expanded with further excavation. The presence of square or sub-square structures is somewhat
exceptional, as is the estimated extent of the site at 4 ha. Until some basic plans
are published, however, it is impossible to consider the implication of such

buildings, or such a large site, in determining the possible origin(s) of those who settled along Cyprus's north coast, in such close proximity to Anatolia.

Overview: Early Aceramic Neolithic

Recent excavations and survey projects have shown that new, and eventually permanent settlers reached Cyprus more than 10,000 years ago, bringing with them cultivated (or domesticated) cereals and herded (or 'managed') animals from the Levantine mainland. Because some sites around the northern and eastern Troodos foothills – *Asprokremmos, Palaeokamina, Kelaïdhoni* – can be dated to a time equivalent to the Levantine PPNA (Manning et al. 2010), they also need to be considered as the background to the island's earliest permanent settlement, perhaps as places where mobile foragers stayed for extended periods of time and made return migrations to other established locations on the Levantine coast (McCartney 2010).

Equally important, and something previously unimagined in the Neolithic of Cyprus, it now seems probable that a coastal, foraging way of life continued to flourish. This possibility is suggested by recent excavations at Nissi Beach that produced two radiocarbon dates (ca. 7750–7100 Cal BC, from limpet shells) in context with a continuing flake-based reduction technology (Ammerman et al. 2008: 12–15, fig. 6). Our ability to place all these sites in the earliest phase of the Neolithic is a 21st-century phenomenon. More significantly, Cyprus must now be regarded as a key island context for understanding mobile foragers and fishers, early farmers, sedentism, developments in seafaring, and all the associated social transformations that occurred within an eastern Mediterranean core zone (similarly McCarthy 2010).

Early Aceramic Neolithic subsistence practices combined the cultivation of plants (and, ultimately, agriculture) and animal husbandry (pig, ovicaprines, cattle) with deer hunting; all these animals, and at least some of the plants, arrived on the island with people from the (northern) Levant, and/or possibly from Anatolia. Based on current radiocarbon data and the extant faunal remains, the pig, goat, sheep and cattle from *Shillourokambos* appear to be as early as any known domesticates from Anatolia and even earlier than those known from the Levant (Vigne and Buitenhuis 1999: 52–55; Vigne et al. 2000: 101; Peters et al. 2005). Debate over the origins and dispersal of the earliest domesticated animals in the Levant and ancient western Asia, indeed even the definition of what constitutes 'domestic' versus 'managed' versus 'wild', seems set to continue for some time (Zeder and Hesse 2000; Vigne et al. 2003: 240; Horwitz et al. 2004; Zeder 2008; 2009; Conolly et al. 2011: 540). On Cyprus, it is now clear that the island's early Neolithic fauna correspond closely to those known from other Mediterranean islands such as Crete, Corsica and Sardinia.

The existence of non-domesticated deer on Cyprus around 8500–8000 Cal BC may point to somewhat earlier herding practices in the northern Levant, but the faunal record overall demonstrates that the island's earliest repeat visitors or settlers transported wild or herded animals by sea from their area of origin. The faunal data from *Asprokremmos* (mainly pig) and *Shillourokambos*, in particular the nearly full range of skeletal parts represented (especially important for cattle) and the kill-off patterns, show that all the species previously attested only in the LAN at Khirokitia were actually present on Cyprus by the mid-9th millennium Cal BC. This is crucially important, as it represents the earliest known, successful introduction of animals by humans to a Mediterranean island. Equally important, it suggests that the people who settled Cyprus not only had mastered seafaring skills, but also had some special – sociocultural or symbolic – relationship with these animals (Vigne et al. 2000: 95–98). The importance of hunted animals, in particular Mesopotamian fallow deer, should not be underestimated: Wasse (2007: 60) argues that hunting actually increased towards the end of the EAN and into the LAN, at a time when such practices became increasingly marginalised in the neighbouring Levant (but cf. McCarthy 2010: 191).

With respect to the floral record, Zohary (1996: 143–144) has postulated that eight founder crops formed the basis of Neolithic agriculture: emmer and einkorn wheat, barley, lentil, pea, chickpea, bitter vetch and flax. Given the rapid spread of agriculture (presumably by demic diffusion) throughout southwest Asia and southeast Europe, he also believes that domestication happened only once, that is, a single domestication event (Zohary 1996: 156). Using phylogenetic evidence, Lev Yadun et al. (2000) maintain – on the basis of the present-day distributions of the wild progenitors of domesticates – that all the founder crops may have been domesticated within a confined area of northern Syria and southeastern Turkey. Others have suggested multiple domestication events for both barley and emmer wheat (e.g. Jones et al. 1998; Nesbitt 2002: 123), whilst McCarthy (2010: 188–191) argues for a lengthy process of 'Neolithisation'. Indeed, a growing number of scholars, including Zeder (2006, 2009), maintains that a long period of time elapsed between people's earliest attempts to manipulate or manage plant and animal resources and the actual appearance of indisputable morphological markers of domestication (see also B.D. Smith 2007). Far from the typical model of a neat and compact 'Neolithic package', new evidence from across the Mediterranean and Near East indicates that most plant and animal species had a unique origin and dispersal story (Zeder 2008).

Willcox (2002: 137) has suggested that cereals may have been domesticated locally on Cyprus. On the one hand, in the earliest phase at *Mylouthkia*, five of these founder crops are present (the vetch and pea may be wild or domestic), which might be taken to support Willcox's position. On the other hand, the wild progentors of emmer and einkorn wheat are not endemic to Cyprus, although wild barley is (Meikle 1985: 1834), and *pisé* impressions of wild barley are present in the earliest phase at *Shillourokambos* (Willcox 2000; Colledge and Conolly 2007: 57–59; Guilaine et al. 2011: 601–603). On present evidence, then, it would seem (1) that the local (Cypriot) domestication of einkorn and emmer would only be possible in the unlikely event that the wild species had earlier been imported to the island, and (2) that the cultivated or domesticated forms found at *Mylouthkia* must have been brought to the island by the agropastoralists who first made repeated visits or settled there.

Once these domestic crops were established on Cyprus, the islanders became – at least for the time being – increasingly reliant on an agricultural (and pastoral) lifestyle, with the founder crops being the most commonly used domestic species throughout the Aceramic Neollithic period. The initially limited diversity of weed species found at Cypriot Aceramic Neolithic sites, including *Mylouthkia*, is a pattern common to emerging Neolithic farming systems throughout central Europe and the eastern Mediterranean. Colledge et al. (2004: S47) attribute this pattern to the greater energy investment early farmers made in maintaining their cultivated fields to sustain and establish grain stocks, essential practice once they had become less attached to their place(s) of origin.

The chipped stone assemblages of *Mylouthkia* 1A and the early phases (A, B) at *Shillourokambos* both demonstrate a primarily bidirectional core technology produced on high-quality translucent chert. The industry at *Shillourokambos* – tools made mainly on prismatic long blades and including Byblos and Amuq points – indicates the full naviform *chaîne opératoire* associated with the Levantine PPNB, and along with the frequency of imported obsidian demonstrates wider links between Cyprus, the (presumed) PPNB interaction sphere and southeastern Anatolia (McCartney 2007: 217). The major implication of the finds from both *Shillourokambos* and *Mylouthkia* is that the Early Aceramic Neolithic on Cyprus resulted from the migration of people to the island, most likely from coastal areas of the northern Levant during the mid-late 9th millennium Cal BC (already foreshadowed by Watson and Stanley Price 1977: 248). Although the push and pull factors behind this very early migration (or series of return migrations) of people to a Mediterranean island remain hypothetical, it seems clear that rising sea levels and the resulting loss of fertile lands along the Levantine coastal shelf must have led to both subsistence shock and social crises, and to the subsequent exploration and possible intentional stocking of the island of Cyprus with wild or 'managed' animals (Horwitz et al. 2004), and cultivated if not domesticated plants.

Such a strategy indicates that these new immigrants to the island were well aware of their own subsistence needs and already had some knowledge of the available natural resources on Cyprus (Colledge and Conolly 2007: 68). In this context, we must consider the full complement of material remains from Ayia Varvara *Asprokremmos*, which now confirm a phase on Cyprus contemporary with the late PPNA in the Levant (so too may the evidence from Ayios Tychonas *Klimonas*, once more fully published). The material record of

Asprokremmos thus far is quite distinct from that of the EAN, with the use of unidirectional blade/bladelet cores and more than 100 complete or fragmentary arrowheads, a wide range of burins, end scrapers, and some microlithic tools including a small geometric component that, along with some bifacially retouched blades, recall Late Epipalaeolithic tool types. Other material parallels with the Levant (chipped stone), and southeast Anatolia or northern Syria (dominance of pig; the small baked-clay figurine from *Ais Giorkis*), suggest that the earliest Neolithic people on Cyprus continued to be entangled with social and cultural developments on the mainland. Whenever they may have wished to return to the Syro-Anatolian mainland, they clearly had the necessary seafaring technology to do so.

Indeed, Peltenburg (2004a: 5–6, and fig. 2) has suggested that there were ongoing transfers of population between related groups of complex hunter-gatherers and farmers living on either side of the straits that separate Cyprus from Syro-Cilicia. In McCartney's (2010: 188–191) view, the large deposits of chipped and groundstone tools and implements, as well as various personal and symbolic items found at Initial Aceramic Neolithic/Cypro-PPNA *Aprokremmos*, and EAN *Mylouthkia*, *Shillourokambos* and *Ais Giorkis* demonstrate the careful organisation by a mobile social group in storing materials or disposing of refuse. For her, both factors – together with the paucity of human burials – point to extended periods of occupation at these sites and delayed or anticipated returns by complex foragers who moved between different, well-established locations. Whether we view these newcomers as mobile foragers or incipient agriculturalists, at some point during the EAN they settled permanently on the island, and established various facilities (dwellings, animal pens, wells, storage bins) that can reasonably be associated with a sedentary way of life.

How did such developments, including an insular way of life, impact on the new settlers' identity? Insularity, as argued earlier, need not necessarily lead to social or cultural isolation, and the sea should be viewed as much a facilitator as a barrier to interaction. If we thus think of a two-way exchange of peoples and practices between Cyprus and the Levant or Anatolia, we can consider how certain symbolic values may have been associated with a new, insular identity (McCartney et al. 2010: 134). In this case, we may note the existence of decorated shaft straighteners (see Figure 14 above) and lozenge points at *Asprokremmos* that reveal a 'shared symbolism' with the Middle Euphrates region (McCartney et al. 2008: 71–75, figs. 2–3); the presence of several non-local white marble stone ring fragments from *Tenta* (Todd 2005: 305–308); and other evidence for social or exchange relations that continued into EAN 3 and the LAN, for example, engraved pebbles from Khirokitia and Kholetria *Ortos* with several Levantine parallels; imported carnelian butterfly beads and small amount of obsidian at Khirokitia and *Tenta* (McCartney 2010: 192, with further refs.). Moreover, the chipped stone technology represented at most early

Neolithic sites is clearly related to that of various Pre-Pottery Neolithic B (PPNB) settlements in the Levant (Briois et al. 1997; McCartney and Gratuze 2003; McCartney 2004; 2005).

The essentially agropastoral economies indicated by finds from the EAN sites of *Mylouthkia* and *Shillourokambos*, as well as those of Kalavassos *Tenta*, Kritou Marottou *Ais Giorkis* and Akanthou *Arkosyko*, are amongst the earliest in western Asia (Bar-Yosef 2001; Peltenburg 2004a; Simmons 2010); they are directly linked to what now seems to be the earliest permanent settlement of Cyprus (or else the repeated, return migrations by complex foragers to well-established locations). Only some 1,000 years later (after ca. 7600 Cal BC), during the latest phase of the EAN, did the chipped stone industry change substantially, at the same time that the round stone structures characteristic of the Late Aceramic Neolithic (LAN) became the norm, and cattle disappeared from the archaeological record, replaced by deer and pig as the basic components of subsistence. The LAN thus no longer needs to be seen as *sui generis*, or as stemming from some 'pre-Neolithic' groups such as those attested at *Aetokremnos*, but rather as a phase during which a uniquely Cypriot culture crystallised after a long period of insular – but not isolated – development and change.

Now that the essential groundwork has been laid systematically, we can begin to investigate to what extent the nature of insularity, the role of distance, the dictates of adjusting to a new climatic and ecological regime, or basic social choices prolonged this period of settlement and adaptation.

CHAPTER 4

EARLY PREHISTORIC CYPRUS 2: LATE ACERAMIC NEOLITHIC AND CERAMIC NEOLITHIC

LATE ACERAMIC NEOLITHIC–KHIROKITIA CULTURE (CA. 7000/6800–5500/5300 CAL BC)

Transition to the Late Aceramic Neolithic

A wide range of material evidence and cultural practices (Peltenburg et al. 2003: 100–103), along with a coherent set of radiocarbon dates (see Table 2; Appendix, Table A2), indicate no interruption in human activity on Cyprus between the Early Aceramic Neolithic (EAN) 3 and the Late Aceramic Neolithic (LAN). In terms of subsistence practices, there is clear continuity in the reliance on the same suite of cereals, legumes, fruits and oil plants (Peltenburg et al. 2003: 69, table 7.5). The major change in the faunal record is the eventual disappearance of cattle, but people continued to hunt (or manage) deer, and, indeed, their reliance on hunting may have increased towards the end of the EAN and into the LAN (Croft 2002: 174; Wasse 2007: 60). Beyond subsistence needs, dog, fox and cat remains – which may have filled social, symbolic or hygienic needs – also continue to appear in LAN cultural deposits.

The use of a unidirectional instead of a of bidirectional core technology and a preference for opaque as opposed to translucent cherts (both factors already evident during *Mylouthkia* Period IB, EAN 3) continued to develop in the classic chipped stone tool assemblages of the LAN (McCartney 2004: 81–82). Similarly, the development of the groundstone industry seen in Well 133 at *Mylouthkia* (EAN 3) continued apace, but the production and decoration of stone vessels became much more elaborate, especially at Khirokitia. Conversely, the occurrence of obsidian fell off sharply during the LAN, a phenomenon already noted in the EAN 3 at *Mylouthkia*, *Tenta* and *Shillourokambos* (Briois et al. 1997; 110–111; McCartney, in Peltenburg et al. 2003: 20–21; Todd 2005: 264, 380).

The somewhat ephemeral signs of curvilinear architecture seen at EAN 1–2 *Shillourokambos* and EAN 3 *Mylouthkia* (Building 340), as well as the impressive stone and mudbrick circular buildings from EAN 3 *Tenta* (Todd 1987:

fig. 20), became the norm during the LAN. Peltenburg (2004c) divides these LAN curvilinear buildings into two types, pillar buildings and radial structures, and points to similar structures at (PPNA) Jerf el-Ahmar in the Levantine Corridor and other (PPNB) Syro-Anatolian sites. Even if the notion of constructing such dwellings derived from overseas, their persistence and elaboration during the LAN, when rectilinear buildings became the standard in the Levant, has often been taken as a sign that contacts with the latter region had fallen off, just as the declining use of obsidian has been seen as an indicator that relations with Anatolia had subsided. Papaconstantinou (2005: 15), however, maintains that the use of space at Khirokitia *Vouni*, at least, shows more commonalities with the use of space in Levantine rectangular structures than in circular structures from that region. McCartney (2010: 191), moreover, contests the notion that the use of circular architecture points to increasing isolation, and notes that at least two nearly contemporary sites in Levantine arid zones (Shaqarat Mazyad, Aswad) continued to use circular stone structures (Hermansen 2004: 37; Cauvin 2000: 39; Stordeur 2004), all part of the wide variation in architectural purpose and design evident across the Near East at this time (Watkins 2008: 153–160). Thus it is no longer possible to argue on architectural grounds for the increasing isolation of those who dwelt on Cyprus. I consider in more detail below issues of foreign contacts, insularity and connectivity during the LAN.

Other apparent continuities include the presence and use of maceheads (pink stone at *Mylouthkia* – see above, Figure 21), schematic human figurines, incised stones and small cylindrical rods ('batons'), and possibly the practice of headshaping (Peltenburg et al. 2003: 101–102). Thus the transition from EAN 3 to the LAN involved both innovation and conservatism. Even so, it is important to emphasise that with the discovery and prompt publication of so much new data on the EAN over the past 15 years, we no longer need to look upon the emergence and development of the LAN (Khirokitia Culture) as something that came about *sui generis*.

The Late Aceramic Neolithic (LAN) extended over a period of some 1,600 years, from about 7000/6800–5200 Cal BC (see Table 2; Appendix, Table A2, and section on Late Aceramic Neolithic [Khirokitia Phase]). The current archaeological record of this period consists of some 30 sites, of which only 10 have been even partially explored. Only Khirokitia *Vouni* and Cape Andreas *Kastros* have been excavated more fully. The large, complex and walled site of Khirokitia stands in stark contrast with the other, smaller and seasonally occupied or special-purpose sites (e.g. Kholetria *Ortos*, Cape Andreas *Kastros*, Kataliondas *Kourvellos*, Limnitis *Petra tou Limniti*, Dhali *Agridhi*). Many LAN sites are distributed along the northern, southern or eastern coasts, where people would have had access to decent arable soils as well as coastal resources (fishing, shellfish, aquatic birds, sea turtles, etc.). Other sites were located in areas where the lowlands (arable soils, agriculture) and uplands (forests, hunting) meet, a common pattern for broad-spectrum subsistence economies. Early agricultur-alists, moreover, may well have preferred areas that gave them access to a range of soil types, from fertile alluvial deposits to lighter, easily tilled soils, an impor-tant consideration before the introduction of animal traction (Seth Button, pers. comm., July 2009; see also Stanley Price 1979a: 62–65). In any case, LAN sites are commonly regarded as agricultural villages where people lived all year round, with an economy characterised by mixed farming and herding, fishing and hunting (Le Brun 2001; Wasse 2007: 60–63). In a recent reappraisal of LAN sites, however, and in particular of Khirokitia, Jones (2008; 2009) argues that they may also have served as necropoleis.

Settlements and Subsistence

The people of the LAN period lived in small village communities, within densely packed stone and mudbrick or *pisé* structures, mainly curvilinear or circular in shape (2–9 m in exterior diameter). Based on recent work at Khirokitia *Vouni*, the excavator has suggested that several of these curvilinear units could have formed a nuclear-family compound around an unroofed 'courtyard' where grinding grain – indicated by fixed querns set in a pebble paving – and other daily activities were carried out (Le Brun 2001: 115; 2002: 25; reconstruction in Le Brun 1997: 26, fig. 18) (Figure 28). Citing the small size of most of these structures (2–3 m in diameter) as well as the mortu-ary evidence found within them, Bolger (2003: 25) has questioned whether they could have served as a residence for nuclear families. Nonetheless, eth-nographic and ethnoarchaeological case studies have demonstrated that, in situations where some family members devote a significant amount of time to procuring resources or to tasks that take place at some distance from the community (e.g. tending flocks, hunting deer, fishing, foraging or seafaring), perhaps only half the family is actually dwelling in the stuctures (Narroll 1962; Kolb 1965).

Some dwellings at Khirokitia may have had small windows (Le Brun 1993: 65). Beyond the entryway, typically about 0.5 m wide and frequently with a paved threshold, the interiors of many dwellings contained earth-plastered floors, hearths, built-in basins, windows or wall niches, and platforms or benches against walls. Small, rectangular hearths found within various struc-tures at Khirokitia may indicate that cooking was done indoors (Le Brun 1997: 22, 25, fig. 17). This was not the case at Cape Andreas *Kastros*, where very few hearths were found inside structures, but several 'firepits' containing burnt material were recovered outside the buildings (Le Brun 1981: 19–20, 114, fig. 6). Whilst a plastered rectangular basin found at Khirokitia may have been used for storing water (Dikaios 1962: 7–9), there are few indicators of large scale or communal storage facilities. Moreover, there are no obvious public or open areas where communal gatherings might have been carried out; the clearest

Figure 28. Khirokitia *Vouni*, reconstruction of nuclear-family compound around an unroofed 'courtyard' (Le Brun [1997] 26, fig. 18). Courtesy of Alain Le Brun and Odile Daune-Le Brun.

indicators of ceremonial activity lie in the mortuary realm (see below, *Mortuary Evidence: Villages of the Dead?*).

Often these structures had a disproportionately large, rectilinear, central pillar (or 'pier', and, at times, double pillars); they have been defined as 'Circular Pillar Buildings' (Peltenburg 2004c: 75–78). Once thought to be roof supports (roofs were probably flat, not domed), some of these pillars have plastered tops, others have traces of plaster coating elsewhere, while a stepped example from Khirokitia (Le Brun 1994: 60, fig. 18) is weakest where it would have needed weight-bearing strength. All this indicates that some of the pillars were freestanding and non-structural. At Khirokitia itself, the plastered walls held some painted decorations but they are too poorly preserved to determine the elements of design (Le Brun 1997: 20, 23, fig. 13). A more symbolic interpretation of at least some of these pillars is suggested by comparable but much more elaborate examples – termed *stelae* – at sites such as Göbekli Tepe and Nevali Çori in eastern Anatolia (Peltenburg 1994c: 76–77, fig. 7.5). Peltenburg (1994c: 74, fig. 7.2, 78–79) also proposes another building tradition with Near Eastern parallels, the 'Circular Radial Building'. In the known LAN examples at Cape Andreas *Kastros* and Khirokitia *Vouni* (an EAN example, Structure 14, exists at *Tenta* – see above, Figure 23), the cells form integral parts of the building but are typically much smaller than the central core; thus they may have served as storage, cooking or other activity areas (but no spatial analyses have been carried out that might demonstrate this to be the case).

Compared to other Neolithic village sites in the Mediterranean, Khirokitia *Vouni*, some 2.5 ha in extent (Le Brun and Daune-Le Brun 2009: 70–71), is relatively large but still an order of magnitude smaller than the largest aceramic

Figure 29. Khirokitia *Vouni*, overview of site along the slope of the hill (*vouni*). View to the northwest. Photograph by A. Bernard Knapp.

Neolithic village sites in the southern Levant (e.g. Kuijt 2000a: 79–87, tables 1–2). Originally excavated by Dikaios between 1936–1946 (Dikaios 1953), the site is perched on the slopes of a prominent hill (*vouni*) in the Maroni River valley (Figure 29), some 6 km from the sea. Khirokitia is divided into east and west sectors by a long wall (Mur 100) running through the site; the eastern sector has nine stratigraphic levels (A–H, J) and the western sector three (I–III) (Le Mort 2008: 24). The densely built-up area of the site – with approximately 65 structures (those excavated by Dikaios are called *tholoi*) or building sequences – has two encircling walls delimiting the site in a southeast to northwest direction (as presently excavated – see Le Brun and Daune-Le Brun 2009: 72, fig. 3) (Figure 30). A sharp meander of the Maroni River more or less completes the circuit of the hill, and originally was thought to have served as a complementary boundary to the wall, if that was the intention (Dikaios 1962: 6, fig. 2; Le Brun 2001: 110, fig. 1). More recent work at the site has suggested to the excavators that the stone-built wall itself may have encircled the entire site, at least during the Level III occupation (Le Brun and Daune-Le Brun 2009: 71–72, fig. 3).

The earlier wall – interpreted by Dikaios (1953: 186–195; 1962: 5) as a 'Main Street' running through the midst of the settlement – was made of *pisé* and

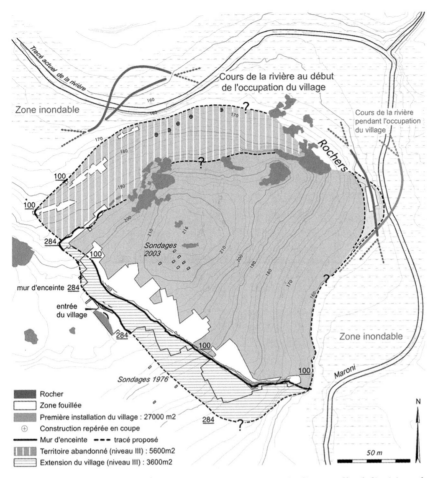

Figure 30. Khirokitia *Vouni*, plan showing two encircling walls delimiting the site in a southeast to northwest direction (Le Brun and Daune-Le Brun 2009: 72, fig. 3). Courtesy of Alain Le Brun and Odile Daune-Le Brun.

faced with stone on its western (outer) side. Once the area within the walls (east sector) filled up with stone and mudbrick structures, a series of new buildings were erected west of the first wall (west sector), and a new wall (Mur 284) was added (excavated by a French team since 1977 – Le Brun 1994: 33–47; 1997: 12–14, figs. 3–4; Le Brun and Daune-Le Brun 2009: 72–73, figs. 3–4). The second wall (Mur 284), 2.5 m thick and preserved to a height of 3 m, was built of stone interlaid with mud mortar; it extends for about 60 m, more or less in parallel with but not nearly so long as Mur 100. Incorporated within this new wall was a gateway that served in part to control access to the site: people had to enter the gate, walk up some steps, and turn at a right angle into the dwelling level (Le Brun 2001: 114, fig. 3). Khirokitia thus seems to have been a village of densely packed mud- and stone-built structures surrounded by a boundary wall whose purpose is uncertain, and whose length – especially in the north and northwest – seems to have decreased somewhat as time passed

(Le Brun and Daune-Le Brun 2009: 71–74, figs. 2–3, 6; for a radically different understanding of the site, see below, *Mortuary Evidence: Villages of the Dead*).

Cape Andreas *Kastros*, 0.17 ha in extent with at least 10 circular structures, is situated on a rocky spur at the easternmost tip of the Karpass Peninsula; the only enclosure is formed by the landscape itself. The site lies within a natural amphitheatre of rock flanked by a steep cliff on the north side that falls abruptly into the sea; its only access point is a passage on the west (Le Brun 1981: 109–110, figs. 1–2, pls. 1–2; 1993: 56). Kholetria *Ortos*, whose surface collection of Neolithic materials extended over 2.4 ha (Fox 1987: 22), is situated on a prominent hill in the Xeros Potamos Valley in the southwest of the island. Despite the ephemeral evidence for architecture (fragments of mudbrick and remnants of pits), there is no indication that the site was protected in any way beyond its hilltop location (Simmons 1996b: 33–34; 2003a: 63–64). Excepting their locations, the sites of Kataliondas *Kourvellos*, on and around a small conical hill (Morrison and Watkins 1974; Watkins 1979), Liminitis *Petra tou Limniti*, on a small offshore islet (Gjerstad et al. 1934: 1–12), and Dhali *Agridhi*, on the upper, southern terrace of the Yialias River (Lehavy 1989), reveal nothing defensive in their physical or material makeup. All these unwalled sites make the enclosure wall at Khirokitia all the more distinctive, its purpose all the more puzzling.

There is little evidence of any rivalry amongst the different settlements, no signs of violent destructions, and very few offensive weapons (e.g. spears and arrowheads are quite rare). As a cautionary tale, however, it may be noted that the massacre of Epipaleolithic foragers near Gebel Sahaba in Egypt was evidently carried out by people using arrows tipped with expedient flakes as points (Wendorf 1968). Moreover, there are signs of violence in the osteological record at Khirokitia: for example, an adult male with a depressed fracture on the left frontal lobe; another with a healed fracture of the left zygomatic arch (Angel 1953: 416); and yet a third who survived traumatic blows to the jaw, right frontal bone, and back of the head (Niklasson 1991: 61). These injuries, however, could have resulted from interpersonal violence rather than inter-village warfare.

With little more than 30 sites known (Held 1992b), site density was low, and it is presumed that population levels were too, with little competition for subsistence or other resources. Perhaps the walls at Khirokitia served to mark out the main community of the island, preserving the social cohesion of that site and helping to curtail any conflicts or limited pressures that existed over subsistence or mineral resources. Walls, of course, obviously serve defensive purposes but they also mark the boundary between the *domus* and the *agros*, between well-fed burghers and hungry outcasts; many modern-day walls, at least, seem to be markers of failed sovereignty (Brown 2010). Although the social organisation of most LAN settlements was quite likely egalitarian (Peltenburg 2004c: 80–84), at Khirokitia the walls may tell part of a different story, of something that separated those within from those without. Tholos 1A, for example, may

represent a communal gathering spot, or perhaps a distinctive household complex. At this stage of our understanding, only Khirokitia seems to reveal signs
of a different social ethos, if not a distinctively different function from the
other, smaller, rural, agricultural communities of the LAN (discussed further
below). At the very least, the walls of Khirokitia suggest that some person or
group could marshall the labour necessary to build and maintain communal
structures.

In terms of subsistence, the hunting of deer (*Dama Mesopotamica*) continued to provide an important source of meat at all sites. Hunting declined at
Khirokitia only in later phases, while it actually increased at Cape Andreas
Kastros (Davis 1989: 195; Le Brun 1993: 75). Pigs, described as a 'large primitive
breed' (Davis 2003: 265), were reared at all LAN sites; their use, like that of deer,
declined through time at Khirokitia (Davis 2003: 262–263, fig. 6) but increased
at Cape Andreas *Kastros* (Davis 1989: 195). At Kholetria *Ortos*, pig totals nearly
30% of the bone fragments identified, while deer makes up just over 20%
(Croft 2003a: 275). At Dhali *Agridhi*, the LAN levels – according to the available 14C dates (Lehavy 1989: 211; questioned by Watkins 1981: 146) – reveal
an overwhelming reliance on deer (nearly 80% of the identified bone fragments), with ovicaprines (nearly 14%) and pig (6.5 %) comprising the remainder (Carter, in Stager and Walker 1989: 247, table 4; Croft, in Stager and Walker
1989: 259, table 1).

Sheep and goat were herded, and as the exploitation of deer and pig
declined at Khirokitia, the proportion of ovicaprines increased, from about
30% to nearly 80% (Davis 2003: 262, fig. 6). As a proportion of the total meat
supply, the use of ovicaprines increased from 18% to 54% (Croft 2005: 356–358,
tables 114–115). At Cape Andreas *Kastros*, exactly the opposite took place: the
numbers of sheep and goat decreased over time from 62% to 19%, while the
remains of deer increased from 19% to 47% (Davis 1989: 195; Le Brun 1993:
75). Of the bone remains reported from Kholetria *Ortos*, ovicaprines represent
nearly 50% of the total (Simmons 1996b: 39, 41, table 3; Croft 2003a: 275). Cats,
dogs, foxes and some rodents were also present at most LAN sites.

Evidence from the coastal site of Cape Andreas *Kastros*, including bone fishhooks and extensive fish remains, indicates that fishing as well as foraging
played a key role in the broad-based economy of the outer Karpass peninsula (Garnier in Le Brun 1981: 93–94; Desse and Desse-Bersot 1994). We may
assume the same for other, north coastal sites such as *Petra tou Limniti* and
Troulli (Gjerstad et al. 1934: 1–12, 63–72). At Khirokitia, an inland site, the limited number of fish bones recovered all came from large fish, but a number of
marine mollusks were also present (Stanley Price and Christou 1973: 30). At
both sites, grouper, sea perch, sea bream (*sargus*) and mullet were present (Le
Brun 1993: 75–76; 1997: 37).

Although the reliance on deer subsided in the diets of those living in the
final LAN phases, most notably at Khirokitia (Davis 2003: 262–263, fig. 6), deer

hunting continued throughout the Neolithic and Chalcolithic periods (Croft 2002: 174). While palynological analyses have thus far indicated no widespread overexploitation of the environment (Renault-Miskovsky 1989), Davis (2003: 263) suggests that the decline at Khirokitia in the use of both deer and pigs – predominantly woodland animals – may signify local degradation around that site. Such an opinion is not contradicted by the evidence of charcoal, which shows a marked decrease in the occurrence of *Pistacia* sp. and sclerophyllous oak (Wasse 2007: 49, 62) alongside notable increases of pine (*Pinus brutia*), almond and juniper – all harbingers of deforestation (Thiébault 2003).

Domesticated plants recovered from Khirokitia, Kholetria *Ortos* and Cape Andreas *Kastros* include wheat (einkorn and emmer), hulled barley and pulses (lentil, pea, horse bean, vetch). Wild fruits and nuts include fig, plum, pear, pistachio, olive and linseed (Waines and Stanley Price 1975–1977; Hansen 1991: 233–234; Miller, in Le Brun 1984: 183–188; Murray 2003: 69, table 7.5; Colledge and Connoly 2007: 57, table 4.1). At Cape Andreas *Kastros*, always atypical, an abundance of rye grass led van Zeist (in Le Brun 1981: 99) to wonder if its grains might have been used as a food source. The people who lived at Dhali *Agridhi*, by contrast, seem to have been collectors of wild plants that grew in the immediate area of the site, although small numbers of hulled barley, lentil, vetch, olive and grape were recovered (Stewart, in Stager et al. 1974: 123–129; Lehavy 1989: 212). Grains were harvested with chert sickle blades, identifiable from the silica sheen on their cutting edges.

Similar palaeobotanical remains have been found at contemporary sites everywhere from southeastern Anatolia through the upper Euphrates to the southern Levant (Hansen 2001; Colledge 2004; Zeder 2009: 29–33; cf. Willcox 2003: 236). Five founder crops – emmer and einkorn wheat, hulled barley, lentil and pea – are the most common domesticated species, and they occur throughout Cyprus's Aceramic Neolithic. Since the numbers and amount of domesticated taxa increase through time (Colledge and Conolly 2007: 61), it would seem that agriculture thrived once established on the island. Thus there is little in the Cypriot floral record to provide support for the notion that agriculture was a subsidiary subsistence strategy (Watkins 1981: 142–145). For the most part, however, and excepting Khirokitia, LAN sites do not reveal clear evidence of agricultural intensification, and the prominence of hunted or herded animals in the faunal record cannot be disregarded (Croft 2002; Wasse 2007: 61–62). Moreover, the gross chronological resolution of most archaeological contexts in which food remains were deposited might have disguised the way that certain plant or animal foods were used in times of higher stress or shortage (Seth Button, pers. comm., July 2009).

For the most part, however, the broad-based economy of the LAN period probably could not prevent occasional crises precipitated by various climatic or environmental factors (e.g. forest clearance, soil depletion or erosion, drier conditions during the mid-Holocene), or by social constraints that arose from

Figure 31. LAN shallow stone bowl. Rectangular in shape, the bowl is decorated with raised dots and chevrons. Height: 10 cm; maximum width 27.5 cm; length 30.5 cm. Courtesy of the Cyprus Museum, Nicosia.

living on an island. Such factors may also have impacted on what has been termed 'settlement drift' (sites seldom occupied for more than one cultural period), and on the demographic or cultural involution posited for the end of the LAN (Held 1992a: 136–137) (discussed further below). Be that as it may, the very length of the LAN suggests that the people who lived on Cyprus at this time had adapted well to the limitations – spatial, social, environmental – imposed by their new, insular home.

The Material Culture of the Late Aceramic Neolithic

The material aspects of the LAN are rich and varied, and typically are found within the curvilinear dwellings, especially those at Khirokitia. Many of these structures had plastered walls or pillars, and recent work at Khirokitia has uncovered green and red (ochre?) painted decoration on a plastered background (Hadjisavvas 2007: 49). One of the LAN's most characteristic material culture features was the production of grey-green stone vessels (Figure 31), skilfully decorated with grooved or ribbed lines (vertical, horizontal, oblique), incised chevrons and dots in relief (Le Brun 2005: 115). One andesite bowl from Khirokitia portrays an individual in low relief (Le Brun 1989b: 78–79, fig. 11.4) and calls to mind the painted pillar from Structure 11 at EAN *Tenta* depicting two human figures in red pigment (see above, Figure 25). Produced mainly from diabase, a hard igneous rock, these vessels contrast with EAN stone vessels from *Shillourokambos, Mylouthkia* and Akanthou *Arkosyko* (Şevketoğlu 2002: 105), all made from a soft chalk or limestone. Diabase vessels first appear at *Tenta* in the EAN 3 period (Todd 2005: 270–281), and (miniature) picrolite vessels are known from both EAN *Tenta* and *Ais Giorkis* (see below); few are decorated until the LAN.

Figure 32. LAN human figure from Khirokitia, with phallic-shaped head and rectangular body. Height: 19 cm. Courtesy of the Cyprus Museum, Nicosia.

Some finely produced bowls and basins were carved from both diabase and soft limestone, while coarser trays and basins were hollowed out from hard limestone or breccia, perhaps in imitation of baskets (Le Brun 2001: 113; Dikaios 1962: 14–35, figs. 5–17; Saliou, in Le Brun 1989a: 137–175; Todd 2005: 270–287, figs. 30–49). Some elaborately decorated and spouted bowls made of diabase, and found only in tombs, may have served a ceremonial function that involved the pouring of liquids (Steel 2004a: 56). Mortuary rituals involving the pouring of liquids could have occurred in several tombs at Khirokitia – III:VI; X (I): I.II.III; XV(II):XV (Niklasson 1991: 19, 26, 28) – that had access channels or were left partly open. Other types of vessel include miniature picrolite cups from *Ais Giorkis* (Fox 1987: 21, ill. 2.5; Simmons 2003a: 66), which recall similar objects from EAN *Tenta* (Todd 2005: 304, fig. 63, 28–29), and others decorated with hatched lines from EAN *Arkosyko* (Şevketoğlu 2006: 125, 134, fig. 16) and *Shillourkambos* (Guilaine 2003b: 334, fig. 2c, 336).

There is a range of human (rarely animal) heads and figurines made of limestone, calcerenite or basalt, mostly lacking indicators of sex but often rendered in an unmistakably phallic form (Dikaios 1962: 48–49, fig. 25/967; Pearlman 1993: fig. 68; Le Brun 1997: 29–31, figs. 23–25) (Figure 32). Most Neolithic and Chalcolithic human figurines from the island appear to be sexually ambiguous; they offer tantalising clues into the nature of sex and sexualities in early prehistoric Cyprus (Knapp and Meskell 1997). At least to our eyes, most figurines seem rather schematic, and most of them come from Khirokitia. One squatting figure from this site reputedly depicts female genitalia pecked out in the stone (Dikaios 1953: 297, pl. 95; 1962: 47, fig. 24/680). At Kholetria *Ortos*, early survey work revealed a broken basalt cruciform figurine (Fox 1987: 23, 37, fig. 6.3), while excavations uncovered a stylised limestone figurine, and two squat, baked-clay figurines (Simmons 1996b: 38, fig. 3). Although not obviously gendered, one of the clay figurines has a pronounced stomach and navel, as well as ample buttocks, and probably represents a female. From Khirokitia comes an exceptional head modeled in clay (Dikaios 1953: 299–300, pl. 98; 1962: 48, fig. 25/1063). All other known LAN figurines are made of (igneous) stone. Le Brun (2005: 115) suggests that the decision to produce vessels, human representations and even engraved pebbles (see further below) in harder igneous stone – in preference to the soft, calcareous stone used for similar items in the EAN – was a distinguishing feature of the LAN; perhaps it was linked to some people's ideology, if not their identity.

In Le Brun's (2002: 30) view, the prominence of the masculine on LAN Cyprus is revealed in the phallic-style representations of most human figures. The rarity of females depicted may be contrasted with material practices in most surrounding Neolithic cultures, from southeast Europe and Greece through Anatolia and the Levant (e.g. Meskell 1998b; Hamilton 2000; Talalay 2000; Nanoglou 2006; Mina 2008). Such (foreign) female figurines often show exaggerated depictions of female sexual characteristics, which have been taken to reflect a concern with fecundity and representation (amongst other possible meanings – Knapp 2009a). If the makers or users of such figurines were actually concerned with fecundity, their absence on Cyprus seems hard to explain, given the high infant mortality reported at Khirokitia and the (presumed) low population density of LAN Cyprus overall.

Nearly all LAN depictions of the human body were found in domestic contexts, whether inside structures or in the occupational debris just outside them (Le Brun 1989b: 79–80). From Mari *Mesovouni*, south of *Tenta*, comes a distinctive quadruped figurine (Todd 1998: 24, fig. 6); only two other animal figurines are known, from Khirokitia, but the species cannot be indentified with any certainty (Dikaios 1962: 48, fig. 25/561, 1252). A great deal of effort went into crafting all these figurines as well as the stone vessels, an effort that seems explicable only in the context of a non-pottery-producing culture, prima facie quite different from those in the contemporary Levant and Anatolia. Scholars often regard them as material signatures of the insularity, intentional or otherwise, that characterised LAN Cyprus.

Small amounts of a light coloured, 'grey ware' pottery were found in the aceramic levels at Khirokitia (Dikaios 1962: 38). This apparent attempt to make bowls with broad flat bases and thick, rounded rims must have been unsuccessful, as it was never repeated. Only from surface layers at Khirokitia, during what Dikaios termed 'phase III', did excavations produce some 2,000 pottery sherds of well-known types – Red Slip, Red Lustrous and Combed wares (Dikaios 1962: 39–43). Dikaios regarded the 'grey ware' to be part of the aceramic occupation, and ultimately decided that the rest of the pottery was a product of the site's reoccupation during the Ceramic Neolithic (or 'Neolithic IB' – see Dikaios 1962: 180), some 2,000 years later. A later reassessment of stratigraphic levels at the site found 'no unambiguous association of pottery with structures assigned by Dikaios to Period III' and concluded that the pottery must have come from later (i.e. Ceramic Neolithic) structures severely disturbed by erosion, more recent cultivation and terrace wall construction (Stanley Price and Christou 1973: 30–32; also Le Brun 1985: 78).

The LAN chipped stone industry is well known from numerous assemblages at most sites across the island. In general, there is a simplification of the core technology and less tool diversity within a general continuity. The *chaîne opératoire* embraced a unidirectional rather than a bidirectional core technology, and there was a further increase in the use of moderate quality (opaque) cherts, as seen already during EAN 3. Blade production from unidirectional cores is seen at Khirokitia, Kholetria *Ortos* and Cape Andreas *Kastros*, but there was less distinction between flake and blade production. Tools from these sites are dominated by backed blades (including 'Ortos crescents' – see below) (McCartney and Todd 2005: 226).

Backed blades, retouched flakes and blades, *pièces esquillées*, denticulates and notches represent the 'classic' tool assemblages of this period (McCartney, in Clarke 2007: 81–82) (Figure 33). Simple utilised flakes and blades dominate, whilst glossed tools (sickles) are frequent, especially in truncated and convex backed forms. Tanged blades are present but in decreased amounts from EAN 3 (*Tenta* Period 4 represents the peak). Various forms of scrapers and awls also were in common use. Burins and perforators, particularly diminutive drill bits, form a significant component of the tool assemblage (McCartney 2003: 145). One variety of sickle blade – a crescent-shaped blank steeply backed or retouched with sickle sheen on the opposing edge – was the most common type among a class that made up nearly 16% of the more than 1,200 tools recovered at Kholetria *Ortos* during the 1992–1993 seasons (Simmons 1996b: 35). Among the *Ortos* tools were four 'thumbnail' endscrapers which, along with an 'exhausted' core type (9% of all cores), recall the tool forms and manufacturing techniques that prevailed at Late Epipalaeolithic Akrotiri *Aetokremnos*, perhaps indicating some degree of technological – but certainly not cultural – continuity (Simmons 1996b: 36).

Overall, then, there was less diversity in the types of tools used during the LAN. The arrowheads characteristic of earlier industries were replaced by large tanged blades (McCartney 2004: 114), more like knives or daggers than projectile points (there is at least one, fragmentary arrowhead from Khirokitia, and other tangs are reported from *Ortos*). At Kholetria *Ortos*, 50% of the tools were produced on blade blanks, 40% on flake blanks, and only 4% on core blanks (Simmons 1996b: 35). All these tools would have been used in a range of agricultural, domestic and craft activities, from harvesting cereals and cutting reeds, to woodworking and scraping animal skins (Le Brun 1996: 4; 1998: 31–32).

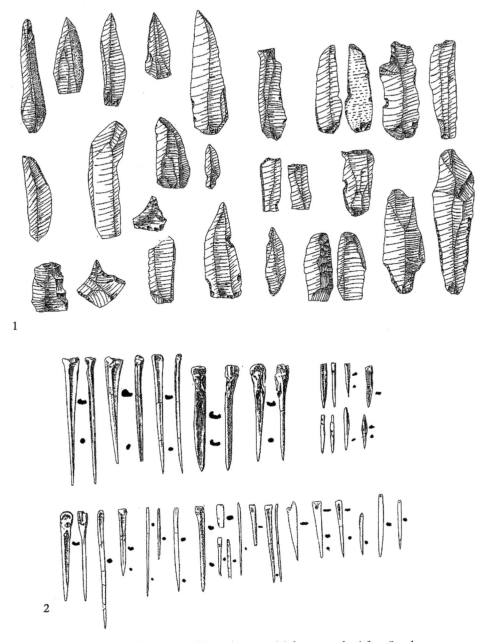

Figure 33. Khirokitia toolkit – (1) chipped stone; (2) bone tools. After Steel 2004a: 55, fig. 3.5). Courtesy of Louise Steel.

In a provactive study of Cypriot Neolithic chipped stone tools and raw materials, McCartney (2002) pointed out that they are dominated by tool types typically associated with domestic (food gathering and preparation) rather than with hunting activities. The evidence, of course, comes from village sites more likely to embed evidence of domestic activities, rather than from hunting camps such as, perhaps, Dhali *Agridhi* (Seth Button, pers. comm., July 2009).

McCartney considers the role of gender in the use of these tools and suggests that task differentiation is more complex than simply assigning particular tool types to either men or women. She concludes that, at least with respect to chipped stone technology, there is no indication of a gendered division of labour; instead she posits an integrated workforce in which both females and males worked together in all aspects of agricultural production (also Bolger 2003: 58–59). Nonetheless, it may be noted that small-scale agricultural societies worldwide exhibit some sexual division of labour, and the association of some groundstone material with female burials at Khirokitia (e.g. Niklasson 1991: 89–94) may suggest that at least some work tasks were separated by sex. Overall, it is likely that both women and men on LAN Cyprus participated in a range of overlapping tasks, even if the chipped stone toolkits were not clearly gendered.

In terms of raw materials, both Lefkara and Moni cherts were well represented at Kholetria *Ortos* (Simmons 1996b: 35). Small numbers of tools were made using chalcedony, jasper and quartz. While the use of obsidian was uncommon, it is at least present at Khirokitia, Cape Andreas *Kastros* and Kholetria *Ortos*. All the obsidian thus far analysed has been sourced to central Anatolia (Göllü Dağ – Gomez et al. 1995; Simmons 1996: 35; see also Cauvin, in Le Brun 1984: 86). That some level of prestige may have been associated with the use of this foreign material seems evident in the fine pressure retouched pointed tang from Khirokitia (Christou 1994a: 664; McCartney 2004: 112–113). Recent comparative analyses of obsidian and chert artefacts from Khirokitia, however, found no differences in their treatment, implying that no special meaning was attached to obsidian as an exotic material (Astruc 2004: 28–29; see also Le Brun 2001: 113). The presence of obsidian and carnelian (at Khirokitia, 50 and 40 pieces, respectively – Le Brun and Daune-Le Brun 2009: 77 n. 26), both foreign materials, may point to some level of low-volume maritime contacts throughout the LAN (Peltenburg 2004c: 83), perhaps in the form of a trinket exchange (McCartney and Grautze 2003: 75). Alternatively, one might view the value of such exchange as the attempt to maintain long-distance kinship networks as a buffer against resource stress (Halstead and O'Shea 1989). Finally, we cannot rule out the possibility that small quantities of obsidian were retrieved from the older, EAN sites, where it was so abundant.

The LAN toolkit also included a narrow range of bone objects, mainly pointed tools such as needles (some with eyes), awls, drills, pins, and other types of perforators (borers) used for piercing, threading and weaving tasks, including basketry (Dikaios 1962: 53–55, figs. 28–29) (see above, Figure 33). Some of the bone tools were fixed in handles made from deer antlers (Le Brun 1997: 32–34, figs. 28–30), while a variety of bone fishhooks was uncovered at Cape Andreas *Kastros* (Le Brun 1981: 61–62, 203, fig. 56).

Groundstone tools included grinders, flat and saddle querns, mortars and pestles (Dikaios 1962: 32–34, figs. 16–17, 44–47, figs. 23–24), all used in

Figure 34. Khirokitia *Vouni* (a) engraved stone pebbles, decorated with incised lines on one or both sides; (b) conical stones decorated with chevrons and chequered or gridded patterns. Courtesy of Alain Le Brun and Odile Daune-Le Brun.

processing cereals or other foodstuffs. Small numbers of pierced circular stones, often called maceheads (e.g. Dikaios 1962: 43–44, fig. 22), also occur but their function is unclear. The most notable of the ground stone tools is the axe (or 'celt'), often highly polished and perhaps used at least occasionally for clearing trees from a heavily wooded landscape in order to expand agricultural production (Dikaios 1962: 45–47, figs. 23–24).

More enigmatic are the various types of engraved flat pebbles, with a grid of incised lines on one or both sides, and conical stones decorated with chevrons on their side and a chequered or gridded pattern on their base (Le Brun 1997: 36, 38, figs. 34–35) (Figure 34a and b). While the engraved pebbles have been found only at Khirokitia and Kholetria *Ortos* during the LAN (Dikaios 1962: 37, fig. 19; Astruc 1994: 236–243, 270–277, figs. 96–99; Simmons 1996b: 37, fig. 2), they are quite similar to patterns seen on engraved and grooved stones from EAN *Shillourokambos* (Guilaine 2003b: 334, fig. 2, discussed above). At least one engraved (sandstone), cross-hatched pebble has now been recovered at the Ceramic Neolithic site of Kalavasos *Kokkinoyia*; it is a surface find and there are no indications of a LAN phase there (Clarke 2004: 59, fig. 3.3). Steel (2004a: 58) has suggested that these pebbles and conical stones might have served either as tokens in a social storage system of mutual obligations or, in functional terms, as weights for fishing nets (perhaps unlikely in these two inland and upland sites?) (discussed below in the overview of the LAN, under *Insularity and Identity*).

Other types of stone – calcite, limestone, picrolite, imported carnelian – and shell (dentalium) were used to make items of personal adornment: pins, pendants, beads, rings and necklaces (Dikaios 1962: 49–52, figs. 26–27; Le Brun 1997: 35–36, fig. 33; Todd 1998: 48–50, figs. 29–30). One curious class of ring-shaped ornaments ('pointed ring pendant', shaped like a question mark), made from picrolite and with one or two points, has been interpreted as dress pins or ornaments (Dikaios 1953: 302–303; Steel 2004a: 58); more importantly, they are seen as representative of incipient craft specialisation (McCartney, in Clarke 2007a: 76). Whatever their purpose, these objects also occur at Khirokitia (and at EAN *Tenta*), often in discard contexts that do not really help to eludicate their purpose (Dikaios 1962: 50–51, figs. 26–27; Astruc 1994: 249–250, fig. 101.6–9; Todd 2005: 302–303, fig. 63, 19–27). Interestingly, they also occur at Cape Andreas *Kastros*, but there are made from chalcedony, an exceptionally hard stone instead of the much softer picrolite (Le Brun 1981: 182–183, fig. 46). This led McCartney (in Clarke 2007a: 76) to suggest an early distinction between the north and south of the island in the types of raw materials used; the south, of course, had much easier access to picrolite. In any case, the working of chalcedony at Cape Andreas *Kastros* may reflect a very specialised kind of craft, given the difficulty of fashioning anything from this stone by grinding rather than knapping (Seth Button, pers. comm., July 2009).

Despite the limited quantities of non-native materials such as carnelian and obsidian in various LAN sites, and bearing in mind that picrolite – found in abundance primarily along the Kouris River bed in the island's south-west – was recovered at both Khirokitia and Cape Andreas *Kastros*, it has been suggested that an exchange or supply network may have existed within and beyond the island during the LAN (Le Brun 1997: 35–36; Steel 2004a: 56), similar to the one proposed for the EAN (Peltenburg et al. 2001a: 42). Alternatively, one might also view these limited quantities of imports as reflecting lower demand in the well-established communities of the LAN for inter-island or external contacts as a buffer against resource stress. However, once we add to these occurrences of foreign or non-local materials the fact that the engraved pebbles ('incised cobbles') from both Khirokitia and *Ortos* have very similar counterparts in both aceramic and ceramic Neolithic contexts in the Levant (Simmons 1996b: 37; McCartney, in Clarke 2007a: 77), it seems clear that we should reconsider carefully the nature of Cyprus's insularity during the LAN. Even more intriguing are the mortuary practices of the LAN, their possible origins, and how they might help us to disentangle long-standing impressions of an insular Neolithic society.

Mortuary Practices: Villages of the Dead?

> ...if the interiors of the large tholoi [at Khirokitia *Vouni*] contained comparatively little evidence of domestic life, they have yielded abundant evidence in connexion with the disposal of the dead. With the exception of tholos XXIV they all contained numerous burials, mostly of adults. (Dikaios 1953: 228)

The rich, diverse and widely published archaeological record of Khirokitia *Vouni* provides a great deal of insight into LAN mortuary practices. The dead, typically single inhumations in a contracted position, were interred in shallow pits beneath the floors of certain buildings, or else in the open spaces just outside them (a practice attested at *Tenta* already in EAN 3) (LeBrun et al. 1987: 294, fig. 12). According to Le Brun (2005: 115), at least some of these pit burials were situated inside of *uninhabited* buildings at Khirokitia. Once the body was in place, the pit was filled with earth and covered with a layer of plaster that then, or later, served as a living floor (Le Brun 1997: 27–28, fig. 19; Moyer, in Todd 2005: 5–6).

At Cape Andreas *Kastros*, the only complete burial of three that were found (with three adults, one child) was in the form of a trapezoidal-shaped pit, and the only possible grave goods were marine shell fragments (Sépulture 540 – Le Brun 1981: 27–28). The unsexed adult in Sépulture 540 and possibly two others had artificially flattened crania (Solivères, in Le Brun 1981: 85; Niklasson 1991: 103–104), a practice also seen at Khirokitia (Le Mort 2003: 322–325), and even earlier at EAN 3 *Mosphilia* (Fox et al., in Peltenburg et al. 2003: 43), *Shillourokambos* (Le Mort 2003: 324 and n. 58) and *Tenta* (one individual – Moyer, in Todd 2005: 4–5). The fragmentary remains of four further individuals found at *Kastros* lacked any burial context. No intact burials have yet been found at Kholetria *Ortos*, and the fragmentary remains of several individuals that do exist provide no direct evidence for intentional burials (Simmons 1996b: 38).

All elements of the population – newborns, infants, children, adult men and women – are represented at Khirokitia, with some 240 'accessible' individuals recorded (Le Mort 2008: 23–24; Le Mort in Le Brun 1994: 157–198). When Niklasson (1991: 11, 57, 174) was writing, Khirokitia's skeletal material totalled 175 individuals, while Le Mort's (2008: 25, table 3.1) most recent tally counts 106 adults, 109 perinates or infants, and 25 'juveniles' (aged 1–19 years). While these accumulative differences are understandable, there are some discrepancies in the numbers generated by other scholars who worked specifically on the skeletal material from Dikaios's excavations (Niklasson 1991: 14–15; Le Mort 2008: 24).

There appears to be a certain level of differentiation in these burials, as some structures contained only male burials (Tholoi V, VII, and Structures 125, 126), others only females (Tholos XV[II] and Structures 117, 122–124), and still others exclusively adults or infants (Le Brun 2002: 26). According to Le Mort's (2008: 26) latest analysis, Structures 89 and 106 in the western sector (French excavations) contained a total of 19 perinatal burials, with Structure 106 including the only case of a double burial recorded at Khirokitia. Three of the *tholoi* excavated in the eastern sector (X[II], XV[II] and XLVII) also held multiple infant burials, mainly perinatal individuals. Amongst a sub-sample of 51 infants under one year of age from the western sector, 50 died before they were six months old (Le Mort: 2000: 67; 2003: 318). This abnormally high infant mortality may reflect demographic anomalies that cannot be explained by uneven archaeological sampling, taphonomic processes or cultural practices such as infanticide (Le Mort 2000: 68; 2003: 321–322). Instead, it may be the result of pathological conditions; Le Mort (2003; 2008: 28) found that porotic bone lesions were quite common amongst infants and juveniles at Khirokitia. Some of the infants and most of the children showed possible signs of genetic anemia, notably β-thalassemia, something noted long ago by Angel (1966; see also Harper 2008: 114). It is also worth mentioning that of seven skeletons (one adult, six subadults) from Khirokita examined for parasitic infections, only the adult showed evidence of the *Tænia* parasite, typically transmitted through foodstuffs (Harper and Fox 2008: 5).

Le Brun (2001: 115–116; 2002: 27), long-time director of excavations at Khirokitia, has distinguished between simple burials with no embellishments (88% of current record) and a more elaborate type where the rim of the pit was lined with *pisé* and pebbles. Within these burials, however, there were no obvious divisions based on age or sex, and only four of seven elaborate burials contained grave goods. The most common objects placed in the burials were pins (bone), pendants, necklaces (dentalium, carnelian) and stone vessels. Burials with some grave goods tend to be evenly distributed between the different structures, with each domestic unit containing at least one example. Occasionally, a large stone was placed on the head, chest or pelvis of the deceased, a practice that seems to have been shared equally among men, women and even some juveniles at Khirokitia (Le Brun 2001: 116). In a few cases, spouted stone vessels were placed on infants in their burials (Le Mort 2008: 27–28). What can this practice possibly have meant: fear of the dead? Whatever the answer, all these factors combined led Le Brun (2002: 27) to suggest that society at Khirokitia was organised on an egalitarian basis, in which each person, male or female, enjoyed a social status that was achieved, not ascribed from birth.

Some women's burials may have received special treatment. First of all, cranial modification (an artifical flattening of the rear of the skull – for which, see Lorentz 2009) is argued to have been more common in women than in men. Of 34 males and 30 females examined by Angel (1953: 416), some 10 males and 15 females showed signs of cranial modification. Niklasson (1991: 168), however, states that only 19 individuals known from Khirokitia showed traces of artificial skull modification. Le Mort (2003: 322–324) adds three more skulls – two female and one male – to this uncertain number. Elsewhere, Le Mort (2007: 154) states that the bones from Khirokitia generally are in poor condition (broken, partial, covered with concretions), and that it is not always easy to separate clearly a deformed from a normal skull. Although some deformations may have been intentional, others – such as those induced by cradle-boarding – would have been unintentional. She concludes that artifical cranial modification was frequent on Aceramic Neolithic Cyprus, and notes that similar practices are attested on the PPN Levantine mainland (Le Mort 2007: 156).

Bolger (2003: 151–152) emphasised that on the basis of the skeletal evidence currently preserved and available for study, it would be imprudent to assume that the practice of artificial cranial modification was a gender-based phenomenon. Lorentz (2009), however, maintains that the people of Khirokitia were intentionally shaping their infants' heads, and that the most extreme cases exemplifying this practice were almost all female. Beyond references to her unpublished PhD thesis (Lorentz 2003), however, she presents no statistical evidence to back up such statements as '…variations in intensity or the degree of headshaping present in the different individuals [at Khirokitia] points to the use of headshaping intensity in gender differentiation' (Lorentz 2009: 24). In fact, because Cypriot crania tend to be short and broad with flattened occipitals, we need to know what a natural cranium looks like before we can say there are extreme cases of headshaping (Nathan Harper, pers. comm., July 2009).

Nonetheless it is clear that female skeletons at Khirokitia were orientated both to the northeast and southwest, whereas those of males faced only northeast. Amongst the grave goods, personal adornments (pins, pendants, necklaces) were restricted to women's burials and, in general, these same burials contained more objects of different types, made of what might be termed more prestigious materials, that is, picrolite adornments, imported carnelian and local dentalium shells, and spouted stone vesssels (Le Brun 2001: 116; 2002: 28). In other words, those burials that appear to be the most prestigious in our eyes belonged to women.

Compare this situation with that at EAN *Tenta*, where 14 human burials with a minimum of 18 individuals were excavated (Moyer, in Todd 2005: 1–17). Once again single, contracted or flexed, fully articulated skeletons were placed on their sides or backs under the floors of two buildings (Structures 9 and 10), or in open areas just outside these and other structures. In only one instance were four bodies, all infants, interred together (Burial 4), in a shallow pit outside Structure 10 (Moyer, in Todd 2005: 6, 10, pl. III). Whereas both adults and infants were buried in close assocation with buildings, all the extramural burials were those of adults (Niklasson 1991: 107). One infant burial (no. 7) had a small limestone cobble placed on top of its thorax. The only grave goods (if such they were) deposited with the dead were two small lumps of worked red ochre, found in a child's burial (no. 11) in Structure 9 (Moyer, in Todd 2005: 6, 12; Todd 1998: 46, fig. 26). Some intact skeletons were placed unceremoniously between buildings together with layers of rubbish. Moreoever, there were no obvious age or sex differences in any of the *Tenta* burials, whether found within or between buildings. Two adult burials, however, received unique treatment. Burial 6 (Structure 42) and Burial 10 (Structure 11) both had been positioned with their heads propped up against the walls of buildings. The skull of Burial 6 lay under a thin limestone slab set vertically against the building wall with a similar slab used to cover it. The skull of Burial 10, covered by a mixed deposit of rubbish, was partially blackened, perhaps by fire (Niklasson 1991: 108–109). Skull flattening was also apparent in female Burial 2 and child Burial 11 at *Tenta* (Moyer, in Todd 2005: 4–5).

In attempting to interpret the mortuary practises of the LAN, we are effectively limited to the remains from Khirokitia *Vouni*; those from Kalavasos *Tenta* are earlier in time. The very limited sample from the latter site – eight adults, eight infants (four interred together in Burial 4), two children and isolated remains of both adults and children – is informative inasmuch as it does not contradict the much more extensive remains from Khirokitia. Worthy of note, perhaps, is the fact that the blackened skull of Burial 10 was placed immediately outside (north) of Structure 11 at *Tenta*, which itself is distinguished by the two stylised, red-painted human figures on one of its internal piers (see above, Figure 25).

At Khirokitia, of approximately 65 structures or building sequences known from the site, 41 contained burials. Many of the *tholoi* had floor layers of plastered surfaces, beneath and between which lay the human remains. Whereas Dikaios (1953: 214) had assumed that the number of burials in any structure was related to the length of time it was occupied, Niklasson (1991: 68) argued that the number of floors in some buildings was related to the (differing) number of burials, perhaps determined or limited by those in the community who were responsible for them (see Kuijt 2000b: 143–145 on collective secondary burial rites in the Levantine Neolithic). There are virtually no distinctions between those buildings that contain burials and those that do not. With few exceptions, the Khirokitia burials were intramural (or 'intradomic' – see Toumazou 1987: 6), a practice standing at odds with that of other early prehistoric sites within and beyond Cyprus, where such inhumations are generally limited to one category of individuals, typically infants (Niklasson 1991: 168).

One common assumption – that all the dead were buried within or beneath the floors of the living – has caught the attention of those scholars who have examined most closely the Khirokitia burials, including Dikaios (1953: 339; also Niklasson 1991: 167; Le Mort 2003: 315–316; Jones 2008: 123–126). Dikaios (1953: 214–215, 340), initially concerned to explain the large number of burials and more limited evidence for settlement activities, noted the possibility that at least some of the Khirokitia evidence might have been associated with (mortuary) ritual or sacrifices. In his final publication of the site, however, Dikaios (1962: 11, 178) maintained that the *tholoi* were used for human habitation, not for burials, and that the hearths, benches, platforms and tools found within them corroborated such a function. Dikaios placed special emphasis on the hearths as habitational elements, but Niklasson (1991: 169–170) insisted that hearths are not as common as Dikaios implied, and at times were placed just above the burials. Moreover, whereas Dikaios (1953: 212) regarded the larger platforms as places to sleep or sit, Niklasson (1991: 169) felt that the platforms in Tholoi V and XVII, at least, could have been highly conspicuous features for burials. Dikaios (1953: 222) scarcely commented on the burials of two complete caprines in Tholoi VII and X(IV), while Niklasson (1991: 170) suggested they might be seen as sacrifices or as substitutes for human burials.

Dikaios singled out Khirokitia's large *tholoi* (e.g. IA, XVII, XXIV, XXV, XLVII) as a special sub-class, and during early work at the site stated that they '…do not seem to have been simple dwelling-houses, but, what is more evident, places for burying important people' (Dikaios 1940: 120; see also Dikaios 1962: 9–11, 13–14). The Tholos IA complex (Le Brun 1997: 46, fig. 41), in particular, sturdily built, with a number of stone tables, fine gypsum-lined recesses on two internal pillars, and quantities of animal as well as human bones and skulls in its successive levels, is difficult to conceptualise as a dwelling (Niklasson 1991: 170, fig. 7; Jones 2008: 75) (Figure 35). Tholos XVII – with its extremely thick walls and platform burials, two of which (II, III) give the impression of display, and one of which (II, a child's burial) contained a finely carved, intentionally broken andesite bowl displayed under the child's pelvic region (Dikaios 1962: fig. 11, 813; fig. XI: 8) – is also rejected as a dwelling by Niklasson (1991: 171, figs. 19, 45–46).

Tholos XLVII, classified by Dikaios amongst the small *tholoi*, has already been noted for its concentration of 25 infant (and 4 adult) burials (Dikaios 1953: 177–183). Among other striking features that set this structure apart are:

Figure 35. Khirokitia 'Tholos' IA, one of the largest and best preserved *tholoi* at the site, with an external diameter of 8+ m, and two large stone pillars within. Photograph by A. Bernard Knapp.

(1) a fiddle-shaped flat stone figurine (Dikaios 1962: 47, fig. 24, 1157β) and a clay human head (Dikaios 1962: 48, fig. 25, 1063); (2) two stone 'seats' (limestone slabs), one built against the structure's wall and another just 0.6 m away from it, with a human burial in the same level; (3) the intentional blocking of the doorway to the structure; and (4) a votive axe-head – 0.375 m in length – found nearby (Dikaios 1953: pl. 91, 1062). In his earliest attempt to interpret Tholos XLVII and its contents, Dikaios (1940: 125 and n. 3, 173) suggested it was a special ritual building holding the remains of sacrificed infants and animals; he linked it directly to the later (Bronze Age) Vounous model of a sacred enclosure. Niklasson (1991: 172–173) views all these features as part of mortuary ritual and practice, whilst Jones (2008: 109) sees them as potential responses to health, fertility or sexual problems that led to increased mortality rates: (1) the figurines as indicative of an ancestor cult; (2) the stone seats as thrones to display the deceased before burial; (3) the blocked doorway as a sign that this particular burial place was full; and (4) the large axe-head and another, phallic-shaped piece of andesite as ritually significant display pieces set outside the *tholos*, itself in a prominent position at the crest of the hill on which Khirokitia is located.

In general throughout the LAN, the simple pit grave, whether within or outside of a building, served as the primary form for burials; a few of these pits at Khirokitia were more elaborate and would have required a greater investment of time to prepare (Niklasson 1991: 191–192). Because intact burials have only been recorded at two LAN sites (Khirokitia, Cape Andreas *Kastros*), it is possible that extramural burial practices were more prevalent than the current archaeological records suggest. Grave goods (marine shells) are scarce at Cape Andreas *Kastros* but at least one-third of the graves at Khirokitia include items such as querns, stone bowls and other stone objects, and unworked stone; chipped stone and obsidian; necklaces and bracelets (with carnelian, onyx and picrolite beads); pointed bone implements (needles, clothing pins?); animal bones and shells (Niklasson 1991: 88–102). Most of the dead – infants, children, adult females and males – received primary burials, although some secondary burial practices may be evident at Khirokitia. Niklasson (1991: 226) believes that the platform burial (II) in Khirokitia's Tholos XVII, where a child was placed on its stomach atop a large fragment of a broken stone bowl, may have been a human sacrifice. Burial VII in Tholos IA, with burnt animal bones, charcoal and ash in its fill, and with skeleton's legs bent backwards from the spine, may also represent a human sacrifice (Niklasson 1991: 228–229).

Other mortuary practices may be attested by constructional features and artefacts contained in the strata intermediate between and beneath the floors of the buildings at Khirokitia. More specifically, these are: (1) a layer of reddish earth between platform burials (II, III) in Tholos XVII; (2) a greenish-painted floor in Tholos XXXVI on which the torso of a figurine was placed; and (3) the sloping extensions (for perishable and other offerings?) to Burials I–III in Tholos X and Burial VIII in Tholos XV, the latter with a hoard of shells in its upper part (Niklasson 1991: 230). Special treatment of the skull is seen in a few burials at Khirokitia (and earlier at *Tenta*), as is the placement of querns or other heavy stones on top of the head or body (Niklasson 1991: 182–185). In this light, it is also worth noting that a fallow deer scapula completely covered the skull of a small child, Burial 538 at Khirokitia (Le Brun 1989a: 68, 117, fig. 40). In Burial 207, where a set of ovicaprid horns was built into the rim of the grave pit, a child's skull was detached from the rest of the body and a quern was placed upside-down on the head (Le Brun 1984: 77–78; Niklasson 1991: 49, fig. 35).

Niklasson (1991: 237) concluded that evidence for interment in the dwellings of the LAN was ambiguous and indeed that the functions of these buildings remain enigmatic. Elsewhere she states that some of the dead were interred beneath the floors of the living, whilst many others were placed in buildings of ritual significance and character (Niklasson 1991: 68, 173). Ultimately she felt that the distribution of the burials as well as different features associated with them demonstrate that the buildings were specifically intended for burials and the ritual practices associated with them. In some cases at Khirokitia, then, we may be dealing with what – on analogy with later Levantine practices – are termed 'charnel houses' (e.g. at Early Bronze Bab edh-Dhra' in Jordan – Schaub and Rast 1989: 548–550), structures for storing human skeletal remains, temporarily or permanently.

Both Niklasson (1991) and Jones (2008) contest Dikaios's (1953: 339) assumption that the hearths, platforms, pits in the main floors, and the intermediary floor levels of the structures provide evidence for their use as dwellings. Jones (2008: 123–126), moreover, has rejected the entire notion of Khirokitia as a sedentary farming village. She argues that it contrasts so dramatically with all other LAN sites that it should no longer be seen as a type site for the LAN (similarly McCartney 2007: 89). Although Jones cites many of the same material anomalies as Niklasson, she interprets them differently, often drawing attention to Levantine parallels associated with mortuary practices. She maintains that hearths, for example, were placed directly above burials not to serve as burial markers but as gateways for the deceased to pass into the afterlife. The association of hearths with burning need not relate to domestic activities, and there is evidence of burning around Grave IA:VII at Khirokitia, with charcoal on the skeleton (Niklasson 1991: 16). Jones (2008: 49) reminds us that some of the human bones from Well 133 at EAN Kissonerga *Mylouthkia* also showed signs of (light) burning. Accordingly, hearths – and burning – could be linked to burials and beliefs surrounding death, practices also evident in the (earlier) Natufian period at el-Wad, Mount Carmel (Boyd 2001: 187, 190).

In Jones's view the platforms, especially in Tholoi V and XVII, may have served as places to exhibit the dead or to wrap their bodies prior to interment; a Levantine analogy may be seen in the platforms found within round stone structures at PPNB Kfar HaHoresh in the Lower Galilee (Goring-Morris 2005: 92). The stone seats, or 'thrones', found in some structures, especially Tholos XVII, could have been used to display revered ancestors; Jones (2008: 119) cites a parallel with a seated female figure from Çatalhöyük that has two felines on either side of her (Hodder 2006: 130, 160 col. fig. 4 – but note that this object was found in a 'grain bin'). The intermediary floors in some tholoi are regarded not as successive habitation levels, but rather as a means to seal in certain burials, thus echoing the practice at Kfar HaHoresh where plastered surfaces were used to seal burials before a structure was erected (Goring-Morris 2005: 92). As to the pits, which occur only in limited numbers and typically in the intermediary levels, no grain or other refuse was recorded from them; here Jones (2008: 124) points out the close association between pits and burials at Natufian Mallaha (Eynan) (Boyd 1995).

The plastered exterior spaces between certain structures at Khirokitia are thought to have served either as public ceremonial areas (Le Brun 1994: 139–142) or as courtyards for grinding grain, which would explain the large fixed querns found in them (Le Brun 1993: 67). Jones (2008: 125), developing the first suggestion, sees them as places where mourners could congregate while awaiting access to the burial structures. The fixed querns she interprets in the light of the limestone mortars found protruding some 20 cm through the top of graves at the Natufian site of Nahal Oren; such mortars have been interpreted either as grave markers or as redundant economic items somehow associated with the deceased. Boyd (2005: 109), however, suggested they might refer to post-mortem transformation of the body from life to death, which segues more smoothly into Jones's view of these spaces. In her opinion, the entire spatial layout of Khirokitia, with its spacious circular structures forming even larger, round 'super-structures', reflects a distant, Levantine social memory, one reworked in Cyprus as a place of the dead, a 'megalithic necropolis' for the ancestors (Jones 2008: 125–126). Jones (2008: 126–128) also regards both EAN Kalavasos *Tenta* and LAN Cape Andreas *Kastros* as belonging to the realm of the dead, but her interpretations of those sites are less compelling. In any case, a more straightforward understanding might be simply that they were charnel houses for the dead.

Stanley Price (1977a; 1977b) also perceived Khirokitia as an exceptional site, but he was never in doubt about its status as an agricultural village. Like Jones, however, he sought to demonstrate that all sites of the Khirokita Culture (LAN) revealed a common cultural heritage with the 8th–6th millennia BC Levant; in so doing, he discussed certain similarities between mortuary practices in the two areas. These included the existence of single primary burials with grave goods, special treatment of the skull, evidence of cranial deformation, placing of querns or large stones on the body, inclusion of stone bowls (often deliberately broken) in burials, and the building of hearths or stone platforms immediately over the body (Stanley Price 1977a: 80–82). That such practices could point to a distant (Levantine) social memory – as Jones suggests – might also be argued on the basis of the skeletal data.

Peltenburg (2004c: 84–85) views LAN Khirokitia as an atypical site, for the following reasons: (1) its large population aggregate (up to 600 people); (2) its overall size (up to 2.5 ha); (3) its rich and diverse material culture, with imports such as obsidian and carnelian pointing to interregional trading links; (4) the independent clusters of *tholoi*; and (5) the elaboration of mortuary practices with common grave goods. Late in the period, at least three Circular Radial Buildings (Structures 82, 83, 111 – Le Brun 1997: 56, fig. 48) were erected at the site (Clarke 2007a: 37). Peltenburg maintains that this type of building could have served as a communal storage facility when, towards the end of Khirokitia's existence, its inhabitants adopted different subsistence strategies and new, less sedentary ways of living. All these factors, as well as the grand scale and sophistication of its architecture, perhaps reflect a level of social organisation beyond the egalitarian. In this respect, McCartney (in Clarke 2007a: 77) notes the differences between Khirokitia and the more complex mega-sites of the contemporary southern Levant. She maintains, however, that Cyprus was involved in 'low intensity interaction' with that region and must have been aware of the material and socio-economic gulf that separated the island from developments elsewhere.

So, given the current state of evidence, can we state unequivocally whether Khirokitia was an agricultural settlement, or a village of the dead, or both? First of all, both quantified faunal and floral data indicate that the people who lived (and died) at Khirokitia, like those at other LAN sites, became increasingly reliant on the exploitation of domesticated plants and animals, in other words the type of agricultural and husbanding practices typical of a mixed farming economy. The longevity of the Aceramic Neolithic period overall, moreover, indicates that the people who initially settled the island not only succeeded in stocking Cyprus with cattle, deer, sheep and goat critical for the well-being of all successive generations, but also adapted well to the natural limitations of an island environment (even if cattle did not).

The chipped stone tools characteristic of the Khirokitia assemblage are typical of those used for harvesting cereals or cutting reeds, scraping animal skins, or working wood and bone (various perforating tools used for threading and weaving tasks, as well as fish hooks). A full range of ground stone tools – including querns, grinders, mortars and pestles – are typical of those used to process cereals or other foodstuffs. The most prominent ground stone tool, the axe, would have been used at least occasionally for clearing trees in order to facilitate agricultural production. All these represent the material conditions of a site whose inhabitants were fully engaged in sedentary agricultural practices. Watkins, Croft and Wasse have all emphasised the importance of deer hunting at Khirokitia, but none have concluded that the site was the exclusive domain of a non-sedentary population. Stanley Price, Le Brun and Peltenburg clearly view Khirokitia as an agricultural settlement, however anomalous its size and however diverse its material remains vis-à-vis those of other LAN sites.

Although Dikaios ultimately reached the same conclusion, he originally felt that Khirokitia might well be a ritual place of the dead, what Jones called a megalithic necropolis for the ancestors, and possibly one used repeatedly by a more mobile population. Indeed, as this section has demonstrated, there is a wide range of mortuary practices largely exclusive to Khirokitia. Both Niklasson and Jones have argued at length that the distribution of the burials within the site, the different features associated with them, the striking number of infant burials, the comparative richness (especially in imports) of female burials, and much more, serve to demonstrate the funerary nature of Khirokitia's buildings and the mortuary practices carried out within them.

In an earlier study, Morrison and Watkins (1974: 74) drew attention to the lack of evidence in Dikaios's site report for a fully established Neolithic economy at Khirokitia, based on agriculture and pastoralism. Instead, they emphasised the continuing importance of deer hunting to the subsistence economy. We now know, however, that there was a decline in the use of both deer and pig at Khirokitia, and Wasse (2007: 62–63) suggests that the shift in emphasis from deer hunting to sheep and goat husbandry may have resulted from increased population density at Khirokitia (or, perhaps, the need for an assured source of meat – and iron – in the diet, to compensate for blood disorders such as thalassemia). Croft (2005: 359), in turn, suggests that the growing reliance on food production at Khirokitia was one response to this growth in population. Finally, as noted earlier, there are signs of deforestation in the charcoal record, and evidence of increasingly drier conditions as the early Holocene humid phase passed its optimum (Wasse 2007: 48–49). Both these factors would have resulted in some level of degradation to the local environment, and a reduction in the range of resources upon which the people of LAN Khirokitia had come to rely.

On their own, it is unlikely that any one of these changes would have led to an irreversible outcome. Taken together, however, such stresses must have had a negative impact on both the subsistence economy and the mentality of those who dwelt at Khirokitia. Such a situation may well have led to a decline in the nature and status of the Khirokitia community, a breakdown in its social system, and perhaps a transformation in its role as a thriving agricultural settlement. In other words, as the social memory of Khirokitia's past grandeur grew amongst the generations of people who suffered through its decline, increasingly the site may have come to function largely as a place to bury the dead, with only certain sectors still inhabited by the living.

Since we cannot refine any more precisely the stratigraphic sequencing in most of the structures excavated by Dikaios, and because the relative chronological placement of most structures – and the floors within them – makes it difficult to trace specific levels of development or decline (Clarke 2007a: 37), we remain reliant on Le Brun's excavations at the west and top of the site to establish or refute such an interpretation. Moreover, the exact stratigraphic relationship between the east and west sectors at Khirokitia remains somewhat unclear, a situation that also affects arguments about subsistence change and environmental degradation. Le Brun (2002: 25–26) has commented generally on the 'constant remodelling that took place within the village network', and stated that while some structures at Khirokitia had very brief spans of occupation, others offer good evidence for long term, continual habitation. Le Brun argues that continuity of occupation by the living in some of these structures corresponds to continuity of occupation by the dead. If by this he means that people were still dwelling in these structures when new burials were dug within them, then we need to see and assess carefully the evidence to which he refers, and perhaps we must rethink yet again the function and meaning of this crucial site. However we understand Khirokitia, our interpretation of it must remain consistent with and coherent within our overall understanding of the Late Aceramic Neolithic.

Overview: The Late Aceramic Neolithic

As the new settlers of the EAN increasingly became adapted to living on an island, there must have been at least occasional crises related to drought, over-exploitation, clearing forests for agricultural expansion, depleting soils and erosion. Nonetheless, site density remained quite low throughout the Aceramic Neolithic and, with limited numbers of people living in each site, there would have been little competition for subsistence or other essential resources. During the LAN, there is no indisputable evidence of conflict or rivalry in the extant material record, and thus it is unlikely that the wall at Khirokitia served any defensive purpose. It may have functioned to mark out the larger community at this site, and thus would have helped to insure cohesion in a society that seems to have been largely egalitarian, and perhaps communal in organisation. Only Khirokitia, by far the largest of the LAN sites, shows evidence of a more complex social organisation, one in which it was possible to summon the labour resources required to build its walls, and maintain the large structures and any possible communal buildings. Even if its function was at least partly mortuary in nature, it is impossible to discount the abundant evidence for agricultural activities at the site.

In interpreting the faunal remains from LAN sites, it is important to bear in mind that in an essentially closed or 'complementary' array of data, any apparent reduction in the proportion of one animal taxon will result in an increase in the proportion of another (Davis 1989: 195; Held 1992: 120; Wasse 2007: 62). On the basis of current evidence, therefore, we can only say that the quantification of faunal remains from LAN sites seems to indicate a shift in emphasis from hunting animals towards their exploitation as domesticates, in other words a shift towards a Levantine-type mixed farming economy. Croft's (2003a: 275–278) suggestion that deer at Kholetria *Ortos* were managed in order to sustain an important source of meat points in the same direction. Newly established sites seem to have relied heavily on pig, and thereafter tended to focus on deer, eventually increasing their investment in domestic animals, especially ovicaprines – perhaps, although not necessarily, as the result of deforestation and other local environmental changes (Seth Button, pers. comm., July 2009).

Watkins (1981: 147–148) suggested long ago, and Wasse (2007: 61–62) more recently, that mixed farming (herding and agriculture) at most LAN sites should perhaps be seen as subsidiary to hunting and gathering as a subsistence strategy; certainly this seems to have been the case at Cape Andreas *Kastros* and Dhali *Agridhi*. During the LAN of Cyprus, with the possible exception of Khirokitia, social organisation remained largely egalitarian and population density remained low. On these bases, however, and despite the obvious importance of hunting deer, it seems excessive to conclude that '...the progress of the Neolithic Revolution came to an abrupt halt soon after it reached Cyprus' during the last half of the 9th millennium Cal BC, and that '...the selective pressures that were driving the process of Neolithisation on the mainland were absent in Cyprus' (Wasse 2007: 63). It is more likely that the faunal remains from Khirokitia and Cape Andreas *Kastros* (less so at Kholetria *Ortos*) reflect subsistence regimes that retained a strong hunting or fishing-foraging component well into, and well beyond the LAN (also Croft 2005: 357). And it is equally likely that the people involved in hunting and fishing or foraging (as social practices) were also in the process of establishing or recreating their identities. Ammerman (pers. comm., June 2009), for example, believes that the ephemeral remains of the Neolithic levels at Nissi Beach represent an expression of a fisher-forager lifestyle that had nothing to do with what is usually deemed to be Neolithic (i.e. sedentary living, agriculture, pottery).

Be that as it may, because the quantity and amount of domesticated plants increased at most known LAN sites as time passed, it seems clear that an agricultural way of life thrived once it was established on the island. Even if the herding and hunting of animals, or foraging and fishing, formed important mainstays of subsistence activities, agriculture cannot be regarded merely as a subsidiary strategy. In terms of ideology, the intentional burial of both ovicaprids and deer, as well as the association of bones from the same animals with human burials, have suggested to some that deer in LAN Cyprus had a symbolic value comparable to that of the bull in other ancient Mediterranean cultures (Le Brun 2005: 116; Vigne 1993; see also Ronen 1995 on deer-oriented ideology). Such suggestions, intriguing as they may be, cannot be demonstrated without much more focused and theoretically informed research.

GENDER/SOCIAL ORGANISATION

The stone and clay figurines, however crude they may appear to modern eyes, have several striking features. Le Brun (2002: 30), for example, highlighted a possible gender-based contradiction between representations of people at Khirokitia and mortuary practices. On the one hand, Le Brun sees in the funerary record evidence suggesting that individuals achieved their social status and that women received at least some level of preferential treatment. On the other hand, he suggests that LAN figurines appear to reflect a masculine 'preeminence', one that (almost) precluded images of women. This masculine preeminence (i.e. phallic shapes – see above, Figure 32) is undeniable, but it must be noted that the extant figurines are highly abstract, few in number and often fragmentary.

Whereas the female form is rarely depicted, a sexual ambiguity seems apparent in many figurines. On the one hand, such ambiguity may be seen as evidence of gender constructs that transcended simple male–female divisions (Hamilton 1994; Knapp and Meskell 1997), or as symbolic of the collectivity of LAN community organisation (as Talalay and Cullen 2002: 191 argue for the Cypriot Bronze Age). On the other hand, taken together with mortuary practices, the ambiguity seen in the figurines may indicate that there was very limited differentiation on the basis of (biological) sex at this time. Perhaps issues of health were also involved: thalassemia – to the extent it affected the people of the LAN – can retard sexual development and the onset of puberty, and may lead to infertility and impotence (Eleftheriou 2003: 70–71; Jones 2008: 103, 109). In this light, given that grave goods and in particular some prestigious personal adornments were limited to female burials at Khirokitia, is it possible that some women, who lost their infants, were accorded such honours in response to the community's situation (Paula Jones, pers. comm., July 2009)?

Careful examination of burials within superimposed structures at Khirokitia revealed that some were reserved exclusively for males (four), others exclusively for females (five) (Le Brun 2001: 115; 2002: 26–27). Perhaps, however, the specific orientation of females at Khirokitia to the northeast and southwest had nothing to do with distinction by biological sex, but instead reflected more subtle preferences of those who were burying them (Jones 2008: 77); for example, the bodies may have been oriented towards the areas where they were born and raised. If the criteria determining the nature of burials within a structure remained constant throughout its period of use, then it seems that some people were interred selectively on the basis of their sex. Does that mean men and women had separate statuses in life, as they did here in death? Recall in this context that certain aspects of the chipped stone technology point to an integrated labour force, while both the ground stone and chipped stone types and forms indicate that people were widely engaged in sedentary agricultural activities. If the vertical sequences of burials do exhibit gender differentiation, representing distinct lineages or kinship ties and achieved rather than ascribed status (Le Brun 2002: 27), then burial practices at Khirokitia contrast even more sharply with those of later periods, when the deceased were placed in large, communal, extramural tombs that were reused for generations and that included people of all ages and sexes (Bolger 2003: 152–153).

INSULARITY AND IDENTITY

Moyer (in Todd 2005: 8–9) suggested that the distinctive cranial morphology, limited phenotypic variation and some level of anemia (thalassemia) in the skeletal data from EAN *Tenta* and LAN Khirokitia indicate that the people of Neolithic Cyprus had little sustained contact with groups on the mainland. In a much earlier study, Angel (1953: 422) also concluded that the people who lived at Khirokitia could have belonged to one or a few small groups who were not at all typical, in biological terms, of the original parent group that first established itself on Cyprus. Comparing limited cranial data sets from prehistoric Anatolia and Syria with those from LAN Khirokitia (brachycranial) and Ceramic Neolithic Sotira (doliocranial), Domurad (1989: 69) concluded that the populations of these two periods had distinctive origins. Craniometric data, then, regardless of the size or representativeness of the samples, stress distinctions within Cypriot populations, and between the populations of Cyprus and those of the surrounding mainlands. Moreover, the comparison of craniometric data from Pre-Pottery Neolithic populations within the Levant suggests that there was considerable morphological heterogeneity among these early agriculturalists (Pinhasi and Pluciennik 2004). In all the analyses conducted, the data from Khirokitia were easily differentiated from those of all mainland groups (some superficial similarity was seen with PPNB Abu Hureyra in Syria and PPNB/C Basta in Jordan – Pinhasi and Pluciennik 2004: S63–S65). Nonetheless, it is possible that the isolation of the population may have been a factor in their ability to discriminate the Khirokitia sample.

In an earlier study, Stanley Price (1977a: 85; 1977b: 33) cited Angel's work and related it to the biogeographical concept of the 'founder effect', in an attempt to explain why the Khirokitia Culture (LAN) continued to use, for example, circular structures and stone bowls whilst contemporary cultures in the Levant had adopted rectangular architecture and pottery. As already noted (in Chapter 2), using biogeographic concepts to study human beings poses certain problems, and viewing islands in isolation is too restrictive. Already during the Late Epipalaeolithic period, people were moving by sea, and exploiting maritime resources along the coasts of Cyprus and the Levant. Both Watkins (2004) and Finlayson (2004) view the permanent settlement of Cyprus during the EAN as a process that opened up new spheres of interaction, not something that led to constricting isolation. More specifically, the repeated appearance of new features in the chipped stone repertoire, the use of circular architecture with its Levantine PPNA heritage, and perhaps the ongoing restocking of the island's fauna (Horwitz et al. 2004: 38; McCartney 2011: 193), all suggest that the earliest Neolithic culture on Cyprus evolved not in isolation but through 'imbedded interactions' with the mainland (also McCartney, in Clarke 2007a: 72–73).

Some level of maritime contacts is surely demonstrated by imported materials such as obsidian (around 100 pieces, much less common than in the EAN but not necessarily a prestige item), carnelian (about 40 beads), and the small engraved pebbles from Khirokitia and Kholetria *Ortos* with counterparts in Levantine aceramic and ceramic Neolithic contexts (Simmons 1996b: 37; Peltenburg 2004c: 83; see further below). Finds of (typically decorated) dentalium shell are found mainly in burials at Khirokitia, just as they are associated mainly with mortuary deposits in Levantine (Natufian) contexts (Boyd 2002: 141). These shells might thus point to some ancestral link, as well as being markers of contemporary exchange. Within the island, an exchange network has been proposed on the basis of the picrolite objects found at Khirokitia and Cape Andreas *Kastros* (Le Brun 1997: 35–36; Steel 2004a: 56). Picrolite is found in abundance only along the Kouris River valley in the south (Xenophontos 1991), and picrolite ornaments may have been used to identify different social groups on the island (as Swantek 2006: 46 has suggested for the following Ceramic Neolithic period).

The production of stone (and miniature picrolite) vessels, and of stone or clay figurines, indicates a notable investment of time and effort; it reinforces the notion that these objects had some symbolic significance (McCartney, in Clarke 2007a: 76). The virtually exclusive use of igneous stone (typically diabase) to carve stone bowls, engraved pebbles and figurines (see above, Figures 31–32, and 34a–b) is also a distinguishing feature of the LAN, one that has been linked to an island ideology (Le Brun 2005: 115). Typically such objects have been seen as indicative of the degree to which the culture of LAN Cyprus had become isolated from those of the surrounding areas (e.g. Ronen 1995: 189–190), but they might also be viewed otherwise. Is it possible that the continuing manufacture of Cyprus's unique ground stone vessels long after pottery had become the norm for production in the Levant was somehow linked to an insular identity? In McCartney's view (in Clarke 2007a: 77), working in stone formed not just a distinctive technological practice but also a potential material signature of Cyprus's LAN people. The inclusion of stone vessels in female burials at Khirokitia, moreover, has been seen as an example of individual achievement (Le Brun 2001: 115–116).

The engraved pebbles found at Khirokitia and Kholetria *Ortos* are seen variously as tokens in a storage system, weights for fishing nets, portable grinders or prestigious symbols. Whatever their purpose, like the stone vessels they may also have signalled ascribed status, or served as indicators of private property, individual persons or families – in other words as material markers of identity (Eirikh-Rose 2004: 158). McCartney (in Clarke 2007a: 77) emphasises that these engraved pebbles, even if taken as hallmarks of identity, should be seen primarily as evidence for interregional interaction (see further below).

There are several other lines of evidence – from mortuary and agricultural practices, to art objects, to chipped and ground stone technologies – that suggest parallels with the Levant during the LAN, if not interaction between Cyprus and that region (McCartney, in Clarke, 2007: 74–79, with refs.). For example: although mortuary evidence from the Levant is thin on the ground during the period of time contemporary with the LAN, burials from Munhata, Sha'ar Hagolan (Garfinkel 1993: 127) and Byblos (Dunand 1973: 29–32) show similarities to those from Khirokitia and elsewhere. The Levantine burials are generally intramural, single, primary and flexed, with intact skulls; those from Byblos are sub-floor inhumations in stone cists or pits, with flexed skeletons (Stewart and Rupp 2004: 167).

The decline in the use of obsidian, often thought to be a sign of Cyprus's isolation in the LAN, is also reflected in the southern Levant: in both cases it may indicate a general decline in supply and/or the realignment of earlier obsidian trade routes. Another possible sign of continuing interaction is the use of green-coloured stone – steatite, green jasper, picrolite – for the production of ornaments such as beads and pendants, parallel with the use of Dabba marble on the Levantine mainland (McCartney, in Clarke 2007a: 76). Although the (occasionally greenish) stone vessels of the LAN are unique objects of high artistic quality, the use of incised decoration, spouts, and the combination of calcareous and volcanic stone in their manufacture also reflect features found in contemporary Levantine sites such as Tell Sabi Ayyad (Syria), Byblos (Lebanon) and Sha'ar Hagolan (Israel) (Akkermans and Schwartz 2003: 141, fig. 4.25; Dunand 1973: 38–42; Garfinkel 1993: 120, 123, fig. 7). Mellaart (1975: 130) even referred to a fragmentary stone bowl of Cypriot origin from Amuq

A (Syria). Moreover, the production of groundstone vessels continued into Levantine Pottery Neolithic at various sites broadly contemporary with the LAN (Akkermans and Schwartz 2003: 99).

To return once again to the engraved pebbles from Khirokitia (106) and Kholetria *Ortos* (51), these provide the clearest evidence for contacts between LAN Cyprus and contemporary sites in the central and southern Levant (Eirikh-Rose 2004; Stewart and Rupp 2004). With a long tradition in the Levant stretching back to the Natufian, mushroom-shaped, engraved conical stones from LAN Khirokitia (seven in number, see above, Figure 34b) show close similarities with examples from Halula (Late Natufian) and some Harifian sites, while the engraved stone pebbles from both Cypriot sites show parallels with Levantine examples from Byblos, Munhata, Sha'ar Hagolan and Ras Shamra (Stewart and Rupp 2004: 166–168). Eirikh-Rose (2004: 152–154) argues that the geometric designs engraved on these pebbles are paralleled on the earliest known seals in the Levant. Whilst the use of engraved pebbles is earlier in date (Late Palaeolithic through Early Chalcolithic) than the first use of seals, such usage overlaps during the Neolithic, until seals finally become the sole type of object bearing these designs during and after the Late Chalcolithic. If these engraved pebbles are regarded as precursors of seals, it is likely they both served a similar function, namely to mark ownership and/or identify individual people or families in a complex but still egalitarian society (Eirikh-Rose 2004: 155). This might also be suggested by the fact that when engraved pebbles are found in burials, with adults of both sexes, each burial yielded only a single pebble (one exception in Tholos XIX – Niklasson 1991: 95; Eirikh-Rose 2004: 152–154).

Alternatively, Stewart and Rupp (2004: 168–171) suggest that the pebbles could have been used in trade transactions – to stamp, count or identify the items exchanged. Equally pertinent here is the fact that pebbles engraved with geometric designs are common and frequent in both Cyprus (LAN) and the Levant (Natufian-Pottery Neolithic). They also overlap in time, perhaps indicating that both regions shared a common symbolic or referential world, and must have been in contact with one another. McCartney (in Clarke 2007a: 77) even suggests that the analogous appearance of engraved pebbles in LAN Cypriot and contemporary Levantine sites – along with the carnelian beads mentioned above – provide good evidence for a regional interaction sphere throughout the coastal eastern Mediterranean. If so, Perlès's (1992) model of a Greek Neolithic seafaring trade in exceptional materials may be applicable to Cyprus as well (Stewart and Rupp 2004: 169).

In both Cyprus and the Levant, then, there seems to have been an exchange of goods and ideas conducted by independent communities within a loosely organised, non-intensive interaction sphere (McCartney, in Clarke 2007a: 79). Diverse aspects of materiality and maritime connectivity indicate that the people of LAN Cyprus not only adapted to their new, insular way of life, but also maintained some level of contact with people in the Levant. Fisher-foragers and farmers alike sought to establish or reaffirm their distinctive identities. Cyprus was never sealed off from the cultures surrounding it during the LAN, even if some degree of isolation is apparent (e.g. in the craniometric data). Was this the result of its geographic position (insularity) or was it the outcome of a conscious and intentional decision related to an insular identity? Social or economic exchanges, as well as the possible existence of gender-based groups during the LAN, are signalled by a wide variety of data: from robust architectural complexes through mortuary practices to picrolite ornaments and engraved pebbles, stone and clay figurines, and intricately carved stone bowls and basins. Even so, more focused, contextual analyses are needed on each class of objects to understand their full significance, and how they might be related to insularity or an island identity.

THE END OF THE LATE ACERAMIC NEOLITHIC

In radiocarbon terms, on the basis of 28 dates, the Late Aceramic Neolithic flourished from about 7200/6800–5200/5000 Cal BC, that is, through the mid-to-late 6th millennium Cal BC (see Appendix, Table A2, and SOM). The end of the LAN is shrouded in uncertainty and debate (see Appendix, detailed discussion under Late Aceramic Neolithic), and interpretations revolve around two opposing notions: (1) the collapse of LAN society and culture was absolute, resulting in the depopulation of Cyprus, a gap of uncertain length in the archaeological record, and a subsequent reoccupation of the island by new, pottery-producing people, most likely from the Levant (e.g. Stanley Price 1977b: 34–37, fig. 3); or (2) there was no break in human occupation of the island, but rather a retraction of settlement towards the end of the LAN, a reversion to a less sedentary way of life, and ultimately the revival of village life, perhaps complemented by new immigrants who brought with them the knowledge of manufacturing pottery (e.g. Watkins 1973: 49).

The inability to resolve this issue stems from several factors, foremost among which are (1) the lack of reliable radiocarbon dates and the ensuing chronological imprecision (Todd 1985: 6), and (2) discontinuities in the stratigraphic records of the best-known archaeological sites. As Steel (2004a: 62) put it: 'Not only is there a discontinuous cultural sequence, there is also a limited chronological sequence'. As far as we can tell, none of the main sites (Khirokitia, Kalavasos *Tenta*, Cape Andreas *Kastros*, Kholetria *Ortos*) were destroyed, but instead were abandoned or at least no longer used as settlements per se, prior to some reoccupation or reuse (Khirokitia) in the Ceramic Neolithic (Stanley Price and Christou 1973: 30–32; Le Brun and Daune-Le Brun 2003; Clarke 2007a: 37–38).

So, when it comes to the end of the LAN, are we dealing with sociocultural decline and 'extinction', or with continuity in the form of a demographic and cultural 'involution', but with a gap in the occupation of Khirokitia and other sites (Held 1992a: 120, 136, 143)? Whereas Knapp et al. (1994: 407, 381, fig. 1) maintained that this radiocarbon gap amounted to no more than 300–700 calendar years, Peltenburg (2004c: 84) argued that it extended for at least one millennium, during which there is no evidence for any sort of occupation on the island. Even if that proves to be the case, this gap need not represent a complete break in the long-term human presence on Cyprus, but rather a dearth of evidence for settlements, as people became detached from earlier subsistence pursuits, and adopted less intensive practices of exploitation in response to environmental pressures. As Wasse (2007: 50) observed: 'If so, the "gap" may be more of an issue of archaeological visibility and reduced site occupation intensity … than a genuine break in the archaeological record of Cyprus'. Clarke (2007: 34) also regards the gap as artificial, created by the lack of relevant sites (mobile population), paucity of material evidence and the small number of radiocarbon determinations. In other words, the break that seems to separate the LAN from the Ceramic Neolithic most likely reflects nothing beyond the existing radiocarbon record. Focusing solely on archaeological sites with architecture, or looking for the earliest sites with pottery at the other end of this notional gap, has perhaps exaggerated it, especially if we are dealing with a society that was becoming more mobile, for whatever reason.

Whereas some material features of the LAN reveal similarities with those of the Ceramic Neolithic (fauna, chipped and groundstone industries, site location – discussed in the following section of this chapter), Legrand-Pineau (2007; 2009) has added another dimension to the debate over a chronological gap with an in-depth study of developments in Khirokitia's bone tool industry. This industry spans both periods, but most evidence for it stems from Aceramic Neolithic levels (only 6% from Ceramic Neolithic). Within the various architectural levels, however, a differential distribution of bone artefacts is evident, and Legrand-Pineau has used a sample of 1,255 items (of a total 2,317) from the most informative levels. The results show that during the early phases of the LAN, expedient techniques (tools made from splinters) were dominant but were replaced over time by more elaborate techniques (use of indirect percussion or grooving), more diversified tools and more specific knowledge about making the best use of what was available (mostly bone from fallow deer).

The two main categories of bone tools from the LAN are needles and points. The needles from LAN levels all have a rectilinear head, a specific type that decreases noticeably in the course of time, being replaced by needles with a round or pointed head (Legrand-Pineau 2007: 119–120, fig. 8). Even so, the function of these various types of needle head seems to have remained the same: working plant fibres. During the Ceramic Neolithic, the same raw material (fallow deer bone metapodials) was exploited and pointed tools continued to predominate. Longitudinal blanks of long bones continued in use and in fact became the most common; and the use of indirect percussion or grooving continued to increase. The needles with rounded or pointed head, the most common types by the end of the LAN, continued to be manufactured into the Ceramic Neolithic, when the rectilinear head type disappeared altogether (Legrand-Pineau 2007: 120–121). Thus, despite some minor technical changes and morphological innovations, overall the technology of bone tool production that began in the LAN – the raw material, the tool morphology and manufacturing techniques, as well as the animal and plant species exploited – seem to have continued in an almost unbroken sequence into the Ceramic Neolithic.

The very length of the Aceramic Neolithic era (some 3,500 years) and the complex social, economic and technological developments that took place during those millennia make it unlikely that a society so well established and so widespread over the island could have collapsed and disappeared completely during the late 7th–early 6th millennium Cal BC, eventually to be replaced by an incoming, pottery-producing group of people at the onset of the Ceramic Neolithic (also Cherry 1990: 157). Having considered several colonisation and extinction episodes for prehistoric Cyprus, Held (1989a: 193–204) concluded that an involution model was much more appropriate than a continuity or an extinction model to explain the transition between the LAN and Ceramic Neolithic.

Arguing the case for insularity, Held (1993: 26) suggested that the collapse of LAN society stemmed from the onset of warmer and drier conditions during the Holocene climatic optimum (broadly dated between about 9000–5000 Cal BP; see also Wasse 2007: 49–50). This warming trend, in Held's view, led to the degradation of arable land, crop failures, the abandonment of village fields systems, the fissioning of larger communities into smaller groups, and an increasing reliance on deer hunting (Held 1992a: 136–137, 162, fig. 6; see also Todd 1985: 11). Not long afterward, an immigrant, booster population (not a recolonisation) may have sparked a turnaround in the decline of the indigenous LAN population, and the 'acculturation' that followed would not, in Held's view, be at odds with the distinctive material signatures of the LAN and the Ceramic Neolithic. Clarke (2007: 33–34) suggests that the adoption of pottery technology was, in fact, a local development that may have been instrumental in the return to village life.

Peltenburg (2004c: 84–85) has presented another scenario for the collapse of LAN society. The large size of Khirokitia and its equally large population, its rich and diverse material culture and sophisticated architecture, and its distinctive mortuary practices all single out the site as atypical, and suggest that its social organisation may have superseded an egalitarian level. As Khirokitia grew to what became an exceptionally large size for a LAN village, Peltenburg suggests that its residents failed to come to terms with the scalar stresses – such as the emergence of autonomous households – inherent in such a community and that, accordingly, the social system collapsed. Le Brun and Daune-Le Brun (2009: 74–77, figs. 7–8) assess this scencario within its archaeological context, noting the abandonment or destruction of Khirokitia in Level II, and the architectural renovations of Level I, when traces of subrectangular structures (S168, 170) appear. Such constructions, of course, became the hallmark of Ceramic Neolithic buildings.

Within such a scenario, it is also worth recalling that Angel's (1953) early analysis of 123 skeletons led him to conclude that the people of Khirokitia suffered a high rate of infant mortality, lived under nutritional stress and had a life expectancy at birth of only 22 years (or, an average age at death of no more than 35 years – Harper 2008: 212–213). Angel's analysis has been confirmed and reiterated by much more recent work (Le Mort 2000; 2008). The dramatic impact on mortality (especially that of infants) also must have had a substantial impact on people's daily life, fertility and sexual development, on their attitudes to death, even on their subsistence choices (Jones 2008: 104–105): those who had become reliant on a cereal diet would have suffered far more dramatically from the continual loss of iron than those with a greater proportion of meat in their diet.

For Clarke (2007: 37–38), the end of the LAN was a time when squatters made use of 'camp sites' such as Dhali *Agridhi* and Kataliondas *Kourvellos*, and when mobile groups met their subsistence needs through hunting. McCartney (in Clarke 2007: 80) notes that Dhali *Agridhi* is a typical, low visibility site with a chipped stone component, wild flora and hunted fauna typical of a mobile community. Radiocarbon data from Dhali *Agridhi*, however, often used to bracket or even fill the gap, are not only of varying quality but are thoroughly confused, from the initial publication through more recent interpolations (Lehavy 1989: 203, 211; Coleman 1992: 224; Knapp et al. 1994: 385–386, fig. 4, 407; Clarke 2001: 69–70). They only serve to underscore the fact, also emphasised in the detailed discussion of all the relevant radiocarbon dates in the Appendix, that we need far more and more high-quality dates for the end of the LAN and the beginning of the Ceramic Neolithic before we can determine their relevance for understanding this era of transition.

Such chronometric and stratigraphic evidence as we have all indicates that Khirokitia and Kholetria *Ortos* were abandoned at some point towards the end of the 6th millennium Cal BC (Le Brun 1994: 27; Simmons 1996: 40; Le Brun and Daune Le Brun 2009: 76–77). The causes proposed for the collapse of LAN society are manifold, logical and in large part unverifiable: climatic change (drier conditions); social and economic stresss (overcrowded settlements, high infant mortality); the lack of a formal hierarchy to control a complex site like Khirokitia; the complexities and contradictions that may have arisen in a mixed herding-hunting economy, in which deer became increasingly important. McCartney (in Clarke 2007a: 79) suggests that Khirokitia's abandonment, at least, was the natural consequence for a society of hunter-farmers who found it difficult to live in a permanently settled village. At the same time, other LAN sites such as Kataliondas *Kourvellos*, Mari *Mesovouni* and Kholetria *Ortos*, which lack any sort of stone architecture, indicate that LAN society was never fully sedentary anyway, again underscoring Khirokitia's distinctiveness.

The continuities that exist with the following, Ceramic Neolithic period suggest that the population may have gone into decline and/or dispersed across the island, perhaps partly due to health problems that hindered population increase. However one views the radiocarbon-based gap, the archaeological record overall conveys an impression of internal coherence and, with the (not long delayed) emergence of the subsequent Ceramic Neolithic (Sotira Culture), we find people who were sedentary, mainly egalitarian farmers, herders and deer hunters that occupied sub-rectangular structures in nucleated settlements often situated in a topographically prominent position – not so very different from those who had recently abandoned a very similar way of life.

THE CERAMIC NEOLITHIC

> ...the 6th to 4th millennia BC have been largely ignored by prehistorians working in Cyprus. This is not solely because of a lack of information or data but because it is a period in the prehistory of Cyprus when nothing much appeared to happen on the island. There is no unequivocal evidence for interaction with the mainland at this time, there is no stylistic or typological evidence for significant cultural change and there are no particularly significant discoveries to excite the imagination of archaeologists. (Clarke 2007a: 5)

Transition to the Ceramic Neolithic

Despite Clarke's honest but grim overview of the Ceramic Neolithic (CN), the emergence of pottery-producing cultures presents intriguing problems for anyone studying archaeology on Cyprus or in the eastern Mediterranean. After the remarkable developments associated with the turn to sedentary living, animal domestication and farming amongst Levantine PPNB cultures, as well as the LAN culture of Cyprus, many sites were abandoned, areas of human habitation changed and new sites were established, some in previously unoccupied and several in coastal areas (Stein 1992; Caneva 1997: 113). This discontinuity of occupation was so widespread in the Levant and Near East that it can only be considered from a regional perspective, and the situation on Cyprus should also be seen in that wider context.

The extent of the Ceramic Neolithic period is still debated, but if we take the widest range of the dates currently available, then we are dealing with a period of about 1,000 years, from about 5200/5000–4100/4000 Cal BC (see Table 2; Appendix, Table A2). This chronology is not without its problems. For example, the 14 most reliable radiocarbon determinations from Ayios Epiktitos *Vrysi* all fall (citing the $\mu\pm\sigma$) between ca. 4222 ± 52–4152 ± 52 Cal BC (see Model 8 in the Appendix) or, looking at the raw 1σ calibrated ranges between

4353–3951 Cal BC (see SOM for details) (Peltenburg 1982b: 112, fig. 12, 460; Clarke 2007a: 17–20, fig. 2.3). Thus they are not relevant to the beginning and possibly not even to the end of the period. Two new radiocarbon dates on charcoal from a chamber and tunnel complex at the CN site of Kalavasos *Kokkinoyia* belong to the mid-to-late 5th millennium Cal BC, and are consistent with the middle phase at *Vrysi* (J. Clarke, pers. comm., December 2009). Most other radiocarbon dates derive from even older excavations and are limited in number: Dhali *Agridhi* and Sotira *Teppes* (two each), Kalavasos *Tenta* and *Pamboules* (one each), and Philia *Drakos* A (one). The possibly relevant *Tenta* date (P-2549) – excluded from the Model 1 analysis in Appendix 1 – offers an overall 1σ calibrated range of 4824–4175 Cal BC, but this is problematic, especially if seen in the context of the associated pottery, which may belong to the Early Chalcolithic (Todd et al. 1987: 178; Clarke 2007a: 19). Eight of nine more recent radiocarbon dates from Kandou *Kouphovounos* cover a wider range, with the start and end boundaries in Model 1 in the Appendix setting a range of ca. 5044±77 to 4071±69 Cal BC (citing the μ±σ) (see also Mantzourani et al. 2009: 241, fig. 1). Kandou thus seems to have had a much longer sequence of occupation than any other CN site on Cyprus. The two radiocarbon dates for the CN at *Agridhi* fall very early (earlier to mid-5th millennium Cal BC), within, or just beyond, the range of known dates for that period (Clarke 2007a: 18 and fig. 2.3). In the reassessment of the radiocarbon dates presented in the Appendix, one of these dates is inconsistent (too early) in Model 1 and in Model 8 the Agridhi phase is placed approximately (citing μ±σ) within boundaries of 4461±91 to 4327±113 Cal BC.

The terminology involved is certainly less confusing than that for earlier periods. Although most scholars in the past have referred to this period as 'Late Neolithic', here it is termed Ceramic Neolithic (CN) in contrast with and as a logical sequel to the Aceramic Neolithic (LAN). Dikaios (1961: 216–217; 1962: 180–184) established the basic chronological terms for what was then the earliest prehistory of the island, defining the Aceramic Neolithic as Neolithic Ia (Khirokitia and Klepini *Troulli* aceramic), the Ceramic Neolithic as Neolithic Ib (*Troulli* ceramic), Neolithic II (Sotira, Kalavasos A – now called *Kokkinoyia*) and Neolithic III (Khirokitia ceramic). The periodisation for the Ceramic Neolithic – based on Dikaios's view that the pottery from *Troulli* was earlier than that from Sotira – was called into question by subsequent excavations at Philia *Drakos* A (Watkins 1970; 1972) and Ayios Epiktitos *Vrysi* (Peltenburg 1978; 1979a). The excavators of both sites, for different reasons but all based on relevant pottery wares, felt that *Troulli* and Sotira were largely contemporary. In fact, the sequences at the two sites overlap but *Troulli* is, as Dikaios argued, somewhat earlier (Clarke 2007a: 28). If the Khirokitia Culture is regarded as (Late) Aceramic Neolithic, then the Sotira Culture should be regarded as Ceramic Neolithic. The suggestion that we should break down the 'Late Neolithic' (a term no longer used – see e.g. Steel 2004a: 63–66) into a

Dhali *Agridhi* phase and a Sotiran phase is helpful only if one wishes to discuss exclusively changes in pottery styles (Clarke 2007a: 28–29 and fig. 2.6, 35–36).

Although Held (1992a: 137) perhaps overstated the similarities in diagnostic traits between the LAN and Ceramic Neolithic (or Sotira Culture), it is nonetheless true that one of the sharpest divide comes in the form of pottery production and in the use of sub-rectangular architecture. It should be noted, however, that a 'sub-rectangular' structure has now been identified at Khirokitia (Le Brun and Daune-Le Brun 2009: 76, fig. 8). Moreover, some sherds of low-fired or unfired, light-coloured, 'grey ware' pottery were recovered from the aceramic levels at Khirokitia (Dikaios 1962: 38), and Clarke (2010: 200) reports that low-fired pottery also occurs in EAN contexts at Kissonerga *Mylouthkia*. The emphasis that archaeologists always place on pottery has enforced the notion of a major social and cultural disruption at the boundary between the LAN and the CN, when pottery was first used widely on the island. When this boundary is reassessed in terms of the chipped stone and groundstone evidence, however, there are signs of continuity within change (McCartney, in Clarke 2007a: 72). Legrand-Pineau (2007; 2009: 120–121), moreover, has now argued for the same kind of continuity in Khirokitia's bone tool industry (already discussed above).

The lithic technology demonstrates clear continuities in time if not necessarily in a sedentary mode of living. Moreover, because it is the main aspect of material culture that spans the supposed temporal gap, it it certainly useful for assessing the level of discontinuity. The chipped stone evidence includes dozens of lithic scatters that need more focused research before their chronological horizons can be further refined (Held 1992b; McCartney, in Clarke 2007a: 80–82). As to the actual material, the proportions of various chipped stone artefact categories closely follow those of the LAN, but there is a greater amount of debris (McCartney in Todd 2005: 207–208). Some of the same raw materials were also used in both periods: there is an increased use of Lefkara basal chert and a slight increase in the use of translucent chert, but a lower percentage of Lefkara dense translucent chert.

In general, there are several continuities in both the blade-based, chipped stone *chaines opératoires* and in the groundstone technology. Specific chipped stone tool types – backed and truncated blades, glossed segments, scrapers, perforating tools, notches, denticulates, unretouched utilised implements – demonstrate similarities in practice. With respect to groundstone, continuities in technology are apparent in a wide range of grinding (querns, rubbers, grinders, pestles, hammerstones, pounders) and cutting tools (axes, miniature polished axes, butts, use of the same basal rocks). Large saddle querns for crushing grains or nuts became particularly prominent. The continued exploitation of picrolite for manufacturing simple beads and other ornaments is also a persistent feature of both the LAN and CN (McCartney, in Clarke 2007a: 82; see also Swantek

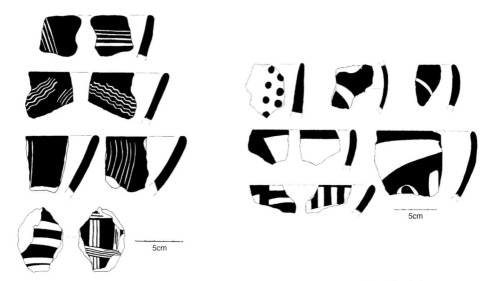

Figure 36. Ceramic Neolithic Combed Ware (left) and Red-on-White (right) pottery. After Clarke 2007a: 102–103, figs. 7.5–7.6. Courtesy of Jo Clarke.

2006: 30–41). The distinctive stone bowls and vessels characteristic of the LAN continued in use but on a more limited scale.

The pottery that first appeared on Cyprus at this time ranges from a locally inspired and produced Coarse Ware, to a dark and/or red burnished mono-chrome ware (Red Monochrome Painted), to a ware with painted designs on a white background (Red-on-White) and ultimately to one with combed decoration (Combed Ware) (Figure 36) (Clarke 2007a: 91, 97–105; 2010: 200). Some dark burnished wares known from the Syro-Cilician region exhibit broad technological similarities to the Dark Face Burnished ware (DFBW, also called Monochrome Burnished Ware) known from Philia *Drakos* A (1), Dhali *Agridhi* II and Klepini *Troulli* (Watkins 1970; 1973: 49). As a result, the onset of the Ceramic Neolithic often has been associated with new immigrants escaping the '…marked increase of population densities in the Syro-Cilician interaction sphere during the 6th millennium cal BC' (Held 1992a: 143; Hours and Copeland 1983: 81–83). Clarke (2007a: 97–98; 2010: 200–201, fig. 23.3), however, feels that 5th millennium BC burnished wares (and their shapes) from Arjoune in Syria represent a regional tradition much closer to that of CN Cyprus.

Whether or not the pottery was indigenous in origin and conception, the people of the CN period rapidly developed a taste for the new product. The change from monochrome to painted pottery (Red-on-White) seems to have come quickly in stratigraphic sequences at Philia *Drakos* A (Watkins 1972; 1973: 50). If the earliest phase there (A1) is equivalent to Dhali *Agridhi* II (Watkins 1981: 11), then we have further indication that the 'gap' between the LAN and the CN is a product of the radiocarbon record. The Red-on-White pottery tradition seen in the north, east and west of the island replaced the DFBW by the mid-5th millennium Cal BC. Although it seems clear that the development of different pottery styles is related to regional rather than temporal variation (Peltenburg 1978), it is likely that the southernmost reaches of Cyprus were not using pottery until the end of that millennium (Clarke 2007a: 99).

During the Ceramic Neolithic, Cyprus was not entirely sealed off from the surrounding Syro-Anatolian cultures, but the paucity of imports cannot be denied. There is a limited amount of obsidian from CN sites such as *Vrysi* (Peltenburg 1982b: 101; 1985b: 94), *Troulli* (see below) and three blades from Kalavasos *Kokkinoyia* (Clarke 2010: 199). Most of the other items noted by Clarke as evidence for continuing, post-LAN contacts (carnelian beads from Khirokitia, white marble stone ring fragments from Kalavasos *Tenta*) actually belong to the LAN, and have been noted above. Nonetheless, we need to consider carefully whether this evident isolation was reinforced by geography (i.e. insularity) and technology, or if it was instead the product of conscious agency and identity processes (i.e. self-imposed). I consider this issue more fully below (*Social Continuity and Social Change*).

Spatial Organisation, Settlement and Subsistence

The landscape of the Ceramic Neolithic (for the sites discussed, see Figure 37) embraced many small village settlements, filled with crowded, single-room, rectangular or sub-rectangular structures (Dikaios 1961; Peltenburg 1985a). Through time, these structures appear to have developed from larger, free-standing buildings to a variety of smaller, subsidiary buildings added to the larger one, perhaps for extended families, or other domestic needs. Some sites lack the usual architectural elements; instead they consist of numerous pits and subterranean features (Clarke 2001: 66), and are often seen as 'squatter encampments' (Clarke 2007a: 22). Of nearly 40 sites identified as Ceramic Neolithic, only about 10 have been excavated even partially, and none enables us to present anything beyond a tentative reconstruction of demographic developments.

Recent survey work has turned up some CN sites, but these have added little to our understanding of settlement organisation during the period. The site of Mitsero *Kriadhis*, for example, with its characteristic chipped and groundstone tools, and Red-on-White and Red Monochrome Painted sherds, stands near the top of a 600 m high, isolated hilltop (Given and Knapp 2003: 265); along with Kalavasos *Angastromeni* (Todd 2004: 35–36), it occupies an unusual position for a CN site. No sites belonging to the CN have been identified in the Troodos Archaeological and Environmental Survey Project, despite the extensive and intensive coverage of three distinctive regions in the northwest Troodos (Given et al. 2002; forthcoming). Along the north coast, a 1973 survey carried out in the Kyrenia district located two CN sites. The first,

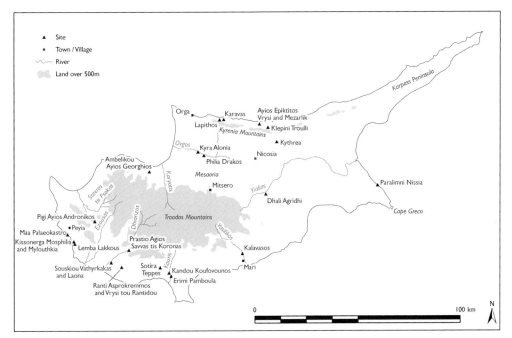

Figure 37. Map with Ceramic Neolithic and Chalcolithic sites mentioned in text. Drawn by Luke Sollars.

Orga *Palialonia*, was identified by its abundant Red-on-White sherds. It may have been a small settlement, situated atop a saddle-shaped plateau with some remains on its western slope, which led down to a stream (Peltenburg 1985b: 100–101). The second site, Ayios Epiktitos *Xylomandra*, had abundant chipped stone (jasper), stone axes and a stone bowl as well as Red-on-White pottery. Situated on an eroded headland not far from CN Ayios Epiktitos *Vrysi* (see below), it may have been a knapping locus associated with that site, but the axes and stone suggest a more diversified status.

The Vasilikos Valley Survey project along the south central coast identified 23 sites with 'Late Neolithic' materials (Todd 2004: 179). These include the well-known Prehistoric Bronze Age (PreBA, Middle Cypriot) sites of Kalavasos *Laroumena* (one Combed Ware sherd) and *Mitsingitis* (a few Combed Ware sherds), as well as Kalavasos *Kokkinoyia*, an important CN site (presented below). Amongst the others, the best known is perhaps Mari *Paliambela*, on the west bank of the Vasilikos River; Dikaios excavated this site briefly in the 1930s and identified a partly sunken dwelling similar to one found at Kalavasos *Kokkinoyia* (Dikaios 1953: 319; Clarke et al. 2007: 48).

In the southwest, the Canadian Palaipaphos Survey Project (CPSP) identified eight sites with 'Late Neolithic' material, four each in the Dhiarizos and Ezousas River valleys. These were cited only in a table or discussed strictly in terms of the associated pottery (Combed Ware and what is likely Red Monochrome Painted Ware), with no indication of their placement in the landscape (Sørensen and Rupp 1993: 3, tables 2–3, following p. 197). Work in the Stavros tis Psokas river drainage, some 4 km northwest of the Ezousas River drainage covered by the CPSP and in an upland zone, was more informative. Four CN ('Late Neolithic') sites were identified and defined as small settlements, with find scatters ranging from 0.28 to 2 ha in extent. In the main, these were situated on gently sloping, good arable land just north or south of the river (Baird 1987: 16–17, fig. 4). Finally, survey by the same team in the northern reaches of the Ktima lowlands identified a key CN site, Peyia *Elia tou Vatani* 1, with finds spread over nearly 3 ha (Baird 1985: 341–343, fig. 1). The homogeneous pottery assemblage included Red Monochrome Painted, Red-on-White and Combed wares, which helped to establish this as the first, unquestionably CN site identified in the west of Cyprus. Situated on the gentle slopes of a dry streambed, this site's location conforms in many respects to that of excavated CN sites such as Sotira *Teppes* and Kandou *Kouphovounos*.

The main excavated sites that offer some data for interpretation are situated along the north coast (Ayios Epiktitos *Vrysi*, Klepini *Troulli*), in the western and central plain (Philia *Drakos* A, Dhali *Agridhi*), along the southern stretches of the island not far from the coast (Sotira *Teppes*, Kandou *Kouphovounos*, Kalavasos *Kokkinoyia*) and on the southeast coast (Paralimni *Nissia*). Based on the Red-on-White pottery (no Combed Ware) found in trial excavations, Pigi *Ayios Andronikos* appears to be the second CN site (after the one at Peyia) found on the west coast. There is also, however, a significant Early Chalcolithic component amongst its ceramics, as well as Bronze Age and classical finds (Ammerman et al. 2009). Some later occupation occurred above LAN levels at Khirokitia and Kalavasos *Tenta*, but in both cases the remains are severely eroded. Kalavasos *Pamboules* and Kissonerga *Mosphilia* also seem to have some very ephemeral CN components. At Klepini *Troulli*, an occupational hiatus seems to have existed between Periods I (LAN) and II (CN) (Peltenburg 1979a: 26).

Some sites of the CN, situated in topographically prominent positions (e.g. Sotira *Teppes*, Klepini *Troulli*) or on remote headlands (e.g. Ayios Epiktitos *Vrysi*), were well protected, perhaps for defensive reasons. Philia *Drakos*, *Vrysi* and notably Paralimni *Nissia* were delimited by a circuit wall or ditch. Unlike other known CN sites, Paralimni *Nissia* was situated right on the seashore with direct access to a natural harbour (Flourentzos 2008: 3). Pigi *Ayios Andronikos'* location is unusual, situated as it is at a much higher elevation (458 m asl) in the interior of the island; however, it lies only 200 m from the natural spring at Pigi, whence the site takes its name, and not much more than 10 km from the west coast (Ammerman and Sorabji 2005: 32–33, fig. 1).

Clarke (2001: 71) identified clusters of CN sites in areas of optimal water and soil resources. The best-known cluster, around the village of Kalavasos (*Tenta*, *Kokknoyia*, *Pamboules* and Mari *Paliambela*), may have formed a single community with different loci serving different functions. Another possible pattern may be seen where two prominent village settlements were located in close spatial proximity. The best-known examples are Sotira *Teppes* and Kandou *Kouphovounos*, and Ayios Epiktitos *Vrysi* and Klepini *Troulli*. Although such settlements might have competed for the available resources, it is also possible that close inter-village relations promoted familial or kin-group networks, mutually beneficial economic links and harmonious social contacts (Clarke 2001: 71). Most sites were chosen for their proximity to water sources (springs or rivers) and show a preference for overlapping environmental zones. In such zones, hunting (deer) could be combined with herding (sheep, goats), farming (raising pigs, growing crops) and collecting (wild fruits, legumes, olives) (also Ammerman and Sorabji 2005: 38). Taken as a whole, the settlement record seems internally coherent, with distinctive spatial patterning and regional expansion developing during the Ceramic Neolithic.

The eponymous type-site of the CN (Sotira Culture) is Sotira *Teppes*, which stands atop a conical hill on a 0.25-ha plateau but has occupational evidence spreading down the south and southeastern slopes of the hill. This site dominates a wide valley ringed by other hills, and offers commanding views of the southern coastal plain all the way to the Mediterranean, some four kms distant (Dikaios 1961: 1–2). The existence of three perennial springs in and around Sotira village originally led Dikaios (in 1934) to explore this area.

Excavations carried out on the *Teppes* plateau uncovered some 47, mainly sub-rectangular structures. Typically these were 3–4 m in diameter, free-standing and single-roomed, although a number of two-room complexes are apparent in the major building phase (Dikaios's Phase III; see Dikaios 1962: 79). The average floor space of these structures ranged from 16–20 m²; some had internal partitions, annexes or subsidiary buildings. Postholes located in the corners of some buildings and irregularly across the floors of others suggest some form of (reed and mud) roofing. Made of irregular stone or rubble foundations and mud-plaster or *pisé* walls, the buildings contained domestic fixtures and fittings such as off-centre platform hearths, *pisé* or stone benches, pits with vessels, grinding installations, socketed stones, stone bowls, and chipped stone and bone tools and implements. Certain groups of houses were arranged around open spaces (see reconstruction in Peltenburg 1978: 57, fig.1) (Figure 38), and some individual buildings may have had courtyards (e.g. Dikaios 1961: plate 35, House 31A). Although it is unclear from the final report whether any domestic installations or facilities existed in open spaces between buildings, some line drawings (e.g. Dikaios 1961: plate 6b) clearly show in situ features (Clarke 2007a: 121–122). Despite the compact arrangement of the houses, people would have been able to negotiate their way through the village along 1-m-wide passageways.

Stanley Price's (1979c: 79) reassessment of the 'household' structure at Sotira *Teppes* identified three stratigraphic phases (1–3) as opposed to the four phases (I–IV) assigned by Dikaios. Early in his Phase 1, structures were thinly spread

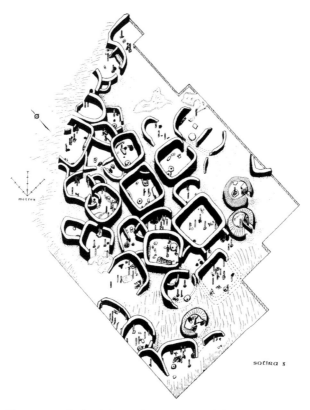

Figure 38. Sotira *Teppes* Ceramic Neolithic site: isometric reconstruction. After Peltenburg 1978: 57, fig. 1.

over the plateau, especially in comparison with the habitational pattern of Phases 2 and 3, when houses, subsidiary structures and cross-walls spread over most of the site, substantially increasing the area of roofed space. During Phase 1b, the settlement's houses were all destroyed by fire, but soon replaced by new ones. Another destruction occurred at the end of Phase 2, perhaps the result of an earthquake, and was followed immediately by reoccupation (Phase 3) and reuse of the largest remaining Phase 2 houses. At this time, a massive retaining wall was built along the plateau's northern edge, evidently to consolidate the northern slope and to remove some of the destruction debris prior to reoccupation. Given various makeshift features and the lack of any major building activity during Phase 3, it seems that this reoccupation was brief. The site was abandoned not long afterwards, and overall seems to have been occupied for no more than two centuries (Stanley Price 1979c: 66–67, 80–81).

The planning and layout of the structures at Sotira *Teppes* is recognisable in the sector plan of the north-coast site at Ayios Epiktitos *Vrysi*, whose close material parallels with the former site Peltenburg (1978) pointed out long ago. Stanley Price (1979c: 80) nonetheless questioned the uniformity of buildings and random distribution of activities that Peltenburg saw as characteristic of both sites, and Peltenburg (1985a: 49–50) himself later drew attention to differences in the way external and internal space was used at *Teppes* and *Vrysi*. Bolger (2003: 26–29) emphasised the segmentation and increasing compartmentalisation of domestic and household space at both sites, although a high degree of standardisation and a general continuity in the internal arrangement of features and fixtures has also been argued for the multifunctional structures at *Vrysi* (Peltenburg 1982b: 97 and fig. 9, 103).

Despite the acknowledged level of intersite variation in CN structures, Steel (2004a: 72–74) presents a case for the archetypal CN household: single room, single-entry, one-storey, sub-rectangular buildings; floor space between 14–30 m²; stone foundations and mudbrick or *pisé* walls with interior plastered surface; flat or conical roofs of reed and mud, supported by timber (pine) posts. Internal features included semi-circular partition walls, off-centre hearths, *pisé* or stone benches, and utensils embedded in the floors (Peltenburg 1978: 56–58). Whereas Peltenburg (1978: 62) felt such households (single-hearth structures) may have been designed for a nuclear family, Stanley Price (1979c: 79) argued that the floor space was inadequate even for a small family. In his view, only the building complexes from Sotira's Phase 2, with one large and several subsidiary structures, could be loosely regarded as households.

In any case, Ayios Epiktitos *Vrysi* is situated on a headland some 14 m above sea level along Cyprus's north central coast, about 9 km east of modern-day Kyrenia and some 2 km from the foothills of the Kyrenia range (see Figure 37 for location). The overall area of the site is about 0.5 ha, but the horizontal extent of the excavations covered only about 500 m², and was confined to the western edge of the promontory (Peltenburg 1982a: 20–21). Four seasons of excavation were carried out at *Vrysi* between 1969–1973, before the Turkish invasion into the northern part of the island brought all archaeological fieldwork there to a halt. The site's well-preserved buildings now lie in ruins, and the excavators were never able to analyse the finds to publication standards. Nonetheless, a final report has appeared (Peltenburg 1982b), as well as a string of articles treating the use of internal space, furnishings and finds at *Vrysi* compared with those of other CN settlements (Peltenburg 1978; 1982a: 37–51; 1985a; 1985b; 2003b).

Occupation within the western area was divided into northern and southern sectors, between which lay a 3–5 m wide central ridge – the natural top of the headland (Peltenburg 1993: 11, fig. 1) (Figure 39). The people who lived at *Vrysi* constructed 4–6-m-deep hollows where they built their houses, effectively semi-subterranean in nature (Mantzourani 2003b: 38–39 suggests the hollows were natural features). Six single-room structures were excavated in the north sector and nine more were partially uncovered in the south; all of them seem to be habitations where various domestic and craft activities were carried out. Given the confines of the hollows in which they were built, these houses were continuously rebuilt or remodelled, one on top of another in

Figure 39. Ayios Epiktitos *Vrysi* Ceramic Neolithic site. View looking east of natural top of headland, showing North and South Sectors and the ridge in between. Courtesy of Edgar Peltenburg.

column-like arrangement (Peltenburg 1982a: 25; 1985a: 46–47 and fig. 1). The buildings vary in size (3–6 m in diameter) and shape (sub-rectangular, oval, triangular); they had an average floor space of 14.4 m². At least one narrow passageway – sometimes paved with pebbles – was identified in each sector. Along these passages, the inhabitants of *Vrysi* occasionally built hearths, in one place associated with querns and rubbers, thus limiting their ability to move easily through the village (Peltenburg 1985b: 94).

During the first phase of occupation at *Vrysi*, a protective ditch and wall was erected at the northern edge of the southern sector; this may have served as the landward boundary of the original settlement to the north (Peltenburg 2003b: 102). During this early phase (the end of an undetermined sequence of earlier occupation), characterised by the presence of Red-on-White pottery, the architectural elements were most likely of timber construction (Peltenburg 1982a: 23–24). During the Middle Phase, people built structures on the remnants of the ditch and wall and expanded into the rest of the southern sector, thus dividing *Vrysi* into two discretely situated groups of buildings, all of which remained subterranean until the final stage of settlement.

Some of *Vrysi*'s Middle Phase structures had discernible but narrow, plank-framed entryways, trampled earth floors and up to 1.5-m-high walls constructed of limestone slabs or rubble, but plastered over and often shored up with timbers (Peltenburg 2003b: 102–103). A few buildings had internal partition walls or standing pillars that created distinctive interior spaces (Peltenburg 1982b:

25–26; Clarke 2007a: 121). Traces of posts and postholes probably indicate roof supports, if not upper levels. Houses typically contained a large, circular, off-centre platform hearth; a stone bench or seats; the occasional walled alcove; a range of stone vessels, lamps, tools, pendants and beads; groundstone tools and implements; a variety of chipped stone tools; bone needles, beads, hooks and other implements; and the ubiquitous Red-on-White pottery. Unique or exotic items include a large, phallic-shaped, grooved stone, and some picrolite pendants (Peltenburg 1982a: 134, pl. 4; 29, 124, fig. 5.12).

Although most buildings at *Vrysi* were similar in construction and internal features, the objects on their floors revealed a great deal of variation (Peltenburg 1985b: 93). House 7 (floor 2), moreover, was quite distinct from the other structures at *Vrysi*, with a plaster basin and large stone bin, as well as an unsually large number of diverse artefacts, flora, fauna and molluscs. By contrast, the lack of ordinary domestic utensils such as rubbers and querns sets this structure apart from the others, and Peltenburg (1982b: 102) suggested that it may have had a communal function. Based on quantitative analyses of all building contents and average floor areas at *Vrysi*, Peltenburg (1985a: 55–62; 1985b: 94–95; 1993: 10–11) felt that some level of asymmetric social relations must have existed between the northern and southern sectors of the site, with the central ridge serving as a natural barrier between the two. Although the northern sector was established at least one generation before the southern, the occurrence of specialised equipment is limited exclusively to buildings in the north. In House 1, for example, a subsidiary wall divided off the northwest corner in which a phallic-shaped grooved stone (noted above) and two other upright, carved stones – all about 60 cm tall – were decoratively wrapped in vegetable fibres (Peltenburg 1985a: 55; 1989: 112 fig. 15.2). Peltenburg (1993: 10–11) links this 'ritual' expression with the older, wealthier sector of the site, and postulates that the founding lineage of the settlement (the elders) actively maintained the exclusive character of the northern sector throughout its span of use.

During the Late Phase, the remaining buildings stood above the level of the old ground surface, and some late occupation (House 16) may have existed in the eastern part of the headland (Peltenburg 1982a: 31–32; 1982b: 108). A few of the buildings may have been destroyed but most seem to have been abandoned, with many portable objects left behind. *Vrysi* seems to have been occupied for no more than two centuries at the end of the 5th millennium Cal BC (between ca. 4222±52–4152±52 Cal BC in Model 8 – see Appendix, caption to Figure 8, and SOM for details). Its excavation, however incomplete in the eyes of its excavators, has proved to be crucial for our understanding of the Ceramic Neolithic period.

Some 10 km east of Ayios Epiktitios, on the south slope of a conical hill not unlike that on which Sotira *Teppes* was established, lies the site of Klepini *Troulli*, often regarded as belonging to the same cluster of CN sites as *Vrysi*

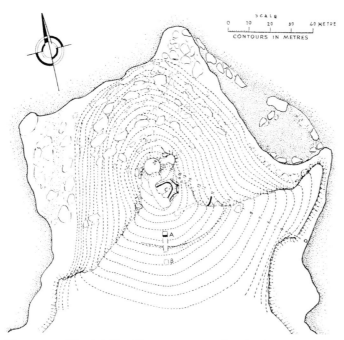

Figure 40. Klepini *Troulli* promontory; sketch plan showing site location on rocky outcrop, with small bay at base to northeast. After Dikaios 1962: 64, fig. 32.

(Clarke 2001: 70–71; 2007: 38). The promontory on which *Troulli* is located ends at a rocky plateau extending east and west, which forms part of the Kyrenia foothills. At the foot of the east slope lay a 'tiny' harbour that could have accommodated small craft (Dikaios 1962: 63–64, fig. 32) (Figure 40).

Dikaios identified two periods of occupation at *Troulli*: an earlier, aceramic level and a later, ceramic one. Peltenburg (1979a: 21) calls these, respectively, Troulli I and II; here we are concerned solely with Troulli II, the CN occupation. Some 40 cm below the surface near the top of the hill (Area C), Dikaios (1962: 64–65, fig. 33) excavated what proved to be one of the largest Neolithic structures known on Cyprus, some 25 m² in size. This building, Hut Γ, had an elongated ground plan with evidence of posts along its longitudinal axis, perhaps roof supports. Outside the apsidal northeastern end of Hut Γ are sections of walls belonging to four other, irregular structures (Peltenburg 1979a: 26). Internal features in Hut Γ included five upright stone slabs with a thick horizontal slab between them (interpreted as a bin); a limited groundstone industry (small stone vessels and implements, including three querns); a few chipped stone tools including a couple of pieces of obsidian; 'Red Lustrous' (Red Monochrome Painted) and Red-on-White Ware pottery (primarily); terracotta discs, nails and a fragmentary object that is possibly a hearth surround; a crescent-shaped piece of steatite; some worked bone and antler (hafting for a chisel); and shell (Peltenburg 1979a: 26–30). The size and prominence of

Hut Γ may signal some level of significance within the community, just as the internal arrangements and proliferation of artefacts suggest some communal function for House 7 (floor 2) at *Vrysi* (Peltenburg 1982b: 102; Steel 2004a: 72). Notwithstanding such occasional evidence for communally organised activities, most archaeologists still regard the architectural and other material indices of the CN as indicators of an egalitarian society.

The sites of Philia *Drakos* A and Dhali *Agridhi* (western and central *Mesaoria*, respectively) have played key roles in discussions of relative chronology and the earliest production of pottery in the CN (usefully summarised in Clarke 2007a: 25–26). Neither, however, has been fully published (but see, e.g., Watkins 1970; 1972 on Phila; Lehavy 1974; 1979 on Dhali). The following description of both sites and their material remains is therefore necessarily general and compatively brief.

Philia *Drakos* A (*Drakos* B is a Late Chalcolithic site) lies on the southern flank of the Ovgos River valley, some 500 m west of the village of Philia and about 20 km inland from the northwest coast. Excavations were conducted there in the late 1960s and published mainly in the annual reports provided by the Director of Cyprus's Department of Antiquities (V. Karageorghis at that time) for the *Bulletin de Correspondance Hellénique* (years 1966, 1968–1971). Early in its history, the site was at least partly surrounded by a rampart of stone with an external ditch; later, as the settlement expanded beyond this perimeter, a larger stone wall was built (as also seems to have happened at *Vrysi* and Paralimni *Nissia*). Several small, sub-circular structures with mud-on-stone foundations and walls composed of crushed lime were constructed within hollows in the bedrock (*Annual Report of the Director of the Department of Antiquities* 1970: 14). Other, sub-rectangular structures with stone foundations had beaten-earth floors with an off-centre hearth.

A series of subterranean hollows, up to 4 m deep and cut into the soft limestone and marl on which the site is located, puzzled Watkins (1972: 167). Gilman (1987: 542), however, has suggested that the presence of such 'pit architecture' indicates storage or seasonal use of a site. The presence of similar phenomena at other CN sites such as *Vrysi* and Kalavasos *Kokkinoyia* now make such features seem less unusual, even if we still cannot comprehend fully the role they played in village life. The ubiquitous pottery ranged from Coarse and Dark Face Burnished Wares in the earliest levels to Red-on-White and Red Monochrome Painted in the most recent. Other notable finds include a not uncommon array of CN materials: abundant chipped stone, ground-stone tools and implements (axes, bowls, lamps, mortars and pestles, querns), and a few bone tools. Faunal remains indicate that sheep, goat and deer were the most common food resources, but pig and (less likely) cattle bones were also recorded. A single, collapsed chamber tomb, with two bodies but lacking grave goods, came to light in the 1969 season (*Annual Report of the Director of the Department of Antiquities* 1969: 12). Further analysis indicated that the two

Figure 41. Kandou *Kouphovounos* aerial photograph (after Mantzourani 2009: fig. 4 (aerial). Courtesy of the Cyprus Museum, Nicosia.

skeletons, both likely females, were of adolescent age; a third skeleton was too fragmentary to determine age (Walker 1975).

Dhali *Agridhi* (with a distinct LAN phase – discussed in the previous section of this chapter) is stituated on the upper, southern terrace of the Yialias River (Lehavy 1989), in an agriculturally rich area. Clarke (2007a: 120) believes that sites such as *Agridhi* were small hunting camps used by mobile farmers and herders who also relied on deer hunting for subsistence. The palaeobotanical remains give no insight here, as only grape and lentil, both likely wild, were recovered. A large concentration of the earliest Dark Face Burnished Wares known on the island was recovered from a circular deposit that reached into the lowest CN levels at *Agridhi* (Lehavy 1989: 209). No structures were identified, and no stone vessels were found in the CN levels; the chipped stone had only been studied in a preliminary fashion at the time of publication. Nearly 100 beads were recorded, made of everything from fossilised fish teeth and seashell to serpentinite, umber and ochre (Lehavy 1989: 211). Although allowing that the people who lived at *Agridhi* collected and utilised wild plant resources, the excavator insisted that this was a sedentary site during both phases of its occupation, arguing that the size and weight of the stone vessels (LAN) and the bulk of the pottery vessels (CN) indicate some level of permanency (Lehavy 1989: 211–212).

Returning to the south of Cyprus, the site of Kandou *Kouphovounos*, often compared or contrasted with its near-neighbour Sotira *Teppes* (some 8 km to the west), was situated atop and along the western and southern slopes of Kouphovounos hill, in close proximity to the Kouris River (Figure 41).

An electromagnetic survey conducted in 1996 revealed scattered architectural remains over an area of some 2 ha, of which about 950 m² were excavated (Mantzourani 2003b: 46, 85; 2009: 21–30). Five architectural phases (I–V) could be distinguished, and there was no evidence of occupation earlier than the CN. Thirty-nine distinctive structures were identified, most with rounded or elliptical and sub-rectangular plans, not unlike those at Sotira *Teppes* and other CN sites. The average internal space of the buildings ranges from 25–30 m² but one building, Structure 3, enclosed 56 m² (Mantzourani 2009: 56–65, fig. 65). This structure was also unusual in having no hearth, but instead two stone benches associated with stone-built pits, a thin dividing wall in its eastern part, and an installation of chipped stone tools (Mantzourani 2003a: 87, fig. 3a, 88).

Most CN sites share this tendency to have a unique structure (or area, as at *Vrysi*), which may suggest more differences in social structure than is usually allowed (e.g. Steel 2004a: 69–72; cf. Peltenburg 1993: 10–11). Clarke (2007a: 122) posits possible social tensions between, rather than within different settlements. In any case, there can be little doubt that all sedentary societies exhibit, to differing degrees, some level of asymmetric relationships (Feinman and Neitzel 1984: 72–77; Peltenburg 1993: 9); I consider this issue in more detail below, in the section on *Social Continuity and Social Change*.

Most of the buildings at *Kouphovounos* appear to be domestic in nature, and are situated within the 'central area' (Mantzourani 2003b: 47, figs. 13–14; Mantzourani and Catapoti 2004: 2–3; Mantzourani 2009: fig. 413). These buildings belong to more than one phase of construction at the site. In general, the lower courses of the buildings' walls, some 35–45 cm thick, were constructed of limestone rubble; the superstructure was of *pisé* or mudbricks. Internal features – benches, platforms, circular off-centre hearths – were made of stone and mud-plaster; there were also grinding installations and pits for diverse uses. During Phase III, when the site reached its greatest extent, Mantzourani (2003b: 48–49; 2009: 188, fig. 414) suggests that groupings of three–four houses may represent separate neighbourhoods and that each habitation likely served several different functions. External space seems to have been more extensive and more heavily utilised at *Kouphovounos* than it was at Sotira *Teppes* and *Vrysi*. There are several open areas with fireplaces and pits (Mantzourani 1994a: 5, 10–11, fig. 6; 2003a: 88–89; Papaconstantinou 2006: 52), and the amount of lithic debris found in open spaces between structures suggests knapping areas (Papagianni 1997: 73; McCartney, in Clarke 2007a: 85).

Beyond the Red-on-White, Red Monochrome Painted and Combed wares typical of most CN sites, other notable finds include a large number of picrolite ornaments (pendants, amulets, beads, pins) and a rare picrolite figurine (Mantzourani 1994b) (Figure 42), a schematic anthropomorphic limestone figurine, and a fragment of a human foot from a large clay statue as well as some cylindrical clay objects (Mantzourani 2003a: 96–97, and fig. 10a).

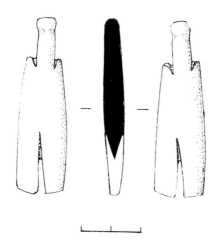

Figure 42. Kandou *Kouphovounos* picrolite figurine. Courtesy of the Cyprus Museum, Nicosia.

Unlike most CN sites but following LAN mortuary practices, at least two intramural burials – one an infant, the other an adult male – were uncovered at *Kouphovounos* within a pit in Structure 15 (Mantzourani 1997: 22–24, figs. 1–4; 2003a: 89).

On the southeastern coast of Cyprus, near Cape Greco and right next to the sea, lies the site of Paralimni *Nissia*. Established on a coastal hillock (*Nissia*) on the southern side of a small bay, with the Potamos tou Lombarti (river) to the west and north, the site was well protected and strategically located, with direct access to the sea (much more so than *Vrysi* and *Troulli* on the north coast). The settlement covered about one-third of a hectare in extent, of which 2,750 m² was excavated (Flourentzos 2008: 3, pl. I, figs. B–C). Forty distinct structures were uncovered during five excavation seasons between 1995–2001, and the excavator sees in their layout a 'primitive', spiral-form urban plan (Flourentzos 1997: 2; 2003: 74) (Figure 43). A notable stone wall, 2 m in width at the most, begins at or near the sea and runs through the settlement's southern sector in an arc, curving back towards the northeast. Constructed of large rough and worked stones, the wall's function is obscure, since several structures were built outside (south) of it. Whether these structures were later in date than the intramural part of the settlement is unclear from any of the reports.

Most structures at *Nissia* are roughly sub-rectangular, whilst a few are clearly circular or elliptical in shape, thus corresponding to other known CN buildings (Flourentzos 2008: fig. B). The walls were constructed up to a maximum height of 1 m with rubble or stone, and had the usual superstructure of *pisé* or mudbrick. Several structures share a common wall, a feature also seen at Sotira *Teppes*, *Vrysi* and *Kouphovounos*. Most of the floors were made of beaten *havara*, that is, the soft limestone that makes up bedrock in this area; some floors also contained an additional layer of pebbles, only partly preserved. A few buildings (e.g. Houses 3, 6, 23, 24) contained small stones fixed

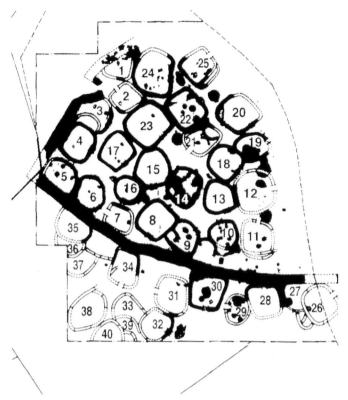

Figure 43. Paralimni *Nissia* Ceramic Neolithic site plan. After Flourentzos 2003: 75, fig. 1.

on the floors with circular depressions; these may have served as postholes to support roofs.

Flourentzos (2008: 16, pls. XIX–XX) regarded sub-rectangular House 22, one of the largest at the site (5.25 × 4.8 m), to be of special interest. Situated at the top of the *Nissia* hillock, this building had the richest assemblage of finds at the site (macehead, chipped and groundstone, stone bowl, phallic amulet, worked shell, etc.), a large circular hearth (ca. 1 m in diameter), a central posthole, a large support base (for a *pithos*?), two small benches constructed of rough stones, and the remains of a pebble floor (Flourentzos 2008: 4, pl. XXd). Such floors are also in evidence outside the houses and in the narrow corridors between them. Many of the structures were equipped with their own, in situ stone mortars; the impressive calcarenite example in House 14 measured 1 × 0.5 m (Flourentzos 2008: pl. XI a, b).

The chipped stone and groundstone assemblages, including some stone vessels, are notable and abundant (see further below, *Material Culture of the Ceramic Neolithic*). Amongst the movable finds were the typical CN pottery wares: Red-on-White, and Red-on-White and Combed, in a limited number of shapes (mainly spouted hemispherical basins, and handleless, spherical jugs or

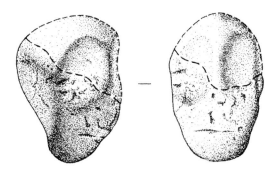

Figure 44. Paralimni *Nissia*, representation of a human head, made of andesite. After Flourentzos 2008: fig. 22, 100.

flasks). One Red-on-White sherd has a painted representation of an animal, a unique occurrence in the CN (Flourentzos 2003: 78–80, fig. 4.4; 2008: pl. CVII, sh. 57). Other notable finds include sixteen anthropomorphic and animal figurines, with seldom-seen pieces such as a human head (Figure 44), a remarkable fish-shaped figurine, and four stone, phallic-shaped images (Flourentzos 2008: 86–87, figs. 22–24). The excavations also produced four terracotta figurines or fragments and other miscellaneous clay objects, imaginatively interpreted by the excavator (Flourentzos 2008: 92–93, fig. 37). This repertoire is rounded out by a variety of other objects: picrolite and other stone amulets, pendants and beads; stone weights and what are reported as loomweights (more likely sinkers for fishing, as the earliest known loomweights on the island are dated some 1,000 years later); and a few objects made of bone and antler (awls, perforator, beads, rods and pins). *Nissia* has one of the richest small find collections of any CN site.

Recent excavations at CN Kalavassos *Kokkinoyia* and nearby, Early Chalcolithic *Pamboules* have helped to expand upon and clarify work undertaken at both sites in the 1940s (Dikaios 1962: 106–112, 133–140). Situated on the eastern side of the Vasilikos valley, some 3 km from Kalavasos village, *Kokkinoyia* lies about 500 m southeast of *Pamboules*. Dikaios dated *Kokkinoyia* (which he called Kalavasos A) to the Neolithic II period (i.e. CN) and *Pamboules* (Kalavasos B) to the Chalcolithic I period (i.e. Early Chalcolithic). More recent fieldwork and survey, and reanalysis of the material collected by Dikaios and stored in the Cyprus Museum (Clarke 2004; 2007b; 2009; Clarke et al. 2007), show that *Kokkinoyia* is primarily a single phase CN site (with secondary use of some features in the Early Chalcolithic), whilst *Pamboules* is a multi-period site, extending from the CN to the Late Chalcolithic period (like Pigi *Ayios Andronikos*, noted above). Here the focus falls on *Kokkinoyia*, a site whose subterranean dwellings, pottery-based stylistic evidence and radiocarbon dates all indicate that it falls quite late in the CN sequence (Clarke 2007a: 105).

Kokkinoyia's position along the eastern edge of a low ridge offers a commanding view of the surrounding coastal lowlands. The site is estimated to have been a maximum of 1.5 ha in extent (Clarke 2007b: 19). With its numerous

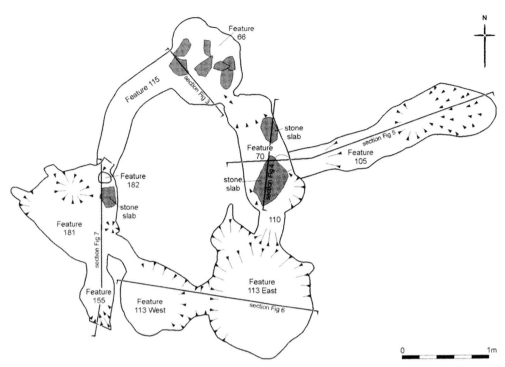

Figure 45. Kalavasos *Kokkinoya* Ceramic Neolithic site; Area U chamber and tunnel complex plan. After Clarke 2009: 49, fig. 2. Courtesy of Jo Clarke.

pit-like features, extensive chamber and tunnel complex, individual chamber-like hollows, a single semi-subterranean structure, and the lack of any faunal or botanical remains, *Kokkinoyia* looks very different from other CN sites, most of which share similar features and materials throughout (e.g. Clarke 2007b: 14–18; 2009: 39–40). The structural feature (136), wide and shallow, had a number of floor levels; its edges and floor were formed from the natural *havara* bedrock. A small, circular, hearth-like installation was situated in its centre, next to a circular pit that might have served as a posthole. This feature contained the highest number of pottery sherds (916) found at *Kokkinoyia* (Clarke 2009: 46). Surrounding feature 136 but not in direct association with it were seven chambers containing only a few distinctive objects (Clarke 2007b: 21). The pits are located primarily in one area of the site, and come in various sizes and different shapes.

The chamber and tunnel complex (Clarke 2007b: 20–21, fig. 9; 2009: 49, fig. 2) (Figure 45) extends over three different levels, and has at least six distinct chambers, each connected to at least one other chamber by an entryway, 'port-hole' or tunnel. One chamber (Feature 70) clearly had a primary deposit, in this case a Combed Ware bottle placed within a spouted, Combed Ware bowl (Clarke 2004: 58, pl. 1.1, 5; 2009: 40, 52, fig. 8a–b); one radiocarbon sample (Wk-26434, pistachio charcoal) came from beneath this bowl (J. Clarke, pers.

comm., December 2009). Just above the base of another, very large chamber (105, linked to Chamber 70 via a tunnel), excavations revealed a triton shell, two pestles and a chalk stone, all part of a secondary deposit (Clarke 2004: 58–59, pl. 1.2); these items may have been placed or rolled into the chamber after a period of disuse.

The main chamber in Feature 205 was one of the largest uncovered at *Kokkinoyia* (2.45 × 1.95 m); it contained several groundstone objects, as well as a moulded, unfired cylindrical 'lamp' (Clarke 2009: 45, 56, fig. 16). Yet another chamber (113 East) contained materials dating to the end of the CN – pottery (typically Red Monochrome), chipped stone and a large cache of groundstone objects – or to the Early Chalcolithic (Glossy Burnished Ware sherds). The excavator suggests this may indicate use of the chamber as a storage facility sometime after its primary use (Clarke 2009: 46–47). Finally, Chamber 215 was distinguished by two distinctive surfaces; against a line of stones dividing the upper from the lower surface lay some chert blades and several sherds (from two pots) of Early Chalcolithic date (Clarke 2009: 46). The lower surface, the base of the chamber, held several pieces of ochre and an ochre-encrusted stone, along with a small Red Monochrome Painted flask of CN date. Some of this material offers tantalising clues that may help us to understand better the purpose and use of the chamber and tunnel complex (see below, in the section *Social Continuity and Social Change*).

Excavations during 2006 also uncovered an intact human burial in a shallow, nearly circular pit – the lower half of a figure-of-eight feature (199) cut into bedrock (Clarke 2007b: 21–22, fig. 10; 2009: 45, 55, fig. 15). The burial held the articulated skeleton of a female interred on her right side in a semi-contracted position. A stone placed under the skull may have served to tilt the head forward, echoing a practice already known from Sotira *Teppes* (Dikaios 1961: 144–145). A number of other bones – perhaps belonging to a previous occupant – had also been placed loosely on top of the skeleton's lower half. The pit in which this burial was placed seems to have been constructed intentionally for mortuary purposes; its form and shape are entirely different from the other pits at *Kokkinoyia*.

The material culture recovered from excavations at *Kokkinoyia* is meagre, and rather different from that of other CN sites. The pottery assemblage is dominated by Combed and Red Monochrome Painted wares (hallmarks of central and southern sites of the CN – Clarke 2007b: 17), but with Coarse ware in higher proportions (up to 30% of the total) than seen at any other CN site (Clarke 2004: 62–63, fig. 6, and pl. 2; 2009: 46). The chipped stone from Dikaios's earlier excavations, at least, is largely blade-based, made from Lefkara basal or translucent cherts, and not dissimilar to other contemporary settlement assemblages (Clarke et al. 2007: 56–59). The quantities of groundstone, many of them expedient tools of domestic type (e.g. pestles, pounders, grinders) elsewhere associated with settlements (Clarke et al. 2007: 53), seem well in excess of what might be expected of a CN site this size. Nevertheless, the absence of botanical and floral data is striking, and there are no bone tools, very few personal ornaments, and only a single figurine fragment of green-veined serpentinite (from Dikaios's excavations – Clarke et al. 2007: 54, fig. 4d; 56). The only other items of note are the ochre pieces and an ochre-encrusted stone (Chamber 215), two triton shells (Chambers 105, 221), an unfired cylindrical 'lamp' (Chamber 205), and a small piece of sandstone with cross-hatched design (Clarke 2004: 59, fig. 3.1, 3).

The purpose and function of *Kokkinoyia* are hard to determine. Clarke (2004: 64–66; 2007b: 23–24) feels that the material found at *Kokkinoyia* is uncharacteristic of domestic production and consumption activities. All features indicate that the site was used for an indeterminate period of time during the latest part of the CN and the transition to the Early Chalcolithic (with no discernible break) (Clarke 2009: 47). Clarke's cautious interpretation is that the single structure (136) was associated with (unknown) activities performed in its tunnels and chambers; the other underground features remain enigmatic. Overall, it is difficult to view such (underground, semi-subterranean) features as belonging to the range of practices associated with everyday activities. Yet whatever took place at *Kokkinoyia* involved the use of quotidian items and it may be pushing the evidence (triton shells, pestles, indicators of pigment processing) to find any extraordinary significance in them.

In terms of subsistence, the limited faunal data for the CN shows a continuing dependence on sheep/goat, a declining use of pig and a heavy reliance on deer. The apparent differences in faunal data from various sites, themselves disparate in terms of actual sample sizes, probably resulted from diversity in local environments rather than from any actual difference in hunting, herding and farming strategies (Peltenburg 1982b: 98; Clarke 2001: 66). Deer nonetheless form large percentages of the rather limited and thus likely biased samples from Sotira *Teppes* (76%), Philia *Drakos* A (71%) and Dhali *Agridhi* (80%) (Clarke 2001: 70). Croft's (2010) recent reassessment of more than 3,000 fragments of animal bones from Philia *Drakos* A confirmed the heavy dominance of fallow deer (66.5%), followed by caprines (22.6%). At Paralimni *Nissia*, deer are said to make up '70% of the nutrition' (Flourentzos 2008: 97); according to Croft (2010: 135), the assemblage of 1,034 large mammal bones at the site comprised 77.1% deer (a 90% contribution to the overall meat supply), again followed by caprines (16.7%). The complete absence of animal bones (or even bone tools) as well as botanical remains from both Dikaios's earlier excavations and the current work at Kalavasos *Kokkinoyia* is thus worth reiterating at this point (Clarke 2007b: 14; Clarke et al. 2007: 72).

Next to Philia *Drakos* A and Paralimni *Nissia*, Ayios Epiktitos *Vrysi* provides the most abundant faunal evidence: ovicaprines (50.4%), fallow deer (37.2%) and pig (10.5%), with lesser numbers of fox, dog and cat, as well as marine turtle, fish and birds (Croft 2010: 133–134, table 16.2). Legge (in Peltenburg

1982b: 81–83) maintained that sheep and goat were herded whilst deer would have been hunted. Although such a view is usually interpreted to mean that CN people were fully sedentary agro-pastoralists who hunted a lot of deer, Croft (1991: 66–69) suggested some time ago that sheep and goat – with no appreciable morphological differences from their western Asiatic ancestors – may have been feral, and if so would have been hunted as well. Nonetheless, the size of deer means that they provide considerably more meat per individual than any other species (Croft 2010: 135). Given that deer hunting seems to have peaked during the CN (Croft 1991: 75; 2010: 136), there is little doubt they provided the primary source of animal protein at that time. Tended sheep and goat nonetheless would have been valuable for other secondary products beyond meat, namely milk, leather and wool (Peltenburg 1985b: 94).

The people who lived along the coasts of Cyprus during the CN also exploited such marine resources as were available. Excavations at Paralimni *Nissia*, for example, produced moderate numbers of fish bones, some crab claws and 16 species of molluscs (Flourentzos 2003: 77). The community at *Vrysi* made generous use of limpets (*Patella*) and topshell (*Monodata*), which together made up 76% of the 36 different marine mollusc species recovered at the site. A number of fragmentary bones from *Vrysi* were identified as marine turtle (similarly at *Nissia* – Croft in Flourentzos 2008: 1–5). Curiously for these coastal sites, however, the limited number of fish bones recovered only represents a few fish (Peltenburg 1982b: 86–87; Croft 2010: 135–136). Nonetheless, bone fishhooks found at *Vrysi* and stone versions of the same from *Nissia* highlight further the importance of marine resources. Significant numbers of seashells turned up at the inland site of Kandou *Kouphovounos*: at least 27 sea species, dominated by murex, oysters and limpets (Mantzourani 2003: 98). Another inland site, Dhali *Agridhi*, divulged fossilised fish teeth and seashells used to make beads; even Sotira *Teppes* contained one fishhook and perforated stones that Dikaios (1961: 202–203) interpreted as sinkers.

Floral data are also quite limited and the most reliable amongst them come from *Vrysi* (Kyllo, in Peltenburg 1982b: 90–93). There, palaeobotanical evidence indicates the cultivation of wheat (einkorn, emmer, breadwheat), barley, rye, oats, lentils and pulses. Olive and fig were present in most samples, with apple and grape less so; there are no clear indications that these fruits were domesticated. At Dhali *Agridhi*, there is evidence of wild einkorn, wild lentil and wild pistachio (Stewart, in Stager et al. 1974: 123–125), and in general the collection of wild grasses, cereals, legumes and fruits no doubt played some role in CN subsistence strategies (Clarke 2001: 70).

Despite the sparse palaeobotanical evidence, the quantities of chipped stone (chert) blades with sickle gloss from cereal grains, alongside abundant finds of mortars, pestles, pounders and grinders from Sotira *Teppes* (Peltenburg 1978: 64), indicate that grain harvesting was a major occupation in CN communities. In turn, the large numbers of axes and adzes that typify the CN material record may have been used to clear wooded areas to generate soils for farming, a strategy also indicated by the reduced number of pig bones (Steel 2004a: 79).

Both Clarke (2001; 2007a: 34) and Wasse (in Clarke 2007a: 61) have cited the large quantities (and percentages) of deer remains in the faunal record to infer the possibility of a more mobile way of life amongst the people of the CN period. The full panoply of evidence presented in this section, however, clearly shows that some CN communities were sedentary in nature (*Teppes, Vrysi, Nissia*), reliant on a mixed economy that heavily exploited hunted deer but also involved farming and herding. Neither the ubiquitous use of pottery nor the abundance of groundstone tools seem consonant with a mobile lifestyle. Even if we interpret some evidence from the end of the period as a sign of environmental deterioration (degraded soils, deforestation), the irregular configuration of *Kokkinoyia* still presents a puzzle; the site nonetheless was well stocked with many accoutrements of everyday domestic life. As Peltenburg (1978: 74) stated more than 30 years ago, '…the advent of the Sotira culture heralds the beginning of scattered, well-defined, mixed farming communities' with 'lively pottery-making customs'. Although evidence for the subsistence base has improved since that time mainly with respect to the faunal record, itself heavily dominated by deer (except for *Vrysi*), we now have a much more extensive and diverse site record that tends to corroborate rather than challenge his statement.

The Material Culture of the Ceramic Neolithic

There is a broad similarity in Ceramic Neolithic material culture throughout the island, including the layout and features of most structures within settlements (Peltenburg 1978: 56–58). Similar if not identical types of stone and bone objects occur commonly in various sites: chipped stone tools, groundstone implements (hammerstones, grinders, mortars and pestles), stone bowls, picrolite and bone ornaments and tools (pendants, amulets, beads; needles, awls, hooks), and pierced discs (Steel 2004a: 74–75, fig. 3.14; Clarke 2007a: 38–39, fig. 3.3) (Figure 46). Axes, adzes and chisels (some hafted in antler) for woodworking or forest clearance also appear at some sites (e.g. Dikaios 1961: 190–195; Peltenburg 1979a: 30).

Pottery shapes (large and small bowls, ovoid jugs or bottles, holemouth jars, small 'thumb pots', shallow flange-based trays) and manufacturing techniques show close similarities in all excavated sites (Clarke 2007a: 100–101). Steel (2004a: 74) suggests that the mode of manufacture is consistent with household production. Vessels were handmade, and decorated in monochrome (red) or bichrome (red, white) finish, or combed design. Clarke (2007a: 40), developing Peltenburg's (1978: 66) original distinctions, differentiates generally between the pottery traditions of the south-central region (Red Monochrome Painted, Combed ware) and those of the southeast, southwest and northern regions

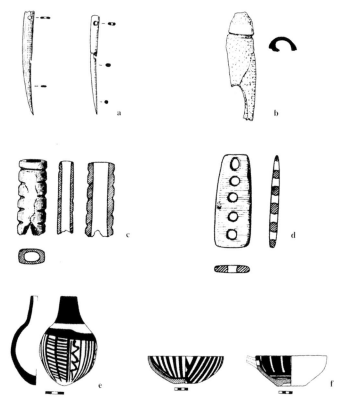

Figure 46. CN material culture: stone, bone and pottery. After Clarke 2007a: 39, fig. 3.3. Courtesy of Jo Clarke. (a) bone needles, Sotira *Teppes* (Dikaios 1962: 97, fig. 49: 810, 657); (b) figurine (?), Sotira *Teppes* (Dikaios 1962: 97, fig. 49: 225 a–b); (c) bone handle, Sotira *Teppes* (Dikaios 1962: 97, fig. 49: 118); (d) stone pendant, Sotira *Teppes* (Dikaios 1962: 96, fig. 48: 672); (e)–(f) Red-on-White pottery: bottle and bowl (Dikaios 1962: 88, fig. 44).

(Red-on-White). Painted and Combed ware is found in small quantities at sites all over the island (Clarke 2007a: 104). Variations in surface treatment and decorative motifs are thought to reflect group identity as expressions of emblemic style (Clarke 2001; 2003: 206; after Wiessner 1983: 257–258).

   Although figurines are rare, and quite schematic, some are singularly expressive in terms of gender and symbolism. From Sotira *Teppes* came a limestone figure (Dikaios 1961: 201, pls. 91.106, 102.106) (Figure 47), whilst a similar example derives from House 7 at Ayios Epiktitos *Vrysi* (Peltenburg 1982a: 124, fig. 5:15). Although both figures are undoubtedly human representations, with legs indicated by a vertical incision and the head by a rounded constriction at the top, their shape is indisputably phallic. Bolger (2003: 85) regards the Sotira figurine as dimorphic, representing both penis and vulva, but another, white limestone figurine from Sotira *Arkolies* (Swiny and Swiny 1983: 57–58, fig. 1) (Figure 48), found near the Ceramic Neolithic settlement at *Teppes*, is much more obvious in this respect (this figurine may date to the Early Chalcolithic).

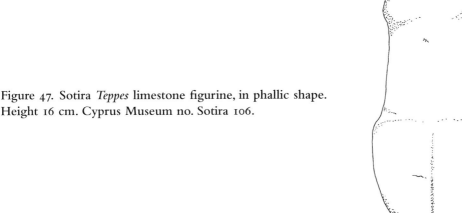

Figure 47. Sotira *Teppes* limestone figurine, in phallic shape. Height 16 cm. Cyprus Museum no. Sotira 106.

Figure 48. Sotira *Arkolies* limestone seated figure. Height 16 cm; length 11.1 cm. Cyprus Museum, No. 1981/VIH-19/1. After Swiny and Swiny 1983, fig. 1. (a) front view; (b) side view; (c) rear view; (d)–(e) top and bottom views.

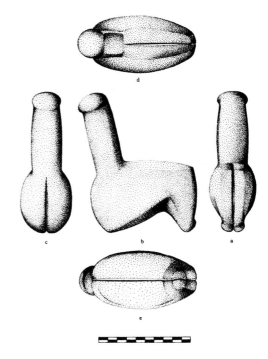

From one angle, this representation seems to render male genitalia (rear view, Figure 48c); from another view (Figure 48e), it resembles female genitalia. Even more schematised but equally phallic in design is the picrolite figurine from *Kouphovounos* (Mantzourani 1994b: 32, fig. 1, pl. V.2) (Figure 42 above);

another abstract limestone figurine from the same site (Mantzourani 2003a: 97, fig. 10a) is less obviously phallic. The most elaborate of three 'pillar' figures from House 1 at *Vrysi* (already noted above) is a tall (58 cm) phallic-shaped grooved stone (Peltenburg 1989: 110, 112, fig. 15.2). The phallic aspect of four stones from *Nissia* (Flourentzos 2008: 87, figs. 22:532 and 114, fig. 23:289 and 311), however, seems less obvious. Nonetheless, the sexual ambiguity seen in most of these anthropomorphic figures becomes increasingly common in Chalcolithic representations of the body (Knapp and Meskell 1997), and suggests that fertility was not the sole concern of those who made and used these figurines or representations (see the next chapter for more detailed discussion).

Both Peltenburg (1982b: 98–101) and Steel (2004a: 73–74) discuss a range of non-specialist, household-based craft activities, including the manufacture of beads, picrolite and bone implements and ornaments (needles, beads, toggles, hooks), pottery, chipped stone, stone bowls and more, all of which took place within the larger structures at CN sites. Chalcedony pebbles found at Sotira may have been used for burnishing pottery surfaces, whilst other stone implements would have been used to grind lumps of iron-rich umbers for use in preparing red slip for pottery or the colouring for wall plasters (Stanley Price 1979c: 76); the ochre pieces and an ochre-encrusted stone from *Kokkinoyia* may also be noted in this context. Parallel types of evidence from *Vrysi* include possible polishers, a waster and haematite pigments and clays (Peltenburg 1978: 59–61). Some pierced or perforated disks from Sotira and *Vrysi* have been identified, probably erroneously, as spindle whorls (Dikaios 1961: 202, pl. 103; Peltenburg 1978: 58–60, fig. 3W). Along with the presence of bone needles, these disks have been interpreted as evidence for textile production based on plant fibres such as flax (Steel 2004a: 74, 80; Barber 1991: 11–15). Crewe (1998: 14), however, points out the difficulties one would face in mounting the purported CN examples on a spindle and thus questions such a function for these objects. She points out, moreover, that similar perforated objects are found alongside spindle whorls during the Bronze Age, the era when she believes spindle whorls, and thus textile production, first began on Cyprus. This does not mean that textiles were not produced at this time, as spinning does not necessarily require spindle whorls, or else the weavers may have used whorls made of wood.

Thirty-three picrolite ornaments – pendants, amulets, beads, one ring – and miscellaneous objects were excavated at Sotira *Teppes* (Dikaios 1961: 200–201). More than 60 ornaments of picrolite (pendants, beads, dress pins), at least 20 miniature picrolite axes and a unique picrolite figurine (mentioned above) were recovered in excavations at Kandou *Kouphovounos* (Mantzourani 2001: 65–66, figs. 1, 3, and 4; Mantzourani and Catapoti 2004: 11, n.17; Swantek 2006: 35–39, figs. 3.9a, 3.9b). From Philia *Drakos* A came at least 10 picrolite objects, including beads, pendants and pebbles (Peltenburg 1991b: 123). Only five picrolite objects – two beads and three pendants – were excavated at *Vrysi* (Peltenburg 1982b: 315). Three picrolite items – a pendant, an incised bead and an 'ithyphallic amulet' – were found at Paralimni *Nissia* (Flourentzos 2008: 87–88, fig. 27, pls. 56: 299, 63: 359, 66: 393).

From the distribution of this material, it is immediately clear that the sites nearest the main picrolite sources (Kouris river in the southwest, Karkotis river in northwest Troodos), namely Sotira *Teppes* and Kandou *Kouphovounos*, have considerably more picrolite objects than other CN sites. Peltenburg (1991b: 115–117) makes a case for a localised exchange system in picrolite during the Chalcolithic period, but during the CN the most we can infer is a pattern of dispersed local production, with the bulk of the evidence confined to the sites nearest the sources. Most picrolite objects from the CN take the form of personal ornaments, including beads, but the unique picrolite figurine from *Kouphovounos* may well represent the start of a tradition that crystallised during the Middle Chalcolithic (Peltenburg 1991b: 113–115). Virtually all picrolite objects were found in settlement contexts, suggesting that the pendants, beads and amulets served as personal ornaments or jewellery for the living, not as heirlooms or grave goods for the dead.

Some continuities between the LAN and the CN in chipped stone and groundstone technologies, raw materials and practices have already been discussed (see above, *Transition to the Ceramic Neolithic*). Innovations in chipped stone technology included the use of a high-quality translucent chert for manufacturing flakes, and a poorer quality Lefkara basal chert for making long blades, especially sickle blades (McCartney, in Clarke 2007a: 83). At Nissia *Paralimni* and Kalavasos *Kokkinoyia*, long blades were subsequently used to make glossed segments, whilst flake tools included perforators, notches and denticulates, *pièces esquillées*, and some scrapers and retouched pieces. At *Kouphovounos*, the most notable feature of the chipped stone industry is the long blade, typically retouched and bearing traces of silica gloss. The rest of the toolkit consists of sickle elements, end scrapers, burins, notches and denticulates, perforators and flakes with marginal retouch (Papagianni 1997: 73). A distinction can also be seen between the *chaines opératoires* of blade and flake production at Kandou *Kouphovounos* and the coarse chert used extensively for producing blades at Ayios Epiktitos *Vrysi* (Papagianni 1997: 74–76; Peltenburg 1978: 59 n. 19). Papagianni (1997: 76) suggests that blades may have been made by specialised knappers (perhaps off-site), flakes by non-specialists (clearly on-site). Tools made on flakes as opposed to blade or bladelet blanks are also a feature of the CN lithics from Kalavasos *Tenta* (McCartney, in Todd 2005: 208–209); these include backed pieces with rectilinear retouch, unretouched glossed tools, single notches and large perforators. Blade-based tools at *Tenta* include scrapers, concave truncations and burins.

McCartney (in Clarke 2007a: 83) argues for the influence of southern Levantine parallels on the diverse glossed tools produced in the CN. For example, the prevalence of flat, inversely truncated segments was unique to this period, whilst one major tool type seen in the largely contemporary Wadi Rabah industry of the southern Levant was a glossed segment with semi-flat, inverse truncation retouch (Barkai and Gopher 1999: 61–66). Another parallel with Wadi Rabah assemblages may be noted in the elongated, inverse retouched blades seen at *Paralimni* and *Kokkinoyia* (McCartney, in Clarke 2007a: 83, 86, fig. 6.2e). Although extremely rare, obsidian does occur in the CN: one nugget from *Vrysi* (Peltenburg 1982b: 101; 1985b: 94) is now accompanied by two blades and a bladelet from *Kokkinoyia*. McCartney (in Clarke 2007a: 83–84) feels that a small amount of obsidian reached Cyprus via what she terms an 'infrequent trinket trade', one that parallels the situation in the southern Levant after the collapse of the so-called PPNB interaction sphere.

Changes in groundstone technology must be seen in light of the newly introduced technology of pottery, in particular the use of decorated ceramics instead of decorated stone vessels (McCartney in Clarke 2007a: 82). Diabase vessels nonetheless continued to be produced on a limited scale, and decorated examples have been uncovered at Philia *Drakos* A and *Nissia* (Watkins 1971: 373–374, fig. 82; Flourentzos 2008: 85–86, figs. 8–9). More notable, perhaps, was the proliferation of specialised cutting tools (adzes, axes, chisels and 'flaked tools'), perhaps for use in woodworking and forest clearance (Peltenburg 1978: 70; Mantzourani 2003a: 90; McCartney in Clarke 2007a: 82–83) (Figure 49). The flaked tools in particular represent a CN innovation and may have been used as scrapers for processing deerskins (Elliot 1983: 16). In the contemporary southern Levant, a similar profusion of such tools has been associated with the practice of building sailing vessels (Galili et al. 2002: 176–177). McCartney (in Clarke 2007a: 83) points to the prominence of woodworking tools in the broadly contemporary Wadi Rabah phase and, whilst emphasising the differences in tool types (e.g. chipped bifacial forms in the Levant), maintains that all these links in material practices suggest the exchange of ideas, and social transformations that must have occurred as new practices were incorporated into local knowledge in the different regions.

In sum, innovations in lithic technologies and practices include the appearance of new woodworking tools (adzes, chisels, flaked tools) in both Cyprus and the southern Levant; the use of lower quality cherts to manufacture long blades; the production of glossed segments with flat inverse retouch and robust inverse retouched long flakes; and an overall decline in obsidian imports. Because many of these features are shared with the southern Levant, McCartney (in Clarke 2007a: 84) maintains that Cyprus must have belonged to an interaction sphere that extended from the region around Byblos in present-day Lebanon to the Esdraelon Plain in southern coastal Israel. Clarke (2007a: 97–98) has also argued for similar links in the ceramic repertoire of both areas (notably with

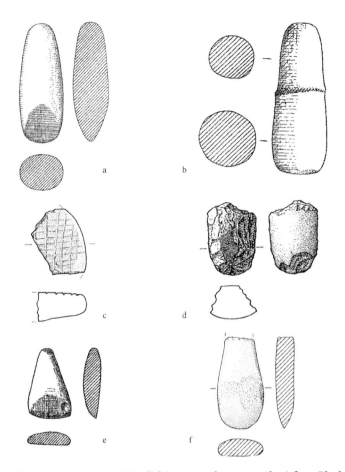

Figure 49. Ceramic Neolithic groundstone tools. After Clarke 2007a: 78, fig. 6.1. Courtesy of Jo Clarke. (a) axe, Sotira *Teppes* (Dikaios 1961: pl. 93: 128); (b) pestle, Sotira *Teppes* (Dikaios 1961: pl. 97: 127); (c) engraved pebble, Kalavasos *Kokkinoyia*; (d) flaked tool, Kalavasos *Kokkinoyia*; (e) adze, Sotira *Teppes* (Dikaios 1961: pl. 94, 94); (f) axe, Kalavasos *Kokkinoyia*

the Syrian site of Arjoune, near the Orontes River in the central Levant). In the next section, I consider these ideas in assessing the nature of insularity on Ceramic Neolithic Cyprus.

Social Continuity and Social Change

Ceramic Neolithic sites and settlements arose in diverse settings: on or near the coast (*Vrysi*, Klepini *Troulli*, Paralimni *Nissia*), on the tops of conical hills (Sotira *Teppes,* Kandou *Kouphovounos*), in the *Mesaoria* (Philia *Drakos* A, Dhali *Agridhi*), in the (southern) coastal lowlands (Kalavasos *Kokkinoyia*), and at a highland site on the west coast (Pigi *Ayios Andronikos*). Most of these sites have a broadly similar settlement layout, architectural forms and associated features;

uniformity if not conformity in pottery, chipped stone and groundstone implements and tools; picrolite and/or bone tools, ornaments and figurines; and a few exotic objects (e.g. triton shells, engraved items, unique figurines). Until recently, there was limited consideration of what all these objects, long-term settlement evidence or the use of space could tell us about social continuity, social change and individual people (but cf. Peltenburg 1993; Clarke 2007a).

McCartney (in Clarke 2007a: 84), for her part, emphasises site diversity, and argues that alongside the small villages with substantial architectural remains (e.g. Sotira, *Vrysi*, *Nissia* and *Kouphovounos*), there are low visibility sites such as Ranti *Vrysi tou Rantidou* (McCartney 2000: 35–38), squatter reoccupations at Khirokitia and *Tenta*, and pit and tunnel complexes at Philia *Drakos* A and Kalavasos *Kokkinoyia*, all of which suggest some level of residential mobility. At *Kokkinoyia*, the low number of cutting and grinding tools, and the numerous ad-hoc, multi-use tools, may also point to a more mobile population, as does the possible storage function of the site (McCartney, in Clarke 2007a: 87). Such distinctions between these low and high visibility sites may indicate nothing more than a 'mosaic of variability' (McCartney, in Clarke 2007a: 89) in Cyprus's economic and demographic patterns.

In terms of demography, evidence from excavated sites such as Sotira *Teppes*, *Vrysi*, *Nissia* and *Kouphovounos*, suggests that population growth may have had a negative impact on village organisation, as carrying capacity was reached and surpassed (Peltenburg 1993: 12). Some division of communities may have resulted, accounting for the wide spread of CN sites over the island. Such growth, however, seems not to have led to surplus wealth, notable amounts of trade or interaction, or larger villages. The people of the Ceramic Neolithic were still mainly egalitarian farmers, herders and hunters, dependent on sheep/goat, pig and especially deer.

On the one hand, simple conservatism in social change may have worked against other developments, or at least against the possibility of concentrating too much power in the hands of a single village, family or individual (Held 1993: 28). On the other hand, having analysed the high densities of in situ finds on the floors at *Vrysi*, as well as the average floor area, Peltenburg (1985a: 55–62; 1993: 10–11) concluded that some degree of 'communal factionalism' may have divided the site's northern and southern sectors, with the elders (founding settlers) maintaining through time the exclusive character of the older and wealthier, northern sector. House 1 in *Vrysi*'s northern sector, distinguished by its central setting and some remarkable features (the three phallic-shaped pillar figures) and substantial fixtures, may have had an exceptional status, whilst House 7 (floor 2) may have been used for central or communal storage. Some other CN sites share this tendency to have a unique structure (or area), for example the size and prominence of Hut Γ at *Troulli*, House 3 at *Kouphovounos* (56 m²), or House 22 at *Nissia* with its commanding position atop the hillock, its size and its rich artefact assemblage. Although most archaeologists still regard the architectural, spatial and material indices of the CN as consistent with those of an egalitarian society, such differences as these may point to some level of asymmetric social relationships (Peltenburg 1993: 9, 11; Feinman and Neitzel 1984: 72–77).

Compared with other CN sites, Kalavasos *Kokkinoyia* may seem peculiar, but perhaps less so when considered alongside the chamber and tunnel complexes at CN Philia *Drakos* A and nearby, Early Chalcolithic Kalavasos *Ayious* (see next chapter). Although *Kokkinoyia* does not appear to be distinctive in either social or ideological terms (cf. Clarke 2007b: 23), in considering its function and purpose it is instructive to consider research carried out on cave sites in the Neolithic Aegean (Tomkins 2009, with further refs.). Usually thought to have served some domestic purpose, the stratigraphic and micromorphological records of these cave sites suggest more episodic activities. At the same time, many cave sequences present good evidence for deep continuity in practice and deposition. The use span of caves tends to be analogous to that of pits or ditches, with alternating episodes of deposition and hiatus. Natural features such as niches, passages, chambers, and so forth. were exploited as a means of separating and structuring activities such as deposition, ritual or burial (Karkanas 2006).

The main constructed features in Aegean caves are hearths, pits and surfaces; the occasional occurrence of walls usually demarcates a simple division of space within or just outside of a cave. The diversity of material found in Aegean Neolithic caves – groundstone tools, obsidian blades and debitage, domesticated animals, shell beads, and so on – is probably not indicative of production activities but rather represents items that had a different biography before deposition (Tomkins 2009: 143–144). Burials are rare (Franchthi and Alepotrypa caves are the best known), and depositions, whether material or skeletal, were often left exposed, sometimes for long periods; at other times, they were reorganised or wholly or partly removed. In these respects, caves seem comparable to pits or other subterranean features left open to repeated access. Tomkins (2009: 136–137) argues that such sub-surface, hidden contexts may have served for ritualised deposition. Neolithic Aegean caves might also have been frequented because of their liminal position in relation to habitational or other resources, or even their neutrality, which would have made them suitable sites for communal gatherings (Nakou 1995: 21–22) devoted to exchange (social or economic), negotiating status or forging new relationships and identities.

If we consider some of these factors associated with Neolithic Aegean caves in relation to the pit-like features, chamber and tunnel complex, hollows, and the structure from CN *Kokkinoyia*, together with its lack of faunal or botanical remains, we might suggest (not unlike the excavator) that this site was used mainly for specific episodes and deposition, or storage, carried out over the long term. Features such as the niches, passages and chambers could have been used to separate and structure activities, ritual or otherwise, that required repeated access. Nonetheless, the diversity of materials found at *Kokkinoyia* – including an intact human burial, the usual range of pottery types, a blade-based chipped stone assemblage, a large cache of expedient groundstone objects, a few personal ornaments (serpentinite figurine fragment, cross-hatched piece of sandstone), two triton shells and an ochre-encrusted stone – would not be out of place in a settlement context.

Excepting the absence of bone tools, and botanical and floral data, what we see is a range of material associated with everyday practices: storage, consumption and deposition are clear, even if evidence for production is not. McCartney (in Clarke 2007a: 87) feels that the pit and tunnel complexes at both *Kokkinoyia* and Philia *Drakos* A may well have been used for planned storage. Finally, it must be noted that Cyprus can be extremely hot in summer, and it is not inconceivable that the people who lived and worked in or around *Kokkinoyia* chose to do so underground, at least during the hotter months of the year. As Todd et al. (in Todd and Croft 2004: 216) have noted: 'In various parts of the world resort has been made to subterranean features or rock-cut chambers purely on the grounds of ease of construction, and the desire to avoid the heat above ground'.

Unlike the situation in the preceding LAN, the mortuary record of the CN is meagre. Although, prima facie, there is no relevant evidence from *Vrysi*, Peltenburg (2003b: 108–113) has suggested that the numerous intact objects found on the floors of certain structures – themselves overlain by thick, sterile deposits – represent deliberate acts that resemble ethnographically documented closure ceremonies. In his view, these ceremonies would have followed the death of an important occupant '...who was buried outside his/her building but whose objects were largely retained in what then became a memorial' (Peltenburg 2003b: 117). Such abandonment events (Tomka and Stevenson 1993) may be seen as a key part of funerary rites, whilst the objects sealed under the sterile deposits could be regarded as foundation deposits for replicate houses built atop metaphoric tombs for the ancestors. In this scenario, CN houses ended their use life by becoming memorials for the dead (cenotaphs), whilst the new structures built over them came to symbolise renewal and continuity, establishing genealogies in which notions of individuals' identities were embedded.

Papaconstantinou (2010: 32–35) points out that the life histories of different structures at *Vrysi* reveal more than one type of abandonment and/ or discard practice, including short resurfacing episodes, partial collapse, and continuous, indistinguishable layers of occupation with no sign of sterile fills. Indeed, she demonstrates that abandonment processes vary from floor to floor within single structures. Nonetheless, she agrees with Peltenburg that all these processes were intentional, and that terminating the life cycle of a house reflects a symbolic connection to its occupants and therefore to their death. The links between materiality (in the CN case, architecture and pottery – see Clarke 2001; 2003), mortuary practices and identity thus seem clear, especially in the relationship between objects (sealed under floors), accelerated notions of possession and property, and the memorialisation of the dead.

At Sotira, excavations in an open area on the eastern slope of the settlement did produce 12 (mainly contracted) burials, all but one of which were adults. All of these were single primary inhumations that had been placed in simple pit graves dug into an ash, stone and animal bone midden, usually covered by stones and largely devoid of anything that could be considered grave goods (Niklasson 1991: 110–116). At *Kokkinoyia*, another intentionally built but very shallow pit contained an intact human burial of a subadult female with a stone placed beneath the skull (as in Graves 3 and 8 at Sotira) (Clarke 2007b: 21–22, fig. 10). Only at Kandou *Kouphovounos* is there evidence of intramural burials (one infant, one adult male) from a pit beneath a dwelling (Mantzourani 1997: 22–24, figs. 1–4). As Steel (2004a: 78–79) has noted, CN mortuary practices tended to remove the dead from any obvious contact with the living; this stands in stark contrast to LAN practices, where the dead were usually buried beneath the floors of houses where people lived, or had lived, or would live. This difference is fully in accord with Angel's (1961: 228) assessment of eight fragmentary skulls from Sotira: these individuals could not have come from the Khirokitia population (Harper 2008: 116).

McCartney (in Clarke 2007a: 89–90), basing her argument mainly on the continuities seen in chipped and groundstone materialities and practices, maintains that a strong Cypriot identity developed during the LAN in reaction to 'an external other', and that this situation continued into the CN (cf. Peltenburg 2004c: 83–84). Because signs of low volume exchange and/or sporadic contact between Cyprus and the mainland are evident, however minimally (Clarke 2010: 199), perhaps the notion of a closed, insular, Ceramic Neolithic culture should be re-evaluated. Even within the island, the highly localised access to picrolite in the southwestern part of the island, and its limited distribution elsewhere, suggest that the main lines of communication may have been along the coast rather than overland.

Whereas the sea has always formed part of everyday life on Cyprus, none of the coastal or near-coastal CN sites, except possibly *Nissia*, can be construed as an archetypal 'Mediterranean Fishing Village' (Galili et al. 2002; 2004; cf. McCartney, in Clarke 2007a: 87–88). On the one hand, such villages seem to have played a more crucial role in the lives of early seafaring people in both the Levant and on Cyprus during the Late Epipalaeolithic and Aceramic Neolithic periods. On the other hand, as McCartney emphasises, this model of the 'Mediterranean Fishing Village' offers an interpretative framework for understanding the evidence (e.g. obsidian, carnelian) of low-scale interaction between Cyprus and the rest of the eastern Mediterranean, as well as a selective adoption of ideas seen in the chipped stone technology (links with the southern Levant) and in pottery form and decoration (links with the central Levant).

Such links prompted McCartney (in Clarke 2007a: 84) to suggest that Cyprus was part of an exchange system extending over the greater part of the eastern Mediterranean seaboard. Summing it up, she stated: 'Cyprus need not be perceived as being quite so far off on the periphery as previously perceived but as [a] regular participant in a coastal *milieu*' (McCartney, in Clarke 2007a: 90). For the most part, and even though most scholars view the villages of the Ceramic Neolithic as being quite isolated, we have to assume that there was always some movement of people, as well as an exchange of goods and ideas. As new practices were incorporated into traditional ways of doing things, society became transformed at some level, however minimal that may seem in comparison with the material and social changes seen on Cyprus during the subsequent Chalcolithic and Bronze Ages.

The End of the Ceramic Neolithic

On the basis of the radiocarbon dates currently available (Appendix, Table A1B, section on Ceramic Neolithic), and recalling their problematic nature, the Ceramic Neolithic could have flourished, at a maximum, from about 5200/5000–4100/4000 Cal BC. It must be emphasised, however, that we lack secure evidence for occupation from ca. 5200/5000 Cal BC to around 4600/4400 Cal BC. The few new radiocarbon dates available (Clarke 2007a: 17–22) do not really help to resolve broader social issues relating to the beginning or the end of the CN: collapse and/or abandonment, settlement discontinuity, the possible influx of new refugees, and so on. We do seem to have a continuous radiocarbon chronology for the transition between the CN and the Early Chalcolithic (Peltenburg et al. 2003: 259–260 and fig. 24.1; Clarke 2007a: 17–21, figs. 2.3–2.4; see also Appendix, and SOM). With the likely exceptions of Kalavasos *Kokkinoyia* or *Pamboules*, however, no site from the end of the CN sequence shows developments that might be seen as forerunners of the distinctive material elements – including the reversion to curvilinear structures – of the following Early Chalcolithic. Older excavations reveal several occupational phases followed by abandonment, while surveys have detected very few sites that might possibly span the Ceramic Neolithic–Chalcolithic juncture.

On the basis of a destruction level at Sotira *Teppes* (Dikaios 1961: 209), it has long been assumed that an earthquake or a series of quakes struck the southern reaches of Cyprus, forcing villagers to abandon their homes and move to subterranean ('squatter') settlements. This time-worn view about earthquake activity as the mechanism that brought an end to the CN, forcing those who survived to live in the subterranean dwellings of the Early Chalcolithic period (the most persuasive discussion is that of Held 1992a: 122), needs to be revised.

Peltenburg's view (in Peltenburg et al. 2003: 257, 273, fig. 24.4) is quite different: '…the dynamics of demographic expansion resulted in the establishment of new settlement patterns, ones that initially involved recourse to timber structures and that consequently lead to less archaeological visibility in the major lacunae' (in the CN–Early Chalcolithic settlement record). The cyclical, three-stage model on which he bases his scenario is as follows (Peltenburg 1993: 16–17):

Stage 1) relatively homogeneous settlement plan ('managed inequalities'), as seen in the early stages at *Vrysi* and Sotira 1 (Stanley Price's phasing)

Stage 2) hierarchically organised settlement plan ('intensified inequalities'), as seen in late stages at *Vrysi* and Sotira 3

Stage 3) abandonment and settlement relocation, or hiatus followed by reoccupation, as seen in the apparent abandonment of both *Vrysi* and Sotira.

In this model, it is assumed that population increased throughout Stages 1 and 2, that differential wealth developed within the expanding communities of Stage 2, and that this unequal wealth lead to social instability and the fissioning or fragmentation of the community into (once again) smaller units during Stage 3 (Peltenburg 1993: 10–12).

In other words, we might reconsider the end of the CN and the transition to the Chalcolithic in terms of some level of settlement dislocation and the shifting nature of settlement. Moreover, there is the likelihood of emerging social differentiation as well as the possibility of environmental deterioration (deforestation, degraded soils) (Peltenburg 1993; Todd et al., in Todd and Croft 2004: 216–217; Clarke 2007a: 118, 122). The problem remains, however, that most scenarios devised to explain the demise of CN society on Cyprus are unverifiable. For example, there is no persuasive supporting evidence to demonstrate that either an earthquake or environmental deterioration was responsible for the cultural retrenchment (i.e. the renewed use of circular architecture; the alleged settlement contraction) associated with the end of the CN and the transition to the Early Chalcolithic (Peltenburg et al. 2003: 272). Earthquakes tend to have a very localised effect, and there is no palaeoclimatic evidence for drought, significant climate change or any other catastrophic factor. The only possible exception is the evidence from (Early Chalcolithic) Kalavasos *Ayious*, where there is some evidence for the depletion or loss of the fertile *terra rossa* and related soils as a result of human impact on the landscape (Todd et al., in Todd and Croft 2004: 217).

The emphasis placed on the change from substantial, stone-foundation, subrectangular houses to pits or subterranean dwellings (Kalavasos *Kokkinoyia*, *Pamboules* and *Ayious*) may also be misleading, as the recurrence of postholes and structural elements made of mudbrick or *pisé* are common features of post-frame wooden buildings, well attested not only at Chalcolithic Kissonerga *Mylouthkia* (Croft and Thomas, in Peltenburg et al. 2003: 117–132) and Kalavasos *Ayious* (Todd et al., in Todd and Croft 2004: 214–215) but also at CN Kalavasos *Kokkinoyia* (Clarke 2004; 2009: 43–44).

As is the case during all periods of Cypriot prehistory, we need to re-examine events within Cyprus on their own terms, not just presume they resulted from migrations, invasions or 'cultural involution'. In order to continue doing so, let us now consider in more detail the material developments of the Chalcolithic, one of the most dynamic periods in all of Cypriot prehistory.

CHAPTER 5

LATER PREHISTORIC CYPRUS: CHALCOLITHIC–LATE CHALCOLITHIC

EARLY–MIDDLE CHALCOLITHIC

Transition to the Early Chalcolithic

The Early–Middle Chalcolithic periods, or Erimi Culture, lasted from ca. 4000/3900–2700 Cal BC (see Appendix, Table A2, and further discussion on the transition between the CN and Early Chalcolithic). Although not all scholars would agree (see below), the passage from the CN to the Early Chalcolithic may be seen as a fairly rapid, indigenous process, one in which there was widespread abandonment, dislocation or fissioning of settlements (Peltenburg 1993). Although we still need a better definition and more nuanced understanding of the economic and social factors (the 'levelling mechanisms') that lay behind settlement discontinuity and communal fissioning (Steel 2004a: 82), from this point onward we find several new or revitalised trends in the material record. Held (1992a: 122) even suggests that '…many of the new features [are] recognizable as cognates of earlier SCU [Sotira Culture, i.e. CN] traits'.

Pre-eminent amongst these features, and continuing developments already seen in the CN, are the evolving tradition in Red-on-White pottery with its new design elements, and a proliferation of regional pottery styles and new pottery fabrics (such as Glossy Burnished Ware); some changes in the ground-stone technology but few in the chipped stone; more intensive use of blue-green picrolite; and a declining importance of deer in the subsistence diet. Amongst the more prominent, new features of the Chalcolithic (Bolger 1988) are the prevalence of curvilinear architecture (vs. the sub-rectangular architecture of the CN) and new uses of internal space, and the manufacture of elaborate stone bowls. By the Middle Chalcolithic (ca. 3600/3400–2700 Cal BC), further innovations may be seen in the use of communal storage facilities (Kissonerga *Mosphilia*); a variety of carved picrolite figurines, beads and pendants; strikingly new (often gender-based) symbolic and ideological conventions; and increasingly complex levels of social organisation (Held 1992a: 122–123; Peltenburg 1997; Bolger 2003: 102–105). Equally important, during the Middle Chalcolithic, we find the earliest, very limited occurrence of cold-hammered copper objects (Peltenburg 2011a: 3–7, fig. 1.1).

New, Early Chalcolithic settlements such as Kissonerga *Mylouthkia* were characterised by (partly) sunken pits and hollows surrounded by postholes. These likely represent post-frame superstructures, with floors that held various fittings (e.g. hearths, pottery vessels, plaster-lined basins), in many respects similar to their CN counterparts (Thomas, in Peltenburg et al. 2003: 123–124). In contrast with the household based society of the CN, the preparation, storage and consumption of food, including feasting, have been argued to represent communal activities during the Early Chalcolithic (see further below, *Ritual and Feasting*) (Peltenburg et al. 1998: 240, 243). In the following Middle Chalcolithic period, however, such factors are thought to be more indicative of individual practices.

The mortuary record presents another contrast with the CN, as most Chalcolithic burials are closely associated with buildings. Otherwise, the burial practices of the two periods show some similarities: inhumations oriented in cardinal directions and in flexed or crouched positions, placed in simple pits without grave goods (Peltenburg 1982a: 53). At the (Middle Chalcolithic) mortuary complex of Souskiou in the southwest, however, we find for the first time in the Cypriot archaeological record cemeteries (*Vathyrkakas, Laona*) physically separated by some distance from the parent settlement, as well as multiple burials placed in deep shaft graves (Peltenburg 2006) (see further below, *Mortuary Practices*).

In the realm of subsistence, there was a gradual decline in the importance of hunting, and a growing reliance on herding and agricultural practices. Deer continued to contribute a significant proportion of the islanders' overall meat supply, but there was a steady fall-off in its consumption relative to pigs and ovicaprines, from as much as 86% in the Early Chalcolithic to as little as 41% in the Late Chalcolithic (Croft 1991: 71, table 3). Deer continued to be the most prominent hunted animal but its declining importance may reflect the growing nutritional demands of an expanding population, and/or increased ceremonial activity involving domesticated animals. The decline in deer consumption was offset by the growing importance of pig in the diet, from as low as 22% in the Early–Middle Chalcolithic to as high as 49% in the Late Chalcolithic (even if some of these remains represent hunted feral animals). Ovicaprines never became a major component of the diet, seldom amounting to more than 10% of the total meat supply (Croft 1991: 71, table 3). Palaeobotanical evidence shows the usual array of cereals (emmer, einkorn, breadwheat, barley), legumes (lentils, vetch, chickpea), wild grasses and fruits (olive, grape, fig, pistachio, juniper berries and capers) (Murray, in Peltenburg et al. 1998: 216, table 11.1).

In terms of social organisation, the mortuary sites of *Vathyrkakas* (Peltenburg 2006) and *Laona* (Crewe et al. 2005) near Souskiou village are exceptional, even with respect to their location – near the edge of a rocky plateau and very narrow ravine in the Dhiarizos River valley. The ravine separates the *Vathyrkakas* cemeteries from the *Laona* settlement on the hillside opposite. With zoomorphic and anthropomorphic vessels, bone pendants, picrolite cruciform figurines and pendants, and copper ornaments, the burials at Souskiou *Vathyrkakas* and *Laona* are thought to represent the development of lineages or families with high social status (Manning 1993). Although one may question whether Chalcolithic sites in general have yielded any real evidence for social hierarchy or a decision-making authority, the distinctive Chalcolithic structures at Kissonerga *Mosphilia* do seem to suggest some structural changes in society (Peltenburg 1991a) (see further below – *Incipient Complexity, Ideology and Identity in the Early–Middle Chalcolithic*).

At the very least, the Souskiou burials hint at social, economic, perhaps even ideological changes unprecedented on prehistoric Cyprus. Much the same is indicated by the prominence of picrolite cruciform figurines or pendants, and other anthropomorphic stone or pottery figurines. The whole notion of a cruciform figure with an elongated neck may represent an attempt at harmonising (or integrating) the sexual characteristics of men and women, if not other genders. The variability amongst Chalcolithic figurines also suggests that they are representations of individual people. Despite the contentiousness of this issue, which presents major challenges to prehistoric archaeologists working anywhere, the Cypriot evidence suggests that we can indeed access individuals in material culture (Knapp and Meskell 1997; Knapp and van Dommelen 2008), thus finding new ways of understanding the body, sexuality and sexual difference.

Spatial Organisation and Settlements: Early Chalcolithic

During the Chalcolithic period, settlement on Cyprus expanded considerably, with at least 125 known sites – and another 48 with material indicators of both the CN and Early Chalcolithic periods (Held 1992a: 122–123). Site location became much more diverse, especially in the island's south and southwest, and the most important excavated settlements – Erimi *Pamboula*, Kissonerga *Mylouthkia* and *Mosphilia*, Lemba *Lakkous* – were all long-lived (for site locations, see above, Figure 37). The site of Ranti *Asprokremmos*, located between Erimi and (modern) Kouklia in the Ranti Forest, is another Early–Middle Chalcolithic site known only from survey work (McCartney 2000: 38–44); it is situated on a prominent hilltop near good chert and two water sources (a seasonal river and a tributary). Sites in other areas of the island are also known mainly from surface survey (Nicolaou 1967; Stanley Price 1979a; Held 1992b; Given and Knapp 2003: 192–197; 265–266), or from small-scale excavations at several of the following, none of which add substantively to the general picture presented below: in the north, Lapithos (Gjerstad et al. 1934: 19–33), Kythrea (Gjerstad et al. 1934: 277–301), Karavas and Ayios Epiktitos *Mezarlik*

(Dikaios 1936: 73–74); in the centre, Nicosia *Ayios Prodhromos* (Dikaios 1935: 12; Nicolaou 1967: 49–50); and in the western *Mesaoria*, Philia *Drakos* Site B, Kyra *Alonia* and Ambelikou *Ayios Georghios* (Dikaios 1962: 141–55). It should be noted that the last three sites have produced material assemblages very similar to those recently excavated at Politiko *Kokkinorotsos* (Webb et al. 2009: 203–205), a site whose radiocarbon dates suggest that it belongs to the very late Middle Chalcolithic, or in a time transitional to the Late Chalcolithic (Webb et al. 2009: see Appendix, caption to Figure A10); in this study *Kokkinorotsos* is treated as part of the earliest Late Chalcolithic period.

The concomitant, steady increase in population along the north coast, in the centre and perhaps even more rapidly in the southwest, is regarded as an aspect of regionalism. If regional social groups (i.e. 'factions') actually existed, we should see variability in the ways that people as well as their material remains were distributed across the island, during all phases of the Chalcolithic, in *spatial* terms. Yet this possibility exists for the most part only in the southwest, where a long-term field enterprise (Lemba Archaeological Project, University of Edinburgh) has carried out an impressive program of excavation and survey over the past 25 years. The notion that Chalcolithic society on Cyprus was broken up into distinct regional groups has long determined how archaeologists think about change and continuity, and how they try to resolve chronological discrepancies. Even if regional factions existed, we must question the notion that pottery is the most important indicator of prehistoric cultural development or change: some pottery styles change through time and space, while others develop much more slowly through time but very rapidly in different places. As Bolger (1987: 75) noted long ago: '…we should recognize the limitations of pottery as a barometer of cultural unity'; other artefactual and bioarchaeological evidence must be brought to bear if we are to understand the '…seemingly erratic patterns of emergence and subsidence of regionalism as a factor in the evolution of Chalcolithic society'. In other words, we would do better to devote equal attention to the total material record.

The most significant change seen in the Early Chalcolithic sites in the south and west of the island is the use of semi-subterranean activity areas with insubstantial features. It is a matter of opinion whether people actually lived in these partly sunken pits and hollows. There are differences as well as broad similarities between Early Chalcolithic features at Kalavasos *Ayious* and *Pamboules* in the south, and the sites of Kissonerga *Mylouthkia* and Maa *Palaeokastro* in the west (Todd and Croft 2004: 220–222). At *Ayious*, for example, pits are relatively small and deep with horizontal work surfaces; at *Mylouthkia* there are mainly wide depressions with sloping surfaces; at Maa *Palaeokastro* the few pits that exist tend to be broad and shallow. The diverse array and different types of pits that occur on all excavated Early Chalcolithic sites probably indicate multiple functions, beyond the obvious ones of storage or discard. Not unlike its CN predecessor (*Kokkinoyia*) in the same area, *Ayious* also has a pit and tunnel complex, and there is no reason to develop alternative explanations for it: planned storage, consumption and deposition, if not periodic habitation almost certainly cover the possible functions of these sites.

Current radiocarbon evidence places the time span of occupation at *Ayious* from ca. 3853±87–3654±184 Cal BC (citing the μ±σ) or perhaps up to a maximum of 50 years later, if allowance is made for an old-wood effect (since all dates are on 'charcoal'; see Appendix Model 8 and SOM for details; see also Todd and Croft 2004: 219). Situated on the eastern side of the Vasilikos valley in an area of high ground, just over 2 km southeast of Kalavasos village (and about 900 m from *Kokkinoyia*), *Ayious* is a very distinctive site, characterised by its wide shallow depressions, a pit and tunnel complex, and more than 100 pits, varying in form from large and deep to small and shallow. The largest have diameters ranging from 1.5–2.75 m, with a maximum depth of 2.2 m (Todd and Croft 2004: 9). Medium-sized pits, around 1 m in diameter and about 30 cm deep, were often filled with lumps of diabase and a few groundstone objects in an ashy matrix; some of these were almost certainly hearths, given evidence of burning and the fire-cracked stones found in them. There are also several bell-shaped pits, 1–2 m deep and quite regular in shape, perhaps used for grain storage (Todd and Croft 2004: 10). There are no standing architectural remains, but evidence for a light superstructure may be seen in the occasional lines of stake holes found in association with pits (Todd and Croft 2004: 10), or in the stones carefully placed in the centre of some pits, perhaps to support central posts for roofing (Clarke 2007a: 122). Todd (1981: 61) noted long ago that 'some slight depressions in the ground may have belonged to structures almost all traces of which have now been erased'. Steel (2004a: 84) suggests that Early Chalcolithic structures would have been made of timber and/or wattle and daub, whilst some pits and hollows may have been used as shelters, if not dwellings.

Amongst many features revealed in the excavations at *Ayious*, a pit and tunnel complex in the northwestern part of the site had two sub-circular shaped pits (25, 27) connected by a low, narrow tunnel. Another tunnel ran from the base of Pit 27 to the small pit (Feature 111.1) that formed a stepped entrance to the entire complex (Todd and Croft 2004: 10, 25–29, figs. 6, 9) (Figure 50). 'Porthole'-like constrictions in each stretch of the tunnels would have impeded movement, as would several distinct changes of angle. In addition, gypsum slabs seem to have been designed to block the portholes. Quite why it was thought necessary to make access and movement so difficult is hard to understand, especially if we consider the amount of labour invested in digging out the complex in the first place, or its contents (fill): potsherds, some chipped stone tools, groundstone artefacts and some 31 ceramic anthropomorphic figurines and fragments.

The largest number (12) of the figurines just mentioned came from the Pit 25 complex, whilst 7 were found in the Feature 129 complex. Because all of

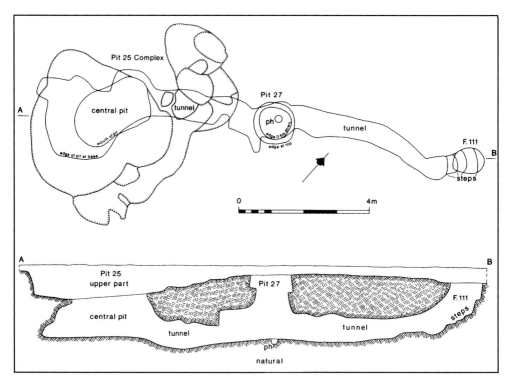

Figure 50. Kalavasos *Ayious* pit and tunnel complex. After Todd and Croft 2004: 10, 25–29, fig. 9. Courtesy of the Cyprus Museum, Nicosia.

them were found either in the bell-shaped pits or in the large hollows associated with deeper pits, South (in Todd and Croft 2004: 193) suggested that their deposition was not random. Whilst others have implied a ritual or religious function for the pits based on varying concentrations of (broken) figurines (e.g. Peltenburg 1989: 113; Steel 2004a: 85), the excavators felt it more likely that their distribution was associated with taphonomic factors (Todd and Croft 2004: 26). Alternatively, South (in Todd and Croft 2004: 193) proposed that the broken figurines might have been dumped into the pits as debris from nearby structures where they had been in use. These figurines and fragments are discussed in more detail below (*Gender and the Individual Body*).

The Early Chalcolithic levels at Kissonerga *Mylouthkia* (periods 2 and 3) have been radiocarbon-dated to the mid-4th millennium BC (from ca. 3641±62–3390±113 Cal BC, citing the μ±σ – see Appendix Model 8 and SOM), slightly later than *Ayious* (Peltenburg et al. 2003: 257–260, fig. 24.1). *Mylouthkia* is a severely eroded site situated very close to the sea and just north of modern-day Paphos on the southwest coast. The Chalcolithic component of the site (EAN wells at the site are discussed in Chapter 3) is limited to an area covering some 200 × 250 m, honeycombed with pits and evidence of likely post-frame structures. In these respects *Mylouthkia* is quite similar to *Ayious*, but the pits of *Mylouthkia* have different shapes – squarish in outline, or shallow concave hollows – and there are no tunnels or tunnel complexes. Whereas the *Ayious* pits have some horizontal surfaces (living areas? activity spaces?), those at *Mylouthkia* are generally sloping. The exception is Pit 1, a large (ca. 7 m in diameter), irregular hollow roughly circular in shape, whose horizontal earthen floor and succession of features in five phases – including possible human burials – indicate that it was used at least occasionally as an activity area (Peltenburg et al. 2003: 261–262 and table 24.3).

Different pits at *Mylouthkia* seem to have had different types of fill, and so perhaps different usages. In Pit 16, for example, finds such as bone needles and points, antler beads and debitage, groundstone spouted bowls, mortars and pounders, ochre-stained stones and jugs, and unfinished axes and adzes may represent craft debris and/or a household midden (Peltenburg et al. 2003: 264–266 and table 24.4). Pit 300, like Pit 1, had several possible surface areas, but more importantly the Pit 300/Building 200 stratigraphic sequence reveals the successive development from a pit to semi-subterranean post-frame structure to a mud-walled Chalcolithic round house with stone foundations (Peltenburg et al. 2003: figs. 40–42; cf. pp. 123–132, where two of the team disagree on the details of this sequence).

Building 200 at *Mylouthkia* contained an impressive quantity and wide variety of material, from pottery and chipped stone to faunal remains (largely deer and pig), charcoal and charred seeds (Peltenburg et al. 1998: 239–240, fig. 14.2; 2003: 264, table 24.4, 267–268, fig. 24.2). In addition to 200 classified objects, there were more than 1,000 pieces of chipped stone, the debitage from working deer antler, dozens of flat pebbles, 40 axes and adzes, antler and dentalium beads, and much more. Building 200 must have served multiple functions, with a much greater concentration of objects than expected from a single household assemblage. The spatial divisions seen in the distribution of artefacts, however, are not significantly different from those proposed for other, conventional, Middle Chalcolithic 'houses' (Peltenburg et al. 2003: 269, fig. 24.3a–d).

The excavator is rightly indecisive: Building 200 represents either a structure that symbolised the prestige and success of a group of elders within the community, or the main room of an extended household (Peltenburg et al. 2003: 271–272). Building 200 ultimately was destroyed by fire and, intriguingly, the burnt level contained the partially charred remains of a six- to eight-year-old child (plus all the objects and materials already noted). The badly preserved remains of the child came to rest in Building 200 at some point soon after the start of this destruction event. If the child was a victim of the fire (rather than an intentional burial), then its remains have little to tell us about Early Chalcolithic mortuary rites. In any case the child's remains, along with all the usable objects that surrounded them in the destruction level, were abandoned after the fire, as was the rest of the settlement; there was no reoccupation.

At Maa *Palaeokastro*, a promontory jutting into the sea just a few kilometres north of *Mylouthkia*, the lack of radiometric evidence, and the more equivocal nature of the usual array of groundstone tools and vessels (axes, adzes, grinders, rubbers, pestles, cupped stones) meant that the excavators had to rely solely on ceramic evidence for dating. Chalcolithic pottery from Maa bears a close resemblance to the Early Chalcolithic assemblages at both *Ayious* and *Mylouthkia* (Bolger, in Karageorghis and Demas 1988: 290–300). Both technically and stylistically, and in the repertoire of vessels shapes, this pottery seems to belong to the earliest phase of the Chalcolithic (e.g. a bridge, trough-spouted bowl similar to those found at Sotira *Teppes* and with direct parallels at *Ayious* – Karageorghis and Demas 1988: 293, 299, fig. 2.1).

Chalcolithic finds at the site are largely restricted to Area III, where the only in situ material was found; large pits in Area I, Courtyard A, also contain some secondary material (Thomas, in Karageorghis and Demas 1988: 282–288). In fact, large open hollows such as Pits C (Unit 61) and G (Unit 48) are very similar to those found at *Ayious* and *Mylouthkia*, and provide the most secure evidence for Early Chalcolithic occupation at Maa. Cuttings for the foundation of a later, Bronze Age building (IV) produced the remains of two bell-shaped pits covered by a layer of reddish soil, in which Chalcolithic material was also found. Three features at the site – Units 1, 3 (Pit K) and 67 (Pit J) – were tentatively classified as tombs, but only on morphological grounds as no skeletal evidence was found in them (Karageorghis and Demas 1988: 269–272, figs. 2–4). Units 1 and 3 are in form very similar to Late Chalcolithic chambered tombs at Kissonerga *Mosphilia* and Kalavasos *Kokkinoyia* (Karageorghis and Demas 1988: 286–287), but this does not prove they had a mortuary nature. Pit J, at least, contains some material in its fill (several broken stone bowl fragments, a female figurine fragment) that might be regarded as grave goods.

From the extreme southeast corner of the excavated area came the remnants of another feature (Unit 69), with five–six irregular postholes delimiting about half its extent (4–4.5 m in diameter) (Karageorghis and Demas 1988: 268, fig. 1, 272–273) (Figure 51). Alongside its counterparts at *Ayious* and *Mylouthkia*, these remnants have been reconstructed as a circular timber (i.e. post-frame) building. Oddly, however, this building (if such it was) contains within it another, much smaller circular feature (Unit 37), consisting of a rock-cut channel, with a series of stake holes on either side of the channel along its entire, approximately 60 m circumference (Karageorghis and Demas 1988: 279, fig. 10). Overall, the Early Chalcolithic remains at Maa are few and problematic, but the limited number of artefacts and pottery recovered are not inconsistent with a small domestic farmstead or similar habitation established during Cyprus's earliest Chalcolithic.

Some 1 km south-southwest of *Mylouthkia* lies the site of Kissonerga *Mosphilia*. Like its neighbour, it is situated on the coastal plain in the Ktima lowlands, some 6 km north of modern-day Paphos. Three radiocarbon dates available for the Early Chalcolithic at *Mosphilia* form an inconsistent set (two of the three yield poor agreement index values in Model 1 in the Appendix – one

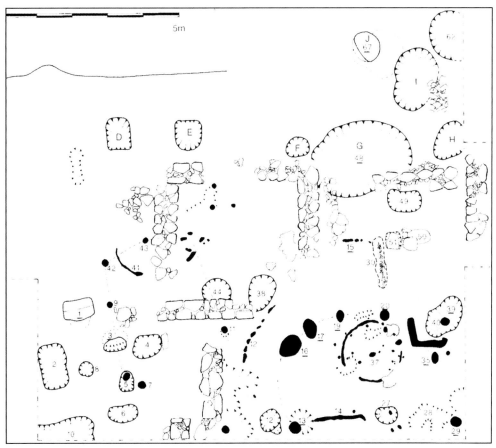

Figure 51. Maa *Palaeokastro* Early Chalcolithic Unit 69 (lower right), perhaps the remains of a circular timber (i.e. post-frame) building; five–six irregular postholes delimit nearly half its extent (4–4.5 m in diameter). After Karageorghis and Demas 1988: 268, fig. 1.

too old, one too recent). The sole remaining date in Model 8 supports an overall (non-modelled) range of 3973–3797 Cal BC at 1σ, while Model 8 places Period 2 ca. 3863±88–3627±160 Cal BC, citing the μ±σ (see Appendix and SOM; see also Peltenburg et al. 1998: 16–17, fig. 2.7), some 200–400 years earlier than the more coherent set at *Mylouthkia* (already mentioned above). The earliest architectural evidence occurs on *Mosphilia*'s 'Upper Terrace', and consists of three curvilinear hollows (Buildings 2178–2180) with a peripheral setting of posts that may have supported a covering of some sort (Peltenburg et al. 1998: 24, 240–241). Building 2178 is described as a work hollow whilst 2179–2180 are thought to be living hollows. Amongst the 73 intra-settlement burials discovered at *Mosphilia*, one notable pit grave (554) – an inhumation covered by an anthropomorphic stone slab, and a piece of malachite (one of the earliest known on the island) placed in bivalve shell – belongs to the Early Chalcolithic (Peltenburg 1991b: 21, fig. 3).

Despite their ephemeral nature, the size (ca. 12 m², Building 2180), sub-circular plan and spatial layout seem well in line with the stone-based buildings and plans of the later, Middle Chalcolithic period, both here and elsewhere. Although the floors held pottery bowls, needles, beads, a figurine and an unworked picrolite pebble, there were neither internal fixtures nor any evidence of large-scale storage within or near these hollows. Food processing and cooking equipment (rubbers, pounders, cupped stones, stone bowl fragments), however, were found in several pits outside these hollows. Furthermore, some odd-shaped pits like those around Building 2178 may have been used to store processed crops (Peltenburg et al. 1998: 240–241). Presuming that these pits served for large-scale, communal, bulk storage (between 10.5 and 16.1 m³) seems a reasonable, if unverifiable assumption. But to infer from presumed bulk storage capacity an estimated village population of 25–50 people, living in 10–27 structures the size of Building 2180 (=12 m²), people who had placed some 25–40 ha of the surrounding landscape under cultivation, which ultimately '… made an initial major impact on the prehistoric landscape' (Peltenburg et al. 1998: 241), puts more of a strain on the available evidence than it can bear.

THE (EARLY–MIDDLE) CHALCOLITHIC HOUSE(HOLD)
The Early Chalcolithic period witnessed an expansion of settlement (especially in the southwest), the beginnings of an enduring circular or curvilinear building form with a discernible interior spatial layout, and continuing developments in the exploitation, production and distribution of picrolite (used in the Early Chalcolithic to manufacture three of four anthropomorphic figurines found at Kissonerga *Mylouthkia* – Peltenburg et al. 2003: 170–171). Evidence from *Mylouthkia* indicates that Building 200 was a long-lived structure; pits at the site were both contemporary with and preceded post-frame structures, which in turn were succeeded by mud-built round houses with stone foundations (Clarke 2007a: 124). At nearby *Mosphilia*, the same development from timber (post-frame) to stone-based structure is clearly seen (Peltenburg et al. 1998: 240–243). Finally, at contemporary (if slightly later) Erimi *Pamboula*, there seems to have been a similar sequence: a depression cut into bedrock contained the floors and postholes of two lightly built, circular structures (Dikaios 1962: 113–115, fig. 57; Todd and Croft 2004: 222).

Clarke (2007a: 124–126) sees a major technological and cultural change in the development from possible pit dwellings to sturdier post-frame structures to curvilinear buildings with stone built foundations. She suggests that climatic deterioration may have led to deep changes in social practices, namely the shift to a more mobile existence based on hunting, with the concomitant transition to less complex building methods and the construction of pits to store collected food for use during the winter months.

By contrast, Peltenburg (in Peltenburg et al. 2003: 272–275) finds no palaeo-climatic evidence around 4000 Cal BC to substantiate such transformations in human behaviour, and instead sees these developments as a practical solution

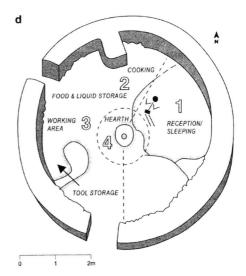

Figure 52. Chalcolithic house layout. After Peltenburg et al. 2003: 266–272 and fig. 24.3 d. Courtesy of Edgar Peltenburg.

to the emergence of new settlements in heavily wooded surroundings, and their eventual consolidation in stone. In his view, the extensive use of timber (assumed from the proliferation of axes and adzes at *Mylouthkia*) and the growth of arable farming practices (based on concentrations of querns in Building 152 at *Mylouthkia* as well as the rich palaeobotanical and molluscan evidence from the site) led to the extensive clearance of a gently sloping landscape, which in turn resulted in serious soil erosion. Such erosion can be seen in the sediment build-up inside and outside of various structures at *Mylouthkia*; it removed most traces of evidence for 'flimsy' post-frame structures. In order to deal with the problems caused by erosion, some people began using stones cleared from arable fields as a means to prevent ground water from affecting structural foundations. Thus, in Peltenburg's view, the major building innovation occurred in the use of timber, not in the stone that simply solidified the existing, curvilinear form. Peltenburg even suggests that many of the pits at *Mylouthkia* were dug as quarries for the mud, *havara* or daub used in these structures' walls.

The emergence of this long-lasting, curvilinear/circular building tradition – beginning in the Early/Middle Chalcolithic and lasting for well over 1,000 years, until the start of the Bronze Age – formed the context for new social practices that emerged during the Chalcolithic period. In Peltenburg's view, the most significant of these practices was the 'definitive materialisation of an ideology of the house' (Peltenburg et al. 2003: 274–275), with its recurring internal spatial divisions and opposing uses of space (Figure 52). The transformation from rectilinear to curvilinear buildings does not necessarily reflect more mobile, corporate societies (as opposed to settled, individualising ones). Rather the curvilinear, post-frame structures represent the consolidation phase of newly settled peoples, part of a wider process of settlement expansion in the Early Chalcolithic.

During Period 3 at *Mylouthkia* (ending no later than ca. 3300 Cal BC), there are signs of more permanency in the pottery (more formal aspects of commensality, varied types of food-processing and nascent intra-mural storage), perhaps even in the sphere of ideology (use of dentalium shell as bodily ornament). These and all the other changes evident in various material and ideological aspects of the Early Chalcolithic (e.g. increasing use of picrolite; greater focus on the house, or household) represent both the media as well as the outcome of social practices. Such practices may be seen as the harbingers of an increasing orientation around the individual in society (see below, under *Gender and the Individual Body*).

Spatial Organisation and Settlements: Middle Chalcolithic

During the Middle Chalcolithic era (ca. 3600/3400–2700 Cal BC), the budding curvilinear building form reached its zenith, whilst novel burial practices also emerged. Production across all sectors of material culture intensified, particularly with respect to picrolite, pottery and the earliest use of copper. There is much greater diversity than ever before not just in pottery types but also in a range of ornamental objects, especially representations of people. The best-known sites are still found in the island's southwest or southern coastal region, where large (3–15 ha) unwalled villages reveal sophisticated and substantial architectural remains, with some evidence that may reflect changes in social structure.

By and large, these villages seem to have shared a common culture, so some sort of social or other exchange relations must have existed amongst them. External relations, however, were still quite limited, and the only known imports (or, more precisely, non-native minerals) are small amounts of carnelian and obsidian. The calcite, marble and ivory (?) artefacts from *Ayious* noted by Todd (Todd and Croft 2004: 219) may be foreign but their origins are unclear. Likewise the exotic materials (chlorite, faience) noted at *Mosphilia* do not really form a sound basis for discussing 'the gradual breakdown of Cypriot insularity' (Peltenburg 1991b: 109). Whether or not this miniscule amount of foreign material should be seen as a continuing, intentional strategy of isolation associated with maintaining a unique island identity is considered further below.

One of the most distinctive developments of the Middle Chalcolithic is the organisation and further development of domestic space in the 'Chalcolithic house' (Peltenburg et al. 1998: 237–240, fig. 14.2; 2003: 266–272 and fig. 24.3 d) (Figure 52). In general, these structures were circular in plan, built of *pisé* on stone foundations, with plastered walls, a hearth in the centre and a roof supported by an interior ring of posts. Internal space was often divided – by means of distinctive partition ridges – into areas for working, storage, cooking, living and reception/sleeping. Burials associated with these structures typically were placed outside the walls, just beyond the living/sleeping area. Some houses contained special purpose, ceremonial areas near the hearth and close to the interface between the living and cooking areas (e.g. Building 994 at *Mosphilia*, discussed further below). Possible oppositions in the use of space may be seen in the sleeping/external burial zone versus an internal working and storage area, or in light (entry) and dark (cooking/food storage) zones, all seen as the expression of a cultural ideal that was sufficiently flexible for negotiating power in society (Peltenburg et al. 2003: 274).

Be that as it may, these new houses point to a renewed permanence in settled village life, one that now revolved more around individual households than the community at large (Steel 2004a: 89). This is perhaps best expressed in the relocation of (formerly communal?) storage and food preparation or consumption activities to the inside of structures. And, as we shall see, Middle Chalcolithic buildings contained a wide variety of material goods, from utilitarian tools to representations of the individuals who lived, worked and likely dined and/or feasted in at least some of these households.

An early locational analysis of Chalcolithic sites by Held (1992a: 138) noted steady population growth along the north coast and in the island's centre, alongside more rapid growth in the southwest and decline in the southeast. Having examined a range of Early–Middle Chalcolithic material (e.g. pottery, domestic architecture, spatial organisation, groundstone industry), Bolger (1987; 1988: 123–134) concluded that no distinctive western region could be identified for those periods; more recently she has suggested that local centres of stylistic production did exist during the Middle Chalcolithic. Held (1993: 28), however, felt that Early–Middle Chalcolithic settlements did not necessarily follow separate regional pursuits; rather communities tended to relocate, providing their inhabitants with access to new agricultural land in thoroughly familiar habitats. The best way to assess these views is to look more closely at the most important excavated settlements of the Middle Chalcolithic period: Kissonerga *Mosphilia* and *Mylouthkia*, Lemba *Lakkous*, Souskiou *Laona* and Erimi *Pamboula*, the last the type site for the Chalcolithic. There is also abundant evidence for examining mortuary practices in the settlement at *Mosphilia* and in the extra-mural cemeteries at Souskiou *Vathyrkakas* and *Laona*.

The site of Erimi *Pamboula* is situated at the northern edge of an alluvial plain, on the east bank of the Kouris River, some 20 km west of modern Limassol. Picrolite, a soft, pale green igneous rock and one of the most characteristic and ubiquitous materials used in craft production during the Chalcolithic, virtually litters the Kouris riverbed in the vicinity of *Pamboula* (Bolger 1988: 15; Xenophontos 1991; Swantek 2006: 4–5). Equally important for understanding the site's location was the abundant water supplied by the Kouris, something that dictated the establishment of sites throughout the river's watershed (Swiny 1981). *Pamboula* was first excavated during three field seasons in 1933–1935

(Dikaios 1936). When Bolger (1988: 1) relocated some of this excavated material in the Cyprus Museum during 1982, it became evident that a wide range of material from Erimi had not been published in the 1936 report, or in the later, revised publication of the site (Dikaios 1962: 113–132). Bolger undertook the task of publishing the newly discovered artefactual material and integrating it with other features at the site.

Dikaios assigned 13 layers to the site at Erimi: period 1 (the earlier) included levels 1–8, and period 2 levels 9–13. The architectural remains, however, were assigned three phases with four building types: Phase 1 (levels 1–4) contained curvilinear buildings outlined by postholes, partly sunk in the bedrock, very similar to the timber, post-frame type of construction noted in Early Chalcolithic buildings. In Phase 2 (levels 5–6), buildings with postholes in a circular pattern continued in use whilst others had a ring of pebbles that served as a foundation course for a light *pisé* superstructure. During Phase 3 (levels 7–13), all the curvilinear buildings had stone foundations (Dikaios 1962: 128; Bolger 1988: 28). These Phase 3 buildings contained many other new features: thresholds, two intercommunicating rooms, partitions (made with rows of small stones), hearths, platforms (workbenches?), and some paved clay areas. Because Dikaios never recorded the precise findspots of artefacts (he simply labelled them with level numbers), it is impossible to define any internal spatial divisions for different kinds of activities. Nonetheless, Bolger (1988: 29) observed that most cooking was done outdoors or in some of the small ancillary units of the two-roomed buildings (VIa, VIIa). In addition to interior finds of chipped stone and bone implements, assemblages of pottery and groundstone tools were found both within and outside of various buildings, perhaps in courtyards. A total of about 500 years is suggested for the duration of both cultural periods at Erimi *Pamboula* (Bolger 1988: 29).

Kissonerga *Mosphilia*, situated on gently sloping ground about 1 km from the present-day coast, is the largest (ca. 12 ha) in a cluster of lowland sites in the Ktima region dated to the Chalcolithic period (*Mylouthkia* is about 6 ha in size, Lemba *Lakkous* 3 ha). People seem to have occupied Early–Middle Chalcolithic (periods 2–4) *Mosphilia* for up to 1,000–1,500 years, within the range ca. 3863 ± 88–2541 ± 47 Cal BC (citing the $\mu \pm \sigma$ for the start and end boundaries from Model 8 in the Appendix; see SOM for details) – perhaps continuously, perhaps not. We are concerned here only with the two main, Middle Chalcolithic periods (3A, 3B). During Period 3A, structures with stone foundations were erected at the site, both in the Main Area (poorly built rectilinear buildings) and on the Upper Terrace (well-built curvilinear buildings). Unique amongst these were Building 1016 with its decorative white orthostats, and Ridge Building 1547, distinctively well constructed with formalised internal divisions of space and a red-tinted floor (Peltenburg et al. 1998: 241–242). Littered with local as well as non-local materials such as picrolite, mother-of-pearl, chalk, pig's teeth and spiny cockle, Building 1547 is regarded as a pendant-maker's workshop (Peltenburg et al. 1998: pl. 36: 7–10).

Successive pairs of structures on the Upper Terrace (e.g. Building 1547/1590, Building 1016/1565) contained hearths, well-demarcated living areas and at least eight discrete burials (including four extra-mural child burials). Interpreted as the domestic dwellings of high-status individuals, these buildings may also reflect the development of property rights and inheritance. Private storage areas (with large storage jars) were now built over earlier, communal (?) storage pits, and some burials were situated immediately outside these dwellings rather than at some distance from them (Peltenburg et al. 1998: 242–243, fig. 14.3). Buildings 1547 and 1016 both show decorative and ornamental features that presage those seen in *Mosphilia* Period 3B: accentuated spatial dividers, painted decoration, pure white plaster polished floors in living areas, walls decorated with white slabs, and large rectangular hearths. Living areas were clearly distinguished from storage or work areas, and the production of pottery (large numbers of bowls, for food presentation and consumption), pendants and ceramic/stone discs intensified, with increased diversity in most artefact types.

Even more significant developments took place at *Mosphilia* during Period 3B, when there are signs it may have become a centrally organised settlement. The Upper Terrace was deserted and the community moved to the Main Area, towards the sea. Settlement expansion is evident in the dramatic increase of roofed space at the site, and in the establishment of separate activity zones, most notably a ceremonial area characterised by its distinctive architectural forms and some of the largest buildings known on prehistoric Cyprus, up to 8.5 m in diameter with interiors up to 77 m² (Peltenburg 1991b: 21–22; Peltenburg et al. 1998: 243–245, fig. 14.5) (Figure 53). Above all, this area was distinguished by its prominent location on a low spur, between a paved track to the west and a ditch to the south, an open space to the east, and a formal approach ('courtyard') to the north, the whole overlooking the (Skotinis) stream below and the sea beyond.

The four structures grouped round this ceremonial area (Buildings 2, 4, 206, 1000 – the last of sub-rectangular form) were constructed of calcarenite (a stone likely transported from the coast nearly half a kilometre west). Spaces described as living rooms in these buildings were distinguished by thick plastered floors (Peltenburg et al. 1998: pl. 5.1), radial partition walls, rectangular hearths and, in Building 206, a red-painted floor and walls. Storage vessels, some of them boldly painted, represent the earliest known *pithoi* used on Cyprus. The excavator has suggested that communal feasting and ritual activities were carried out in the open area between these buildings (see further below, under *Ritual and Feasting*). Other, less substantial rectilinear buildings near the larger calcarenite structures may have served as more specialised units. At least two smaller, more basic contemporary structures (Buildings 494, 855) were situated

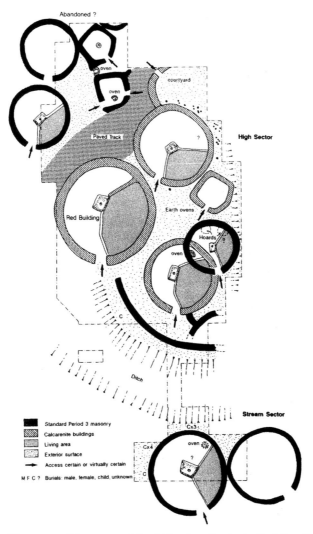

Figure 53. Kissonerga *Mosphilia* plan, Period 3B. After Peltenburg et al. 1998: 243–245, fig. 14.5. Courtesy of Edgar Peltenburg.

on a lower terrace to the southeast, which led the excavator to conclude that *Mosphilia* may have been a community divided socially as well as spatially (Peltenburg et al. 1998: 244–247).

The architectural elements, the provision of open areas that may have been used for ceremonial activities, and controlled access to those areas are also features of spatial organisation evident at Lemba *Lakkous*. The site is situated on a series of terraces overlooking a narrow coastal plain at the northern limit of the Ktima lowlands; *Mylouthkia* lies some 2 km to the north. There are two distinctive areas at Lemba (I, II, separated by some 100 m); the earliest traces of settlement are best represented on the Lower Terrace of Area I (Peltenburg 1982a: 76) and at the base of the Area II stratigraphic sequence (Peltenburg et al. 1985: 314). The excavators made clear the limited chronological resolution (especially for Periods 1 and 2) concerning graves and some extra-mural areas (Peltenburg et al. 1985: 16–18, 313–318). Period 1 occupation at Lemba (the radiocarbon dates are problematic – see Appendix, section on Early–Middle Chalcolithic – but indicate a calendar range somewhere in the late 4th to very early 3rd millennia Cal BC) is represented mainly by nine small circular structures built of *pisé* and stone, densely arranged against the back edge of the Area I terrace (Peltenburg et al. 1985: fig. 10). The settlement at this time was thus very crowded, and seems to have had a prolonged existence, as some structures, such as Building 5, were rebuilt once or twice and repaved at least four times.

Period 2 occupation at Lemba *Lakkous*, found in both Areas I and II (Peltenburg et al. 1985: 316, fig. 6.2), is again difficult to date. There is only one datum, which is inconsistent (too late in Model 1 in the Appendix), but presumably lies in the early 3rd millennium Cal BC. Lemba periods 1–2 are modelled by the surrounding data in Model 8 as extending from ca. 3151±266–2846±141 Cal BC (see Appendix and SOM for details). In general, the buildings are larger and more substantial, and many have walls made of stone instead of *pisé*. Building 20 (Area II) contained an exceptional concentration of some 40 cup-sized bowls and three flasks, all well used and placed around a central hearth. The excavators felt that all these utensils were designed for individual portions, and thus suggested this building might have served for the consumption of liquids (Peltenburg et al. 1985: 111, 326). Building 1 (Area I), the most prominent of all the Period 2 structures, stood in an isolated position on the tip of the Upper Terrace, widely separated from the six or seven smaller Period 2 structures in Area II. Only the eastern portion of Building 1 has survived, but its sturdily built wall forms the arc of a circular structure nearly seven m in diameter with an internal space of some 28 m² (Peltenburg et al. 1985: 35, and fig. 11) (Figure 54). With a floor plan typical of most Middle Chalcolithic structures, the remaining two internal segments of Building 1 were divided by a pebble-lined groove. Both segments contained several Red-on-White storage jars, bowls and flasks, and caches of axes (Peltenburg 1982a: 77).

In the northern sector, just beyond the pebble-lined groove, lay a shattered Red Monochrome Painted storage jar (F7) that seems to have been filled with animal bones. Sealed beneath its 244 sherds was the most distinctive object found in Building 1, a large (nearly 40 cm tall), fiddle-shaped, limestone female figurine that has come to be known as the 'Lemba Lady' (Peltenburg et al. 1985: 35–36; Figure 55; see inset in Figure 54 for locus). This now-famous lady shares many features in common with picrolite cruciform figures, including an elongated neck, elliptical head, slanting nose and outstretched arms (discussed in more detail below, under *Gender and the Individual Body*).

Two burials (23, 28) were placed, respectively, at the southern and northern terminals of Building 1's existing walls, and immediately to the north was a dense concentration of graves. Burials, in fact, are found throughout the

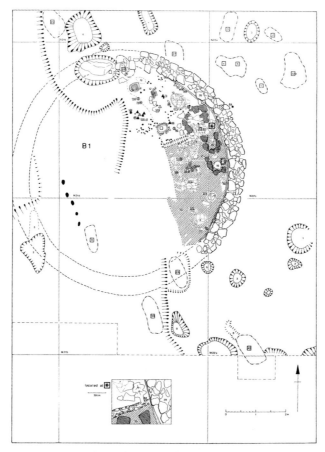

Figure 54. Lemba *Lakkous* Building 1, Period 2, Middle Chalcolithic, with surrounding pits and tombs. Inset shows details of the find spot of the 'Lemba Lady'. After Peltenburg et al. 1985: fig. 11. Courtesy of Edgar Peltenburg.

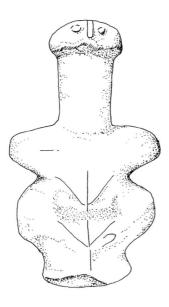

Figure 55. Lemba *Lakkous* – Middle Chalcolithic limestone female figurine, the 'Lemba Lady'. From Building 1 (see Figure 54 for locus). Height: 36 cm. Cyprus Museum no. LL 54.

settlement at Lemba *Lakkous*. Lemba, however, was most likely a multi-period site, not a sequence of continuous occupation. Thus, wherever burials are stratified in the specialised units of Area II (including Grave 20 below Building 2, with a picrolite cruciform figurine), they were found sealed beneath the floors and walls of Period 3; thus they are regarded as belonging to Period 2, along with the remnants of Period 2 structures such as Building 10 (Peltenburg et al. 1985: 316, fig. 6.2), or even earlier.

The latest known site in the Middle Chalcolithic sequence, albeit one with early Middle Chalcolithic components, is Souskiou *Laona* (Peltenburg et al. 2006; Peltenburg 2011b). Because excavations at the site are ongoing, the discussion here must be regarded as tentative and subject to change. Dated generally to about 3000 BC, *Laona* is situated on a prominent, narrow ridge, within an elongated arc of five discrete Middle Chalcolithic sites, four of them cemeteries (see below, Figure 57). Palaipaphos (modern Kouklia) lies about 2.5 km south, and the modern coastline is some 4 km distant. Perched near the entry to the Dhiarizos River valley, with its chain of Chalcolithic sites leading inland and upland, *Laona* may have served as a regional centre in the southwest. According to a viewshed analysis, the site was oriented towards the sea, the Ktima lowlands and the *Vathyrkakas* cemeteries, not towards the Dhiarizos valley (McCarthy, in Peltenburg et al. 2006: 102). The mortuary remains recovered from the Souskiou *Vathyrkakas* and *Laona* cemeteries – including their remarkable concentrations of cruciform figurines – are discussed in more detail below.

Following up a series of trial trenches and on-site survey, both of which hinted at the unusual nature of the *Laona* settlement and its well-preserved remains, excavations began in 2005. The site, overall about 2 ha in size, stands atop a long narrow ridge, with components on two parts of the ridge (east, west), and on the (south) slope and saddle between them (Peltenburg et al. 2006: 78–83, figs. 2–6). A stone-built construction one–three courses tall and up to 1 m wide may have served as an enclosure wall (Peltenburg et al. 2006: 96). On the relatively flat south slope, curvilinear structures were built on discrete terraces stepped down the hillside, with certain buildings – richer in material culture – situated on the ridge. One such structure, Building 69, was made of large cobbles or boulders laid in (five) rough courses. In the centre of the building was a raised area stained red from burning, most likely a hearth. Lying on the hard plaster surface of Building 69 were more than 100 stone tools, most of them arranged around the base of the wall (Peltenburg et al. 2006: 94–95, figs. 17–18). Despite the central hearth, the activity zones in this building do not conform to those of the standard 'Chalcolithic house' (Peltenburg et al. 1998: 239, fig. 14.2). Another curvilinear structure, Building 34 (at the top of the south slope), with an interior diameter of 6–7 m, had three preserved courses of stone and at least two building phases; several striking objects were found within it (see below). More recent work (2008) on the west ridge has uncovered at least three more curvilinear structures (Peltenburg 2011b: fig. 6).

Nearly 300 picrolite wasters, roughouts and debris found at the site (Peltenburg et al. 2006: 84–85, fig. 10; Peltenburg, pers. comm., August 2010), and the dominance of abrasion tools found in the site survey (Sewell, in Peltenburg et al. 2006: 87–88, fig. 16), provide evidence pointing to the manufacture of the iconic cruciform figures so well known from the nearby cemeteries. Within some dark ashy material in Building 34, excavations produced a unique, double-armed figurine, found in context with seven dentalium shells and two finely made chert blades; another picrolite cruciform figurine came from the surface overlying Building 34 (Peltenburg et al. 2006: 97–99, figs. 19, 22). From an ashy, oval pit in the centre of Building 34 came yet a third cruciform figurine, as well as a spiral-form copper ornament, perhaps a pendant (Peltenburg et al. 2006: 85, 98, fig. 21). At least two further metal objects are reported, a small mineralised fragment and a flat fragment from a blade-like object. Together with the spiral object (also a pendant?) and six curved fragments of copper found in Tomb 158 at the nearby *Laona* cemetery (Crewe et al. 2005: 51–52, 65, figs. 16.2, 16.3), and another copper spiral from the cemetery of Souskiou *Vathyrkakas* (Peltenburg 2006: 99–100), the material from *Laona* represents the earliest known evidence of copper almost certainly produced from Cypriot ores and used in the manufacture of metal artefacts.

The chipped stone assemblage is typically Chalcolithic, and the tools include an abundance of flake scrapers made primarily from the local, dark-coloured Moni chert. This may indicate that *Laona* played some role in the production and distribution of these items within and perhaps even beyond western Cyprus (McCartney, in Peltenburg et al. 2006: 89). Overall, and based on the material collected thus far, there is a low percentage of glossed tools associated with agricultural activities, whilst a concentration of perforators in what seems to be a specific activity area may be associated with the working of picrolite at *Laona* (McCartney, in Peltenburg et al. 2006: 92–93, tables 4–5).

The pottery, recovered from both survey and excavation during the 2005 season, was primarily Middle Chalcolithic but with a small component of Late Chalcolithic sherds (Bolger, in Peltenburg et al. 2006: 100–101). The principal pottery types were Red-on-White ('Parallel Band') and Red Monochrome Painted wares, mirroring the case at both Kissonerga *Mosphilia* and *Mylouthkia* during the Middle Chalcolithic. The pottery shapes (e.g. platters, deep bowls, spouted bowls, trays and flasks) and the infrequent occurrence of storage jars, suggest that the site belongs mainly to the Middle Chalcolithic. The same time frame was also suggested by the absence from excavations at *Laona* of Red and Black Stroke-Burnished Ware, the principal Late Chalcolithic pottery type. Both Clarke (in Rupp et al. 1992: 298) and Bolger et al. (2004: 112), however, recorded small numbers of this ware in survey at *Laona*. Moreover, recent radiocarbon dates (unpublished, from short-lived barley, grape, lens and pistacia seeds, ca. 2888–2700 Cal BC – Peltenburg 2011b: fig. 10; these dates are not used in the Appendix and analyses) and further finds of 'transitional' Middle–Late Chalcolithic pottery would now seem to establish occupation at *Laona* right down to the beginning of the Late Chalcolithic period.

In the view of the excavator, Souskiou *Laona* should be seen as a production centre for picrolite cruciform figurines, which promoted a mortuary ideology instrumental in integrating communities throughout the lower Dhiarizos River valley and the coastal plain beyond it (Peltenburg 2011b). By promoting this ideology, some members of these communities may have attained a unique social status, one that seems fully evident in some of the more prominent tombs at nearby Souskiou *Vathyrkakas* and *Laona* (see further below, under *Mortuary Practices*).

SUBSISTENCE STRATEGIES

The people of the Ceramic Neolithic had exploited deer heavily, a practice that continued into the Early Chalcolithic. Limited faunal data from Early Chalcolithic sites such as *Mylouthkia* and *Ayious* (and possibly Lemba *Lakkous* although the dating is problematic) show that the frequency of deer relative to other species was between 63–78% (Keswani 1994: 264, table 2). The only possible signs of ritual practices associated with animals at this time are the presence of deer antlers in graves at Erimi *Pamboula* and Karavas *Gyrisma* (Dikaios 1936: 12, 74; Toumazou 1987: 101, 104).

By the Middle Chalcolithic, there is a clear rise in the consumption of pigs at the expense of both deer and ovicaprines (Croft 1991: 71, table 3). Faunal evidence from Kissonerga *Mylouthkia*, for example, shows that between the Early and Middle Chalcolithic deer declined from nearly 55% of the sample to 40%, whilst pig rose from 24% to 51.5%; ovicaprines (mainly goats) also declined over the same period, from 17% to 5.3%. Adjusting the raw counts in order to estimate the relative contributions of these fauna to the meat supply, Croft (in Peltenburg et al. 2003: 235, table 20.12) suggests that deer declined from almost 75% (Period 2) to 56% (Period 3), ovicaprines from 8% to 2.2%, whilst pigs rose from 17% to 41%.

Similar calculations from Kissonerga *Mosphilia* reveal that the contribution of deer to the meat supply declined from 73% (Period 3A, Middle Chalcolithic) to 56.8% (Period 3B, Late Chalcolithic), ovicaprines from 8% to 6%, whilst pigs rose from nearly 19% to 37.2% (Early Chalcolithic faunal remains from *Mosphilia* Period 2 were too limited to compare in this manner). Although the faunal remains from Kalavasos *Ayious* are much more limited because of poor bone preservation at the site, deer still seem to have provided the main contribution to the meat diet in both the early and late phases (above 80%), whilst the (apparent) contribution of both pig and ovicaprine remained limited (Croft, in Todd and Croft 2004: 202, tables 39a–b, 207–208, table 43).

Finally, at Lemba *Lakkous*, the consumption of deer fell from 71.4% (Period 1) to 59% during Period 2, whilst pigs rose from 22% to 29% and ovicaprines rose from about 6% to nearly 12% (Croft 1991: 71, table 3).

This evident shift during the Chalcolithic towards domesticated or herded livestock (pigs, ovicaprines), alongside the declining importance of (hunted) deer, may reflect the increasing nutritional demands of an expanding population; it is even possible that increased settlement density reduced deer habitat, leading to a decline in their numbers (Croft 1991: 73). Alternatively, it may be that the intentional ritual consumption of animals favoured domestic livestock, which itself could be related to population increase (Keswani 1994: 265). Expanding communities thus would have developed formal social networks as well as ceremonial rituals to mediate conflicts and to facilitate social reproduction. Indeed, an intensification in ritual activities and the increasing consumption of domesticated animals may be seen in the evident decrease through time of the culling ages for both deer and pig during the Early–Middle Chalcolithic (Croft 1991: 70–73).

In the past, it was reported that the fill of Souskiou Tombs 21–23 (= Cyprus Department of Antiquities Tombs 1–3 – Peltenburg 2006: 13–14) contained bird and animal bones in thick ash layers, perhaps pointing to the use of animals in mortuary ritual (Christou 1989: 84, 85, fig. 12.3; Keswani 1984: 267–268). More recent excavations in dozens of other tombs, however, have failed to produce similar remains, so this suggestion remains inconclusive. The only other, related evidence is the unusual Red-on-White painted quadruped vase with a human head (Maier and Karageorghis 1984: 26, fig. 3) and the unique zoomorphic picrolite pendant found with dentalium shells in Tomb 23 (= Cyprus Department of Antiquities Tomb 3 – Peltenburg 2006: 14, pl. 10).

The slight preponderance of female over male caprine remains at *Mylouthkia*, *Mosphilia* and Lemba *Lakkous* (seen in fused skeletal elements) made it possible to sex these animals. Assessing the results, Croft (1991: 74) felt that the nearly equivalent ratio of male to female caprines at *Mosphilia* (0.95) and Lemba *Lakkous* (0.73), and even earlier at *Mylouthkia* (0.79), was inconsistent with efficient meat or milk production, and might best be explained in symbolic terms. In his view, such animals may have symbolised social values or aspirations, whilst the massive and graceful horns of mature male goats – a powerful symbol even today in rural Cyprus – may have boosted the status or wealth of their owners.

Turning to the palaeobotanical record, there is evidence of domesticated cereals such as emmer, einkorn, breadwheat and barley, along with oats and rye. Legumes such as lentils, peas, chickpeas, vetch and grass pea were also exploited. Other floral remains from Kissonerga *Mosphilia*, possibly domesticated, include olive, grape, fig and pistachio, whilst wild grasses and fruits such as juniper berries and capers also formed part of the Chalcolithic diet (Murray, in Peltenburg et al. 1998: 216, table 11.1). At nearby *Mylouthkia*, charred plant remains from three pits comprised much the same range of domesticated crops: emmer and einkorn wheat, hulled barley, rye and oats; legumes (lentils, chickpeas, bitter vetch and peas) and fruits (fig, grapes, olives and possibly pistachios – Colledge, in Peltenburg et al. 2003: 241–243). The very poorly preserved remains from Kalavasos *Ayious* indicate the use of domesticated barley and emmer wheat, wild barley and oats, and lentils (Hansen in Todd and Croft 2004: 200).

Food production is also attested by the increased numbers of groundstone tools used in crop processing, including querns, rubbers, pestles and pounders as well as polished sickle blades. Although it is speculated that some of the pits from *Ayious* may have been used for grain storage (Todd and Croft 2004: 214), nothing from any of the excavated pits confirms this suggestion. At *Mylouthkia*, the concentrations of charred plant remains in certain pits led the palaeo-botanist to conclude that they were used for waste disposal rather than grain storage (Colledge, in Peltenburg et al. 2003: 244).

The dual subsistence strategy of hunting and agropastoralism adopted by the people of Chalcolithic Cyprus probably neutralised any possible economic repercussions of an increasing population (Knapp et al. 1994: 412). As Stanley Price (1979a: 75–77) noted, dual strategies such as these offer a very effective use of natural and social resources. The growth and intensification of animal husbandry, moreover, seems to have been accompanied by intensified ritual practices, whilst the high ratios of male to female caprines may well reflect ideological as well as economic concerns (Keswani 1994: 267). And, as the fau-nal evidence from Souskiou *Vathyrkakas* hints, mortuary rituals were one form of ceremonial activity that became much more elaborate during the Middle Chalcolithic.

Mortuary Practices

In contrast to the preceding Ceramic Neolithic, mortuary practices are quite well attested during the Chalcolithic. The most common form of burial was in a pit grave, with or without a capstone. In the settlements, burials were closely associated with buildings, although few were placed inside them. During the Early Chalcolithic there is little indication of any formalised location within or beyond the settlement for burying the dead. At *Mylouthkia*, the largely frag-mentary and disarticulated remains of 10 people were recovered from various pits or fill from pits, hearths and general deposits; only one individual was found in a structure (Building 152). Because human remains were thrown into these pits with all sorts of domestic rubbish and animal bones, they have been termed 'trash burials' (Peltenburg et al. 2003: 221–224, 263). No complete skeletons were recovered from *Ayious* and none of the pits containing disar-ticulated remains seem to have been dug specifically for mortuary purposes (Todd and Croft 2004: 198–199). The skeletal remains from *Ayious*, fragmen-tary and poorly preserved, consist of only three individuals: one adult found in a surface deposit and two children, the first recovered from a pit, the other from a shallow depression. At Erimi *Pamboula*, only one (pit) burial belongs to the earliest period, but all four burials excavated at Erimi – two adult males, one child and one adolescent or young adult female – were single inhumations associated with a particular building or succession of buildings (Niklasson 1991: 119–122).

Beginning in the Middle Chalcolithic, more formal and quite likely differential mortuary practices become evident. One of the most unique is the multiple burial of at least five individuals in an ossuary cut into the face of a small gulley at Prastio *Agios Savvas tis Koronas* (Rupp and D'Annibale 1995: 39). Whilst only one individual was identified from Middle Chalcolithic Building 200 at Kissonerga *Mylouthkia*, at nearby *Mosphilia* 73 intra-settlement graves and tombs make up the largest set of mortuary data from the Chalcolithic period (Peltenburg et al. 1998: 64–92). Most of these burials (52–55 individuals) are dated to the Late Chalcolithic (Period 4) whilst those from the Middle Chalcolithic (periods 3A–3B) number 24; only a few stem from the Prehistoric Bronze Age 1 (Period 5) (Peltenburg et al. 2003: 83 table 4.8). The mortuary record extends over a period of nearly 1,000 years, and is discussed here in its entirety to give an overview of burial practices at the site through time.

Five tomb types were identified at *Mosphilia*: pit graves (10 in number), pit graves with capstone (19), pot burials (2), scoop graves (14) and chamber tombs (13), the last introduced during Period 4, fully within the Late Chalcolithic. In general, pit graves held only single inhumations, whilst the chamber tombs were designed to hold both single and multiple adult burials. Beyond this apparent correlation between chamber tombs and collective burial rites, even more striking is the intentional (?) practice of having separate burials for adults (in chamber tombs) and children (in pit burials), although children were present in chamber tombs 505 and 566 (Peltenburg et al. 1998: 70–71). The scoop burials, irregular cuts made in the loose fill of an existing pit or depression, were introduced in Period 4 and were used mainly for the primary but informal burial of children. The only two pot burials (Graves 504, 530 – both Period 5) contained infants and were likely sub-floor burials.

Most interments – 89 individuals in total, including those found outside of specific mortuary features – were inhumations and included single and multiple burials. A number of Middle Chalcolithic interments involved more than one individual, and perhaps were intended for members of the same family, household or clan; when such graves became full, the bones were removed to make room for newcomers (Peltenburg 1992: 31). The most common burial position was flexed on the right side, facing inland (northeast), with both hands placed in front of the face (Peltenburg et al. 1998: 65, pl. 22.5). Some concentrations of disarticulated human skeletal remains within the settlement must represent secondary deposition (Niklasson 1991: 188–189). In the ceremonial

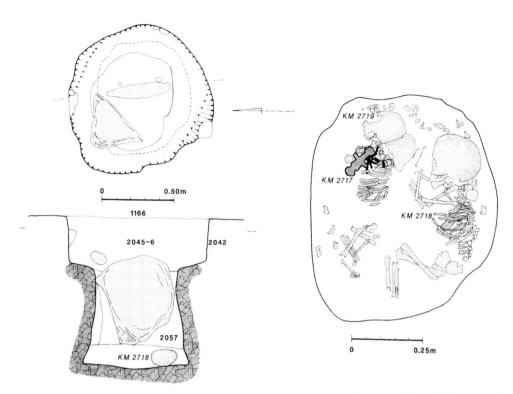

Figure 56. Kissonerga *Mosphilia* Burial 563, of a one-and-a-half-year-old child (KM 2719) interred with a dentalium necklace and picrolite cruciform figurine. After Peltenburg 1992: 28, fig. 1. Courtesy of Edgar Peltenburg.

area at *Mosphilia* (Main Area, high sector), there may have been two, intramural adult burials (inferred from the size of Graves 503 and 568, but both were empty); one child's burial (Grave 560) was placed just outside a building's wall. Overall, the low proportion of adult burials at the site is a striking feature of the Middle Chalcolithic mortuary record. During Period 3, for example, 66.7% of the burials at *Mosphilia* were neonates or infants below the age of three years (Peltenburg et al. 1998: 74–75, table 4.3). At least some adults from this community may have been interred in separate cemeteries, such as that at Souskiou *Vathyrkakas* (see below).

Although the number of grave goods deposited with the deceased remained low throughout *Mosphilia*'s lifetime, the amount is highest during Period 3B, when all known burials were those of children. These same burials also contain a high proportion of dentalium shell as well as non-local picrolite, usually in the form of pendants. Burial 563 provides a striking example of this practice (Figure 56): a one-and-a-half-year-old child (KM 2719) was buried with a dentalium necklace and picrolite cruciform figurine whilst another, three and a half years of age (KM 2718), was interred with a single piece of dentalium – several other pieces of dentalia and at least two anthropomorphic pendants came from the fill of this pit burial (Peltenburg 1992). Because a 48-cm-long necklace with 17 dentalia and a 10 × 5 cm cruciform figurine were too large and too heavy to be worn by a one-and-a-half-year-old infant, it may have belonged to a family member. Such practices suggest preferential treatment for selected children (or adults) buried with these types of goods. It is worth noting in this context that picrolite cruciform pendants seldom accompanied adult male burials. The repeated association of picrolite with children or adult women may indicate that certain families or social groups enjoyed some level of social status (ranking?) and had differential access to picrolite (whether raw material or finished ornaments). Women, in turn, may have been involved somehow in the production and exchange of picrolite (Peltenburg 1992: 32–33; Bolger 2003: 156–157).

Beyond picrolite beads, pendants and figurines, and dentalium shell beads and necklaces, other common grave goods at *Mosphilia* included Red-on-White or Red and Black Stroke-Burnished flasks, jars, bottles and bowls; groundstone discs, bowls and tools; conical stones; chalk bowls and beads; and a single metal spiral hair-ring (KM 1182 in Grave 529, likely Period 4). This last item is one of only six metal objects found at *Mosphilia* (the others are all tools), along with some fragments of pure smelted copper (Peltenburg et al. 1998: 188–189). Such objects and materials mostly belong to types commonly found in the settlement levels as well, suggesting that they may have been personal, everyday items that accompanied their deceased owners to the afterlife. As we shall see, much more specialised types of pottery, picrolite and other material things were deposited in the Souskiou cemeteries.

Fifty-six graves of Chalcolithic to Prehistoric Bronze Age date were uncovered at nearby Lemba *Lakkous*. Of the 56 individual burials identified in these graves, single infant or child inhumations predominate, although all age groups are represented (Peltenburg et al. 1985: 43–53, 134–149). All burials except one were placed in pit graves: Grave 46 in Area II was an isolated child's skull found sitting upright in the ground (Niklasson 1991: 126). There were two types of burial pit, one roughly oval or rectangular in shape and cut into the bedrock, the other of similar shape but situated at the base of a shallow, roughly circular depression cut through softer material. More than half the graves had some kind of covering, usually a capstone. Twenty-two graves were found in Area I, and 34 in Area II; in the latter area, at least, the graves were closely associated with buildings. An unusual complex of pit graves equipped with 'libation holes' – surely the focus of some sort of ceremonial activity – was found in Area II, beneath Late Chalcolithic Building 2, the largest structure found at the site (Peltenburg et al. 1985: 116–118, 327–328; Keswani 1994: 266). The dating of all burials is problematic for the same reason that stratigraphic sequences were difficult to establish at Lemba: erosion, shallow deposits and modern agricultural disturbances. In Area II, most buildings belong to Period 3 (Late

Chalcolithic) although most burials, found beneath these buildings, have been dated to Period 2 (Middle Chalcolithic).

There is only one known case of intramural burial: Grave 45 in Area I belonged to an infant whose remains were placed next to an interior wall of Building 15 (Niklasson 1991: 124). The rare multiple burials were made up almost exclusively of infants and/or children buried with other children; only in Grave 30 (Area I) is it possible that two adults were buried together (Peltenburg et al. 1985: 49, 142). Thus no female adults were interred with an infant or child, and no family groups were ever buried together. Mortuary goods were sparse at Lemba: only 13 of the 56 burials contained materials such as querns, unworked stones, a basalt axe, some shells, one cruciform female figurine made of picrolite (from the fill of Grave 20), and three dentalium shell necklaces, two of which had picrolite pendants (Niklasson 1991: 138–140). A Red Monochrome Painted bowl was found in a small circular pit cut from the same layer as Grave 38, and the two features thus may have been connected. Various types of artefacts – potsherds, bone, stone and terracotta objects, some shells, chipped stone and faunal remains – were found in the fills of several graves.

Finally, it is worth recalling here the distinctive ceremonial, if not specifically mortuary aspects of Building 1 at Lemba (noted above), where two burials were recovered at the ends of the extant walls, and a concentration of graves was placed immediately to the north of the structure. Peltenburg (1982a: 78) suggests that the association of burials and the large limestone figurine (Lemba Lady) reflect to some extent mortuary practices at Souskiou, where picrolite cruciform figurines often accompanied the deceased. Let us now take a closer look at this impressive necropolis complex in the Dhiarizos River valley, first identified at the site of *Vathyrkakas* (Cemetery 1) situated near the edge of a flat, rocky plateau and a deep (80 m at this point), very narrow ravine.

The Souskiou complex of sites – located some 4 km from the southwest coast – includes four discrete Middle Chalcolithic cemeteries (three at *Vathyrkakas*, one at *Laona*) and a settlement bisected by the Vathyrkakas ravine, a tributary of the Dhiarizos. Of the three distinct mortuary areas at *Vathyrkakas*, Cemetery 1 has about 80 tombs (many of them looted), whilst Cemetery 2 (some 450 m to the south) and Cemetery 3 beyond it are only small concentrations of completely looted graves. The recent identification of some further, truncated graves at the edge of the plateau between Cemeteries 1 and 2, however, may indicate that the distinction between these two cemeteries is meaningless and that many more tombs once existed there (Peltenburg 2011b).

The cemeteries were physically isolated from the only known settlement (Souskiou *Laona*, a Middle Chalcolithic site with possible Late Chalcolithic component – mentioned above), on the hillside opposite (Rupp et al. 1992: 297–299; Bolger et al. 2004: 112; Peltenburg et al. 2006; Peltenburg 2006: pl. 1.3)

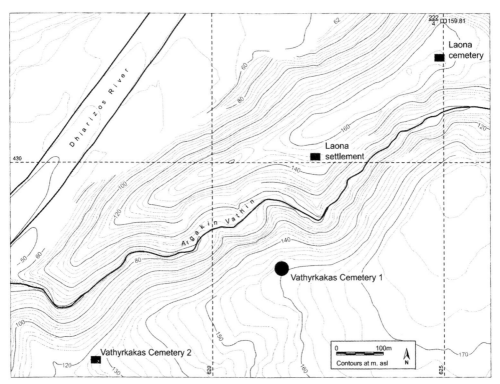

Figure 57. Souskiou *Laona* and *Vathyrkakas* – topographic plan with locations of three cemeteries and one settlement (*Laona*) on a prominent, narrow ridge near the entry to the Dhiarizos River valley. Courtesy of Edgar Peltenburg.

(Figure 57). The major distinctions, indeed innovations, in the Souskiou complex are the spacious mortuary facilities and elaborate tomb types; the repeated use and reuse of shaft tombs over several generations; the multiple inhumations; unequivocal examples of secondary burial practices; and the large numbers of material goods accompanying the deceased (Crewe et al. 2005: 43).

The long and tumultuous tale of looting at these sites, together with the final publication of four separate excavation projects at Cemetery 1, are presented in admirable detail by Peltenburg (2006, with several specialists). Despite the lack of radiocarbon dates, the careful correlation of Red-on-White pottery found in the tombs with similar wares from *Mosphilia* Period 3B and Lemba Period 2 suggest that the cemetery was in use during the later Middle Chalcolithic, towards the end of the 4th millennium BC (Peltenburg 2006: 158). Extending over an area of about 30 × 60 m, Cemetery 1 at *Vathyrkakas* contained deep (up to 3 m), bell-shaped shafts with multiple burials. These shaft burials comprise almost half the known sample of tombs, but are otherwise unknown in the mortuary record of the Neolithic and Chalcolithic periods. Another entirely new type is the 'square pit-and-shaft' tomb, distinguished by a large hollow above for the capstone, and described as an 'incipient dromos' (Peltenburg

2006: 160). Tombs 29 and 73, the largest and deepest of the eight square pit-and-shaft type, had single steps leading down into the flat base of the tomb. Other, smaller pit-and-shaft tombs, and uncertain types of graves make up the remainder of the sample from *Vathyrkakas* Cemetery 1 (Peltenburg 2006: 157 and fig. 12.3).

Tomb 73 is by far the largest extant mortuary feature in Cyprus before the Bronze Age; its upper pit measures 43.5 m³ with a floor area of 19.35 m² (Peltenburg 2006: 161; Peltenburg 2011b: fig. 5). This upper area could well have served as a spacious setting for mortuary ceremonies. The walls of the shaft were coated with plaster, and lined with stones set on their edges. A long row of slab stones (2.25 m) that had fallen into the pit may represent the remnant core of a kerbed tumulus that once covered this tomb.

The approximately 200 individuals buried in the 82 known graves from Cemetery 1 contained a significantly higher proportion of adults to children; in the deep, bell-shaped shaft tombs, that proportion reaches 10:1 (Peltenburg 2006: 162). Having noted above that the mortuary remains from *Mosphilia* Period 3B were made up almost exclusively of infants and children, it was suggested that the deceased adults at *Mosphilia* might have been moved the 20 km to *Vathyrkakas* for secondary burial. Certain well-built and richly endowed tombs at *Vathyrkakas* (Tombs 29, 58, 86), however, also contain the remains of children that equal or outnumber the adults, so there seems to be no one-to-one correlation between intramural child burial and extramural adult burial. Moreover, at least one adult was buried in a grave (814) within the settlement at *Laona* (Peltenburg 2011b: fig. 7). There is also some question about the social rank or familial status of both the children and adults buried in the *Vathyrkakas* shaft tombs. Of the 13 tombs with children's (and adult's) burials, 10 contained anthropomorphic figurines; of the 12 tombs that held exclusively adult burials, only 2 had such figurines (Peltenburg 2006: 163).

The burials in *Vathyrkakas* Cemetery 1 were accompanied by a rich and distinctive array of mortuary offerings (Christou 1989: figs. 12.4–10; Vagnetti 1980; Peltenburg 2006: passim): zoomorphic and anthropomorphic vessels, including (1) a Red-on-White pottery vessel in the shape of a pregnant female, whose striking decoration includes a necklace, from which another painted human figure hangs (Peltenburg 2006: pl. 30.1, colour pl. A: 2–5); (2) a Red-on-White painted quadruped vase with a human head; and (3) the somewhat bizarre ithyphallic male figurine now in the Pierides collection (the last two in Maier and Karageorghis 1984: 26, fig. 3, 28, fig. 8); picrolite pendants and (eight) cruciform figurines, including an exquisite polished, mottled pale green example with an oblong, flat, featureless face (Peltenburg 2006: colour pl. B: 5–6) (Figure 58); numerous dentalium shells including two necklaces with dentalium spacers and variously shaped pendants (Peltenburg 2006: pl. 10); a beautifully crafted groundstone macehead made of gabbro with large quartz inclusions (Peltenburg 2006: pl. 27.4); a small but highly specialised corpus of

Figure 58. Souskiou *Vathyrkakkas* (Cemetery 1): polished, mottled pale green picrolite figurine with an oblong, flat face. Height 12.5 cm; greatest width 8.25 cm. Courtesy of Edgar Peltenburg.

chipped stone tools, many made of distinctive Moni chert; pig-tusk, antler or bone needles, beads and pendants.

The extensive use of picrolite for pendants, beads and cruciform figurines at Souskiou *Vathyrkakas* and *Laona*, as well as at Lemba *Lakkous*, Kissonerga *Mylouthkia* and especially *Mosphilia*, has wider ramifications for the study of ideology and identity during the Chalcolithic era (see below – *Incipient Complexity, Ideology and Identity*). Quite unusual amongst this striking set of grave goods, although not unexpected in the Chalcolithic, are some objects of copper and faience. The sole metal object from *Vathyrkakas* is a copper spiral ornament (or bead), very similar to another spiral found at Souskiou *Laona* Tomb 158 (Crewe et al. 2005: 51, fig. 16.2; Peltenburg 2006: 99–100, pl. 10.5); together they provide the earliest known evidence for copper working on Cyprus. Although faience has heretofore proved to be very rare in contexts prior to the Bronze Age, the shape, size, form and technology of the *Vathyrkakas* examples point to local production and contemporary deposition, a conclusion made even more probable with the discovery of securely dated segmented faience beads from the contemporary cemetery at Souskiou *Laona* (Crewe et al. 2002: 21–22, fig. 3; 2005: 52, 63, fig. 14.4, 64, fig. 15.2). Both sets of beads belong to the 'same, self-glazing faience tradition' and should be dated towards the end of the Middle Chalcolithic, making them what are, on current evidence, the earliest known faience objects not only on Cyprus but also in the Mediterranean (Peltenburg 2006: 95; 2011: 6).

Some interesting but very tentative correlations have been drawn between the mortuary assemblages of goods and tomb types, and between various types of objects and the people buried in the Souskiou tombs (Peltenburg 2006: 163–170). For example, whereas the bell-shaped shaft tombs have a higher proportion of anthropomorphic figures and dentalium shell, the square pit-and-shaft tombs have a greater diversity of burial goods and materials. Dentalia, cruciform figurines and pendants frequently adorned adult interments, and there is some indication that females wore pendants (including large cruciform figurines) whilst males were at least occasionally buried with cruciform pendants (Tomb 59) (cf. Bolger 2003: 156). At least one (unsexed) adult, perhaps along with a child, was interred in the lowest layer of bell-shaped shaft Tomb 86 with a large number and diverse types of grave goods: the pottery vessel in the shape of a pregnant woman, a picrolite pendant and three picrolite figurines, dentalium beads, a stone cup and palette, and various painted pottery vessels. Peltenburg (2006: 29–30, 166) sees this as clear evidence for individual, high-status burials at *Vathyrkakas*. More generally, Manning (1993: 43) sees in the cemetery plausible evidence for the development of lineages or families who possessed certain social rights and high social status, something unprecedented in the material record of prehistoric Cyprus.

Excavations carried out between 2001–2005 at the cemetery of Souskiou *Laona* (Crewe et al. 2005; Peltenburg 2011b) have helped to substantiate several assumptions made on the basis of poorly documented or unprovenanced finds – especially cruciform figurines and pendants – said to be from *Vathyrkakas*. The *Laona* cemetery is situated approximately 500 m northeast of Cemetery 1, on a discrete limestone outcrop on the same narrow ridge but on the opposite side of the ravine (see above, Figure 57). Of the 137 tombs recorded at *Laona*, all but 15 had been partially if not totally looted. Most intact tombs contained one primary burial in the form of an articulated skeleton, along with a stack of bones from secondary burials. There are a few instances of double burials and one example of a triple burial (Tomb 207). As is typical elsewhere in Cyprus, the preservation of the human skeletal remains is quite poor.

Amongst the notable mortuary goods placed in the tombs at *Laona* were distinctive Red-on-White pottery vessels including one anthropomorphic example; picrolite pendants with dentalium shell beads; a large (13 cm tall) picrolite figurine found on a ledge cut for the aperture of Tomb 168 (Crewe et al. 2005: 50–51, fig. 11); the segmented faience beads and copper object noted above from Tomb 158. Six additional curved fragments of copper, perhaps all part of one annular pendant or pin, were also recovered from the same tomb (Crewe et al. 2005: 51, 65, fig. 16.3). In general, these tomb assemblages from *Laona* are quite similar to those excavated systematically at *Vathyrkakas* Cemetery 1, but it is still unclear if these were contemporary or successive burial grounds. Equally important, these extra-mural cemeteries and multiple-stage mortuary practices – involving both primary and secondary burials, exhumation and reburial, and the conspicuous consumption of exceptional grave goods – can now be seen as the Chalcolithic forerunners of later Bronze Age mortuary practices, as Keswani (2004: 41–42) had already predicted.

The mortuary sites of Souskiou *Vathyrkakas* and *Laona* – with an estimated 1,200 people buried in them (Peltenburg 2011b) – provide dramatic and unequivocal evidence for the use of extra-mural cemeteries, each spatially separated by a few hundred metres from the only known contemporary settlement at *Laona*. Elsewhere, in Area I at Lemba *Lakkous*, one group of burials was situated in a distinct area on slightly higher ground (the Upper Terrace) but only a few metres distant from the contemporary buildings. And, as pointed out earlier, the burial zone on the eastern slope of the CN settlement at Sotira also demonstrates the practice of extra-mural burial in a discrete part of the site (not necessarily a 'corporate burial ground' or 'bounded precinct for burial' – Peltenburg 2006: 180).

Peltenburg (2011b) regards the abandonment of Souskiou and the cessation of the mortuary practices associated with it as '…a major disjuncture in the development of Cypriot society *c.* 2700 BC'. Indeed, the cemeteries at *Vathyrkakas* and *Laona* represent a fundamental break in Cypriot mortuary practices, one that looks ahead to the Bronze Age, not back to the Ceramic Neolithic. Other innovations seen at Souskiou that might be seen as harbingers of later, Bronze Age practices include the marked variation in the size of tombs (and thus in the labour required for their construction); larger tombs designed for multiple inhumations; the sealing of tomb entrances with a stone slab and wedges after successive interments; the secondary treatment of skeletal remains; the under-representation of children and infants; the use of the 'capstone hollow', an expanded space around some shaft tombs that might have provided space for those involved in funerary rituals (like the *dromoi* of Bronze Age tombs); and the lavish if somewhat variable quality and range of gifts buried with the deceased (Crewe et al. 2005: 59).

Along with the disarticulation of some skeletons and their movement to bone stacks, Peltenburg (2006: 181) sees here a 'shift in ideology from the individual to the corporate that corresponds to the increased importance of houses/households'. By corporate he means segregated social groups, such as Keswani's (2004: 11–13) descent groups, not the community as a whole. On the contrary, and as argued elsewhere (e.g. Knapp and Meskell 1997: 199), and reiterated below (under *Gender and the Individual Body*), several novel material features of the Middle–Late Chalcolithic – including the distinctive mortuary practices treated here – seem instead to reflect the emergence and growing importance of individuals within the social spectrum of prehistoric Cyprus.

In general, the mortuary practices of the Chalcolithic period are notably variable, ranging from burials in ditches, below and within buildings, on the perimeter of various structures interpreted as domestic dwellings, in a somewhat discrete area (the Upper Terrace at Lemba *Lakkous*), and in extramural cemeteries. At Kissonerga *Mosphilia*, there are a few adult burials but those of children and infants predominate, and during Period 3B children were interred with a wealth of grave goods. Several graves from *Mosphilia* and Lemba *Lakkous* contain incomplete and/or disarticulated human remains with indicators of special processing, including skull treatment, many of which belong to infant or child burials (Niklasson 1991: 186–190; Keswani 1994: 266). In sum, there is solid evidence for multistage burials, multiple inhumations, special treatment associated with infant or child burials, and secondary treatment of the dead during the Middle Chalcolithic, indicating the complexity of mortuary rituals. The meaning and significance of the picrolite cruciform figurines typically found in mortuary contexts (especially at Souskiou) raise other issues about mortuary practices (discussed below, under *Gender and the Individual Body*).

By the Late Chalcolithic, the evidence is limited once again to burials inside settlements, with no evidence for secondary treatment. Because the use of formal cemeteries for mortuary rituals was taken up anew in Prehistoric Bronze Age Cyprus, it may be that the current Late Chalcolithic material record, largely limited to the southwest of the island, is incomplete. Alternatively, as Peltenburg (2006: 181) suggests, we should not focus on gaps in the material record, thus treating cemeteries as independent variables, but instead see them '…as the materialisation of fluctuating social and political agendas of members of prehistoric communities'. Indeed, we need to consider within the wider material context of the Chalcolithic just how these changing mortuary practices relate to the emergence and negotiation of an island identity, whether individual, corporate or communal, and whether the same or similar mortuary practices may have served different social agendas. Let us turn, then, to engage a range of other material and social features of the Early–Middle Chalcolithic in the attempt to disentangle issues related to island ideology and identity.

Other Material and Social Practices

The Chalcolithic period was a time of impressive developments in pottery production, the extraction and crafting of picrolite and (most likely) the earliest mining and smelting of copper. Let us look at each of these in turn, before considering a few other aspects of the Chalcolithic, specifically ritual and feasting, gender and the body, and the probable emergence of 'the individual'.

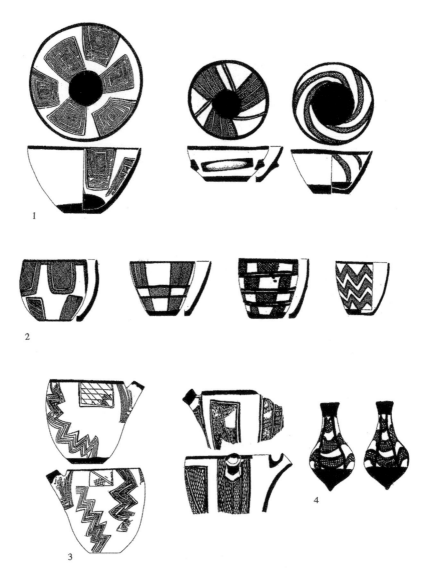

Figure 59. *Mosphilia* Red-on-White pottery. After Peltenburg et al. 1998: figs. 63–66. Courtesy of Louise Steel. (1) Hemispherical bowls, (2) deep bowls, (3) spouted bowls, (4) bottle.

The Red-on-White pottery that first appeared during the Ceramic Neolithic continued to develop and diversify, and the 'Close Line' style seems to have been in use over the entire island already in the Early Chalcolithic (Bolger 1991). Although more detailed geometric design schemes became common, and the range of shapes increased, pottery continued to be produced at the household level. In addition to new and different kinds of bowls (deep, spouted, hemispherical) (Figure 59), the presence of trays, flasks, platters and *pithoi* indicate that the storage and more formal consumption of food (what is increasingly understood as 'feasting') had become important. If the *pithoi*

Figure 60. Souskiou *Laona* copper spiral ornament (SL 428), from Tomb 158; metal strip is 3 cm wide with nine twisting spirals. After Crewe et al. 2005: 51, 55–56, 65, fig. 16.2. Courtesy of Lindy Crewe; with permission of Edgar Peltenburg.

are taken as the material marker of the change from communal storage in pits to autonomous household storage (Peltenburg 1998: 243), then we have an example of how a shift in socio-economic patterns also impacted on pottery production. During the Middle Chalcolithic, the motifs that decorate Red-on-White pottery become more distinctive at different sites, which may indicate the emergence of local production centres (Bolger 1991: 85–92). Moreover, some of the finest of these decorated vessels, and in particular large serving bowls, were recovered from some special purpose structures such as Building 1 at Lemba *Lakkous* or Building 206 at Kissonerga *Mosphilia* (Bolger 1994: 13), already discussed above. By the Late Chalcolithic period, Red-on-White pottery virtually disappeared, to be replaced by a monochrome tradition that persisted until well into the Prehistoric Bronze Age.

The Middle Chalcolithic period witnessed the earliest attested use of copper on Cyprus. From Souskiou *Vathyrkakas* (Tombs 23, 78) came a spiral ornament and a corroded piece of copper. From Souskiou *Laona* Tomb 158 came a spiral ornament ('bead') and pendant (?), whilst Building 34 at the same site produced a blade, a unique spiralform pendant and two 'amorphous' fragments (Peltenburg 2011a: 4, table 1.1; see also Crewe et al. 2005: 51, 65, fig. 16.2; Peltenburg 2006: 99–100, pl. 10.5) (Figure 60). Together with some nearly contemporary copper pieces from Erimi – a chisel, two 'needles', and two uncertain pieces ('blade', 'narrow band'? – Peltenburg 2011a: 4, table 1.1; Bolger 1985: 180–186; Balthazar 1990: 92–93), these objects represent the earliest evidence of copper almost certainly produced on Cyprus.

Around the time of the transition between the Middle and Late Chalcolithic (early 3rd millennium, ca. 2800–2700 Cal BC), several metal items found abroad are reportedly (based on lead isotope analysis) made of copper consistent with a Cypriot ore source. From Pella in Jordan came an axe and two daggers (Philip et al. 2003); and from the Cretan site of Hagia Photia came a fishhook, and an awl (Stos-Gale and Gale 2003: 91–92, table 5). Both of the findspots are dated roughly to ca. 3000 BC: at Pella, a well-dated EB II hoard of ca. 3000; on Crete an EB I cemetery (Davaras and Betancourt 2004: 4; Day et al. 1998). Nothing else in the contemporary archaeological record (neither exports nor imports) indicate the production and export of Cypriot copper at this early date. As Peltenburg (2011: 6) points out, however, much of our information on the extraction and/or production of copper at this time comes from the copper-poor south and west of Cyprus, not the copper-rich north.

From the Late Chalcolithic period on the island, excavations at Kissonerga *Mosphilia* provide some indicators of indigenous metalworking and casting activities. Six metal objects, two lumps of ore and two possible crucibles suggest that the exploitation of local copper ores was underway before the mid-3rd millennium BC. Three chisels (KM 694, 986, 2174), an awl (KM 416), a buckle or clasp fragment (KM 539, not listed in the most recent tally of objects – Peltenburg 2011a: 4, table 1.1), and some flakes of oxidised copper belong to Period 4 (Late Chalcolithic), whilst a spiral hair- or ear-ring (KM 1182) from Grave 529 probably belongs to Period 5 (Philia phase, Prehistoric Bronze Age), since it is described as a 'typical Philia ornament' (Peltenburg et al. 1998: 188: Peltenburg 2011a: 4, caption to table 1.1). The butt of an axe or adze (KM 457) also comes from a Period 5 context. There are also two Late Chalcolithic metal objects from Lemba *Lakkous* (Building 3): a chisel (LL 134) and a thin fragment (LL 209) that may be part of a blade (Peltenburg 2011a: 4, table 1.1).

At *Mosphilia*, the association of copper ore, two possible crucibles and two chisels in and around the Pithos House makes it feasible to suggest that local copper was worked during Period 4 (Late Chalcolithic). More specifically, fragments of unalloyed, oxidised copper from Building 834 (Period 4a) could be from metal objects, or else may represent the residue of metalworking. Ore lumps with bright green corrosion (KM 701) were found in association with a chisel (KM 694) and a copper-laden stone 'dish' (KM 693, possibly serving as a crucible) from Building 706 (Period 4b at *Mosphilia*). This concentration of copper objects, waste products (?) and a possible crucible around Building 706 (successor to the Pithos House – discussed further below) thus may indicate a local knowledge of copper ores and the small-scale working of copper. Finally, because Webb and Frankel (1999: 31) had argued that all Late Chalcolithic metal objects might be associated with 'intrusive' Anatolian peoples during the (later) Philia phase, Peltenburg (2011a: 7) emphasised that the chisel (KM 2174) and flakes of oxidised copper (C 384) from Building 834 belong to Period 4a at *Mosphilia*, thus antedating Period 4b, the earliest point at which indigenous and intrusive groups may have coexisted on the island.

Lead isotope analysis (LIA) of a lump of copper ore (KM 633, Period 4) and a copper axe/adze (KM 457, Period 5) from *Mosphilia* indicated that whilst the ore was consistent with production from Cypriot sources, the isotopic composition of the copper axe fell beyond the so-called Cypriot field, or 'ellipse' (Gale 1991a). The use of such ellipses has now been discredited as a means of identifying ore sources (Gale and Stos-Gale 2002: 278). Moreover, copper ore and minerals such as chalcopyrite and malachite are present along the west coast of Cyprus (Zwicker 1988: 427–428), and in principle would have been easily accessible to those who lived at *Mosphilia*. Thus the ore used at the site need not have come from the Troodos sources used to establish the lead isotope field for Cyprus, and could have a different lead isotope composition from the Troodos ores. Moreover, Peltenburg et al. (1998: 189) note that ores from a source nearby (Akoursos) have lead isotope compositions that seem similar to those of the *Mosphilia* axe/adze and other PreBA coppers. This factor alone may account for the distinctive LIA signature of the *Mosphilia* axe. Peltenburg further noted that the form of this axe/adze (Period 5, PreBA 1) could conceivably link it to other examples of PreBA 1 metal artefacts thought to be consistent – in LIA terms – with production from northwest Anatolian ores (Stos-Gale and Gale, in Knapp and Cherry 1994: 212). The bottom line, however, is that the lead isotope field used to exclude axe/adze KM 457 was inadequately defined. It could well lie within a Cypriot field defined by a Kernel Density Estimate, reputedly a better gauge of a parent lead isotope field's true extent (Pollard 2009).

Instrumental Neutron Activation Analysis (INAA) carried out on six Chalcolithic metal artefacts (from Erimi, *Mylouthkia*, *Mosphilia* and Lemba) indicated they were made of metal smelted from copper ores, not from native copper (Gale 1991a: 47–52). Despite its recognised accuracy for provenancing clays used in pottery, INAA is much less accurate – as an isolated technique – to determine metals' provenance. Nonetheless, and even though metallographic analyses demonstrated that those who made the Chalcolithic artefacts analysed were well acquainted with cold-working and annealing, Gale (1991a: 54) concluded that Chalcolithic metallurgy on Cyprus was 'primitive and provincial'. If the indigenous Cypriotes of the early 3rd millennium BC are to be granted any agency at all, we should assume it was they who produced these metal objects, not foreigners who in any case are otherwise scarcely attested in the Late Chalcolithic material record. If local people were so 'provincial', how did they have the wherewithal to conduct trade in the first place?

In this light, Peltenburg (1982c: 54–56, figs. 3a–b; 2011: 6) proposed a link between the early exploitation and working of copper and the intensified procurement and production of picrolite. Although he is treating the use of native copper rather than the mining or smelting of copper ores, he noted that the distribution of native copper ores overlapped to some extent that of picrolite sources, and that native copper might have been collected alongside the picrolite. This soft, easily workable stone – especially the blue-green variety, not dissimilar to oxidised copper ores – was increasingly exploited during the Chalcolithic to make a diverse array of ornaments, notably the diverse pendants and cruciform figurines that are a hallmark of the Middle Chalcolithic (see further below). Despite the evident social and symbolic value of picrolite, Peltenburg (1991b: 116–117) maintains that its extraction and use to manufacture ornaments and figurines were decentralised endeavours, in the hands of highly localised, part-time craftspeople. Bolger (1994: 14–15) too argues for the household production of picrolite, and suggests that contextual evidence – linking women and picrolite pendants – indicates female involvement both in procuring picrolite and producing pendants. Whatever the answer, the production and distribution of picrolite seems to have been closely controlled, not least because it was used to underpin a new ideological and conceptual system, with connotations of rank or social status (Steel 2004a: 95).

At the present time, no more than 20 metal artefacts (ornaments, tools) can be dated to the Chalcolithic period (Muhly 1991a: 358–359; Peltenburg 2011a: 4, table 1.1), whilst at least 450 picrolite objects (mainly ornaments and figurines) have been tabulated (Peltenburg 1991b: 114). If any correspondence actually existed between extracting picrolite and collecting copper, then the primary focus clearly fell on the picrolite. In turn, and given the social and ideological significance of picrolite during the Chalcolithic, it may be that a more developed and controlled system of exchange was in operation than Peltenburg has allowed. Although this exchange 'network' continued into the Late Chalcolithic, its demise thereafter was soon followed by the emergence of an entirely new social and economic system involving the production and exchange of metallic (not native) copper. Quite different from that which preceded it in terms of sources, extractive technology and trade routes, this new system of production and exchange took on not just local but interregional aspects by the mid-3rd millennium BC (Webb et al. 2006; Stos-Gale 2001: 200–201, fig. 10.2), all discussed in greater detail in the next chapter.

RITUAL AND FEASTING

Most material relevant for a discussion of feasting during the Middle Chalcolithic derives from the site of Kissonerga *Mosphilia*. It is worth recalling, however, that around a central hearth in Building 20 (Area II) at Lemba *Lakkous*, the excavators found a striking concentration of three flasks and some 40 cup-sized bowls, perhaps intended for consuming liquids during special gatherings. Also in Area II, beneath the large, Late Chalcolithic Building 2, a series of pit graves with 'libation holes' may also represent some sort of drinking ceremony associated with the deceased (Peltenburg et al. 1985: 116–118, 327–328; Keswani 1994: 266).

At *Mosphilia* (Period 3B), the excavators found a unique deposit of representational art – including a Red-on-White painted building model (a bowl, see further below) and 18 anthropomorphic figurines – within an architecturally distinctive area (Peltenburg 1991a: 21–27; Peltenburg 1991c). Situated on a low but distinctive rise at the site, this area was accessed by a paved track leading in from the north; it was enclosed by the four calcarenite structures (Buildings 2, 4, 206, 1000) discussed above (see Figure 53 above for reconstructed area plan), and by another, somewhat later structure (Building 994). The excavators have argued that this open area between these buildings – with a series of densely pitted surfaces interpreted as the remnants of large earthen ovens – may have served as an arena for competitive ritual feasting (Peltenburg 1993: 14–15). Peltenburg regards Building 206, with its red-painted floors and walls (the 'Red Building'), as the property of an élite group who distributed quantities of food during public feasting ceremonies, and whose status dictated that they preside over other communal ceremonies. In this respect, it should be noted that the surrounding buildings held a concentration of highly decorated, large bowls used for serving foodstuffs, and several holemouth storage jars (Bolger, in Peltenburg et al. 1998: 118, 246, figs. 14.6–14.7).

Below the floor of Building 994, which somewhat postdates Building 206 and the other calcarenite structures (Peltenburg et al. 1998: 248), were two pits – Units 1015 and 1225. The latter contained three stacked Red-on-White bowls along with 350 heat-cracked and blackened stones and cobbles, as well as a dozen fragmentary groundstone artefacts, all embedded in an ashy silt. Unit 1015 held an even more unusual deposit of more than 50 objects, likewise embedded in an ashy matrix together with more heat-cracked and blackened groundstone, cobble/pebble and pottery fragments, as well as bone and shell (Peltenburg 1991a: 23–26; 1991c: 12–27, 39–55). This remarkable deposit has been interpreted by the excavator as evidence for purposeful, communal ritual activity, once again accompanied by feasting (Peltenburg et al. 1998: 247).

For most other archaeologists working on Cyprus, however, what has attracted the most attention is the deposit found at the base of Unit 1015. Here lay 18 anthropomorphic figurines (10 stone, 8 pottery), an anthropomorphic pottery vessel, a terracotta stool and triton shell, and various groundstone pebbles and tools, all packed in and around a Red-on-White bowl modelled in the form of a typical Middle Chalcolithic building (Figure 61). Although the bowl has painted designs on its interior and exterior, the paint had been concealed by a layer of whitish clay applied before its final, surely deliberate deposition (Peltenburg 1991a: 24–25; 1991c: 12–27, frontispiece, pl. 1:5, 6). With one exception, the stone figurines were not freestanding and likely

Figure 61. Kissonerga *Mosphilia* Red-on-White bowl/building model, with 18 anthropomorphic figurines and several other items packed in and around it. Courtesy of Edgar Peltenburg.

were intended to hold in the hand, perhaps as talismans or charms (Goring, in Peltenburg 1991c: 52–55). Only two of the stone examples show clear indications of (female) sex, but at least four others have phallic-shaped necks or heads (Peltenburg 1991c: figs. 21–22).

All the pottery examples are freestanding and depict females with elaborately painted decoration; some are standing, others squatting or kneeling, and three are sitting on stools. The stool of one figurine (KM 1451) was broken away, but still visible is an anthropomorphic pendant painted around her neck and the schematic rendering of a baby (arms and head) emerging between her legs (Peltenburg 1991c: fig. 24) (Figure 62). It is widely believed that these figurines were associated with childbirth (or birthing rituals) and used in ceremonies to promote female fertility (e.g. Peltenburg 1991a: 24; 1991c: 98–102; Bolger 1992: 155–156; 2003: 104–105) (discussed further below, under *Gender and the Individual Body*). More specifically, Peltenburg and Goring (1991: 21–22)

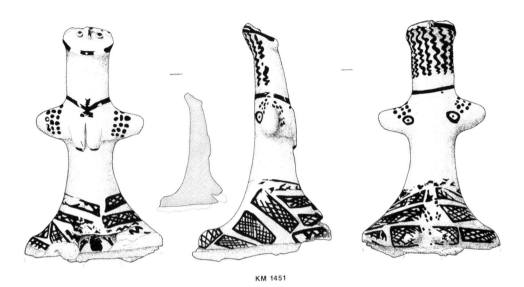

KM 1451

Figure 62. Kissonerga *Mosphilia* 'birthing figurine' (KM 1451). Height 20.3 cm; width 11.5 cm; thickness 11.3 cm. After Peltenberg 1991c: fig. 24. Courtesy of Edgar Peltenburg.

maintain that the Unit 1015 at *Mosphilia* is a special deposit whose total find context points to a place where steam or heat generated from fire-cracked stones would have been used at the time of parturition or in postnatal care. Certainly all this symbolism surrounding childbirth had some social significance for the people who lived in the small communities of Chalcolithic Cyprus, where the spectre of infant mortality always stalked family life (Lunt 1995; Peltenburg et al. 1998: 82–83; Steel 2004a: 106).

The precise nature of the activities that took place within and/or amongst these buildings can only be a matter for speculation (Keswani 1994: 267). Rituals associated with birth, death, agricultural activities (planting, harvesting) and rites of passage may have been of considerable importance for the agropastoral communities of Chalcolithic Cyprus. Nonetheless, there is some tension in these interpretations that spin off various scenarios concerning ceremonial rituals that involved feasting (Building 206 and the ceremonial area) and childbirth (Building 994 and Pit 1015).

On the one hand, it would be fatuous to deny some link with childbirth, given all the representational evidence seen there. On the other hand, Bolger (1996) has suggested that Chalcolithic figurines such as these were related not only to birthing but also to fertility, and further that this female sphere of influence reflects the presence of an egalitarian society. Chalcolithic is thus seen as synonymous with female and egalitarian and, by a strictly binary extension, the subsequent Bronze Age is equated with male and a patriarchal regime, when '…centralised authorities created structures in which women's roles were increasingly restricted and social and economic inequalities became institutionalised' (Bolger 1996: 371). Bolger thus seeks to explain the origin of female oppression through changes seen in figurine representations. Male and female are polarised and non-ambiguous; women are stigmatised as fertile birth-givers whilst men drive society to ever more complex and socially strat-ified levels. As this notion has already been critiqued (Frankel 1997), I leave it to one side here but consider alternative interpretations below (*Gender and the Individual Body*).

Regarding the so-called ceremonial area and Building 206, the case for feasting may be somewhat overstated, as the definition and understanding of this phenomenon – in material terms – have become a very precise undertak-ing (e.g. Twiss 2008; Ben-Shlomo et al. 2009: 130–131). Many of the material aspects of feasting – unusual amounts or types of food residues/animal bones, special consumption/disposal areas, ovens or hearths for preparing food, over-size serving vessels or large numbers of standard-sized vessels, distinctive food storage facilities, ritual or prestige objects – could equally apply to other phe-nomena. Intriguingly, during Period 3B at *Mosphilia*, there was a notable fall-off in the amount of food preparation equipment, in the numbers of axes and adzes recovered, and in the amount of charred seeds retrieved (Peltenburg et al. 1998: 244). Moreover, neither in the 'ceremonial area' nor in the structures sur-rounding it was there any noticeable concentration of animal bones or plant remains to indicate a place set aside for cooking, and the same holds true for Unit 1015 (Peltenburg and Goring 1991: 21). In other words, the concentration of remarkable (ritual or prestige) objects found in and around the 'ceremonial area' contrasts with the scarcity of materials related to food preparation and consumption. Nonetheless, we must bear in mind that in addition to the ritual deposit of representational figures from Pit 1015, most of the cruciform figu-rines from *Mosphilia*, and virtually all figurines from the Main Area, including the largest known example in picrolite, belong to Period 3b (Peltenburg et al. 1998: 246).

The most we can surmise, then, is that the combination of features seen in and around the 'ceremonial area' and in the pits beneath Building 994 at *Mosphilia* make it likely that these assemblages served ceremonial purposes, which might have included feasting, drinking or entertainment. Peltenburg (1991a: 25–26; also Peltenburg et al. 1998: 247–248), however, also maintains that Unit 1015 was a deliberate deposit of exceptional material representing a closure ceremony involving the entire community at *Mosphilia*. The building model with all its unique contents indeed may have formed part of an intentional act carried out by one or more members of the community. However, it is surely stretching the evidence to suggest that these 'ceremonial pits' were part of a specific '… communal feast [that] signalled an end to Chalcolithic birthing ideologies and associated gender constructs' (Bolger 2003: 105), even more to argue that '… the Kissonerga deposit can serve as a case study in which emerging élite groups attempted to dominate the power of individual performers by appropriating, destroying, and concealing their ritual symbols' (Bolger 2003: 121).

It seems just as reasonable to suggest that this special deposit – that is, the building model, its context as well as its contents – represents nothing more than an elaborate domestic structure (Bolger 1992: 158; 2003: 104; Knapp and Meskell 1997: 192) whose occupants used (handled, displayed, broke) the figurines found within it. Even if the collecting and deposition of these objects are seen to represent communal practices, it seems obvious that the figurines themselves were used by individual people. Moreover, the stone figurines, despite their simplicity, appear quite individualised (Goring, in Peltenburg 1991c: 53, 55), whilst the elaborate decoration on the pottery examples also makes them individually distinctive (similarly Bolger 2003: 108, 120). In other words, there is sufficient variability amongst these Chalcolithic figurines to suggest characterisations of the individual self, a topic that requires further consideration.

GENDER AND THE INDIVIDUAL BODY

Until recently, the study of gender and the body in Cypriot archaeology was devoted largely to describing and classifying a diverse array of anthropomorphic clay, stone and – especially for the Chalcolithic period – picrolite figurines (e.g. Merrillees 1980; 1988; Orphanides 1988; Mogelonsky 1991; Goring 1991). Despite a maturing interest in gender issues amongst Cypriot archaeologists (e.g. Hamilton 1994; 2000; papers in Bolger and Serwint 2002; Bolger 1992; 1996; 2002), classifications remain mainly binary (male/female) and most interpretations revolve around ritualistic usage or the notion of a 'mother goddess' (following J. Karageorghis 1977; 2005). Dividing humanity into mutually exclusive and oppositional male and female categories, however, is not exclusive to research on Cyprus; indeed it typifies a diverse range of archaeological approaches (discussed by Conkey and Gero 1997; Voss 2008). The sexing of figurines traditionally has followed this universalising ethos (Hamilton 2000), and the ritual, mortuary or divine interpretations that follow are the logical outcome.

Such figurines, however, may have little to do with ritual and certainly should not be seen exclusively as representing goddesses (Knapp 2009a). What they do offer is an important source of visual information on the ways people dressed and marked their bodies; they provide intriguing clues to questions of sex, gender and identity in prehistoric Cyprus. Yet the complexity of different forms, the differences between picrolite pendants and figurines, and the multiple find contexts (where they exist) all make it difficult to understand just what their diverse meaning(s) and function(s) may have been – for example, ritual, ideological, funerary, fertility, pregnancy/birth or the life cycle (Vagnetti 1974: 29–30; Steel 2004a: 101–102).

In contrast to the limited, rather schematic repertoire of the Neolithic period, representational art becomes a common feature during the Chalcolithic, particularly in clay and stone figurines. Even in the Early Chalcolithic, the images are more readily recognisable as people, with individualised features depicted (eyes, nose, fingers, toes), and occasionally with detailed modelling of anatomy. Of 31 ceramic anthropomorphic figurines and fragments found in pits within the Northwest Area at Early Chalcolithic *Ayious*, only two examples were complete; these, along with some more distinctive fragments, seem to have had a basic cruciform shape. If so, they might reasonably be interpreted as reflecting an early stage in the development of the more elaborate terracotta and picrolite types found at later, Middle Chalcolithic sites such as *Mosphilia*, Lemba *Lakkous* and Souskiou *Vathyrkakas*. Some remnants of painted geometric decoration are preserved on the *Ayious* figurines and the sex, whenever apparent, is female (Todd and Croft 2004: 191–195, figs. 57–60, pls. 51–53).

By the Middle Chalcolithic, a quantitative and artistic revolution is evident in the production of figurines: clay, limestone and especially picrolite. Quite varied in style as well as size, these representations range from schematised pendants only a few centimetres tall, to small portable figurines from 5–15 cm high, to larger examples standing between 35–40 cm in height (Steel 2004a: 99). The largest known example (39.5 cm tall) is a limestone cruciform figure, reportedly from Souskiou, with breasts clearly indicated and markings (a cape? tattoo?) carved on the arms (Maier and Karageorghis 1984: 34–35, fig. 16). By this time, there was a renewed emphasis on the human form, more obvious indicators of sex, and detailed attention given to facial features (excepting the mouth).

Many of the human representations in stone and clay are shown wearing jewellery, whilst the bodies of the clay figurines are often richly decorated with painted or incised decoration. Whilst some figurines are shown squatting or giving birth, others are depicted in triangular form, but the most common and striking shape is the cruciform (cross-shaped). Although clay and stone examples are frequently represented in this manner, the picrolite cruciforms seem to us the most compelling, not least because of the exquisite material from which they were made. Notable amongst them are the mottled dark and light green example from Souskiou *Vathyrkakas* (Peltenburg 2006: colour pl. B.5–6; see above, Figure 58), and the soft, almost marble-like model from Yialia (15 cm tall) that now graces the reverse of the one- and two-euro Cypriot coins (Figure 63). Depicted in typical bent-leg pose with arms outstretched, the latter figurine has a smaller representation of itself hanging round the neck (Vagnetti 1974: 28–29, pl. V.1).

In contextual terms, the extensive use of picrolite for pendants, beads and cruciform figurines, and the number of picrolite cruciforms typically found in mortuary contexts (notably in the shaft graves at Souskiou), raise various issues concerning their meaning and significance. By and large, these figurines were found in the graves of women or children; Bolger (1994: 15) suggests that women may have produced them. Such figurines seldom accompanied adult male burials but Tomb 59 at *Vathyrkakas* is one case in which they did

Figure 63. Yialia picrolite cruciform figurine. Height 16 cm. Courtesy of the Cyprus Museum, Nicosia.

(Peltenburg 2006: 165). Children outnumber adults in some of the richer tombs at *Vathyrkakas* (Tombs 29, 58, 86), and anthropomorphic figurines were found in 10 of the 13 tombs that held child and adult burials; amongst exclusively adult burials, however, only two held figurines. At Lemba *Lakkous*, the three Middle Chalcolithic graves (21, 44, 46) that contained a picrolite pendant belonged to children whilst the one grave with a picrolite figurine had no occupant (Bolger 2002: 72 and table 3). The majority of Middle Chalcolithic burials from Kissonerga *Mosphilia* were those of children, and the highest proportion of picrolite (mostly pendants, a few cruciform figurines) came from those same burials (Peltenburg et al. 1998: 66–68).

Does the common association of picrolite with children or (adult) females point to preferential treatment and/or some level of social status for certain individuals, families or social groups? Considerations of source, distribution, context and use once led Peltenburg (1991: 116) to argue for the decentralised, non-specialist production of picrolite pendants and figurines, even if the dissemination of picrolite as a raw material was carefully controlled. More recently, he has suggested that the settlement at Souskiou *Laona* may have served as a production centre for picrolite figurines (Peltenburg 2011b). In the Souskiou cemeteries, at least, there seems to have been scope for people to emphasise their individuality within the developing ideological system symbolised by the picrolite cruciform figurines (Peltenburg 2006: 168). For example, the quantity and diversity of grave goods found in *Vathyrkakas* shaft Tomb 86, along with three picrolite figurines, suggest this was the tomb of a 'highly privileged' individual (Peltenburg 2006: 166). Amongst all the opulent grave goods buried in the *Vathyrkakas* tombs, the anthropomorphic picrolite figurines seem to encapsulate best the growing importance of individuals – and individual identities – on Chalcolithic Cyprus.

The 36-cm tall figurine known as the Lemba Lady (see above, Figure 55) may also tell us something about individuals as well as sexual ambiguity on Chalcolithic Cyprus. Peltenburg (1977: 142) first noted this ambiguity, describing the figure as hermaphroditic; he thus focused on a dualism he also sees in certain picrolite cruciform figurines (see below) whose phallic-shaped arms transform them into another figure of indeterminate sex. The Lemba Lady, an incised, violin-shaped figurine made from limestone and modelled with arms outstretched in cruciform fashion, has an elongated neck and a back-tilted, flat head with the eyes and nose depicted in relief. The incised female breasts and genitalia, as well as the broad hips and swollen stomach, contrast with the roughly phallic-shaped head. Recovered in a very distinctive context in Building 1 at Lemba initially regarded as a sacred place (Peltenburg 1977: 141; 1989: 122), this figurine was originally seen as a possible (Middle) Chalcolithic deity (Bolger 1992: 155). Yet its form, attributes and bisexual nature need have nothing to do with a divinity (Budin 2003: 115–116, 119), and Bolger (2003: 87) more recently has suggested it represents a pregnant female.

In a variation on this theme, Reitler (1963) regarded the head and neck of cruciform figurines as phallic representations, and the lower part with bent knees as a woman giving birth. Another interesting and equally ambiguous example is the white limestone figurine found at Sotira *Arkolies* and discussed above (see Figure 48) (Swiny and Swiny 1983). Although generally regarded as Ceramic Neolithic in date, on stylistic grounds it might equally be attributed to the (Late) Chalcolithic (Knapp and Meskell 1997: 193). Depending on one's chosen viewpoint, this unique figurine could be regarded as either male or female, or both (Swiny and Swiny 1983: 57–58). Its sexual ambiguity becomes clear when compared to obviously phallic examples such as another limestone figure from Sotira *Teppes* (Dikaios 1961: 201, pls. 91.106, 102.106) (see Figure 47), or to the bone pendant from Kouklia (Osaki and Harris 1990: 37, fig. 21).

The Lemba Lady and the *Arkolies* model clearly incorporate both phallic and vulvic qualities. Often it has been assumed that all Chalcolithic cruciform figurines are female and should be understood to have breasts, even if the representation lacks them (a Campo 1994: 134; Budin 2003: 114; 2011: 224 n.12). Amongst the corpus of 83 Chalcolithic cruciform figurines examined by a Campo (1994: 128, table 10), only 12 (14%) had breasts and only one, a picrolite figurine from Kissonerga *Mylouthkia* (KM 52), has the genitals rendered ambiguously: it has been interpreted as either male or female (Morris 1985: 128; Goring, in Peltenburg et al. 2003: 170, fig. 61.5).

A further glance at several other Chalcolithic figurines indicates that few are demonstrably female: the exceptions are two terracotta 'lactating' figurines (Caubet 1974: 35–36, pl. VII.1, 4; Morris 1985: 133, figs. 173–174), and three further examples from Souskiou with breasts in prominent relief (Vagnetti 1974: 29, pl.V.3; Osaki and Harris 1990: 42–43, figs. 32–33; Peltenburg 2006: pl. 28.3 [tomb 86]). At least one, more abstract example from Tomb 31 at Souskiou *Vathyrkakas* is clearly male (Peltenburg 2006: pl. 15.3). Another, allegedly from Souskiou and now in the Pierides Collection in Larnaca, depicts an ithyphallic male, seated on a stool with his head tilted back and his mouth wide open (Karageorghis and Vagnetti 1981). Despite its evident maleness, seen by some as representing an ejaculating figure broadcasting male fertility (Morris 1985: 134–135, fig. 175), Hamilton (1994: 305, 309–311) contends that the viewer's attention is drawn not to the penis but to the grimacing facial features. She maintains, not altogether convincingly, that the figure may reflect the custom of *couvade*, which prescribes how and to what extent males can be involved with pregnancy and childbirth.

Hamilton's multiple- and/or cross-gender approach to the study of sexually ambivalent Cypriot figurines offers tantalising clues about the nature of sex, sexuality and the individual. If we want to understand better how a gendered approach can provide insights into the nature and purpose of Chalcolithic figurines, it is important to view sex as socially constituted and to move beyond notions of a female–male dichotomy. Even the notion of multiple genders does little to advance our quest unless we take into account the full spectrum of possible variation.

The whole repertoire of cruciform figurines with outstretched arms and/or an elongated neck – taken to an extreme in examples where the arms have become virtually a second body as fully detailed as the standard cruciforms (e.g. Morris 1985: 131, figs. 167–170; Peltenburg 2006: pl. 28.8 [tomb 86]) – may represent an attempt to harmonise, or at least to incorporate in one object, the sexual characteristics of males and females. By the same token, however, the androgynous nuances evident in various cruciform representations (Osaki and Harris 1990: 41–44, figs. 29–33, 36, with further refs) may have nothing to do with sexual dualities. Rather than seeing these representations simply as males or females, or harmonising their sexual characteristics, that is, in terms of gender or sex per se, perhaps what is being formulated is the construction of the individual (Knapp and Meskell 1997: 199–200).

The subject of individuals in prehistory is a contentious issue, and has been discussed and debated at length elsewhere (Knapp and van Dommelen 2008). The only point to reiterate here is that we are not dealing with the contemporary, socially conscious, fully interiorised notions of the modern individual, but rather to possible ancient Cypriot notions of the self. To experience oneself as a living individual is a basic feature of human nature, and in this respect Chalcolithic Cypriotes were no different than anyone else. Early–Middle Chalcolithic society overall was small in scale, agriculturally oriented, with a largely egalitarian social structure organised at the household or village level. In such societies, individuals always had a social or political dimension, but it is rare for any individual, or even a single group, to assume a permanent level of social prominence.

Nonetheless, we find several novel features in the Chalcolithic era that may be relevant to an emerging individual status: the dramatic increase in the production and use of picrolite pendants and figurines (in particular the cruciform and 'birthing' examples); greater focus on individual households and ancestors (the latter evident from burials associated with building sequences); intensified agricultural production; household (vs. communal) storage, food preparation and consumption; elaborate burials with individualised grave goods and the attention given to children; the earliest decorative use of metals (the copper spirals). All of these material developments may be linked to structural changes in society (Peltenburg 1993: 20) and perhaps point to the development of individual rights or status, within distinct lineages or amongst élite families (see further in the following section, *Incipient Complexity, Ideology and Identity*).

Chalcolithic figurines served, at least in part, to characterise individuals rather than to delineate social categories. The figurines show varying degrees of differentiation, especially in their facial features and hairstyles, the shape of their hands and feet, and their bodily ornamentation – necklaces, bracelets, clothing or tattooing (Swantek 2006: 99). Bailey (1994) made a similar argument for Chalcolithic figurines from Bulgaria; based upon their form, context and perceived social role, he suggested they are the outward expressions of prehistoric individuals. Beyond emphasising their sexual ambiguity, most Cypriot figurines, pendants and modelled figures defy straightforward sexual interpretation. This does not mean, however, that sex had no bearing on Chalcolithic society. The apparent paucity of male figurines may indicate that masculinity, as understood in the strictly Western sense (Knapp 1998a), lacked any social significance, or that male fertility had little relevance to Chalcolithic society. Alternatively, and equally likely, it could suggest that male authority was so firmly embedded in society that there was no need to signify it. Even if some figurines were intended to represent multi-sexed or cross-gendered individuals, this presumes that there were clear gender boundaries to cross (Hamilton 2000: 28).

There seems little reason to question the notion that the striking terracotta figurines from Unit 1015 at *Mosphilia* involved some ceremony, or possibly even an ideology surrounding childbirth, especially in a society where a child's life expectancy was low. It is also well to recall here that once the contents of Unit 1015 had been deposited in the pit, there is no further evidence for the production or use of pottery figurines in the subsequent, Late Chalcolithic period, even if picrolite continued to be used to make cruciform birthing figurines at Lemba and *Mosphilia* (Bolger 1996: 369).

Interpretations that revolve solely around issues of fertility, divinity and ritual seem suspect, not least because they implicitly reflect modern concerns or viewpoints. They take little account of the fact that these figurines – however symbolic and abstract they seem to us – formed an integral part of the material and sensual factors of everyday life. Attempts to interpret them must engage their social, spatial, ideological and economic contexts, all of which were intimately linked in prehistoric societies such as that of Chalcolithic Cyprus. We should not think of these striking human representations exclusively in sexual terms (and certainly not as binary representations).

In this corpus of female, male, hybrid, trans-, cross- or third-gender representations, we may be seeing images that moved in and out of traditional sexual categories. Once we dismiss the deeply held notion that these figurines connote fertility or divinity, it becomes possible to consider them as representations of individual women or men, of feasting or other types of celebration (e.g. rites of passage), of ceremonial activities, even of cultic practices. The use of binary or essentialist categorisations will never deepen our understanding of prehistoric society. Each one of the images or individuals represented in these Chalcolithic figurines served to shape gendered practices and performances in society; in turn they were imbricated in the formation of people's social identity. In that light, I now turn to consider in more detail various other aspects of identity, ideology and social complexity on Early–Middle Chalcolithic Cyprus.

Incipient Complexity, Ideology and Identity in the Early–Middle Chalcolithic

Peltenburg (1993: 17–18) viewed the fractal nature of Chalcolithic settlements as the result of 'communal fissioning' (i.e. abandonment, relocation, reoccupation), a factor that also served as an important check on the excessive accumulation of power by any one individual or group. The unstable sociopolitical configuration of communities in southwest Cyprus, he suggested, might best be equated with a segmentary society, that is, a polity made up of small, autonomous, egalitarian villages that show no evidence for *institutionalised* forms of inequality. Held (1993), writing several years before the final published reports of sites such as Kissonerga *Mosphilia* or Kalavasos *Ayious*, adopted a similar, minimalist view of Chalcolithic social developments; he questioned whether the relevant sites had yielded sufficient data to justify arguments for the existence of power differentials or decision-making authorities during the Early–Middle Chalcolithic.

More recently, Peltenburg (2006: 175; n.d.) has modified his viewpoint. He now sees the High Sector and Upper Terrace structures at *Mosphilia* (and by extension structures elsewhere such as Building 200 at *Mylouthkia* or Building 1 at Lemba *Lakkous*), as well as the mortuary evidence from Souskiou and *Mosphilia*, as signalling the emergence of a higher status group, one that promoted its position within the community through feasting, location, access to special resources (picrolite) and control over an ideological system. Held (1993: 28) argued that these distinctive structures might indicate at most 'some consensual caretaker' or possibly 'rudimentary social rank' amongst elders at *Mosphilia*. In his view, even if some degree of social hierarchy existed during the Chalcolithic, this need not indicate regionally empowered élites or social stratification but rather the side effects of ecological and subsistence strategies designed to perpetuate a largely egalitarian social and economic system.

Although it would thus seem that unstable, transient forms of social or economic ascendancy were characteristic of the Middle–Late Chalcolithic (Peltenburg 2006: 175), the evidence of emulation and competitive display at Souskiou *Vathyrkakas* is exceptional, at least compared to that from most contemporary settlements. Manning (1993: 43), it may be recalled, regards the multiple burials from *Vathyrkakas* and the attention given to juvenile burials during the Chalcolithic generally as indicative of distinct lineages that had the ability to formalise certain rights and social status over the long term (see also Peltenburg 2006: 166). Within Chalcolithic settlements, structures with private storage areas and burials just outside their walls (e.g. Buildings 1547/1590 and 1016/1565 on *Mosphilia*'s Upper Terrace) might point to the emergence of property and inheritance rights. Thus people's motivations and in particular their aspirations towards social status or privileges, alongside certain environmental and social constraints, certainly could account for the discontinuities seen in the material record. In addition to disruptions and dispersals, however, there must also have been continuities and interconnections. Indeed, communities with expanding populations probably developed networks for communication and participated in certain common rituals in order to mediate conflicts and to ensure their social reproduction.

The distinctive mortuary practices and rich grave goods from the Souskiou cemeteries, together with several other, novel material aspects of the Early–Middle Chalcolithic, seem to point to the emergence of individual identities on Chalcolithic Cyprus. Peltenburg (2006: 175, fig. 12.9, 176–177), for example, suggests that Tomb 73 at *Vathyrkakas* – by far the largest mortuary installation ever seen on the island up to this time – represents the mobilisation of labour to create a facility far exceeding any basic or practical requirements of burial. Two possible males were interred in shaft 73.6 on a floor with an area of 1.17 m^2, thus commanding much more space than is usual in these graves. Although the grave goods are not otherwise remarkable, they include a pointed-base, Red-on-White flask decorated in four horizontal registers, the lowest of which has the earliest known painted depiction of a human being on pottery (Peltenburg 2006: 103–104, pl. 23.3, colour pl. B.8). Although highly schematic, this figure does appear to be anthropomorphic and of a very elongated cruciform shape, not unlike those seen on the picrolite figurines. In Peltenburg's (2006: 176) own words: 'It may be that quite specific individuals rather than an extended sub-group were so outstanding in MChal society'. Indeed, taken together with increasing household autonomy and food storage, feasting, grandiose buildings, increased production and consumption of picrolite if not metal, and the new attention given to representational art, these elaborate burials with unique, individualised grave goods certainly offer material witness of the steps taken in the attempt to overcome resistance to structural inequalities in society.

The extensive use of picrolite in producing distinctive, new representational objects, and the earliest occurrences of copper tools and objects, have other ramifications for the study of identity and ideology during the Chalcolithic. Bolger (1994: 15), for example, suggests that women were intimately linked with the procurement of picrolite and the manufacture in a household context of at least some picrolite pendants. Quite how this squares with Peltenburg's (2011b) more recent view of the settlement at Souskiou *Laona* as a centre for the production of picrolite figurines remains to be seen. The occurrence at various Chalcolithic sites of exotic materials such as picrolite, faience, malachite and several species of shells may reflect the growth of regional exchange, through which wealth would have been generated for ceremonial use, feasting, social payments or other requirements of the networked village system (Keswani 1994: 267, with refs.).

The 'foreign' artefacts from *Ayious* and 'exotic' materials (chlorite, faience) from *Mosphilia and Vathyrkakas*, however, do not constitute sufficient evidence to indicate that Cyprus's isolation from the surrounding world had come to an end. Even Peltenburg (2006: 168–170), who emphasised the close relationship between metals and faience, and considered whether both might have been imported to the island at this early date, found the evidence equivocal. Elsewhere, he has suggested that Cyprus remained in what he termed a 'dynamic of stability' right up to the final phases of its earlier prehistory (Peltenburg 2004c: 84). We have to consider the possibility that Cyprus's insularity at this time points to an intentional strategy of maintaining a distinct island identity. By the early to mid-3rd millennium BC, however, during the Late Chalcolithic and the early phases of the Prehistoric Bronze Age, this isolation – if such it was – came to a definitive end, as Cypriot contacts with Anatolia, the Aegean and perhaps even the southern Levant increasingly come to the fore.

LATE CHALCOLITHIC

Throughout its long duration, the Chalcolithic way of life remained rural and self-sufficient, factors that may have minimised if not inhibited the emergence of central places or hierarchical social relationships. From the mid-4th millennium Cal BC (i.e. Middle Chalcolithic), however, there are possible signs of wealth, surplus and social differentiation: (1) a two-tiered intra-site hierarchy, larger and better-built (calcarenite) structures, wealthy children's burials, birthing figurines and a house model at *Mosphilia* (Period 3b), perhaps even public, ceremonial feasting (Peltenburg et al. 1998: 244–249); (2) the prestige-laden picrolite figurines (Peltenburg et al. 1998: 189–192); (3) the materiality of emulation and competitive display evident at Souskiou *Laona* and *Vathyrkakas*, hinting at some level of social or economic ascendancy (Peltenburg 2006: 175); and (4) finds of metal and faience from contexts both mortuary (e.g. Souskiou *Laona*) and domestic (*Mosphilia*, Souskiou *Laona*) (Peltenburg et al. 1998: 188–189; Crewe et al. 2005; Peltenburg et al. 2006: 98).

By the end of the Middle Chalcolithic, however, some see indicators of a society in the throes of a demographic crisis, for example the high rates of infant and child mortality (Lunt 1995: 58, table 10.1; Peltenburg et al. 1998: 73–75, table 4.4) and the low average life expectancy of Chalcolithic women (Bolger 1993: 37; Keswani 2004: 147). And yet, with little evidence to compare from other periods, earlier or later, these factors cannot be regarded as decisive. It is clear nonetheless that the prior emphasis on sexuality and procreativity, expressed through a variety of figurines, virtually disappeared. Moreover, the thriving community at *Mosphilia* came to an end, and possibly lay abandoned for up to 200 years (Peltenburg et al. 1998: 249). The picture is less clear at Lemba *Lakkous* but a gap in occupation between Periods 2 and 3 is possible (Peltenburg et al. 1985: 18; Peltenburg 2007a: 144 now calls this 200-year gap an 'informational hiatus').

In a new development, excavations at Politiko *Kokkinorotsos* (née *Phournia*) in the north central Troodos have revealed a small, intermittently used hunting station with low intensity occupation, something quite unusual in the Chalcolithic settlement record (Webb et al. 2009). The dating of this site (ca. 2820–2750 Cal BC, see Appendix, caption to Figure A10) seems to fall in the 200-year occupational hiatus seen at *Mosphilia* and Lemba *Lakkous*. Webb et al. (2009: 195) also report that the settlement at Souskiou *Laona* has produced radiocarbon dates similar to those from *Kokkinorotsos*; Peltenburg (2011b: fig. 10) comments generally on these unpublished radiocarbon dates, which seem to confirm a late Middle or early Late Chalcolithic occupation at *Laona* between ca. 2888–2700 Cal BC (see above, p. 215).

All these factors and more point to a significant change between the Middle and Late Chalcolithic periods. In Peltenburg's (1993) view, the occupational or informational hiatus at *Mosphilia* (possibly also at Lemba) likely indicates the outcome of a reaction to the increased centralisation of power that seems evident at that site towards the end of Middle Chalcolithic. In such a scenario, Politiko *Kokkinorotsos* would represent yet a further reaction, namely a reversion to a more mobile, hunting-oriented way of life. But we also need to consider an alternative scenario, namely that periodically used hunting villages may always have formed part of the (late Middle or early Late) Chalcolithic landscape (Webb et al. 2009: 233). Like other site types in the central lowlands and foothills of the island, they may thus far have been poorly reported, or overlooked, in the archaeological record (further discussion below).

During the Late Chalcolithic phase (ca. 2700/2600–2500/2400 Cal BC), occupation levels at Kissonerga *Mosphilia* (Periods 4a, 4b) and Lemba *Lakkous*

(Period 3) reveal, to differing extents, smaller structures (circular in plan, and lacking spatially divided interiors); an absence of cruciform figurines; a decline in the use of picrolite, metal and faience; and a new, technically proficient and standardised type of pottery (Red and Black Stroke-Burnished, an unpainted monochrome ware). Elaborate burials continue in use but now with the dead (adults only) placed in newly developed chamber tombs (Period 4b at *Mosphilia*). There are also clear indicators of intensified agricultural production (pig-rearing, food processing, perhaps centralised storage) and possibly of increased external contacts, all of which may well reflect some level of structural change in Cypriot society (Peltenburg et al. 1998: 251–258). Before we can determine to what extent such changes represent resistance to established power structures, we need to take a closer look at Late Chalcolithic materiality and settlement evidence.

Settlement, Society and Materiality

In recent years, the material sequences from settlement sites of the Late Chalcolithic through Early Cypriot periods have become much better documented and dated (e.g. Manning and Swiny 1994; Peltenburg et al. 1998: 18–21). The traditional chronological phases – Late Chalcolithic, Philia, Early Cypriot I–II – now appear to be sequential and to some extent overlapping, with the Late Chalcolithic and Early Cypriot components incorporating certain material features previously linked exclusively to the Philia phase. Material, cultural and social factors alike became much more complex by the mid-3rd millennium Cal BC, in a newly transformed set of sociopolitical and economic circumstances. The Late Chalcolithic was a time of change, a period transitional to the initial stages of the Early Bronze Age on Cyprus (i.e. PreBA I – Knapp 2008: 68–74). Some material developments in both the settlement and mortuary spheres foreshadow those of the PreBA, and are taken up again, with different emphases, in the next chapter.

Assuming that there was indeed a break in occupation at the end of the Middle Chalcolithic, at Lemba *Lakkous* (Period 3) we can see a clear reorganisation of the settlement. A linear band of six habitational structures was terraced into the slope in Area II (Peltenburg et al. 1985: 318, 326–329, fig. 6.6). All except one of several burials in this area are sealed beneath the floors and walls of structures. Two of these structures (Buildings 2, 3) contained a distinctive storage area around their inner walls, circular hearths, and a range of tools, animal bones (especially pig) and stone vessels. Building 2 also contained some distinctive personal items: pendants, beads, a figurine, pierced discs, and some small conical and grooved stones. Building 7 housed 4 elaborate groundstone basins, 16 rubbers, a built-in mortar and some spouted flasks, all suggesting some kind of specialised food and/or drink preparation. This terraced row of buildings might best be seen as a family compound, with specialised activity areas related to the preparation and storage of consumables.

At Kissonerga *Mosphilia* (Peltenburg et al. 1998: 3), those who established the new settlement moved into a landscape with upstanding ruins (Peltenburg et al. 1998: 249). Here we find evidence for communal food storage, metalworking and specialised craft activities. During Phase 4a, only a few, isolated structures were identified. Amongst them, the most important was Building 3, christened the 'Pithos House' and designated an élite structure on the basis of finds within it. According to the excavator, the community at Late Chalcolithic *Mosphilia* reached its maximum extent in Period 4b, with population estimates ranging between 600–1,500 (Peltenburg et al. 1998: 255).

The Pithos House of Period 4a revealed, amongst others things, (imported?) faience beads, triton shells, annular shell pendants, evidence for the working of shell, picrolite and red pigment, a cache of 47 stone axes and adzes, a concentration of conical stones similar to west Asiatic tokens (Schmandt-Besserat 1994), possible evidence for an oil press, vessels for food preparation, and at least 37 storage vessels with a capacity of up to 4,000 litres (Peltenburg et al. 1998: 37–43, fig. 3.9, 252–254) (Figure 64). From what we might call 'recycled' contexts in the subsequent Building 706 (Period 4b) came a stamp seal (KM 597), five of the six annular pendants found, and evidence for copper working (a possible crucible, KM 693, and ore KM 701) (Peltenburg et al. 1998: 37). According to the excavator, Building 706 represents a reoccupation of the underlying Pithos House (Building 3), a temporary roofed or unroofed area where the occupants prepared to rebuild their lives in 'a re-possession of Pithos House property space' (Peltenburg et al. 1998: 48–49). This space was used for cooking, metalworking, caching and curating of high value material originally associated with Building 3, and building operations for the succeeding Building 86. Although it is argued that the seal (a possible 'administrative device') and evidence of metalworking originated in the earlier, Period 4a building, the seal and the ore, and a possible crucible and chisel actually derive from the later, Period 4b, Building 706. At the very least this has an impact on the earliest uses of sealing and metalworking at *Mosphilia* (i.e. no earlier than about 2500 Cal BC).

Be that as it may, the Pithos House (Building 3, Level 4a), nearly 10 m in diameter, is somewhat larger than other contemporary structures but also shows features (e.g. a central hearth) known elsewhere. Completely atypical for this period, however, is this level of storage capacity (about 4,000 litres), which common sense dictates is well beyond the household level. Moreover, the dense concentrations of standardised bowls and small conical stones (tokens for exchange?) may have been associated with the redistribution of surplus agricultural products (Peltenburg et al. 1998: 253). In addition, the unusually large number of deer bones found in the Pithos House, at a time when pig had become the staple of the meat diet, may also hint at some special status for the residents of this building (Peltenburg et al. 1998: 213–214, 253). Taken together with the evidence (discussed below) for specialised deer hunting at

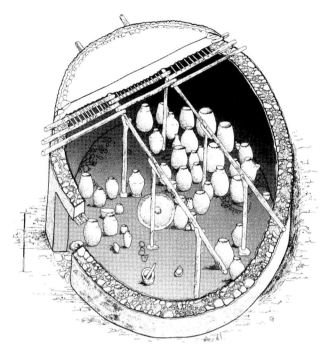

Figure 64. Kissonerga *Mosphilia* 'Pithos House', reconstruction. After Peltenburg et al. 1998: 37–43, fig. 3.9. Courtesy of Edgar Peltenburg.

the site of Politiko *Kokkinorotsos*, we might consider whether (a) deer hunting was an élite activity, a type of social storage developed as a response to occasional shortfalls in agricultural production, or if (b) it was associated with more regular centralised storage and redistribution practices (Jennifer Webb, pers. comm., June 2010).

Steel (2004a: 112–113) also suggested that evidence from the Pithos House might constitute an example of social storage (Halstead 1981; Halstead and O'Shea 1982). She pointed out that storage strategies had become increasingly sophisticated throughout the Chalcolithic, and that the Pithos House might represent a highly developed response to sustained shortfalls in agricultural production, or to other economic uncertainties. Peltenburg (1993: 15), too, originally proposed that the Pithos House served as a central storage and redistribution centre where surplus production represented wealth. In the final publication of *Mosphilia* (Peltenburg et al. 1998: 252–254), however, the Pithos House is regarded as a special, élite residence with bulk storage facilities, a house whose occupants had more wealth and greater control over production and distribution than any other community household.

A severe conflagration destroyed the Pithos House, and a group of smaller, less substantial structures was built over and to the south of it (Peltenburg et al. 1998: 250, fig. 14.8). In addition to Building 706 (noted above), there was a large, stone structure (Building 86) that seems to have shared both physical (hearth, entrance) and perhaps social continuity with its predecessor. Overall, however, the new and final, Period 4b, Late Chalcolithic settlement was distinctively different, lacking communal facilities or public works as well as prominent structures (excepting possibly Building 86); its social structure is regarded as egalitarian (Peltenburg et al. 1998: 250–251). The new settlement layout had three distinct zones, each with compounds of independent households that perhaps shared economic and social resources; adult men and women were buried both within and beyond the confines of the structures themselves.

Zone 1 included Building 86 and some ancillary structures, all with very similar building fills, whilst Zone 2, to the south, had a series of at least seven buildings in two opposing blocks facing onto an east–west passage. Zone 3, the southernmost, had two successive pairs of functionally different structures, one (Building 1165) with multiple pits and another (Building 200) with a sturdy cobbled floor. By the final phase of the Late Chalcolithic, it would seem that new, horizontal social structures had replaced the more complex social regime(s) of the Middle Chalcolithic. In such a setting, small groups of households would have shared in agricultural and craft production, most likely through close kinship links and social exchanges. Period 5 at Kissonerga *Mosphilia*, the subsequent Philia phase level (PreBA 1), was severely disturbed, with no upstanding architectural remains. Late Chalcolithic type pottery – Red and Black Stroke-Burnished, Coarse Painted Ware – probably ceased to be produced after Period 4 at *Mosphilia*, but recycled jars of the former type were used for the pithos burials of Period 5.

In material terms more generally, we see during the Late Chalcolithic the continuation of the basic Chalcolithic house form (no rectilinear structures), but the disappearance of the hard floors, floor ridges and partition walls that divided interior space. Although the formal division of space is therefore no longer apparent, the house interiors still served the same range of functions (Peltenburg et al. 1998: 237–240, 251); food production, storage, eating and sleeping now took place in less formally segregated areas. The central rectilinear hearth went out of use, and was replaced by circular platform hearths. Walls began to be plastered with mud instead of lime, and calcarenite was no longer used as building material, perhaps indicating a decline in building standards. Thus although one can see some overall level of continuity in the use of domestic space, the changes suggest fairly deep-seated alterations in Late Chalcolithic society.

The recently excavated site of Politiko *Kokkinorotsos* (Webb et al. 2009: 193, fig. 4) (Figure 65) – less than 0.5 ha in extent – provides another perspective on change, but whether this concerns actual transformations in Late Chalcolithic society or, more likely, in altering the way we view that period, remains to be seen. In radiocarbon terms, *Kokkinorotsos* sits ambiguously, either at the transition to the Late Chalcolithic or, as treated here, during its earliest part. It is the only Chalcolithic site currently known in the immediate area, but survey work

Figure 65. Politiko *Kokkinorotsos* site (Webb et al. 2009: 193, fig. 4). Courtesy of David Frankel and Jennifer Webb.

has identified other sites 15–20 km to the west: for example, Kato Moni *Kambia* and *Monarga*; Orounda *Stavros tou Koundi* (Given and Knapp 2003: 265).

At *Kokkinorotsos*, fallow deer form the major component (74%) of the substantial faunal sample (with caprines at 24%); the chipped stone repertoire also points to intensive exploitation of meat resources. The floral remains (predominantly cereals, nuts, legumes and fruit) as well as the most common types of groundstone tools (see below) indicate that domesticated plants and wild fruits were processed and consumed at the site (but probably not harvested – only five glossed sickles are present amongst 1,510 tools). There is no formal architecture at *Kokkinorotsos* and little evidence of activity areas, beyond traces of hearths or oven-pits. Three roughly circular pits of various size and shape (3–5 m wide; up to 1 m deep), filled with pottery, faunal remains and other debris, may represent dumping episodes rather than structural or living components. A large, natural hollow (more than 200 m² in area; up to 1.5 m deep) containing stones, bones and potsherds indicates the same. There were no human remains and no traces of burial pits.

Amongst nearly 55,000 potsherds recovered from the site, typical Middle Chalcolithic fabrics such as Red-on-White (6.7%) and Coarse ware (1%) were easily recognisable, but were noticeably outnumbered by five unpainted varieties of pottery. The dominant pottery tradition was an unpainted style with both bichrome and monochrome variations; three of the four remaining fabrics are quite similar, but some have a more limited range of shapes. Closed vessels, whether large or small, are much more common than open vessels. Spouted jars and bowls predominate, suggesting that the storage and consumption of liquids were common activities (Webb et al. 2009: 231). The excavators argue that these five unpainted fabrics are better seen along a continuum rather than as separate wares: they show some similarities to other, Chalcolithic wares known from the central region of Cyprus (e.g. Red Lustrous, Red and Black Lustrous, Black Polished, Red Monochrome). The similarities between the pottery from *Kokkinorotsos* and that found at the central Cypriot sites of Ambelikou *Ayios Georghios*, Philia *Drakos* B and Kyra *Alonia* may point to a common technological tradition.

In terms of dating, it is worth emphasising that, in pottery assemblages from the island's south and southwest during the later phases of the Middle Chalcolithic, painted fabrics dominate; where they occur in what are defined as Late Chalcolithic contexts, however, they are regarded as 'residual'. The low proportion of Red-on-White pottery at *Kokkinorotsos* and in the central region generally (i.e. at Ambelikou, Philia and Kyra) may indicate that these sites too should be regarded as late Middle Chalcolithic or transitional to the Late Chalcolithic (recall that the radiocarbon dates from *Kokkinorotsos*, ca. 2820–2750 Cal BC, place it at the same time – discussed above). Within the central region, there appears to be a preference for monochrome vessels, red- and black-burnished fabrics and the use of relief knobs and ridges – all features that seem to precede their appearance in the southwest of the island.

Peltenburg (2007a: 147–152; Peltenburg et al. 1998: 256–258) and to a lesser extent Bolger (2007) regard these and other distinctive material and social practices seen at Kissonerga *Mosphilia* and Lemba *Lakkous* after 2700 Cal BC as the result of emerging external contacts, especially with western Anatolia. The fact that precursors of some of these elements appear at *Kokkinorotsos* and Ambelikou *Ayios Georghios*, however, suggests the possibility of an indigenous source, and hint that the centre of the island may have played a more prominent role in the material developments of the Late Chalcolithic than has been recognised previously (Webb et al. 2009: 205). Alternatively, if sites in the central region were contemporary with those in the southwest, then we may simply be observing regional variations (Frankel 2009), wherein painted wares were unpopular in the island's central area. Whatever the answer may be here, the 'Anatolianising' elements that become increasingly apparent in various material aspects of the PreBA 1 period are considered further in the following chapter.

Amongst the other material components of *Kokkinorotsos*, the groundstone repertoire (Figure 66a and b) is largely oriented towards grinding or pounding activities (rubbers, querns, pounders, pestles, hammerstones), less so towards

Figure 66a and b. Politiko *Kokkinorotsos* groundstone tools and vessels – pounders, hammerstones, pecking stone, burnisher. After Webb et al. 2009: 207, figs.25–26. Courtesy of David Frankel and Jennifer Webb.

cutting and chopping work (axes, adzes, chisels) (Webb et al. 2009: 206–209). Groundstone bowls make up 11% of the 112 groundstone objects recovered. Personal ornaments included a perforated limestone pendant and a cylindrical, blue picrolite bead; earlier intensive surface survey at the site recovered another, disk-shaped picrolite bead (Given and Knapp 2003: 197, 213, pl. 35). Lefkara basal chert (79%), followed by jasper (7%) dominate the chipped stone assemblage of 5,704 artefacts, itself made up largely of *pièces esquillées* (for splitting bone?), scrapers (for treating hides) and burins (for grooving bone or antler) (Webb et al. 2009: 213, table 9). There is little evidence for a blade core technology at *Kokkinorotsos*, which contrasts strongly with other Middle–Late Chalcolithic chipped stone assemblages, and sets the site apart as having a more specialised industry.

The materials recovered from *Kokkinorotsos* also include 2 cruciform figurine fragments more than 100 modified potsherds, (Red-on-White ware), 7 dentalium shell beads, 2 worked marine shells, 10 pieces of worked antler and 7 bone tools (Webb et al. 2009: 218–219, fig. 33). The unique composition of the tool sample from *Kokkinorotsos*, the site's small size, its lack of formal architecture, the exploitation of a forested piedmont region, and the emphasis on hunting deer points to a highly specialised, less permanent (i.e. seasonal) occupation than we see at the Late Chalcolithic, lowland, coastal settlements of *Mosphilia* and Lemba. The excavators define *Kokkinorotsos* as '…a seasonally or intermittently occupied hunting station', one that was used intensively for consuming meat or processing hides, and where the final deposition of material resulted from a single, rapid episode, perhaps of feasting involved in the formal closure of the site (Webb et al. 2009: 231–232).

In Late Chalcolithic society generally, notable social, cultural and economic changes – including overseas contacts – become apparent in virtually every class of material culture: pottery (new fabrics); chipped stone assemblages (more varied, new sources exploited); copper exploitation and production (on the increase); faience disk beads, conical and grooved stones, and stamp seals (newly appear); stone bowl and picrolite production (both declined); changing fashions of personal ornamentation (dentalium necklaces simplified, new disc bead necklaces). There was a transformation in the use of space, especially within the household (formal divisions and the use of a rectangular central hearth disappeared) but also within the settlements themselves (lack of communal architecture). Peltenburg et al. (1998: 252) see the decline of figurative art (picrolite figurines), the move away from communal activities (decline in public works, ritual activities, communal feasting) and the emergence of new mortuary practices (see next section) as indicators of a more egalitarian social organisation.

Red-on-White pottery all but disappears during the Late Chalcolithic, and the most prominent new fabric to appear – at least in the southwest – was Red and Black Stroke-Burnished ware (Bolger 2007: 173). As the painted style decreased in popularity, potters began to use relief work, differential firing and pattern burnishing to decorate their vessels. Elsewhere on the island (e.g. at Kyra *Alonia*, Ambelikou *Ayios Georghios*), pottery types known as Red (or Red and Black) Lustrous were in use (Dikaios 1962: 143, 152–153); at Kyra *Alonia* and other sites in the north and northwest, Late Chalcolithic type wares were eventually replaced by a monochrome pottery known as Red Polished (Philia). *Mosphilia* is the only site thus far where the materiality of the Late Chalcolithic and the Philia phase overlaps, and some sherds of Red Polished (Philia) and Black Slip and Combed ware appear already in Period 4b, increasing during Period 5, the Philia horizon (Bolger 2007: 173–175).

Several different vessel shapes were produced in the new Red and Black Stroke-Burnished ware: conical, hemispherical and deep bowls, spouted bottles, flasks and holemouth jars. Some of the larger versions of the holemouth jars – up to 1 m tall – served for storage; many such vessels were produced in two other new fabrics: Coarse Painted Ware and Red Monochrome Painted. Bolger (1994: 13) suggests that this emphasis on storage may reflect the production of agricultural surpluses and perhaps the (re-)emergence of a redistributive exchange system. There were also technological improvements in this new pottery style, including its higher firing temperature, thinner walls and harder fabrics, experimenting with new clays and surface finishes, more standardised vessel sizes, and higher volume of production (Peltenburg et al. 1998: 251–252; Bolger 2003: 222). In Bolger's (2007: 173–175) view, these factors, especially the standardisation in Red and Black Stroke-Burnished wares, may point to centralised production and the involvement of specialist potters. Some of the new pottery forms – such as spouted bottles – show some affinities with pottery types from southern and western Anatolia, but this does not necessarily mean that they came to the island with Anatolian migrants or colonists. In my view they represent the outcome of hybridisation practices, as the people of Cyprus increasingly came into contact with foreign merchants, traders and travellers, perhaps even migrants (see following chapter).

Middle–Late Chalcolithic metal ores, a possible crucible and some artefacts have already been discussed above; here I only summarise the material from the Late Chalcolithic. From Period 4a and 4b (Late Chalcolithic) at Kissonerga *Mosphilia* came six metal objects, fragments of oxidised copper, lumps of copper ore, and two possible crucibles. Amongst the metal objects, some chisels and an awl came from settlement contexts, where we might not expect to find weapons, personal ornaments or other, higher status, symbolic items; an ear/hair-ring came from a grave. The other materials most likely represent the by-products of metallurgical production and suggest that local Cypriot ores were being extracted and used in the local production of metal artefacts during the early–mid-3rd millennium BC. The concentration of material in levels just above the Pithos House points to the precocious development of small-scale metallurgy, perhaps even to the manipulation of a new technology to promote what Peltenburg et al. (1998: 254) term 'the politics of exclusion'.

There is no question that the excavations at *Mosphilia* have produced a range of distinctive material objects. Amongst them are 132 pendants, including picrolite anthropomorphic examples, and a range of other, pierced and unpierced types (Peltenburg et al. 1998: pls. 36:7–14, 37:6). The spurred annular shell pendant, unattested before this time, typically takes the form of a flat, oval or circular ring with a small hole drilled at the top, and a spurred or arrow-shaped projection at the bottom (Frankel and Webb 2004: 1–3). Peltenburg (2007: 145) sees these 'newly prized objects' as a source of social power during the Late Chalcolithic, and notes that they must be distinguished from Philia period examples, which have been seen as personal identity markers (Frankel and Webb 2004: 7). The somewhat unique but later examples from Sotira *Kaminoudhia*, with an elongated top and a slight swelling below, led the excavator to identify them as anthropomorphic (Swiny et al. 2003: 236, fig. 6.16). Although a new feature of the Late Chalcolithic, the spurred annular pendant becomes a very diagnostic, Philia-type object.

Frankel and Webb (2004: 6) discuss the spurred annular pendants in the context of what they regard as overlapping exchange networks between indigenous Chalcolithic communities and intrusive groups of people during the later, Philia phase. They maintain that these objects played a crucial role in proclaiming an (intrusive) 'Philia identity', whilst their production and use during the Late Chalcolithic at *Mosphilia* reflect the appropriation by indigenous Chalcolithic communities of personal Philia identity markers. That may be so, but the timing here is problematic, and in any case I see different processes at work: in my view (and terminology), these annular (picrolite or shell) pendants represent a striking example of the material, social and cultural ambiguity involved in hybridisation practices (pace Bolger 2009: 550), a point to which I return in greater detail in the next chapter.

Another type of personal ornament, the globular faience disk bead, also appears first during the Late Chalcolithic (Peltenburg 1995). Segmented faience beads are attested in the Middle Chalcolithic cemeteries at Souskiou *Laona*, and spherical, cylindrical, ring- and disk-shaped faience beads are found at contemporary *Vathyrkakas*; together these are amongst the earliest examples of faience known in the Mediterranean world (Peltenburg 2006: 93–95). At (early) Late Chalcolithic *Kokkinorotsos*, survey and excavations produced one example each of a cylindrical and disk-shaped picrolite bead. Most of the 21 faience beads found at *Mosphilia*, however, are globular in shape, which becomes the most common type used during the Prehistoric Bronze Age. These faience beads occurred mainly in or near chamber tombs at *Mosphilia*, and were probably used for small, single-strand necklaces interred with adults or children.

Peltenburg (in Peltenburg et al. 1998: 193) once argued that the use of faience required a radical departure from earlier traditions of bead making, and thus believed it unlikely that this technique developed independently on Cyprus.

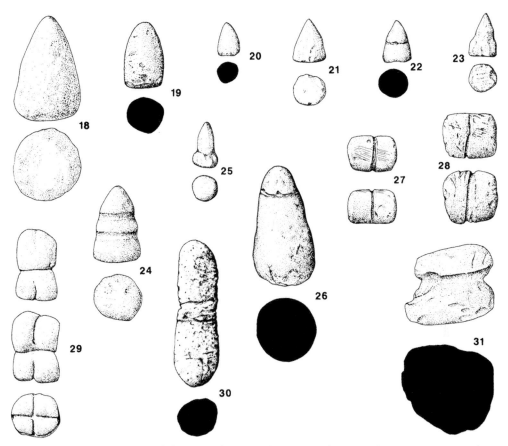

Figure 67. Kissonerga *Mosphilia* conical stones (18–25) and grooved stones (26–31). After Peltenburg et al. 1998: fig. 99. Courtesy of Edgar Peltenburg.

More recently, he seems inclined to link the technological traditions involved in producing metals and faience, thus implying they may both have been indigenous developments (Peltenburg 2006: 168–170). In this light, it is worth noting that nearly 80% of the 500 recorded beads from *Mosphilia* were made from dentalium shell which, like the marine shell and other types of beads found (chert, chalk, pig-teeth), were manufactured on-site (Peltenburg et al. 1998: 192–193). Despite the array of possible reasons Peltenburg (1995: 36–40) once proposed for the non-local production of these beads, the technique of their manufacture cannot be pinned down to a specific area within the only possible external source regions – the Levant or Egypt (Peltenburg et al. 1998: 193–194). Is it not possible that local craftsmen – who were producing hundreds of beads from other materials – could have adapted their skills to this new medium of faience?

The large number of grooved and conical stones found at *Mosphilia* (36 grooved, 345 conical) and Lemba *Lakkous* (12 grooved, 28 conical) form another class of object introduced in the Late Chalcolithic (Peltenburg et al. 1985: 288–289, fig. 85; 1998: 195–197, fig. 99: 18–31) (Figure 67). They are so similar in terms of their material (usually made of chalk), size, shape and date that they may be considered together. At *Mosphilia*, such stones were found most commonly inside of buildings but at least two were recovered from tombs. Whilst their proposed functions (gaming stones, cosmetics grinder, counting tokens) are plausible, their proposed relationship with stamp seals is based both on context and on the conical shape, size and material. Two Late Chalcolithic stamp seals have been identified, one from Building 706 (Period 4b) at *Mosphilia* (Peltenburg et al. 1998: pl. 37.13 – KM 597) and another from Area II at Lemba (Peltenburg et al. 1985: 289, fig. 85.5, pl. 47.11). At this early date, these 'stamp seals' may well have been used as personal ornaments rather than sealing devices. Even so, they might have been used for simple administrative tasks, and it is possible that the conical stones could have served as counting devices, as they had been earlier on the Levantine mainland (Schmandt-Besserat 1992: 35–39).

Mortuary Practices

Several changes are evident in the mortuary practices of the Late Chalcolithic: the earliest use (*Mosphilia* Period 4b) of the chamber tomb, a vertical, circular shaft descending to one or two smaller chambers; a decline in grave goods; and an increase in multiple interments and group burials made up of women, men and children. At Souskiou *Laona* (whether late Middle Chalcolithic or early Late Chalcolithic is unclear), mortuary practices involved multistage burial rites and possibly secondary treatment of the interred (Crewe et al. 2005). At the same time in *Mosphilia* (Period 4), adults once again are found buried inside the settlement, and differential mortuary practices become evident in some new tomb types – chamber tombs, pot burials and scoop graves (Peltenburg et al. 1998: 70–73). At both Lemba *Lakkous* and *Mosphilia*, adults and children were buried together (Bolger 2003: 153–155). In other words, differently sexed and aged individuals (family groups, including children) were now interred in the same tomb. The new chamber tombs were largely used for adult burials; at *Mosphilia* children were placed unceremoniously in hastily built pits or scoops with few grave goods. For the most part adults were also buried simply, accompanied only by utilitarian bowls and spouted vessels. The special treatment (e.g. libation-hole graves) and illustrious grave goods accorded to children during the Middle Chalcolithic were a thing of the past (Peltenburg et al. 1998: 85, 91; Niklasson 1991: 186–187).

In an attempt to assess phenetic changes between the Middle and Late Chalcolithic periods, Parras (2006) conducted a comparison of dental (non-metric) morphological traits based on 1,887 teeth – representing the human remains of 138 individuals from Middle Chalcolithic Souskiou *Vathyrkakas*, 55 from Kissonerga *Mosphilia* and 42 from Lemba *Lakkous* (both the latter from Middle and Late Chalcolithic levels). The data were analysed in two stages: (1) non-metric data were compared by site for an overall representation of the biological variation for southwest Cyprus; (2) the traits from Kissonerga were divided by time period (3A–3B, Middle Chalcolithic; 4, Late Chalcolithic;

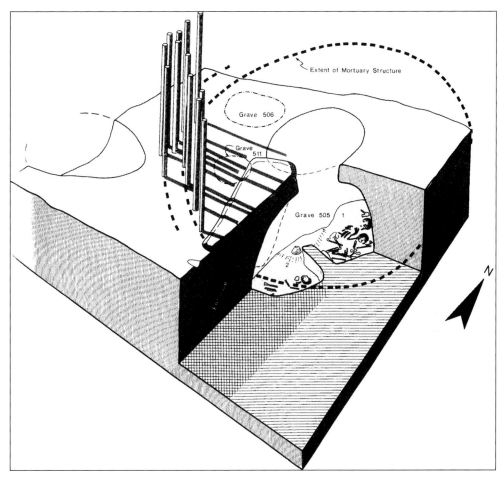

Figure 68. Kissonerga *Mosphilia*, reconstruction of mortuary enclosure 375. After Peltenburg et al. 1998: 47, fig. 3.14. Courtesy of Edgar Peltenburg.

5, Philia phase), in an attempt to identify biological changes through time. Whilst the sample was quite limited, and whilst phenetics (based on morphological classification) has largely been superseded by cladistics for research into evolutionary relationships among species, statistical comparison of the Middle Chalcolithic data from Souskiou and Lemba with those of the Late Chalcolithic from Kissonerga (Period 4) indicate that all traits appearing in the Late Chalcolithic had been present in southwest Cyprus during the Middle Chalcolithic. Bearing in mind that these data pertain only to the southwestern part of Cyprus, the author suggests tentatively that the biological population represented by these data was of local rather than foreign origin (i.e. no 'new' traits that might have belonged to a foreign population are evident).

An unusual structure at *Mosphilia* (Building 375) features a double line of about 10 postholes defining an arc that has been interpreted as the remnants of a large, approximately 8 m² mortuary enclosure (Peltenburg et al. 1998: 46–47, fig. 3.14) (Figure 68). Nine burials (five adults, four children) – a succession of large graves and tombs – were placed within this (reconstructed) feature, which also included a unique rectangular platform, standing 20 cm high with a flat top and bevelled edges. The skeletal evidence (adults died by the age of 20; children died from thalassemia) suggested to the excavator that a consanguine (descent) group had created a distinct, bounded zone to bury its dead (Peltenburg et al. 1998: 88–89). Steel (2004a: 116) suggests this enclosure may have belonged to a non-agnatic social group, building on the notion that a mortuary ritual involving a special bounded area for disposal of the dead provides a means of demonstrating lineal descent from specific ancestors (Goldstein 1981).

Peltenburg sees these changes in mortuary practices as further evidence for a 'major ideological shift' in the Late Chalcolithic period at *Mosphilia* (Peltenburg et al. 1998: 84; Crewe et al. 2005: 58–59). From a gendered perspective, these changes are thought to indicate (1) new, more complex social and economic conditions that reinforced familial bonds, and (2) new gender and age constructs that impacted on male–female relationships (Bolger 2003: 155–158). In addition, Peltenburg feels that these changed mortuary phenomena indicate some level of indigenous social differentiation linked to other '… fashions, technology, eating and drinking habits' of foreign inspiration or derivation (Peltenburg et al. 1998: 252, 257). I return to consider such notions in the next chapter, and at this point emphasise only that the Middle Chalcolithic trajectory towards social differentiation had now levelled off, if not disappeared altogether (cf. Bolger 2003: 158).

Transition to the Bronze Age

Whether by chance or intentional design, once the Early Aceramic Neolithic period came to an end (ca. 7000 Cal BC), people living on the island of Cyprus seem to have had somewhat limited contacts with the surrounding peoples and cultures of the eastern Mediterranean. During the Late Chalcolithic period, at least based on evidence from Kissonerga *Mosphilia*, this apparent isolation began to break down, although there are no direct imports (unless the faience beads were not locally produced), only materials, designs, traits and features that suggest inspiration and/or material connections with Anatolia and the eastern Aegean. Peltenburg (2007a) has pointed to various changes in the materiality of the Late Chalcolithic – pottery production (and associated drinking habits), copper metalworking, spurred annular pendants and faience beads, stamp seals and conical stones – as reflecting non-native material practices. He thus suggests that we are dealing with an insular selection and adaptation of certain material traits, not imports, which he views as the result of initiatives taken by the Cypriotes themselves (2007a: 154).

Understanding the transition between the Late Chalcolithic and Early Bronze Age periods on Cyprus has been a contentious undertaking, and discussions of this period still elicit lively debate (e.g. Manning 1993; Peltenburg 1993, 2007; Webb and Frankel 1999; Knapp 2001, 2008: 103–130; Bolger 2007). In a long and continuing series of publications, it has been argued that Anatolian colonists or migrants (both terms continue to be used as if they were interchangeable) came to Cyprus during the earliest phase (Philia) of the Prehistoric Bronze Age, bringing with them a series of material innovations and establishing communities entirely separate from the local one (Frankel et al. 1996; Frankel and Webb 1998, 2004; Webb and Frankel 1999, 2004, 2007, 2011; Frankel 2000, 2005). In material terms, this notion of an ethnic migration or colonisation from Anatolia to Cyprus is compelling, and has been taken up by several specialists in both the Chalcolithic and Bronze Ages (e.g. Peltenburg et al. 1998: 256–258; Steel 2004a: 117–118; Peltenburg 2007a; Bolger 2007: 164–170).

The materials, objects and technologies in question involve some items already discussed (e.g. stamp seals, shell annular pendants, copper spiral pendants or earrings, faience disk beads) and others still to be considered (e.g. pottery shapes, relief decoration and manufacturing techniques, spindle whorls). The links seen are primarily with Anatolia and the eastern Aegean, and it is argued that these innovations demonstrate major social and organisational changes in the daily aspects of people's lives: for example, diet, dress, personal ornamentation, work and administration, storage and mortuary practices, ideology and technologies (pottery, metals) (Peltenburg et al. 1998: 256–257; Steel 2004a: 117–118).

It is crucial to rethink and reassess the social and material encounters that took place between Cyprus and various overseas polities during the transitional PreBA 1 era. There is no reason to dispute the notion that some people from southern Anatolia and the eastern Aegean, if not the Levant, had developed and maintained contacts with people on Cyprus by the mid-3rd millennium Cal BC (e.g. Şahoğlu 2005; Webb et al. 2006; Peltenburg 2007a: 144–151; see also Philip et al. 2003 for possible earlier contacts). But we still need to consider carefully the view that the communities of PreBA 1 Cyprus were divided into two distinctive groups: (1) Anatolian migrants or colonists (the 'Philia' facies) who brought themselves and their technologically transferable practices to bear upon (2) the indigenous Cypriotes (Frankel and Webb 2004: 6–7; Webb and Frankel 2004: 135–136; 2007, 2011).

If we accept the notion that there are two distinct social groups dwelling on Cyprus at this time, we still need to consider how the co-presence of indigenous people and newcomers, and the material connections that developed between them, were necessary preconditions for the emergence of all the innovations we see in PreBA material culture. In their latest contribution to this debate, Webb and Frankel (2011: 29–30) revert to the problematic notion that the Anatolian ethnic group in question was made up of colonisers, not migrants; they maintain that '…it would be naïve to assume that this was necessarily an evenly bidirectional process'. In other words, they still seem to assume unidirectional power dynamics between a dominant, colonising group from Anatolia, imposing their lifeways and materiality on the indigenous people of the island. I revisit these arguments at the outset of the following chapter, and attempt to reassess Late Chalcolithic as well as PreBA 1 materialities in terms of hybridisation practices rather than as the result of exchange relations, an ethnic migration or, least likely, an Anatolian colonisation of the island.

CHAPTER 6

PREHISTORIC BRONZE AGE CYPRUS

Like their Neolithic and Chalcolithic predecessors, the people of Prehistoric Bronze Age (PreBA) Cyprus (ca. 2400–1700 Cal BC) relied on a mixed agro-pastoral economy. At the same time, however, we see what has been described as a 'wholesale change in the island's material culture' (Steel 2004a: 119; see also Swiny 1997: 185–205; Knapp 2008: 68–102): sub-rectangular and often multi-cellular architecture; the introduction of the plough and equids, and the reintroduction of cattle; several distinctive pottery wares (in particular Red Polished); a variety of mould-cast copper tools, weapons and ornaments (Balthazar 1990); 'gaming stones' (Swiny 1980); a growing use of spindle whorls and loomweights (Crewe 1998), pointing to new types of textiles (portrayed to some extent on figurines); and new types of symbolic representations and mortuary practices. Subsistence evidence indicates a decline in the exploitation of deer, a rise in the use of cattle, the introduction of screw-horned goats (at Marki *Alonia*), and a change in the way that animals were integrated into the island's ideology and economy (Keswani 1994).

Settlement size as well as the actual number of sites increased from the Middle–Late Chalcolithic periods onward (for PreBA sites, see Figure 69, below). Both factors involved more than simple population growth. The costs of subsistence production grew, placing some stress on available land resources. The people who lived in these PreBA communities may have restructured themselves through (managerial) specialisation or perhaps even fissioned off into new communities (Peltenburg 1993; Manning 1993). Settlement expanded into areas previously unoccupied, and most areas of the island became inhabited. On the plains and closer to the coast, sites typically lent themselves to the use of intensified plough agriculture, whilst those in the Troodos foothills were ideally situated to exploit specific kinds of mineral, clay, timber and other natural resources.

The 'Secondary Products Revolution' (Sherratt 1981; Knapp 1990a; Greenfield 2010), as well as the intensified production of copper from Cypriot ores, ultimately would transform island society from an isolated, village-based culture into an international, town-centred polity. Interpretations of these developments have differed radically in the past. One school of thought holds that a 'focal migration', or colonisation, of Anatolian people with new technologies made a major impact on Cyprus's PreBA culture (e.g. Webb and Frankel 1999; 2007; 2011; Frankel 2000; 2005; Webb 2002a: 27). Another viewpoint long maintained that local responses to social pressures and economic demand (e.g. prestige-goods exchange) provided the stimulus for change (Stewart 1962; Swiny 1986b; Knapp 1993a; 2001), to which Manning (1993) added the significance of 'aggrandizing' behaviour by emerging élites, most evident in mortuary practices and foreign imports.

More recently, these differences have become more muted, although Webb and Frankel (e.g. 2007; 2008; 2011) still maintain there was a 'population movement' or 'colonisation' from Anatolia, whereas I tend to view all 'Anatolianising' features in PreBA 1 material culture as the result of hybridisation practices (Knapp 2008: 110–130). Such practices certainly do not exclude a movement of people, and the likely co-presence of different social groups on the island. The rich and diverse material record of PreBA Cyprus thus has been 'read' in diverse ways, at different times, but when it comes to the later phase of this period (PreBA 2, ca. 2000–1750/1700 Cal BC), none of these readings engages the material evidence with relevant, contemporary (19th–17th centuries BC) cuneiform records from the Levant to develop a more holistic, sociohistorical approach (the relevant texts were presented and discussed in Knapp 2008: 307–308). As bookends at either end of the Bronze Age, the notions of an (Early Bronze Age) Anatolian and an (Late Bronze Age) Aegean *colonisation* of Cyprus cannot be substantiated in a material record that instead portrays vividly hybridisation practices at work between different peoples and cultures (Knapp 2008; Voskos and Knapp 2008). Because the concept of hybridisation is complex and goes against the grain of most archaeological thinking on cultural contact and cultural change on Cyprus, I return repeatedly to discuss it in the following sections (but see already Knapp 2008: 57–61).

MIGRATION OR INDIGENOUS DEVELOPMENT?

This debate essentially has revolved around two contrasting positions concerning the origins of the diverse material, social and cultural innovations of the PreBA:

(1) an ethnic migration, or colonisation, and 'technology transfer' from Anatolia, along with some movement of goods and ideas;

(2) internal changes and developments on Cyprus, tied to external demand for copper and a prestige goods economy, not excluding the movement of goods and ideas.

To be clear, it is important to distinguish between the concepts of migration and colonisation. Migration, or at least human migration, refers to the physical movement by people from one geographical area to another, sometimes over long distances or in large groups. Colonisation, by contrast, refers to the establishment of settlements, colonies, trading posts or the like by foreign people in an area some distance from their place of origin, often but not always with the intention of establishing political domination over, and/or carrying out economic exploitation of, the inhabitants or resources of the region (van Dommelen 1998: 15–16). Colonists almost always migrate, but migrants are not always colonists. Cyprus received many migrants throughout its prehistory and protohistory, but in my view it was never colonised before the Romans did so.

The material records of mid-to-late 3rd millennium BC Cyprus (PreBA 1), and of southern, if not western Anatolia (Early Bronze II), leave no doubt that these two regions were in contact. The cultural contacts and social mixings involved were once explained in terms of Anatolian invaders (Dikaios 1962: 202–203) or refugees from Anatolia (Catling 1971a: 808–816). Dikaios (1962: 190–191), moreover, believed – correctly as it turned out – that the Philia culture preceded the Early Cypriot (EC) period and stood at the very beginning of the Bronze Age cultural sequence. Stewart (1962: 269, 296), by contrast, felt (1) that the intrusive 'Philia culture' was a contemporary, regional variant of EC I-II; (2) that both cultures derived from a common, Cypriot Chalcolithic source; and (3) that the Anatolian influences apparent in the material culture were superficial and ephemeral when taken into account alongside the strikingly different material culture of the EC period. In his view, '…the development [of EC culture], no matter what influences brought it about, was essentially a Cypriote affair and due to the genius of the islanders' (Stewart 1962: 296; Webb 2002a: 11–19 provides a good general discussion of this debate). Based almost exclusively on excavated evidence from the sites of Kissonerga *Mosphilia* (Peltenburg et al. 1998), Marki *Alonia* (Frankel and Webb 1996; 2006a) and Sotira *Kaminoudhia* (Swiny et al. 2003), it is now clear that the traditional chronological phases – Late Chalcolithic, Philia, Early Cypriot I–II – are sequential and to some extent overlapping.

In other words, subsequent research on matters both material and chronological (e.g. Manning 1993; Manning and Swiny 1994; Webb and Frankel 1999; 2007; see also the Appendix to this volume) have rendered Stewart's proposal untenable. Indeed, this stream of research led me to recast my own, earlier scepticism over the impact of Anatolian influences, but not that over a colonisation from Anatolia (e.g. Knapp 2001). Some of the cultural innovations of the PreBA – spindle whorls, new pottery types and decoration, metal and shell products, spurred annular pendants, pithos burials, metalworking activities, the use of stamp seals – have been seen as 'adaptations' of (western) Anatolian traditions (Peltenburg et al. 1998: 256–258). More recently, Peltenburg (2007a: 142) has argued forcefully that (offshore?) contacts with western Anatolia pre-date the Philia horizon, and that even with respect to the latter we still cannot determine from the material evidence whether migration, indigenous appropriation of innovations, or some combination of these two factors were responsible. Bolger (2007: 181), in turn, argues for the 'differential reception' of non-indigenous artefacts and lifestyles by the Late Chalcolithic communities at Lemba and Kissonerga.

The timing of these changes is crucial for understanding whether there were pre-Philia contacts of any sort with Anatolia. Frankel and Webb (Frankel 2005; Webb and Frankel 2007: 199; 2011: 33–35) accept that there were limited, separate Late Chalcolithic contacts with Anatolia but feel that the Philia phase innovations represent a complete break with earlier practices. Moreover, as already noted and argued at length by Webb and Frankel (2011: 34), it is likely that the earliest evidence for sealing and metalworking practices at *Mosphilia* belong to the Level 4b Building 706, and should be dated no earlier than about 2500 BC, that is, contemporary with the Philia phase (here dated to 2400/2350–2250 Cal BC). Webb and Frankel (2011) also feel that these and other Philia-type 'innovations' are likely to be evidence of a local (Late Chalcolithic) response to a contemporary, foreign-derived, Philia presence on the island. In other words, the jury is still out determining both the extent and the exact chronological placement of the earliest Anatolian 'influences' on Cyprus.

In their excavations at Marki *Alonia*, situated in the central plain and thus quite distant from any possible entry point of Anatolian migrants (and one or two generations removed in time from such an event), Frankel and Webb (1996; 2006a) found no direct correlations between the various classes of material or technologies (Anatolian originals, Cypriot derivatives) used in their arguments. In various other studies, they have argued that the innovations seen in the material record of PreBA Cyprus could be explained neither by stimulus diffusion nor by a prestige-goods economy driven by external demand. Having attributed the lack of direct material correlations to a process of acculturation, they use notions of 'technology transfer' and 'everyday practices' to explain the appearance of what they see as new skills, crafts, technologies and a series of associated social patterns (most recently, Frankel 2005; Webb and Frankel 2007; 2011). The transfer and development of new technologies, they suggest, are most easily realised by the movement of experienced workers (Frankel et al. 1996: 41), indeed the migration of a distinct, independent, ethnic community (Frankel 2000; Webb and Frankel 2011) made up of men, women and children; of farmers, herdsmen, cattle, donkeys, goats and sheep; of potters, metalsmiths, cooks and weavers (Webb 2002a: 27; Webb and Frankel 2007: 206).

Webb and Frankel (1999; 2007; 2011; Frankel et al. 1996) have vacillated over how they wish to define the movement of people they associate with the Philia 'facies', from an outright Anatolian colonisation of Cyprus, to an ethnic migration or a more vague 'population movement'. What remains constant is their view that some people from Anatolia intermixed with an indigenous Chalcolithic group, inciting them through the adoption and adaptation of new technologies to 'acculturate' and assimilate. At first, Anatolian contact with local Cypriot communities was limited, but incoming Anatolians and indigenous Cypriotes somehow coexisted, living and carrying out their daily tasks in distinctive ways (Frankel 2000: 178). It must be noted, at the very least, that this is not the case with technologies associated with the exploitation of Cyprus's copper resources: there is no sign of two distinctive sets of metal artefacts (Muhly 2002: 81), nor of different metalworking tools.

In Frankel's (2005) view, quantifiable changes in material culture were tied directly to 'acculturation' processes and to a change in *ethnic* identity (also Bolger 2007: 177–179). Despite the diverse and impressive array of material evidence presented – pottery, textiles, culinary traditions and agricultural practices, architecture, metallurgy, mortuary customs, discard strategies (most recently Frankel 2005; Webb and Frankel 2007; 2008; 2011) – there is no sign of the non-random, discontinuous distribution of material evidence that might plausibly be associated with an ethnic identity. Despite the long-standing hope of many archaeologists to discern distinctive material boundaries ('bounded cultural practices' in the words of Webb and Frankel 2011: 29) that separate human social groups from one another, pots still don't equal people (Terrell 2010: 4), and these skilfully contextualised trait lists of material culture can never provide an adequate basis for establishing an ethnic identity (Cusick 1998: 137–138).

As pointed out previously (Knapp 2008: 106), any transfers of technology must consider how migrants (in this case arguably Anatolians) and indigenous peoples (in this case local Cypriotes) interact and exchange ideas, ideologies and sociocultural practices, and in the process adopt new cultural traits and new forms of material culture. Webb and Frankel (2007) have addressed these issues explicitly, examining the 'archaeology of everyday practice' to underpin their arguments for the Anatolian origin of what is defined as the Philia culture, or 'facies'. According to them (Webb and Frankel 2007: 191):

> These migration episodes … were followed by adaptation, stabilisation and development, while indigenous Chalcolithic communities underwent parallel processes of reaction, acculturation and eventual assimilation, leading ultimately to the development of a Bronze Age system across the island.

Most recently, Webb and Frankel (2011: 30) state that the mid-3rd millennium BC 'colonisation' of Cyprus:

> …involved a 'transported landscape' – that is, incoming groups brought with them resources which they knew were not available on the island (cattle, donkeys) and targeted a specific resource (copper) which they knew was available. The establishment of an integrated Philia settlement system involved the founding of new villages with a remarkably homogeneous material culture near copper ore bodies and along communication and transport routes…

I see the social and interactive processes involved quite differently, and have already argued at length against the usage of terms such as 'colonisation' and 'acculturation', the latter a top-down and now largely discredited concept in the social sciences (Knapp 2008: 53–55). To be sure, Webb and Frankel's arguments are not always presented in 'top-down' terms, and recently they have suggested that Anatolian 'colonists' may have been seeking new sources of raw materials (i.e. copper) for exchange in a 'prestige goods' network that included Anatolia, the Aegean and the Cyclades (Webb and Frankel 2011). Involvement in the 'Anatolian Trade Network' (Şahoğlu 2005; Webb et al. 2006 – discussed elsewhere in this chapter) surely provides one reason for migrants arriving from Anatolia, but this explanation revolves entirely around metallurgical technology and trade, and Anatolia in no way lacks metal resources (de Jesus 1980; Yener 2000). We need to understand more about the background to this migration, beyond the possible earlier presence of certain 'Philia' traits in the Late Chalcolithic (Peltenburg 2007a; Bolger 2007).

In any case, migrants tend to break with their original culture and, when adapting to a new culture or cultural area, to produce new material and cultural forms. Migration, in other words, irrevocably alters the idea of 'home', weakening old bonds and creating new ones (Papastergiadis 2005: 55). Rather than talking of (Anatolian) adaptation, stabilisation and development, versus (Cypriot) reactions, acculturation and assimilation, we should try to assess the effects of multiple cultural meetings and mixings on both the incoming and indigenous groups. With respect to all the everyday behaviours and technologies discussed by Frankel and Webb, I believe they may be considered more usefully in terms of hybridisation practices. In what follows, I review briefly the material innovations and associated social changes, both from Frankel and Webb's perspective and my own: understanding what lay behind these changes is crucial for any interpretation of PreBA society on Cyprus.

Hybridisation and Everyday Practices in the Prehistoric Bronze Age

The concept of hybridisation has been introduced, defined, contextualised and applied in several case studies involving Mediterranean archaeology (e.g. van Dommelen 2005; 2006; Counts 2008; Vives-Ferrándiz 2008; Russell 2009). I have discussed this concept and defended its use at some length previously (e.g. Knapp 2008: 110–130); calls to restrict its usage in archaeology, or to replace it with terms such as 'entanglement' (Stockhammer 2011; Yasur-Landou 2011), have been argued too rigidly, or with too narrow an understanding of the concept. Here, we need only emphasise that hybridisation refers (1) to the practices in which cultural differences are either naturalised or neutralised when distinct cultures meet and mix, and (2) to the visible manifestation of difference, in terms of both material culture and identity, as a consequence of incorporating foreign elements. Previously, and at some length, I have discussed in terms of hybridisation practices the material bases used to support Frankel and Webb's proposed ethnic migration from Anatolia (Knapp 2008: 103–130). Below I summarise (*in italics*) seven of the innovations and 'everyday practices' recently outlined by Webb and Frankel (2007: 193–204) and based mainly on their excavations at Marki *Alonia*, followed by my own views on these innovations and how they might better be seen as representing hybridisation practices. Finally, I try to place such differences of opinion in the wider history of scholarship on Bronze Age Cyprus.

(1) *Animal husbandry and agriculture: the remains of cattle, donkeys and screw-horned goats appear in Philia levels at Marki Alonia and in later levels at the site are represented in a few, very fragmentary terracotta figurines. These animals were not present during the Chalcolithic era, and the pattern of animal exploitation overall is strikingly different (deer and pig predominate in the Chalcolithic, cattle and sheep in PreBA 1). A new form of backed sickle blade found at Marki in Philia levels may be indicative of new harvesting techniques, whilst the use of the 'single-handled sole-ard plough' (as seen on a clay model and a Red Polished jug with modelled decoration, both from Vounous and dating some 400–500 years later – Dikaios 1940: 127–129, pls. 10a, 17), as well as a notable increase in cereal grinding equipment, may indicate an increase in the production and consumption of cereals.*

There is no question that cattle, donkeys and screw-horned goats are new to the PreBA 1 period (cattle reintroduced after their demise during the EAN), but there is no evidence to link any of these animals – or the single-handled sole-ard plough – directly to Anatolia. Although it is uncertain where donkeys were first domesticated (Africa or Asia), if indeed they ever were (Milevski 2011: 178), Sherratt (1981: 274 and fig. 10.11) argued that they were already in use as a pack animal in both the southern Levant and Egypt during the early 3rd millennium BC (Grigson 1995: 258 suggests the late 4th millennium BC). Likewise Sherratt (1981: 266–269, fig. 10.7) regarded the sole-ard plough as represented on the clay model from *Vounous* as part of a much broader European – as opposed to Near Eastern – tradition (see also Greenfield 2010: 39); in Anatolia, however, it remains unknown what form was used as there is no evidence for it. From their own discussion (Webb and Frankel 2007: 195–196), it is also clear that the new chipped stone (backed blade) and bone (rib points) tools discussed are widely distributed throughout the Levant and western Asia (including Anatolia) during the Late Chalcolithic. In sum, although we may indeed have new patterns of animal exploitation, new tools and increased production and consumption of grains, there is nothing that ties any of these innovations specifically to Anatolia.

(2) *Architecture: Philia levels at Marki contain rectilinear multi-roomed structures built of mould-made mudbricks and standing on stone footings, with semi-enclosed*

rectangular courtyards. Such structures are notably different from the circular buildings and compounds of the Chalcolithic period, and point to changes in the nature of households and the use of domestic space. Frankel and Webb (2006a: 314–315) also suggest that demographic growth resulting from migration was a major factor in the evolving (rectilinear) architectural tradition at Marki Alonia.

The differences cited by Webb and Frankel between PreBA rectilinear buildings and Chalcolithic circular structures are self-evident. But there are no precise parallels between the architectural features seen in PreBA Cypriot structures and those in Anatolian buildings, mainly because of the variety of Bronze Age designs and the generalised nature of any similarities. The ongoing development throughout the PreBA of rectilinear, multi-roomed, shared-wall structures built of mudbricks shares various 'generic' similarities (Frankel 2000: 175) with contemporary Anatolian, Levantine and even Aegean buildings (Swiny et al. 2003: 66–71). Whilst the fundamental changes in house form and design may well signal changes in social organisation (Flannery 1972; Swiny 1989: 21; Frankel and Webb 2006a: 311–315), there may also have been functional reasons for adopting new building materials. Using mudbricks to construct the earlier, circular structures of the Chalcolithic, for example, would have been counterproductive. Although more effort is required to make mudbricks than mudwalls, replacing bricks in a rectangular structure is far easier than replacing or repairing entire mud-walls.

Narrowly viewed, then, one could argue that the change from round to rectangular houses demanded a change in building technique (from mud-wall to mudbrick), and that any accompanying social changes resulted from gradual, internal developments and change, not from external influences or ethnic migrations. Indeed, Frankel (2000: 175) acknowledged the functional aspects of these architectural developments but questioned them as the by-product of a changing social order, instead attributing the introduction of new architectural traditions and techniques to an intrusive Anatolian group. All the new features in PreBA architectural form and design are indeed strikingly different from those of the Chalcolithic; they may have been influenced to some extent by alternative, Anatolian construction traditions and technology, especially those seen at Early Bronze II Tarsus in Cilicia (fuller discussion in Knapp 2008: 121–125). In sum, the many ambiguous building features of the PreBA – variously seen as 'Anatolianising', locally derived or some combination of the two – indicate that some were recombined into new material elements as the result of hybridisation practices.

(3) *Mortuary practices: most Philia-phase burials (multiple inhumations with significant numbers of grave goods) were placed in rock-cut chamber and pit tombs in extramural cemeteries, whereas most Late Chalcolithic burials were single inhumations placed in intramural pit graves. The exception here, and it is a significant one, is the practice of placing multiple burials in rock-cut tombs in the extensive*

Middle Chalcolithic cemetery at Souskiou. Pithos (or 'pot') burials, said to reflect west Anatolian practices, are also in evidence at the sites of Kissonerga, Marki, Philia and Vasilia.

The extramural cemeteries and *pithos* burials – seen as hallmarks of PreBA 1 mortuary practice and as indicative of incoming Anatolian people – have precedents or contemporary parallels throughout the Early Bronze Age Levant and Anatolia. Keswani (2004: 81), who accepts some level of Anatolian influence, noted that the cemeteries at Middle Chalcolithic Souskiou established local, albeit not direct precedents for later, PreBA mortuary practices, and that such practices could not be traced to any specific region of western Anatolia. She concluded that PreBA mortuary practices might best be seen as '...an *evolving fusion of mainland and local practices*, elaborated by indigenous and immigrant communities in the context of ongoing social competition and gradual cultural assimilation' (Keswani 2004: 81, emphasis added). Such factors, in sum, are precisely what I would define as key elements of hybridisation practices.

(4) *Metals and metalworking: Marki has produced remarkable evidence for the casting and smelting of local ores (three chalk casting moulds, one in a secure Philia context). Together with a wealth of mould-cast, copper-based artefacts (weapons, tools, various implements, jewellery), the local production of metal artefacts from Cypriot ores is now evident, but was likely present already on a smaller scale at contemporary (Period 5) or slightly earlier (Late Chalcolithic, Period 4b) Kissonerga Mosphilia. Excepting the chisel, all other metal items appear for the first time on Cyprus, and several show parallels with western and central Anatolian tools and implements.*

In fact, similar metal items were produced throughout the eastern Mediterranean during the mid-3rd millennium BC. Based on chemical and lead isotope analyses conducted on 16 PreBA 1–2 metal artefacts found in Cypriot tomb or hoard deposits (notably at Vasilia), Webb et al. (2006) argued that metallurgical developments on mid-3rd millennium BC Cyprus emerged within a very complex regional interaction sphere (the 'Anatolian Trade Network') involving the sea-borne movement of metals and metal artefacts between coastal Anatolia, the eastern Aegean and Cyprus. Metalworkers from all these areas, including Cyprus, would have had access to the same metal sources. Because only the north-coast site of Vasilia (PreBA 1) can be seen to have participated directly in this trade network (Webb et al. 2006: 283), Cyprus's role remains unclear. The raw materials and finished artefacts analysed could have been acquired in Anatolia by Cypriote élites, obtained through seaborne trade conducted by Cycladic or Anatolian (or Cypriote) merchants and mariners, or brought to Cyprus by Anatolian migrants or metalsmiths. In sum, there is no clear solution to the problem of who inspired or 'pushed' local metallurgical developments, but equally there is no question that they occurred at this time in the context of widespread interaction networks (e.g. Şahoğlu 2005), where the meeting, mixing and co-presence of different peoples – their ideas, technologies and material goods – inevitably led to hybridised cultural practices.

> (5) *Pottery: new pottery forms (flat-based, ovoid-shaped jugs/juglets with tall cutaway spouts, flat-based, conical, hemispherical or ovoid bowls with pierced vertical or horizontal lugs, amphorae, flasks, storage jars) and new production techniques (disk bases, rod handles, surface treatment, differential firing) portray changes from earlier forms, fabrics and practices. Some innovations – new flask shapes, increased use of small bowls, surface blackening and burnishing – were already in use at Late Chalcolithic Kissonerga (Period 4a). Recent excavations at Politiko Kokkinorotsos, however, show that non-calcareous monochrome fabrics with occasional relief decoration were used in central Cyprus prior to Period 4 at Kissonerga (Webb et al. 2009: 205). Whilst Webb et al. would still contend that such wares ultimately may be derived from Early Bronze I Anatolia, they were present in the ceramic record on Cyprus before 2700 Cal BC and do not necessarily provide evidence for long-distance contacts at Kissonerga during Period 4a. All these practices are associated with the movement of Anatolia potters having particular knowledge and skills, whilst the range of pouring, mixing and serving vessels in Red Polished Philia ware is also linked to the introduction of alcoholic drinks and feasting activities (Webb and Frankel 2008).*

It has long been acknowledged that the innovative forms and techniques evident in these new pottery wares are 'Anatolianising' rather than a specific Anatolian product or type (e.g. Swiny 1986b: 35–37, figs. 1–2; Mellink 1991: 172–173). The breakdown in established pottery traditions, especially in the wares that characterise the PreBA 1 period, involved experimentation with pottery shapes, fabrics and surface treatments, as well as a '…tendency toward hybridization among the full repertoire of ware types' (Bolger, in Peltenburg 1986a: 39). More recently Bolger (2007: 183) has suggested: '…it is essential that we begin to approach the Philia phenomenon from a Chalcolithic perspective, within the framework of traditions antedating the arrival of migrant groups from the mainland'. Although it is clear that new pottery-producing practices were adopted in the initial phases of the Bronze Age, and that some of these innovations 'replicate' pottery-producing practices known earlier in Anatolia, Bolger (2007: 182) maintains that other innovations resulted from increased local demand and greater efficiency in production techniques on Cyprus itself. Moreover, because Red and Black Stroke-Burnished Ware (RB/B) appears earlier than Philia Red Polished wares, it is possible that some features of Late Chalcolithic pottery were incorporated into Philia wares, rather than vice versa. She concludes: 'The term "innovation" … should be regarded in this instance as *a multi-pronged, bi-directional set of interactions between indigenous and foreign elements*' (Bolger 2007: 182, emphasis added), precisely what would be defined as hybridisation practices in most colonial or postcolonial contexts.

(6) *Domestic technologies and practices: Philia levels at Marki have produced new hearth and oven types, and new cooking equipment, including horseshoe-shaped hearth surrounds ('hobs' or pot stands), baking pans, tripod braziers and direct fire-boiling vessels, each reportedly with antecedents and contemporary parallels in central and western Anatolia. Together with new types of food (meat, cereals), these objects imply new ways of preparing and consuming foodstuffs. The same (Philia) levels at Marki also have produced early evidence for the use of terracotta spindle whorls and clay loomweights on Cyprus. These two items are said to demonstrate the presence of the vertical, warp-weighted loom and the practice of low whorl spinning technology, both of which are argued to have originated in Europe and/or Anatolia (as opposed to Egypt and the Near East, where the horizontal ground loom and high whorl spinning technology were used). Finally, unlike Neolithic-Chalcolithic discard practices in which a wealth of in situ artefacts were deliberately abandoned on house floors, PreBA 1 practice – at least at Marki – was to clear the floors whenever buildings were abandoned.*

Turning first to textiles, loomweights and spindle whorls, evidence from several PreBA sites is consistent with the production of flax and wool, both of which were used not just on Cyprus (Åström 1964: 112 and fig. 1; Pieridou 1967: 26–28; Flourentzos 1989: 67) but throughout northwest Europe and indeed in Anatolia too (Barber 1991: 250, fig. 11.1). Textile production on Cyprus thus clearly formed part of a broader Euro-Anatolian tradition, but there is no material basis to argue that this particular craft technique was *imported* from Anatolia (Webb 2002c; Frankel 2000: 172; Frankel and Webb 2006a: 177). Rahmstorf (2005: 157–158), moreover, argues that evidence for the origin of the warp-weighted loom used throughout the eastern Mediterranean during the later Bronze and Iron Ages is ambiguous, and doubts that loomweights can tell us anything about *ethnic* groupings.

Horseshoe-shaped cooking hobs made of unbaked or low-fired clay are known throughout Anatolia and the southern Levant as well as on Cyprus (Frankel and Webb 2006a: 18; Falconer et al. 2010). The earliest examples from Marki are undecorated and of different form than the later hobs at the site, which are decorated with dashed and zigzag lines (see Figure 71 below) and small dots that recall facial markings seen on contemporary (PreBA 2) Red Polished 'plank' figurines (Frankel and Webb 1994: 52, figs. 1–2; Frankel and Webb 2006a: fig. 2.5). Objects such as hearths and hobs are obviously associated with everyday practices, and make unlikely items for trade (Frankel and Webb 1996: 183). The hobs found at Marki in particular reveal similarities in form, function and meaning with Anatolian or Levantine examples, but as they evolve they lose some of their distinctive foreign features and become decorated with distinctively Cypriot designs. In sum, although the style of these hobs developed over the longer term, they still bear striking witness to both the material and social aspects of hybridisation practices.

(7) *Childcare practices: at Marki, three of five human skulls examined (including an infant from a Philia jar burial) reportedly show signs of headshaping, and are argued to be consistent with the regular use of cradleboards, some examples of which are seen on later (PreBA 1–2) terracottas (mostly plank figurines) (Lorentz 2006). Although headshaping does have Late Aceramic Neolithic precedents on Cyprus, there is no evidence for this practice during the Chalcolithic.*

As was the case with the much larger skeletal sample from LAN Khirokitia (Lorentz 2003; 2009), analysis of the five human skulls from Marki (Lorentz 2006) presents no statistical evidence to demonstrate the degree of cranial modifications that exist in those individuals. Because Cypriot crania are naturally short and broad with flattened occipitals, it is important to establish what a natural cranium looks like before one can argue for clear evidence of headshaping. It may be granted that infant crania could well have been modified by the constant use of cradleboards, which seem to be depicted on several later Cypriot terracotta plank figurines (PreBA 1–2) (Karageorghis 1991: 77–81, pls. 44–47). Bergoffen (2009), who suggests that the plank figurines might be regarded as abstract representations of cradleboards, points out that the unintentional flattening of the back of an infant's head depends entirely on how long and in what position the head has been fixed against the board. The use of cradleboards, then, would not necessarily result in cranial modifications (Bergoffen 2009: 69). Given the uncertainties over the way cradleboards were used on PreBA Cyprus, the link that Webb and Frankel (2007: 203) propose between headshaping and the 'regular use' of cradleboards at Marki must be regarded as equivocal. Moreover, the comparative Anatolian evidence (Ubaid, Early Bronze Age) for headshaping practices cited by Lorentz (2006: 301) also lacks statistical verification and thus cannot be used to demonstrate any direct link between these (assumed) practices, in Anatolia and/or on Cyprus. Finally, as Lorentz (2006: 301–302) herself notes, purported evidence for headshaping exists throughout the Near East (Turkey, Iraq, Iran, Syria, Lebanon, Palestine), Greece and Crete from the 10th millennium BC to the present day, and the lack of any viable comparative study on these materials makes it impossible to link the Cypriot evidence directly to any other area.

Finally, Parras's (2006) statistical comparison of dental non-metric traits on 235 individuals from (Middle Chalcolithic) Souskiou *Vathyrkakas* and Lemba *Lakkous* with those from (Late Chalcolithic, Period 4) Kissonerga *Mosphilia* (noted in the previous chapter) revealed that all traits from the later remains were already present in the earlier ones. If new colonists or ethnic migrants first arrived on Cyprus during the Late Chalcolithic (Peltenburg 2007a; Bolger 2007), then we might expect to find evidence for them amongst this kind of sample. Whilst Parras (2006: 63) cautiously speculated in her summary that '… the impetus behind the beginning of the Bronze Age was a local phenomenon rather than initiated [sic] by external contacts', it must be pointed out that these data could also be taken to indicate that (foreign) Philia people did not intermarry or otherwise become involved with those at Kissonerga during the Late Chalcolithic.

In summarising their study of all these 'everyday practices', Webb and Frankel (2007: 204–205) state:

> …Philia artefacts and innovations were not components within a broader system but form an entire cultural inventory: a set of material markers and attendant behaviours that constitute habitual practice at every level. … Each of these reflects an embedded set of technologies and corresponding skills, motor habits and cultural preferences.

They see the advent and rapid spread across the island of all these new practices, related artefacts and 'embedded cultural preferences' as evidence for the arrival of new settlers (and their families, animals and materials), skilled specialists and practitioners who operated within a new and interactive social and material context, different from everything that preceded it (except, perhaps, the more casual interactions between Cyprus and Anatolia seen at Late Chalcolithic Kissonerga *Mosphilia*).

That some new people or practices arrived on Cyprus at the onset of the PreBA is not in question. However, it is one thing to see these practices as the result of a colonisation (or ethnic migration) and technology transfer which, by their very nature, assume a dominant and a receptive group, quite another to view them as reflecting the co-presence of multiple cultural meetings and mixings involving incoming and indigenous groups of people. Whilst such interactions are necessarily structured by differential relations of power, the outcome is never predetermined: instead it is contingent on the specific social and cultural context as well as the imperatives of local agents.

To put all these arguments into the context of past scholarship on Cyprus, it is useful to recall Catling's (1971a: 819–820) views on 'the identity of the earliest Bronze Age settlers', published some 40 years ago in the third edition of the *Cambridge Ancient History*:

> The E.C. [Early Cypriot] episode in the development of Cyprus resulted from the arrival from Anatolia of bands of refugees, who had escaped from the destroyers of E.B. [Early Bronze] 2 culture in that region. They appear to have mixed with, and not to have destroyed the sparse Chalcolithic II [Late Chalcolithic] population they encountered in the area of Morphou bay, their first landfall. They introduced metallurgical skills, new types of pottery and methods of decorating it, particularly incision; they were also responsible for new ways of treating the dead. All this is clear from their graves and grave-offerings; *the future, when their occupation sites begin to be excavated, will no doubt show other innovations for which they were responsible.* (emphasis added)

Few archaeologists who have worked on Cyprus were as adept as Catling in predicting the outcome of future fieldwork on the island. Likewise few were as predictable in downplaying the role of the indigenous population in any 'innovations' or cultural developments seen in the island's material record (see above, p. 29):

> It is tempting … to infer that the bearers of the Philia culture came from a considerably more sophisticated environment than that of the residual Chalcolithic culture which they encountered on their arrival in Cyprus. They and their descendants coalesced with the native population, succumbing to their influence sufficiently to adopt changed standards in many aspects of their lives; it was not to be the only time that such a process took place. (Catling 1971a: 812–813)

Excavations in an area unforeseen by Catling, that is, in the island's southwest at Kissonerga *Mosphilia*, have provided some insights into the sequence of the latest Chalcolithic *and* early Philia phases (4a, 4b and 5) (Peltenburg et al. 1998: 256–259), whilst excavations there and at Politiko *Kokkinorotsos* (Webb et al. 2009) have rendered some information on the 'sparse Chalcolithic II population' whom any incoming people would have encountered. Long-term excavations at Marki *Alonia* (Frankel and Webb 1996; 2006a) have produced a range of material – much of it unique – upon which the colonisation/migration model for the Philia phase is based. Various materials and mechanisms thought to explain the arrival of immigrants have been identified as well as (in Catling's words) the 'other innovations for which they were responsible'. Whereas Peltenburg (2007a) and Bolger (2007) remain sceptical about the extent to which Anatolian migrants (or 'refugees', or 'invaders') were responsible for the changes seen in the relevant levels at *Mosphilia*, Frankel and Webb's work at Marki *Alonia* has gone some way to fulfilling Catling's prophecy.

Most of the differences highlighted between the purported intrusive Philia group and the indigenous (Late Chalcolithic) communities of Cyprus, and thus the essence of the argument for an Anatolian colonisation or ethnic migration during the Prehistoric Bronze Age, are based on material stemming from overlapping sequences at Kissonerga *Mosphilia* (disturbed top of site) and Marki *Alonia* (preserved base of site). Both of these sequences were short-lived in comparison with their much longer Chalcolithic (Kissonerga) and PreBA (Marki) levels. Because no settlement site, therefore, yet offers substantial stratigraphic evidence for the transition from the latest Chalcolithic to the earliest Bronze Age sequence, the interpretation of the archaeological data involved is bound to be contentious, however robust the analyses of the data may seem. This is particularly the case when that evidence has been used to postulate an ethnic migration or colonisation, and the social, economic and demographic factors that lay behind it, or resulted from it.

On the one hand, Frankel and Webb maintain that the crucial factors in 'becoming Bronze Age' (Frankel 2005) were a focal ethnic migration and an associated transfer of technologies and everyday practices, most of which were 'directly introduced' from Anatolia. On the other hand, the social, material, technological and behavioural markers they see as distinguishing Anatolian (Philia) migrants have no direct manifestations in the archaeological record, not least because they must be several generations removed from the time of the presumed migration(s). In Frankel and Webb's (2006a: 305) own words:

> There is no current evidence for any of these Bronze Age migrants and it must be assumed that they underwent a relatively rapid adaptation in both technological and social systems to adjust to a different environment and succeed in establishing viable communities.

In sum, all these material witnesses of daily life, family circumstances, food production, feasting and ritual, right down to burial practices, seem to lack direct Anatolian parallels. Moreover, we must now take into account what Peltenburg (2007a; see also Bolger 2007) regards as the earlier presence of certain 'Philia' traits during the Late Chalcolithic although, as noted above, such traits may well belong to Period 4b at Kissonerga *Mosphilia*, and would thus be nearly contemporaneous with the Philia phase.

In their focal article on the Philia 'facies', Webb and Frankel (1999: 40) suggest that all those 'things' – pottery, metal goods, spindle whorls, hobs, figurines and discard practices, spurred annular pendants, the built environment – that distinguish an intrusive Philia group from an indigenous Cypriot group resulted from '…a transformation process of acculturation and adaptation to new geographical, ecological, and social circumstances'. In my view, the validity of this argument is diminished, but certainly not invalidated, by the use of problematic concepts such as ethnicity and acculturation. Beyond the new goods and practices introduced, it is also necessary to consider how the co-presence of different cultural or social groups in a common space actually works, or how people on the move from one place to another might identify themselves in material terms. These issues are crucial in evaluating the likelihood of a PreBA 1 Anatolian migration to (or colonisation of) Cyprus. However one views this growing body of evidence, in terms of (ethnic) migration(s) or hybridisation practices, which in any case are not mutually exclusive, in order to gain a fuller picture of PreBA Cyprus it is also important to consider other material, spatial and social aspects of this period.

SPATIAL ORGANISATION, SETTLEMENT AND SUBSISTENCE

During the Prehistoric Bronze Age, settlement expanded at an increasing rate through time into areas previously unoccupied (Figure 69): good agricultural land such as the western *Mesaoria* (the plain between the Troodos and Kyrenia mountain ranges) or the fertile plain along the north coast; the foothills of the Troodos near the upper reaches of the Kouris, Pedhaios and Yialias Rivers, and around the eastern rim of the Troodos; along (but not on) the south and west coast and the surrounding hinterlands. Several other concentrations of PreBA materials or sites around the island have been identified through survey work

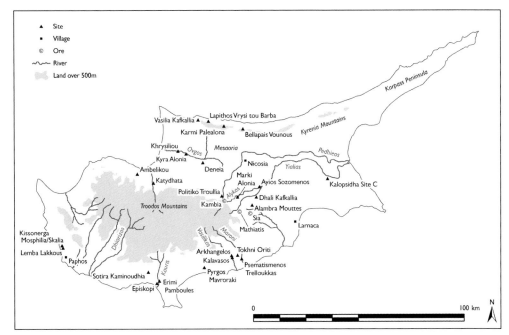

Figure 69. Map of PreBA sites mentioned in text. Drawn by Luke Sollars.

(Catling 1962: 138–139, 148–154; Knapp 2008: 74, table 2). The most recent and by far the most reliable survey of PreBA settlement (Georgiou 2007) identified 44 sites of PreBA 1 (Early Cypriot [EC] I–II) date, which increased eight-fold during PreBA 2 (EC III-Middle Cypriot [MC] II) to 345 sites. Such a dramatic expansion in the number of sites suggests that the population also grew to an unprecedented extent during the late 3rd millennium BC. Most sites situated in the plains were well suited to agricultural pursuits, whilst those in the Troodos foothills were ideally placed to exploit the copper deposits of the Lower Pillow Lavas. In the near-coastal zones, new sites emerged first in the north and south, somewhat later in the east and west (and into the foothill zone).

The material and chronological sequences of the PreBA 1 period (Philia phase-EC I, II; see Table 2; Appendix, Table A2 and section on Prehistoric Bronze Age) have now been established securely on the basis of excavations and radiocarbon dates from three sites: Kissonerga *Mosphilia* (Peltenburg et al. 1998), Marki *Alonia* (Frankel and Webb 1996; 2006a; Webb and Frankel 1999) and Sotira *Kaminoudhia* (Swiny et al. 2003). At *Mosphilia*, as already mentioned several times, Periods 4a–4b belong to the Late Chalcolithic while a very thin and disturbed level, Period 5, is attributed to the Philia phase. *Mosphilia* and Kyra *Alonia* (Dikaios 1962: 152–155) have both mortuary and settlement evidence from the Philia phase, whilst *Kaminoudhia* has only mortuary remains. Local Philia-style pottery is reported from Kissonerga *Skalia*, but not in a stratified context (Crewe 2010a: 71). Other sites with notable burial remains include

(EC I–II) Bellapais *Vounous* (Stewart and Stewart 1950; Dunn-Vaturi 2003), Lapithos *Vrysi tou Barba* (Gjerstad et al. 1934), and Karmi *Palealona* (Webb et al. 2009); (Philia phase) Philia *Laxia tou Kasinou* (Dikaios 1962: 160–176); and (Philia phase-EC I/II) Nicosia *Ayia Paraskevi* (Hennessy et al. 1988).

At Marki, stratigraphic evidence demonstrates without question that the Philia phase predates the EC I–II sequences; occupation at Marki lasted for some 500 years, into the PreBA 2 (MC II) period. At Sotira *Kaminoudhia*, the remains date from PreBA 1 (Philia phase, burials only) through PreBA 2 (EC III). Philia pottery from several tombs serves to support the stratigraphic sequence developed at Marki. This sequence also demonstrates that Dikaios's (1962: 192–203) view of the Philia culture as preceding the EC was correct, and that the traditional pottery phases (Philia, EC I–II, EC III–MC I) are sequential and overlapping.

Sites of the Philia phase are situated in the central and western *Mesaoria*, around the Troodos massif and on or near the northern, western and southern coasts. Webb and Frankel (1999: 7–13) have identified securely 19 Philia phase sites, and questioned the identification of a further 14 (all of which, however, belong to the PreBA 1 period). Most well-documented sites of this phase are cemeteries, albeit with much inter- and intra-site variability; tomb groups have been documented at Vasilia (and perhaps Bellapais) on the north coast; at Philia, Kyra, Khrysiliou and Deneia in the Ovgos Valley; at Marki and Nicosia in the central plain; and at Episkopi, Sotira and Kissonerga in the south and southwest (Webb and Frankel 1999: 7–13, fig. 1; see also Swiny 1997: 177–185). Based on current evidence, it seems that the Philia phase was marked by the establishment of new settlements in agriculturally productive areas, along routes of transport and close to coastal outlets (Webb n.d.). Because several Philia phase sites are found in rather close proximity to copper ore sources in the Troodos foothills, whilst some others (e.g. Vasilia, *Bellapais*, Episkopi, Kissonerga) are located near the coast, it may be that access to metal deposits and proximity to the sea were important factors in choosing where to live (Webb and Frankel 1999: 7–8). Swiny (1981; 1997: 195), however, argued that good arable land and proximity to reliable water sources were the most important considerations.

The subsequent stages (EC I–III) in the settlement of Cyprus involved the expansion of sites into most parts of the island: near the north coast and on both sides of the Kyrenia range, even into the Karpass peninsula; in the central and western *Mesaoria*, less so in the southeast; into the foothill zone of the northwest and northeast Troodos; all along but not directly on the south coast, and very little in the southwest (but cf. Crewe 2010a on Kissonerga *Skalia*). By the turn of the millennium (PreBA 2), clusters of settlement also appear at the interface between the mineral-rich Troodos foothills and the arable lands of the *Mesaoria*, perhaps indicating the increased exploitation of the island's copper resources (Marki *Alonia*, of course, is in this zone but dates much earlier). Several other PreBA 1–2 sites have been identified by survey (Knapp 2008: 74, table 2; Bombardieri 2010a, for the Kouris Valley) and a few settlement sites have been partially excavated or intensively surveyed: for example, Kalopsidha Site C (EC I–MC III – Crewe 2010b: 65), Pyrgos *Mavroraki* (Philia, EC I–II), Psematismenos *Trelloukkas* (EC III) and Ambelikou *Aletri* (MC I). Stratified deposits at Pyrgos *Mavroraki* have been dated to a late phase of PreBA 2, but the role and function of this important site remain unclear (Belgiorno 1999; 2002; 2004). None of these sites is presented in detail here, but rather are discussed in contexts where their location or finds become relevant.

There is little evidence to indicate how long sites of the Philia phase were occupied, but many of the period's distinctive material traits (pottery, metallurgical production, agricultural and mortuary practices) continued to develop throughout the PreBA. The excavations at Marki *Alonia*, with human-made deposits between 1.5–2 m deep, reveal that this site, at least, enjoyed a long stretch of human occupation (Frankel and Webb 2006a: 318). Although most material developments of the Philia phase currently are documented only at Marki, they may be inferred to apply – for the time being – to other settlements as well (Webb n.d.). The estimated population of Marki's earliest phase is only a few dozen people (Webb and Frankel 2004: 129–130; Frankel and Webb 2006a: 310). If this were extrapolated to all of the Philia phase's dispersed communities, it might help to explain the marked homogeneity seen in material culture (pottery, spurred annular pendants, distinctive metal artefacts, biconical spindle whorls) across widely dispersed sites (Webb and Frankel 1999; 2008). These material patterns, in particular the distinctive types of Red Polished pottery (MacLaurin 1985), increasingly took on regional characteristics, but by the time of the population expansion during the PreBA 2 period, these communities had developed into a broadly based sociocultural system with island-wide networks of communication and exchange (Frankel and Webb 2006a: 307; Webb 2012).

The only PreBA 1–2 settlements (or phases within settlements) excavated to any extent are Kissonerga *Mosphilia*, Marki *Alonia*, Sotira *Kaminoudhia*, Alambra *Mouttes*, Pyrgos *Mavroraki* and Politiko *Troullia* (*Troullia* is thus far dated only by pottery sequences to PreBA 2 [EC III–MC II], with possible extension into ProBA 1 [MC III–LC I] – Fall et al. 2008: 197; Falconer et al. 2010). Disturbed deposits with PreBA 1 pottery are reported at Kissonerga *Skalia* (Crewe 2010a: 71), but further excavations are required to demonstrate if this material is in situ. At Kissonerga *Mosphilia* in the southwest, the final phase of the Chalcolithic settlement (Period 4b), with its three distinct zones of 'household compounds' – but no prominent structures, communal facilities or public works (possibly excepting Building 86) – was notably different from everything that preceded it (Peltenburg et al. 1998: 250–251). During the subsequent, Philia phase level at Kissonerga *Mosphilia* (Period 5, PreBA 1 in date), two infants were buried in recycled Red and Black Stroke-Burnished Ware jars, the only Period 4 pottery found in Period 5. This level was severely disturbed, and there were no architectural remains.

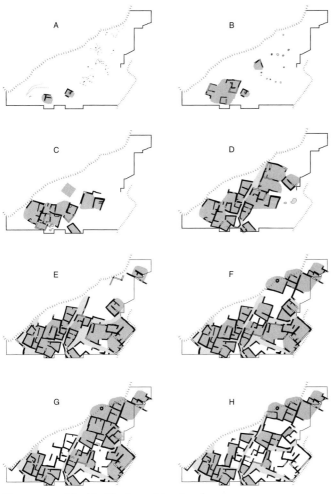

Figure 70. Marki *Alonia* architectural sequence over 500 years (Frankel and Webb 2006a: 308–315, text fig. 11.3). Courtesy of David Frankel and Jennifer Webb.

Marki Alonia

The site of Marki *Alonia* is situated just south of the Alykos River in central Cyprus, some 15 km south of modern-day Nicosia and only a few kilometres from the northeastern foothills of the Troodos mountains. Surface remains at Marki were spread over 5–6 ha of sloping fields; within this extent, some 2,000 m^2 were exposed during eight field seasons between 1991–2000. The excavated area constitutes the largest settlement exposure of the PreBA 1–2 periods on Cyprus (Frankel and Webb 1996; 2006a: 1–3). Nine phases of Bronze Age habitation (from A, the earliest, to I, the latest) were established (Frankel and Webb 2006a: 36–37). The excavators provide a detailed reconstruction of the site's built environment over nearly 500 years of occupation (Frankel and Webb 2006a: 308–315, text fig. 11.3; 2006b; Webb 2009) (Figure 70). The standard building form was a rectilinear, multi-cellular, mudbrick structure with substantial stone foundations. Most of the 33 compounds ('households') excavated had two or three covered rooms set within a larger, partly or fully enclosed courtyard.

During the Philia phase at Marki (internal Phases A–B), this household lay-out is already apparent; Compounds 3 and 4 were two-room units set within a common courtyard, where chipped stone, deer antler and shell were worked, pottery produced and food cooked in a large oven. Sets of postholes may represent the remnants of animal pens (or roof supports?), whilst a single room in the southeast may have served as a storage facility. In Phases C–D (EC I–II, PreBA 1), the built area of the site and presumably the population expanded; the courtyards of Compounds 6 and 7 (which replaced 3 and 4) were now enclosed by a stone wall on three sides. During Phase D, as the inhabited area continued to expand, a narrow lane running north–south was developed to provide access into and between compounds, whether old, restructured or new: Compounds 9 (three rooms), 14 and 15 (two rooms) and 13 (two inner rooms and courtyard) were all entered from this lane. In Phases E–F (EC III, PreBA 2), major and minor changes marked new development: rooms were enlarged or added (Compound 8, to the west of the lane), and new lanes appeared in the east. To the north, new compounds (22, 25–27) were laid out, and a large new structure (Compound 28) was erected in the centre of the site, leaving some standing ruins. Two new, single-room compounds (23, 24) also arose at this time. During Phases G–H (MC I–II, PreBA 2), the settlement began to decline as some compounds were reduced in size, others abandoned and never rebuilt. At least one new, large compound (29), however, was built in the northern part of the site. By the time of Phase H, several compounds stood in ruins, and by Phase I (MC II), only three compounds (22, 26–27) in the northern sector remained in use.

The excavated remains at Marki *Alonia* reflect a gradual growth in popu-lation, and a gradual expansion of the site's original small settlement. During the Philia phase, courtyards were defined by light fences or informally demar-cated by animal pens, large ovens, free-standing storerooms and outhouses or lean-tos, all of which the excavators see as evidence for resource-sharing and cooperative relationships between kin-related households (Frankel and Webb 2006a: 313–314). In time, these buildings become more segregated: stone walls enclosed courtyards on three sides, leaving a wide entrance into the com-pounds from public lanes. These developments possibly reflect the need for inter-household privacy. By the beginning of PreBA 2 (EC III), courtyards became smaller and fully enclosed with only narrow entrances or internal pas-sageways giving access to the buildings, whilst the interior rooms themselves grew in size and number. The changing nature of the courtyard and the activi-ties carried out within the rooms of the compounds may point to an increased specialisation in production and maintenance activities, and more diverse household behaviours (Frankel and Webb 2006a: 313). By the later phases of

Figure 71. Marki *Alonia* hob, P2000 (Frankel and Webb 1996: pl. 32a). Courtesy of David Frankel and Jennifer Webb.

PreBA 2 (MC I–II), expansion and intensification gave way to abandonment and contraction, even if some of the standing ruins were used as animal pens or for other, non-residential purposes (Frankel and Webb 2006a: 309).

Discrete house compounds with two–three rooms at the rear of a courtyard represent the most common form of buildings at Marki, from the first to the final occupation of the site (Webb 2009: 260). As time passed, the interiors of these compounds progressively became subdivided and lanes were built to facilitate movement throughout the village. Within the compounds, at least one of the interior rooms typically contained a hearth built against a low mudbrick or plaster bench, with semi-circular or rectangular plaster 'fenders', and often equipped with a 'hob' (clay hearth surrounds or pot supports) (Frankel and Webb 1996: pl. 32a; 2006a: 17–21) (Figure 71). A few ovens, distinct from hearths, were also found in the interior rooms; these had a narrow chamber enclosed by vertical mudbrick slabs on one side and the house-wall on the other. Several units had mudbrick or stone work benches set against the interior walls, whilst rectangular wall bins – built on or set into floors – may have been used for short-term food storage (along with some Coarse Ware 'mealing bins'?). Most courtyards were furnished with hard, pebble-based floor emplacements (supports for *pithoi*, mortars for preparing cereal grains before pounding), animal pens and informal working areas (Webb n.d.). Between 80–90% of the artefacts recovered (all phases) came from the interior rooms (not the courtyards), and in particular from the area in and around the hearths (Frankel and Webb 2006a: 312–313). Thus it would seem that a wide range of social activities and interaction took place in and around the fire, with other interior spaces most likely used for storage and sleeping. The courtyards, by contrast, seem to have been kept clean, perhaps reflecting routine maintenance activities but resulting in the loss of *de facto* refuse and other residual materials (Webb 1995; 1998).

There is little evidence of large scale or long term planning in any of these buildings, but there is a general continuity in size (around 100 m²) and structure through time. On the one hand, none of the compounds is better built than the others, and whilst there is some variation in the number or size of the rooms or the facilities and fittings within them, there is nothing to indicate significant differences in the wealth or status of those who dwelt in them. On the other hand, by Phases C–D, certain changes in the layout of space – enclosed courtyards, absence of animal pens and work stations within the compounds, relocation of ovens and screen walls built to conceal hearths from exterior view – may indicate a trend towards increased privacy and security, perhaps linked to notions of heritable property and the control and manipulation of space and household resources. Moreover, Frankel and Webb (2006a: 314) suggest that the longevity of use (300–400 years) seen in Compounds 6 and 7, whose occupants may have been the descendants of the 'pioneer' dwellers in Compounds 3 and 4, may indicate well-established families who exercised some social dominance in the community (also seen in a private access passage to Compound 6, and its capacity to establish and maintain another household, in Compound 8). As the population and the size of the village increased, the social organisation of the community also must have changed, perhaps giving rise to mechanisms of social cohesion and control. By Phase E (EC III), the appearance of anthropomorphic (mainly female or infant) and zoomorphic (cattle) figurines may indicate an attempt to control sources of labour (reproductive females) and capital or social storage (cattle) in an increasingly intensified agricultural economy (Webb 2009: 261–264).

Despite all these internal developments, Marki remained a small agricultural village whose inhabitants relied on the usual faunal triad of cattle, sheep and goat, along with less frequent use of pig and deer. Donkeys as well as cattle would have provided animal traction, whilst sheep, goats and cattle were used not just for meat, but also for milk and other secondary products (Croft 2006). Whilst the faunal evidence is extensive and lends itself well to interpretation, the floral component was less substantial, and consisted of wheat, barley, olives, pulses, figs and grapes (Adams and Simmons 1996). The large number of groundstone tools used for harvesting and processing grain nonetheless indicates a heavy reliance on cereal cultivation, whilst cattle seem to have provided the bulk of the meat consumed. All in all, the inhabitants of Marki had access to a broad spectrum of diverse food resources to meet their subsistence requirements.

Sotira Kaminoudhia

The site of Sotira *Kaminoudhia* is situated on a series of sloping terraces, 5 km from Cyprus's south coast and some 15 km west of modern-day Limassol. It lies just west of a track leading up to the Ceramic Neolithic site of Sotira *Teppes*, which stands above the surrounding territory and the southern coastal plain. The impetus behind the long-term and repeated use of this area (the modern village lies only 200 m south) is a series of three perennial springs, something that first drew Dikaios to excavate here. To the north of the site, at about 100 and 150 m respectively, lay Cemetery A (21 tombs) and Cemetery B (three rock-cut, looted chambers) (Swiny et al. 2003: 3–6, and fig. 1.3). Preliminary soundings carried out at *Kaminoudhia* in 1981 indicated a PreBA settlement that covered at least 1 ha. Two further excavation seasons followed, in 1983 and 1986, and two field surveys associated with the project were conducted (Held 1988; Swiny and Mavromatis 2000). Three further seasons of excavations began in 2004 but are largely unpublished (cf. Swiny 2008). Twelve individual radiocarbon dates from the site (uncalibrated) range between ca. 2500–1950 BC (PreBA 1–2 periods, or EC I–III). But when the site dates are modelled as a Sequence with two Phases (I and II) within the overall Cyprus Prehistoric Sequence as in the Appendix, then the start and end 'Boundaries' of the radio-carbon dates for the site cluster much more closely in time or, if allowance is made for an old-wood TPQ since all the samples are on charcoal (we use 50±50 years as a rough measure as in the original study by Manning and Swiny 1994), between ca. 2270–2080 Cal BC (see Appendix, caption to Figure A11).

Architectural remains were uncovered in three areas; the largest exposure was in Area A in the northeast, with less substantial remains uncovered in Area B (to the west) and Area C (to the south) (Swiny et al. 2003: pl. 1.3) (Figure 72). A trial trench between Areas A and B revealed architectural remains throughout; this was not the case to the south, between Areas A and C, where bedrock rises to the present ground level. Two phases (I, II) were identified in Area A, where several narrow passages or lanes separated a series of mainly rectilinear, stone-built, domestic structures. Building plans, however, were by no means standardised: there is considerable variation and complexity in the shape, layout and proportions of the structures. Rectangular structures stand beside square or even triangular ones, whilst other buildings incorporate curvilinear walls (Swiny 2008: 44, with plan of Area A) (Figure 73). Some building units had two or three rooms, others were single room, multi-purpose structures, whilst still others were fronted by a courtyard (as at Marki *Alonia*). The walls of these structures – made of fieldstones bonded in mud – were about 60 cm wide and set directly on the bedrock; only a few floors, made of lime plaster, were preserved (Swiny 1997: 186–187). Although virtually all buildings were constructed with the locally abundant tabular limestone, some sun-dried mud-bricks were found at the site (Swiny et al. 2003: 59).

Within the buildings, rectangular hearths abutted the walls, whilst counter-sunk stone mortars and lime plaster bins were found on several floors. Low, narrow benches that held a range of stone and antler artefacts were laid out along some walls, and often ran their entire length. Several entrances had high, monolithic thresholds as well as pivot holes to support doors (Swiny et al. 2003:

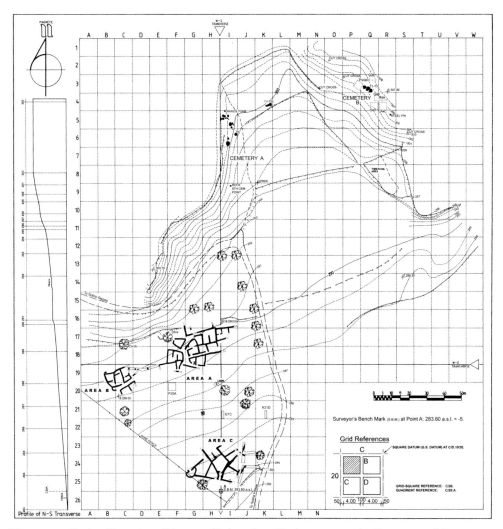

Figure 72. Sotira *Kamminoudhia* overall site plan (Swiny 2008: 45). Courtesy of Stuart Swiny.

5). Finds within these structures were numerous and included groundstone tools (querns, rubbers, pounders, etc.), chert sickle blades, a broad range of Red Polished pottery vessels (bowls, jugs, amphorae, a few storage jars), terracotta spindle whorls and loom weights, a few copper-based metal objects (knives, chisels, an axe, needles and awls, personal ornaments), and picrolite beads, pendants and 'tubes'. The debris that accumulated on the floors of domestic structures in use seems repeatedly to have been swept away, into the passageways just outside the houses (Swiny et al. 2003: 30–31, 37).

Excavations in Area A uncovered one, large building (Unit 1) of Phase 1, and some 15 additional structures ('units') of Phase II, excluding corridors and other units found in the trial trench between Areas A and B (Swiny et al. 2003: 10–34). Unit 1 (Phase I) was a large structure (almost 50 m²), subdivided during

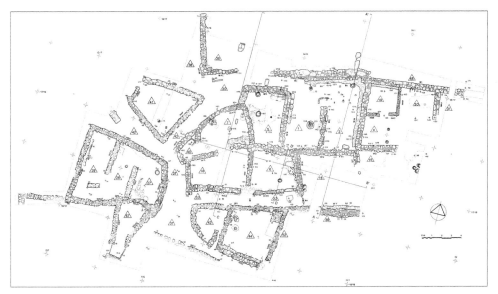

Figure 73. Sotira *Kaminoudhia*, plan of Area A showing diverse building plans (rectangular, triangular, curvilinear) (Swiny 2008: 44). Courtesy of Stuart Swiny.

Phase II by a low partition wall into two rooms (Units 2 and 3) (Swiny et al. 2003: 77–78, figs. 2.1–2.2). The use of dividing walls and the construction of low benches largely took place in Phase II. Groundstone tools, a cockleshell pendant and a fragmentary Red Polished pot stand (like the hobs found at Marki *Alonia*) make up the main finds from this building. In the southwestern corner of Area A, the single-roomed, nearly square Unit 44 (Phase II) yielded an array of intact or restorable Red Polished bowls and jugs placed on a low bench or resting against the walls (Swiny 2008: 45–46). Near the centre of the building lay the skeleton of a young woman with no discernible grave goods and nothing demarcating a proper burial space; she may have been the victim of an earthquake, evidence for which may be seen in the collapsed wall debris from Area B (Swiny 2008: 48).

In Area C (Phase II only), eight more structures came to light, the most notable of which was Unit 2, a large (34 m²), roughly square space entered through a narrow corridor on its southern side (Swiny et al. 2003: 39–42, 87, fig. 2.11). There are low benches along the two eastern walls, and a large stone threshold at the wide entryway from the corridor (Unit 25). A hearth in the northern corner, and a lime plaster bin with a stone mortar incorporated in its base in the southeast corner, are the only notable internal fittings. Unit 2 contained the densest array of potsherds at the site (including the rim sherds of up to 92 small Red Polished bowls), as well as seven intact or restorable vessels (Red Polished, Drab Polished Blue Core), groundstone tools and weights, two gaming stones, two pieces of worked picrolite, one bone needle, four spindle whorls, a copper awl and a similar copper tool. The size of the enclosed space – with the interior walls rendered in lime plaster – suggests that it was unroofed, thus a courtyard, throughout which a thick deposit of 'ash-rich occupation debris' had accumulated on all the floor surfaces (Swiny et al. 2003: 40–41). This structure's function is uncertain, but it is worth emphasising that a spacious, white-walled interior courtyard with a concentration of pottery vessels for holding or pouring liquids contrasts sharply with all the other buildings at Sotira *Kaminoudhia*; it may have served as some sort of communal space.

In Area B (Phase II only), four further structures were uncovered, the most notable being the large (80 m²), D-shaped, Unit 12 Complex, with a rectangular courtyard separated by parapet walls from three smaller rooms (Swiny 2008: 48 with plan of Area B). From the wide doorway leading off the street, the courtyard sloped upward towards a heavy, shallow stone trough set in the midst of a low wall, delimiting a narrow space in front of three large stone boulders. These boulders formed the backdrop to a tall, white plastered wall that would have towered over the courtyard. Unit 12 lacked some of the features typical in the buildings at *Kaminoudhia* (bins, benches, hearth) but contained a large stone basin in the courtyard and, in the small southwest room, a unique grinding platform still supporting a pair of saddle querns, next to which was an even larger, deep limestone basin holding an intact Red Polished juglet (Swiny 2008: 49, with illustration of the Unit 12 Complex).

Found throughout the Unit 12 Complex were a large number of groundstone tools, a copper chisel and small lumps of copper ore and slag, several Red Polished pottery vessels and sherds, five gaming stones, some picrolite artefacts, a cattle scapula and a fragment of a bone needle. Together with the striking architectural feature at the north end of the courtyard, the diversity of these finds initially suggest that this building might have served some public or ceremonial purpose (Swiny et al. 2003: 34–37).

During the more recent excavations, a probe just beyond the northwestern corner of the Unit 12 Complex uncovered a young woman buried against the north face of the wall and covered by a stone bench. There were no mortuary goods, but nearby lay some debris left over from the production of annular shell pendants (Swiny 2008: 49). Given the atypical architectural plan, the presence of unique installations (e.g. the tall, white-plastered wall backing the courtyard), several striking objects (e.g. the cattle scapula, gaming stones) and the atypical distribution pattern of finds, along with a carefully planned burial (the only known inhumation within the settlement), Swiny (2008: 49–50) now suggests that this complex may well have served for the performance of ceremonial activities and display, if not the consumption of food and drink. Indeed, it is an unusual structure for a PreBA 1 site, and like Units 2/25 in Area C, must have had some special, likely communal purpose.

Despite these architectural anomalies *Kaminoudhia*, like Marki *Alonia*, must be regarded as a typical PreBA 1 village whose inhabitants relied for their meat on cattle (30% of the faunal record), sheep and goat (38%), but also on deer (18%) and pig (13%) (Croft 2003b: 439, table 11.1). Cattle, along with equids, provided animal traction, but like sheep and goat also yielded important secondary products, especially milk. Donkeys may also have served as pack animals (see the unprovenanced clay model with saddle bags illustrated in Morris 1985: 204–205, fig. 327). Taking bone weight rather than bone frequency into account, Croft (2003b: 440, table 11.2, 446) concluded that cattle formed the basis of the animal economy at Sotira *Kaminoudhia* (and Marki *Alonia*) throughout the PreBA. Amongst the botanical remains recovered at *Kaminoudhia* (Hansen, in Swiny et al. 2003: 449–453), emmer wheat, grape, olive and almond formed the primary species; wild pistachio and pear were also present. Like other PreBA 1 sites, relatively few plant remains were found at *Kaminoudhia*, but when taken into account alongside the faunal remains there is no reason to doubt its status as an agro-pastoral village.

Alambra Mouttes

Located less than 10 km southeast of Marki and about 20 km south of Nicosia, Alambra *Mouttes* is situated on the flanks of a ridge, one of a series of low hills that rise above the surrounding plain (Coleman et al. 1996: 1–2). This location, at the interface of the igneous and sedimentary geological zones, provided easy access both to the copper sulphide ore deposits of the Pillow Lava formations in the Troodos (south and west of the site), and to the more fertile, agricultural soils of the surrounding plain (north and east of the site). Of two major rivers that flow within a few kilometres of the site (Yialias to the north, Tremithos to the southeast), only a small tributary, the Kalamoudhia, passes near it, just south of the *Mouttes* ridge.

A preliminary surface survey of the Alambra area took place in 1974, excavations began in 1978, and successive field seasons were carried out from 1980–82, with study seasons from 1983–85. Three surface surveys were also conducted on the site and its environs, in 1974, 1980 and 1984 (Coleman et al. 1996: 7–10). Earlier, 19th-century explorations in the area by Lang, Cesnola and Ohnefalsch-Richter opened at least 100 tombs, so it is likely that most mortuary deposits around the *Mouttes* settlement have been thoroughly disturbed. A series (termed 'clusters') of both chamber tombs and pit graves was documented on the slopes and ridges to the east, west and south of the site, and six tombs were excavated (Coleman et al. 1996: 113–128, figs. 6, 8). Although the precise date of all the mortuary evidence found in or reported from the vicinity of the site is of uncertain Early–Middle Cypriot date (Keswani 2004: 47, 187, table 3.1), *Mouttes* itself has been more narrowly dated. Based on pottery and four radiocarbon dates (only three survive to the final Model 8) within the Cypriot prehistoric sequence analysed in the Appendix (see caption to Figure A11), these dates fall in a range between limits (start and end Boundaries) of about 2090–1800 Cal BC (PreBA 2, or MC II).

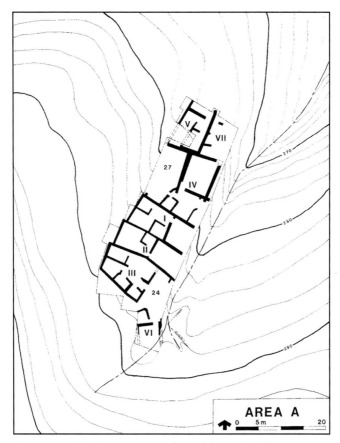

Figure 74. Alambra *Mouttes*, plan of Area A with structures and surrounding topography. After Coleman et al. (1996: fig. 9b). Courtesy of John Coleman.

The settlement at *Mouttes* is believed to have extended over a minimum of 6 ha, but the main focus of the excavations was in Area A (Figure 74), at the bottom of a shallow ravine sloping down to the northeast of the *Mouttes* ridge. Here the stubs of walls and Bronze Age potsherds had already been noted during the 1974 survey (Coleman et al. 1996: 18–19, figs. 9–11, 75). The excavations uncovered a terrace of houses – with common walls and entrances opening off a street – cut into the hillslope and built directly upon bedrock. This seems to represent a more deliberate and formal layout of settlement than those at Marki *Alonia* or Sotira *Kaminoudhia*, perhaps because the bedrock terraces were devoid of soil cover, and the surfaces thus would have required little preparation for building activities (Coleman et al. 1996: 21). Each of the seven structures (I–VII) excavated had a major wall dividing the house into front and rear sections; the rear was often subdivided so that each house had three to five rooms. The foundation courses of these buildings were largely built of sedimentary stone, laid only roughly in courses, and joined by a bedding of mortar. The upper courses were undoubtedly mudbrick, but only one, five-course stretch was found in situ (Building IV); other, fallen stretches or fragments of mudbrick walls were found in Buildings I, II and VII. On the lower surface of some better preserved, standing, interior walls, and on a few exterior wall surfaces, there was evidence of a rough, mud-plaster coating (Coleman et al. 1996: 24–25).

Entrances to the buildings in Area A measure between 0.6–1.3 m in width; threshold stones were found only in the stepped entrances to rooms in three of the buildings. There is no evidence for windows or roofing at the site. Three hearths were identified (Buildings I, IV and VI), the most distinctive of which was in the south corner of Room 8 in Building IV (Coleman et al. 1996: 28, pl. 13e–f). The bedrock floors frequently revealed what appear to be hollowed out, roughly circular, shallow cavities, seven of which were lined with mud-plaster. These may have been used as stands for round-bottomed jugs and jars, as mortars for grinding grain, or perhaps for the temporary storage of grains or other foods. The only other interior features identified were low benches or platforms, small stone-built enclosures and a single masonry pedestal; ledges left in the bedrock near the edge of some rooms would have provided useful surfaces (Coleman et al. 1996: 27–30). As was the case at Marki *Alonia*, there was little or no accumulation on the floors of use or discard deposits, perhaps because the bedrock surface is crumbly and would have required frequent sweeping.

Excavations in a series of test pits (Areas C, D and E) revealed little evidence of architecture but substantial amounts of contemporary (and later) pottery (Coleman et al. 1996: 109–110). No remains of the 'house' excavated almost 90 years ago at Alambra *Asproyi* are visible today, although Coleman et al. (1996: 24, fig. 4) pinpointed its location some 160 m southwest of *Mouttes*. In that earlier excavation, Gjerstad identified two separate, rectangular rooms set within an L-shaped courtyard that surrounded the house on three sides. The obvious similarities between the layout of this house and the compounds at Mark *Alonia* should be noted (Webb 2009: 263; cf. Wright 1992: 71–72). The northern room was interpreted as a working and living space (cooking, eating, sleeping), the southern room – with several benches and a 'grinding place' – as a work and storage area. Gjerstad suggested that this was the house of a rural shepherd, and he dated it to EC III. Subsequent study of the sherd material, however, revealed similarities with the pottery assemblage found in Area A at *Mouttes* (Coleman et al. 1996: 522–523; see also Barlow 1985: 48–49, 52), and the house is now also dated to the MC I period.

With the possible exception of Building IV (see below), all structures at *Mouttes* probably represent the households of small family groups. Different rooms were given over to various domestic activities (based on the finds within them): food storage and preparation, weaving and perhaps metallur-gical production. In Room 9 of Building III and elsewhere in that structure, there is some evidence for copper working: two terracotta crucible fragments, slag and pieces of ore or gossan (Coleman et al. 1996: 73–74; Swiny 1989: 20). Building IV, and within it Room 8, may have served communal if not cere- monial purposes. This structure has four separate, interconnected rooms, and its size (ca. 135 m²) and plan differ noticeably from other buildings at *Mouttes*. Room 8 was the largest enclosed area excavated at *Mouttes* (Coleman et al. 1996: 77), and it also contained the largest hearth: it had more and better pre- served pottery vessels (with a high proportion of juglets and small bowls), and more burnt animal bones in stratified levels, than any other room in the settlement. All this material may indicate a space that served groups larger than an individual family, one in which feasting or other ceremonial activities took place.

Beyond this, perhaps fanciful portrayal of feasting, evidence for the sub- sistence economy at *Mouttes* is uneven, with no direct botanical evidence, only the impressions of a grape leaf on a griddle and an olive leaf on a Red Polished juglet (Coleman et al. 1996: 325). The large number of ground- stone implements found at the site, however, surely points to the grinding and processing of grains. Faunal remains, by contrast, were abundant (nearly 9,000 bone fragments), and demonstrate that the people who lived at *Mouttes* relied for their dietary and other everyday needs primarily on sheep/goat (44% of the faunal sample), deer (22%), cattle (21%) and pig (11%), follow- ing a pattern similar to but distinctive from that known at other PreBA set- tlement sites. Two small dentalium and murex shells found at the site were probably used as ornaments or jewellery, the four triton shells as vessels or (one, with open apex) as a shell 'trumpet' (Reese, in Coleman et al. 1996: 475–486, table 8.2).

The absence of any clear indicators of authority, wealth or status differences (excepting the possible public or ceremonial nature of Building IV) suggests that PreBA 2 society at Alambra *Mouttes* was egalitarian. Production and con- sumption activities – based on analytical evidence of pottery, groundstone and terracotta (figurines, spindle whorls, etc.) – indicate that most materials were manufactured at or nearby the site. The relative paucity and condition of the metallurgical remains likewise indicate that any copper produced or consumed was destined to fill the needs of the village's inhabitants alone. Like Marki *Alonia*, Alambra *Mouttes* seems to have been abandoned entirely. Coleman et al. (1996: 331) suggest this phenomenon might reflect the absence of private ownership of land and resources during the PreBA. In contrast, Frankel and Webb (2006a: 308) see it as part of a wider development in which some PreBA 2 sites were abandoned (Deneia), whilst others (e.g. Ayios Sozomenos, Nicosia *Ayia Paraskevi*) rapidly expanded at the transition to the ProBA 1 period (MC III–LC I), when a major social and economic, if not ideological reorganisation occurred across the island. As we shall see in the next chapter, the latter expla- nation is the more likely one.

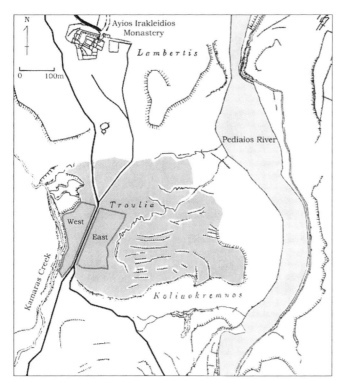

Figure 75. Politiko *Troullia* cadastral map, showing areas defined as Troullia West and Troullia East. Grey area indicates the distribution of Bronze Age pottery on the surface of the site. Drawing by Sid Rempel. Courtesy of Steven Falconer and Patricia Fall.

Politiko Troullia

Recent excavations at Politiko *Troullia* are beginning to shed additional light on the nature of PreBA village sites (Falconer et al. 2005; 2010; Fall et al. 2008). Like Marki *Alonia* and Alambra *Mouttes*, the site of *Troullia* – some 8 km east of Marki and about 25 km southwest of Nicosia – sits astride the border between the copper-rich foothills of the Troodos and the fertile *Mesaoria* plain. Bounded by hills to the north and south, and situated on an alluvial terrace between the Pedhaios River to the east and a smaller tributary (Kamaras Creek) to the west, *Troullia* forms part of an area repeatedly inhabited since the Early Aceramic Neolithic (Given and Knapp 2003: 182–183, 264–266).

By means of both pedestrian and soil resistivity survey carried out in 2004, and topographic survey conducted in 2005–2006, surface remains were found distributed discontinuously over approximately 20 ha, whilst the densest concentrations of domestic material – in the areas defined as Troullia West and Troullia East – likely represent the 2-ha core of the settlement (Falconer et al. 2005: 70, fig. 1, 72–73, 75) (Figure 75). Trimming one of a series of nine buried

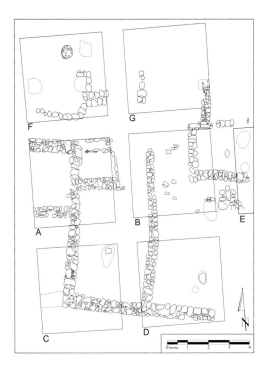

Figure 76. Politiko *Troullia* East, plan of Areas A–G (Fall et al. 2008: 194, fig. 13). Courtesy of Steven Falconer and Patricia Fall.

Figure 77. Politiko *Troullia* East, architecture in Areas A–G, view to southeast; note stone-lined bin near centre of photo. Photo by Sid Rempel. Courtesy of Steven Falconer and Patricia Fall.

stone walls eroding out of the east bank of Kamares Creek revealed a foundation surface at least 3 m below the modern surface, as well as five stratified use surfaces (Falconer et al. 2005: 72–73, fig. 2), all indicating habitation at the site over a long period of time. Topographic mapping carried out in 2005 and 2006 identified three further concentrations of material, two just north of Troullia West and another some 200 m east of Troullia East (Fall et al. 2008: 187, fig. 4). Excavations at the site began in 2006, and have continued each season through 2011; three preliminary reports have appeared, covering the 2004–2008 seasons (Falconer et al. 2005; 2010; Fall et al. 2008).

Using the results of topographic mapping (2005) and targeted soil resistivity survey (2006) to guide excavation, work first concentrated in Areas A–G in Troullia East (Fall et al. 2008: 191–193, figs. 9–11) (Figures 76 and 77). At least one multi-room, possibly roofed compound was uncovered, along with lanes ('alleyways'), storage bins and external buildings. Possible courtyards lie to the north and east of the main complex (Fall et al. 2008: 194–195, figs. 12–13). Deep postholes dug into the bedrock presumably served as roof supports. Excavations in Area L, some 50 m to the south, uncovered a substantial stone foundation, as well as the collapse of a stone wall. Excavations at the western end of the lane in Troullia West (Areas U and Z) in 2009 and 2010 have revealed 4 m of cultural deposits associated with three stratified walls totalling 2.5 m in height (Falconer, pers. comm., October 2010).

According to the published reports, pottery found in association with the building remains from Areas A–G and L consists of Red Polished III and White Painted wares dating to the very end of PreBA 2 and the beginning of ProBA 1 (MC II–III). Stratified pottery from Troullia West dates somewhat earlier in PreBA 2 (EC III–MC I), and includes Red Polished II–III and what are termed 'White Polished Handmade' wares, as well as some Red or Black Slip wares (Fall et al. 2008: 197, 205). In Areas Q–Y, adjacent to Area Z and excavated in 2008 (see below), the pottery – Red Polished III bowls and incised vessels, Black Topped bowls, White Painted II–III sherds – also points to this slightly earlier date. Limited amounts of later Protohistoric Bronze Age (ProBA 1) pottery wares – White Slip, Red-on-Black, White Painted III–IV – were recovered in deposits from the latest levels associated with the building remains in Troullia East. This suggests that *Troullia* continued to be inhabited on some level into the Late Bronze Age. There are as yet no radiocarbon data published to confirm these relative dates.

In 2008, new excavations adjacent to Area Z, in Areas Q–Y, uncovered a large central courtyard surrounded by structures on its east, west and northern sides (Falconer et al. 2010: fig. 5). To the south of the courtyard (Areas X, Y), parallel walls running east–west delineate a narrow street – with further buildings to the south – that led down to Kamares Creek, presumably a primary water source for those who lived at *Troullia*. The structures surrounding the central courtyard, with stone foundations and mudbrick walls, were built on a terrace partially levelled from bedrock. The spatial layout of the settlement at *Troullia* thus appears to be one in which dwellings were built on a gentle hill slope in a series of different levels, recalling to some extent the layout at Alambra *Mouttes*.

Concentrations of pottery, faunal remains, charcoal fragments and metallurgical equipment provide further evidence of spatial patterning at the site. Dense amounts of pottery sherds and animal bones (ovicaprines, cattle, pig, deer, a few equids) were found in the east–west running lane just south of the central courtyard in Areas Q–Y, as well as in the courtyard itself. Copper slag, copper tongs and fragments of a limestone casting mould recovered from a lane in Areas B and D may point to some level of metallurgical production; a small, clay, anthropomorphic figurine fragment was also recovered there (Fall et al. 2008: 195–196, figs. 14–16). Less dense concentrations of cultural materials were found in building interiors, hinting that house floors were kept cleaner than exterior spaces (as was the case at Marki *Alonia*). Other noteworthy finds from the 2008 field season include some gaming stones (with both linear and spiral patterning), a cooking hob with anthropomorphic features, and the hafted end of a copper-alloy dagger blade (Falconer et al. 2010).

The carbonised plant remains thus far recovered from *Troullia* include olive (the most frequent), grape, fig, pistachio and caper, along with some cereals and wild taxa, as well as substantial amounts of wood charcoal. Archaeobotanical analyses of charcoal and charred seeds from *Troullia* thus suggest intensive cultivation of orchard crops (less so of cultivated cereals), and point to the likelihood of a wooded landscape around the site (Klinge and Fall 2010: 2626–2627), one that would have provided fuel for various household and industrial tasks. The faunal record thus far is dominated by ovicaprines (70% of number of individual specimens) and deer (18%), but also includes cattle (9%) and pig (4%) (Falconer et al. 2010). It remains to be seen from the ongoing excavations, however, whether the subsistence economy at *Troullia* differs to any significant degree from those seen at the other agricultural villages of the PreBA.

On present evidence, then, Politiko *Troullia* appears to have been another PreBA rural agrarian community, with households of farmers and herders who shared a central, communal space, which may later have evolved into a situation of more discrete, independent households. These villagers enjoyed good access to arable land, a spring-fed stream and one of the most dynamic river regimes (Pedhaios) on Cyprus. At the same time, they were situated in close proximity (about 1 km distant) to the copper ore resources at *Kokkinorotsos* (Knapp and Kassianidou 2008). Such resources meant that the inhabitants of *Troullia* were intimately involved in the two most dynamic aspects of the PreBA economy on Cyprus (Knapp 1990a).

Overview

Looking at the sites of the PreBA period in general, people seem to have established their settlements to differing extents throughout the island. Most were in agriculturally productive areas, along rivers and/or routes of transport, including coastal outlets, or near mineral resources. None of the known sites shows any evidence of a perimeter wall, although some sites are situated on low plateaus, or on the slopes of low hills. Defence, then, seems to have been of minimal concern in choosing a place to live (Swiny 1989: 17). It should be noted that well-known, fortified sites such as Krini and Dhikomo, or Korovia *Nitovikla* and Dhali *Kafkallia*, belong to the subsequent, ProBA 1 period (MC III–LC I), and are not considered here.

Because copper resources were already being exploited (Knapp 1990a: 159–160; Keswani 2005: 385–391), several sites were situated close to the copper-rich foothills of the Troodos, or between the foothills and the *Mesaoria* plain. The only known settlement located along the north coast was (EC I–MC I) Lapithos *Vrysi tou Barba* (Gjerstad et al. 1934; Swiny 1989: 17), although (Philia phase) Vasilia is said to 'command an excellent harbour' (Webb et al. 2009b: 247). Even so, the wealthy north-coast cemeteries – in addition to Lapithos and Vasilia, Bellapais *Vounous* (Stewart and Stewart 1950; Dunn-Vaturi 2003; Keswani 2004: 63–67), Karmi *Lapatsa* and *Palealona* (Webb et al. 2009) – must bear witness to nearby settlements. Webb and Frankel (1999: 7–8) have suggested that Bellapais *Vounourouthkia* may have been a PreBA 1 settlement and cemetery site, and Manning (1993: 47) also predicted the discovery of one or more PreBA sites in the fertile northwest. Moreover, recent studies by Webb et al. (2006) and Şahoğlu (2005) suggest that the north coast likely participated in a maritime interaction sphere that linked Cyprus, Anatolia and parts of the Aegean as early as 2400 Cal BC, and involved the possible export of copper ingots as well as copper and bronze artefacts. However, because virtually no excavations have been conducted on the north coast since 1974, we have a very incomplete picture of Cyprus's external relations in the mid–late 3rd millennium BC (Webb n.d.).

The PreBA 1–2 buildings uncovered at Marki *Alonia*, Sotira *Kaminoudhia* and Alambra are largely rectilinear in plan with a single entry, many with several rooms and shared walls, and with some similar interior features. Yet there are also some notable differences amongst them (Frankel and Webb 1996: 53–54). At Sotira *Kaminoudhia* (Swiny et al. 2003: 54–66), for example, one can see significant variation and complexity in the shape, layout and proportions of different rooms, and less regularity in the orientation and placement of buildings than is evident at Alambra, with its more deliberate and formal layout of terrace houses cut into the hillslope and built directly upon bedrock. At Marki *Alonia*, the rectilinear, multi-roomed house compounds can be seen as an artefact of time, with a more or less standard architectural form: two or three room houses set at the rear of a larger, enclosed courtyard. Limited work carried out thus far at Politiko *Troullia* reveals house forms like those of Marki, some of which were built directly on bedrock (and on a hillslope) like those at Alambra. In the end, it may be that the main differences in domestic architecture seen at all these sites result from their distinct topographies, diverse settlement histories and the vagaries of excavation (Webb 2009: 263). This is particularly the case at Alambra *Mouttes*, where limited excavations focused on one small, relatively short-lived sector (and one 'house', excavated by Gjerstad) of a longer inhabited and much larger settlement (Frankel and Webb 2006a: 314).

We still have much to learn about both the internal and external relations of these PreBA settlements on Cyprus. Ongoing excavations and further reports from more recent fieldwork at Sotira *Kaminoudhia* and Politiko *Troullia* – the latter most likely a site with deep layers of anthropogenic deposits representing long-term settlement – will help to elaborate and refine our understanding of internal developments, as will the publication in English of Georgiou's (2007) PhD thesis. Equally intriguing is the multi-terraced site of Erimi *Laonin tou Porakou*, which preliminary reports assign largely to the PreBA 2 period, with continuation into ProBA 1 (e.g. Bombardieri 2010a: 39–43; 2010b). Although at present there is scant evidence (mainly in the north), at least some coastal sites must have functioned as key outlets for external trade and communications. Above all, we need to reconsider carefully the notion that PreBA 1 society was mainly insular and minimally differentiated in socio-economic terms (e.g. Frankel 1988; Baxevani 1997; Davies 1997). The next section, in which I examine the evidence for internal production and external relations in more detail, takes another step in that direction.

METALLURGICAL AND AGRICULTURAL PRODUCTION

Metallurgical Production

Recent excavations in PreBA settlements and cemeteries have provided important new data relevant to the earliest stages of indigenous metalworking and casting activities on Cyprus. From Kissonerga *Mosphilia* – Periods 4 (Late Chalcolithic) and 5 (Philia phase) – come six metal objects, a few fragments of pure smelted copper, ore consistent with production from local sources, and two possible crucibles, all indicating that extractive metallurgy and metalworking from local ores had begun no later than the mid-3rd millennium BC (Peltenburg et al. 1998: 18–20, 188–189) (discussed above, pp. 230–231). An early lead isotope analysis (LIA) of a lump of copper ore (KM 633, Period 4) and a copper axe/adze (KM 457, Period 5) from *Mosphilia* indicated that the ore was consistent with production from Cypriot sources (Gale 1991a). Although the lead isotope composition of the copper axe fell beyond the so-called Cypriot

Figure 78. Marki *Alonia*, chalk casting moulds (Frankel and Webb 2006a: 216–217, fig. 6.19) Courtesy of David Frankel and Jennifer Webb.

field (or 'ellipse'), local ores from the region around *Mosphilia* conceivably also could account for the distinctive LIA signature of the axe. Moreover, the lead isotope field used to suggest that axe/adze KM 457 was not a local, Cypriot product is now seen to have been inadequately defined (Pollard 2009: 184–186, fig. 1; cf. Gale 2009).

If any native copper deposits had existed during the Chalcolithic period on Cyprus, they had been exhausted by the PreBA. By definition, native copper is nearly pure; it is one of the few metallic elements to occur in uncombined form as a natural mineral. Accordingly, the impurities seen in analytical work on several PreBA copper-based artefacts (e.g. Craddock in Swiny 1986a: table 2; Balthazar 1990: 105, 161) must indicate – like the materials from *Mosphilia* – that copper was now being mined and smelted locally (Swiny 1997: 200), arguably by local metalsmiths. Whereas new types of metal items showing parallels with Anatolian tools and implements also appeared on Cyprus at this time (Webb and Frankel 2007: 199), the evidence for a local metallurgical technology is unequivocal, and continues to increase throughout the PreBA – not least during the Philia phase with its numerous mould-cast, copper-based artefacts (Webb and Frankel 1999: 31–33).

Excavations at Marki *Alonia* have provided the best evidence thus far for the smelting and casting of local ores during the PreBA: three chalk casting moulds, one of which stems from the earliest, Philia phase wall excavated at the site (Frankel and Webb 2006a: 216–217, fig. 6.19) (Figure 78). Used to make axes (or axe-shaped ingots?) with parallels in Philia metalwork, these moulds demonstrate well the local production of metal artefacts from Cypriot ores (Fasnacht and Künzler Wagner 2001: 38–41, fig. 11). Frankel and Webb (2006a: 217) make a similar point: 'there can be no doubt that the smelting and casting of copper were among the earliest activities undertaken at Marki, which may have owed its foundation to its proximity to the ore sources at Mathiatis, Kampia [Kambia] and Sia'.

Both archaeological and archaeometallurgical (EDXRF analysis) evidence from Sotira *Kaminoudhia* provide additional proof of local metalworking during the PreBA, including the knowledge of alloying metals (Swiny et al. 2003: 380; Giardino et al. 2003: 392). Of the 31 catalogued metal finds from *Kaminoudhia* (daggers, axes, chisels, awl, needle, earrings), 2 from Cemetery A may be singled out for discussion. The first is a dagger (M18, from Tomb 15), of 99% pure copper, forged from locally smelted copper ore and diagnostic of the Philia phase; it is likely to be contemporary with the mould from Marki. The second object is a small 'billet' casting of a dagger blade (M12, from Tomb 6), produced in an open mould but placed in the burial before forging (Swiny et al. 2003: 370–373) (Figure 79). Its proportions are identical to the dagger (M18), and so it too may be dated to the Philia phase. The unfinished state of this casting offers further evidence of local metalworking during the PreBA, as does the surface discovery of a crucible fragment at the nearby PreBA site of Paramali *Pharkonia* (Swiny and Mavromatis 2000: 435).

Excavations at PreBA 2 Alambra *Mouttes* produced fragments of 3 moulds and 16 crucibles, 38 pieces of ores or gossans and at least 16 pieces of slag (Coleman et al. 1996: 129–137), suggesting that the extraction, smelting and casting of local copper ores continued as the PreBA progressed. Twenty-three metal artefacts were recovered: 4 surface finds, 8 from settlement contexts and 11 from tombs. Of 12 artefacts and 9 slag samples subjected to LIA, 2 bronze rings (A34, A36) and a lead ring (A1) fell '…well outside the Cypriot field'; they were interpreted as being foreign in origin or as made of imported copper or lead (Gale et al. 1996: 397–398, 423, table 2.24). As already noted, however, the analysis and interpretation of LIA data no longer involves ellipses, or statistics, but rather relies on the use of two bivariate plots and point-by-point comparisons (Gale 2009: 192). Until these metal rings from Alambra are reanalysed using today's standards and techniques, they can no longer be regarded as foreign objects.

Further evidence for PreBA 2 metalworking comes from the following sites: Ambelikou *Aletri* (Merrillees 1984 – see further below), Episkopi *Phaneromeni* (Swiny 1986a: 68, 87), Kalopsidha 'C' (Åström 1966: 25–28), Dhali *Kafkallia* (Overbeck and Swiny 1972: 8, 21–23), Politiko *Troullia* (Falconer et al. 2010) and possibly Kalavasos *Laroumena* (Todd 1988: 135, 139–140) (see also Gale and Stos-Gale 1989). All this material demonstrates that Cyprus's copper sulphide orebodies were first exploited from the very beginning of the PreBA period at various points around the island: *Mosphilia* in the southwest, Marki *Alonia* in the northeast Troodos foothills and *Kaminoudhia* in the south central region. The internal demand for copper was such that a range of both utilitarian and prestige metal items entered the archaeological record. Many of these objects were removed from circulation and deposited in burials like those along the north coast at Lapithos *Vrysi tou Barba*, Bellapais *Vounous* and Vasilia *Kafkallia*, and at *Kaminoudhia* in the south (Keswani 2004: 63–71). Of course, the types of metal objects involved and the intensity of their deposition varies considerably between sites of the same phase (e.g. Vasilia and other Philia phase tombs), and between phases (e.g. a significant increase in numbers towards the end of EC III and into MC I at Lapithos) (detailed discussion in Webb et al. 2009b: 247–255). Whatever the time period, mortuary displays using metal objects must have been costly, and together with the attendant costs of heritable property (Keswani 2005: 385–394) would have stimulated increased production of copper.

Turning to consider possible external demand for copper at this time, recent analytical work by Webb et al. (2006) on 16 PreBA (EC–MC) metal artefacts found in Cypriot tomb or hoard deposits indicates that the early stages in metalworking practices on Cyprus developed in the context of a much broader regional interaction sphere. These interactions involved the seaborne movement of metals and metal artefacts between Cyprus, coastal Anatolia and the eastern Aegean, if not (even earlier) the southern Levant (Philip et al. 2003; Şahoğlu 2005; Peltenburg 2007a: 144–151); metalworkers from all these areas must have had access to very similar metal sources. In a related study, Stos-Gale (2001: 200–201, fig. 10.2) argued that 25 of 118 copper-based metal artefacts from various tomb contexts in Pre-Palatial Crete (ca. 2600–1900 BC) were consistent with production from Cypriot ores. Stos-Gale's study does not make clear the actual number of items from Pre-Palatial Crete that date to the earlier stages of the PreBA. The implication nonetheless is that during the same time period in which Webb et al. (2006) find closely similar objects (rod- or ring-shaped ingots) being exchanged throughout the eastern Mediterranean, other metal artefacts from Crete consistent with production from Cypriot copper ores may also have been involved. Cyprus's role in this interaction sphere remains uncertain, as only the site of Vasilia appears to have been directly implicated (Webb et al. 2006: 283). It also remains uncertain how ores likely to have come from Cyprus made their way to Crete during the Pre-Palatial period, but it now seems that the southern Aegean may have been part of this interaction sphere as well.

Such developments transformed the economy of Cyprus, and made it possible for those who managed production to answer a growing external demand for Cypriot copper. Evidence for Cypriot contacts with the wider eastern Mediterranean during the PreBA remains limited (see below, *External Contacts/Influences*), but the material records show that contemporary polities in the Aegean, the Levant and Egypt exchanged a range of different goods: for example, cedars from Lebanon (or Cyprus?), gold from Egypt, copper from Cyprus (Runnels and van Andel 1988; Knapp 1994: 280–282 and fig. 9.4). Equally important, cuneiform documents from Mari in Syria dated to the 19th century BC (PreBA 2) offer supportive evidence for the export of Cypriot (*Alašiyan*) copper at that time (further discussion and refs. in Knapp 2008: 307–308).

As a result of the increase in communications and seaborne trade between Cyprus and the surrounding regions, some people on the island began to emulate or adopt as their own certain material innovations that characterise the PreBA. Even if distance and isolation had limited Cyprus's overseas contacts during the preceding, Chalcolithic period, increasingly the demand for copper and the production and trade in raw materials and metal goods broke down old barriers. In turn, new foreign ideas and objects became part of a new and very different kind of Cypriot identity, one that looked outwards as well as inwards.

The intensification of copper production and the manufacture of metal goods may well have dictated why some people chose to locate PreBA sites at or near the agricultural-mineral interface (e.g. Marki *Alonia*, Sotira *Kaminoudhia*, Alambra *Mouttes*, Politiko *Troullia*, Ambelikou *Aletri*). The last, Ambelikou *Aletri*, is the sole site of the PreBA (MC I) for which we have some limited evidence for the actual mining and extraction of copper. Excavated in 1942, 2 areas and 10 restricted trial trenches produced fragmentary wall sections and some stone foundations, along with much debris (Dikaios 1946; Merrillees 1984: 3–4, figs. 2–4). Some 250 m distant from *Aletri*, in modern mining shafts explored during the 1940s, workers found groundstone tools and pottery (Red Polished III sherds, 19th century BC) 19 m deep inside the Stoa 2 shaft and 2 m deep inside the Kekleimenou 1 shaft (accessible only from the former shaft). No formal excavations were conducted in these shafts, but the artefacts were obviously in situ. From this we can surmise that seams of quality ore were being exploited nearly 4,000 years ago, deep inside mines near Ambelikou. At Pyrgos *Mavroraki*, Belgiorno (1999; 2000) has reported a range of metallurgical activities (washing, smelting, casting), identified copper slags and argued that four, sub-circular structures served as furnaces for smelting copper. Because the association between these reputed archaeometallurgical finds and structures, and the dated pottery, remains unclear (Muhly 2002: 81), the role and function of this crucial site in Cyprus's early metallurgical history continues to be obscure.

The wealth of copper-based metal artefacts (weaponry, tools, pins and other personal ornaments; toiletry items such as needles, razors, tweezers) found in the cemeteries along the north coast, as well as the more utilitarian copper objects found in the agricultural villages situated near the copper sources, suggest that different groups of people held different social attitudes towards metals. Spearheads are more numerous from the north-coast cemeteries, especially at Karmi *Palealona* (Webb et al. 2009b: 233, fig. 4.32, 235), but they also appear in tombs in the centre and south of the island – for example, at Nicosia *Ayia Paraskevi*, Episkopi *Phaneromeni*, Psematismenos and Kalavasos (J. Webb, pers. comm., July 2011). More metal objects in a wider range of types have been found in burials than in settlements, which may suggest a higher rate of re-use in household contexts (Frankel and Webb 2006a: 190). Some metal artefacts (e.g. gold earrings from Tomb 6 at Sotira *Kaminoudhia*) found in mortuary deposits have a distinctive composition and style that may well indicate their value as objects for prestigious display (Giardino et al. 2003: 392). On analogy with Levantine traditions, Philip (1991: 91, 95) suggested that the larger 'hook-tang' weapons might have served as status symbols, not least because their shape and manufacturing tradition barely changed over nearly 800 years. Swiny (1997: 205–206), in turn, suggested that the people buried with such symbolic objects were members of an emerging élite.

Those settlements situated near the mineral resources available in the Troodos foothills were certainly self-sufficient with respect to metals. But did they produce only the amount needed locally? If, as Frankel and Webb (2006a: 217) have argued, the people at (Philia phase) Marki were already producing axe-shaped ingots with holes in the butt that could have been used to string them together for distribution, then some PreBA 1–2 sites must have been producing metal for off-site distribution. Keswani (2005: 391) maintains that the rich metal assemblages in the north-coast cemeteries resulted from the responsiveness of copper producers to ceremonial demand, as well as to the effectiveness of *internal* networks of exchange (further discussion of Keswani's views is presented below, under *Material Culture and Mortuary Practices*).

Crewe (2007b: 158–159) interpreted these rich finds of copper-based metal artefacts in the north-coast cemeteries somewhat differently. She suggests that the extensive use of copper artefacts in these (MC) tombs implies that the north-coast sites were exporting copper in *external* trade networks at this early date, a pattern she sees continuing into the Protohistoric Bronze Age (MC III–LC I). Crewe's suggestion was posited in order to sustain her somewhat contentious argument that copper production at Enkomi during the LC I period was neither intensive nor extensive (discussed further below). Be that as it may, the overall picture remains one of small-scale, localised production and the internal, interregional consumption of metals. That picture was to change dramatically in the course of only a couple of centuries (pace Crewe 2007b: 18, who argues that the small-scale production of copper and metal goods continued at most sites until the 13th century BC).

Agricultural Production

Alongside this intensified but still local-level production of the island's copper resources, the adoption of several aspects of the so-called Secondary Products

Revolution brought about other changes in PreBA society (Knapp 1990; Sherratt 1981; 1983). The material markers of this transformation include terracotta models of the elbow plough and bullock, of pack animals, and of other pastoral or agricultural scenes; the reappearance of cattle (and their remains); pottery shapes perhaps linked to the use of milk products (Red Polished 'milk' and 'cream' bowls); a faunal record that shows, amongst other things, a prominence of young female ovicaprines and very mature species (suggesting a milk-, wool- and hair-producing herd); an increase in the number of domesticated (as opposed to hunted) animals; a large number of querns, grinders and pounders in the remains of most settlements; copper-based axes and stone axe-adzes (the latter already seen in Middle Chalcolithic); the development of a metals' toolkit related in part to forest clearance; an increase in household-based storage capacity (lime-plastered bins and perhaps Coarse ware 'mealing' bins); and the appearance (PreBA 2) of 'plank' figurines, with patterned decorations that might symbolise new types of (woollen) clothing or other goods (Knapp 1990a: 156–158, table 5, for refs. and full discussion).

All of this material is consistent with the growth and intensification of an agro-pastoral economy or, perhaps, its 'extensification' (Halstead 1987; Manning 1993: 44). The use of the axe (or axe-adze) for clearing land and the adoption of the plough (and cattle for traction) for cultivating greater stretches of land, transformed subsistence production. At the same time, these factors enabled the increased agricultural yields necessary for a surplus and the means to transport that surplus. The use of the plough in agriculture, moreover, tends to result in increased areas of settlement and often a dispersed pattern of settlement, as well as more extensive cultivation (Shennan 1986: 117; Greenfield 2010: 30, 46). As already noted, there was an eight-fold increase in the number of sites (345) during the PreBA 2 period, and an unprecedented spread in settlement throughout the island (less so in the very southwest and southeast, which would be filled in during the subsequent, ProBA period). This increased level of agricultural activities enabled new types of specialised production (Manning 1993: 47), well represented in the material record: metal weapons, tools and ornaments; bead and shell ornaments and pendants; gold and silver jewellery; terracotta and antigorite figurines; new pottery shapes and styles, as well as terracotta models.

Faunal remains from Marki *Alonia* and Sotira *Kaminoudhia* (PreBA 1–2), as well as Alambra *Mouttes* and Politiko *Troullia* (PreBA 2), indicate a preponderance of sheep and goat, cattle, wild deer and pig, more or less in that order (deer are more numerous than cattle at Alambra and thus far also at *Troullia*). Donkey, fox, dog and cat make up the remainder of the PreBA faunal record. Sheep and goat dominated the faunal resource (up to 61% at Alambra and 70% at *Troullia*), followed by cattle (up to 32% at Sotira), deer (15–20% at all sites) and pig (from 3% at Marki to 12% at Sotira) (Reese 1996a; Croft 2003b: 439–440; 2006: 277–281). Analysing the faunal remains from Marki and Sotira by weight rather than frequency, Croft (2003b: 440, table 11.2, 446; 2006: 279–280, table 9.1) argued that cattle formed the mainstay of meat consumption at both sites throughout the PreBA. Because the bones of cattle and deer are much heavier than those of ovicaprines, deer may have been as important as sheep and goat to the economy. It is also crucial to point out that in assessing the relative values of these animals to food consumption, there is a tendency to forget that cattle, sheep and goat all yield important secondary products (Croft 2003b: 446–447). Moreover, faunal resources typically are exploited within a yearly cycle in which hunting, the slaughter of juveniles and the dispatching of older animals take place in different seasons.

Spigelman (2006), having analysed the species diversity of ovicaprines, cattle, deer and pig, and the kill patterns of sheep and goat at Marki, Sotira and Alambra during the PreBA, draws two important conclusions about the people who raised and herded these animals:

(1) they practiced a diversified faunal strategy, using a suite of domesticated and wild animal resources that provided buffering mechanisms against resource failure, obviating the need for communal or large-scale storage;

(2) based on kill patterns, they used their herds of sheep and goats for both meat and secondary products, in particular milk and wool or hair.

The kill patterns from Marki and Alambra show that 45–60% of ovicaprines reached full maturity (i.e. beyond three years; the Sotira assemblage was too small to indicate the percentage of animals that lived to maturity). Mature animals not only provide secondary products, but also tend to be used for traction (with the plough); in addition, they have the reproductive capacity so essential for maintaining a herd. Similar exploitation strategies at all three settlements indicate that they were self-reliant communities whose inhabitants exploited sheep, goat and cattle for meat, milk, wool and hair products (Spigelman 2006: 122–124).

The rise in importance of cattle, sheep and goat in the economy of PreBA villages, coupled with the less frequent use of pig and deer, is clearly linked to all the social, material and environmental changes involved in the Secondary Products Revolution. The adoption of the plough and other secondary products typically leads to a change in social organisation and a shift in the basis of power relations, including kinship and gender relations. Had land/labour and gender relations remained fixed, it is likely that technological innovations would have been resisted. Unlike agriculture based on the use of the hoe (the norm for earlier periods), farming based on the plough typically involves more intensive work cycles, more and different kinds of effort over a larger area and – as a consequence – more people involved in the harvest, typically family members or relations, including women and children (Boserup 1965; Sherratt 1981; Bolger 2003: 38–39). Thus, in addition to any domestic and parenting tasks associated with the household (Hodder 1990: 44–99), some women at least must have been engaged in the intensified and compartmentalised labour necessitated by the Secondary Products Revolution. Ethnographic research, moreover, indicates that domestic work increases along with the development of intensive agricultural practices (Ember 1983). In this case, the division of labour amongst men and women seems to have been a cultural solution to the problems that arose in the face of intensified agricultural practices (Bolger 2003: 39).

These intensified practices would have required clearing trees from the landscape, preparing new ground for crops, and tending and herding new types and larger numbers of animals. Such a compartmentalisation of labour practices, and the need for wider participation in farmwork at specific times in the annual cycle, would have freed at least some people – at certain times – from the relentless labour demanded by hoe agriculture. Such developments would also have fostered population growth, the production of surpluses and possibly corporate control over land (Manning 1993). Increased emphasis may have been placed on the hereditary transmission of property (and draft animals), with family groups becoming attached to specific fields or landscape sectors. Social phenomena such as these may find spatial reflection in the well-known pattern of site clustering in the PreBA (Swiny 1981; Knapp 1990a: 158–159). The changes in labour practices wrought by the Secondary Products Revolution precipitated further changes not only in the amount of time invested and the types of animals needed, but also in the social organisation of PreBA communities. Formerly communal households now likely became extended family households in which a great deal of cooperation was involved.

The layout of the new rectilinear, multi-roomed domestic structures seen at PreBA 1 settlements such as Marki *Alonia* and Sotira *Kaminoudhia* has led some scholars to view the basic social unit as the nuclear family (Swiny 1989: 21; Bolger 2003: 35–36, 134) or the patriarchal family (Bolger 1996: 371). Webb (2002b: 88), however, challenges these notions, arguing that we need not equate hierarchical gender relations with increasing levels of social complexity and economic inequality. She maintains that the household is the most appropriate analytical unit for carrying out a gendered examination of individual men's and women's lives. Furthermore, both Webb (2002a) and Keswani (2005: 342 and n. 9) acknowledge that the concept of community is also crucial for a better understanding of PreBA 1 social organisation (see Frankel and Webb 2006a: 311–313; Webb and Frankel 2011, for overviews of community and household at Marki *Alonia*).

If individual households replaced communal groups as the basic unit of PreBA society, each household may be expected to have developed its own storage facilities within or nearby their home, thus promoting the accumulation of private wealth (Keswani 2004: 148–149). Indeed, basic storage facilities are found in various structures at Marki *Alonia* (Philia phase–EC) (Webb

2002b: 92–93), Sotira *Kaminoudhia* (EC) (Swiny et al. 2003: 189–191) and Alambra *Mouttes* (early MC) (Coleman et al. 1996: 282–283). The tendency to enclose domestic activity areas during the PreBA may point to attempts at household privacy (Keswani 2004: 148). In contrast to at least some level of communal storage during the Late Chalcolithic (i.e. the Pithos House at *Mosphilia* – Peltenburg et al. 1998: 41–42, fig. 3.9), most excavated PreBA buildings have small rooms or other spaces (structural installations and plastered bins) that could have been used to store household items or perishable foodstuffs, fodder and fuel. Evidence for large storage *pithoi* is quite limited (Pilides 1996: 107; 2005: 172; Swiny et al. 2003: 44). At Marki *Alonia*, however, one large Red Polished (Philia) *pithos* was reused to hold a child's burial, and the room beneath the floor where it was found contained the bases of several other, very large but poorly preserved *pithoi* (Frankel and Webb 2000: 71, fig. 4, 74–75; 2006a: 71–72, 285, pls. 64a–b).

Like the conspicuous wealth seen in PreBA mortuary evidence (see below), all this evidence implies that new alliances were built, new exchange patterns created and new power strategies developed. Social relations between workers (farmers, shepherds, miners), specialist producers, and managers or élites thus were restructured. In strictly agricultural terms, specialised animal husbandry, the exploitation of larger tracts of arable land, facilities for (household) storage, and an increased level of control over production and distribution all resulted in a more intensified agro-pastoral economy, and provided a surplus that élites could mobilise or manipulate: these factors would have helped to meet the socio-economic if not ideological needs of producers and élites alike. Alterations in the organisation of production that followed the adoption of plough-based agriculture also led people to change how they identified themselves, and the ways they communicated within and beyond the island.

EXTERNAL CONTACTS AND INFLUENCES

Because various material aspects of the Secondary Products Revolution are apparent in the Cypriot archaeological record, the corollary is that some sort of communication and contacts existed with other areas of the eastern Mediterranean. On a broader scale, there is little reason to question the existence of a regional interaction sphere involving the seaborne movement of metals and metal artefacts between Cyprus, the coast of western Anatolia and the eastern Aegean (Webb et al. 2006). On the local scale, however, only a limited number of goods was exchanged between Cyprus and its Aegean or Levantine neighbours during the PreBA 1–2 periods (Knapp 1990a: table 3). The find contexts of these goods, moreover, do not allow good chronological resolution. Since most goods exchanged were used or reused over long periods, or were distributed so widely as to limit their value in establishing cultural synchronisms, it remains difficult to determine the precise chronological horizon, much less the actual nature of foreign contacts during the PreBA. Nonetheless we need to keep in mind not just the more obvious prestige goods involved in exchange relations, but also the quest for raw materials and the acquisition of intangible types of knowledge, as Wengrow (2009: 157–158) recently argued in reconceptualising Egyptian goods found in contemporary Crete (ca. 2300–1850 BC).

The scarcity of land and resources that resulted from extensive plough agriculture and increased exploitation of copper, as well as the natural circumscription of the island of Cyprus, had long-lasting social and economic consequences (ultimately, in the Protohistoric Bronze Age, the concentration of resources and centralisation of authority on the island). Constraints both natural and cultural may have limited foreign contacts during the PreBA, but constraints may also be seen as potentials. Distance in and of itself, as well as (coastal or inland) location, seems to have had little or no impact on Cyprus's external contacts at this time, a pattern that holds true even with the island's much more intensive involvement in interregional trade during the Protohistoric Bronze Age (Portugali and Knapp 1985). In addition to the mid–late 3rd millennium BC 'Anatolian Trade Network' (Şahoğlu 2005; see also Mellink 1986; 1993), there are also material indicators of intensifying foreign contacts during the early 2nd millennium BC (PreBA 2). Moreover, documentary evidence for the use of Cypriot copper in Mari and Babylon at this time (Sasson, in Knapp 1996b: 17–19) points to maritime trading ventures in the eastern Mediterranean that must have involved some people from Cyprus, whether producers or distributors.

To begin at the beginning, however, from at least six PreBA 1 (Philia phase) sites around the island (Webb and Frankel 1999: 25–28 and fig. 18) come examples of Black Slip and Combed ware, long associated with Red and Black Streak-Burnished ware sherds found in Early Bronze II levels at Tarsus in Anatolia (Goldman 1956: 112–113, 130; Swiny 1986b: 35; Mellink 1991: 170–172). Stewart (1962: 231) long ago maintained that the larger Cypriot shapes were simply variants of Red Polished Philia wares, and thus felt that any relationship between the two wares was entirely fortuitous. Peltenburg (1991a: 31, 33 n. 5), however, re-examined both sets of wares and felt that they were diagnostically the same; he concluded that the Tarsus examples were imported from Cyprus. From a somewhat earlier level at EB II Tarsus came a Red Polished ware bottle and jug (Swiny et al. 2003: 68, with further refs.). Other, more general similarities have been noted between various EB II vessels from Anatolia (Tarsus, Karataş-Semayük) and some Philia-phase pottery shapes (further discussion and refs. in Knapp 2008: 115–116).

Links with Anatolia also seem evident in some Philia phase metal objects. Two spearheads, probably from tombs around Vasilia on the north coast, are unique in Cypriot metalwork but similar in form to examples from Cilicia and north Syria; they are said to be 'the first objects of direct Anatolian origin to be identified in Cyprus' (Webb et al. 2006: 265). One of the spearheads (from the Museum of Antiquities, University of New England, Armidale, Australia – UNEMA no. 74/6/4), and a rat-tang sword from the same collection (UNEMA 74/6/5), are made of tin bronze, otherwise attested in Philia metalwork only in the case of four small spiral earrings from Tomb 6 at Sotira *Kaminoudhia* (Giardino et al. 2003: 388–390). Since tin does not occur on Cyprus and is also absent from Cypriot copper ores (Bear 1963; Muhly 1985a), it must have been imported in some form or other. Lead isotope analysis also indicates that the tin-bronze spearhead and rat-tang sword – as well as a knife from the same collection (UNEMA 74/6/6) – are consistent with production from copper ores found in Anatolia's central Taurus Mountains (Bolkardağ) (Webb et al. 2006: 271–273). Four other UNEMA artefacts (a ring-ingot, a perforated axe, two knives) are reportedly derived from Cycladic copper ores. Thus both compositional and lead isotope analyses suggest that copper and tin, as imported artefacts or raw materials, reached Cyprus during the PreBA 1 period.

Two alloyed gold, silver and copper spiral earrings from Sotira *Kaminoudhia* Tomb 6 (Swiny et al. 2003: 376–379), and other examples reportedly from Vasilia *Kafkallia* Tomb 1 (Hennessy et al. 1988: 26), also have close parallels in Early Bronze II Tarsus in Cilicia (Goldman 1956: fig. 434.2). The shape of these earrings, however, finds reflection in other, arsenical copper and bronze examples found at *Kaminoudhia* (Swiny et al. 2003: 376–379; see also Giardino et al. 2003: 391–392) and at several other PreBA sites (Webb and Frankel 2006a: 187). Beyond these, some 20-odd (utilitarian or luxury) imports – pottery, metal daggers and a razor, faience pendants and beads, calcite or gypsum vessels – arrived in Cyprus during the PreBA: from Crete, the Levant, Anatolia and Egypt. Beads and pendants made of faience and shell, found at Marki *Alonia*, also may have been imported at this time (Frankel and Webb 1996: 215–216). Merrillees (2009a) recently argued that three gypsum vessels – two bowls and a jug – from Vasilia *Kilistra* Tomb 103 were most likely imports from Egypt.

Although spread over a period of at least 400 years, all these objects were recovered primarily from the north-coast cemeteries at Vasilia *Kafkalla*, Bellapais *Vounous*, Lapithos *Vrysi tou Barba* and Karmi *Palealona* (Knapp 1994: 281, fig. 9.4; on the Kamares ware cup from *Palealona*, see Webb et al. 2009: 252). More recent study of objects exchanged between Cyprus and Crete finds only 5 Minoan objects in 'secure' PreBA contexts on Cyprus, and 10 Cypriot objects in Pre- or Protopalatial contexts on Crete (Sørensen 2006: 156; by contrast Knapp 1994 listed, respectively, eight and one objects). Unfortunately Sørensen provides no further information on the objects she cites or their findspots. The scarcity of imports, their deposition wherever known in mortuary contexts, and their aesthetic qualities (e.g. the faience beads and pendants, calcite vessels, Kamares ware cup, metal earrings) may imply some special status (Merrillees 1977: 36) or social significance: certain people may have sought to identify themselves or their ancestors by displaying exotic goods or symbols.

The quantities of copper and bronze weapons and implements deposited in some PreBA 2 (EC III) tombs at Lapithos (Keswani 2004: 208–213, tables 4.11b–c) may represent not only internal consumption but also a growing external demand for Cypriot copper (Knapp 1990a: 159–160; Knapp and Cherry 1994: 161–162). The manufacture after ca. 2000 BC of bronze objects alloyed with tin (Balthazar 1990: 161–162) also points to Cyprus's involvement in regional interaction spheres that brought tin to the island (Yener 2000: 75). Lapithos, with its coastal location in a protected bay, was ideally situated to take part in an expanding system of seaborne trade (Webb et al. 2009: 251–252). Along with the Minoan Kamares ware cup from Karmi *Palealona* Tomb 11B (already noted), Tomb 806A at Lapithos also contained a Minoan spouted jar (Grace 1940: 24–27, pl. IA).

Although both objects from Crete have been taken as evidence that the Minoans actively sought copper from Cyprus (e.g. Betancourt 1998; Peltenburg 2008: 153), Kouka (2009: 40) suggests that the few known Minoan objects found on Cyprus at this time arrived indirectly, via Minoan outposts in the southeast Aegean. The return trade, extremely limited, may be seen in a PreBA 2 (EC III or MC I) vase from the 'palace' at Knossos (Catling and MacGillivray 1983). The White Painted IV juglet from a Middle Minoan (MM) III context at Kommos (Rutter 2006: 654–655) is too late to be relevant here, whilst the Cypriot sherds mentioned by Watrous (1985: 12) from a MM III context are neither mentioned nor discounted in the final report on the Cypriot pottery found at Kommos (Rutter 2006: 653–658, tables 3: 104–105). Peltenburg (2008: 153) has suggested that the minimal evidence for imports, including those from Crete, presumably in return for Cypriot copper, may be attributed to the 'passive' engagement of local Cypriot communities in these long-distance exchange systems.

Nonetheless, as copper increasingly came into demand, whether for internal consumption in funerary displays or for external distribution and exchange, some people eventually gained control over access to one or more of the island's copper ore deposits. At the same time, social and organisational changes that followed in the wake of the Secondary Products Revolution were linked to the increased production of copper and metal goods that served internal needs and answered external demand. Internally and externally, therefore, the demand for copper resulted in the intensification of metallurgical production and the technologies associated with it (metal alloys, weapons), which in turn enhanced the ability of local individuals or groups to become involved directly in overseas trade. The very practice of metallurgy involves some level of participation in mobility networks. Skills and technologies, ideas and objects, perhaps even some of the metalworkers themselves moved along and through these networks, exposing local craftspeople to far-reaching regional practices (Russell 2011).

All these factors – internal social and economic changes, external demand and contacts – required new and different levels of communication, a new social infrastructure that involved the emergence of social alliances as well as socially differentiated groups or individuals. As these people came to control agricultural surpluses, access to copper ores and metallurgical production, they would have been able to manipulate the output of other social groups (farmers, smiths, artisans), and exclude them from metal or other precious goods that not only symbolised élite membership (Keswani 2005: 392–393), but also served as material representations of how these islanders viewed and identified themselves. And yet, because the excavated settlements of this period have yet to produce material evidence of any striking differences in wealth within PreBA communities, it would appear that mortuary ritual and practices served as the main showcase for displaying or affirming social or status differences amongst the islanders (Swiny 1997: 206; Keswani 2004: 153–154; 2005: 384).

MORTUARY PRACTICES

Like all the other changes seen in the material record of the PreBA, mortuary practices too were transformed. Most people were now buried in large, formal, extra-mural cemeteries, often situated on hillslopes within sight of a settlement (e.g. at Sotira *Kaminoudhia* and Alambra *Mouttes*, less so at Marki *Alonia*). Pit or rock-cut chamber tombs were the most common types throughout the PreBA, although bodies occasionally were disposed of within settlements (Frankel and Webb 2006a: 283–285). The chamber tomb (already seen in the Late Chalcolithic) typically consisted of three parts: (1) the *dromos*, an open entrance passage or hollow of varying depth; (2) the *stomion*, a narrow, often circular passage or opening running off the *dromos* and giving entry to the chamber; and (3) a domed, irregular chamber roughly hewn into the bedrock. In graves on hillslopes, the *dromos* was cut into the hillside; on flat ground, it was sunk into the rock (Stewart 1962: 215–221, figs. 86–89) (Figure 79). The *stomion* was usually blocked by a stone slab or a rough wall of stone rubble, and it is assumed that – once the chamber was filled with successive interments – the *dromos* would have been closed off as well. Chamber tombs regularly contained one or more burials accompanied by a range of grave goods: pottery (most common), metal weapons, implements and jewellery, and smaller numbers of spindle whorls, shell and stone pendants and beads, and picrolite.

From the Philia phase (Period 5) at Kissonerga *Mosphilia* came two pot burials only. Swiny (1997: 195) felt that three of the (Late Chalcolithic) chamber tombs at *Mosphilia* – with their flexed burials and limited numbers of grave goods – heralded the typical PreBA funerary practices seen in southern Cyprus. At Sotira, excavations in a narrow valley some 100 m northeast of the PreBA 1 settlement at *Kaminoudhia* revealed a series of chamber tombs cut into

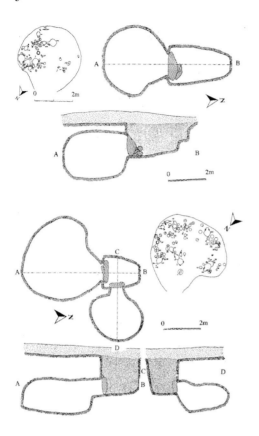

Figure 79. Vounous chamber tombs; top Tomb 11, bottom Tomb 3 (Steel 2004a: 140, fig. 5.8. After Dikaios 1940: 9 fig. 3; 25, fig. 9). Courtesy of Louise Steel.

the hillsides, as well as some pit and cist graves (Swiny 1997: 189–191; Swiny et al. 2003: 103–144). It is possible that these burials formed part of a mortuary complex that stretched across the valley, from Cemetery A in the west to Cemetery B in the east (Swiny et al. 2003: 6, fig. 1.3, 104) (see above, Figure 72). Cemetery B contained three rock-cut chamber tombs, long since looted. Cemetery A, by contrast, held 21 tombs (including Tomb 1, dated to the Philia phase, already excavated by Dikaios), of which 17 contained at least some human remains and funerary goods.

Most of the chamber tombs held a single, contracted burial, but multiple burials were also recorded, always in a disturbed condition. Tombs 6, 10 and 15 may be dated to the Philia phase, along with a few Red Polished Philia pottery vessels and an earring found outside the Cemetery A tombs (Swiny et al. 2003: 137–139). All well-preserved burials contained grave goods such as Red Polished pottery (bowls, basins, jugs, bottle, amphorae), some spindle whorls, stylised anthropomorphic shell and stone pendants, multicoloured stone beads and picrolite spacers (from necklaces), metal implements (a dagger, some awls, a needle), and several arsenical copper and bronze spiral earrings, plus one pair made of gold, silver and copper (Swiny et al. 2003: 376–378). It may be recalled here that the skeletons of two young women recovered in the settlement at

Kaminoudhia both lacked a proper burial space as well as any discernible grave goods (noted above).

At least five separate cemeteries of looted chamber and pit tombs were located within 1 km of Marki *Alonia* (Frankel and Webb 1996: 11–15). Of more than 800 tombs identified (Sneddon 2002), only three extra-mural burials were excavated. All three were located in the cemetery at Marki *Davari*: two were Philia-phase (PreBA 1) pit tombs and one was a PreBA 2 chamber tomb. The two pit tombs (Davari Tombs 6–7) were both shallow and roughly circular; they contained some fragments of human bone alongside numerous fragmentary pottery vessels and hundreds of sherds. The chamber tomb (Davari Tomb 5) was cut into soft, sloping limestone, and had a relatively shallow, vertical shaft with an oval or rectilinear *stomion* closed by a large, limestone block; the chamber itself was roughly circular with a flat floor and domed roof. The only mortuary goods found, in the fill of the chamber along with a few fragments of human bone and a sickle blade, were some 1,200 pottery sherds of largely PreBA 2 date (Frankel and Webb 2006a: 285–286). Within the settlement at Marki, the excavations uncovered six further burials, simple inhumations in a variety of contexts – mainly abandoned or ruined structures – and mostly from the later phases of the site's occupation (Frankel and Webb 2006a: 283–285). Of the nine individuals buried, at least six were women and young children; one small child was placed at the base of a pithos in a purpose-built pit (Unit XCIX-12) (discussed further below). Beyond a few pieces of pottery and a dentalium shell bead, no other mortuary goods were found in association with these intra-mural burials.

Along the northern coastal plain and in the foothills that arise from it lie a series of cemeteries with striking mortuary remains: Bellapais *Vounous*, Lapithos *Vrysi tou Barba* and Karmi *Lapatsa* and *Palealona* (Webb and Frankel 2010: 186, fig. 1) (Figure 80). The cemetery at Bellapais *Vounous* (Sites A and B) lies on a low but prominent hill above sloping ground in the northern foothills of the Kyrenia mountain range, some 4 km southeast of Kyrenia village (Stewart and Stewart 1950: 40). Early excavations carried out by Cypriote, French and British/Australian teams (Schaeffer 1936; Dikaios 1940; Stewart and Stewart 1950; Dunn-Vaturi 2003) in more than 150 tombs produced a sequence of burials covering much of the PreBA (EC I–MC II) (Webb and Frankel 2010: 186–187). Three of the early Vounous chamber tombs (114, 116, 117) had their *stomion* facades carved with representations of wooden doorways (Stewart and Stewart 1950: 152–165, figs. 111, 120, 123, 124). These decorated doorways may mark the tombs as shrines (Keswani 2004: 56) or perhaps, as is the case in the southern Levantine Early Bronze Age, as (charnel) houses for the dead (Chesson 1999; 2001).

The oldest, single-chamber tombs usually contained one burial, but as time passed the size and depth of the *dromoi* increased, often giving access to two or

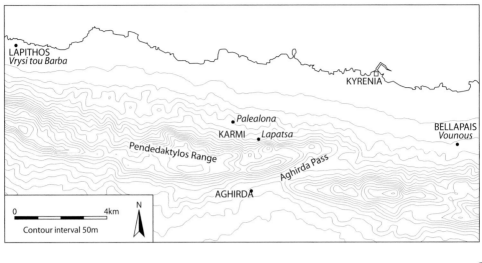

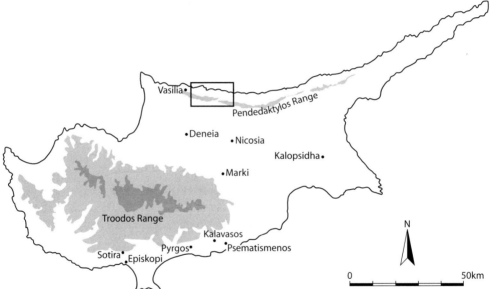

Figure 80. Cemetery locations along Cyprus's northern coastal plain: *Vounous*, *Vrysi tou Barba*, Karmi *Lapatsa* and *Palealona* (Webb and Frankel 2010: 186, fig. 1). Courtesy of David Frankel and Jennifer Webb.

more chambers, each with multiple burials (e.g. *Vounous* Cemetery B, Tomb 70 – Schaeffer 1936: fig. 10). Burials were accompanied by diverse mortuary goods such as the ubiquitous Red Polished pottery (some vessels with elaborate incisions and modelled human or animal representations attached to the rim or handle), spindle whorls, models of various items (e.g. a dagger and its sheath, a brush) and a range of metal items: daggers, knives, axes, razors, chisels, tweezers, dress pins, awls and four broken fragments of sheet gold (Stewart and Stewart 1950: 370, pls. 102–107). Pieces of woven cloth adhering to a copper-based sword or dagger from Tomb 26 at *Vounous* (Dikaios 1940: pl. 42:

C), along with similar impressions on three other metal weapons of PreBA date (Pieridou 1967: 25–26, pls. IV–V), suggest that the dead may have been wrapped in a shroud (Swiny 1997: 192).

Several tomb chambers at *Vounous* contained quantities of animal bones: cattle (the majority), sheep and goat; these were often placed at the skeleton's feet (Stewart and Stewart 1950: 122, 130, 141). All these bones were present not only as cuts of meat, but also as cranial and facial bones, mandibles, and wrist and foot bones, suggesting that the animals were dispatched at *Vounous* itself. Webb and Frankel (2010: 196–197) thus propose that mortuary ceremonies at *Vounous* involved the slaughter and likely consumption of adult cattle and other animals. Moreover, the presence of ceremonial vessels in nearly 50% of the chamber tombs at *Vounous* Site A (Keswani 2004: 64, 197, table 4.7a) may indicate that feasting formed part of the mortuary rituals here (Webb and Frankel 2010: 195). Because the presence of animal bones, decorated vessels and food presentation bowls is notably lower at other, PreBA 1 (EC I–II) northern cemeteries (Karmi and Lapithos, discussed below), and because complex (ritual) vessels are entirely absent from those sites (Webb et al. 2009: 209–211, tables 4.3–4.4, fig. 4.8; Herscher 1997: 32), it may be that *Vounous* was the dominant regional centre of an 'ancient social territory' extending from Lapithos in the west, through Karmi, to *Vounous* in the east (Webb and Frankel 2010: 204–206).

At Lapithos *Vrysi tou Barba*, British, Swedish and American teams excavated 96 tombs, primarily of PreBA 2 date (some are EC II), between 1913–1931 (Gjerstad et al. 1934: 33–162; Grace 1940; Herscher 1978: 2–3). Whilst the chamber tomb is the most common type, pit graves and burials placed on *pithos* sherds are also attested (Keswani 2004: 44–45). The *dromoi* of the chamber tombs gave access to anywhere from one–four chambers, and some tombs were elaborated with steps, recesses, diverse decorative elements and 'cupboards' (small niches cut into the *dromoi*, occasionally with child burials, as in Tomb 804F – Herscher 1978: 703). Mortuary goods entombed with the deceased include a range of PreBA pottery (e.g. Red Polished, Red Slip, Black Polished, Black Slip, White Painted), one Cretan jar and two Cretan daggers, concentrations of metal objects (daggers, knives, swords, 'hook-tang' weapons, axes, razors, tweezers, pins, rings), ornaments of gold and silver, spindle whorls, several figurines, the bones of cattle and equids (horse?), some groundstone (a gypsum 'idol') and bone objects, and faience necklaces and beads.

More than 700 copper-based metal objects were concentrated in a relatively small number of tombs at Lapithos. Although 63 tombs contained metal goods, 9 chambers held almost 65% of them; burials associated with 7 of 59 *dromoi* yielded 70% of all metal finds (Swiny 1989: 27). Keswani (2004: 67–71) breaks down the percentage of metal wealth in the Lapithos tombs through time, from 40% (14 of 35 chambers) during EC II–III to 96% (22 of 23) during MC I–III. The two richest collections of mortuary goods stem from (Pennsylvania)

Tomb 806A and (Swedish) Tomb 322B. The former, which held the skeletal remains of three individuals, contained 110 pottery vessels (several of composite type often interpreted as ceremonial in nature), 14 copper-based items (pins, knives, a 'hook-tang' weapon, tweezers), a Minoan bridge-spouted jar, cattle bones (from feasting?), and several small ornaments of silver, gold and faience. Nearby Tomb 322B, which held the skeletal remains of an 18–24-year-old female, contained 20 pottery vessels (2 of ceremonial type), a fragmentary plank figurine, equid bones (imported?) and small ornaments of silver and faience.

The chambers in which this wealth of metal goods was placed are larger than most others in the cemetery. Because they contained multiple burials, however, the number of mortuary goods associated with each individual may not have been extraordinary (Swiny 1989: 27). Keswani (2004: 69–71, fig. 4.5, 214–215, tables 4.12–4.14) makes a similar point, based on statistical analyses of 'wealth indices' (the display and disposal of metals): whilst broadly available throughout the community, differentials in the distribution of prestige goods appear to be quantitative and graded rather than qualitative and discontinuous. Nonetheless, several scholars – including Keswani (2004: 71) – have interpreted these concentrations of metal items in a limited number of chamber tombs as indicating the emergence of individuals or groups of high status (Swiny 1989: 27; Knapp 1990: 158–159; Manning 1993: 45, 48; Webb and Frankel 2010: 205) (discussed further below).

The cemeteries at Karmi *Lapatsa* and *Palealona*, located about 5 km southwest of Kyrenia (see above, Figure 80), are nestled in moderately sloping land within the relatively steep northern foothills of the Kyrenia mountain range; they lie about 3 km apart. Twenty-seven tombs excavated by Stewart in 1961 (Stewart 1963) have now been published fully, and are dated to the end of PreBA 1–beginning PreBA 2 (EC II–MC I) (Webb et al. 2009: 201, fig. 4.1). Differences between the tomb assemblages from *Lapatsa* and *Palealona* are probably largely chronological in nature: *Palealona* was used longer, to the end of PreBA 2 (MC I–II). The tombs regularly had a single (oval) chamber, approached by a square or oblong *dromos*; the chambers themselves, rather smaller in area than the *dromoi*, were sealed with large stone slabs or stone walls packed with earth. Cut into the walls of some *dromoi* were small burial 'cupboards', for example at Karmi *Palealona* Tomb 10B, typically used for infant or child burials (Webb et al. 2009: 257–266). Mortuary goods from the tombs at Karmi include the following (953 items inventoried in 1961): 840 complete and fragmentary Bronze Age pottery vessels (including a Kamares ware cup from Crete); 7 terracotta figurines (including 2 of the largest known Red Polished anthropomorphic plank figurines); 39 clay and 1 stone spindle whorl; a clay lamp and 2 pierced clay disks; 39 copper-based artefacts; 9 paste (faience?) beads; and several other clay or stone items (Webb et al. 2009: 207–214). In addition, large quantities of potsherds were recovered from both chambers and *dromoi*.

Figure 81. Karmi *Palealona* Tomb 6, relief figure and pilasters (Webb and Frankel 2010: 189, fig. 3). Courtesy of David Frankel and Jennifer Webb.

Tomb 6 at Karmi *Palealona* has three striking features: (1) a standing anthropomorphic figure in relief flanked by one if not two relief pilasters to the right of the chamber's entrance, with another two relief pilasters on the opposite wall (Figure 81); (2) a unique carved pilaster in the centre of the chamber topped by a pair of horns; and (3) the carved stomion façade with three broader pilasters, topped with a horizontal row of V-shaped incisions (Webb and Frankel 2010: 189–190, figs. 3–4). Although similar buttressed chambers were found at Lapithos and are thought to have served as supports for the curved roofs (Gjerstad et al. 1934: 86), most of the Lapithos examples were much smaller, and Herscher (1978: 706) suggested that the truncated, pilaster-like examples (such as that in Tomb 6) had a ritual purpose. The construction, use and sealing of this elaborately decorated tomb, which the excavators believe may be a mortuary shrine, is attributed entirely to the PreBA 1 (EC I–II) period (Webb et al. 2009: 131–133). Most skeletal material from both *Lapatsa* and *Palealona* was in poor condition, but age determinations, at least, were made on 30 individuals (Webb et al. 2009: 237, table 4.10; cf. p. 255, which notes only 28 individuals).

The extensive cemeteries at Deneia in the Ovgos River valley of northwest Cyprus are spread over 6 ha; they are situated atop and just below extensive hard limestone plateaux in this region (Frankel and Webb 2007: fig. 1.2 for locations). A total of 1,286 tombs has been documented and, indeed, the Deneia mortuary complex far outstrips in size and number all other Bronze Age cemeteries known on Cyprus. The few early tombs (*Kafkalla*) date to the Philia phase, whilst the majority (at *Kafkalla* and *Kafkalla tis Malis*) – at least 764 tombs – belongs to PreBA 2 (EC III–MC II, ca. 2000–1750/1700 Cal BC). Most tombs are larger than those found elsewhere on the island, and they likely contained more burials as well (Frankel and Webb 2007: 149–151).

The Deneia tombs take different forms, depending upon the particular topography. Atop the plateaux, tomb *dromoi* generally have vertical shafts, rectangular or circular in plan, about 1 m across and typically about 1 m deep. The tunnel-like, oval entrance (*stomion*) cut from the base of these shafts extends down into chambers hollowed out from the limestone; in several cases, these tombs were blocked by large stone slabs, following patterns known elsewhere during the PreBA. Below the plateaux, simple shafts were cut horizontally into the steep slopes of the hillside, forming relatively small chamber or pit tombs. All the tombs investigated were single-chambered but some had smaller side chambers or niches. In one extraordinary case at *Kafkalla* (the 'tomb complex'), at least 10 primary shafts gave access to a complex system of interconnected subterranean caverns (Frankel and Webb 2007: 34–35, text fig. 3.60) (Figure 82).

Skeletal evidence was rare, not unsurprising given the long history of tomb looting in the area around Deneia (Frankel and Webb 2007: 3–12). In the case of Tomb 789, however, the fragmentary and commingled remains of 46 individuals revealed an exceptionally high number of children aged 12 years or less (29, 62%); of these 19 (41%) were foetal or perinatal burials (Frankel and Webb 2007: 148, table 8.1). It should be noted that this was the only example of a larger tomb at Deneia where the deposits were carefully excavated and fully sieved. Nonetheless, such mortuary practices seem quite unusual for the Bronze Age (Keswani 2004: 30).

Burial goods are dominated by pottery, in particular by various Red Polished and Black Polished wares. The latter, seen in a limited array of small, finely decorated vessels, is far more common at Deneia than at any other PreBA site, whilst the former includes vessels with elaborate and very distinctive relief decoration as well as a range of unusual forms. The excavators believe such vessels demonstrated an assertive, idiosyncratic community style and were specifically designed to communicate a localised, corporate identity (Webb and Frankel 2009; Webb 2010). Other burial goods included shell and metal annular pendants (Philia phase); 3 fragmentary plank figurines and 1 bull figurine; 30 spindle whorls; 11 copper-based objects (mostly small and fragmentary); 9 faience beads; more than 900 tiny disk-shaped, white, grey or pale blue beads (probably from one necklace); and a small, cylinder seal of pale blue faience (probably imported from Syria, LC I in date). By the PreBA 2 (late MC I) period, the energy expended in constructing Deneia's large and elaborate

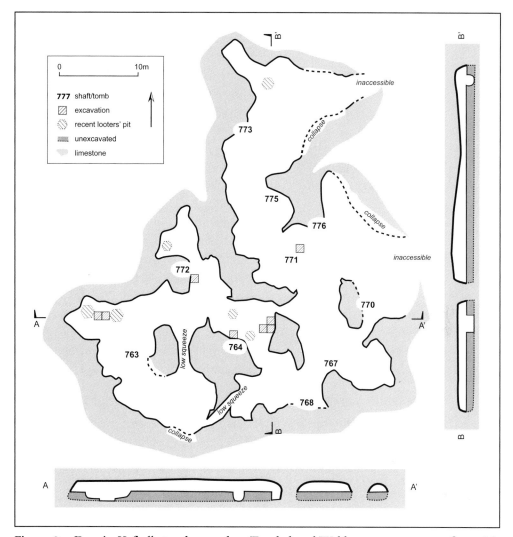

Figure 82. Deneia *Kafkalla* tomb complex (Frankel and Webb 2007: 34–35, text fig. 3.60). Courtesy of David Frankel and Jennifer Webb.

chamber tombs with private entrance shafts suggests they were owned and used by specific family groups.

One further mortuary site may be treated more briefly (see Keswani 2004: 52–62 for fuller coverage of this and other sites). At Nicosia *Ayia Paraskevi* in the central *Mesaoria*, several British, Cypriote and Australian teams have excavated – over the past 130 years – close to 200 tombs dated to the Bronze and Iron Ages, some to the Hellenistic era (Kromholz 1982: 2–9). Of the 10 Bronze Age tomb groups published by Kromholz (1982), 1 (Tomb 7) is dated to the Philia phase, and 7 more to the PreBA (EC–MC generally). At least 9 of the (18?) graves excavated by Stewart at Nicosia *Ayia Paraskevi* (Stewart 1957; 1962: 384; Hennessy et al. 1988: 12–24) produced diagnostic PreBA pottery (Philia phase, EC III). These tombs were so badly eroded they appeared to be simple, oval pit graves, but Swiny (1997: 194) felt they might well represent the standard chamber type with *dromos*. Despite the condition of the *Ayia Paraskevi* tombs, the burial goods included some distinctive items: for example, two bronze shafthole axes (Buchholz 1979: 78–79, perhaps imports, from the very end of PreBA 2), and an imported Syro-Cilician jug with painted decoration (Tomb 9). Tomb 8 contained nearly 300 pottery vessels, a few metal items (copper-based dagger, knife and toggle pins, 20 spiral ring fragments made of lead) and 8 faience beads (Kromholz 1982: 32–39; Keswani 2004: 72).

Although the evidence is slim, it may be that certain individuals were excluded from extra-mural burial on the basis of age, sex, manner of death or other social factors. Of the nine burials found within the settlement at Marki *Alonia*, for example, at least six were those of women and young children (Frankel and Webb 2006a: 283). Keswani (2004: 40) suggested that these burials may have resulted from the suspension or postponement of the standard interment practices in chamber tombs, a point that raises certain issues related to secondary burial practices. As already noted, Keswani (2004: 40–42, 50–55) regards secondary treatment of the dead as standard PreBA mortuary practice, but her views are complex, and have now been contested. The large number of subadult burials in one tomb at Deneia should also be recalled here, as this stands at odds with most other known PreBA mortuary practices.

In examining the fragmentary pottery vessels, disarticulated human remains and chronologically mixed assemblages of PreBA mortuary deposits, Keswani (2004: 150–153) argued for the prevalence of a multi-stage burial program that sometimes involved temporary burial in shallow pits or other features, eventually followed by exhumation and reburial in the chamber tombs. Based on their detailed study of the same suite of evidence – remnant assemblages of sherds, broken vessels and human bone fragments – from Karmi *Lapatsa* Deposits 3 and 13, Webb et al. (2009: 240) maintain that primary burials during EC I–II (and into EC III) routinely took place in chamber tombs, followed by the removal of old skeletons and the redeposition of both bones and grave goods, sometimes in shallow pits or scoops elsewhere in the cemetery area. In their view, PreBA mortuary practices, at least at Karmi, involved sequential primary interments; whenever these tombs were reused, the human remains and grave goods already present were removed and placed in other types of mortuary facilities. This is effectively the opposite of what Keswani has argued. During EC III, however, this practice gave way along the lines envisioned by Keswani, that is, the long-term retention of human remains and grave goods within the chamber tombs, which themselves became larger in size or elaborated with additional chambers and other, associated features. Webb et al. (2009: 240) feel that this may be related to a change in the concept of a tomb, from a temporary resting place for a single person to one of permanent burial for a specific social or ancestral group.

In either case, at least some extended families or other social groups adopted new mortuary rituals to underpin their status and highlight their identity, arguably by throwing feasts to revere and celebrate their status-laden ancestors. Manning (1993: 45, 48) has argued that the prestige goods found in the collective burials of the PreBA belonged to an élite, hereditary aristocracy. Some of the distinctive serving vessels, he suggested, could have been used by these élites for drinking alcoholic beverages at feasts. Herscher (1997: 31–34) also felt that the various funerary customs and distinctive artefacts, extensive faunal remains, and the positioning of certain skeletons seen at *Vounous* were indicators of special rituals in honour of élite ancestors (similarly Webb and Frankel 2010: 202–204). Bolger (2003: 159–160) too regards the continuous use of the mortuary grounds and rituals over several generations as reflecting a reverence for ancestral links.

We may suggest, therefore, that certain PreBA cemeteries became focal points for competitive display, the possible emergence of social inequalities, the negotiation of social identities, and the veneration of ancestors that would have helped establish the rights of specific social groups to land (Keswani 2005: 348–349, 363, 392). PreBA mortuary practices were thus linked to a broad complex of socio-economic (Secondary Products Revolution) and ideological developments. Moreover, these competitive mortuary celebrations would also have provided stimulus within the island for the intensification of copper production (Keswani 2005: 388–389). The mortuary display of costly local metalwork, not to mention other types of luxury imports, somehow may have attracted the attention of foreign merchants or visitors, thus broadening the exposure of Cypriot culture and its rich copper resources to the wider eastern Mediterranean world, and/or enhancing its involvement in the regional exchange network(s) that operated during the late 3rd millennium BC.

The social groups or élites who instigated these elaborate mortuary practices may have done so in the context of diminishing agricultural land that followed in the wake of the Secondary Products Revolution (Knapp 1990; Keswani 2004: 151; 2005: 349). They laid claim to specific resources or regions (such as the north coast – Webb and Frankel 2010: 204–206) by constructing chamber tombs in formal, extra-mural cemeteries, which helped to perpetuate the links between specific groups, their ancestors and communal connections to the land. These emerging élites, who had stimulated production by creating an internal demand for increased amounts of copper goods for mortuary deposition and display, would also have been well placed to respond to the growing external demand for Cypriot copper.

In sum, PreBA mortuary practices highlight new economic and ideological activities underpinning a new and more elaborate social organisation involving an élite group (or groups) (Keswani 2005: 370, 382–384). In contrast to those who take a minimalist approach to understanding the social implications of all the striking changes in mortuary and material practices during the PreBA (e.g.

Davies 1997: 22; Frankel 2002: 174; Steel 2004a: 139–142), I would argue that some social group maintained a significant amount of control over an increasingly status-oriented society. The mortuary practices of this group demonstrate the individuality of its members and the idealised links between the living, the dead and their collective ancestors. Mortuary practices involving both primary and secondary burial likely served as community events where collective as well as individual memories were negotiated, and celebrated (similarly for the southern Levant – Kuijt and Chesson 2005: 175). The allure of the luxury goods and imports they were able to acquire and display, some of which would have emulated foreign élites and ideologies, served not only to deepen social distinctions but also to establish and legitimate new élite identities on Cyprus. Meanwhile, the social memories created in and elicited by these mortuary practices may well have impacted on other material and social practices, from pottery, chipped stone and spindle whorls to the meanings embedded in the distinctive figurines, 'genre scenes' and other human representations of the PreBA.

OTHER MATERIAL AND SOCIAL PRACTICES

Many types of (mainly household?) production are attested in the PreBA archaeological record, from spindle whorls (Crewe 1998), to picrolite, groundstone and chipped stone (Swantek 2006: 116–144; Webb 1998), to pottery and terracotta models (e.g. Barlow et al. 1991; Vandenabeele and Laffineur 1991). The terracotta models and scenic compositions in three-dimensional form found on certain types of Red Polished pottery vessels, as well as the distinctive plank figurines, are discussed in a separate section below (*Representations*).

Turning first to pottery production, the most characteristic ceramic style of the PreBA is Red Polished ware. Not only are there a wide range of fabrics and many different types and shapes of vessel (e,g. see Steel 2004a: 133, fig. 5.5; Frankel and Webb 2006a: figs. 4.16–4.47) (Figure 83), there are also considerable regional differences (especially in EC I–III) and changes through time (see, e.g., the discussion in Webb et al. 2009b: 215–223). All Red Polished ware is handmade, and many vessels tend to have incised decoration (mainly geometric motifs, such as hatching or zigzag lines), often filled in with a white, lime-based paste. Amongst the different types of vessel produced in Red Polished fabric and found throughout PreBA settlements are the following: bowls, from large and spouted varieties to small hemispherical ones; basins; cooking pans and ladles; multiple kinds of jugs and juglets; jars and amphorae; and storage vessels. More specialised shapes are also known, largely from funerary contexts: bowls and jugs decorated around the rim and shoulder with what are known as 'genre scenes' (or 'scenic compositions'); zoomorphic vessels with representations of bulls, deer or donkeys; elaborate composite vessels, at least some of which also have attached, modelled figures, animals or miniature pottery

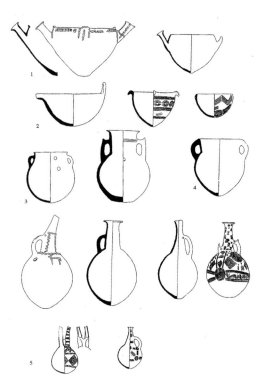

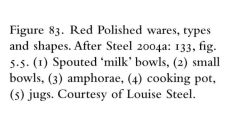

Figure 83. Red Polished wares, types and shapes. After Steel 2004a: 133, fig. 5.5. (1) Spouted 'milk' bowls, (2) small bowls, (3) amphorae, (4) cooking pot, (5) jugs. Courtesy of Louise Steel.

vessels; large jugs with double or otherwise exaggerated spouts (e.g. see Morris 1985: 85–112).

White Painted II ware forms another, not uncommon pottery tradition that belongs fully in the PreBA 2 period. White Painted III–V variants probably belong to the ProBA, that is, to MC III or later, but the high degree of subjectivity involved in these classifications (Maguire 1991: 59–60) makes it impossible for anyone other than pottery specialists to draw firm conclusions. Although White Painted ware has long been seen as a marker of the Middle Cypriot period islandwide, it is actually a regional variant most characteristic of the north coast, in particular of the cemeteries at *Vounous* and Lapithos (Gjerstad 1926: 148–151; Samuelson 1993: 106–107). This ware turns up only in very limited numbers at the settlement sites of Marki *Alonia* and Alambra *Mouttes* (Frankel and Webb 1996: 160–161; 2006a: 141–143; Coleman et al. 1996: 254), and in the Deneia cemetery (Frankel and Webb 2007: 70–71); even this material may well have originated on the north coast. The White Painted style of decoration – linear or geometric motifs painted in a lustrous, reddish-brown colour – is most commonly seen on jugs, juglets, small bowls, spouted bowls and cups.

Frankel (1974; 1988) has long argued for the household-based, non-specialised production (or at most 'elementary specialisation' – Frankel and Webb 2001: 126–127) and localised consumption of White Painted (and Red Polished) wares in different regions of the island. He has also suggested that women potters who married outside their own village may have transmitted specific motifs seen on White Painted wares, although it has never been demonstrated satisfactorily that the potters of the PreBA were women (Bolger 2003: 121). Moreover, analytical work on the limited amount of White Painted ware from Alambra *Mouttes* (Coleman et al. 1996: 255, 437–446), and a more detailed study of all White Painted I wares (Samuelson 1993: 115), suggests some level of specialised, perhaps even workshop production.

In general, Frankel has always doubted the existence of specialised production or interregional exchange networks at any point before the beginning of the ProBA. This minimalist view may well be right as far as kinship-based pottery production at the household level is concerned, but innovative and wide-ranging developments in agrarian production, metallurgical technology and overseas exchange suggest significant organisational change elsewhere in the society and political economy of PreBA Cyprus. Moreover, Webb's (2010: 179–180) recent discussion of the PreBA 2 pottery industry at Deneia – in terms of identity formation (and differentiation from neighbouring groups), place making and community-level organisation – presents an alternative to Frankel's view. Her detailed analysis of several Red Polished vessel forms and stylistic attributes uncovered at Deneia suggests clear changes in the social dynamics of this site (the 'deliberate crafting of a corporate identity', 'the institutionalisation of internal hierarchies') by the beginning of the 2nd millennium BC.

One of the more interesting, recent interpretations of the large quantities of often complete pottery vessels found in mortuary contexts suggests that they were not burial goods or possessions of the dead, but instead the residues of feasting carried out by the living to celebrate or recognise the passage of the deceased (Webb and Frankel 2008). During the Philia phase, a range of incised, fine-ware pouring, mixing and serving vessels (amphorae, jugs with cutaway spouts, small jars and flasks, small bowls) may have been used for the shared consumption of alcoholic beverages (see also Manning 1993: 45). During the EC I–II phases of the PreBA 1 period, at least along the north coast, there is more emphasis on individually distinctive drinking vessels ('tulip bowls', 'ear-lug' pots, spouted bowls and flasks) or ceremonial wares (deep or large pedestalled bowls, often with modelled figures attached to the rim) (Webb and Frankel 2010: 196–202). Large and medium bowls from the cemetery at Bellapais *Vounous* suggest that food as well as drink was consumed during mortuary celebrations. The same is suggested by the quantities of animal bones (mainly adult cattle) found in the tomb chambers at *Vounous*.

By the PreBA 2 period (EC III–MC I), there are changes in mortuary consumption practices, with a notable increase in the number of small, plain bowls and juglets, along with the decreased use of jugs. Moreover, the ceremonial-type vessels disappear from the mortuary inventory, whilst more complex or composite bowls and juglets become prominent. The increasingly elaborate decorations are now confined primarily to jugs and complex vessels, widely distributed

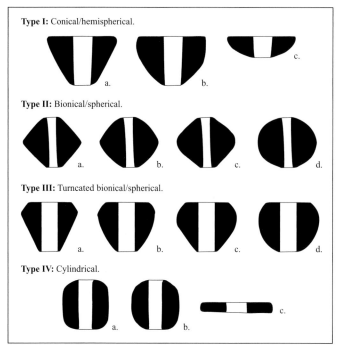

Figure 84. Spindle whorls: typological divisions of Bronze Age examples. After Crewe 1998: 21–22, fig. 4.1. Courtesy of Lindy Crewe.

throughout the *Vounous* cemetery and indeed more broadly throughout Cyprus. Thus they may have formed part of a widely shared, symbolic system in which larger numbers of people were involved in the commensal and drinking aspects of mortuary practices (Webb and Frankel 2008: 293).

There are, of course, many other wares that belong to the PreBA ceramic tradition, typically named after their most characteristic feature(s) in a bewildering range of monikers known best to pottery specialists: Red Polished Philia, Philia Red Slip, White Painted Philia, Black Slip and Combed, Red Polished Coarse, Red Polished South Coast, Brown Polished, Black Polished, Drab Polished, Black Slip and so forth. Perhaps the most accessible descriptions and discussion of all these wares is that provided in the final publication of the Marki *Alonia* excavations (Frankel and Webb 2006a: 90–143; see also various papers in Barlow et al. 1991).

Turning to the production of textiles, the earliest evidence available dates to the beginning of the PreBA. Alongside the ubiquitous pottery vessels, figurines, metal objects and jewellery found in mortuary deposits, spindle whorls (but not loom weights) are a common occurrence. There are two model spindles made of clay from Bellapais *Vounous* (Crewe 1998: 8, fig. 2.2), but the only known, actual spindle is a copper-based object, 29 cm in length (Webb 2002c; Lubsen-Admiraal 2003: no. 601). Spindle whorls come in a variety of different shapes, including conical, biconical, spherical, hemispherical, truncated and cylindrical (Crewe 1998: 21–22, fig. 4.1) (Figure 84). The incised, linear or geometric decorations on many spindle whorls are also quite distinctive, but through time there seems to be a trend towards less decoration, which culminates in the ProBA (Crewe 1998: 43; Frankel and Webb 2006a: 174). Some of the PreBA design elements have been compared to those seen on contemporary pottery (Crewe 1998: 45–50), and there are even suggestions of individual artisans (e.g. Coleman et al. 1996: 211; Crewe 1998: 52). Most spindle whorls have a reddish- or orange-brown slip similar to that seen on Red Polished pottery vessels or figurines, but they are not normally classified with ceramic wares.

Whilst these objects are known from several sites, the excavations at Marki *Alonia* produced a corpus of 154 spindle whorls or whorl-shaped objects, by far the largest number known from any PreBA settlement site, including examples from the Philia phase (Frankel and Webb 2006a: 159–175). Sixty-five examples are recorded from Alambra *Mouttes* (Coleman et al. 1996: 205–217) and 31 from Sotira *Kaminoudhia* – the last number may be minimal, as the excavators classified any whorl-shaped object weighing less than 15 g as a bead (Swiny et al. 2003: 401–406). There is a great deal of variation in the height, weight, diameter and perforation diameter of these ubiquitous objects. At Marki *Alonia*, for example, the mean sizes and weight of spindle whorls increase over three time periods; mean height ranges from 22–29 mm; mean diameter from 28–40 mm; mean weight from 16–48 g; and mean size of the perforated hole in the whorl from 4.6–9.3 mm (Frankel and Webb 2006: 171, table 5.17). The point of providing all these measurements is that the different weight groups of the whorls were probably related to different types of fibre spun by PreBA weavers: fine sheep's wool (light whorls), goats' wool (medium), flax/linen (heavy).

Walz and Swiny (in Swiny et al. 2003: 405) suggest that the homogeneity seen in the incised decorations on spindle whorls may be the result of work by a tight-knit group of artisans, perhaps from one extended family. Frankel and Webb (2006a: 175) also have argued that the repetitious patterns seen in the decoration of spindle whorls and the intrasite distribution of related designs may point to their production by specific kin groups through several generations. Their movement over significant distances within the island is thought to imply a concomitant movement of (women) spinners. Later, more detailed evidence (ProBA 1–2 periods, prior to LC IIC (late 14th–13th centuries Cal BC), indicates that spindle whorls are often associated with female burials, thus suggesting that spinning and weaving indeed may have been largely in the hands of women (Smith 2002a; Bolger 2003: 75). The large number of spindle whorls found in individual burials of the PreBA (but not in the metal-rich, high status chamber tombs) has led some scholars to posit the existence of a special class of textile producers (Crewe 1998: 36–37; Steel 2004a: 141). It must be reiterated, however, that the loomweights and spindle whorls so common in many PreBA sites provide no material basis to argue that Cypriot textile production was a craft technique derived from Anatolia (see above; cf. Webb 2002c; Swiny et al. 2003: 405–406).

Evidence for picrolite, chipped stone and groundstone production is also prominent at most PreBA sites. Turning first to picrolite, the quantity of small objects and personal ornaments, blanks and debitage found at Sotira *Kaminoudhia* – 178 pieces in all stages of manufacture – indicates that the production if not the distribution and exchange of picrolite formed important activities at this site (Swiny 2008: 47–48). This comes as no surprise, since one of the island's primary sources of picrolite is the Kouris River bed, situated only 5 km east of *Kaminoudhia*.

Amongst the personal ornaments found at *Kaminoudhia* are 11 pendants – carved in a range of shapes and mostly perforated towards one end. Like the pendants, three cylindrical or tubular beads, all perforated, were most likely worn hanging from a necklace or bracelet (Swiny et al. 2003: 233–234, 253, fig. 6.15). Other picrolite objects include a necklace spacer, a pierced disk and an elongated pebble that may have been used for burnishing. Forty-seven, various-sized pieces of worked picrolite – unidentifiable as specific objects – were also recovered from diverse contexts at the site (Swantek 2006: 124–134).

From Cemetery A at *Kaminoudhia* came seven, quite small (1.28–1.46 cm high), 'anthropomorphic ornaments' (Swiny et al. 2003: 276, and fig. 6.16); elsewhere such objects are termed 'spurred annular pendants' (e.g. Frankel and Webb 2006a: 242). Six of the *Kaminoudhia* ornaments are made of picrolite, the other of shell (S471/7). All seven are vaguely anthropomorphic in shape, whilst another, made of picrolite, is a miniature cruciform figurine (S144); all have suspension holes drilled through the 'head' (Swiny et al. 2003: 236, 253, fig. 6.15 [S144], 254, fig. 6.16). Some 850 miniature beads, cylindrical or disk-shaped with perforations, and made of quartz, calcite and jasper, were also found at *Kaminoudhia*. Of these, 132 came from Tomb 15, along with 7 of the 8 pendants – they were probably all strung onto necklaces.

Two very similar spurred annular pendants were found in PreBA (Philia phase) tombs at Philia *Laksia tou Kasinou* (Dikaios 1962: 174, fig. 84: 23–24), and a further 43 examples were recovered at Nicosia *Ayia Paraskevi* – 37 of these came from Tomb 4, an undisturbed pit grave with a single burial (Hennessy et al. 1998: 14–17, figs. 17, 25; see also Stewart 1962: 261, fig. 105: 10–12). Although Swiny suggested that these 'figurines' (spurred annular pendants) must have served as mortuary offerings (Swiny et al. 2003: 236), one *Kaminoudhia* example (S469) was found in Area A of the settlement. Moreover, the recovery from occupational deposits of eight such pendants at Kissonerga *Mosphilia* (Peltenburg et al. 1998: 189, figs. 97.29, 98.1) and a further eight examples (four of picrolite) at Marki *Alonia* (Frankel and Webb 2006a: 242–243, fig. 6.46) indicate that these ornaments were also in everyday use.

The only other picrolite objects from Marki are what is likely a pendant (S239, without perforation), a pierced disk (S855) and two unstratified finds – a nodule and what appears to be a torso fragment (S291) of a cruciform figurine (Frankel and Webb 2006a: 243–244, 247, fig. 6.37). Only three unidentifiable picrolite objects, two of which might be pendants, were found at Alambra *Mouttes* (Coleman et al. 1996: 173–174). Two plundered cemeteries from the south coast – Paramali *Pharkonia* (south) and Lophou *Chomastsies* (south) – have also produced five picrolite objects (Herscher and Swiny 1992: 77, 80–81). Whilst the dating of the settlement-cemetery complex at Episkopi *Phaneromeni* is problematic, much of the published lithic industry from the site (Swiny 1986a: 1–31) belongs either to PreBA 2, or to the following, ProBA 1 period (MC III–LC I). Given the uncertainties, and the fact that the use of picrolite virtually disappeared in the Late Bronze Age, we can at least mention *Phaneromeni*'s picrolite assemblage here: 3 spindle whorls; 6 other buttons or 'toggles'; several personal ornaments (pendants, beads, earrings); and 12 unidentified pieces that may represent manufacturing debris (see Swiny 1986a: 14–15, 17–18, 28–31, where picrolite is termed 'serpentine [antigorite]'; Swantek 2006: 140–143 provides a useful summary).

Swiny et al. (2003: 237–238) are probably correct in thinking that *Kaminoudhia* played a central role during the PreBA in the production and/or distribution of picrolite objects in the southern part of the island (see also Swantek 2006: 152–155). It may be recalled here that Peltenburg (2011b) believes the settlement at (Late Chalcolithic?) Souskiou *Laona* may have served as a production centre for picrolite figurines, a few centuries earlier than *Kaminoudhia*. The presence of picrolite in some quantity at Nicosia *Ayia Paraskevi* (more than 40 ornaments), less so at Philia *Laksia tou Kasinou* in the *Mesaoria* (but within striking distance of another primary source of picrolite, the Karkotis River valley – Xenophontos 1991: 136–137), suggests localised production both north and south of the Troodos. The distribution of picrolite at so many PreBA sites in different regions of the island, including Marki *Alonia* in the eastern Troodos foothills, perhaps indicates a pattern of small-scale interaction between sites rather than long-distance exchange from one, primary production centre (similarly, Frankel and Webb 2006a: 243).

Any discussion of the PreBA chipped stone and groundstone repertoire must be based largely on the analyses and discussion of the assemblages recovered at Marki *Alonia* (Webb 1998; Frankel and Webb 2006a: 197–248; Smith, in Frankel and Webb 2006a: 249–256). Significant amounts of material from both Sotira *Kaminoudhia* (Swiny et al. 2003: 221–368) and Alambra *Mouttes* (Coleman et al. 1996: 143–196), however, have also been published in detail. In order to analyse groundstone tools, it is useful to think of them as expedient and curated items (Webb 1998; Frankel and Webb 2006a: 197). Expedient tools are opportunistic, show minimum technological effort and were made to address immediate needs, for example pounding, grinding and hammering

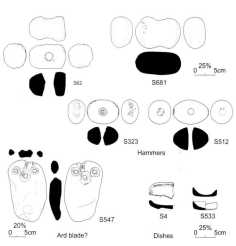

Figure 85. Marki *Alonia* groundstone tools (axes and adzes, hammers, dishes, ard blade?) (Frankel and Webb 2006a: fig. 6.1). Courtesy of David Frankel and Jennifer Webb.

jobs. Curated tools, by contrast, are designed for specific tasks, have formal shapes and were manufactured, maintained and reworked until worn out; examples include axes and adzes, hammers, mortars, querns and rubbers.

The groundstone assemblage from Marki consists of 1,017 artefacts: 676 curated and 223 expedient; 44 gaming stones; 40 architectural elements; 21 ornaments and 13 miscellaneous items (Frankel and Webb 2006a: 197–200; fig. 6.1, table 6.1) (Figure 85). The most common types of groundstone artefacts were rubbers and querns (31% and 14%, respectively, of the total), and mortars (10.1%) and pounders (9.7%; an expedient tool): these were most likely sets used in domestic food processing (grinding cereals and grains). The number of cutting tools (seven axes, three adzes) is remarkably small (about 1% of the total), a situation that probably reflects the increased use of metal tools. This is a complete turnaround from the Chalcolithic, where axes and adzes regularly made up more than 35% of the curated assemblages (Frankel and Webb 2006a: 198, fig. 6.1, with further refs.).

Like other classes of material at Marki, most groundstone artefacts were found in the interiors of structures, albeit not usually in specific activity areas as seems to have been the case in Chalcolithic houses. Querns found in close conjunction with Coarse Ware mealing bins, or placed on wall benches and

Figure 86. Marki *Alonia*, black serpentine macehead (Frankel and Webb 2006a:
fig. 6.3, pl. 55 [S610]). Courtesy of David Frankel and Jennifer Webb.

against central roofing posts, may be an exception. So too may be the pebble-
lined 'emplacements' located in courtyards and perhaps used to prepare cereal
grains for grinding. Deep stone mortars were frequently set into the floors of
interior rooms, whilst pestles, hammers, weights and (expedient) handstones
were often associated with (interior) wall benches. Such factors would seem to
indicate that preparing grains took place outdoors whilst their further pounding and grinding were routinely carried out indoors.

The most common raw materials used to manufacture these groundstone
implements were diabase and vesicular lava (both igneous rocks), which served
for a variety of tool types (e.g. rubbers, pestles, grinders). Calcarenite and chalk
(both sedimentary rocks) were also used, the former mainly for querns and
architectural elements (Frankel and Webb 2006a: 201–202, fig. 6.7). One striking find was a macehead made of black serpentine (another igneous rock)
(Frankel and Webb 2006a: 211–212, fig. 6.3, pl. 55) (Figure 86), which must
have travelled some distance to reach the site, as sources are known only atop
Mount Troodos or in the Limassol forest area. Overall, there seems to be a clear
tendency to use particular types of rock for specific functions: that is, igneous
rocks for grinding, hammering, rubbing and cutting; sedimentary rocks for
abrasion, shaping and sharpening, or for gaming stones and basins. Virtually all
the main groundstone materials used (excepting calcarenite and black serpentine) were available locally, and thus it is likely that most tools and implements
were manufactured at or very near the site. The quality of craftsmanship was

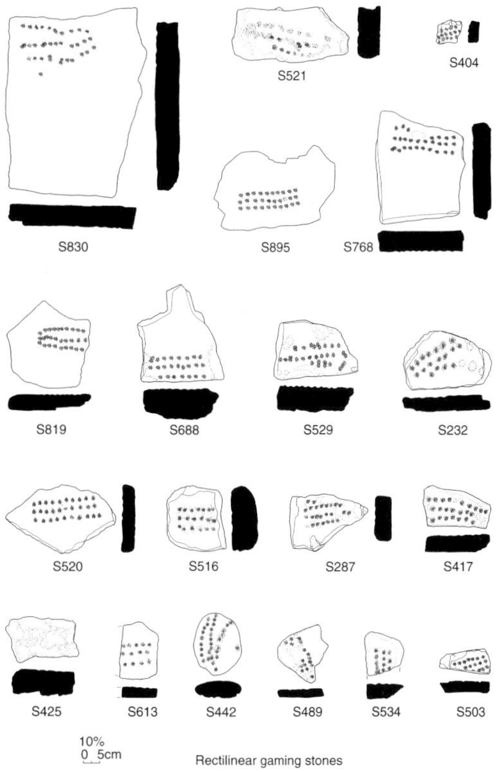

Figure 87. Marki *Alonia*, rectilinear gaming stones (Frankel and Webb 2006a: fig. 6.34). Courtesy of David Frankel and Jennifer Webb.

not high, nor was there much standardisation of form or technique, factors that lead the excavators to assume household-level production (Frankel and Webb 2006a: 203).

Forty-four gaming stones, both rectilinear and spiral-shaped, have been found at Marki (Frankel and Webb 2006a: 244–246, figs. 6.48–49) (Figure 87), 35 at Sotira *Kaminoudhia* (Swiny et al. 2003: 231–233) and 8 at Alambra (Coleman et al. 1996: 174–176). Several others are now reported from Politiko *Troullia* (Falconer et al. 2010). Long identified with the Egyptian board games of Senet (rectilinear) and Mehen (spiral) (Swiny 1980; 1986a: 32–64, figs. 33–42), these gaming stones – more than 200 currently known – are widely distributed throughout Bronze Age settlement sites (and a few burials) within and beyond the island; they have even been found during field survey. Also worthy of mention here are the three, fragmentary, chalk casting moulds from Marki *Alonia*, all recovered as recycled parts of stone walls (Frankel and Webb 2006a: 215–217) (see above and Figure 78).

A few, heavy stone pounders, classified as expedient tools, may have been used in metalworking activities at Marki (Frankel and Webb 2006a: 233–235). Recent survey work by the Troodos Archaeological and Environmental Survey Project (TAESP) also recorded some of these heavy pounding tools at Phlasou *Koutroullis*, which appears to be another PreBA settlement site, based on several examples of very early Red Polished Ware, possibly Red Polished Philia.

The commonality of querns and rubbers – as well as numerous pounders and grinders – demonstrates a focus on food processing and in particular grain-grinding activities so prevalent in domestic contexts at other contemporary settlement sites. The predominance of tools used in rubbing and pounding activities, and the absence of pestles and cutting implements, is also common in other PreBA assemblages.

Looking at the wider picture of groundstone production, the assemblages from (EC III) Sotira *Kaminoudhia* and (MC I–II) Alambra *Mouttes* seem to have a comparable structure and to have served a similar range of functions, in particular those associated with the preparation and grinding of grains. Rubbers, querns, expedient pounders (which largely replaced pestles), mortars and basins are common on most sites, as are (suspension) weights, perhaps used on (vertical) warp-weighted looms (Frankel and Webb 2006a: 203). Stone vessels and figurines are seldom seen in PreBA assemblages, and there are fewer cutting tools – especially at Marki *Alonia* – than there were in Chalcolithic sites. No doubt some cutting implements were replaced by their counterparts in metal, but stone axes, adzes and flaked tools still make up a notable proportion of the curated assemblages at Alambra *Mouttes* (20% – Coleman et al. 1996: 147–154) and Sotira *Kaminoudhia* (18% – Swiny et al. 2003: 222–223, 290–291). Although rubbers, querns and curated tools in general appear to be more common at Marki than at Sotira or Alambra (Frankel and Webb 2006a: 206, fig. 6.9), such patterns may be related to distinctive fieldwork and recording strategies rather than to economic differences.

All these sites were agricultural settlements, clearly reflected in the large numbers of groundstone implements for food processing and cereal grinding (rubbers, querns). This is also evident in the high incidence of (backed) sickle blades amongst the chipped stone tools, especially at Marki *Alonia* (Smith, in Frankel and Webb 2006a: 252–254, fig. 7.2, table 7.5) and Sotira *Kaminoudhia* (Swiny et al. 2003: 290, 333). Sickle blades and convex scrapers make up the bulk of the chipped stone tools from Marki, followed by end scrapers, drills (or borers), notched implements and a range of informal, expedient tools. The composition and structure of chipped stone assemblages at other PreBA sites does not differ significantly, and (backed) sickle blades are always the main tool type. The distinction from earlier, Chalcolithic assemblages, however, is notable: the best-represented tools in those collections – burins, rectilinear retouched tools, denticulates – are virtually absent from PreBA settlement sites (Smith, in Frankel and Webb 2006a: 256). Clearly the harvesting and processing of cereals, grains and perhaps even pulses were of primary importance to the people who lived in the village communities of PreBA Cyprus. All this ties in well with the introduction to Cyprus of the plough, the use of cattle as draught animals, and all the other material and social aspects of the Secondary Products Revolution (Knapp 1990).

Figure 88. *Vounous* Red Polished model (Dikaios 1940: 50–51, pls. VII, VIII). Courtesy of the Cyprus Museum, Nicosia.

Representations

How were social identities, whether group or individual, signified in PreBA material culture? Turning first to what was likely the top of the social spectrum, Peltenburg (1994: 159) has suggested that weapon-bearing élites from the north of Cyprus sought to stabilise their position through the use of ritual authority. He argues that a well-known Red Polished pottery bowl from the cemetery at Bellapais *Vounous* (Dikaios 1940: 50–51, pls. VII, VIII) (Figure 88), dated ca. 2000 Cal BC (EC III–MC I), represents an attempt to legitimise this new élite regime, and to symbolise new social conventions of power and exclusion. Inside this modified bowl rendered with an entryway (an 'enclosure model'), 19 human figures and 4 penned cattle are depicted. Only one of these figures, holding an infant, is obviously female (two are of indeterminate sex). Whilst the men appear to be active participants in whatever is happening, the woman is depicted in what Bolger (2003: 39–41) defines as a confined, maternal role. Overall, the figures are represented in what seems to be a hierarchical, social manner – from animals, infant and female, through individual males, to a seated male of some prominence.

Figure 89. Pyrgos Red Polished jug with female figure crushing grapes?
Courtesy of the Cyprus Museum, Nicosia.

Although there are other, often-contradictory interpretations of this extraordinary object (see Knapp 2008: 88 for fuller discussion), it clearly held a specific meaning for those who placed it in the *Vounous* tomb. Manning (1993:
45–46) suggested that the main figure in this model represents an 'aggrandiser'
surrounded by images of power, wealth and institutional authority on PreBA
Cyprus. Keswani (2004: 78), however, maintained that any social differences
represented by this scene had not become institutionalised into a rigid social
or political hierarchy. Most scholars regard the *Vounous* model – and three
abbreviated, plank-like versions from the areas around Kalopsidha and Marki
(also likely to be of EC III date – Dikaios 1940: 118; Åström 1966: 14–15;
Karageorghis 1970) – as depictions of open-air sanctuaries. Peltenburg (1994:
162), however, rightly maintains that this model represents a special building,
the emergence of male élites, perhaps even a specifically gendered ideology
that separated male from female in PreBA Cypriot society.

Other scenic representations ('genre scenes') of PreBA 2 date depict what
also may be regarded as gendered practices. Whenever women are depicted
in these genre scenes, they are represented consistently as parents, partners or
labourers involved in food-processing activities associated with the household
(Webb 2002b: 93–94; 2009: 264). For example, a 'wine production' scene on
a Red Polished jug from Pyrgos (PreBA 2, MC I) depicts a centrally placed,
female figure in the round (Karageorghis 2002b: 72, fig. 7, 75–76) (Figure 89).

Figure 90. 'Pierides Bowl' (from Marki?). Red Polished bowl, with genre scene of life cycle. Courtesy of the Pierides Museum–Laiki Group, Larnaca.

She stands in a small trough, identified as a grape-crushing vat, below which is another (male?) figure holding a large basin. The repeated performance of such socially constructed activities (here, making wine?), suggests an embodied division of labour in which the identities of both women and men were gendered with respect to their productive roles in society (see further below). Four other PreBA vessels with scenic compositions, and a model from a private collection (Karageorghis 2002b: 69–74, figs. 1–5, pl. II), have also been interpreted as representations of grape pressing scenes (Herscher 1997: 28–30). A similar scenario – making wine and bread – has been proposed for the modelled figures placed below the rim of a Red Polished III mottled ware deep bowl from Tomb 36 of the Bronze Age cemetery at Kalavasos (Cullen in Todd 1986: 151–154, fig. 25.2). All these scenes seem to represent vignettes of agrarian life idealised for inclusion in burials. Beyond the Pyrgos jug and Kalavasos bowl, however, none reveal quite so unambiguously the sex of the figures depicted.

The scene depicted on the Red Polished III 'Oxford Bowl' (Morris 1985: 269–274, pls. 292–302) may show gendered activities segregated by placement on opposite sides of the bowl. The actual interpretation of the scene is problematic (Swiny 1997: 203–204): although only males are clearly depicted, class or age might equally have dictated the differentiation of tasks. Two further Red Polished bowls from Marki (PreBA 1–2) also depict people at work, but have been interpreted quite differently. The vessels in question are the 'Marki Bowl' (Karageorghis 1991: 120–121, pl. 80; Morris 1985: 274–275, fig. 488) and the 'Pierides Bowl' (Karageorghis 1991: 120, pls. 78–79; Morris 1985: 277–278, fig. 490) (Figure 90). The people depicted on the Marki Bowl may have been engaged in grinding corn (Karageorghis 1958) or making bread (Morris 1985: 275), whilst the men, women, infants, animals and various other objects or installations shown on the Pierides Bowl seem to be arranged in temporal sequence (Morris 1985: 278), perhaps representing a life-cycle narrative – from pregnancy to childbirth, marriage (partnering), parenting, working and death (Swiny 1997: 204–205; cf. Bolger 2003: 115–117, where the name and provenance of the two bowls are transposed).

Using as examples 10 pottery vessels with attached human figures, Ribeiro (2002: 204–206) pointed out that scenic compositions typically lack explicit sexual indicators. In her view, the unsexed figures depicted on PreBA scenic compositions may have been intended to represent a distinct gender group, or a prepubescent third sex. In turn, Bolger (2003: 135–138) felt that taphonomic factors combined with the fragile state of the actual appliqué figures could account for the lack of sexual markers in these scenic compositions. Using as examples six, Red Polished ware vessels with genre scenes, she also shows that there is a far higher proportion of unsexed figures than of identifiable males and females. If Ribeiro is correct, children or adolescents would have contributed more to a wider range of domestic activities than adults did, and thus would have provided a crucial source of labour beyond the usual gendered categorisations. If Webb (2002b) is correct, however, in arguing that these modelled vessels represent people who were gendered according to the performance of a specific task, and if all members of society were aware of this division, there would have been little need explicitly to sex the figures.

Citing both archaeological and ethnographic evidence, Bolger (2003: 37–39) points out that women in intensive agricultural societies spend more time working indoors than their counterparts in more simple farming systems. Thus she suggests there may be a correlation between the increasing segmentation of domestic space and the intensive agricultural regime that characterised PreBA Cyprus, as well as a gender-based division of labour. The repeated portrayal of women involved in food-processing activities on PreBA Red Polished pottery vessels, and the apparent distinction in men's and women's tasks as seen on these same vessels, led Webb (2002b: 93–94) to infer a sexual division of labour associated with their respective roles within the household. More recently published data from Marki *Alonia* indicate that tasks such as grinding, pounding and baking – as well as flint-knapping, groundstone tool production and woodworking – were mainly conducted in rooms that contained hearths (Frankel and Webb 2006a: 312). Accordingly Webb (2009: 264–265) now suggests that a wide range of domestic tasks involving both men and women can be linked to household space, but that gender segregation or seclusion is unlikely.

Wherever one can observe clearly gendered persons in these scenic compositions (e.g. the various-sized standing males, and a prominently seated one,

Figure 91. Plank figurine; provenance uncertain. Cyprus Museum 1963/IV-20/12. Courtesy of the Cyprus Museum, Nicosia.

on the *Vounous* model [see above, Figure 90]; the centrally placed female figure on the Pyrgos jug [see above, Figure 91]), it is likely that we are seeing not only socially constructed activities, but also distinctively gendered identities for women and men somehow related to their maintenance roles in an insular society. If so, perhaps the unsexed figures discussed by Ribeiro and Bolger should be seen not as marking a distinctive gender, but rather as representing another (class-based?) aspect of their social identity. Thus we may conclude that the diverse and lively genre scenes modelled on Red Polished vessels served, informally, to reproduce gender differences as a 'social fact' (Webb 2002b: 94). They demonstrate how the body, and bodily performance, may serve as the site of gendered difference.

The final category of representational evidence to consider is that of human figurines, most of which appear early in PreBA 2 (EC III), and many of which depict females and infants. On the one hand, most discussions of anthropomorphic clay or stone figurines on Cyprus tend to be descriptive and classificatory, whilst the main criteria used in their interpretation revolve around notions of ritual or fertility, and the binary (male/female) division of human society (e.g. Merrillees 1980: 172, 184; Bolger 1992; 1996). On the other hand, Knapp and Meskell (1997) have argued that these figurines provide crucial evidence not only for discussing issues of sex and sexuality, but also for considering changing ideologies and emerging individual identities on PreBA Cyprus.

By the PreBA period, characterisations of individuals can be seen in a wide range of material. Frankel (2005: 24) questioned the likelihood of singling out individuals in PreBA Cyprus, and he is correct inasmuch as this presents a real challenge to archaeological interpretation, one that has been resisted strongly in prehistoric studies (e.g. Thomas 2002; 2004; cf. Knapp and van Dommelen 2008). Frankel's argument for the 'enculturation' of Anatolian migrants, however, is somewhat contradictory, based as it is on the active involvement, movement, training and learning of individual people. As he notes: 'Each generation – each individual – had to learn to become a Bronze Age person, socialised into patterns of behaviour and social relationships and trained in many specific skills' (Frankel 2005: 24). For his part, Manning (1993: 45) suggests that the earliest import of prestige goods into northern Cyprus (seen in mortuary deposits) may have prompted a 'key individual' to organise or institutionalise politico-economic control over increased levels of production and consumption in Cypriot society.

In considering how and why representations of individual people become so visible in PreBA Cyprus, and the ways in which they might have constructed their identity, Knapp and Meskell (1997) analysed a range of Chalcolithic and PreBA Cypriot figurines and modelled figures. We adopted contemporary discourses on the body and sought to engage these figurines in constructing an archaeology of the individual. Whilst we maintained that individuals, or individual characteristics most likely had emerged in Cypriot material culture already during the Middle Chalcolithic, we suggested that representations of individuals became more prominent during the PreBA (Knapp and Meskell 1997: 192–199).

Prior to recent excavations carried out at PreBA settlement sites, most well-provenanced anthropomorphic figurines had been found in burials; thus it was assumed that their main purpose was mortuary, ceremonial or ritual in nature. More than 50 such figurines, or more correctly figurine fragments, have now been recovered from PreBA settlement contexts; evidence for their prolonged use, mending and discard indicates that they formed part of people's everyday practices. For the sake of completeness, I note here seven anthropomorphic clay figurines from Period 4 (Late Chalcolithic) at Kissonerga *Mosphilia* (Peltenburg et al. 1998: 154–158, table 6.8).

The corpus of fragmentary examples from PreBA habitational contexts includes: 35 anthropomorphic figurines in red monochrome and 1 (or 3?)

example(s) in White Painted (Philia) ware from PreBA 1–2 Marki *Alonia* (Frankel and Webb 2006a: 155–157); 1 small (Red Polished) fragment of a (cruciform?) figurine from PreBA 1 Sotira *Kaminoudhia* (Swiny et al. 2003: 399–400, fig. 9.2 [TC22]); 11 fragmentary Red Polished ware figurines, of which five were plank types, from PreBA 2 Alambra *Mouttes* (Coleman et al. 1996: 202–203, and fig. 49); and 1 anthropomorphic figurine from PreBA 2 Ambelikou *Aletri* (Belgiorno 1984: 19). Frankel and Webb (1996: 187–188) documented several other examples of fragmentary anthropomorphic terracotta figurines from PreBA mortuary contexts (see also Stewart 1962: 236–238, 347–348; Karageorghis 1991: 3–40, 52–102; Mogelonsky 1991).

Plank figurines of various types and subtypes, which do not appear until the PreBA 2 period, became the most common way of representing people (Morris 1985: 135–62; Karageorghis 1991: 49–101) (Figure 91). Forty plank figurines out of a corpus of 78 (a Campo 1994) came from tombs in and around the north-coast villages of *Vounous* and Lapithos (Merrillees 1980: 184), in particular from the cemetery at Lapithos *Vrysi tou Barba*. Eleven of the figurines from Lapithos had been placed in large, elaborately furnished tombs with a wealth of metal objects, whilst the remainder were also found in context with metal objects (knives, daggers, axes, pins and rings) and/or prestige goods made of gold, silver and faience (Talalay and Cullen 2002: 185). Thus there is a clear contextual association between the plank figurines and exclusive burials (Keswani 2004: 74–80, 146–150), whether of family groups or perhaps of individuals within a collective whole, as the Lapithos mortuary practices suggest (Talalay and Cullen 2002: 189; see also Herscher 1997: 31–33; Sneddon 2002: 105–109).

In her detailed analysis of plank figures published up to about 1990, a Campo (1994: 145) pointed out that these typically flat, rectangular figures have a roughly human shape and a recognisable face, but often lack sexual characteristics (34% have breasts). Amongst the figurines that depict a person carrying a child (16% of her corpus) (i.e. the *kourotrophos* variants), some have breasts and others do not; one unprovenanced example depicts an individual with a penis holding a child (Morris 1985: 148, fig. 233). Various patterns and designs engraved on the body may represent clothing or weaving, scarves round the neck and headgear of various sorts (a Campo 1994: 146, pls. X–XXII). About 65% of the plank figures have markings on the face, which have been interpreted as tattoos, face-paintings or masks; the diversity of these marks suggests they represented an individual's social status or personality (Lubsen-Admiraal 1994: 29, 31). Thus the facemarks may represent identity or status: 'the individuality in design might be due to the personal choice of the artist, or be used to stress the individuality of the person' (a Campo 1994: 150). In fact, and despite alternative opinions (see below), one of the most distinctive features of the plank figures is their individualised dress, ornamentation and face-marks; they most likely represent specific people wearing their own distinctive apparel.

Most interpretations of plank figurines were conducted at a time when scholars had no exposure to an archaeology of gender; ancient people were universally regarded as being either female or (typically) male, with little scope for gender or sexual differentiation. For example, a White Painted Ware plank figurine from Nicosia *Ayia Paraskevi* has been interpreted either as a bearded man with breasts, or a long-faced woman (Morris 1985: 157, fig. 250; Hamilton 2000: 26, fig. 2.6b). Another example depicted with breasts and a penis (Knapp and Meskell 1997: 196, fig. 6) (Figure 92), was described as being hermaphroditic ('of double sex'), or else as a male whose breasts were an 'insignificant sexual characteristic' (Karageorghis 1991: 178 no. 10, 180, pl. CXL.8). Some plank figurines are portrayed with two or three heads (Morris 1985: 144–145, figs. 218–227) that themselves sometimes display different facial features. Karageorghis (1991: 91) suggested that one variety of this group of figurines might represent a male–female couple, whilst Morris (1985: 145) fancied they might have held some magic powers for families seeking twins or triplets.

The plank figurines, like many of the modelled figures and genre scenes discussed above, challenge straightforward sexual categorisation or interpretation. Indeed, excepting breasts, sexual characteristics are uncommon, genitalia are rare and infants represent only a small portion of the extant corpus (Merrillees 1980: 174–176). Talalay and Cullen (2002) concurred that a binary approach to the sexuality of Cypriot plank figurines is untenable. They propose multivalent and ambiguous meanings, and regard the plank figurines as symbols of social prestige. They concluded, however, that these figurines most likely represented collective or group (as opposed to individual) identities, and served as ancestral ties for the people living in PreBA Cypriot communities (Talalay and Cullen 2002: 187, 191). On the basis of their two-dimensional form and stylised character (Merrillees 1980: 183), Bolger (2003: 108) also maintains that the plank figurines did not represent individuals, any more than their Chalcolithic forerunners did. And yet, whilst the flattened aspect of these figurines indeed may appear to simplify the human form, they are certainly not 'reductionist' (Talalay and Cullen 2002: 183). MacLachlan (2002: 367–368), whilst acknowledging the highly stylised nature of the plank figurines, suggested that their bisexual aspect or dual sexual symbolism might reflect the social tensions of individuals trying to redefine their identity in the rapidly changing world of the PreBA.

The plank figurines, it must be reiterated, bear richly incised geometric patterns revealing highly distinctive eyes and eyebrows, mouths, noses, hair and ears. Their bodily ornamentation most likely represents some kind of dress (shawls, scarves, necklaces, headbands and waistbands) or decoration (paint, scarifications, tattoos) (Knapp and Meskell 1997: 196). Multivariate statistical analyses

Figure 92. Plain Ware terracotta figurine depicted with breasts and a penis. Ht: 17.5 cm; width at arms 4.2 cm, at hips 2.9 cm. Unknown provenance. Glasgow Museums, Kelvingrove, No. ARCH NN 548 (Knapp and Meskell 1997: 196, fig. 6).

of the figurines' diverse decorative features led to the conclusion that (1) such features portray individual dress and ornament; (2) the face-marks distinguish different people and point to an individual's place in society; and (3) the form of the plank figurines represents specific, individual women (a Campo 1994: 150, 165–166, 168). More generally, Talalay and Cullen (2002: 189–190) concluded that the plank figurines most likely symbolise an emerging social élite, and that their schematic form and ambiguous sexuality could accommodate singular male, female or other identities during a period of increasing social complexity. After a thorough reconsideration of the plank figurines, especially the kourotrophic examples (woman holding a child), Budin (2011: 229–259), concluded that they represent the identity, status and possibly the reproductive potential of the individual women portrayed, within a society that was becoming increasingly stratified and oriented towards centralised control over property and resources.

In addition to other PreBA representations of the human form already noted above (the modelled figures on pottery rims and the 'genre scenes', the figure carved in low relief in the dromos of Tomb 6 at Karmi *Palealona*, perhaps a precursor to plank figurines), there are also several figures modelled in the round or freestanding figurines (Merrillees 1980: 177–178, types IA2 and IB2). Finally, we should include here the 'sanctuary' models from Kotchatis and Kalopsidha (Karageorghis 1970; Frankel and Tamvaki 1973; Åström 1988), as well as the unusual, human-shaped vases (*askoi*) or vessel-shaped figures, often decorated with designs similar to those seen on the plank figurines (e.g. Morris 1985: 162–164; Stewart 1992: 36 [class III]; Karageorghis 2001a).

Why do so many of these human representations, not least the plank figurines, turn up in burials on north-coast sites, and why at this particular time? Webb and Frankel (2010) have suggested that some tombs at Karmi *Palealona* and Bellapais *Vounous* were the loci of ongoing ritual activities, possibly serving as mortuary 'shrines'. Such forms of patterned mortuary behavior, in particular at *Vounous*, may have underpinned new forms of social or ritual authority linked to ancestral groups. The elaboration of tombs, feasting and other mortuary practices may have served as vehicles for ideological exchange 'in contexts designed to validate emerging claims to social and ritual authority' (Webb and Frankel 2010: 185). Add to this Manning's (1993: 45) view that the imported prestige goods found in these same north-coast burials may have led to the emergence of an individual exercising politico-economic control over increased levels of production and consumption in Cypriot society, as well as the clear contextual association between plank figurines and exclusive burials in these tombs, we may posit that a social group of some status appropriated the plank figurines to mark their identity and symbolise their individual status.

What else can all these diverse representations of the human form tell us about the people who lived on PreBA Cyprus? Were they used in the attempt to establish distinctive, insular identities? Did the plank figurines represent a major ideological shift in women's roles on prehistoric Cyprus (Bolger 1993; 1996)? Although Hamilton (2000: 28) has argued that we should not be forcing prehistoric figurines '…into preconceived sex and gender pigeonholes, and then using the results to interpret social structures', it is not clear exactly what she thinks we *should* be doing. In a comparable recent study, Morris (2009) explores the potential of viewing anthropomorphic figurines from Bronze

Age Crete, especially those showing special attributes and gestures, as representations that played an active role in constructing and projecting individual human identities within Minoan culture.

The function(s) of female anthropomorphic figurines, as well as their sex or gender, are typically assigned on the basis of formal or stylistic attributes. They are most often regarded as representations of a fertility goddess, or as specialised grave goods (Lubsen-Admiraal 1994: 28–30). Webb (1992: 90), however, pointed out that female anthropomorphic figurines appear in fewer than 10% of the interments in a sample of more than 300 PreBA (EC–MC) burials; it thus seems unlikely they were designed only for the mortuary realm. Instead, they may well represent the valued possessions of individual people, only occasionally placed in burials. The assumption that PreBA 2 female and infant figurines served a mortuary function has in turn led to their identification as a fertility goddess who could restore life to the dead, as effigies of mortal women, or as symbols of the continuity of human existence (Bolger 2003: 93–122; Webb n.d.). The recovery of all the fragmentary examples noted above, however, makes it clear they were also used in everyday life. Although their function and identity remain issues for discussion, Webb (n.d.) suggests that their increasing numbers throughout the PreBA 2 period may reflect the need to control the reproductive potential of adult females in an economy based on intensive agricultural production.

Bolger (1996: 371; cf. Frankel 1997) went so far as to suggest that the origin of female oppression was the result of social changes (centralised authority restricting women's roles and institutionalising socio-economic inequality) reflected in the figurines. Following a Campo (1994), Bolger assumed that all plank figurines were representations of females, an assumption that ignores their sexual ambiguity and overlooks the likelihood that sex per se may have had little relevance for the people who produced and used these figurines (Hamilton 2000: 18–23, 28). Even if the social structure of PreBA Cyprus were more patriarchal than that of preceding eras, I would argue that Bolger has underestimated women's social roles. For example, the repeated appearance in genre scenes modelled on PreBA pottery of socially constructed, gendered activities – often highlighting women as well as their life cycle – suggests that both female and male identities were gendered in line with their social roles.

Rather than regarding the often standardised shapes and flattened form of the plank figurines as representing collective or group identities, these features could be seen as providing a platform for individual owners to impose upon them their own sexual or gendered identities (Talalay and Cullen 2002: 186), or to adapt or transform their identity throughout their life cycle. The contextual associations of these plank figurines link them to an emerging, high status group that used such representations to announce and reinforce their individual status, and to mark their distinctive identities within this island society.

OVERVIEW: PREHISTORIC BRONZE AGE

Stuart Swiny (2007: 171) began his masterful overview of the Early Bronze Age of Cyprus in the Ιστορια της Κυπρου with the following observation: 'Indeed, the transition from the Chalcolithic to the Early Bronze Age represents the most radical cultural discontinuity to occur during the long span of Cypriot prehistory'. To be sure, the remarkably rich and increasingly diverse material record of the PreBA served as a prelude to social and cultural developments that would unfold over the following 1,500 years. Unfortunately, no settlement site or cemetery yet shows detailed stratigraphic sequences that illuminate clearly this 'radical' period of transition. Furthermore, because several aspects of the evidence have been taken to support the possibility of an ethnic migration or 'colonisation' from Anatolia, with all the attendant economic, demographic and social consequences, interpretations of the relevant material record have long been a source of contention.

Whilst many of the material witnesses of daily life, food production, feasting and ritual, and mortuary practices cited by Webb and Frankel to support a migration or 'colonisation' are intrusive in the Cypriot context, none can be shown to have *direct* Anatolian parallels. In my own view, all these material and social changes are better treated in the trajectory of 'third space' (Bhabha 1994: 53–55; van Dommelen 2006: 107), another aspect of hybridisation practices. Neither Cypriot nor Anatolian, they represent the outcome of still unknown or at least ambivalent interactions between these two groups of people; such interactions occur both within and against the binary structures of culture and identity. People involved in hybridisation practices renegotiate their identities at least in part by revamping their material culture. Thinking about migration in terms of hybridisation practices also helps us to understand better the dynamics involved in the emergence of the Prehistoric Bronze Age culture of Cyprus, in most ways distinctively different from everything that preceded it in both material and social terms. If we were to understand all these innovations and changes in terms of the meeting and mixing of different sociocultural groups – including various levels of migration – that resulted in entirely new material forms and social practices, without assuming any form of technological or cultural superiority, and leaving aside the missing evidence of foreign presence, we would stand on much firmer ground in attempting to interpret this complex period of transition.

Unlike the town and village sites that make up the landscape of the contemporary Levant (e.g. Tell Umm el-Marra, Tell es-Sweyhat), there is no evident site hierarchy on PreBA Cyprus, no evidence of a social organisation in which regional or urban centres dominated agro-pastoral villages or received from them tribute or agricultural surpluses. Within the villages of PreBA Cyprus, the introduction of the plough, an increase in the size and number of implements for grinding grain, and the likelihood that cattle (at least from Marki *Alonia*) served as draught animals all suggest an increasing dietary reliance on cereal crops (Frankel and Webb 2006a: 207). As far as storage facilities are concerned, however, they seem to be confined to what was necessary to support and feed each household. The size and structure of house compounds, the presence of limited storage containers within them, and the lack of evidence for communal enterprises all indicate that the agropastoral villages of the PreBA were autonomous communities inhabited by extended family units or households that owned both the land and its products (Frankel and Webb 2006a: 314–315; Webb n.d.).

The villages of PreBA Cyprus thus may be seen as open communities, internally well integrated and perhaps interdependent. They had lower population densities and were more dispersed than their contemporary, Levantine counterparts. The lack of an urban-based socio-economic organisation may also help to explain the stability of sites such as Marki *Alonia* over the long term (in this case more than 400 years). This stability also seems evident in the lack of fortifications (and the location of settlements in non-defensive positions), the paucity of weaponry (at least until the end of EC III – Keswani 2004: 77, table 4.15), and the absence of evidence for violent destruction or forced abandonment (except possibly an earthquake at Sotira *Kaminoudhia*) (Webb 2012).

The rise of foreign demand for Cypriot copper, the entry of prestige goods into the politico-economic or ritual sphere, the intensified production of copper and control over access to its sources, all led to new social dynamics of communication, negotiation and interaction. The material indicators of these developments can be seen – increasingly as time passed during the PreBA – in the wealth and status differences postulated amongst certain PreBA households and compounds, a range of new types (and technologies) of mould-cast, copper-based implements, tools and jewellery, anthropomorphic and zoomorphic figurines, and a small but notable array of imports seen primarily but not exclusively in mortuary deposits on the north coast. New means of communication and exchange, new types of competition and display, changing mortuary practices focused on the ancestors, indicators of capital or social storage in an intensified agricultural economy, and labour practices that seem to reproduce gender as a social fact, all become apparent during the PreBA (Manning 1993: 48–49; Webb 2002b: 93–94; 2009: 261–264; Bolger 2003: 193; Keswani 2005: 382–384).

Several remarkable changes took place during the PreBA in the way tombs were constructed, and in the mortuary practices associated with them (Keswani

2004: 37–62; see also Toumazou 1987: 203–207; Webb and Frankel 2010). The deceased were now usually interred in large extra-mural cemeteries clearly demarcated from their associated settlements, typically in chambered tombs that at times contained more than one person and were characterised by many new types of grave goods. Mortuary rites became increasingly elaborate and costly if not competitive during the course of the PreBA, as indicated by both the decorative features of the actual tombs and the grave goods found within them. Excavations at sites ranging in date from the Philia phase to MC II – *Vounous*, Lapithos, Karmi *Lapatsa* and *Palealona*, Deneia *Kafkalla* and *Kafkalla tis Malis*, Sotira *Kaminoudhia*, Nicosia *Ayia Paraskevi* and several other mortuary sites – have produced hundreds of copper weapons, tools and ornaments, and more limited numbers of imports (Minoan and Syro-Cilician pottery, Minoan daggers, faience beads and necklaces, perhaps horses), as well as other luxury items (shell and stone pendants, 'hook-tang' metal weapons, earrings made of copper, bronze and precious metals, gold and silver ornaments, a gypsum 'idol', terracotta figurines, woven clothing, distinctive and elaborate pottery vessels). Keswani (2005: 348–349, 363, 388–389, 392) rightly links such changes in PreBA mortuary practices to various economic (Secondary Products Revolution, intensified copper production and exchange) and social developments: ancestor veneration, the possible emergence of social inequalities, and the negotiation of social identities. PreBA cemeteries thus became places for competitive display, helping certain social groups to establish land rights, perhaps even control over the production of copper.

The strikingly new material culture that characterises the PreBA points to the presence of certain individuals or groups of higher social status. Whilst the most obvious material markers of this new social group are their elaborate mortuary practices with sumptuous burial goods, we also see an intensification in agricultural practices, the expansion of local and long-distance trade, and the personal use of metal items (hair-rings and earrings) if not seals. The involvement of this group in social and material exchanges within and beyond Cyprus certainly must have prompted changes in social structure on the island (Manning 1993: 46; Peltenburg 1993: 20; Knapp et al. 1994: 413–414). By developing and intensifying metallurgical production and exchange, and taking advantage of a prestige-goods system that emerged in response to external demand, an élite group or some élite individuals were able to assume a focal position in PreBA society (Knapp 1994: 279–280).

The Prehistoric Bronze Age marks a clean break with the earlier prehistory of Cyprus, evident not only in the material culture (pottery, metals, human representations, figurative art, architecture) but also in the dramatic economic and social changes associated with intensified agrarian practices and metallurgical production. The landscape of the island was transformed as forests were cleared to provide more land for the 'cattle and plough complex' and to fuel the production of copper (Steel 2004a: 148). Above all, Cyprus now took the first, halting steps towards involvement in the emerging systems of trade and interaction that enveloped the entire eastern Mediterranean world. All these developments peaked in a dramatic, punctuated fashion towards the end of the PreBA and at the outset of the ProBA (17th–16th centuries Cal BC), when the earliest, major urban polities emerged on Cyprus.

CHAPTER 7

PROTOHISTORIC BRONZE AGE CYPRUS

The people of Cyprus's Protohistoric Bronze Age (ProBA) (ca. 1750/1700–1100/1050 Cal BC) retained the agro-pastoral base that had underpinned the PreBA economy, but their orientation increasingly – and rapidly – became industrial in nature, town-centred and integrated within the wider Levantine and Mediterranean worlds. The exchange of bulk goods, luxury items, organic products and raw materials with other, often historically dated cultures of the eastern Mediterranean (Egypt, the Levant) and the Aegean, has made it possible to establish a sound relative chronology for the ProBA. In turn, this chronology meshes reasonably well with the absolute chronology adopted in this volume and elsewhere, in which MC III begins ca. 1750/1700 Cal BC, and Late Cypriot IA ca. 1680/1650 Cal BC; the duration of the Late Cypriot IIC period is ca. 1340/1325–1200 Cal BC (see Appendix, Table A2, and captions to Figures A12 and A13; see also Manning 2001; Manning et al. 2001).

As was the case with the PreBA, several striking changes appear in the ProBA archaeological record, but at an entirely different level and scale (Knapp et al. 1994: 224–229; Knapp 2008: 134–201):

(a) town centres with monumental architecture;
(b) burial practices showing clear distinctions in social status;
(c) writing (Cypro-Minoan) on clay tablets, cylinders and other materials;
(d) intensified and widespread production and export of copper;
(e) extensive regional and interregional trade (especially with the Levant and Aegean);
(f) newly built fortifications, weaponry in burials, warriors depicted on pottery.

Such changes indicate that Cypriot society was no longer egalitarian, isolated, cooperative and village-oriented but rather socially stratified (heterarchical or hierarchical?), international, competitive and town-centred (Keswani 1996; Webb 2005). The commercially successful exploitation, production and trade of Cyprus's copper resources, together with the generation of agricultural surpluses, fuelled the emergence of a politico-economic élite and the centralisation of sociopolitical authority (Knapp 1996a; 2008; Peltenburg 1996), at least initially at the site of Enkomi (Webb 1999: 292–294; Knapp 2008: 324–341; cf. Crewe 2007b: 159–160). During the course of the ProBA, the intensified production and trade in copper made Cyprus the main provider of this metal throughout the Mediterranean, if not the Levant and parts of the Near East – a situation that endured for at least 2,000 years, until the fall of the Roman Empire.

During the 2nd millennium BC, the eastern Mediterranean and Aegean, if not the central Mediterranean, became a single zone of maritime innovation, mobility and connectivity (Bietti Sestieri 1988; Sherratt and Sherratt 1991; Cline and Harris-Cline 1998; Broodbank 2010: 256). Cyprus's involvement in this élite-driven international trade, and the ideological and iconographic exchanges – spurred by notions of distance and the exotic – that typified this era (e.g. Feldman 2006; Knapp 1998; 2006; Schon 2009: 229–235), surely triggered some of the other striking changes that appear for the first time in the Cypriot archaeological record. About the time these changes first became evident on Cyprus, Middle Bronze II urban sites in the Levant had reached their apex, not least amongst them the coastal emporia at Ugarit, Byblos and Tell el-Ajjul (Stewart 1974; Marcus 2002b; Akkermans and Schwartz 2003: 321–325; Yon 2006a: 16). Finds of Middle Cypriot pottery at these and many other Levantine and Egyptian coastal or near-coastal sites (Maguire 2009) suggest that the internationalism which became such a prominent feature of the ProBA had already emerged by the end of the preceding, PreBA 2 period.

Overseas associations are equally clear from the mortuary record, which shows the increasing consumption of Levantine and other, western Asian élite ideology and paraphernalia. These involved in particular military equipment or warrior symbolism, which seem to have been important factors in negotiating and constructing a new, élite, island identity. An informative documentary record broadens the evidential base and facilitates a more integrated discussion of this protohistoric period (Knapp 1996b; 2008: 308–341). In what follows, other, related factors – settlements and subsistence, metallurgical and agricultural production, monumental architecture, gendered practices, sociopolitical organisation – are reassessed in the light of the themes that structure this volume: insularity and connectivity, island identity and hybridisation practices.

SPATIAL ORGANISATION AND SETTLEMENT

From household goods to mortuary enclosures, the material culture that typified the last stages of PreBA 2 (MC I–II, ending about 1750/1700 Cal BC) became increasingly homogenous. Such homogeneity suggests a society where people shared beliefs, sought social alliances and merged economic activities, in particular as they were related to the burgeoning trade in copper and

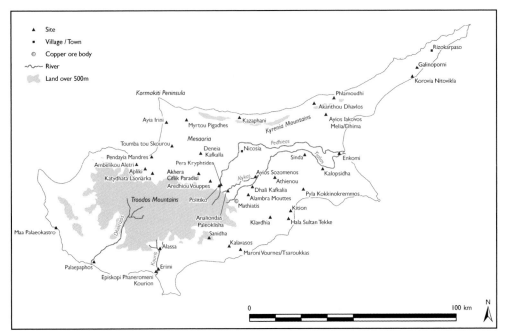

Figure 93. Map of ProBA sites discussed in text. Prepared by Luke Sollars.

the spread of communications throughout the island (Frankel 1974: 10–11; Herscher 1991; Knapp 1994: 279–280). These trends suggest that regionalism, and the regional factions or groups that lay behind them, no longer played such an important role in the island's economy. Settlement evidence from the end of the PreBA reveals that people now lived throughout the island, from the Karpass peninsula and the foothills along either side of the Kyrenia range in the north and northeast, to the lower river valleys of the northern Troodos where they met and crossed the *Mesaoria*, to the southern and eastern rims of the Troodos and farther east (e.g. Kalopsidha – see Crewe 2010b); this holds true but to a lesser extent in the south and southwest (Knapp 2008: 134, with further refs.) (Figure 93).

By the end of the PreBA, the size of settlements as well as their locations had begun to change in ways that had major consequences for both the economy and social organisation of ProBA Cyprus. Within the Vasilikos Valley along the south central coast, for example, there are several sites of exceptional size, unusual for the PreBA 2 period: Kalavasos *Mitsingites* (6.25 ha), *Lourca* (8.25 ha), *Alonia tou Pano Zyou* (9 ha), *Laroumena* (10 ha) and *Arkhangelos* (14–16 ha), and *Khorapheri/Vounaritashi* (36 ha) (Todd 2004: 39–40, 58–61, 67–75, 85–87). *Arkhangelos* and *Laroumena* appear to have formed one huge (late) Middle Bronze Age 'complex', more than 77 ha in extent, on the western side of the valley (Todd 2004: 40). The *Khorapheri/Vounaritashi* complex (36 ha) lies not quite 1 km west of *Mitsingites*, and Todd (2004: 59) suggests these two sites should also be considered in relation to one another, even if they were distinctive. Both have large numbers of Middle Cypriot and scattered amounts of Late Cypriot wares (thus likely ProBA 1 in date). The site of *Spilios* in the farther, northwestern part of the Vasilikos Valley is also extensive (40 ha), with Middle Cypriot sherds widely scattered throughout; its size, however, may be associated more with its importance during the Archaic and Roman periods (Todd 2004: 101–104).

At *Laroumena*, courses of walls are evident in different parts of the site, and more than 160 groundstone artefacts – querns, pounders, hammerstones and more – were collected from its surface; clearly food processing was one main activity here. Several clay spindle whorls and fragments were recovered from *Laroumena*, as were a crucible and several slag pieces of unknown date. A large number (88) of groundstone tools and implements was also found at *Arkhangelos*, along with a significant quantity of chipped stone (mostly retouched flakes). A general scatter of chipped stone and a few groundstone items were found at *Khorapheri/Vounaritashi*, along with some Late Cypriot sherds, a spindle whorl and a fragmentary clay animal figurine.

Opposite *Laroumena* and *Arkhangelos* on the eastern side of the valley lay a chain of (distinct) Middle Bronze Age sites, stretching some 2 km from *Pervolia* in the north (itself a direct continuation of the large site complex at Tokhni *Oriti* – see below), through *Alonia tou Pano Zyou* (9 ha, across the river from *Laroumena*), and south to *Lourca* (Todd 2004: fig. 20). *Lourca* and *Alonia tou Pano Zyou* are both large Middle Cypriot sites with significant sherd scatters (Red Polished, White Painted), the former with a series of tombs, the latter with some occasional Late Cypriot pottery (White Slip, Base-ring, *pithoi*) (Todd 2004: 33–34, 73–75). If *Kokkinokremos* (3 ha) indeed forms the 'lower component' of the *Lourca* site (Todd 2004: 62), it is possible there was another 'mega-site' here, to the southeast of Kalavasos village. Also in the eastern Vasilikos Valley and north of Kalavasos village lies another major Bronze Age site complex, at Tokhni *Oriti* North (on a ridge with a commanding view) and South. At Tokhni *Oriti* North, 27 groundstone artefacts were collected, mainly querns and pounders, and a single piece of slag. Together this complex extends over some 10–11 ha (Todd 2004: 137–139), and both sites have significant quantities of Middle Cypriot material as well as some Late Cypriot coarse ware and pithos sherds.

Why do we find such a concentration of large, contemporary sites (late PreBA 2, or ProBA 1) in this single river valley? How do 'mega-sites' such as *Laroumena/Arkhangelos* (77 ha) or *Khorapheri/Vounaritashi* (38 ha) measure up to the more typical, small (5 ha or less), locally oriented Middle Cypriot villages? Do these sites overlap temporally with Politiko *Troullia*, another site that dates in part to the end of PreBA (with some Late Cypriot pottery already identified), with material spread over about 20 ha? Until some level of field excavation is carried out at these extensive site complexes, any answers would be premature. Even so, it must be recalled that copper production and (possibly) export are regarded as having been instrumental in the accumulation of élite wealth at the best-known site in the Vasilikos Valley, the ProBA 2 town of *Ayios Dhimitrios* (some 3 km south of Kalavasos village) (South and Todd 1985; South 1989: 322; 1996: 41–42). A likely coppersmith's workshop (Building IX) was also uncovered at this site, as were 11 bronze and 3 hematite weights (Building III) (Courtois 1983). Finally, the large (20 ha) Late Cypriot II industrial site (White Slip pottery production) of Sanidha *Moutti tou Ayiou Serkou* (Todd 2004: 161–171), which lies some 10 km northwest of Kalavasos village, was underlain by a small ProBA 1 forerunner. In other words, some of the key mineral resources that propelled the dynamic economy of the ProBA were available in the upper Vasilikos Valley: it may be that the large site complexes of the late Middle Cypriot period had already begun to exploit these resources on more than a purely local scale.

Throughout the ProBA, there was a major expansion of settlements and an overall increase in site size; the population must have grown accordingly. Only the mountainous zone of the Troodos seems to have remained underpopulated during the ProBA. As was the case in later periods (Given 2002), however, it was likely exploited for timber and various mineral resources. The current settlement record of ProBA Cyprus numbers well over 300 sites (Catling 1962: 160–169; Knapp 1997: 46–52), several of which – Enkomi, Kition, Alassa, Kalavasos *Ayios Dhimitrios*, Maroni *Vournes*, Hala Sultan Tekke *Vyzakia* – have been excavated extensively and provide detailed stratigraphic sequences. With this comprehensive body of excavated material, alongside new evidence from regional survey projects, it is possible to provide a detailed overview of material, cultural and spatial developments during the ProBA, and to draw some tentative social conclusions.

The best-known settlements are widely scattered in different regions of the island. One of the hallmarks of ProBA settlement patterns is the expansion into the south and southeast of the island, as opposed to the formerly prominent north-coast sites. Indeed, some of the best-known and prosperous coastal towns of the ProBA were established in the east and southeast – Enkomi (the earliest), Hala Sultan Tekke and Kition (Schaeffer 1971; 1984; Dikaios 1969–1971; Karageorghis and Demas 1985; Åström 1986; 1989). Along the south central coast, new town centres arose at Maroni *Tsaroukkas/Vournes* (Cadogan 1996; Cadogan et al. 2001; Manning and DeMita 1997; Manning et al. 2002) and Kalavasos *Ayios Dhimitrios* (South 1996; South et al. 1989). Deep in the foothills behind Kalavasos, a pottery production village was established at Sanidha *Moutti tou Ayiou Serkou* (Todd 2000; Todd and Pilides 2001). In the southern Kouris River valley, some earlier settlements continued in use (e.g. Episkopi *Phaneromeni*, Erimi *Laonin tou Porakou*) whilst new ones appeared (e.g. Episkopi/Kourion *Bamboula*, Alassa *Pano Mandilares* and *Paleotaverna*, Erimi *Pitharka*); farther west in the Dhiarizos River valley, Kouklia *Palaipaphos* was established (Weinberg 1983; Maier and Karageorghis 1984; Swiny 1986a; Maier

1987; Hadjisavvas 1996; 2006; Vassiliou and Stylianou 2004; Bombardieri et al. 2009a; Bombardieri 2010b).

In the northwest, settlements such as Morphou *Toumba tou Skourou* (Vermeule and Wolsky 1990) and Myrtou *Pigadhes* (Du Plat Taylor 1957), as well as the cemetery at Ayia Irini *Paleokastro* (Pecorella 1973; 1977), demonstrate population growth in and around the Kormakiti peninsula. The excavators of *Toumba tou Skourou* maintain that it was a specialised industrial site devoted to the production of fine ware pottery (White Painted, Proto-White Slip, White Slip 1, Base-ring 1), *pithoi* and bricks (Vermeule and Wolsky 1990: 19–22). Along the north coast and east of Kyrenia, commercial traffic from abroad probably touched at sites such as Kazaphani (Nicolaou and Nicolaou 1989), Phlamoudhi *Vounari* and *Melissa* (another pottery production site – Smith 2008a: 49), and near Akanthou or Dhavlos. At the interface of the *Mesaoria* plain and the igneous zone of the northern and eastern Troodos, several smaller agricultural settlements (e.g. Aredhiou *Vouppes*, Analiondas *Paleoklichia*) and mining sites or communities (e.g. Politiko *Phorades*, Apliki *Karamallos*) were established at different times during the ProBA (Webb and Frankel 1994; Knapp and Kassianidou 2008; Steel and McCartney 2008; Steel and Thomas 2008).

From the general constellation of sites and the wide array of local and imported material found in them, it would seem that a maritime location (especially in the east and southeast), a rapidly growing overseas market orientation, and the intricacies involved in establishing social groups and political alliances were all factors at least as important as resource orientation in choosing where to locate a site. Ultimately they were instrumental in all the socio-economic developments and changes that characterise the ProBA.

Perhaps the most striking feature of the settlement record is the establishment of new, good-sized towns along the coast, many of them ports. Already during the ProBA 1 period (ca. 1700–1450 Cal BC), prominent new settlements were established at Enkomi *Ayios Iakovos* and Hala Sultan Tekke *Vyzakia* (east and southeast), Episkopi (Kourion) *Bamboula* and Kouklia *Palaipaphos* (south), and Morphou *Toumba tou Skourou* (near the northwest coast) (Keswani 1996; Knapp 1997: 46–48). Proximity to the sea and access to the copper ore sources in the Troodos seem to have been important in the location of these sites (Portugali and Knapp 1985: 50–61). Although a few key sites of the earlier, PreBA had been established on or near the north coast, almost certainly to facilitate overseas contacts (e.g. settlements associated with the cemeteries at Lapithos, Karmi, Vasilia), the newly established coastal sites of the ProBA – in the east and southeast, south and northwest – were oriented decisively towards the connecting sea. They served to answer foreign demand for Cypriot copper and other goods, and to bring prestigious Near Eastern and Aegean products into Cyprus (Merrillees 1965: 146–147; Knapp 1998; Crewe 2007b: 12–14). No doubt Cypriot élites were instrumental in establishing these coastal centres, in order to promote politico-economic and ideological alliances with other,

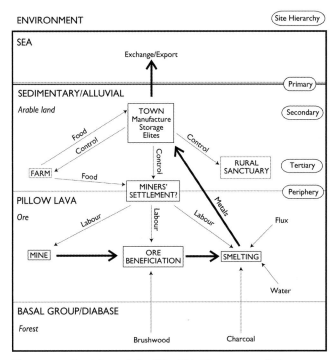

Figure 94. Social model of ProBA Cyprus, outlining some of the
environmental, agricultural, metallurgical and politico-economic processes at
work in the landscape. The proposed site hierarchy is indicated on the right.
Prepared by Michael Given.

more powerful polities in the Aegean and eastern Mediterranean (Keswani
1989; Manning et al. 2002).

In her study of the patterns of town life and the internal spatial configuration
of the major coastal centres at Enkomi, *Toumba tou Skourou*, Hala Sultan Tekke
and Kition, Keswani (1996; 2004: 154–156) suggests that they may have been
established by groups of people from outlying communities. As they settled in
these towns, differences in access to productive resources may have fostered
hierarchical social relations. In contrast, the more nucleated populations of
town centres in the south and southwest – Maroni, Kalavasos *Ayios Dhimitrios*
and Alassa *Paleotaverna* – may have been local in origin, with administrative
structures that were more centralised, perhaps the result of easier access to and
control over copper ore sources. Some smaller centres founded during the 13th
century BC may have served as outposts for these larger town centres: Maa
Palaeokastro for Kouklia *Palaipaphos*; Pyla *Kokkinokremos* for Kition; Episkopi
(Kourion), the smallest of the town centres, for Alassa *Paleotaverna* (on the last,
Bombardieri 2009: 288–289; Bombardieri et al. 2009b: 117).

Building on earlier work by Catling (1962) and Keswani (1993), and based
on a growing corpus of spatial and archaeological data from survey work and
newer excavations, I argued the case for a ProBA settlement hierarchy during
the ProBA (Knapp 1997). Because the archaeological record is much fuller for

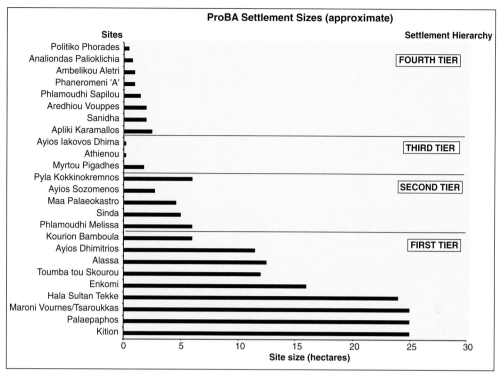

Figure 95. ProBA site size approximations; the proposed site hierarchy is indicated on the right. Prepared by A. Bernard Knapp.

the 14th–13th centuries BC (ProBA 2–3) than it is for the 17th–15th centuries BC (ProBA 1), the proposed settlement patterns and politico-economic systems are much better substantiated for the 13th century BC. The distinctions proposed for the four tiers of settlement are based on the differing types and arrays of material culture found at the various sites in each tier, and thus on their presumed functions, which in turn seem to reflect hierarchical social or political processes and structures (Figure 94):

(1) coastal centres (commercial, ceremonial, administrative, production);
(2) inland towns (administrative, production, transport, some storage);
(3) smaller inland sites (ceremonial, production, transport, some storage);
(4) agricultural and pottery-producing villages, mining sites (production, storage, transport).

The primary coastal (or near-coastal) centres were the largest sites; all but one of them (Episkopi *Bamboula*) range from 12–25 ha in extent. Iacovou (2007) recently, and rightly, criticised earlier estimates (in fact 'guess-timates') concerning the size of ProBA sites. Unfortunately, she offered nothing in the way of more reasonable estimates. Taking her arguments seriously, however, Figure 95 (ProBA site size) offers new 'guess-timates', accepting that the size of the four largest sites (Kition, *Palaipaphos*, Maroni and Hala Sultan Tekke) probably represents the maximum area of dispersed settlement in and around the actual excavated or surveyed areas. The estimates for Enkomi and *Ayios Dhimitrios* are based on the actual excavated area; in my view (*contra* Iacovou), it seems reasonable to assume that Alassa *Pano Mandilares* and *Paleotaverna* form one site, whilst modern farming operations have made it impossible to determine whether *Toumba tou Skourou* was about equal in size to these other 'primary' sites. Regarding Phlamoudhi *Melissa* (probably a second tier site), once again we have no idea of the actual size of the site, but rather than assume that it was equivalent in size to Enkomi or *Ayios Dhimitrios* (Smith 2008a: 49–53), I would suggest that its function was more like that of Episkopi *Bamboula* and thus estimate its size accordingly. With respect to Iacovou's (2007: 11–12) comments on the sizes of Pyla *Kokkinokremos* and Maa *Palaeokastro* (both second tier sites), the excavators stated that a surface survey showed the entire (27 ha) plateau of Pyla had been inhabited (Karageorghis and Demas 1984: 4–5). Whilst renewed work at Pyla continues to uncover additional habitational elements away from the edge of the plateau, Brown (2009: 67) states flatly that *Kokkinokremos* was about 6 ha in extent. Moreover, geomorphological work has identified what appears to be a harbour and a palaeocoastline below the plateau (Caraher et al. 2005: 246–248): both these factors suggest an area of dispersed but associated settlement beyond the plateau.

Found within the first tier sites were varying amounts of some key material features: ashlar masonry, prestige goods and imports, metallurgical products, impressed *pithoi*, Cypro-Minoan inscriptions, seals and weights (Knapp 1997: 54–55, table 2, with full refs.). Even if size is discounted as a factor in determining a site's politico-economic organisation or function, location may have assumed strategic as well as commercial importance (Merrillees 1992a: 316–319, 328, appendix 1). Stanley Price (1979a: 80) first suggested that such primary centres could have exercised some level of economic if not political hegemony over sites in their immediate hinterlands. Centralised production in the coastal towns served an élite strategy to ensure the cooperation and to control the output of the agricultural, mining and pottery-producing villages. In turn, this increased the rural sector's dependence on specialised goods and services available only in the town centres (Aravantinos 1991: 62). The variety and quantity of local and imported goods found in the primary centres, along with the differences in site size, distinguish them markedly from the other three levels of the site hierarchy.

The primarily administrative, secondary towns, and mainly ceremonial, tertiary sites typically were located at strategic nodes where the production or flow of copper, agricultural products and imports or prestige goods could be controlled. Whether these sites were administered by the primary centres or by local élites in alliance with their coastal counterparts is uncertain; nonetheless they served at least partly as transhipment points where local resources and exchange articulated with broader regional systems. The location of rural 'sanctuaries' (third tier) also may have served to demarcate regional territorial claims (Alcock 1993: 202).

The productive sector of ProBA Cypriot society forms the final tier in the site hierarchy: mining sites, pottery-producing and agricultural support villages. Mining-related sites tend to be concentrated in or near the igneous zone of the Troodos foothills, whilst the agricultural support villages are typically found in the *Mesaoria* close to the interface between the igneous and sedimentary zones. In addition to Aredhiou *Vouppes* (Steel and Thomas 2008) and Analiondas *Paleoklichia* (Webb and Frankel 1994), two further agricultural sites are (1) Phlamoudhi *Sapilou* (Symeonoglou 1972: Catling 1976), located near the north coast, and (2) Episkopi *Phaneromeni* 'A', situated on the southern coastal plain (Swiny 1986a). The pottery-producing site of Sanidha *Moutti tou Ayiou Serkou* lies in the upper Vasilikos Valley in an area rich in the type of clays used to produce the typical White Slip wares of the ProBA (Courtois 1970: 83). Most sites involved in production activities may be differentiated both spatially (inland periphery) and materially (Troodos mineral zones) from the primary coastal and secondary administrative centres.

The primary centres of Kalavasos *Ayios Dhimitrios* and Alassa *Pano Mandilares/Paleotaverna* not only served multiple functions (overlapping with those of secondary and tertiary centres) but also had inland locations closer to the mines. These sites would have exercised some level of control over the mining, production and transport of copper, were involved in agricultural production (olive oil), and functioned commercially as administrative and transhipment points. If such places were engaged strictly in administrative, production and ceremonial activities, then it is possible that their commercial functions were carried out by, for example, Maroni *Tsaroukkas* (for *Ayios Dhimitrios* and Maroni *Vournes*) and Episkopi *Bamboula* (for Alassa *Paleotaverna*). Interestingly, Smith (1994: 316) notes that the functions and contexts of seal-impressed *pithoi* from Alassa indicate centralised control over storage facilities, whilst those at *Bamboula* suggest more individualised control. More recently, she has clarified that *pithoi* from both *Paleotaverna* and *Bamboula* were impressed with a wooden cylindrical roller representing a series of griffins, perhaps demonstrating administrative connections and a regional site hierarchy (Smith 2008a: 61; Keswani 2009: 122–123).

On present evidence, the sites of Maa *Palaeokastro* and Pyla *Kokkinokremos*, situated, respectively, on and near the coast, do not really conform to the proposed settlement hierarchy. Karageorghis (1998a: 127–130) argues that they served defensive functions, and Steel (2004a: 188–190) seems to agree, suggesting that both Pyla and Maa were local 'strongholds'. Keswani (1996: 234; 2004: 155; 2009: 123), similarly, suggests they may have served as outposts of Kouklia *Palaipaphos* (or even Alassa) and Kition. Smith (1994: 274), by contrast, wondered whether Maa, at least, might have been a centralised storage facility. Stanley Price (1979a: 80–81) long ago suggested that sites like Pyla could have served as inland, support settlements for a nearby port. Recent geomorphological investigations in the lowland around Pyla have provided some support for this suggestion: Caraher et al. (2005: 246–248) identified what they term 'the definitive characteristics of a prehistoric to historic harbour' and a palaeocoastline some 150 m inland from the present-day beach near Pyla (see also Brown 2009: 67). Thus we might suggest that Pyla *Kokkinokremos* could have served to facilitate the movement of traded goods from coastal ports to inland settlements (similarly Sherratt 1998: 300–301 n. 15).

In this context, it is interesting to note that imported goods have been recovered not just from second tier, inland centres but also from third tier, sanctuary sites and fourth tier, remote agricultural villages. Late Helladic ('Mycenaean') pottery, for example, has been found at Athienou *Bamboulari tis Koukounninas* (Dothan 1993: 132–133), Myrtou *Pigadhes* (Catling 1957), Ayios Iakovos *Dhima* (Steel 2004b: 76–77), Mathiati (along with finished metal products – Hadjicosti 1991), in the hinterlands west of Larnaca (Leonard 2004), and in smaller amounts all over the island's interior (Pacci 1986). It is uncertain whether such imports reached these sites directly via regional trade networks or more indirectly, through informal and/or individual encounters (Merrillees 1965: 146–147; Webb and Frankel 1994: 17; Webb 2002d: 130).

Looking at settlements in terms of their storage facilities provides an interesting contrast between coastal and inland sites. On the one hand, the four (near) coastal emporia at Enkomi, Kition, Hala Sultan Tekke and Morphou *Toumba tou Skourou* contain virtually no evidence for storage (or does this simply reflect the nature of the current archaeological record? – Keswani 1993: 78; cf. Fischer 2011: 84, 87–88). On the other hand, storage facilities are prominent in the primary centres of Kalavasos *Ayios Dhimitrios*, Maroni *Vournes* and Alassa *Paleotaverna*, and in agricultural support villages as well as other inland sites (Webb 2002d: 130–131; Smith 2008a: 59). It may be that agricultural goods and surpluses were produced and stored in the countryside, then redistributed on demand to governing élites or specialised producers. In attempting to explain possible redistributive components of the ProBA settlement system, Keswani (1993) considered how subsistence needs and institutional structures might have been integrated into staple (rural) and wealth (urban) finance systems (after D'Altroy and Earle 1985).

Beyond settlement location and patterning, several other factors must be taken into account in order to gain a better understanding of (1) the social, political and ideological shifts that resulted in Cyprus's rapid transformation from an insular polity to an international player, and (2) the processes through which the economy expanded from a local, cooperative, village-based system (PreBA) to a more competitive and comprehensive, interregional, town-based system (ProBA). Even within the ProBA, we must consider how the early polity established at Enkomi – in part to ensure the direct procurement of copper ores via a network of forts set up at critical transport junctures (Peltenburg

1996: 30–35) – eventually was replaced by more subtle, ideological sanctions expressed through ritual paraphernalia, the circulation of symbol-laden goods, and the widespread presence of monumental architecture (see below) (Knapp 1988; 1996: 81–94). Moreover, factors of transport and issues related to internal versus external communications and connectivity require deeper analysis, as they will have impacted on any perceived or real social or spatial hierarchy. Beyond such factors of transport and exchange, we must also consider the complex, ever-changing relations of production and consumption – all subject to the individual or collective human behaviour – that linked sites of different size, function and location. Anyone who attempted to impose coercive force, establish economic hegemony or cement political alliances had to have the ability to manipulate social relations and, more importantly, the capacity to control access to resources in demand.

In the sections that follow, I consider each of these factors – and others – in some detail before attempting to elaborate on the sociopolitical organisation of ProBA Cyprus. Unlike earlier chapters, with the ProBA it is impossible to present a detailed discussion of each key site. Not only are there far too many, I have also discussed at length elsewhere the monumental constructions of most ProBA sites, as well as other, special-purpose sites and constructions (Knapp 2008: 211–249). Here I summarise all this evidence for (architectural) monumentality in terms of its relevance to the emergence of a new social order, and a changing island identity (see also Knapp 2009b).

Monumentality

The monumental nature of ProBA Cypriot architecture has been the subject of both traditional (e.g. Dikaios 1960; Wright 1992; Hadjisavvas and Hadjisavva 1997) and not so traditional analyses (e.g. Webb 1999; Fisher 2007; 2009). With respect to the latter, Webb treats a combination of material elements related to the 'ritual' architecture and iconography of ProBA Cyprus without specifically treating their monumental aspects. Fisher, by contrast, presents an entirely new, socio-spatial analysis of the construction, elaboration and meaning of monumental architecture. Although many scholars define certain ProBA monumental buildings as 'temples' (see further below), only Wright argues for the existence of 'palaces' (with the rider that there were no 'non-religious public buildings' – Wright 1992: 273–278). On the one hand, the existence of true palaces in western Asia and facsimiles in the Aegean (e.g. van de Mieroop 1999; Galaty and Parkinson 2007), alongside cuneiform documentary evidence related to *Alašiya* (Yon 2006b), might lead us to expect palatial structures on ProBA Cyprus. On the other hand, in terms of size and splendour, such expectations are never met in the archaeological record (this issue is treated further below, under *Sociopolitical Organisation – The Documentary View*).

As already noted more than once, Cyprus's material culture differs markedly from that of the surrounding regions throughout much of its history and pre-history; thus there is no reason to think that we shall ever find Near Eastern or Aegean-type 'palaces' on Cyprus. And yet, as we shall see, structures such as Building X at Kalavasos *Ayios Dhimitrios* or Building II at Alassa *Paleotaverna* were exceptional in terms of their size, layout, contents and likely functions. Some areas of these structures certainly could be regarded as 'public' in nature, and so may have served some of the same functions as Near Eastern palaces. Attempts to distinguish between 'public' and 'private' buildings in prehistoric contexts, however, are fraught with difficulties; in any case, it's most unlikely that the people of prehistoric Cyprus made such distinctions. Indeed it has proved difficult to distinguish between public and ceremonial space on ProBA Cyprus (Knapp 1996a: 75–80, 92–94), although Fisher (2009: 184, 201–202) makes a strong case for seeing certain rooms in ProBA monumental buildings as crucial for élite 'place-making' and as contexts for social events that centred on ceremonial activities such as feasting. Overall, there is no building or build-ing complex on ProBA Cyprus that conforms readily to binary categories such as public/private or secular/ceremonial. Most of the structures treated in this section are not only architecturally complex but also served multiple purposes: residential, administrative, industrial and ceremonial (see also Knapp 2008: 211–233).

In discussing monumentality on ProBA Cyprus, it is important to consider not only how people – in this case élites – used monumental constructions to establish their authority and to reproduce asymmetrical power relations, but also how the buildings themselves profoundly affected the social lives of those who constructed and used them (Fisher 2009: 205; see also Villamil 2008: 184). In other words, the monumental buildings of ProBA Cyprus, especially during the 14th–13th centuries BC, were not simply places where social interactions (from daily encounters to feasting) were carried out; they were also dynamic participants in the actions through which people negotiated and displayed their power and social status, constructed their identity and sought to make sense of their world.

These new élites began to make a permanent impression on the Cypriot landscape already at the outset of the ProBA 1 period (MC III–LC I). At this time, a series of 'forts' was constructed in the central and eastern *Mesaoria*, along the southern flanks of the Kyrenia range and in the Karpass peninsula (Peltenburg 1996: 31, fig. 4). The most prominent of these was the so-called 'fortress' in Area III at the northern entrance to the town of Enkomi (Dikaios 1969–1971: 16–21). Thus began a trend of 'place-making' by emergent élites, designed to control people's movements and interactions by appropriating, enclosing and monumentalising space (Fisher 2009: 204–205). This trend cul-minated in the construction of the monumental, court-centred buildings of the ProBA 2–3 periods (LC II–III), built wholly or partially of ashlar masonry – in itself a strong indicator of élite control over technical knowledge as well as

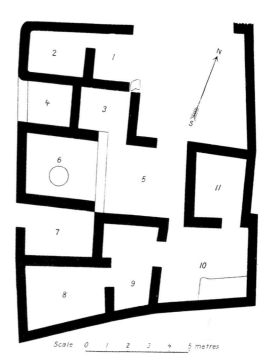

Figure 96. Kalopsidha Site C, plan of Gjerstad's 'House'. After Gjerstad 1926: fig. 3.

labour (Trigger 1990: 127). At most sites, these 14th–13th century BC buildings cannot be shown to have monumental forerunners in earlier periods, nor even that they had the same form or function. Nonetheless, given the long-term development of most ProBA settlements, it may be suggested that some significance must have been attached to the specific, earlier places where the later, monumental buildings were erected.

In what follows, monumentality refers to the construction and use of large, multi- or special-purpose, usually ashlar-constructed buildings or building complexes. By 'large', Wright (1992: 273) understood a substantial 'public' building at least 500 m² in extent. In this study, 'large' refers to structures ranging from 250 to nearly 1,500 m² in size. The main sites with such structures are Kition, Enkomi, Kouklia *Palaipaphos*, Kalavasos *Ayios Dhimitrios*, Maroni *Vournes*, Alassa *Paleotaverna*, Hala Sultan Tekke *Vyzakia*, Myrtou *Pigadhes*, Morphou *Toumba tou Skourou*, Athienou *Bamboulari tis Koukounninas*, Pyla *Kokkinokremos* and Maa *Palaeokastro* (for locations, see above, Figure 93). Whilst an early (ProBA 1) and somewhat controversial, 10-room structure from 'Site C' at Kalopsidha (about 180 m² in size) has become a standard part of the literature (Gjerstad 1926: 27–37, fig. 3; Swiny 1989: 20; Åström 2001b), it can only be mentioned in passing here (Figure 96). Another structure may have adjoined it on the east, and a road is said to have run along its southern edge. Frankel and Webb (1996: 54) have questioned whether 'Gjerstad's house' was a single structure (see also Crewe 2010b: 63–66).

The earliest, true monumental structure of the ProBA is the approximately 550 m², Level IA 'fortress' at Enkomi, already mentioned above

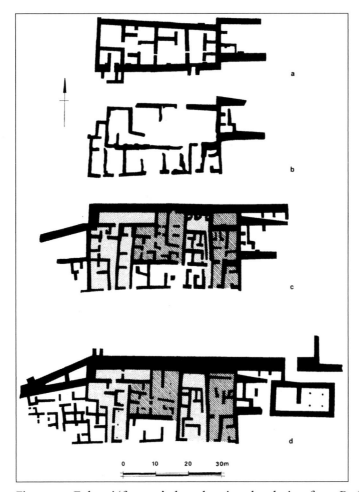

Figure 97. Enkomi 'fortress' plan, showing devolution from ProBA 1 to ProBA 2. From top: Levels IB, IIA, IIB, IIIA. After Pickles and Peltenburg 1998: 89, fig. 2. Courtesy of Edgar Peltenburg.

(Figure 97). This was a free-standing, rectangular building of massive construction, with at least 16 rooms including a central courtyard (Room 111), another large courtyard in the east (Room 119) and rooms for working copper in the west. The evidence for archaeometallurgical activities is not extensive on the ground in this early phase, but the melting and casting activities that took place were likely not limited to this one area (Kassianidou 2012); in any case, the role of Enkomi as a centre for the production and export of Cypriot copper is not in doubt (Peltenburg 1996: 31; cf. Crewe 2007b: 17–18, 156). This early fortress was destroyed and rebuilt (Level IB), with more rooms (101–109) in the western sector now devoted to copper smelting, whilst those in the eastern sector may have been used for residential purposes (Dikaios 1969–1971: 21). The central and eastern courts continued in use, whilst a 'stoa' was built along the building's southern façade.

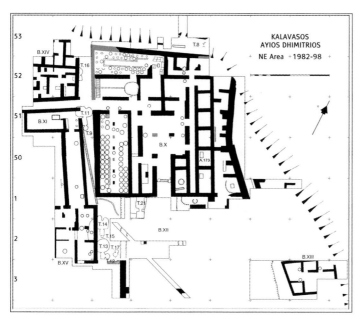

Figure 98. Kalavasos *Ayios Dhimitrios* Building X plan. Approximately 1,000 m²
in extent, with a 'Pithos Hall' for storage and ashlar masonry used for different
features. Courtesy of Alison South and the Cyprus Museum, Nicosia.

This fortress dominated the early town at Enkomi and its physical presence
has prompted everyone from Dikaios (1969–1971: 510–511) to Wright (1992:
275) to Pickles and Peltenburg (1998: 87) to view it as a special-purpose structure that housed a 'powerful citizen' or 'overarching authority'. Even Crewe
(2007b: 158), who feels there is little evidence at this time for institutionalised power at Enkomi, acknowledges the monumentality of this structure,
noting that both its construction and destruction reflect people competing
and negotiating for power. Peltenburg (1996: 29), however, has better captured
its essence: 'This enormous building and its contents is a material isomorph
of an hierarchically organised society, profoundly at odds with the architectural remains from preceding small-scale settlements on the island'. Enkomi's
monumental fortress flourished throughout ProBA 1, and likely served as an
economic and administrative centre for newly emerging élites.

Monumental construction thus became a prominent material feature of
the Cypriot landscape already during ProBA 1. By the following, ProBA 2
period (ca. 1450–1300 Cal BC), monumental ashlar-built structures had been
erected in several other urban centres. The overlay of later constructions, however, makes it difficult to trace the full extent of architectural elaboration in
15th–14th century BC buildings at Alassa *Paleotaverna*, Maroni *Vournes*, Kouklia
Palaipaphos, Myrtou *Pigadhes* and Athienou *Bamboulari tis Koukounninas*.

Although several other notable structures have been unearthed at Kalavasos
Ayios Dhimitrios, in terms of size, construction and contents ashlar Building X
is by far the most impressive, monumental structure (Figure 98). Approximately

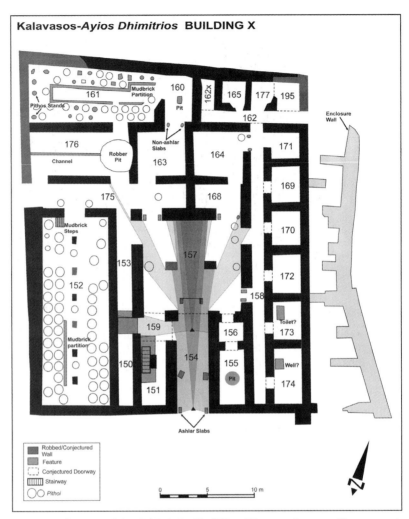

Figure 99. Kalavasos *Ayios Dhimitrios* Building X central court (Room 157), where various social gatherings were held (Fisher 2009: 196–198, figs. 7–8). Courtesty of Kevin Fisher.

1,000 m² in size, this building contained a 'Pithos Hall' (A. 152) that held some 50 large, highly standardised storage jars with a capacity estimated at 33,500 litres (Keswani 1993: 76). With a western façade of large ashlar blocks, and an entry hall ('vestibule', Room 154) bordered by ashlar slabs, Building X presented a striking face to passersby. The entry hall gave way, via a few steps, to the central court (Room 157) where feasting events were likely conducted (Fisher 2009: 196–8, figs. 7–8, 201–202) (Figure 99). Perhaps the remnants of just such a feast were found in Room 173 in the eastern corridor of Building X, with a deposit of meat-bearing sheep/goat bones and some 85 pottery vessels, including a range of imported Mycenaean tablewares (South 1988: 227). Building X also contained a concentration of stamp seals and several diverse types of Cypro-Minoan inscriptions (South 1996: 42; Masson, in South et al.

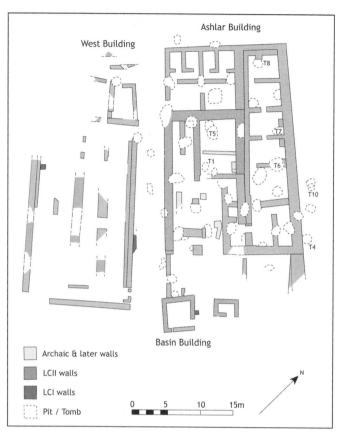

Figure 100. Maroni *Vournes* plan, showing the Ashlar, West and Basin Buildings. After Manning 1998b: 52, fig. 4. Redrawn by Luke Sollars.

1989: 38–40, pl. 13, figs. 60–63). Immediately west of Building X lay Tomb 11, with its abundant gold jewellery (see below, Figure 116), imported goods and luxury items, all demonstrating the accumulated wealth and long-distance connections of local élites at *Ayios Dhimitrios* (South 2000). The size, layout and contents of Building X suggest that it served centralised administrative and storage functions, and played a prominent role in the life of the community and surrounding region.

At Maroni *Vournes*, the 600 m² 'Ashlar Building', with a tripartite plan, had walls up to 2 m thick, and various rooms that contained an olive press, a construction with a sunken *pithos* and a central area likely used for storage. Standing on a low hillock, the Ashlar Building would have been visible far and wide, 'designed to impress' as the excavator put it (Cadogan 1996: 16–17). Both the Ashlar Building and its near, also monumental neighbour, the 'West Building' (Figure 100), revealed a range of evidence for storage and production activities – metalworking, olive-oil processing, weaving, writing (Cadogan 1989; 1996). The 'Basin Building', at the southwestern end of the Ashlar Building, contained some copper debris and possibly had an industrial function. Because

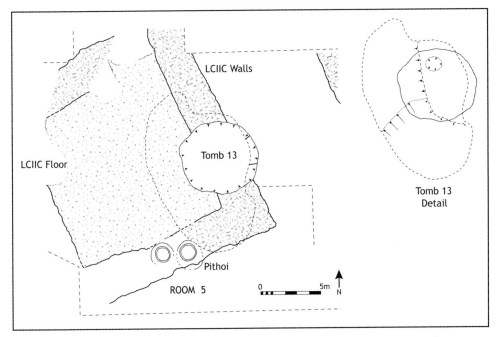

Figure 101. Maroni *Tsaroukkas* Tomb 13 (ProBA 2) and overbuilt structures. After Manning 1998: 48, fig. 3. Redrawn by Luke Sollars.

both the Basin and Ashlar buildings were constructed during ProBA 2 in areas previously used as cemeteries, Manning (1998b: 51) suggested that a dominant social group may have sought to legitimise their authority by erecting monumental structures over the tombs of other, competing groups, thus appealing to ancestral authority (Figure 101). All these buildings, perhaps even the tombs beneath some of them, may be regarded as monumental constructions that served élite administrative, industrial, storage and possibly ceremonial functions.

Building II At Alassa *Paleotaverna* is a massive, 1,400 m², π-shaped structure with north, south and west wings enclosing an inner courtyard and portico (Figure 102). It was constructed of large, well-preserved ashlar blocks, and its northern, outer wall contains two courses of ashlar orthostats with towing bosses (Hadjisavvas 2003: 31–33 and fig. 2) (Figure 103). The internal layout of Building II is unique amongst the excavated remains of ProBA Cyprus. In the south wing was a pair of small rooms (one designated a 'bathroom') that opened onto a large rectangular space termed the 'Hearth Room' (Hadjisavvas 1996: 32; 2003: 33); this room had a monolithic square block (the hearth) and the remnants of fine, slender pillars. The central placement of this hearth in such a monumental setting gives it a certain level of symbolic cachet; Fisher (2009: 200, 202–203, fig. 9) regards this hearth-centred setting as an 'ideologically-charged space' where high-level, 'public-inclusive' interactions would have taken place.

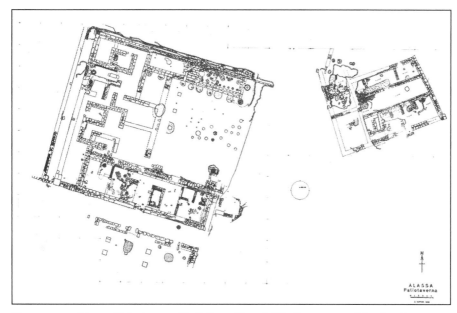

Figure 102. Alassa *Paleotaverna* Buildings II and III. Courtesy of Sophocles Hadjisavvas.

Figure 103. Alassa *Paleotaverna* Building II, showing northern, outer wall with two courses of ashlar orthostats and towing bosses. View to the east-southeast. Photograph by A. Bernard Knapp.

Figure 104. Alassa *Pano Mandilares* seal impression (on *Pithos* sherd), showing a horse-drawn chariot and bull-hunting scene. Courtesy of Sophocles Hadjisavvas.

The large central court of Building II, just to the north and nearly 400 m² in size, would have been an appropriate venue for such interactions. In the north wing was a long, rectangular storage area with a double row of at least 16 large *pithoi* resting on stone bases set in circular depressions in the floor. Several *pithos* sherds impressed with chariot and hunting or combat scenes were recovered from Building II (Figure 104). Due east of Building II and directly associated with it lay Building III, another large, at least 400 m² structure. A long narrow storage room in its northern sector, with a probable wine press and more *pithos* sherds (some impressed with bull and chariot scenes), suggests that Building III functioned as a production and storage annex or 'subsidiary' to Building II (Steel 2003–04: 96–97; Hadjisavvas 2009: 130, 133, fig. 3). The monumental structures at *Paleotaverna* reveal clear evidence for the production of wine and the storage of olive oil; their impressive size, layout and contents also point to administrative, industrial and likely domestic functions.

Enkomi *Ayios Iakovos* is a key site in all discussions of the ProBA, from town planning and origins, to international connections, to monumental architecture (Wright 1992: 85–86) (Figure 105). Beyond the ProBA 1 fortress already discussed above, two other prominent, monumental buildings, ProBA 2 in date, lie in the heart of the excavated area: (1) the 'Ashlar Building' in Quartier 4W (Dikaios's Area I) and 'Batiment 18' in Quartier 5W (Schaeffer 1952: 239–369; Dikaios 1969: 171–220; Courtois et al. 1986: 18–20). Both buildings had a central entrance hall with spacious rooms on either side, and both have been interpreted as élite dwellings (Wright 1992: 87, 103). Batiment 18 (about 1,800 m²) appears to date to the very end of the 13th century BC (ProBA 2), when its rebuilders incorporated some finely dressed stone masonry into the structure

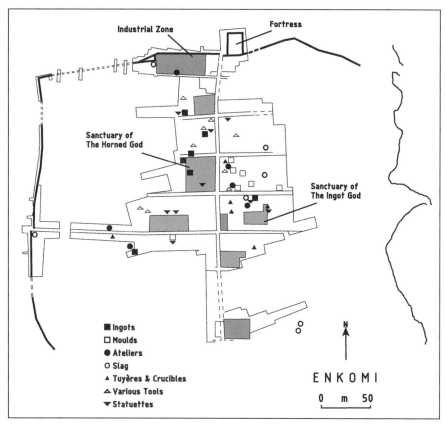

Figure 105. Enkomi site plan showing various architectural and archaeometal-lurgical features. After Courtois 1982: 156, fig. 1. Redrawn by Luke Sollars.

(Courtois et al. 1986: 20); a series of massive ashlar blocks adorns its south façade (Fisher 2009: 193, fig. 4).

The Ashlar Building (925 m²) was rebuilt during the ProBA 3 period (LC IIIA) with the extensive use of cut-stone masonry, a change that prompted its now widely known name (Figure 106). Fisher (2006: 127–128; 2009: 200) has argued convincingly that the ashlar-built, residential and administrative sectors of this structure were grouped around a central hall (Room 14) that contained a large, formal hearth. This elaborately constructed and ideologically charged space was likely used by élites for important social occasions ('public-inclusive' interactions).

In the southern part of the building were two 'sanctuaries', named after figurines found within them (Sanctuary of the Horned God; Sanctuary of the Double Goddess); both belonged to Level IIIB. The Horned God sanctuary (or 'West Megaron') was a large pillared hall (Room 45, 60 m²) embellished with hearths (Dikaios 1969–1971: 194–199). Leading off this hall to the east were two small, interconnected rooms (9, 10), the latter and easternmost of which contained the statue of the Horned God (for a discussion of

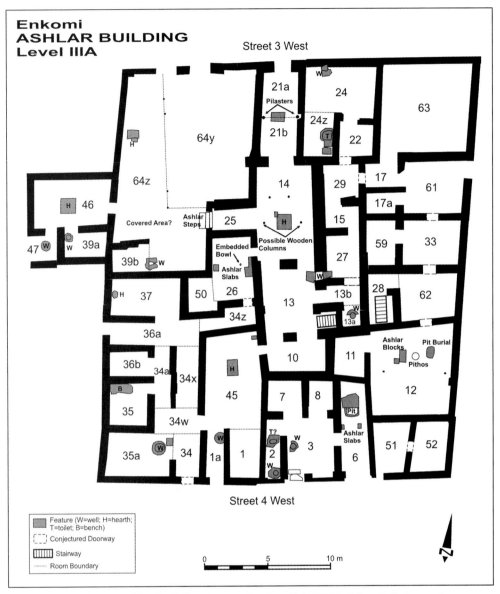

Figure 106. Enkomi Ashlar Building isometric plan (LC IIIA). After Dikaios 1969–1971: pls. 274, 277. Courtesy of Kevin Fisher.

the complex stratigraphy involved here, see Webb 1999: 98–99 and fig. 40) (Figure 107). Fisher (2009: 190–191, fig. 3, 194–195) suggests that the main hall in this part of the structure (Room 45) would have hosted 'public-inclusive' ceremonies associated with the Horned God, whilst Room 10 was a 'private-exclusive' place entered through the liminal space of Room 9. Just east of Room 10 but entirely separate from it lay Room 11, entered via the large 'East Megaron' (Room 12) or 'Sanctuary of the Double Goddess' (Dikaios 1969–1971: 199–200). A shallow pit in Room 11 held the 'double goddess', a small (5.5 cm high), double-sided bronze statuette depicting a nude female

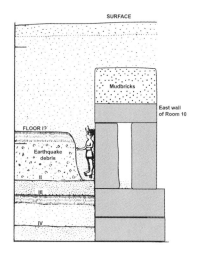

Figure 107. Enkomi, locus of the 'Horned God' in the sanctuary of the same name (Webb 1999: 98–99 and fig. 40). Courtesy of Jennifer Webb.

Figure 108. Enkomi, 'Ingot god' figurine (Quartier 5E). Cyprus Museum, Nicosia; French Mission 1963, no. 16.15. Courtesy of the Cyprus Museum, Nicosia.

with hands held to her breasts (Dikaios 1969–1971: 721, no. 271, pl. 171:52; Webb 1999: 233, fig. 80.4).

The Sanctuary of the Ingot God – centrally situated in Quartier 5E at Enkomi – was erected at some point during ProBA 3 (Webb 1999: 102; 2001: 77–80). Its special-purpose nature is based more on its contents and élite associations than on building materials, as all its walls were built of rubble. Near the centre of the hall was a large stone block identified as a sacrificial table, just northwest of which was a pierced block that could have been used for tethering sacrificial animals. This structure produced the largest, most diverse array of objects found in any ceremonial structure on Cyprus (Webb 2001: 69), including the eponymous statue of the Ingot God (Figure 108). The rich variety of material goods found in the Sol ('floor') III horizon of this structure, alongside extensive evidence of animal sacrifices, led Webb (2001: 78) to conclude that '…ritual practice was in the hands of an established urban élite intent upon conspicuous display and the manipulation of unique objects and images'.

Excavations by multiple teams over nearly 50 years at Enkomi (before 1974) produced several monumental, special-purpose structures that served a multitude of functions. Webb (1999: 91–149) believes that only the three 'sanctuaries' discussed here – those of the Horned God, the Ingot God and the Double Goddess – are accurately identified. Within these complexes, large formal hearths bear witness to food preparation and feasting activities, important elements in the creation of monumental places and the promotion of social occasions that supported Enkomi's élites (Fisher 2009: 200–201). Both the Ashlar Building (ProBA 3) and Baitement 18 (ProBA 2) have been interpreted as élite residences, whilst the fortress (ProBA 1) is thought to have served administrative, domestic and industrial functions. No excavated site exemplifies better the diversity of functions served by the monumental structures of ProBA Cyprus.

The only monumental structure known at Kouklia *Palaipaphos*, in the island's southwest, is 'Sanctuary' I, founded late in LC IIC and thus dated to the ProBA 3 period (Maier and Karageorghis 1984: 53, fig. 28; Rupp 1981: 256; Maier 1986: 313). Excavated by a Swiss-German team between 1973–1978 (Maier and von Wartburg 1985: 149–150; see also Maier and Karageorghis 1984: 81–102), the remnants of Sanctuary I consist of a hall (250 m²) to the north, with two parallel rows of six square stone bases (probably for pillars to support a roof). Inside this hall were two rock-cut pits and a rectangular basin. To the south stood an open courtyard (approximately 400 m² in extent) enclosed by a substantial wall of large, dressed limestone orthostats raised on a pediment of rectangular blocks (Figure 109). A shallow limestone basin, directly aligned with the western entry, was the only intact feature in the courtyard; other finds included some fragmentary stepped capital blocks, two pairs of horns of consecration, a terracotta basin, a large *pithos* with wavy-line decoration and a seal-impressed handle, some local pottery and a small Canaanite jar.

A few terracotta female figurines (Type 'B' – Karageorghis 1993: 22) are reported from the sanctuary itself (Maier and von Wartburg 1985: 150 and pl. V:3), whilst excavations some 35 m to the west produced three other female figurines (Webb 1999: 61). The long association of Cyprus's southwest with the Greek goddess Aphrodite, and the foundation of her temple by the mythological Kinyras, the first high priest of the goddess (Maier 1986), has ensured that the site's main monumental structure would become known as a sanctuary. The limited number of finds and features associated with this complex, however, suggest diverse functions: industrial, storage and ceremonial. Above all, Sanctuary I at *Palaipaphos*, with its fine ashlar masonry and diverse monumental features (the dressed limestone orthostat blocks, stepped capital blocks,

Figure 109. Kouklia *Palaipaphos*, 'Sanctuary' I (ProBA 3), with dressed limestone ortho-stat blocks of the courtyard. Photograph by A. Bernard Knapp.

pillared hall), displays architectural elements as impressive as those found in any of the other monumental structures on ProBA Cyprus.

In the southeastern part of the island, Hala Sultan Tekke *Vyzakia* and Kition *Kathari* likely served as major ports, but were situated in such close proximity that they must have served multiple or different functions. Kition, to be sure, contains far more extensive evidence of monumentality; Hala Sultan Tekke has only one notable ashlar structure (Building C) in the area excavated (another, even larger structure is reported from recent, 2010 and 2011 excavations at the site – see Fischer 2011: 78–80).

Taking Kition first: its monumental architecture is imposing and quite complex. There were two main sectors of excavation (Areas I and II) with a series of occupation levels (Floors I–IV). Area I, first occupied towards the end of ProBA 2 (Floor IV), produced evidence of residential and industrial use (Karageorghis and Demas 1985[I]: 4–10). Area II is regarded as a 'sacred precinct' that was reorganised extensively at the outset of ProBA 3 (Floor IIIA, early 12th century BC) (Figure 110). Spread over about 5,500 m², this precinct embraced 'Temples' 1, 2, 4 and 5, as well as '*Temene*' A and B (Floors IIIA, III and II – Webb 1999: 66, fig. 22 provides a useful illustration). Workshops in the northern (metallurgical) and western (weaving and textile manufacture) areas

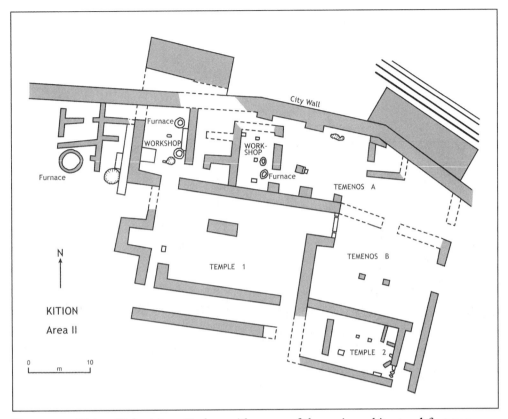

Figure 110. Kition *Kathari* Area II plan, with some of the main architectural features (Temples 1, 2, *Temene* A, B) and archaeometallurgical installations. After Karageorghis 1976: 63–64, fig. 11). Redrawn by Luke Sollars.

of the site were clearly associated with Temple 1 and Temenos A but the nature of that association is uncertain (Smith 2009: 34–51).

Temples 1 and 2 were both ashlar-based or -enhanced constructions, whilst *Temene* A and B formed an integrated unit in the western sector of the precinct (Karageorghis and Demas 1985[1]: 38–65; for a detailed discussion of these buildings and their contents, see Smith 2009: 51–70). Temple 1 (some 500 m²), oriented east–west and built with long stretches of large ashlar blocks, contained a main rectangular hall with three narrow rooms to the west, a long narrow room to the south, and a grand, ashlar-decorated entryway in the northeast corner, leading to Temenos B. Temenos A (350 m²), linked directly to the northern workshops, lies northeast of Temple 1 and between (north of) Temenos B and the city wall. Temenos B (260 m²), immediately south of Temenos A and providing access on its west to Temple 1, contained a large open courtyard with three pillar bases running down its centre, and a grand porch to the east enclosed by ashlar walls and threshold (see Callot's somewhat embellished reconstructions, in Karageorghis and Demas 1985(I): 237–239, figs. 67–71).

Figure 111. Hala Sultan Tekke *Vyzakia* site view, looking northeast. The modern town of Larnaca is in the background. Photograph by A. Bernard Knapp.

Temples 4 and 5 at Kition were situated in the eastern sector of the precinct, and were separated from the other structures by a street and a large open area (Courtyard A) just inside the northern city wall (Karageorghis and Demas 1985(I): 65–77, 108–112, plan XXIV). Like Courtyard A, Temple 4 was also built against the city wall: it is a small (125 m²) ashlar structure, with a large central hall in the west and three smaller rooms to the east. A doorway in its southwest corner gave access to Courtyard A, whilst another in the southeast led to Room 39, a large open area, possibly a courtyard paved with stone slabs. Just south of Temple 4 lay Temple 5 (235 m²), which contained another large, main hall, a narrow inner room to the west, and courtyards to the east and south. The special-purpose, élite nature of the entire 'sacred precinct' (Area II) at Kition seems clear enough, but this area also served industrial (copper refining, weaving) if not administrative functions (also Smith 2009: 53, 67), whilst Area I was devoted to both residential and industrial uses.

Hala Sultan Tekke *Vyzakia*, by contrast, appears to be a well-organised, grid-planned settlement with distinctive houses. Directly accessible from the sea during the ProBA, this settlement site served as a prominent international harbour (Figure 111), attested by an array of imported goods from the Aegean, Anatolia, the Levant and Egypt (Åström 1996). Within Area 8 several structures open onto a 4-m-wide, north–south street; some show a selective use of ashlar masonry. Building C (approximately 135 m²), by no means 'monumental' in size, is the most prominent, with a large forecourt (and well) that gave access to an inner courtyard onto which rooms opened from the south and west. The full building complex contained a range of imported Mycenaean and Canaanite pottery, lead ingots and plaques, a bronze arrowhead and crushed murex shells; a silver bowl with an Ugaritic inscription was recovered nearby (Åström 1985; 1986: 11–13, figs. 11–14). The excavator suggested that Building C might have been a merchant's house (Åström 1996: 12).

Whilst the domestic, industrial and mercantile nature of most structures in Area 8 at Hala Sultan Tekke seems evident, two room complexes – one immediately west of Building C, the other in the southernmost part of Area 8 – have been singled out as possible 'sanctuaries' (Webb 1999: 127–130). Renewed excavations at the site, begun in 2010, concentrated on Area 6 (north and east of Area 8), where no complete structures had been found during earlier test soundings (Åström et al. 2001; Fischer 2011: 69). A large building complex, approximately 600 m² in area, was uncovered, with an external wall some 25 m in length, 0.8 m wide and preserved in places to a height of 0.7 m (Fischer 2011: 78, 76, fig. 8). Within this structure, parts of nine walled rooms – with some ashlar architectural elements including a threshold – have been uncovered; these appear to be both working and living areas. Amongst the many reported finds are spindle whorls and loomweights; copper slag and lead; jewellery, tools and weapons of bronze; two lead sling bullets; many examples of locally made fine wares, a Canaanite jar and a few Mycenaean imports (Fischer 2011: figs. 9–17). According to the excavator, the wide range of material culture found in these rooms points to habitational, industrial, storage and administrative activities.

Excavations carried out at Myrtou *Pigadhes* in the island's northwest between 1949 and 1951 uncovered a large complex of rooms with a major courtyard area (Du Plat Taylor 1957: 3–23, 103–112). This complex was categorised as a 'sanctuary' and cult centre, dated to the ProBA 3 period but with ProBA 2 antecedents (Webb 1999: 35–37, 44–53, figs. 8, 13–14). Largely rubble-built, this complex was divided by a north–south running street (Figure 112). To the west, a spacious rectangular courtyard (230 m²) enveloped by a series of smaller rooms contained a monumental, stepped stone, ashlar-dressed construction identified as an 'altar' (Du Plat Taylor 1957: 12–18, figs. 8–11); this feature was crowned with a reconstructed, and thus hypothetical set of horns of consecration (Ionas 1985). East of the courtyard and across the street lay a large, freestanding, multi-roomed but integrated structure, approximately 320 m² in size. This building was centred on an internal courtyard (Rooms 12–14, 21), entered through a corridor to the east (Rooms 25, 15) and divided by a partition wall from three other rooms (10, 11, 23) to the west.

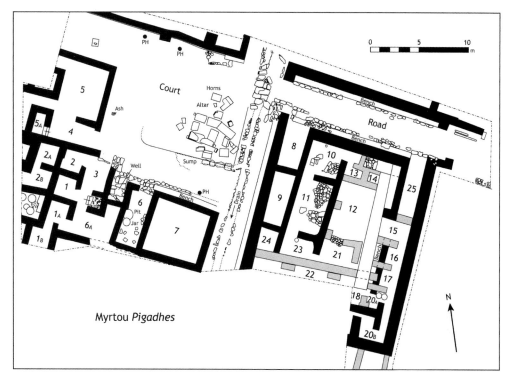

Figure 112. Myrtou *Pigadhes* 'sanctuary' complex, Periods V–VI (ProBA 2). After Du Plat
Taylor 1957: 11, fig. 7. Redrawn by Luke Sollars.

The excavated finds from *Pigadhes* are striking; from the western sector came
some Late Helladic IIIB/C imports, a small bronze bull and two complete terracotta bulls, many wall brackets, three cylinder seals (one of Mitannian style),
a fragmentary 'offering stand', a faience bowl, several groundstone tools, two
bronze daggers and two bronze knives (Webb 1999: 47–53 provides a useful
summary). One room (16) in the eastern sector contained some evidence of
metallurgical activity (Du Plat Taylor 1957: 20, fig. 12), and Muhly (1989: 302)
mentions the existence of furnace conglomerate amongst the material from
Pigadhes stored in the Cyprus Museum. The eastern sector was equally rich in
finds, which ranged from Mycenaean pottery to human and animal representations, to cylinder seals and a range of metal goods. Hadjisavvas (1992: 21–23,
fig. 38) noted that one of a series of rooms lying just south of the eastern sector
contained an olive-oil press.

Given the wide array of local goods and materials, several special imports,
evidence for metallurgical and other industrial activities, as well as the grand
stepped-stone construction, the monumental complex at Myrtou *Pigadhes*
clearly served multiple functions – storage, production and transport – and
it would be too restrictive to define it strictly as a ceremonial site. In fact
Keswani (1993: 81 n. 4) once suggested that *Pigadhes* might also have served as

Figure 113. Phlamoudhi *Melissa* site view, looking north (Smith 2008: 48, fig. 25). Courtesy of Joanna S. Smith for the Columbia University Expedition to Phlamoudhi Photo Archive.

a copper ore transhipment point, whilst Webb (1999: 287) argued that its monumentality, diversity of finds and 'cultic' equipment may point to an inland primary centre, not unlike those at *Ayios Dhimitrios* and *Paleotaverna*.

Excavations at the site of Phlamoudhi *Melissa*, near the north coast at the base of the Karpass Peninsula, were conducted during the 1970s; they have only been published recently, thanks to the efforts of a research team led by Joanna Smith (2008a) that was not involved in the original excavations (Figure 113). Despite the difficulties imposed by this situation, it seems clear that the ProBA 2 (LC IIC) 'courtyard building' measured somewhere between 500–900 m². It was thus similar in size to either the Ashlar Building at Maroni *Vournes* or Building X at *Ayios Dhimitrios*; it may also have served a similar storage function, as fragments of more than 35 large *pithoi* were found (Smith 2008a: 52–53, 59). The preserved parts of the building during Phases 5–7 (ProBA 2–3, LC IIB–C) show limited use of ashlar masonry, in specific parts of the building (pillar supports, ends of walls, thresholds, alongside the pebble floor, parts of a carved capital) (Smith 2008a: 57–58). Through time, this structure served more than one function, but most were industrial or administrative in nature: storage (olive oil?), pottery manufacture

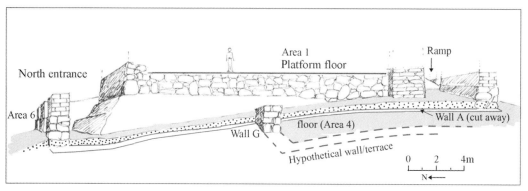

Figure 114. Phlamoudhi *Vounari*, reconstruction of platform and associated structure, Phase 5 (ProBA 1) (Smith 2008: 77, fig. 49). Drawing by M.T. Horowitz. Courtesy of Joanna S. Smith for the Columbia University Expedition to Phlamoudhi Photo Archive.

(Red-on-Black/Red, Black Slip), metallurgical and textile production (Smith 2008a: 61–64). The small, approximately 250 m² platform and associated structure at nearby Phlamoudhi *Vounari*, built in a conspicuous setting on a hilltop, is no longer regarded simply as a 'sanctuary' but rather as a 'multi-function', tertiary-level site focused on storage, distribution and perhaps some 'feasting' activities (Horowitz 2008: 80–82) (Figure 114).

The remains at Athienou *Bamboulari tis Koukounninas* (Dothan and Ben-Tor 1983) in the southeast *Mesaoria* defy easy interpretation. Within Stratum III (ProBA 2), excavations uncovered a large architectural complex (some 2,500 m² in extent) with a rectangular court (320 m²) flanked by two smaller rooms to the northwest and northeast; beyond these were some pits and metallurgical debris. The same complex continued in use during Stratum II (ProBA 3) but with structural modifications, including the addition of platforms to the east and northeast, defined by the excavators as copper working installations (Dothan and Ben-Tor 1983: 140). Maddin et al. (1983: 136–138; also Stech 1982: 107), however, argued that primary copper smelting never took place at Athienou, only secondary processing and refining. Moreover, at least 11 large *pithoi* found on or near the eastern platform suggest that this was an olive-oil storage area, and storage thus may have played a major economic role at Athienou (Keswani 1993: 78). At least 2,000 intact pottery vessels, and fragments of up to 8,000 more, were found within the Stratum III courtyard and small northwest room. Both miniature and full-sized vessels (typically Base-ring I jugs and White Shaved juglets) were recovered, but the miniatures predominate: a small number imitate regular-sized Late Cypriot and Late Helladic types but a much larger group (handmade, coarse ware juglets) has no counterparts amongst typical Late Cypriot wares (Webb 1999: 22). Åström (1987) suggested that the votive vessels might have been used in ritual feasting ceremonies.

Whatever the differences of opinion held by the excavators and the archae-ometallurgists who worked at Athienou (for which see Knapp 2008: 234–235), it seems evident that most metalworking activities at Athienou took place during ProBA 2, less so during ProBA 3, a situation that holds true the island over (Muhly 1985b: 34 and nn. 93–98; cf. Webb 1999: 29). The thousands of (mostly miniature, votive) pottery vessels from Stratum III (ProBA 2) were found in association with an array of other specialised objects, including the bronze model of a chariot (Schaeffer 1969: 276, pl. 21b). From contemporary pits to the east of the main complex came more exotic objects: an elaborately decorated ivory rhyton, cylinder seals, an Egyptian scarab, a fibula and a situla handle, and beads of faience, carnelian and steatite. Overall, the large archi-tectural complex (whether or not a 'monumental' structure) and special finds suggest specialised industrial and ceremonial activities at Athienou. Moreover, the spatial association between metallurgical installations and special-purpose structures is hard to deny (Knapp 1986b: 43–56).

Although no monumental structures were found at Pyla *Kokkinokremos* or Maa *Palaeokastro*, some structures at Maa – Building I, Area II, an ashlar con-struction, and Building II (80 m²) – have been interpreted as élite residences (e.g. Wright 1992: 322). All construction at Pyla was of traditional, rubble type, and no ashlar masonry was found in the approximately 400 m² area excavated in the 1980s (a new campaign began in 2010). Sherratt (1998: 300–301 n. 15) suggested that Pyla and Maa may have been 'bypass and outflanking centres' serving mercantile élites who had broken away, respectively, from Kition and *Palaipaphos* in an attempt to set up their own power bases. And, as already noted, Karageorghis (1998a) believes that Maa and Pyla served as strongholds. Pyla, at least, more likely served as a transport centre to ensure the movement of imported goods – of which it contained several – from coast to inland. Whatever their functions may have been, with the possible exception of Building I at Maa, the excavated structures at both sites lack the typical mon-umental features seen at other ProBA sites.

Monumental structures can express power as well as mask it; they serve as physical manifestations of social order and collective will (Parker Pearson and Richards 1994: 3). The building of large, complex structures required a long-term commitment as well as the ability to control resources and coordinate substantial investments of labour (DeMarrais et al. 1996: 18–19, 31). On ProBA Cyprus, the time and energy invested in monumental architecture, tomb con-structions, feasting, mortuary practices, and producing or consuming exotic goods reflect the central importance to Cypriot élites of establishing a corpo-rate identity and perpetuating the group's social memory. Certain ceremonial or symbolic places were crucial for Cypriot élites in establishing and express-ing their identity, in wielding politico-economic power and authority, and in reinforcing social institutions and social memory. Like shrines or sanctuar-ies, monumental buildings and tombs were social spaces where ceremonial activities were carried out, memories established and social identity made manifest.

The social interactions that took place within the monumental structures of ProBA Cyprus were instrumental in the ways that people within the towns negotiated their identity and formed their individual or collective social memories (Fisher 2009: 204). Like identity and memory, ideology represents a key aspect of everyone's social reality. Not all members of a society share the dominant ideology, and people's identities, memories and practices may result in further social divisions. The material markers of ideology, memory and identity include first and foremost monumental architecture, but also exotic pottery, textiles, costumes, regalia and colour symbolism (in narrative sculptures, wall paintings, metals) (Barber 1991: 373–376; Hosler 1995; DeMarrais et al. 1996; Jones and MacGregor 2002: 12–15). Such 'things' indicate how symbolism and material design meet in archaeological contexts, linking monumental architecture, imagery and human action in marking social identity and creating social memory.

During the ProBA on Cyprus, élite identity and ideology were intimately linked to monumentality, tomb construction, mortuary ritual and the consumption of exotica. Much of the symbolism evident on ProBA figurines, seals, metal goods and pottery is associated with copper production and distribution (Knapp 1986a). All of these material and social practices – erecting monumental buildings, constructing tombs for elders and ancestors, making and using figurines and seals, producing copper, olive oil and textiles – formed part of the islanders' social memory and fed into the construction of a unique, Cypriote, island identity. Let us now look in more detail at some of these material and social practices, before turning to consider the islanders' wider social world.

MATERIAL AND SOCIAL PRACTICES

Mortuary Practices

Several different scholars have treated at length the materials and monuments associated with mortuary practices during the ProBA (e.g. Goring 1989; Bolger 2003: 165–182; Keswani 2004: 84–144, 154–160). The extramural, collective burials seen during the PreBA diminished as social divisions between different groups widened in the ProBA. Intramural burials became much more common, and grave goods much richer. The inclusion in various ProBA burials of luxury items, precious metals and exotic imports (ivory, glass, faience, ostrich egg containers), many of which bear regal imagery from Egypt, western Asia or the Aegean, points to their use in accentuating identities (élite or otherwise), establishing social or political hierarchies, and perpetuating ancestral memories.

Mortuary rituals continued to reproduce status differentials, but mortuary practices themselves no longer served as the only way to express one's (élite) identity; nor were burial grounds the only or even the preferred venue for expressing social reproduction. With the centralisation of political authority came the possibility of using other ways and other media to express wealth, power and social status: monumental architecture, luxury goods and imports, élite representations, seals and sealings. By the end of the 13th century Cal BC (transition to ProBA 3, LC IIC–LC IIIA), burials show considerable variation in wealth or status, and small groups or even individuals came to be interred in shaft graves (Keswani 2004: 159). These new trends in mortuary practice perhaps followed inevitably from the collapse of long-standing economic links and sociopolitical patterns that undermined the stability of polities throughout the Aegean and eastern Mediterranean.

On Cyprus, however, these same events seem to have created new opportunities for redefining one's identity, establishing social status and accumulating wealth. By the 11th century BC (LC IIIB), extramural cemeteries once again became common, along with new, more elaborate forms of chamber tombs. Cremation as well as inhumation burials are attested, and communal burial grounds took on new significance, at least to judge from the large deposits of metal, ceramic and luxury goods deposited within them (Steel 1995; Raptou 2002; Keswani 2004: 160). Mortuary rituals and display thus once again assumed crucial importance in negotiating island identities during the early Iron Age.

Looking more closely at various aspects of ProBA mortuary practices, the most striking change was the shift from extramural to intramural burials. Whilst a few earlier, extramural cemeteries continued in use (e.g. Deneia – Åström and Wright 1962; Frankel and Webb 2007; Katydhata – Åström 1989; Boutin et al. 2003), new ones were established at Ayia Irini *Paleokastro* (Pecorella 1977), Myrtou *Stephania* (Hennessy 1964) and Akhera *Çiflik Paradisi* (Karageorghis 1965a). Older practices of collective burial and secondary treatment continued, albeit on a larger scale, at Enkomi (Swedish Tombs 6 and 18 – Gjerstad et al. 1934: 491–497, 546–549), Ayios Iakovos *Melia* (Gjerstad et al. 1934: 325–355) and Pendayia *Mandres* (Karageorghis 1965b). In a walled area just east of the 'fortress' at Korovia *Nitovikla* lay a unique arrangement of at least 15 tombs (Hult 1992: 43–47). Although some of the shaft graves that made their appearance during ProBA 3 contained wealthy, élite burials (e.g. at Enkomi, Swedish Graves 11a, 15 and 16 – Gjerstad et al. 1934: 510–525, 537–540, and Cypriot Grave 24 – Dikaios 1969: 433–434; Niklasson-Sönnerby 1987), in general there seems to have been a decrease in the number of burial goods and in the time expended on tomb construction (Keswani 2004: 85, 119–120).

One obvious change from all earlier periods is the variety of tomb types characteristic of the ProBA. This is most evident at Enkomi (Keswani 1989: 52–56) where there are rock-cut chamber tombs (most common), *tholos* tombs (ProBA 1–2 in date – Courtois et al. 1986: 49–50), rectangular, ashlar-built

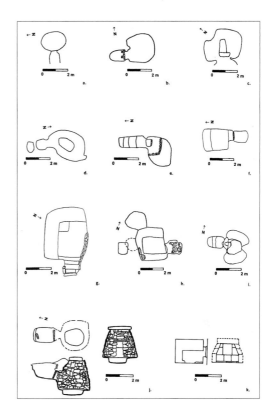

Figure 115. Enkomi, multiple tomb types of the ProBA (after Keswani 2004: 111, fig. 5.3).

tombs (all ProBA 2 in date – Courtois et al. 1986: 24–26), as well as pit graves, pot burials of infants and shaft graves (ProBA 3 only – Keswani 2004: 93) (Figure 115). Enkomi British Tomb 66 (=French Tomb 1322), the only ashlar-built tomb found intact, contained numerous gold, bronze, faience and other exotic items. Fragmentary gold finds from two *tholos* tombs (looted before excavation – Enkomi Swedish Tomb 21, British Tomb 71) also must have held high status burials.

Situated in various sectors of Enkomi, the *tholos* tombs are unlikely to represent the burials of any specific residential or social group. They seem to be variations on the standard Cypriot rock-cut chamber tomb, but they might also represent Cypriot adaptations of Aegean, or even Levantine prototypes. By contrast, because all the ashlar-built tombs at Enkomi were found in Quartiers 3E and 4E in association with well-built residential structures, Keswani (2004: 115) suggested they may have belonged to a single élite group. Both the *tholos* and ashlar-built tombs may have been inspired by foreign designs, the latter by the larger and more elaborate ashlar tombs found beneath élite households in Ugarit (Salles 1995). Nonetheless, rock-cut chamber tombs in other parts of Enkomi (e.g. French Tomb 2 – Schaeffer 1952: 111–135; British Tombs 19, 67 and 93 – Murray et al. 1900; Swedish Tomb 8 – Gjerstad et al. 1934) have comparable if not wealthier burial assemblages than their foreign counterparts, suggesting that neither the ashlar-built nor the *tholos* tombs were built solely for the use of élites.

Intramural tombs are found in most excavated ProBA settlements, and are situated in diverse contexts: residential, administrative, even in workshops (Keswani 2004: 85, 87–88). For example, at Enkomi (Dikaios 1969–1971: 418–434), Alassa *Pano Mandilares* (Hadjisavvas 1989: 35, 39–40; 1991: 173–176 and fig. 17.3) and Episkopi *Bamboula* (Benson 1972: 3–4, 9), various tombs were placed either beneath streets or in domestic courtyards. The four élite tombs excavated at *Ayios Dhimitrios* (nos. 11, 14, 13 and 21) were also constructed below a street just west of the monumental Building X (South 1997: 161; 2000: 348) (see above, Figure 98). Because excavations at *Ayios Dhimitrios* have shown a continuous stratigraphic and architectural sequence throughout the ProBA 2 period, the juxtaposition of this élite public structure and the élite tombs seems to have been planned. Moreover, the regular alignment of these tombs along a north–south running street, the Mycenaean kraters found in Tombs 11, 13 and 14, and the segregation of male and female burials may all hint at the mortuary program of a distinct élite group, spatially differentiated from others at the site (Bolger 2003: 172).

Tomb 11 at *Ayios Dhimitrios* – which held three young women, the bones of a three-year-old child and three newborn infants – was exceptionally rich (Goring 1989; South 1997: 159–161; 2000: 349–353). The remains of the three women had been placed on two benches cut into the rock on either side of the entry to the tomb chamber, whilst the bones of the child and infants were found on the floor, near the benches. The skeleton of one young female was fully articulated and covered with gold, silver and glass jewellery (Figure 116). Whilst the other two women's skeletons were disarticulated and incomplete, they too were adorned with jewellery, ivory and other precious items. Bolger (2003: 172) emphasised the sexual segregation in the mortuary deposits at *Ayios Dhimitrios*, and argued that Tomb 11 was one of the most prestigious female mortuary deposits known on prehistoric Cyprus. In addition to these remains, a small niche in the *dromos* of Tomb 11 contained the partial remains of another infant and an adult, together with a large bronze ring and a Base-ring I juglet (South 2000: 352). A small chamber near the entrance to the tomb (separately designated Tomb 9), held a nearly complete infant's skeleton and a few ivory fragments.

The women interred in Tomb 11 were accompanied by some of the most exquisite and extraordinary grave goods known from prehistoric Cyprus. Amongst the 177 registered items were 12 gold earrings (six each found with the women on the two benches, and nearly standardised in weight, at 10.8 grams), two gold finger rings with Cypro-Minoan signs and other motifs, two silver toe rings, four gold spirals, and a double-sided stone stamp seal. Ceramic evidence includes 'sets' (of two) Mycenaean kraters and piriform jars, pedestalled Base-ring bowls and almost identical Base-ring bull-shaped vessels; a

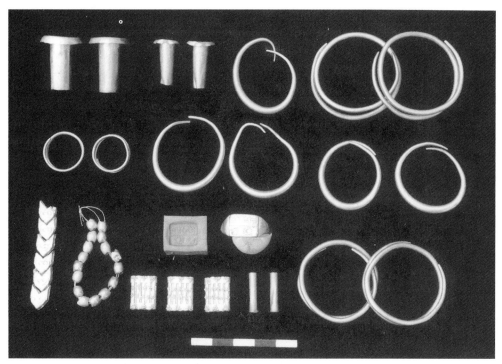

Figure 116. Kalavasos *Ayios Dhimitrios* Tomb 11, miscellaneous gold jewellery accompanying the burials. Courtesy of Alison South and the Cyprus Museum, Nicosia.

group of three very similar White Slip II bowls; and at least 17 Red Lustrous spindle bottles and five lentoid flasks. Other notable items include Egyptian glass jars and duck-shaped ivory vessels. Much of the gold jewellery showed signs of prior use, suggesting that these items were worn in life as well as in death, most likely as paraphernalia pointing to the wearer's social status and élite identity.

Yet another sumptuous female burial (a 36-year-old woman) of the ProBA was found in Enkomi's Swedish Tomb 18, a rock-cut chamber tomb. Interred with her were an array of gold jewellery, a bronze mirror and some bronze vessels, an ivory comb and several fragments of an ivory box (Fischer 1986: 36–37; Keswani 2004: 126). The latest burial in a multiple-chambered, ProBA tomb at Morphou *Toumba tou Skourou* belonged to a 25-year-old female (Vermeule and Wolsky 1990: 247–248); she was interred with gold beads, fragments of ivory boxes, a lapis lazuli cylinder seal with gold foil caps and Mycenaean pottery. The remains of earlier burials in this tomb had been moved to make way for hers.

Keswani (2004: 85–86) has suggested that ProBA burial practices reflect new urban attitudes to mortuary rituals, in which status differentials increasingly were based upon differential access to copper, traded goods and sociopolitical position. The evident fall-off in the amount of gold in ProBA 2–3 mortuary contexts at Enkomi (Keswani 1989: 66) seems to have been offset by an increase in the number of gold items used in ceremonial contexts within the settlement (Area I – Antoniadou 2004: 174, tables 156, 160). Although mortuary rituals thus continued to represent one means of reproducing status differentials and expressing social identity, mortuary practices themselves were no longer the only way, or the main venue, for such expressions.

Manning (1998b; Manning and Monks 1998), for example, has argued that as new production, craft and storage facilities developed at ProBA 2 Maroni (*Vournes* and *Tsaroukkas*), several earlier, élite tombs were emptied, destroyed or built over by new structures (the 'Ashlar Building' at *Vournes*, and Buildings 1 and 2 at *Tsaroukkas*) (see above, Figure 101). He sees such changes as the deliberate attempt by those who erected these new buildings to erase earlier memories and appropriate ancestral authority (Manning 1998b: 48–53). Similarly, Webb (1999: 287–288) interprets the destruction of ancestral burial plots such as those at *Vournes* or *Tsaroukkas*, and the 'conspicuous consumption' associated with it, as reflecting processes of domination and resistance between élites competing for political legitimacy. In Manning's (1998b: 51–54) view, these new constructions over earlier tombs and buildings suggest that the social authority associated with various ancestral groups now came under the control of a single ruling élite headed by a 'key individual in Cypriot prehistory', perhaps the king of *Alašiya* as known from contemporary cuneiform documents.

From yet another perspective, Keswani (1996: 236–237; 2004: 87–88) suggests that ProBA mortuary practices were linked to the social circumstances involved in the founding of new population centres. As already noted above, in coastal towns such as Enkomi, Morphou *Toumba tou Skourou* and perhaps Kition, the new settlers consisted of heterogeneous descent groups from different ancestral villages who lacked the sense of corporate identity that might be associated with communal, extramural burial grounds (Keswani 2004: 87). Thus they buried their dead close to their own houses or work areas, setting themselves apart from other, unrelated groups in the community. In inland towns with continuous sequences of prior occupation, however, the residents either built new ashlar structures directly above earlier tombs (as at Maroni *Vournes* and Kalavasos *Ayios Dhimitrios*), or else built new tombs along or beneath streets and open areas in everyday use (as at Episkopi *Bamboula*, Alassa *Pano Mandilares* and Kalavasos *Ayios Dhimitrios*).

The variety and quality of grave goods found in ProBA burials throughout the island, including imported items, indicates that mortuary practices and rituals still played an important role in establishing social status, signalling people's identity and maintaining the memory of ancestral groups. There is some disparity between the numbers and types of luxury or imported goods found in burials within the town centres and those from inland communities, of whatever type (Keswani 2004: 143). On the one hand, mortuary assemblages from towns such as Kition, Hala Sultan Tekke, *Ayios Dhimitrios*, Kourion, Kouklia

Palaipaphos, *Toumba tou Skourou* and Ayia Irini *Paleokastro* contain luxury goods of comparable quality, albeit in smaller amounts than those from Enkomi. On the other hand, mortuary finds from rural sites – such as (PreBA 2–ProBA 1) Erimi *Laonin tou Porakou* (Bombardieri 2009: 286–288; 2010; Bombardieri et al. 2009a: 138–140), (ProBA 1) Nicosia *Ayia Paraskevi* (Georgiou 2009), (ProBA 2) Politiko Tomb 6 (Karageorghis 1965c) or (ProBA 2–3) Akhera *Çiflik Paradisi* Tombs 2 and 3 (Karageorghis 1965a) – are made up of local pottery types, a few Mycenaean or Syrian vessels, limited amounts of ivory, faience or picrolite, some spindle whorls, locally made cylinder seals, and bronze weapons and ornaments. The recovery of a single fragmentary Mycenaean krater from Pera *Kryptides* (Åström 1972: 317) and a gold Hittite seal from nearby Politiko *Lambertis* (Buchholz and Untiedt 1996: 71, fig. 14a) only serves to highlight the paucity of higher order valuables in rural tombs of this period. Most prestige goods flowing into the hinterland probably involved subordinate exchange relationships, and were not the same as those involving higher status groups in the coastal centres (Keswani and Knapp 2003).

Grave goods from the town centres are quite remarkable, and include gold jewellery (earrings, hair-rings, finger rings, necklaces, diadems, etc. – Goring 1989), numerous metal objects (bronze spatulae and mirrors, silver bowls), as well as ivory, glass, faience and ostrich egg containers. Whilst some jewellery may have been made exclusively for funerary consumption (e.g. Lagarce and Lagarce 1986: 117–122), most items show signs of longer-term use (Keswani 2004: 138). Sets or single occurrences of balance weights from ProBA 1–2 tombs at Enkomi, Maroni, *Toumba tou Skourou* and Ayia Irini *Paleokastro* suggest some link with metallurgical factors. Also worthy of mention are the elaborately decorated Mycenaean chariot kraters found in high status tombs, which may have formed part of élite drinking sets (Steel 1998: 294–296). One very distinctive krater from Tomb 13 at *Ayios Dhimitrios* shows a woman standing in a building viewing a chariot group, with horses and fish flanking a structure topped by five pairs of 'horns of consecration' (Steel 1994b: 206, fig. 4) (Figure 117). From Tomb 21 at the same site came another Mycenaean krater depicting women exclusively; it was found in association with ivories, five gold diadems (or mouthpieces?) and some local pottery (South 2000: 362). The implication follows that women were closely associated with funerary activities, although this is no less than we would expect.

Imported Mycenaean alabastra and stirrup jars, as well as (locally made?) Red Lustrous ware spindle bottles or arm-shaped vessels are also found with some frequency in mortuary contexts; such vessels were likely used in ritual practices that involved anointing the deceased's body or the pouring of libations (Steel 1998: 294–296; cf. Webb 1992: 89). Other striking or unusual vessels – Mycenaean conical and zoomorphic rhyta, Base-ring bull rhyta, faience zoomorphic rhyta and cups – have been found in both ceremonial and mortuary contexts (Keswani 2004: 137). The striking ProBA 2 (LC IIC)

Figure 117. Kalavasos *Ayios Dhimitrios* Tomb 13, krater showing a woman looking out from a building. After Steel 1994b: 206, fig. 4. Courtesy of Alison South and the Cyprus Museum, Nicosia.

Figure 118. Enkomi British Tomb 58, relief-carved ivory gaming box. British Museum, London, Inventory 1897,0401.996 AN256187. © The Trustees of the British Museum.

faience rhyton from Kition *Chrysopolitissa*, depicting hunting scenes, bulls, a goat, stylised flowers and two hunters in Egyptian, Orientalising and Aegean styles, was found next to partly looted tombs (Peltenburg 1974: 116–126, plate XCIV) (see below, Figure 131). From British Tomb 58 at Enkomi came the well-known ivory gaming box portraying horned and hoofed animals in flying gallop, fleeing before an archer-driven chariot (Murray et al. 1900: 12–14, pl. I) (Figure 118). Taking into account this array of specialised vessels and exotic objects, alongside the faunal remains from tombs at *Ayios Dhimitrios* (South 2000: 361) and *Toumba tou Skourou* (Vermeule and Wolsky 1990: 169, 245), it seems likely that feasting and libation ceremonies played a notable role in ProBA mortuary practices (Steel 2004a: 174). Such concentrations of higher order prestige goods – richly designed gold jewellery, Mycenaean pictorial kraters, bronze vessels and tools, personal and toiletry items, weaponry – point to a stratified society with status differences closely linked to hereditary social rank and tomb group affiliation (Keswani 2004: 142).

All this diversity in mortuary practices, rituals and beliefs, as well as the quality and number of grave goods, become evident as ProBA Cypriot communities increasingly were exposed to wider regional and external horizons, in the process becoming more heterogeneous and socially complex (Keswani 2004: 103–104). It is also worth emphasising the extent to which all these mortuary practices, as well as the actual tombs, had become integrated into people's daily lives: encountering the tombs of their élite ancestors on an everyday basis must have fostered in people a strong sense of their own social identity, testaments to their own, hereditary legitimacy.

Finally, with respect to gendered aspects of mortuary patterns and practices, Bolger (2003: 165–182), argues that women's and men's role became more sharply differentiated during the ProBA than in any previous period. For example, ProBA tomb groups at Ayios Iakovos *Melia*, Kourion *Bamboula* and Enkomi *Ayios Iakovos* reveal a disproportionate, 2:1 ratio (nearly 4:1 at *Ayios Iakovos*) of male to female osteological remains (see also Keswani 2004: 31, 220, table 5.3; Fischer 1986: 12). Moreover, males and females were spatially segregated into different tomb groups at Akhera *Çiflik Paradisi*, Morphou *Toumba tou Skourou* and Kalavasos *Ayios Dhimitrios*. At the last site, and to some extent at Enkomi and *Toumba tou Skourou*, there is a contrast between the high-status, female burials and the apparent lack of lower-status female burials. Intriguingly, Bolger (2003: 175–182) sees possible evidence – in the form of elaborate clothing, jewellery and a cosmetic box interred with males – for third gender or transgendered individuals buried at Hala Sultan Tekke (Tomb 23), Enkomi (Swedish Tomb 17), Ayios Iakovos (Tomb 13), *Ayios Dhimitrios* (Tomb 14) and Lapithos (Swedish Tomb 29). Whilst her argument is solidly based on social scientific literature related to gender and identity, the fact that males were 'dressing for death' doesn't necessarily make them transgendered.

As I have emphasised before, engendering material objects presents real challenges to archaeologists, at least to those who are willing to try and meet them. I turn now to consider other aspects of a gendered prehistory, notably some ProBA figural representations.

Representations of Gender

As Bolger (2010: 156) recently emphasised: 'Without explicitly considering gender, … we are more likely to base our interpretations of past societies upon unmediated assumptions reflecting modern western beliefs and practices'. Determining the nature and purpose of figurines and other gendered representations found on ProBA Cyprus is no mean feat. And whilst the link between these representations and social identity may seem obvious, those archaeologists who have devoted the most attention to ProBA figurines have reached no consensus about their purpose or function in Cypriot society.

Elsewhere I have written extensively on the ways that gender currently provides an important focus for archaeological analysis and interpretation, in particular with reference to Cypriot figurines (Knapp and Meskell 1997; Knapp 1998a; 2008: 173–186; 2009a). Other Cypriot archaeologists also have been closely involved in this area of study, and their contributions mark an important change of direction for the archaeology of this island (e.g. various papers in Bolger and Serwent 2002; Bolger 2003; 2009; 2010; Steel 1994b; 2002). Taking a wider view, the archaeology of gender today no longer needs rationalisation or justification (see most recently Joyce 2008; Voss 2008). Current archaeological research regards gender as a vital aspect of people's identities, and engages issues of sex, sexuality and the body in order to consider the roles and statuses of women and men in the past (e.g. Hamilakis et al. 2002; Meskell 2001; 2002b). An archaeology of gender thus enables us to examine material culture in its social context, and so to attempt to interpret people's beliefs, bodies, sexualities and identities more holistically.

Although representations of prehistoric people – figurines, drawings, appliqué mouldings, seal impressions – at times appear to be abstract or unrealistic, they clearly formed an integral part of the materiality of everyday life (Barrett 1991: 6). Here, using a selection of (mainly) ProBA 2–3 female figurines whose iconography, form and function are quite different from those of their Chalcolithic and PreBA counterparts, I discuss the link between gendered representations and island identity. Most ProBA figurines portray nude females and exhibit some other features seen on Chalcolithic and PreBA figurines; like those earlier examples, they too are typically viewed as representations of a deity or some form of 'mother goddess' (e.g. Karageorghis and Karageorghis 2002; Budin 2003: 177–179). Instead of viewing these figurines as goddesses or even servants of a deity, we should consider alternative interpretations (Bolger 2003: 99), for example how they might represent other roles or daily practices on protohistoric Cyprus – mothers and motherhood, priestesses, sexual objects, dancers or celebrants.

The earliest, 'spindle shaped' figurines, dated to ProBA 1 (Karageorghis 1999b: 84–90, figs. 57–61; Budin 2003: 131–132), were executed in Plain White, Red Slip or Black Slip fabrics, and foreshadow later styles. They depict naked women wearing tight necklaces and having perforated ears, with emphasised sexual features and hands placed on the body beneath the breasts. Many ProBA 2 (LC II) examples were manufactured in a fabric similar to Base-ring ware (defined as 'Brown ware' – Karageorghis and Karageorghis 2002: 271). The two main ProBA 2 figurine categories, Type A ('bird-faced') and Type B ('normal faced') (Karageorghis 1993), are also known as 'Astarte' figurines or 'pubic triangle figurines' (Morris 1985: 166).

Figure 119. Female figurine, Type Aii, holding an infant (ProBA 2). Cyprus Museum Inventory No. 1934/IV-27/23. Courtesy of the Cyprus Museum, Nicosia.

Typically produced in a Base-ring II-type fabric, the Type A figurines portray standing women with a small, beaked nose, vertical ears and large earrings, with arms placed on, below or between small pointed breasts (Figure 119). Their genitals are usually marked by incised or punctured patterns (Karageorghis 1993: 3–5, pls. I–III); occasionally these markings seem to depict some kind of woven garment, like a kilt. The Type Aii variant holds an infant (Karageorghis 1993: 5–10, pls. III–V; Merrillees 1988), whilst other, sub-variants hold a tambourine or clap their hands (Karageorghis 1993: 10, pl. VII: 2–3). Concerning the last, Karageorghis (2006: 86) suggested that these figurines represent women playing (or being accompanied by) music in sanctuaries, and '…may represent priestesses or simply worshippers of the Great Goddess' (similarly Kolotourou 2005: 188–189, 192). There is, however, no contextual, material or even iconographic reason to support such an interpretation (Knapp 2011).

Webb (1999: 209 and 235 n. 28) lists 48 known examples of Type A figurines depicted with an infant and 65 without. Both Merrillees (1988: 55) and Karageorghis (1993: 21) argue for the Cypriot origin of these figurines, emphasising their wide distribution on the island. Budin (2003: 140–144) too acknowledges their local origin, but feels that the Type A examples were modelled on figurines ('divine' images) from mid-2nd millennium BC northern Syria. Both Morris (1985: 166) and Begg (1991: 11–12) find the figurines rather schematic and lacking in individuality. Whilst Karageorghis (1993: 1, 21) felt that their mode of production and decoration were so similar that they must have been mass produced, Merrillees (1988: 56) noted differences in the modelling and finish of the figurines with infants, and thus suggested they were produced over a wide area during the 15th–14th centuries BC.

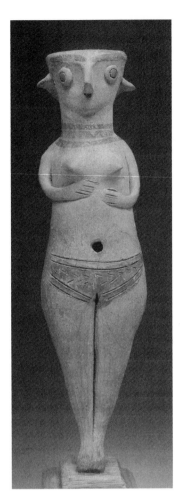

Figure 120. Female figurine Type B, with painted pubic triangle. Cyprus Museum Inventory No. A 53. Courtesy of the Cyprus Museum, Nicosia.

Type B figurines have the same, Base-ring II type fabric, and are similar in form to those of Type A (Figure 120). Stylistically, however, they are quite different (Karageorghis 1993: 22), and may have been modelled after Mycenaean *tau*, *phi* and *psi*-type painted figurines (Karageorghis and Karageorghis 2002: 272; Budin 2003: 145). This type of figurine displays a triangular, flat-topped head with painted facial features, pointed-down ears, pierced navels and genitals with incised or punctured patterns, sometimes painted; only one example holds an infant (Karageorghis 1993: 10–13, pls. VII–IX). The other main category of female figurine (Type C) depicts a nude woman seated on a stool, with legs joined together and arms curved across the chest, or with hands placed on the chest or stomach (Karageorghis 1993: 13–14, pl. X). In terms of numbers (Type B), Webb (1999: 256 n. 31) notes 100 standing examples, 20 seated examples and 23 fragments of uncertain variety. She dates the Type B figurines to the 13th–12th centuries BC, perhaps with some continuity into the 11th century (Webb 1999: 209–211; see also Courtois 1984: 79–80).

Opinions about the contexts of both Type A and B figurines are bewildering, and have been described at length elsewhere (Knapp 2008: 178–179; 2009a). Suffice it to note here that they have been found in mortuary (both high status and less sumptuous burials) as well as domestic contexts, even in 'residual' ceremonial contexts. When some clear indications of numbers are provided (Webb 1992: 90; 1999: 211), it would seem that these figurines were used and discarded primarily in settlement (rarely 'ritual') contexts, less often in mortuary contexts. Thus they would have been used in life as well as in death, and no doubt were valued possessions of all who owned, used or displayed them.

As to their function and meaning, the notion that these figurines were produced as grave goods stems partly from the mortuary bias of the Cypriot archaeological record (Talalay and Cullen 2002: 184), and partly from the fact that many earlier, PreBA 2 figurines with good contexts were recovered from burials (Frankel and Webb 1996: 188). Begg (1991: 53) felt the ProBA 2 figurines might have been used as personal charms, but Webb (1999: 211) noted that their prominence in domestic contexts wouldn't have excluded their use in ceremonial or cultic contexts. Most scholars presume that both Type A and Type B figurines represent some sort of female fertility deity worshipped in households, sanctuaries and cultic buildings, or placed in tombs during mortuary rituals (cf. Morris 1985; Budin 2003: 140). For her part, Budin (2003: 199–241) sees iconographic similarities and possible literary links between various Levantine goddesses (Ishtar, Ishara) and Cypriot figurines. She maintains that (bird-faced) representations of Ishtar or Ishara (or both) from the region around Alalakh in north Syria should be seen as the inspiration for Cyprus's bird-faced figurines (Budin 2003: 241).

Another notable female figurine, widely discussed for differing reasons, is the so-called Bomford Figurine (Catling 1971b; Hulin 1989; Webb 1999: 211; Budin 2003: 156–159, 215) (Figure 121). Catling (1971b: 29) believed this figurine to be the 12th-century-BC version of a long-established Cypriot female fertility goddess whose origins lay in the Near East. Bolger (2003: 97–100) and Budin (2002) both disputed the association of this figurine (or 'goddess') with fertility, as well as Morris's (1985: 166) more general interpretation of female figurines as sexual playthings. For Budin, this ancient 'goddess' embodies sexuality in its own terms, not as it relates to maternity or fecundity. Bolger (2003: 99) argues that the standard view of these figurines as deities has precluded alternative interpretations. Like Bolger and Budin, I cannot agree with the assumption that all these Cypriot figurines represent a fertility goddess; indeed I remain sceptical whether most of these figurines represent a deity at all. The Bomford statuette seems exceptional, but in my view it should be considered more in terms of the ideological rather than the sexual (Knapp 1986b: 4; 2008: 182; cf. Budin 2002: 319–320, who highlights the sheer sexuality of this figurine). Both the 'Ingot God' (Knapp 1986a: 9–14; see above,

Figure 121. Bronze statuette of female figurine, depicted standing on an oxhide ingot. Bomford Collection, Ashmolean Museum, no. AN1971.888. Courtesy of the Ashmolean Museum, University of Oxford, UK.

Figure 108) and the Bomford Figurine – whether representing the human or the divine – stand as materialisations of political authority and élite identity during the ProBA.

Another new type of figurine – modelled on Mycenaean-type *psi* figurines and termed 'the goddess with upraised arms' (or 'snowman figurines' – Morris 1985: 174–181, figs. 288–292) – first appears on the island during the late 12th–11th centuries BC (Karageorghis 1993: 1, 58–61, Type GA[i]) (Figure 122). Webb (1999: 213–215, fig. 75) presents differing views on the dating and floruit of these figurines, and concludes they became common by the end of the 12th century BC. The early Iron Age examples (LC IIIB), executed in Proto-White Painted ware, have cylindrical bodies, arms raised to either side of the head, painted hair, jewellery and clothing; the eyes, nose and breasts are rendered in relief. A concentration of more than 150 small, fragmentary examples was found in the western sector of the Ingot God 'sanctuary' at Enkomi; others stem from various areas at Kition (Karageorghis 1985b: 98, 103, 105, pls. CIX, CX; Webb 1999: 213). These smaller versions, designated Type GD

Figure 122. 'Goddess with upraised arms', from Limassol *Komissariato*. Limassol Museum, no. 580/8. Courtesy of the Cyprus Museum, Nicosia.

by Karageorghis (1993: 64–65), have cylindrical bodies, upraised arms, painted clothing and jewellery, with indented eyes and mouths. Most examples depict females with flattened heads, although a few males are represented, wearing pointed caps or helmets.

Most scholars feel that the large number of LC IIIB, *psi*-type figurines found in ceremonial structures ('sanctuaries'), as well as their more schematic style, indicates they were offered as votives (never the case with the ProBA 2 figurines). Karageorghis (1993: 1, 60–61), for example, suggested that these figurines were used as votive offerings to a divinity or else as votive gifts for the dead. Webb (1999: 215), similarly, maintained that they were used in rituals for worshipping female deities, whilst D'Agata (2005: 14) regards them as prestige objects related to ritual practices. Webb's (1999: 209–215) presentation of all these figurines is the most coherent: she concludes that, prior to the early Iron Age when they had more widespread use, none of these female representations played a major role in public cult; they were only used occasionally as votives. Because no anthropomorphic female figurines of any type have been found in Enkomi's Ingot and Horned God 'sanctuaries', Webb suggests that their use was restricted to the worship of one or more female deities (also Karageorghis 2003: 216).

The diverse contexts in which ProBA 2–3 figurines were produced and displayed suggest that they had multiple functions. At least some of these representations, female or male, served a performative role involving music and dance (also Webb 1999: 215), whether in cultic, ritual or other, unknown ceremonial practices. For example, two decorated bronze stands of ProBA 3 date but lacking provenance depict three musicians – two harp players and a lyre player (Karageorghis 2006: 82–83, figs. 68–69, nos. 58 and 59). On one stand (no. 58),

Figure 123. Kourion (?), four-sided bronze stand with figural decoration (harp player). British Museum, London, Inventory 1920,1220.1 AN513250. © The Trustees of the British Museum.

a harp player sits on a stool in front of a stylised tree (Figure 123); on the other (no. 59), a harpist seated on a stool faces a standing figure playing a lyre, whilst behind them another figure is depicted, holding a *kylix* in his left hand and a jug in his right. Both scenes have been interpreted strictly in ritual terms, as a feast or religious festival in which music and the ceramic vessels were offered to an unspecified deity (Karageorghis 2006: 82). To take another example: in his interpretation of a decorated bronze bowl depicting a bilateral procession of women approaching a figure seated on a throne (Markoe 1985: 171–172, 248–249 [Cy3]), Karageorghis (2006: 113) states: 'The seated figure may be a goddess, probably Astarte herself, or her priestess. It is important that all figures of participants in the ritual feast are female, servants of the Great Goddess, who is entertained with music, dancing, and is offered food and drink'. Such interpretations are found in virtually every publication dealing with female figurines or representations of women, and more specifically with those treating music and musical practices on Cyprus (e.g. Averett 2002–2004; cf. Knapp 2011).

Bolger (2003: 99–100) has forcefully argued that we should not see god-desses or divinities in every female figurine or other human representation. Moreover, to suggest that all Cypriot figurines were involved in 'cultic' prac-tice is overly restrictive: both females and males are depicted as well as images that defy placement in traditional sexual categories. Thus we must also con-sider what kinds of gender information may have been broadcast by the pos-tures, gestures, dress, ornamentation and colour used in these representations, and whether their use was restricted to certain practices, whether domestic, public or more generally ceremonial. Were certain kinds of activities associ-ated specifically with women, or men? As Talalay (2005: 137–139) suggests, it is important to develop a better awareness of the possible *performative* roles of these figurines in ProBA Cypriot society. The fact that these figurines were produced, used and displayed in a variety of contexts argues against any single function or use.

Anthropomorphic representations such as these ProBA 2–3 figurines raise a whole series of questions concerning the meanings, strategies or rules of social and ceremonial behaviour: from female rites of passage, perhaps reflecting same-sex relations (Rehak 2002), to androgynous figures (Hitchcock 2000), to multiple if not contradictory images depending on who made, viewed or used them, and who controlled their use (Brumfiel 1996). In a strictly material setting such as that of ProBA Cyprus, it is difficult to determine what kind of people were being portrayed, taking part in unknown events. Context is all-important, but many of the objects treated in this section lack specific prov-enance. Those whose provenance we know often come from burials, or from buildings that have been identified, seldom with good reason, as 'sanctuaries' (Knapp 2008: 206–211). In sum, we should no longer think of ProBA Cypriot figurines simply in sexual terms, and nor should we assume they were all involved in 'religious' practices. Most figurines treated here represent females, but males are not absent. More detailed and focused analyses would certainly reveal hybrid or more ambiguous representations – images that move in and out of traditional sexual categories, the same kind of ambiguous or multiple genders seen in PreBA and indeed in earlier human representations on the island (Knapp and Meskell 1997).

PRODUCTION, TRADE AND THE 'EXOTIC'

From Corsica and Sardinia in the west to Egypt and Mesopotamia in the east, archaeological evidence old and new reveals a significant expansion in the dis-tribution and trade of a wide range of goods and products during the ProBA (Sherratt and Sherratt 1991; Cline 1994; Laffineur and Greco 2005; Phillips 2008). The circulation of pottery from Italy and Sardinia, the Aegean, Cyprus and the Levant is striking, as is the exchange of copper oxhide ingots and sev-eral types of metal goods, faience and glass products (e.g. Crielaard et al. 1999;

Peltenburg 2007b; Lo Schiavo et al. 2009). Prestige goods made of ivory, gold and amber, as well as pictorial pottery, are less common but nonetheless significant (e.g. Feldman 2006; Feldman and Sauvage 2010), as are all manner of organic goods. The remains of coriander, caper, safflower, fig and pomegranate seeds, olive pits, cereal grains, almond shells and terebinth resin were all recovered from the Uluburun shipwreck (Haldane 1993). An often invisible trade in resins, oils, fibres, wine and other foodstuffs helped to fuel the subsistence economies of Cyprus and other eastern Mediterranean lands (Knapp 1991; Martlew 2004; Reese 2006–07). Cyprus was also a rich source of wood – for example, pine, oak and cypress – used in shipbuilding, mining/metallurgy and pottery production (Raptou 2002). During the ProBA 2 period, the king of Cyprus asked the Egyptian pharaoh to pay what he owed for '…my timber that the king of Egypt received from me' (Amarna letter [EA] 35: 27–29, for which see Moran, in Knapp 1996b: 22). The nearly Mediterranean-wide scope of trade in the international era of the Late Bronze Age brought bulk goods and prestige objects to ruling élites, raw materials to craftspeople, and food supplies and other basic products to rural peasants and producers.

Although powerful élites seem to have managed most local economies throughout the Aegean and eastern Mediterranean at this time (Monroe 2009; Schon 2009; Tartaron 2010), the dynamics of distribution and exchange freed up resources for individual enterprise within a loosely structured political economy. Let us now consider various aspects of production, consumption and exchange in turn, bearing in mind how these factors must have stimulated a burgeoning economy such as that of ProBA 1 Cyprus, eventually propelling the island and its inhabitants into the mobile, highly connected world of the Late Bronze Age Mediterranean.

Agricultural Production/Consumption

Alongside all the dramatic developments in international trade, agricultural and pastoral production on ProBA Cyprus apparently continued on much the same level as before. Currently published evidence reveals no components or strategies beyond that expected for a Bronze Age Mediterranean agro-pastoral economy (Knapp 1994: 283–287, fig. 9.5). Although the limited evidence available means that any conclusions drawn must be provisional, the concentration of people in the new, ProBA town centres surely required a more intensified production of crops and an increased use or exploitation of animals. The urban-oriented economy of the ProBA involved systems of production and social reproduction flexible enough to feed and support a number of specialists.

Excavations at several ProBA sites suggest that ovicaprines (sheep and goat) were the species of preference (Knapp 1994: 283–287; Reese 1996a: 476–481). Domesticated cattle, however, were kept at most sites: at Episkopi *Phaneromeni* and Maa *Palaeokastro* the percentage of their remains nearly equals that of ovicaprines (Swiny 1989: 23; Croft 1988: 452, 454, table 1). By contrast, pig is found much less frequently than in earlier periods, an exception again being Maa *Palaeokastro*, where it amounts to about 10% of the faunal record (Croft 1988; 1989). This enigmatic site also shows a higher frequency (about 20%) of fallow deer, whilst the high incidence of deer from Kouklia (about 22%, found in a well, TE III) may represent nothing beyond élite dietary preferences (Halstead 1977: 261, 271). The high numbers of deer at Kouklia, and the high proportion of deer and nearly equal percentages of cattle and caprines (about 30%) in the faunal record at Maa, may indicate that southwestern Cyprus was more wooded than other inhabited areas on the island (Croft 1988: 453; Miksicek 1988: 470). Whilst cattle and ovicaprines would have provided meat and secondary products (milk, wool), horses and donkeys were probably kept as draft animals (traction).

Although we lack evidence for the kind of animal sacrifices associated with ritual and feasting during the PreBA (Keswani 1994: 259, 268–272), notable faunal components have been found in 'sanctuary' contexts at Enkomi, Kition and Myrtou *Pigadhes* (Webb 1999: 44–53). At the last site, at least 41 fallow deer antlers recovered around the well-known 'horns of consecration' may point to feasting activities (Zeuner in Du Plat Taylor 1957: 97–101; Webb 1999: 47, 53, 250–252). At *Toumba tou Skourou*, sheep, goat and deer were recovered from various contexts along with ash and charcoal (Vermeule and Wolsky 1990: 169, 245), which suggests cooking if not feasting activities. The prominence of Mycenaean jugs, bowls and kraters in certain, relatively rich mortuary deposits may suggest they played some role in mortuary rituals that also involved feasting (Steel 1998: 291–292; 2004c: 174).

Amongst domesticated plants, the key staples in the diet continued to be cereals, pulses, nuts and fruits (Miksicek 1988; Hansen 1991; 2003). The presence of grape, fig, olive and almond suggests cultivated orchards (Helbaek 1962; South et al. 1989: 92–93; Dammann in Smith 2008a: 104–107, 109); olive-oil production is well attested during the ProBA (Hadjisavvas 1992: 21–26). But the most obvious change related to Cyprus's mixed farming economy involves the evidence for storage facilities.

At Kalavasos *Ayios Dhimitrios*, some 50 massive, terracotta *pithoi* from Building X almost certainly held olive oil, in amounts estimated at some 50,000 kg (Keswani 1992); the adjacent Building XI contained a stone tank that may have been used to produce olive oil (South 1992: 135–139). The storage facilities at Alassa *Paleotaverna* are also impressive: the remnants of at least 16 enormous *pithoi* and stone bases for others were found in the northern sector of Building II; four more *pithoi* on stone bases were retrieved from a storage cellar between its north wall and the vertically cut bedrock, and at least eight more were found outside the south and east walls of this storeroom (Hadjisavvas 2001:

212; 2009: 130, 133, fig. 3) (see above, Figure 103). Quantities of *pithos* fragments from Building III (directly east of Building II), as well as a large, nearly two-m deep *pithos* sunk into a rock-cut pit in its northern sector, suggest that this structure too served as a storage facility. In the eastern sector of Building II was an installation thought to be a wine press (Hadjisavvas 2009: 130). Just down the hill at *Pano Mandilares*, the courtyards of several dwellings contained pits likely used as receptacles for storage *pithoi* or basins (Hadjisavvas 1996: 25).

At Maroni *Vournes*, the Ashlar Building contained an olive press with several large *pithoi* and stands for others. Two rooms at the rear of this structure had stone drains built into the wall, evidently intended to move liquids (olive oil?) from the inside out (Cadogan 1996: 16–17). Keswani (1993: 78) has suggested that the 11 large *pithoi* found beside a large architectural complex at Athienou *Bamboulari tis Koukounninas* are likely indicators of olive-oil production and storage. The storeroom in House A at Apliki *Karamallos*, perhaps an official's residence, contained some 15 large *pithoi* with a storage capacity of up to 7,500 litres, presumably for olive oil (Keswani 1993: 77). The fragments of up to 35 large *pithoi* in Phlamoudhi *Melissa*'s large 'courtyard' building (Phases 5–7), and a pebbled area nearby that may have been part of an 'oil pressing workspace', also indicate a considerable capacity for storage at this site (Smith 2008a: 57, 59–60).

To this evidence from excavated sites, we must also add the numerous *pithos* sherds documented through survey work at agricultural support villages such as Analiondas *Paleoklichia* or Aredhiou *Vouppes* (Webb and Frankel 1994; Knapp 2003: 572–573). More intensive survey at the latter site also indicated a predominance of *pithoi* amongst the pottery recovered (Steel and McCartney 2008: 14, table 1). Some of these *pithoi*, however, were small, short-necked vessels that might point to household use rather than centralised storage (Steel and McCartney 2008: 32–33). Subsequent excavations at *Vouppes* have produced fewer examples of *pithoi* than might have been expected, given their abundance on the surface (Steel and Thomas 2008: 232). The site of Alassa *Paleotaverna* has produced more than 50 impressed *pithos* sherds, and 38 more sherds are known from eight other sites (Hadjisavvas 2001: 213). Not only do such impressions provide evidence for élite storage, they also open up the possibility that grain or olive oil was transported between production sites and consumption centres. The impressions may have indicated the contents of the *pithoi* (Smith 1994: 282–289), if not the identity of those involved in such transactions (Webb 2002d: 131).

Pottery Production/Consumption

The mention of sealing impressions on *pithos* sherds raises issues related to the production and consumption of the pottery vessels themselves. Although the best-known, new wares that appeared during the ProBA 1 period – White Slip,

Base-ring, Plain Monochrome (Merrillees 1971) – were handmade, there was no shortage of wheelmade wares on the island during this period. The majority of wares for which the wheel was adopted, however, were produced in both handmade and wheelmade versions (Crewe 2007a: 210). The distinction between handmade and wheelmade pottery assumes some significance at this historical juncture, inasmuch as the introduction of a wheelmade technology is often associated with mass production, economic specialisation and more complex levels of society (e.g. Rice 1981; Arnold 1985: 208–210; Wattenmaker 1998: 928). Ethnographic work has even suggested that craft specialisation may be correlated with a political strategy to legitimise and maintain élite authority, and as such is not strictly an economic or artistic activity (Peregrine 1991). Such correlations have been questioned on both technological and economic grounds (e.g. Knappett 1999; Loney 2000): the adoption of new technologies – such as the manufacture of wheelmade pottery – involves a suite of complex, interlinked, cultural, behavioural and even motor-related skills that are neither predictable nor rational (Roux 2003; Loney 2007; Roux and de Miroschedji 2009).

In the case of ProBA Cyprus, Crewe (2007a: 209–210) has argued that economic considerations are irrelevant to the adoption of the potter's wheel, and that the introduction of a range of multi-purpose plain wares (including wheelmade wares such as Plain White, White Painted, Red/Black Slip, earlier produced only in handmade versions) should be seen instead as a deliberate choice to produce what she terms 'urban style' pottery. The adoption of such pottery wares involved both stylistic and technological changes, and was likely influenced by increasing contacts with town centres in the contemporary Levant.

In her recent study of ProBA pottery production, Steel (2010) relates the changing dynamics of pottery manufacture to sociopolitical and demographic changes, which may be characterised as follows:

ProBA 1: increasing specialisation in regional workshops;
ProBA 2: widespread, decentralised distribution of pottery styles islandwide;
ProBA 3: increasing standardisation and specialisation indicative of mass production.

Sherratt (1991) also argued that pottery production became increasingly standardised during the 13th–early 12th centuries BC, as shown especially by the wider use of the potter's wheel and the decline of Cyprus's handmade fine wares; she too links this change to an increasingly urbanised and centralised polity. Crewe (2007a: 216), however, maintains that whilst pottery production throughout the ProBA period was always specialised, it remained largely decentralised and in the hands of local, village potters.

Provenance studies on a wide range of Cypriot wares (Knapp and Cherry 1994: 159–161), however, call Crewe's views into question. Analytical and typologically derived divisions indicate regional production centres in the east, north coast/northeast (including the Karpass Peninsula), southwest (and south central?), and central/northwest of the island. Certainly sites such as Morphou *Toumba tou Skourou* and Sanidha *Moutti tou Ayiou Serkou* served as specialised pottery production centres. At *Toumba tou Skourou*, where little evidence of habitation was preserved, the excavators identified a specialised structure – the 'Basin Building' – where fine ware pottery (White Painted, Proto-White Slip, White Slip I wares), *pithoi* and bricks were produced (Vermeule and Wolsky 1990: 20, 55–57, 76–78). Other evidence for pottery production includes remnant 'sacks' of clay, pits with potters' clay, clay 'dumps', ceramic slag, misfired and misshapen vases and quantities of *pithos* sherds. At Sanidha, excavations revealed not just an enormous amount of White Slip wares, but also unslipped White Slip sherds, fragments of 'fire-bars' (bricks from a kiln?), ceramic wasters and pebbles probably used as burnishing tools (Todd 2000; Todd and Pilides 2001).

The production and distribution of pottery may well have been centralised in at least some of the major urban centres – for example, Enkomi (Keswani 1991; Gunneweg et al. 1992), Morphou *Toumba tou Skourou* (Vermeule and Wolsky 1990), Episkopi (Kourion) *Bamboula* (Daniel 1938: 266), Kition and *Palaipaphos* (Knapp and Cherry 1994: 160–161). The case for centralised production is less clear at Alassa *Pano Mandilares* and *Paleotaverna* (Jacobs 2009), although Keswani (2009: 121) has suggested that regional production centres may have served Alassa and Kalavasos *Ayios Dhimitrios*. Regionally based pottery workshops seem evident at Athienou *Bamboulari tis Koukounninas* (Dothan and Ben-Tor 1983; Keswani 1993: 78), Kalopsidha (Åström 1966: 8), Phlamoudhi *Melissa* (Smith 2008a: 49) and possibly Erimi *Pitharka* (Vassiliou and Stylianou 2004). Provenance studies on Base-ring ware led Vaughan (1994: 89) to postulate regional production centres over most of the island. Various studies on White Slip production, moreover, and the diversity of White Slip forms seen in the south-central area and the southwest (e.g. Kalavasos, Maroni, Kourion, *Palaipaphos*), suggest regional production centres, perhaps overseen by élites (Steel 2010: 110–111). Analytical, stylistic and morphological studies all demonstrate the increasing uniformity of Cypriot pottery production island-wide by mid-to-late 13th century BC, whilst the 'Aegeanising' White Painted Wheelmade III wares of ProBA 2–3 provide another indicator of centralised, mass produced pottery (Sherratt 1991: 191; Steel 2010: 112–113, fig. 13.4; see further below).

Steel (2010) has also provided a definitive discussion of how pottery production was organised throughout ProBA Cyprus. Although the manufacture of pottery seems to have been coordinated at different times on different levels (local, regional, centralised), it seems always to have been a specialised endeavour. Red Polished pottery, in use for more than 500 years, was replaced by several new wares during ProBA 1 (MC III–LC I). Most prominent amongst

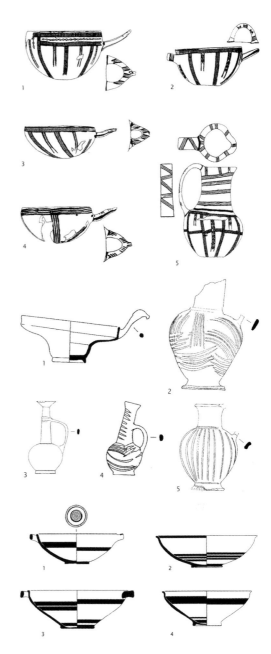

Figure 124. White Slip, Base-ring and White Painted pottery styles. After Steel 2010: 110, fig. 13.2; 111, fig. 13.3; 113, fig. 13.4). (a) White Slip: (1, 3, 4) hemispherical bowls (WS II); (2) spouted bowl (WS II); (5) jug (WS II). All examples come from Kalavasos *Ayios Dhimitrios*. (b) Base-ring: (1) carinated cup (BR II); (2) jug with painted decoration (BR II); (3) juglet (BR I); (4) juglet with painted decoration (BR II); (5) Bucchero jug. (c) White Painted: (1–4) shallows bowls, all from Kalavasos *Ayios Dhimitrios*. Courtesy of Louise Steel.

these were the fine wares that became hallmarks of the period: White Slip, Base-ring and Monochrome (Figure 124a–c). The production of both Base-ring and White Slip wares – with their highly refined clays, thin walls and elaborate shapes (Base-ring) – would have required potters with very specialised, technical skills. These canonical ProBA wares emerged first in the northwest and centre of the island (Merrillees 1971); in the east and against the backdrop of a more conservative tradition, new styles also developed: Red on Black,

Red on Red, Bichrome (White Painted in the *Mesaoria*). At the same time, certain features of traditional vessels became transformed: for example, the use of softer clays and flat or ring bases instead of rounded bases on jugs and jars; Levantine influence on shapes such as the krater; new, individual serving vessels such as small bowls and cups (Merrillees 1971: 62; Crewe 2007a: 227–229). Two distinct stylistic trajectories have been identified (Crewe 2007a: 223): (1) Red/Black Slip and White Painted wares, with a traditional Cypriot form and finish; and (2) Plain White and Bichrome wares, with a 'foreign' form and finish. By the end of the ProBA 1 period, however, the production of traditional wares/finish using the new (wheelmade) technology had ceased, which left only the manifestly 'foreign' Plain White and finer wheelmade lustrous wares alongside the new, finely produced handmade wares, notably White Slip and Base-ring.

The first use of these new wares seems to have been associated with mortuary practices, including feasting activities; only gradually were they absorbed into everyday, living contexts (Merrillees 1971: 57; Crewe 2007a: 214). The Plain White handmade jars, for example, were adopted to implement new storage strategies, whilst the Bichrome and Red Lustrous Wheelmade wares may reflect new social practices and interactions associated with the (communal?) preparation and consumption of food and drink (Crewe 2007a: 228; Steel 2010: 108–109). Specialist potters, exploiting clay beds in the Troodos (Courtois 1977), became proficient at manufacturing these new wares, using the wheel or turntable for certain elements, and a kiln-based technology to achieve higher firing temperatures (Aloupi et al. 2001; Crewe 2007a). Some of the new wares reveal foreign practices: for example, Syrian and/or Cycladic influences on Bichrome Wheelmade wares, Anatolian or Syrian influence on Red Lustrous wares (Åström 2001a; Artzy 2002; Knappett and Kilikoglou 2007).

During the ProBA 2 period (Late Cypriot IIA–IIC early), pottery production became increasingly standardised, although regional variations are still evident. For example, whilst White Slip II pottery – in particular the hemispherical bowl with wishbone handle – appears to be uniform islandwide, there is an exceptional diversity of form and decoration in the south central region, as seen in material from Kalavasos *Ayios Dhimitrios* and Maroni *Vournes* (South and Steel 2001; Steel 2010: 109–110, fig. 13.2). Other regional variations in White Slip II styles are evident stylistically and have also been demonstrated by chemical analyses (Artzy et al. 1981: 44–45; Knapp and Cherry 1994: 57–59). These regional variants were most likely associated with workshops in or near Kalavasos, Kourion or Kouklia, near sources of basaltic clays consistent with the White Slip fabric. Such regional production centres were most likely controlled by urban élites who would have been able to distribute these wares efficiently within and beyond the island, especially to the Levant where they were in great demand (e.g. Gittlen 1975; Hatcher 2002; various papers in Karageorghis 2001b).

As the more elaborate forms of both Base-ring and White Slip wares went out of use, increasingly the ceramic repertoire was dominated by a few standard shapes – hemispherical bowls, carinated bowls and small juglets (Base-ring) – and more uniformity in the size of vessels (Steel 2010: 109–112). The potters who produced Base-ring wares achieved a remarkable standardisation in the shape and decoration of these vessels, whose appearance islandwide always suggested some level of regional if not centralised production as well as an extensive distribution network. Detailed chemical, petrographic and statistical analyses of Base-ring data by Vaughan (1991; 1994, mentioned above) identified at least three regional production centres – one in the north, two in the south – run by highly skilled, technically proficient potters, but perhaps coordinated by urban élites who managed the circulation of these wares throughout the island and beyond (see various papers in Åström 2001a).

In some 16th–14th century BC Cypriot burials, elaborate 'drinking sets' – kraters, jugs, tankards, large spouted bowls – of White Slip, Base-ring and Bichrome Wheelmade wares became prominent. In mortuary (and feasting) contexts of the ProBA 2 period (14th–13th centuries BC), Mycenaean pictorial style imports – especially cups, chalices and kraters – were widely adopted as drinking sets, largely replacing the use of local wares (Steel 1998: 290–292, and n. 43; 1999; Feldman and Sauvage 2010: 97–99). One very characteristic vessel, the krater, was mainly limited to wealthy burials in the large coastal centres. These imported Mycenaean wares, used for feasting and drinking, thus had a notable impact on both the material culture and social practices of the ProBA 2 period: their distribution was restricted and they were emblematic of élite status. At the same time, it is evident that these luxury imports, which clearly had little mortuary meaning or relevance in their original (Aegean) context (Mountjoy 1993: 73), had been integrated into an existing (élite) burial custom; they thus portray an interesting example of hybridised material and social practices.

By the ProBA 3 period (Late Cypriot IIC late–IIIA), technological, morphological, stylistic and analytical data alike indicate an increasing uniformity in pottery production within an urban context (Knapp and Cherry 1994: 161; Sherratt 1991: 191). White Slip and Base-ring wares were now mass-produced for local and overseas consumption (Steel 1998: 292; 2010: 112). White Slip hemispherical bowls and Base-ring carinated cups became the exclusive focus of manufacture in those wares; even the decoration of White Slip wares became standardised whilst Base-ring vessels were no longer burnished or polished.

Mycenaean imports had decreased markedly by this time, alongside a striking increase in the local production of Mycenaean-type wares. Included in this category are several wares – Rude or Pastoral Style, Late Helladic IIIB and IIIC:1b, Decorated Late Cypriot III – that specialists now widely refer to as White Painted Wheelmade III (Åström 1972: 276; Kling 2000: 281–282; Sherratt 1991: 186–187; Steel 1998: 288). These wares became increasingly prominent in LC IIIA (ProBA 3) and also appear to have been mass-produced, most likely in centrally organised workshops in Enkomi, Kition and *Palaipaphos* (Jones 1986: 606–607). Comprised mainly of kraters and bowls, White Painted Wheelmade III vessels were formed on the wheel, and decorated (mainly with straight, horizontal lines) on turntables – 'the ultimate rapidly produced ceramic product' (Steel 2010: 112). By the beginning of the following, LC IIIB phase (early Iron Age), a new type of wheelmade, decorated pottery – Proto White Painted ware – was being mass-produced in a homogeneous style on an islandwide scale (Iacovou 1988; Sherratt 1991: 191; Steel 1994a).

Diachronic developments in pottery manufacture on ProBA Cyprus reflect to varying degrees sociopolitical changes and population dynamics. In general, the organisation of pottery production often tends to be decentralised at the local (household, community) level, and more structured on a larger, regional or urban level; this simply reflects the ability of a larger polity to attract specialised labour, provide the necessary materials and services, and support the manufacture of prestige goods for élite consumption (Berdan 1983: 87). During the ProBA 1 period, the manufacture of new types of wares necessitated technological innovations and the exploitation of new clay and mineral resources. Demographic shifts to new town centres and a growth in population probably meant new levels of demand, and increased specialisation beyond the household level, within local or regional workshops. By the 14th century BC (ProBA 2), as political élites tightened their grip regionally if not centrally, White Slip and Base-ring wares, with regional variants, circulated throughout the island. During the 13th–12th centuries BC (ProBA 3), when a wide range of material culture features as well as contemporary documentary evidence point to centralised political power in all the key urban centres (Knapp 2008: 335–341), there emerged a standardised class of wheelmade, painted pottery – White Painted Wheelmade III ware – that lent itself well to specialised, and almost certainly centralised mass production.

Metallurgical Production / Consumption

The production, distribution and consumption of copper played a major role in the economy of ProBA Cyprus, and external demand for Cypriot copper was instrumental in the rise of the urban coastal centres. Installations used in the mining, smelting and final production of copper ores are attested throughout the island (e.g. Knapp 1986b: 39–46, table 1; Muhly 1989; 1996; Kassianidou 2004). Based on currently available evidence, the intensification of copper production occurred initially (ProBA 1) at Enkomi (Muhly et al. 1988: 294–295; Muhly 1989: 299–300), Kalopsidha *Koufos* (Watkins, in Åström 1966: 115) and perhaps at Hala Sultan Tekke (Åström 1982). During the 16th century Cal BC, copper (matte) was being smelted at Politiko *Phorades*, a primary production centre, perhaps for onward shipment to the coastal centres where it was further refined. During the subsequent, ProBA 2 period, there is abundant evidence for the production and/or refinement of copper at several key sites across the island: Kalavasos *Ayios Dhimitrios*, Maroni *Vournes*, Myrtou *Pigadhes*, Kition, Alassa *Pano Mandilares*, Morphou *Toumba tou Skourou*, Episkopi *Bamboula*, Athienou *Bamboulari tis Koukounninas*, Apliki *Karamallos*, Pyla *Kokkinokremos* and Maa *Palaeokastro* (Knapp 1986b; 1988; Muhly 1989: 301–302; 1991).

Although it has been argued that the production of copper may have been controlled locally in the initial stages of the ProBA (LC IA) (Stech 1985), Enkomi is widely seen as the dominant site in this newly developing copper industry (Courtois 1982; Muhly 1989: 299; Pickles and Peltenburg 1998: 87; Kassianidou 2012). However, following her re-examination of metalworking paraphernalia from Enkomi stored in the Cyprus Museum, Crewe (2007b: 17–19) suggested that the best evidence for copper working at Enkomi dates no earlier than the mid-16th century BC (LC IB), and that there is no secure evidence for centrally organised, intensive production for another 250 years, that is, until LC IIC. Both suggestions may be challenged, not least because the formative years of the Cypriot copper industry during the ProBA period need to be seen in a longer-term context (Kassianidou 2008).

From the earliest phase of Enkomi's 'fortress' (Area III, Level IA, Room 101), Dikaios's excavations produced tuyère and crucible fragments, as well as remnants of copper oxidation and charcoal, all of which he associated with the localised smelting of copper (Dikaios 1969–1971: 18). Muhly (1989: 299), furthermore, pointed out: 'It is particularly significant that one of the elbow or bent tuyères (that from tray 2295D) comes from a deposit below Floor IX (Area III, Room 101, Level IA), indicating that the type was in use right from the beginning of the history of Enkomi'. These elbow tuyères are very characteristic of Enkomi's metal-producing industry through time, and this very early find suggests long-term continuity in metallurgical practices at the site (see further below).

Crewe rightly states that the metallurgical evidence from Level IB at Enkomi is more substantial than that of Level IA (Dikaios 1969–1971: 23–24, 500, 516), but there are other issues to consider regarding the level and significance of Enkomi's earliest evidence for the production of metal. Crewe (2007b: 18, 156) bases her argument at least in part on the limited number of metallurgical finds from Level IA at Enkomi as compared to those from (nearly contemporary) Politiko *Phorades* (Crewe 2007b: 17). As Kassianidou (2012) points out, however, such a comparison is inappropriate, since the Enkomi workshops were situated inside a building continuously used over a long period of time within an urban centre, whilst Politiko *Phorades* was strictly a copper smelting site that operated over a brief period of time in the 16th century BC; after 100 years or so, it was abandoned together with all its metallurgical waste (Knapp and Kassianidou 2008). Moreover, Courtois (1982) carefully recorded all instances of metalworking installations at Enkomi through time, from both the French

and Cypriot excavations. In addition to some 1,200 m^2 of Level IA–IB deposits from Dikaios's Area I, he also notes several French exposures of LC I more
generally, and shows that in later periods there is evidence for copper working
throughout the town.

Given the plentiful, long-term evidence for metallurgical production at
Enkomi, there is no reason to presume that this was not the case from the
beginning (Kassianidou 2012). Crewe has also minimised the fact that from
the outset of the ProBA, smelting technology on Cyprus was already highly
developed, and the use of tuyères as attested in the earliest levels at Enkomi was
one of the crucial technological developments in the fledgling Cypriot copper
industry. Along with improved furnace design, the use of tuyères and bellows
enabled those who worked copper ores to achieve higher temperatures and a
better reducing atmosphere, whilst fluxing agents produced a lower melting
point to achieve more fluid slags and a better separation between the metal and
the slag (Kassianidou 2008: 258).

By the ProBA 2 period (14th–13th centuries Cal BC), there is indisputable
and widespread evidence for copper production at Enkomi. By that time, the
coastal towns of Hala Sultan Tekke and Kition were also involved in copper
smelting or refining (Muhly 1989: 301–302), and further metalworking installations have been uncovered at Alassa and Atheniou. Slag from smelting copper is plentiful at sites such as Hala Sultan Tekke, Enkomi and Kition, at the
smelting site of Politiko *Phorades* (ProBA 1), and at the mining village of Apliki
Karamallos (ProBA 2). Both the latter sites are situated very close to the rich
copper ore deposits of the Lower Pillow Lavas in the Troodos, and add another
dimension to what we know about final production processes carried out in
the coastal towns.

Evidence for the smelting or remelting of metallic copper in the major
coastal centres (Stech 1982: 112–113; Kassianidou 2009) indicates that copper
for export was crucial to the Cypriot economy; it also suggests that a centralised authority regulated that economy. Such an authority is also indicated by
the common systems of measurement in use (Courtois 1983; Alberti and Parise
2005: 382, 389; Michailidou 2009: 100–106), and by the roughly standardised
weight, shape and purity of the oxide ingots. Although these ingots are found
distributed widely throughout the Mediterranean, from Marseilles, Corsica
and Sardinia in the west to the Black Sea and Babylonia in the east (Muhly et
al. 1988; Lo Schiavo 2003: 23–25; Lo Schiavo et al. 2009), very few have been
found on Cyprus: this is exactly the situation we would expect if centralised
copper production were geared mainly for export.

Archaeologists working on Cyprus have always assumed that incompletely
processed copper ores were brought from primary production centres near
the ore sources to the coastal sites for further refining (e.g. Stech 1982). Once
the processed ores arrived in the coastal centres, specialist metalworkers would
have carried out the secondary smelting, melting and refinement of these ores,

and produced oxhide ingots for internal or external distribution. The problem in corroborating this scenario has always been the complete lack of evidence from a primary smelting site. The closest thing was a small village – Apliki *Karamallos* – whose inhabitants were almost certainly involved in the mining or production of copper. In the 1990s, however, excavations were finally conducted at a primary production centre, Politiko *Phorades*, where copper ores were processed. Let us look more closely at these two sites.

Situated on the high slopes of the northwestern Troodos foothills, Apliki *Karamallos* lay in the heart of what is arguably the richest mining district on Cyprus (Constantinou, in Kling and Muhly 2007: 339). The site was excavated during two seasons in 1938 and 1939 (Du Plat Taylor 1952; Muhly 1989: 306–310). The materials recovered pointed to a time during the 13th–12th centuries BC (ProBA 2), now confirmed and refined by radiocarbon dating: House A at Apliki – one of several structures fully excavated – was in use between ca. 1300–1200/1156 Cal BC (Manning and Kuniholm 2007: 328; see also Appendix). In terms of the overall radiocarbon sequence and data in Model 8 of the Appendix, the final cereal data from Apliki lie at 1216–1130 Cal BC at 68.2% probability ($\mu\pm\sigma$: 1184±41 Cal BC) and the subsequent Boundary marking a terminus ante quem for the Apliki data lies at 1245–1103 Cal BC at 68.2% probability ($\mu\pm\sigma$: 1127±104 Cal BC). Some metal objects (bronze, lead, a gold earring) were recovered and some faunal remains were stained green, perhaps with metal 'salts'. Based on a detailed study of the groundstone tools, Kassianidou (in Kling and Muhly 2007: 277) concluded that Apliki was not just a settlement with storage facilities but also an industrial site where copper metal was extracted from sulphide ores. In her last word on the site, however, Du Plat Taylor (1952: 150) had expressed concern that '…the evidence for the mining of copper ore by the occupants of this site is tentative'.

Although no traces of furnaces were recovered at the archaeological site, explorations by the Cyprus Mines Corporation found remnants of discarded furnaces on the 'North Hill' of Apliki, at that time covered in slag heaps (Du Plat Taylor 1952: 152). Moreover, at Apliki itself, tuyères were found in House A and in a pit nearby, together with fragments of crucibles, stone hammers and abundant slag. These finds strongly suggest that those who lived at Apliki were involved in processing ores, whether within or beyond the village itself. Most importantly, several large blocks of a black ropy slag were present in all the rooms of House A (Du Plat Taylor 1952: 142). Muhly (1989: 306–307, fig. 35.1) argued that these slag blocks, along with the massive size of the tuyères found at the site (Muhly 1989: 307–308, fig. 35.2), confirmed that '… extensive mining and smelting operations were carried out at Apliki during the 13th and 12th centuries BC'.

The excavations at Politiko *Phorades* (Knapp et al. 2001; Knapp and Kassianidou 2008) indicate that metalworkers operated smelting furnaces on an artificial working platform constructed from river channel deposits. On

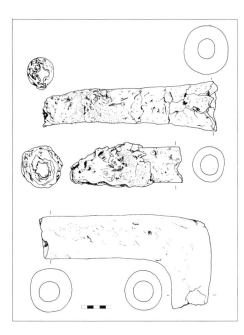

Figure 125. Politiko *Phorades* tuyères: cylindrical (top), double-walled (middle), elbow (bottom). Drawn by Glynnis Fawkes.

Figure 126. Politiko *Phorades* slag heap, during the course of excavation. Photograph by Vasiliki Kassianidou.

this artificial bank lay a stone-lined cavity, within which were several tuyère fragments, and around which were several almost complete tuyères (Figure 125). This cavity was most likely a tapping pit associated with smelting rather than an actual smelting furnace. The slag left over from smelting (more than 3.5 tons recovered) eventually formed a small heap (Figure 126). There was no definitive evidence of ore beneficiation or the actual roasting process, but concentrations of broken tuyères and furnace fragments, and the large amount of slag recovered, indicate that copper ores were being smelted at *Phorades*. The close dating to the ProBA 1 period of pottery found at the site – White Slip I and II (early), Base-ring I, Red Lustrous Wheelmade, Black or Red Slip Wheelmade and Plain White Handmade wares – was eventually confirmed by AMS radiocarbon analyses conducted on charcoal found within the furnace walls and the slag (Period IIIb). These dates demonstrate a calendar age range especially in the 16th–15th centuries Cal BC (Figure 127).

The excavations at *Phorades* produced more than 6,000 fragments of furnace rims, walls and bases, 50 almost complete tuyères and up to 600 tuyère fragments. The *Phorades* tuyères are all quite similar in material and shape (mainly cylindrical, a few double-walled tuyères, one elbow-shaped tuyère like those from Enkomi and Apliki). A detailed chemical and mineralogical study of the furnaces and tuyères revealed that local clay deposits were used in their manufacture (Hein and Kilikoglou 2007; Hein et al. 2007). Copper sulphide ores were smelted in the furnaces, using as fuel charcoal almost exclusively derived from *pinus brutia*, a tree that still dominates the landscape today.

The 3.5 tons of slag from *Phorades* came in the form of large plano-concave cakes that weighed approximately 20 kg (Figure 128). The *Phorades* slag – with a copper content averaging 2.7% – differs from all other Late Bronze slags excavated on Cyprus, whether the large tap slags from Apliki (Muhly 1989: 306) or the plano-convex slags from Kition (Tylecote 1982: 89). Based on the presence of matte prills within the slag matrix, as well as a small piece of silver-blue matte (73.5% copper, 2.6 % iron, 23.9% sulphur), we concluded that this was the form of metal produced at *Phorades*. An intermediate product in the production of copper metal, matte has always been quite rare in archaeological excavations. Its presence here indicates that *Phorades* was a primary smelting workshop. The excavations at *Phorades* go some way towards supporting the notion that the initial stages of the copper smelting process on ProBA Cyprus took place near the ore sources (at *Phorades*, only 500 m distant), whilst secondary smelting, refining and final production (of oxhide or other ingots, finished products) took place at the coastal centres.

Before turning to consider broader issues of *Connectivity and Exchange* (next section), it will be helpful to consider first the extensive work that has gone into sourcing the copper oxide ingots found throughout the Mediterranean and widely assumed to have been produced on Cyprus. Lead isotope analyses on ingots from Sardinia, mainland Greece and the Cape Gelidonya and Uluburun shipwrecks indicated that they were made from copper consistent with an origin in Cyprus's sulphide orebodies (e.g. Gale 1991b; Stos-Gale et al. 1997; Gale and Stos-Gale 2005; cf. Begemann et al. 2001). In an earlier study (Knapp 2000), I noted that many of the copper oxhide ingots analysed had remarkably consistent lead isotopic abundance ratios. Some 50 ingots

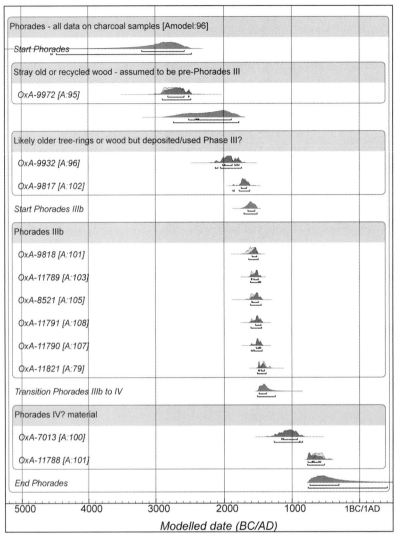

Figure 127. Politiko *Phorades* calibrated calendar ages of radiocarbon dates (run separately as a stand-alone model, but similar age ranges found in Models 1–8 in the Appendix). The upper and lower horizontal lines under each distribution indicate the 68.2% and 95.4% probability calibrated calendar age ranges respectively (modelled). The Phase IIIb grouping is stratigraphically defined; assessments of earlier phases represent judgements made on common-sense grounds; this is also the case for a more recent post-Phase IIIb, perhaps Phase IV, grouping of what is substantially more recent material (OxA-7013, OxA-11788). The main Phase IIIb grouping of six dates forms a clear and tight chronological grouping, which best reflects the ages of the wood/charcoal employed at the site during Phase IIIb activities. All samples are charcoal (*Pinus brutia*) and thus represent *terminus post quem* estimates for actual human use. An old-wood adjusted estimate (50±50 years) for the *Pinus brutia* tree-rings would revise the start and end dates to ca. 1556±71–1350±88 Cal BC (see Appendix). Calibration employs OxCal 4.17, using IntCal09 (Reimer et al. 2009) with curve resolution set at 5. Analysis and illustration by Sturt W. Manning.

Figure 128. Politiko *Phorades* slag cake, base fragment. Photograph by Christopher Parks.

from Cyprus, Sardinia, the Aegean, the Levant, and the Cape Gelidonya and Uluburun shipwrecks indicate a spread of only 0.5% on a conventional plot of lead isotope data (Budd et al. 1995: 13–15, and fig. 5; Gale 1989: 257, fig. 29.18). Most scholars involved interpreted these results as proof of a common Cypriot origin for these ingots but felt that they must have come from multiple ore sources (a process known as 'pooling'). For example, based on the evidence from *Phorades*, we would assume that the primary smelting of raw copper ores at multiple, similar small sites across the island produced matte or a similar end product. Then, in the secondary smelting work carried out in the coastal centres, the products of primary smelting at various sources would have been pooled to produce 'black copper' (rich in iron) which, when further refined, was cast into copper oxhide ingots.

Extrapolating from the results of lead isotope analyses carried out on some of the oxhide ingots from the Cape Gelidonya and Uluburun shipwrecks

(Gale 1991b: 227–231; 2005; Pulak 2000: 146–150), to all the ingots recovered
from these two wreck deposits (Pulak 1997: 235–238; 2001: 20–21), results in
a total of about 380 ingots – up to 10 tons of metal – consistent with production from Cypriot ores. Although the combined weight of archaeological and
compositional evidence might suggest a process of recycling (Budd et al. 1995;
see also Muhly 1991b), further metallographic and chemical analyses indicated that the composition of the copper oxhide ingots from the Uluburun
shipwreck was not affected by remelting scrap metal or by the use of several
different ingots (Hauptmann et al. 2002). Yet these same Uluburun ingots are
most unlikely to have derived from a single batch of copper from one smelting
process (Hauptmann et al. 2002: 18).

The international trade of bulk copper in the form of standardised ingots
represents a growing commodification of metals, a process in which the metals'
original sources increasingly became irrelevant. If the motivation was to maintain or expand the already vast scale of the interregional trade in metals, there
must have been every economic if not social incentive to use mixed sources of
copper ores, or even recycled metals, in producing the copper oxhide ingots.
The results of chemical and metallographic analyses at the very least call into
question the assumption that all the primary smelting copper that went into
any single oxhide ingot derived from a single source.

Nonetheless, the research team from Oxford University that set up a
comprehensive and long-term programme of lead isotope analysis to study
Mediterranean metals, ores and oxhide ingots has insisted – repeatedly over
the years – that the copper used for producing *all* oxhide ingots dated after
1250 BC (some 180 examples) came from a single mine near Apliki (Stos-Gale
et al. 1997; Gale 1999: 116; Gale and Stos-Gale 2012). At the same time, this copper was almost never used to make bronze or copper artefacts. As Kassianidou
(2001: 110; 2009) has emphasised, many archaeologists found this suggestion
hard to accept.

As already noted, the copper ore deposits in the region around Apliki,
Skouriotissa and Mavrovouni in northwest Cyprus are the most substantial on
the island and amongst the largest in the Mediterranean region. Nonetheless
there are countless other copper deposits scattered throughout the Lower
Pillow Lavas of the Troodos (Constantinou 1992), and it seems inconceivable
that none of them were exploited to produce oxhide ingots. Apliki, of course,
is the only ore deposit currently known that is also associated with an excavated ProBA 2 settlement (*Karamallos*). *Phorades*, an excavated copper smelting site of the ProBA 1 period located only 500 m distant from an orebody
at *Kokkinorotsos*, must be regarded as but one (possibly the only remaining)
example of a type of site that was once ubiquitous throughout the mining
areas that encircle the Troodos mountains (Knapp 2003: 564). It is difficult to
imagine that those who controlled the production of copper in an export-
oriented economy so well developed as that on ProBA Cyprus would have

limited their activities to one mine (Apliki), even if they might have preferred it above all others.

Moreover, as Kassianidou (2009) recently argued, Apliki's location is not favourable for such an export-oriented economy: it is located too far from the sea and its ores lie at a level so deep that it could not have been easy for ancient miners to work. Furthermore Apliki, as well as all the other mines around the 'Solea Axis' and those at Limni, are situated farther than any other deposits from the coastal workshops where the ultimate refinement of copper ores took place (cf. Gale and Stos-Gale 2012). If the Apliki ores were used exclusively to produce ingots, while ores from other mines (local or foreign) were used to manufacture copper or bronze artefacts (Apliki copper was almost never used to make metal artefacts), how are we to understand the oxhide ingots or ingot fragments found in archaeometallurgical installations or hoarding contexts at Enkomi, Maroni *Tsaroukkas* and *Vournes,* Kalavasos *Ayios Dhimitrios*, Pyla *Kokkinokremos* and Maa *Palaeokastro,* or in less secure contexts at Mathiatis and Skouriotissa? Were all metalworkers around the island supplied with copper oxhide ingots coming from Apliki? Whatever its overall benefits may prove to be, in this case lead isotope analysis has raised as many questions for archaeologists as it has answered.

When it comes to provenancing artefacts, lead isotope analysis provides a characterisation of the source(s) of lead in them, not the source of the copper. In Muhly's (2003: 145) view, this conundrum '…constitutes the fatal flaw in all the research published by the Gales, going back to 1982'. Muhly also points out in the same study that lead isotope analysis of some Late Minoan I artefacts (i.e. 16th century BC) from Khania on Crete were made from Apliki copper (Stos-Gale et al. 2000: 209). Yet the Oxford team that produced these results have insisted in all their publications that Apliki copper only came into use ca. 1250 BC (Gale and Stos-Gale 2012 have now modified their views in the face of such criticism, stating that all 'post ≈1400 BC' oxhide ingots were made of ores from Apliki).

How and why do such inconsistencies arise? How are archaeologists untrained in science-based techniques supposed to understand such contradictions? Most archaeologists who have attempted to understand the role of Cyprus in the Late Bronze Age metals trade within and beyond the Mediterranean would acknowledge that the data derived from LIA are 'objective'. The problems arise with the consistency of these analyses, and the archaeological interpretations inferred on the basis of lead isotope data, in particular concerning ingots, or artefacts made of alloyed copper. Perhaps the most egregious of these problems is a recent 're-evaluation' of LIA data that argues – with little sense of space, time, mobility or connectivity – that a large number of some 375 metal artefacts from both PreBA and ProBA Cyprus derive from ores in the Aegean, Anatolia, Sardinia, southern France and southwestern Spain (Stos-Gale and Gale 2010).

This debate is not exclusively archaeological in nature. Pollard (2009) now insists that for multiple archaeological and analytical reasons, there is little point in attempting to trace the exact source of copper ores to particular mines. It is exceedingly difficult in any case to obtain ores that reflect with any accuracy those used in antiquity. In turn, Gale (2009) charges Pollard with a failure to engage with the data, and reiterates that the majority of Mediterranean oxhide ingots dated after 1250 BC ('post ≈1400 BC') and analysed by lead isotope analysis were made exclusively of copper from the Apliki ore deposit. On the one hand, the 'scientific' evidence that suggests *all* oxhide ingots produced on Cyprus after 1250 BC had to come from Apliki seems as contrary to the material, social, economic and spatial evidence as it did more than 10 years ago (Knapp 1999b: 106). On the other hand, many of the lead isotope analyses carried out on copper oxhide ingots have tended to confirm that they are *consistent with production from* Cypriot ores. Moreover, ingots of unalloyed copper have a lead isotope signature that is not only remarkably consistent within and between different laboratories, but also indicates a Cypriot ore source (Muhly 2003: 150). There are multiple analytical, archaeological and documentary reasons to argue for Cyprus's key role in copper production and trade in the Late Bronze Age Mediterranean, and lead isotope analysis has provided one of the more prominent. Until the discrepancies involved in applying this technique to sourcing copper ores have been resolved, however, and until quantitative data are analysed and interpreted in tandem with archaeologists and/or together with archaeological reasoning, it remains a frustratingly weak link in the chain of provenance studies.

Analytical issues aside, there is little doubt that the copper industry was instrumental in propelling Cyprus into the politico-economic sphere of eastern Mediterranean production and exchange systems. The market potential of Cypriot ports such as Enkomi, Hala Sultan Tekke, Kition and Maroni ensured access to various domestic products, such as pottery or copper ingots, and to imported goods such as ivory, tin ingots, gold and silver, amber, Aegean and Levantine pottery, Egyptian faience and alabaster, Hittite statuary and a whole range of organic products. Let us now consider in detail some of the raw materials and goods exchanged, the meanings and intentions that lay behind them, and the mechanisms by which they were imported to or exported from Cyprus.

Materiality, Connectivity and Exchange

Late Bronze Age polities in the Aegean and eastern Mediterranean were intricately engaged in one of the most prominent and extensive systems of international trade known in a prehistoric setting. Merchants, mariners and monarchs alike were all involved, on different scales and in different ways, in the production, distribution and consumption of raw materials (copper, tin, silver, gold), utilitarian products (pottery, metal artefacts), luxury items (ivory, faience, amber, precious and semi-precious stones), and a range of textiles and organic goods (olive oil, wine, honey, spices) (Knapp 1991; Sherratt and Sherratt 1991; Haldane 1993; Rehak 1996; Cline and Harris Cline 1998; Sherratt 2003). Cypriot and Aegean pottery was exported widely throughout the Mediterranean, from the Levant and Egypt in the east (Snape 2003; Bergoffen 2005; Dabney 2007; Maguire 2009) to Sicily, the Aeolian islands, Sardinia and Spain in the west (Martín de la Cruz 1988; Knapp 1990b; Almagro-Gorbea and Fontes 1997: 345–347; D'Agata 2000; Alberti 2005; Jones et al. 2005; Vianello 2005). Copper oxhide ingots, as we have already seen, turn up in diverse contexts within and beyond the Mediterranean (most recently, Lo Schiavo et al. 2009). The extraordinary cargo of the Uluburun shipwreck – copper and tin ingots, glass and cobalt ingots, gold and silver jewellery, metal vessels, ivory, wood, spices and condiments, terebinth resin, ostrich eggshells, Cypriot and Mycenaean pottery – offer an unprecedented view into the objects and subjects of Late Bronze Age trade (Pulak 2001; 2008: 290–297; Yalçin et al. 2005; Monroe 2009: 10–12).

A group of exquisite gold, silver, ivory and faience objects dated to the 14th–13th centuries BC in the eastern Mediterranean reveals the iconographic and design elements of an 'international style' that not only symbolised the social and exchange relations of ruling élites, but also facilitated diplomatic contacts between them (Feldman 2006; Feldman and Sauvage 2010). The quality, design and manufacture of these luxury goods reflect the labour intensive, technologically sophisticated output of craft specialists attached to the households or courts of the major powers of the day, all part of an interconnected system that linked ideology, iconography and traded goods with social and political status. The Late Bronze Age thus was a truly 'international era' (e.g. Cline 1994): ships from the Aegean, Cyprus, Anatolia, the Levant and Egypt, if not the central Mediterranean, were actively involved. But in order to discuss how this trade actually worked, its 'mechanisms' in other words, we must consider not just the nature and types of goods traded, but also evidence for mercantile cooperation and competition, the ideology of exchange and material and social connections ('connectivity') more generally (e.g. Webb 2005; Monroe 2009; van Dommelen and Knapp 2010).

Connectivity, in its broadest sense, refers to modes of travel, mobility, social exchange and communications – all mechanisms that helped to establish, motivate or modify the outlooks and identities of merchants, mariners and migrants. In Skeates's (2009: 556) view, connectivity '…refers to the social and geographical interdependence of small-scale, locally specific phenomena (including micro-regions, places, peoples, economic strategies, and interactions) with[in] a dynamic network of relations enjoyed by them with the wider world'. Connectivity via the sea – maritime mobility – has been a key feature of island life in the Mediterranean throughout prehistoric and historic times:

Horden and Purcell (2000: 224–230) ascribe various aspects of Aegean island production to '*all around* connectivity'. Islanders and coastal dwellers formed open ('imagined') communities linked by the sea (Gosden and Pavlides 1994: 163). Most coastal and island communities, especially those settled in large ports, harbours or entrepôts, were not only oriented towards the sea but also relied on its connecting role to fulfil the demands of a broader system created by maritime contacts. Connectivity and maritime trading both condition and compel the mobility of island and coastal communities, and impact on the level and intensity of contacts they enjoy.

In the Late Bronze Age eastern Mediterranean, there was a notable and significant increase in connectivity amongst Levantine, Egyptian and Aegean polities that also embraced Cyprus (Knapp 1990b: 118–128). During the ProBA I period, some people on the island began to import and use Egyptian or Levantine pottery (e.g. Tell el-Yahudiyeh ware – Kaplan 1980; Merrillees 2007; Syrian Black Burnished and Plain wares – Georgiou 2009), and to display elaborate military equipment, in particular bronze 'warrior' belts and bronze notched chisel axes ('socketed axeheads'). Both types of equipment – common in Levantine burials (e.g. Tell ed-Dab'a, Ugarit, Kültepe, Jerusalem, Jericho, Tell el-Far'ah North) – have been found in Cypriot mortuary contexts at Dhali *Kafkallia*, Politiko *Chomazoudhia*, Nicosia *Ayia Paraskevi*, Ayios Iakovos *Melia*, Klavdhia *Trimithios*, Kazaphani *Ayios Andronikos* and elsewhere (Overbeck and Swiny 1972: 7–24; Masson 1976: 153–157; Keswani 2004: 80, 121–124). Even in the unlikely case that such bronzes were produced locally, they were clearly inspired by Near Eastern prototypes (Philip 1991: 78–83; 1995).

Levantine and Near Eastern ideas or ideologies may also be seen in equid burials from Politiko *Chomazoudhia* Tomb 3 (Buchholz 1973), Kalopsidha Tomb 9 and Lapithos Tomb 322B (Keswani 2004: 80). Based on a detailed new study of the pottery from Kalopsidha, including several innovative vessel types of 'Levantine style' or 'Syrian inspiration', Crewe (2010b: 68) is of the opinion that the site enjoyed 'privileged access to imported goods and trade relations'. Several other imported or exotic items – Syrian and Old Babylonian cylinder seals, faience ornaments, worked bone and ivory, ostrich eggs, gold jewellery and other precious metal objects, semi-precious stones – that first appear during ProBA I served as potential markers of status and identity (Courtois 1986; Keswani 2004: 136).

During the same period of time (ProBA I), Cypriot pottery increasingly was exported to Egypt (Merrillees 1968) and the Levant (Johnson 1982). From Tell ed-Dab'a in the eastern Nile Delta, for example, came a substantial assemblage of Cypriot wares – White Painted (the majority), Red on Black, Black Slip, Red Slip, Red Polished, Bichrome, Plain White Handmade, Proto White Slip and White Slip (Maguire 2009: 26–37). Most of these take the form of closed vessels, that is, small jugs and juglets, but several types of bowls, small jars and amphorae are also present. Cypriot wares of this period are also widely

Figure 129. 'Lustrous' Base-ring I krater from Alalakh, restored. Ht: 33 cm. After Bergoffen 2005: 88, 121, pl. 13. Courtesy of Celia J. Bergoffen.

distributed – albeit with significant differences in types – along the Levantine coast or its near hinterland, from Alalakh and Ras Shamra in the north to Ashkelon and Tell el-'Ajjul in the south (Bergoffen 2005; Maguire 2009: 22, fig. 2a, 47–66). These wares derive from both mortuary and settlement contexts. Although bowls and storage jars have been found, narrow-necked jugs and juglets – 'precious commodity containers' for perfumed oils (Maguire 2009: 53, 61, fig. 21) – dominate the Cypriot pottery assemblages found in both the Nile Delta and the Levant.

During the ProBA 1 (LC I) period, new types of Cypriot wares – Base-ring, Red Lustrous (tall, narrow-necked 'spindle bottles'), Black Lustrous, White Slip – begin to replace the older exports, but small jugs and juglets continue to appear (Maguire 2009: 62–64, figs. 22–23). The best-known ProBA 1–2 wares (White Slip, Base-ring, Monochrome) are found in significant quantities throughout the Levant (e.g. Gittlen 1981; Artzy 1985; Bergoffen 1991; Badre 2003: 85–86) and in Egypt (e.g. Merrillees 1968; White 2002; Snape 2003), and increasingly so in Anatolia (Mielke 2007). One example, and one of the most striking of these objects is a 'lustrous' Base-ring I krater from Alalakh, a vessel that must have been used for special, drinking or banqueting occasions (Bergoffen 2007: fig. 1) (Figure 129). The large quantities of ProBA 2 Cypriot wares found at Ugarit in the north (Yon 2001) and Tell el-'Ajjul in the south (Bergoffen 2001a; 2001b) suggest that these sites served as transit points for the receipt and further transport of imports; other important harbour towns, such as Byblos, also had their fair share of Cypriot imports (Karageorghis 2008).

In Egypt, excavations at Kom Rabia (Memphis) have produced a Black
Lustrous juglet handle, Red Lustrous sherds and a Base-ring I body sherd in
an early 18th Dynasty context, and Cypriot Base-ring II sherds in early 19th
Dynasty contexts (Bourriau n.d.; 1987: 10–11). In western Egypt, excavations in
Late Bronze Age levels (15th–13th centuries BC) at Marsa Matruh uncovered
abundant examples of imported pottery, largely Cypriot but also including
Aegean and Levantine wares. The most frequently attested Cypriot wares are
White Slip I and II hemispherical bowls, Base-ring I and II juglets, flasks and
cups, White Shaved ware juglets; there are a few examples of Monochrome,
Red Lustrous, Bichrome Wheelmade, and Plain Ware jars, as well as various
coarse ware *pithoi*, storage vessels and Canaanite jars (Russell, Hulin, in White
2002: 8–15, 28–38)

Some 25 km west of Marsa Matruh (and today 1 km inland from the sea)
lay the massive fortified enclosure of Zawiyet Umm el-Rakham, dated to
the time of Ramesses II in the 13th century BC (Snape 2003). Whilst the
bulk of the imported pottery identified thus far comes from 15 whole and
several other, fragmentary Canaanite jars (amphorae), there are also at least
five, tall, coarse-ware stirrup jars (two with Cypro-Minoan marks on their
handles), some Mycenaean fine wares and Late Minoan jugs. Amongst the
Cypriot wares are some 'Cypriote flasks, white shaved [sic] and Base Ring
II wares' (Thomas 2003: 524); the only items illustrated are some curiously
drawn strainer jugs, perhaps of Base-ring ware (Snape 2000; 2003: 67–68, fig.
5; Thomas 2003: 527, fig. 4). In Snape's (2003: 67) view, this material may have
found its way to the site as an unofficial 'custom's duty' paid by seaborne traders en route to/from Egypt, who re-fitted or restocked their ships at Umm
el-Rakham. White (2003: 77), however, suggests that the lack of any suitable
anchorage along the coast north of Umm el-Rakham counts against its role
as a trading post; he suggests instead that the transport and storage containers
found there represent provisions offloaded at Marsa Matruh and carried overland to Umm el-Rakham.

The meaning(s) of such southern and southeastern exports, as well as the
identities of those who shipped or received them, still awaits meaningful social
interpretation. For example, even if the Base-ring jugs and juglets widely found
in mortuary contexts in the southern Levant were designed and decorated in
imitation of an opium poppy (Merrillees 1962; 1969; Merrillees and Evans
1989), who was producing and who was consuming that drug, and why? In
which ways would the use of opium have intensified, or elaborated mortuary
rituals? Those scholars most qualified to consider such questions seldom ask
them. One exception, at least, comes from the work at Marsa Matruh.

In the final report of work at Marsa Matruh, Hulin (in White 2002: 174)
suggests only that the extensive number of imports at the site may relate to
an 'informal/tramping/sailor's trade' in 'relatively value-less' items. White
(1986: 83–84; 2003: 75), however, originally proposed that this unique site

may have served as a summer revictualing station for merchants or traders en route from the Aegean to the Egyptian delta, the Levantine coast and Cyprus. The numerous ostrich eggshell fragments found at the site suggest the same (White 1999: 933–934). Clearly those who lived or worked at Marsa Matruh had close connections to Cyprus (Cypriot pottery predominates amongst the imports), although the metal items and metallurgical debris (slags and crucible) seem more in keeping with small-scale local production for local use (White 2003: 74). And whilst Marsa Matruh may have something to tell us about the relationship of its inhabitants to indigenous Libyan peoples (Knapp 1981; White 2003: 75–76), in the present discussion its significance lies in its unique location and the unexpected connectivity role it played within Bronze Age Mediterranean exchange systems.

One of the material hallmarks of Late Bronze Age trade in the eastern Mediterranean is the widespread occurrence of Aegean pottery, in particular Minoan and Mycenaean wares. Noticeable amounts of Aegean pottery in particular have been found on Cyprus, beginning with a few Late Minoan I and Late Helladic (Mycenaean) I–II imports during the ProBA 1 period (16th–15th centuries BC). Most of these have been found in the island's northwest, at sites such as Morphou *Toumba tou Skourou* and Ayia Irini *Paleokastro* (Pecorella 1973; Vermeule and Wolsky 1990: 381–385; see also Portugali and Knapp 1985: 71–72). Mycenaean pottery imports increased in number during the 15th–early 14th centuries BC, but in the later 14th and 13th centuries (ProBA 2) this earlier 'trickle' turned into a 'flood' of Late Helladic IIIA2–IIIB wares (Catling 1975: 199–200; Cadogan 1993; Steel 2004b: 70). Finds of Mycenaean pottery on Cyprus are concentrated in town centres along or near the southern and eastern coasts – for example, Enkomi, Kition, Hala Sultan Tekke, Maroni, Kalavasos and Kourion (Steel 2004b: 71–72), but are also found in lesser amounts throughout the island's interior (Pacci 1986). Mycenaean imports turn up most frequently in mortuary or ceremonial contexts, whether in the coastal centres or at inland 'sanctuary' sites: Myrtou *Pigadhes*, Athienou *Bamboulari tis Koukounninas* and Ayios Iakovos *Dhima* (Steel 1998: 286; 2004b: 74–78).

The most typical, or at least the most striking types of Mycenaean imports were the stirrup jar and the pictorial krater. The stirrup jar is a small container for perfumed oil or other precious substance, whilst the krater is a large vessel most likely used to serve wine (Leonard 1981: 94–96; Steel 1998: 291–294). Mycenaean pictorial style kraters of the 14th–13th centuries BC served as drinking sets, and clearly had a major impact on both the material culture and social practices of the ProBA 2 period. Feldman and Sauvage (2010: 110) suggest that Mycenaean 'chariot' kraters were prestigious military objects, with strong social signification. By the end of and especially during the 12th century BC, Mycenaean imports decreased significantly as the local production of Mycenaean-type pottery increased. The range of names given to these wares (Rude or Pastoral Style, Late Helladic IIIB and IIIC:1b, Decorated Late Cypriot III) in earlier literature is no longer used: they are now all referred to as White Painted Wheelmade III wares (Kling 2000: 281–282; see also Sherratt 1991: 186–187; Steel 1998: 288).

Cypriot exports westward, to the Aegean and central Mediterranean, typically receive less attention but they too tell us a great deal about mobility and connectivity in the Late Bronze Age Mediterranean. Amongst numerous imports found at Kommos on Crete (from Egypt, the Levant and the central Mediterranean) were 76 Cypriot items spanning the Middle Minoan III through Late Minoan IIIB periods (ca. 1750–1200 BC) (Manning 2010: 23, table 2.2; Rutter 2006: 653–658). The earliest material cited in early reports, from late Middle Minoan contexts, consists of fragments from a Middle Cypriot, White Painted IV Cross Line Style jug, a 'large Cypriot flask' and 'many more fragments of Cypriot pottery from soundings' (Shaw 1998: 13–14, 23, and fig. 1). From the Late Minoan IA(final)–III periods came the bulk of the Cypriot imports: Red Slip and Proto Base-ring jugs, White Slip II bowls (31 pieces, the majority), Base-ring II jugs (14 pieces), juglets, carinated cups and a bowl, Plain White *pithoi* and amphorae, White Painted Wheelmade I jugs or tankards, White Shaved juglets and a Red Lustrous spindle bottle (Watrous 1992: 156–159; Rutter 2006: 654–656, tables 3.104–105). The bulk of these fragments belong to medium-large size pouring vessels, and they may be associated with drinking ceremonies held within Building T at the site (Rutter 2006: 656). In addition, two, three-holed stone anchors from a Late Minoan IIIA 2 context (ca. 1390–1330 BC) at Kommos are of a type common in both Cyprus and Ugarit (Shaw 1998: 15–16).

INAA (Instrumental Neutron Activation Analysis) was used in the attempt to determine the provenance of 48 presumed Cypriot imports at Kommos. Forty of these proved to be related to known Cypriot analytical groups, four to Cretan groups, with another four unprovenanced (Tomlinson et al. 2010). Most White Slip II 'milk bowls' imported to Kommos were made from clays consistent with production from the (inland) southern coast of Cyprus, possibly from the White Slip production centre at Sanidha (Tomlinson et al. 2010: 217–218; Todd and Pilides 2001). It is worthwhile mentioning that the single example of a Red Lustrous spindle bottle from Kommos could not be associated with any known Cypriot ceramic reference group. Tomlinson et al. (2010: 218), however, did not have access to the INAA and petrographic analytical data on 95 samples of this ware from seven sites in Anatolia, Cyprus and Egypt (Knappett and Kilikoglou 2007); these data indicate that the examples from all sites have a very similar fabric composition, that the ware most likely stems from a single source, and that the area around Kazaphani in northern Cyprus remains the most likely source, even if southern Anatolia cannot be ruled out.

From the Greek mainland, Cline (1994: 60) recorded 40 Cypriot objects 'in good LBA contexts', and 20 more from Rhodes (see also Portugali and Knapp

1985: 77–78). Most of these are White Slip hemispherical bowls, followed by Base-ring juglets, terracotta wall brackets, Red Lustrous 'spindle bottles', White Shaved juglets, terracotta figurines, faience and lapis lazuli cylinder seals, haematite and steatite seals, and diverse objects of gold, silver and bronze (Cline 1994: 268–270, table 66). Taking the site of Tiryns as an example, excavations over the years have produced a notable corpus of Cypriot material: White Slip II milkbowls (Kilian et al. 1981: 170, 184, fig. 40:5; Kilian 1988: 121, 129, fig. 25:11); a White Shaved ware juglet (Kilian 1983: 292, fig. 15:14, 304); a large 'transport jug' (Maran 2008: 58–59, fig. 41); Cypro-Minoan graffiti on local and foreign vessels (Maran 2008: 56; see also Hirschfeld 1996); fragments of at least two, animal-headed faience vessels which may be of either Cypriot or Levantine origin (Maran 2008: 52, 57, fig. 38; 2009: 247; Kostoula and Maran 2012); various objects from the 'Tiryns treasure', whose authenticity has now been demonstrated (Maran 2006: 130–140); and an ivory rod with six cuneiform signs, argued on contextual grounds to have been used by Cypriote or Levantine craftspeople (Maran 2009: 247; Cohen et al. 2010). Recent work indicates some 15 wall brackets found at Tiryns were not Cypriot imports with high 'distance-value', as Cline (1999) maintained, but instead were locally made, even if clearly of Cypriot inspiration (Maran 2004: 11–13). Stockhammer (2007: 156–157) has even tentatively suggested that some Cypriotes may have been resident in Tiryns early in the 12th century BC.

As excavations or reassessments of material from earlier excavations in southern Italy, the Aeolian islands, Sicily and Sardinia increasingly single out material of Aegean or Cypriot form, fabric, or appearance (e.g. Marazzi et al. 1986; Militello 2004; Alberti 2005; Tanasi 2005; 2009), the number of central Mediterranean sites that contain eastern Mediterranean material grows steadily (on that growth, compare Smith 1987, with Vianello 2005). Much of the data discussed in what follows stems from Anthony Russell's (2011) recent research.

Prominent amongst these finds, at least in attempting to assess the nature and extent of contacts between the eastern and central Mediterranean, are copper oxhide ingots and ingot fragments. These objects have been found at 34 sites across Sardinia (Lo Schiavo 1998; 2008: 263–268), and in varying numbers in Sicily, Lipari, Corsica and southern France (Lo Schiavo et al. 2009). The fact that more oxhide ingots and fragments have been found on Sardinia than anywhere else in the central Mediterranean inevitably has led to suggestions of Cypriot involvement in local metallurgical developments (e.g. Lo Schiavo et al. 1985; Lo Schiavo 1990; 2001; see also Bietti Sestieri 1988: 49). The evidence for such involvement, however, is rather limited.

Although lead isotope analyses conducted by the Oxford Isotrace Laboratory on oxhide ingots from Sardinia suggested that they were consistent with production from Cypriot ores (Stos-Gale et al. 1997; cf. Knapp 2000: 39–40), more recent analyses of three (out of a total of seven) fragments of oxhide ingots found in a hoard from Sedda Ottinnèra di Pattada (Sassari) indicate that they are consistent with production from a Sardinian source (Begemann et al. 2001: 57). Another, founder's hoard from Nuraghe Funtana, also in Sassari but about 50 km west of Pattada, produced 24 oxhide ingot fragments, in context with 10 'bun' ingots and another 10 ingot fragments too small to identify (Begemann et al. 2001: 47 and fig. 3; Lo Schiavo 2005a: 320). Given that Sardinia is rich in copper ores, and had been exploiting them for some time, and because oxhide ingot fragments are not infrequently found together with typical Sardinian bun-shaped copper ingots, the mixing of local and foreign ores or metals may have been standard practice.

I have already rehearsed in some detail (pp. 413–416) various problems in accepting at face value the quantitative results of lead isotope analysis, and have written at length elsewhere about specific problems with various data sets (Knapp 1990b; 2000; see also Muhly 1995; 2003: 145). Here I only wish to question the assertion that the copper in oxhide ingots found on Sardinia derived exclusively from Cypriot ore sources. Given that most oxhide ingot fragments found on Sardinia had been grouped together in 'hoards' with other metal objects and tools, whole or fragmentary, all of them must have been regarded as useful sources of metal rather than as special objects with a non-intrinsic value (Begemann et al. 2001: 67).

However one regards the profusion of copper oxhide ingots and ingot fragments found throughout Sardinia, other objects have been put forward as corroborating evidence for a close relationship between Sardinia and Cyprus. These include pottery, weapons, tripod stands, double axes, figurines, a cylinder seal, and most significantly, metallurgical tools such as hammers, tongs and shovels (Lo Schiavo 1985: 7–9; Lo Schiavo et al. 1985: 22–28; Knapp 1990b: 141, 145). Such tools are very limited on the ground: from a total of three hammers, three charcoal shovels, one shovel mould, and seven pairs of tongs (Lo Schiavo 2005b: 294), only four of the tongs have reliable contextual information. Lacking datable contexts, any association of these objects with Cyprus rests strictly on typological grounds. Moreover, none of these tools was found in context with the oxhide ingots. Only one oxhide ingot, from the Pattada hoard, was found together with finished objects (double axes and axe-adzes) thought to indicate some kind of a link to Cyprus: Lo Schiavo et al. (1985: 18–22, figs. 7–8) compare them to examples from hoards at Enkomi, although lead isotope analysis indicates they were likely made in Sardinia (Begemann et al. 2001: 70, table 4, 72). One of the three charcoal shovels – from Sa Sedda 'e Sos Carros (Nuoro) – also seems to be have been produced locally (Begemann et al. 2001: 50, 73). Although the Sardinian tongs are similar to but slightly smaller than their Cypriot counterparts, the function of tongs is such that there is little variety in their shapes; indeed, the fact that the Sardinian tongs are compared with 'Levantine' instead of Cypriot types underscores their generic nature (Lo Schiavo et al. 1985: 23–25).

Amongst the few finished bronze objects from Sardinia thought to portray Cypriot affinities are two hook-tanged daggers from Ottana (Vianello 2005: 142). Although these resemble Cypriot 'rat-tail' tang weapons (Catling 1964: 56–59, pl. 2a–b), formal differences between them suggest that the Sardinian versions were locally made (Lo Schiavo 1985: 7). Three miniature tripod stands and two figurines found on Sardinia have also been cited as evidence for connections with Cyprus (Lo Schiavo et al. 1985: 42, 54–55). Two of the tripod stands are regarded as Sardinian imitations of the Cypriot form, but only the fragmentary, third example (lacking provenance) is regarded as an actual import because of its close resemblance – albeit on a smaller scale – to Cypriot examples (e.g. those in Catling 1964: pls. 27–29).

However much weight we allow for links between Sardinia and Cyprus (or the Aegean) with respect to metalwork, when it comes to pottery, the evidence of Cypriot or Aegean-style wares at various sites in the central Mediterranean is actually quite limited; it certainly lends itself well to reinterpretation (e.g. Russell 2010). Moreover, we see an apparent distribution trend: larger amounts of eastern material occur earlier in southern Italy and Sicily, whilst more limited amounts of later material occur in Sardinia and southern Italy, or even as single sherds in central or northern Italy (Knapp 1990b: 124–128). At Antigori on Sardinia, in addition to numerous Aegean or 'Aegean-style' sherds, excavations uncovered some 30 *pithos* sherds (from a single vessel) of presumed Cypriot origin (Ferrarese Ceruti and Assorgia 1982: 170), a few Cypriot wavy-banded *pithos* fragments, and a fragment of what the excavator described as a Cypriot Base-ring wish-bone handle (Ferrarese Ceruti 1997: 439). Vagnetti (2001: 80) regards the last item as a 'desurfaced' White Slip II handle whilst petrographic analyses of this and another Base-ring sherd only indicated that their origin was non-local (Jones and Day 1987: 259, 268 sample 74); it was not specifically Cypriot (Vagnetti 2001: 80–81, 86). Based on petrographic and physico-chemical analyses of 61 non-local sherds from Antigori, only one – from a wavy-banded pithos – proved to be of Cypriot origin (Jones and Day 1987: 259, 268, sample 62). Finally, there is a small amount of possibly Cypriot pottery from San Giovanni di Sinis/Tharros in Oristano (Vianello 2005: 165); and from a tomb at Su Fràigu near San Sperate (16 km north of Calgiari) comes a wishbone handle and a carved cylinder seal, both of which may be of Cypriot origin (Lo Schiavo 2003: 16–17, fig. 2b, 20–21).

Beyond the oxhide ingots, therefore, the evidence for Cypriot contacts with Sardinia is as follows: 13 smithing tools (3 with published archaeological contexts), a charcoal shovel mould, 15 other bronze objects (3 with contexts), 3 sites with a small amount of possible Cypriot pottery, and a cylinder seal. In my view, this does not qualify as a corpus 'so incredibly rich in LC II/LC III elements and connections' (Lo Schiavo 2001: 134). For the sake of completeness, I note here the highly unlikely suggestion, based on lead isotope analysis, that some very fragmentary tin bronze or lead objects found in 12th

century BC sites such as Kition, Pyla *Kokkinokremos*, Hala Sultan Tekke and
Maa *Palaeokastro* were made with metal from the Cambrian ores of Sardinia,
or with ores from Monte Romero, Huelva, in Spain (Stos-Gale and Gale 2010:
398–399, table 5).

Elsewhere in the central Mediterranean, on the Italian mainland, there are
a few sherds of 'Cypro-Mycenaean' ware from Scoglio del Tonno (Apulia)
and Eboli (Campania) (Vagnetti 2001: 78–83, 86, figs. 1.1, 2.1; Alberti 2005:
343–344). In Sicily, some Cypriot, or Cypriot-looking wares have been found
in Thapsos (two White Shaved juglets, two juglets of Base-ring shape), Siracusa
(Base-ring II juglet – Vianello 2005: 179) and Cannatello (two White Slip II
sherds, some wavy-banded pithos sherds, three handles of Late Helladic or
Late Minoan transport stirrup jars engraved with signs resembling those of
the Cypro-Minoan script). Two large storage jars from Cannatello are listed
as having a Cypriot provenance, although no reference is provided for the
analysis (Levi 2004: 235). Graziadio (1997: 683–684) identified another, fragmentary Base-ring jug from Tomb 7 at Thapsos, whilst Karageorghis (1995:
94–95) and Alberti (2005: 344) identified local imitations of Base-ring bowls at
Thapsos, Cozzo del Pantano and Matrensa (all sites in southeastern Sicily close
to Siracusa). Alberti (2005: 345) also suggests that some local types of jugs and
bowls from this same region are similar to Cypriot wares, but these comparisons stretch his already questionable points that 'there is something Cypriot
in the air' (Alberti 2008), and that Cypriot traders were in direct contact with
Sicilian élites.

From a tomb at Capreria (near Agrigento on the south coast of Sicily)
comes a Late Cypriot IIIA cup in reddish-yellow clay and two bronze bowls,
very similar to some ceremonial bronze basins found at Enkomi (Vianello
2005: 157; Catling 1964: 153–154, fig. 17.10). There are also some bronze mirrors
found in the burial grounds at Pantalica (some 40 km northwest of Siracusa)
that have been compared with both Cypriot and Aegean prototypes (Leighton
1999: 178). Oxhide ingot fragments have been found at Cannatello (1) and
Thapsos (1), and on Lipari (dozens of small pieces) in the Aeolian islands, just
northwest of Sicily. Even so, the most recent, detailed study of oxhide ingots
in Sicily suggests that their scarcity is as notable as their presence (Lo Schiavo
et al. 2009: 135). Giardino (1992: 307–308), at least, wonders whether they
might represents links with Sardinia rather than Cyprus. Certainly this could
be the case at Cannatello, where Sardinian pottery – both imported and locally
made – has also been found (Levi 2004: 238).

Finally, suggestions concerning direct Aegean or Cypriot influence on the
physical design of buildings (such as at Thapsos in Sicily – Tomasello 2004: 206;
Militello 2004: 318), or on tombs of tholos-type construction (also in Sicily –
Leighton 1999: 168), are little more than *ex Oriente lux* views that still crop
up in the writings of some local prehistorians (e.g. Alberti 2008; Tanasi 2009).
Such interpretations create more problems than they resolve: for example, *why*

would Bronze Age Sicilian builders even wish to emulate buildings they had never seen? There is not enough Aegean or Cypriot material of any kind in any Sicilian site to indicate the actual presence of foreigners, so I forego further discussion here (but see Russell 2011).

PRESTIGE GOODS AND THE ORGANISATION OF EXCHANGE

So, what do all these intriguing but quite limited Cypriot finds or imitations in the central Mediterranean actually mean? Interpreting and understanding the nature of Late Bronze Age trade and the organisation(s) that lay behind it are exercises fraught with difficulties. Minimalist interpretations caution that we should not overemphasise the importance of imported goods, and instead simply aim to identify them, record their spatial and temporal contexts (whether individual objects or classes of objects), and determine where possible their places of origin (e.g. Catling 1991: 10; Snodgrass 1991: 19).

In turn, Manning and Hulin (2005: 271) argue that many current perceptions of Bronze Age Mediterranean trade are imbalanced in the way they highlight the production and distribution of 'exotic' imports, instead of considering their social life, biographies, relative values and localised contexts of consumption. In commenting on Cline's (1994) corpus of 'Orientalia' found in Late Bronze Age Aegean sites, for example, they note that these 1,118 imports of differing certainty and context amount to the exchange of 0.5 objects per year, averaged over the period of 600 years with which the study was concerned (Manning and Hulin 2005: 283). From their perspective, the assumed volume of trade or level of interaction can hardly be correlated directly with the actual impact or importance of the objects traded. Moreover, it overlooks the possibility that many of these objects could have arrived simultaneously, that is, in a few shipments, rather than piecemeal over the longer term. Whilst Cherry (2009: 112) comments on this same issue with reference to Prepalatial Crete, Parkinson (2010: 17–18, table 2.1) takes an even closer look at the foreign contacts of the Late Bronze Age Aegean: he argues that they were '…infrequent, sporadic, and consisted primarily of the importation of small prestige items'. The number of foreign items that would have entered different areas of the Aegean if tabulated *per decade* is instructive: 6.78 for Crete, 5.85 for the Greek mainland and 1.60 for the Aegean islands.

Focusing on the origins of objects tends to obscure their meaning(s) and significance in a new context (Burns 2010: 16). Goods and materials obtained from afar – whether 'luxury' or 'utilitarian' in nature – may take on social and symbolic values that can be manipulated in various strategies of competition and power in their new context. Objects themselves may be embedded with 'agency' (Feldman 2010; González-Ruibal et al. 2011), and thus carry their own messages of power and prestige, beyond exoticism. Objects made of rare, exotic or precious materials (e.g. on Cyprus – gold, ivory, faience) not only would have invoked wonder but also could have represented important paraphernalia of power, whether as a result of the external connections they represent or because of their intrinsic value or agency. The conspicuous consumption of foreign objects, materials, symbols and ideas thus may reflect not just their mere acquisition but also all sorts of intentions and aspirations difficult to grasp.

'Object diasporas' make it possible to trace the movements and encounters of diverse types of people and social groups (Gkiasta 2010: 87), including traders and migrants. The circulation of objects across spatial, economic and cultural boundaries represents not just physical movement but a social transaction entangling givers and receivers in wider relations of alliance and dependence, prestige and debt (Thomas 1991: 123–124). An impressive range of material, documentary and analytical evidence makes it clear that seaborne trade within and beyond the Late Bronze Age Mediterranean was diverse in structure and complex in nature, embracing state-dominated and entrepreneurial trade as well as gift exchange on the royal or state level (Knapp and Cherry 1994: 126–151). The driving mechanisms behind trade were complex, multidimensional and always in a state of flux, as distinctive goods or new opportunities presented themselves to those most intimately involved in long-distance trade. Even if interregional trade in the Late Bronze Age eastern Mediterranean was largely palace-centred (Sherratt and Sherratt 1991: 370–373), wider factors of consumption and demand for specific imports or exports meant that there was plenty of scope for entrepreneurial initiative.

On ProBA Cyprus, élite groups adopted and in time assimilated various aspects of foreign technologies and iconography; the hybridisation of local and imported motifs or symbolism becomes fully apparent in ProBA material culture (Voskos and Knapp 2008: 664–673). By the ProBA 2 (LC IIA–IIC early) period, these élites began to use, wear or display imported ivory, gold and faience objects, and to use ceremonial, funnel-shaped vessels (*rhyta*) similar to those found in the Aegean and the Levant. Such *rhyta*, along with fine golden utensils and other items, are mentioned as items of exchange between Cyprus (*Alašiya*) and the Hittite court in an Akkadian document from 14th–13th century BC Hattusha (Boğazköy) in Anatolia (Knapp 1980; Beckman in Knapp 1996b: 29). Several gold, metal and stone objects, found at Enkomi and decorated with sphinxes, real animals, hieroglyphics and other images reveal a 'cosmic symbolism' and suggest a close association with or manipulation of Near Eastern political ideologies (Keswani 1989: 69–70).

Faience vessels appear widely on Cyprus, but also throughout the Levant and Egypt, in contexts ranging from wealthy tombs to common households (Peltenburg 2002; 2007b: 379). On Cyprus, there are concentrations of these vessels in Kition Tomb 9 and Enkomi British Tomb 66. Tombs 1 and 9 at Kition *Chrysopolitissa* contained 12 faience vases of various shapes – juglets, bowls, flasks, a *pyxis* – that may be either Egyptian or western Asiatic in origin (Peltenburg 1974: 105–144). From Tomb 1 came the lower half of a small stirrup vase or juglet that betrays Aegean inspiration in its shape; this vessel

Figure 130. Kalavasos *Ayios Dhimitrios* Tomb 12: silver kilted male figure with conical headdress standing on a stag, ProBA 2 date. Ht: 6.2 cm. Cyprus Museum, K-AD 1599. Courtesy of Alison South and the Cyprus Museum, Nicosia.

and others like it may be Cypriot or north Syrian products (Peltenburg 1974: 107–108). Another striking faience bottle in the form of a pomegranate (Tomb 43, 1896 British excavations at Enkomi – Buchholz and Karageorghis 1973: 157, 456 no. 1678; Smith 2009: 98–99) is decorated with horizontal bands of zigzags that may also exemplify Aegean influences. Egyptian faience bowls turn up in several other Cypriot sites during the 13th–12th centuries BC (Peltenburg 2007b: 384–385). These faience vessels, all from mortuary contexts, depict everything from lion and bull hunts to heraldic designs: they are luxury objects exemplifying an international artistic koiné that admits of no single source (Feldman 2006: 41–43).

Other prestige items that might be mentioned in this context include a faience sceptre-head with the cartouche of the 13th century BC Egyptian pharaoh Horemheb, found at Hala Sultan Tekke (Åström 1979), and a silver figurine from Kalavasos *Ayios Dhimitrios* (ProBA 2) with a kilted male figure in a tall conical headdress standing on a stag (South 1997: 163, pl. XV.1) (Figure 130). The same kind of intricate imagery is also portrayed on certain ivories, faience vessels and cylinder seals. These artistic and iconographic elements of Near Eastern, Egyptian and Aegean political systems or cosmologies were incorporated into Cypriot symbolic and ideological systems. They reflect a conscious strategy of consumption geared to enhance status and authority, and as such served both to legitimise new power relations within Cypriot society and to mark out the social identity of the ruling élite (Keswani 2004: 136–139, 157).

On a broader scale, Feldman (2006) has portrayed a small number of prestige goods from Ugarit – made of ivory, gold, faience and alabaster – as symbolic resources that served to identify and enhance the status of élites throughout western Asia and the Levant, as well as on Cyprus and in the

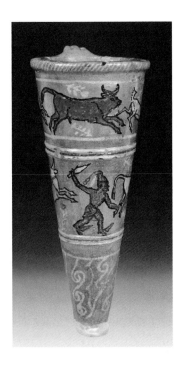

Figure 131. Kition *Chrysopolitissa* faience rhyton, ProBA
2 in date. Preserved ht: 26.8 cm. Courtesy of the Cyprus
Museum, Nicosia.

Aegean. These items share hybrid motifs and compositional devices, and form
part of a wider range of 'International Style' luxury goods found throughout this region (Kantor 1947; Vercoutter 1956; Smith 1965; Crowley 1989).
Feldman (2002: 17–23; 2006: 10–11, 30–31) isolates two basic themes – com-
bative and heraldic – that resonate deeply with an iconography based on the
ancient Near Eastern concept of kingship. In discussing certain prestigious
items from Ugarit, she cites some faience and ivory objects from Cyprus
that depict similar themes or compositions. The well-known faience conical
rhyton from Kition *Chrysopolitissa* (ProBA 2–3, LC IIC), for example, is decorated with a combination of Aegean, Egyptian and Orientalising motifs –
hunting scenes, bulls, a goat, stylised flowers, two hunters with short kilts
and tasselled headdresses (Peltenburg 1974: 116–126, pl. XCIV; Karageorghis
2002a: 49–50, fig. 98) (Figure 131). Another example is the equally famous
ivory box from British Tomb 58 at Enkomi (ProBA 3, LC IIIA), which depicts
various horned and hoofed animals in flying gallop, fleeing before a chariot
holding an archer, as well as a large bull with lowered horns facing the chariot (Karageorghis 2002a: 100, fig. 205) (see above, Figure 118). Feldman (2006:
65 and pl. 8) compares the bull and vignette of a hunter spearing a charging
lion on this ivory box with similar features on a gold plate from Ugarit. This
object from Enkomi thus not only reveals direct iconographic links to exotic
items from Ugarit, but also forms part of the wider eastern Mediterranean
sphere of luxury goods.

Finally, amongst the more striking examples of luxury goods found on
Cyprus, dated to the 12th century BC, are the six gold rings with cloisonné

Figure 132. Kouklia *Evreti* Tomb VIII: gold finger ring with cloisonne bezel. British Excavations, 1952. Diameter: 2.2 cm. Courtesy of the Cyprus Museum, Nicosia.

bezels from Tomb VIII at Kouklia *Evreti* (Karageorghis 2002a: 110, fig. 229; Pini 2010: 40–43, nos. 64–69) (Figure 132). These gold rings have a broad hoop and round bezel decorated in filigree, with a central *cloison* ('compartment') filled with molten glass or an inset of cut stone or clay (Pini 2010: 67). Although these are the earliest known examples of enamelling found on Cyprus, earlier cases using this technique are known from the Aegean (Pini 2010: 58–59). There are some similarities between the Cypriot rings and various Aegean examples, but these horseshoe-shaped rings and many aspects of the design seem to be uniquely Cypriot; the concentration of gold rings at Enkomi may suggest the presence of a specialist workshop there.

The richness and diversity of Late Bronze Age exchange systems, the motivations of merchants and mariners, and the expectations and perceptions of those who received imported goods blur the differences amongst traders, trade and the actual mechanisms involved (Skeates 2009: 565–566). Within the Late Bronze Age Mediterranean, there were so many different kinds of resources and types of transport, so many different kinds of luxury and utilitarian goods exchanged, that no single system of trade or level of exchange predominated. Any analysis that extends beyond the strictly local or regional demonstrates that Aegean, Canaanite or Egyptian 'thalassocracies' are modern constructs based on myth and tradition, not ancient realities (Knapp 1993b). Late Bronze Age trade in the Mediterranean most likely consisted of open-ended, multistage journeys (Kemp and Merrillees 1980: 276), in which many places of both primary and secondary importance participated, all linked by coastal or open-sea routes of various lengths and diverse destinations.

On Cyprus, the island's natural circumscription, with limited agricultural land but a metal resource in constant demand during the Late Bronze Age, ensured and indeed promoted the concentration of power, production facilities and exchange transactions in the hands of an overarching political authority. By the end of the 14th century BC, the material culture of Cyprus – architecture, pottery, figurines, finished metal products, and the iconography and imagery seen on everything from ivory carvings and faience objects to jewellery, seals and sealings – appears to be as homogeneous as the single polity that governed the island (see next section, *Sociopolitical Organisation*). The rich and diverse documentary record of ProBA Cyprus (Knapp 2008: 307–341) equally points to a diverse, highly specialised and well-organised polity that coordinated if not controlled transport, communication and exchange within and beyond the island.

SOCIOPOLITICAL ORGANISATION

The Material View: Heterarchy or Hierarchy?

By the onset of the ProBA, Cyprus had begun to undergo the transformation from an insular polity to an international player, one in which the economy expanded from a stable, village-based system to a more competitive, socially divided, urban–rural system. This transformation has been attributed, variously, to processes of urbanisation, secondary state formation, heterarchical or peer polities, and intensified (copper) production combined with overseas trade. Assessing the nature of 'all these imponderables' (Merrillees 1992a: 324), and proposing a sociohistorical reconstruction, is a formidable task. Elsewhere I have set forth my own views (Knapp 2008: 144–159, 324–341), which to some extent have already been challenged (Peltenburg n.d., see below). Here I present the basic data, and provide some differing views concerning the sociopolitical structure(s) of ProBA Cyprus.

Attempts to interpret long-term changes in the sociopolitical organisation of ProBA Cyprus (ca. 1750/1700–1100 Cal BC) are hampered by the archaeological evidence, which derives chiefly from settlements and tombs or burials dated between about 1450–1200 Cal BC (on the sparser material and settlement records of the centuries between 1700–1450 Cal BC, see Knapp 2008: 148–151). The material record of the 13th century BC, in particular, is manifestly richer and more diverse than that of the previous centuries. One must be cautious, however, in extrapolating evidence from the 13th or 12th centuries BC (ProBA 2–3) back to the 16th and 15th centuries BC (ProBA 1) in order to gain some perspective on the sociopolitical structure(s) of the ProBA overall. As Peltenburg (1996: 28) pointed out, the so-called urban expansion of the

13th century BC may represent a distinctive period of political change, a '…
devolution of central authority, perhaps related to the increasing pre-eminence
of Aegean traits in Cyprus' (cf. Voskos and Knapp 2008).

Peltenburg's understanding of the earlier, ProBA 1 period (ca. 1700–1450
Cal BC), however, was quite different. He argued for the rapid emergence
at that time of a secondary state modelled on the western Asiatic political
systems surrounding Cyprus (Peltenburg 1996: 27–28). Only at Enkomi do
we have a detailed archaeological record for the earliest phase of the ProBA.
Peltenburg (1996: 29; also Muhly 1989: 299) laid out the evidence for the
large-scale production of copper in the massive Enkomi 'fortress' (Level IB, see
Dikaios 1969–1971: 21–24), stating that it represents a major labour investment
'by a centralised authority intimately concerned with copper production'.

Crewe (2007b: 17–19, 156–157), as already noted, questioned Enkomi's primary role in producing copper for export at this time. Basing her argument on
the abundance of metal artefacts found in north-coast tombs of the preceding
period (PreBA 2, for which see Keswani 2005: 382–384), Crewe (2007b: 158–
159) suggests that north-coast sites – closer to the ore sources – may have been
involved in the export of copper. Beyond the problems with Crewe's interpretation of the archaeometallurgical evidence (already discussed above), it must
also be noted that (1) no known settlements are yet associated with these north-
coast tombs (*Vounos*, Lapithos *Vrysi tou Barba*), which are in any case PreBA 1–2
in date and were never used during the ProBA (some Lapithos tombs extend
into MC III, but no later), and (2) there is no material sign that any inland site
closer to the ore sources was involved in the export of copper, much less any
significant scale of production during the 16th–14th centuries BC (e.g. as at
Politiko *Phorades* – Kassianidou and Knapp 2008: 144–145; Kassianidou 2012).
Peltenburg (1996: 31), moreover, had already pointed out that the desertion of
those very same north-coast cemeteries, 'whose earlier prosperity was so closely
linked with copper exploitation, mirrors the rise of Enkomi'.

Crewe's citation of Keswani in support of her argument is curious, since the
latter maintains that (1) the frequency and volume of overseas trade (and the
trade in copper) was limited before MC III, 'more sporadic than systematic',
and (2) the metal wealth of the north coast, PreBA tombs was based more
on producers' responsiveness to ceremonial demand and internal exchange
networks, rather than on the export trade (Keswani 2005: 387, 391). Elsewhere,
and in reference to the ProBA 1 period, Keswani (1996: 222) suggests that the
prominence of the Enkomi fortress may reflect its involvement in centralised
exchange transactions. Finally, it may be noted that just outside this fortress,
Enkomi Tomb 1851 (ProBA 1 in date) contained a balance pan, a rock crystal
weight and an 'exotic' ostrich egg (Lagarce and Lagarce 1985: 8, 47–48), evidence that directly relates metals' production to luxury imports.

Crewe's argument is certainly not faulty on one point: the copper ore sources
upon which Enkomi's well-being relied lay almost 60 km inland, and in order

to secure the delivery of ores from the mining district to their final processing and transhipment point, some sort of transportation infrastructure – road network, communications, staging posts – would have been necessary. Peltenburg (1996: 31–35, fig. 4) suggested that those who controlled production at Enkomi secured the movement of ores through a network of forts along the Alykos and Yialias River valleys, within the *Mesaoria*. These forts, nearby the modern villages of Eylenja (near Nicosia), Yeri, Dhali *(Kafkallia)* and Ayios Sozomenos, as well as others in the northwest and northeast of the island, were once seen as material reflections of unsettled conditions on the island, as refuges or places of defence against enemies from within or without (Hyksos; people from the Levant) (e.g. Catling 1973: 168; Merrillees 1971; Fortin 1983: 217–218). Crewe (2007b: 65–66) argues that the distribution of the forts may represent a series of regional responses to external and internal pressures, at once strengthening older regional ties and helping to solidify links with the new, mainly coastal town centres. This argument, of course, supports Crewe's broader thesis that no single site (i.e. Enkomi) established control over Cyprus's production and distribution system(s) during ProBA 1.

Merrillees (1982: 375) first suggested that the *Mesaoria* fortifications might have been linked strategically with the intensified production and overseas trade in copper. It was Peltenburg (1996), however, who presented a detailed argument on how all forts around the island were linked to the rise of Enkomi as a 'secondary state' and the attempt to stabilise its economic bases of power. Thus these forts were part of a 'hinterland strategy' developed 'by expansionary Enkomi' (Peltenburg 1996: 33, 35) in order: (1) to secure the transportation route from the copper mines to Enkomi and ensure the cooperation of local groups along that route; (2) to protect Enkomi from hostile elements within and beyond the island; and (3) to reconfigure settlements in the countryside for mobilising agricultural surpluses used to support all the industrial specialists and personnel required to maintain this elaborate system. More recently, Peltenburg (2008) has pointed out some similarities between the Cypriot forts at Korovia *Nitovikla* and Dhali *Kafkallia*, and the fortified compound at the Lebanese coastal site of Tell el-Burak (Sader and Kamlah 2010). Thus he infers a possible Levantine origin for the Cypriot forts, but more importantly suggests that those responsible for building the forts on Cyprus were emulating mainland behaviour, both before and during the process of secondary state formation that took place at Enkomi.

From the early 16th to mid-14th centuries BC, Enkomi offers substantial evidence for intensified, uninterrupted copper production, for the consumption and emulation of imported prestige goods from Egypt and the Levant (Keswani 1989; Peltenburg 1996: 35–36; Knapp 1998b), and for the emergence of a centralised, hierarchical, state level, sociopolitical organisation (note that the 14th century BC Amarna letters from *Alašiya* first document the existence of a single 'king' on Cyprus – Knapp 2008: 335–341).

Enkomi, moreover, has the only substantial claim to being a centre of glyptic production throughout the ProBA. Its abundant seals (some 200 cylinder seals; several stamp and signet rings) and the symbolic images engraved on them may well have served as mechanisms for ideological and organisational control (Webb 2002d: 139–140). Élites at Enkomi not only dominated the local production and overseas distribution of copper, they also had direct access to foreign markets and to the luxury goods that first appeared on the island during ProBA 1. Such close interactions with overseas polities and/ or individuals in the Levant and Egypt helped to enhance a distinctive new identity for the island's élite(s), and ultimately to legitimise élite positions of power (Knapp 1998b; 2006).

By the 14th–13th centuries BC (ProBA 2), however, most specialists involved in the study of protohistoric Cyprus seem to agree that the existing geopolitical configuration had changed. The details of this change are widely debated (e.g. Merrillees 1992a; Keswani 1993; 1996; Knapp 1994: 290–293; Webb 1999; 2002d), but the general assumption is that Enkomi's dominance – if such it was – finally gave way (by the 13th century BC at the latest) to a series of local polities administered by regional élites who had gained control over the production and distribution of copper. Some scholars, myself included, have viewed the unprecedented urban flourishing of the 13th century BC (Negbi 2005) as reflecting a process of political fragmentation and the collapse of centralised rule (Muhly 1989: 301–303; Peltenburg 1996: 28, 36; Knapp 1997: 66–68). Others view the material record of the entire ProBA as reflecting decentralised rule under a number of heterarchical polities (e.g. Keswani 1996; Manning and DeMita 1997; South 2002; Bolger 2003: 194).

Most prominent amongst the latter is Keswani (1993; 1996: 236–237; 2004: 154–155). Citing evidence from settlement patterns, architecture, iconography, burial practices and storage jar capacity, Keswani maintains that several regional polities operated at the same time on ProBA Cyprus, what she terms a heterarchical system of social organisation (after Ehrenreich et al. 1995). Although noting that Enkomi may have risen to prominence early, she feels it was later marginalised by polities centred at sites such as Kition or Hala Sultan Tekke (Keswani 1996: 234). The competing factions she envisions took form initially during the ProBA 1 period in order to gain access to resources in demand or to control transport and trade critical to their own polities (Keswani 2004: 154–157).

Such independent polities are assumed either to have been integrated through corporate alliances, sanctions and tributary or gift relations, or else to have been maintained by a quasi-independent central authority and linked by market-oriented exchange. Coastal centres such as Enkomi, *Toumba tou Skourou*, Hala Sultan Tekke and perhaps Kition emerged when heterogeneous kin groups from communities near and far converged at a locale advantageous for exploiting foreign trade: here Keswani sees the presence of diverse if not competing élite groups. By contrast, inland and/or southern centres such as Maroni, *Ayios Dhimitrios* and Alassa were established in areas that had long sequences of prior occupation, where earlier, corporate identities were replaced by new urban identities: here Keswani sees a more centralised, highly prestigious social élite without political or economic peers. In effect, Keswani sees a hierarchical social system operating in the southern part of Cyprus, and a heterarchical system in the east and far west, thus implying variation in sociopolitical organisation within different regions of the island.

Other scholars also have argued against the notion of centralised authority on ProBA Cyprus, and thus implicitly for a heterarchical form of social organisation. Stech (1982: 103; 1985: 112–113), for example, maintained that different towns exercised either secular or 'religious' control over copper production and exchange. A detailed study and analysis of seals led Smith (1994: 163–164, 314–315) to conclude that the polities of ProBA 2–3 Cyprus, at least, were a series of complex chiefdoms lacking administrative records and controls (cf. Smith 2009: 246). South-Todd (2002: 65–68) also suggested that the polities of ProBA Cyprus were independently organised, and essentially equal in size and complexity.

By contrast, yet others see some degree of centralised (hierarchical), sociopolitical authority on ProBA Cyprus (e.g. Webb 1999; 2005; Knapp 2008: 144–159, 324–341). Webb (1999: 305–308; 2005: 180) first adopted an 'archaic' state model, citing several material indices of a common iconographic system and common ritual or ceremonial practices, from the 15th century BC onward. These include: (1) close similarities in the style and content of seal iconography (14th–12th centuries BC), with frequent depictions of specific motifs and divinities drawing on the Near Eastern ideology of kingship; (2) Base-ring bull rhyta in mortuary contexts; and (3) standardised female terracotta images in both settlement and mortuary contexts (see above, *Gendered Representations*).

Webb emphasised the role of seals whose motifs – presentation scenes, horned divinities, regal animals (lions, griffins) – were drawn from Near Eastern cosmologies related to kingship. Seals are highly mobile devices that could serve as mechanisms for organisational control; their common symbolic elements may also be related to expressions of centralised power and prestige (Webb 1999: 307). In Webb's (2005: 180–181) view, secondary state formation on ProBA Cyprus emerged abruptly, triggered by direct contact with overseas powers, and by entrepreneurially oriented long-distance trade: the export of Cypriot copper and the import of foreign exotic goods. This rapid development of a hierarchical, sociopolitical organisation on ProBA Cyprus spurred local élites to adopt very similar material goods – prestigious foreign objects – to display their social position, broadcast their political authority and legitimise their newly established regime(s) of power.

Several scholars, in fact, including Keswani (1996; 2004), have cited the emulation of Near Eastern ideologies of kingship as a key structuring principle in the emergence of more complex, hierarchical *or* heterarchical forms of sociopolitical organisation on ProBA Cyprus (e.g. Knapp 1998b; 2006; Webb 2005). This notion, of course, is based on the highly influential work of Helms (1988: 148), who maintains that 'kingship was at least partly legitimized by association with foreign political ideologies derived from outside polities'. Thus prestigious foreign symbols, reflecting foreign models of political ideology, provided Cypriot élites with a 'blueprint' for domination (Webb 2005: 181).

My own views on the sociopolitical organisation of ProBA Cyprus have changed over time. Having recently reconsidered the entire range of material and documentary evidence for the ProBA (Knapp 2008), I stood my ground concerning the role of Enkomi, which must have served as the dominant political authority on Cyprus during the ProBA 1 period. Although Crewe (2007b) has sown doubt about the extent of Enkomi's authority on the island at that time, the polity centred at Enkomi nonetheless seems to have been instrumental in developing and first exploiting the advantages of foreign trade; thus it must also have played an important role in the intensified production and export of Cypriot copper. However, in contrast to my previous interpretations of the ProBA 2 period (local polities run by local élites – Knapp 1997: 66–68; 2006: 52), I would now argue that a single unified polity emerged on the island by the 14th century BC, headed by the leader (*šarru* or 'king') of a dominant élite group, perhaps with a second-in-command (*rābiṣu*) (Knapp 2008: 335–341).

This brings us to yet a third series of views, neither strictly heterarchical nor hierarchical, on the sociopolitical organisation of ProBA Cyprus. Merrillees (1992a) long ago argued that economic, not political élites dominated the administration if not the government of ProBA Cyprus. Having denied any possibility of a unified state, Merrillees suggested that autonomous settlements – differentiated by size and wealth, and in particular by the level of commercial activities they enjoyed – held sway in different parts of the island. The distinction Merrillees makes between economic and political organisation may well have had some basis in reality (cf. Knapp 1986b; 1994: 282–290), but why should one pattern – economic or political – prevail over another? Manning and DeMita (1997: 108–109) proposed yet another, essentially economic interpretation: independent, entrepreneurial foreign merchants – 'aggrandisers' in their words – served as the administrative force that organised production and distribution in each region. In their view, there were no bureaucrats, no élite iconography and no dominant ideology on ProBA Cyprus (see further below). More recently, Peltenburg (n.d.) has set forth another interpretation, political as well as economic in approach. He revisits the notion of an archaic state, and explores the interface between text and materiality. More specifically,

Peltenburg considers closely the disjunction between the textual evidence related to *Alašiya* and the material record of ProBA 2 Cyprus, which thus leads us to consider documentary views on the sociopolitical organisation of ProBA Cyprus.

The Documentary View: Hierarchy or Households?

First of all, an alternative and entirely independent view has emerged from scientific analyses conducted on the Akkadian cuneiform letters sent from *Alašiya* (Cyprus) to Amarna in Egypt, and on another letter sent from the king of *Alašiya* to the king of Ugarit (Goren et al. 2003; 2004: 48–75). Inductively Coupled Plasma Spectroscopy (ICP) and petrographic analyses indicated that the clay used to make these tablets derived from sources in the southeastern Troodos mountains: thus Goren et al. suggest that either Alassa *Paleotaverna* or Kalavasos *Ayios Dhimitrios* may have became the political and administrative centre of *Alašiya* during the 14th–13th centuries BC. The validity of these analyses, in particular the petrographic work, has now been called into question by Merrillees (2011), but it must be born in mind that his primary aim is to discount the Cyprus-*Alašiya* equation.

Other, recently published cuneiform documents from Ugarit pertaining to *Alašiya* (Bordreuil and Malbran-Labat 1995: 445; Malbran-Labat 1999; Yon 2007: 17–24) show that royal as well as diplomatic exchanges between these two centres lasted from at least the mid-14th century BC (Amarna letters) into the late 13th century BC. During all this time, a period of more than 150 years, Cyprus was ruled by a 'king' – whatever his/her stature and prominence may have been, from wherever s/he may have ruled (Knapp 2008: 335–341). We even know the name of one 'king', Kushmeshusha, who ruled on Cyprus at the same time as Niqmaddu (III), of Ugarit, late in the 13th century BC (Ras Shamra tablets RS 94.2177 + 2491, RS 94.2475 – Yon 2007: 18–19).

Thus it became crucial to reconsider the prevailing view of political fragmentation on 13th century BC Cyprus (Goren et al. 2003: 248–252): either the 'king' of *Alašiya* was a paramount king, or else he served as a *primus inter pares*, that is, the leader of several competing regional polities during the 14th–13th centuries BC (ProBA 2). A third possible political configuration is that the 'king' (*šarru*) shared power with an important official, the *rābiṣu* ('senior prefect'). We know the names of three of these officials from ProBA 2 Cyprus, all of whom were in direct contact with the king of Ugarit: Eshuwara (RS 20.18), Shinama (RS 94.2173) and Shangiwa (RS 94.2447+) (note that Amarna letter EA 40 was also sent by the *rābiṣu* of *Alašiya*, but to his counterpart in Egypt). In whatever capacity the 'king' of *Alašiya* may have ruled, it now seems that the reading from the material record – of regional, heterarchically organised polities – is either exaggerated or incorrect, or else must be viewed in an entirely different manner.

Peltenburg (n.d.) has now set forth this new view, suggesting that ProBA 2 Cyprus fell under the control of a 'devolved authority' held by different (patrimonial) households but united under a *primus inter pares* who managed foreign relations. Several aspects of Peltenburg's 'model' for ProBA Cyprus had already been proposed by Manning and DeMita (1997: 106–113) but attracted little attention. Given Cyprus's size, ecological and resource diversity, and the presence of several potential ports in reasonable proximity to surrounding mainlands, Manning and DeMita (1997: 107) argued that it would be extremely difficult for a centralised authority to emerge, whether in the form of a nascent state or a paramount chiefdom. To achieve any sort of monopoly over such broadly spread resources (copper, wood, olive oil) and factors of transport (ports, forts), a centralised authority would have needed impressive force and/or a very powerful ideology. In their view, such an ideology or potentially coercive force cannot be demonstrated in the material record: there are no palatial centres with craft specialists, no 'clear-cut hierarchy' of sites, no iconographic representations of a dominant ideology or ruling élite.

Thus any 'king' of Cyprus would at best have had '…nominal control over what seem to be largely independent élite groupings elsewhere on the island' (Manning and DeMita 1997: 108). In their view, the Amarna letters from *Alašiya* in particular show the use of diplomatic discourse to mask what are 'baldly economic and political transactions' (Manning and DeMita 1997: 108). Thus they argued that a scenario with the king of *Alašiya* as paramount over other, regional kings or 'chiefs' is not just attractive but rooted in the structural history of Late Bronze Age Cyprus, that is, with Enkomi as the first and foremost centre not just for copper production but for interregional trade, and with other regional groupings emulating and competing with Enkomi from at least 1450 BC onward (ProBA 2). So, rather than any form of a centrally administered state controlling and coordinating production and exchange, ritual practice and ideology, Manning and DeMita (1997: 113) held that ProBA Cyprus was managed by a highly evolved administrative structure, with mechanisms of economic control expressed through '…a highly intertwined web of political and kin alliances'.

For Manning and DeMita (1997: 112–115), economic control revolved around the substantial influence and impact of foreign merchants, a professional merchant class with different members linked directly to the various regional polities that (purportedly) dominated ProBA Cyprus. In their view, these traders served as 'brokers' for Cypriot commodities in demand abroad (especially copper), and at the same time provided in return the prestigious foreign goods that local rulers needed to maintain and legitimise their authority. Although Peltenburg (n.d.) treats several issues that Manning and DeMita used to define the politico-economic organisation of ProBA 2 Cyprus, his analysis and reconstruction of devolved authority on ProBA Cyprus are entirely different.

First of all, Peltenburg (n.d.) maintains that the term 'state' as applied to Late Bronze Age Cyprus is problematic. He sees a conflict between documentary evidence that portrays *Alašiya* as comparable to other ancient Near East states, and the archaeological record that lacks many features seen in those neighbouring states, in particular the material paraphernalia of formal governmental institutions. He thus raises once again issues related to the emulation of Near Eastern 'valuables', the material insignia of high status, as well as the manufacture of prestigious goods (seals) engraved with complex iconographic features portraying foreign models of political ideology.

Turning to documentary evidence in the attempt to understand how all these materials may be related to the sociopolitical structure of ProBA Cyprus, Peltenburg singles out the use of the term 'household' in the salutation by the Cypriot 'king' to the Egyptian pharaoh in Amarna letter EA 35 (note that this term – *bit*, literally 'house', not 'household' – is also used in EA 33–34, 37–39). He suggests that in Egypt, or in any other contemporary state in ancient western Asia, such a term would signal a palace. There are, however, no palaces of Near Eastern dimensions known on Cyprus, nothing for example that matches even the 7,000 m² palace at nearby Ugarit, nothing with living quarters for dependent labourers or administrative officials (but cf. Fisher 2009, discussed further below). Sealings used for administrative purposes, another characteristic material signature of the state, are also missing from ProBA Cyprus (but not seals – see above and Smith 2002b; Webb 2002d).

Thus in Peltenburg's view, the material apex of Late Bronze Age state hierarchy (the palace) is missing on Cyprus, as are the dynastic paraphernalia and ideological iconography that characterised centrally administered polities in the Levant and western Asia (also Manning and DeMita 1997: 109; but cf. Webb 1999: 307, and see above, for details concerning just such insignia and 'regalia'). Thus Peltenburg feels that Cyprus, an acknowledged member of the closely interconnected regimes that made the Late Bronze Age a truly international era, is lacking many material signifiers of centralised power found in those Levantine or Near Eastern sites with which it was so well connected, and by whom it was so deeply influenced.

As I have noted, however, here and elsewhere, such connections and influences do not mean that Cyprus must share the materiality of its neighbours, to the east or west, south or north. In virtually all periods, prehistoric or historical, the material culture of Cyprus is predictably and demonstrably quite different from that of the polities that surround it. One may thus regard it as 'insular' in the geographic sense, but it is crucial that we don't overemphasise Cyprus's differences with other cultures and societies of the Mediterranean and Near East; in so doing we lose track of the internal perspective. In the present case, Peltenburg discounts the possibility that Cyprus's always-different material culture is reflective of a 'centrally administered state'. Yet he emphasises that those same kinds of states in western Asia recognised – through their textual evidence – such a polity on Cyprus. In my view, whilst there is indeed a 'disjuncture' between the documentary and material evidence, it is one to be expected, not just in the case of Cyprus but also in similar protohistoric contexts elsewhere (Knapp 1992: 84–85). Although the Late Bronze Age Aegean world had 'palaces', and the Mycenaeans certainly had kings, they also lacked certain features associated with the 'state' in western Asia and Egypt: for example, royal iconography (or the iconography of kingship), royal gifts analogous to Egyptian gifts sent to Byblos, and so on. In other words, from a Near Eastern perspective, the Aegean kingdoms appear almost as anomalous as Cyprus (Louise Steel, pers. comm., June 2011).

Having demonstrated through various examples from Middle–Late Bronze Age Syria, Mesopotamia and Anatolia that the concept of the 'state' needs reconsideration (citing Stein 2001: 369), Peltenburg (n.d.) suggests we should regard the situation on Cyprus in terms of corporate forms of political action and agency (e.g. authoritative councils, groups of elders). In such corporate bodies, elders held equal sway with the king and the exercise of power had to be negotiated. In particular, he draws attention (1) to 'locally empowered households' and cites the influential 'Patrimonial Household Model' model of Schloen (2001) as applied to contemporary Ugarit, and (2) to another recent study (Routledge and McGeough 2009), also applied to Ugarit but designed to show the interdependence between royal and private economic transactions.

Both studies, based on evidence from Ugarit, essentially argue that the royal household was the first among many, or that the palace operated as the most prominent in a network of households. Surely, however, Schloen's monolithic model (criticised at length by others, e.g. Fleming 2002; Monroe 2002) cannot be applied uncritically to Cyprus, nor should we forget that, in addition to 'households', the concepts of 'brotherhood' (*ahhutu*) if not 'fatherhood' were also crucial in negotiating one's way through the maze of international relations that typified Late Bronze Age ancient western Asia and Egypt (Liverani 1990: 197–202). We cannot presume that political authority (in the Levant, as per Schloen, or on Bronze Age Cyprus, as per Peltenburg) was only expressed in terms of a 'simple, nested hierarchy of individual patriarchal households, with a king at its top' (Fleming 2002: 79).

The relevance of McGeough's (2007; Routledge and McGeough 2009) network model in demonstrating that exchange transactions are informal, socially embedded, neither strictly royal nor independent and entrepreneurial, is more apropos in this case. It leads Peltenburg (n.d.) to suggest that we might consider the ProBA political economy less in strictly monolithic, hierarchical terms, and more along the lines seen in Levantine polities, that is, with devolved economic and judicial powers exercised at the household level. He also suggests, citing Monroe (2009: 246–247), that we should not expect the stereotypical royal ideology noted in the documentary evidence to convey the complexities of political organisation as implied by the patterning of

Cypriot material culture. Indeed, this is precisely the point: we cannot expect material culture to provide anything other than a 'disjuncture' with the documentary evidence, anything beyond the 'parallel realities' between object and text. The real dilemma here, and one unlikely to be resolved any time soon, is how different archaeologists interpret the same body of material culture (I return to discuss this issue below).

In Peltenburg's scenario, the term *šarru* as used in the Amarna letters from *Alašiya* was indeed used for a person of authority on ProBA Cyprus. That person's position, however, had been adapted to suit local conditions – namely a 'kin-based society' that resisted Near Eastern notions of hierarchy and social stratification. This begins to sound more like the 'resistance to complexity' that Peltenburg (1993) has long used to characterise the social structure of Chalcolithic Cyprus (if not the 'Chalcolithic household' – Steel 2004a: 87–89). It is also somewhat misleading in this context to give such prominence to discussion of how Prehistoric Bronze Age Cyprus differed so fundamentally from that of its mainland neighbours, with its 'small scale communities' lacking in 'institutionalised hierarchies' and its emphasis on deer-hunting, as opposed to the urbanism and sheep–goat pastoralism in the Levant (Peltenburg n.d.). These economic and subsistence strategies belong to an era that precedes the ProBA by at least 1,000 years, and have little bearing on the new and unprecedented sociopolitical and economic circumstances of the mid-2nd millennium BC.

Indeed, Peltenburg acknowledges the changes wrought by the move to key coastal localities during the ProBA 1 period, to take advantage of the emerging systems of long-distance exchange. In his view, aggregated kin-based households in these newly established, outward-looking centres would have competed for resources and trade partners, and developed new economic practices as well as sociopolitical institutions with strong corporate and mercantile bases. Because existing exchange relationships in ancient western Asia and the Levant revolved so closely around diplomatic connections between royal households, Peltenburg suggests that the new coastal centres on Cyprus required a similar institution or personage, a representative leader, if they were to conduct foreign relations and become part of this international world of commerce. In such a way, the role and office of the 'king' of *Alašiya* emerged; in other words, 'kingship' on Cyprus was at least partly geared to expedite the island's engagement with and involvement in already existing systems of exchange (in all this echoing the model of Manning and DeMita 1997).

The various regionally based groups that became involved in this enterprise would have sought the material exotica and luxury goods that came to be disseminated so widely on the island, beginning even before the 14th century BC. Thus if *Alašiya* functioned as a devolved, decentralised polity, we need not expect to find royal palaces and tombs, royal seals and sculptures, or monumental royal inscriptions (Peltenburg n.d.). It must be countered, however, that certain 'arenas of power' may be seen in the open, three-sided courts such as the 440 m², π-shaped example at Alassa *Paleotaverna*, suitable for large assemblies of people, or other, similar examples at *Ayios Dhimitrios* (Building X) and Enkomi ('Fortress' complex, Ashlar Building) discussed by Fisher (2009, and already noted above). According to Peltenburg, the wealth that can be seen in all these centres should not be equated with political independence. The ideology of power and unity worked through consensus, not coercion, whilst integration was fostered and achieved through ritual practices and ritual paraphernalia (Knapp 1986a; Webb 1999).

Peltenburg (n.d.) emphasises that the Amarna letters from *Alašiya*, like those from trade-oriented Assyria, stand out from others in the corpus because of their strong commercial tenor (also Manning and DeMita 1997: 110–111). Having made overseas trade – in particular with the Levant and western Asia – the focus of its economy, the best way for local élites to stabilise and secure Cyprus's economy was to adopt the concept of kingship, modelled on those interregional examples they knew best. According to Peltenburg, and following the models of Schloen (2001) and McGeough (2007), the political ideology of western Asiatic states was based on the authority of households imbricated in regional structures of power that inhibited singular, personalised leadership. On Cyprus, adopting such an ideology would have ensured the continuity of the island's distinctive traditions. Thus the domestic power of the king of *Alašiya* was constrained, his/ her authority circumscribed by being only the central household in a social network of privileged households. Peltenburg argues that the economic role of the *šarru*, combined with the political role of the *rābiṣu*, reflects a 'dual power-sharing arrangement' within dispersed networks of power and different (spatial) centres of authority. Within Cyprus, therefore, the king was a *primus inter pares*; beyond Cyprus, he was yet another *šarru* but one whose copper and timber resources enabled him to 'punch above his weight'. And so, instead of anything we might regard as a unified state apparatus, the configuration of power on ProBA Cyprus involved one premier household in a network of enduring élite households.

I have already suggested, above and elsewhere, that one possible sociopolitical configuration for the ProBA would have involved its 'king' (*šarru*) sharing power with the *rābiṣu* ('senior prefect'), albeit with the latter serving as the second most powerful official in the political hierarchy (also Moran 1992: 113 n. 1; Sürenhagen 2001: 254). Specifically, I stated (Knapp 2008: 336):

> Taken together with the rest of the *Alašiya* correspondence, these written sources dealing with state-level diplomacy and trade demonstrate that a single, internationally recognised king – perhaps with a high official who served as his second in command – ruled Cyprus during the mid-14th century BC (Amarna tablets) and at the end of the 13th century BC (archive of Urtenu at Ugarit).

Of course, in my view, 'kingship' on Cyprus, even if held by a *primus inter pares*, involved a more absolute kind of authority, not the kind of devolved system portrayed by Peltenburg. Once Enkomi's position as the focal point of political power had passed, that is, by the late 15th or early 14th century BC, sites such as Alassa *Paleotaverna* or Kalavasos *Ayios Dhimitrios* would have served as regional centres for the production, storage and distribution of agricultural products, raw materials and metallurgical surpluses. All three centres – Enkomi, *Paleotaverna* and *Ayios Dhimitrios* – may have filled some of the diverse needs of Cyprus's ruling élite, who may have used these sites at different times over the long-term political cycle of the ProBA. If the 'senior prefect' (*rābiṣu*) of *Alašiya* was second-in-command to the king (Sürenhagen 2001: 254), then s/he too may have dwelt, at different times and for unknown reasons, in one or the other of these centres.

Peltenburg's overall argument is thoughtful, well argued, even compelling in many aspects. There is a fundamental difference, however, between seeing the politico-economic organisation of ProBA Cyprus as vested in a singular institution of (absolute?) power, as I do, and as being shared through devolved authority amongst kin-based households. Just as others see problems in the notion that patrimonial or networked households dominated Levantine Late Bronze Age polities, I feel that these models cannot explain several socio-economic or political realities on ProBA Cyprus.

For example, how could such a 'devolved' authority command all the resources necessary to produce, transport and organise for export more than 900 copper oxhide ingots (the Amarna letters do not make clear the exact weight of these ingots, but when they do, more than 100 'talents' are mentioned, and a talent weighed on average 28 kg – Knapp 2008: 309–310, 312–313)? If we take this average weight of 28 kg for an oxhide ingot, then over the period of no more than 50 years to which the Amarna correspondence belongs, there are recorded single shipments of Cypriot copper ranging from 140 kg (5 ingots) to 14,000 kg (500 ingots), or in total over 25,000 kg of copper (on average, then, 500 kg per year). The documentary evidence is also quite explicit about the level of control Cyprus's king wielded over the economic sphere. In Amarna letter EA 39: 14–20, for example, sent from *Alašiya* to the Egyptian pharaoh, the king of Cyprus states: 'These men are *my merchants* ... let them go safely and prom[pt]ly. No one making a claim in your name is to approach *my merchants* or *my ships*' (emphasis added). Moreover, if Pulak (2008: 291–292; 2009) is correct in suggesting (based on lead isotope analysis) that the 10-plus tons of copper found on the Uluburun shipwreck were made from Cypriot ores, then we have a material reflection of the textual evidence, also demonstrating the organisational and productive capacity of this insular polity. Such a scale of production for export necessitated the mobilisation of and control over a well-organised, full-time and specialised workforce, one whose subsistence needs would have to be met through the labour of others equally well integrated into the overall system.

Because I do not necessarily expect Cyprus to have the same type of 'royal palaces' that characterised Near Eastern or even Aegean polities, I see instead various 'arenas of power' materialised in the monumental, special-purpose structures at several Cypriot sites. Such buildings, with material, ideological and spatial settings distinctively different from those of neighbouring polities, served a multiplicity of functions. Their remains (large formal hearths, ashlar masonry, grand entryways and halls/courts, viewing portals, sunken constructions) bear material witness to social gatherings, feasting activities and ritual performances, all important elements in creating monumental places and promoting social occasions – public or private – that helped to support and legitimise élite groups as new, unequal power relations came to be institutionalised (Fisher 2009: 190–195, 200–201).

Amongst these structures, those that stand out are the monumental Buildings II and III at Alassa *Paleotaverna* (see above, Figure 102), whose material remains and architectural elements point to production and storage facilities, and administrative, industrial and domestic functions that in the Near East would be regarded as palatial in nature. At Maroni *Vournes* and *Tsaroukkas*, the buildings if not the tombs beneath (some of) them should also be regarded as monumental constructions that served 'palatial' administrative, industrial, storage and ceremonial functions. Building X at Kalavasos *Ayios Dhimitrios* (see above, Figure 98), approximately 1,000 m² in size, is one of the most impressive monumental structures ever uncovered on Cyprus: amongst other features it contains a 'Pithos Hall' for large storage jars, a western façade of large ashlar blocks, an entry hall (Room 154) bordered by ashlar slabs, and a distinctive central court (Room 157) that would have hosted various ceremonial and feasting events. With its concentration of stamp seals and several diverse types of Cypro-Minoan inscriptions, Building X could well have served centralised administrative, industrial and distributive functions on a par with many of the palatial-based polities of the surrounding eastern Mediterranean regions.

Peltenburg is technically correct to say there are no seals, sculptures, tombs or monumental royal inscriptions that we can pinpoint as being 'royal' in the Near Eastern sense. In my view (and that of Webb 1999: 307), however, it is misleading to argue that we have no material counterparts of the dynastic paraphernalia or the iconography of ideology that were characteristic of centralised polities in the Levant and western Asia. But here I must preface my remarks by reiterating that the real dilemma we face is the inherent ambiguity of the material record, and the way different archaeologists understand the same or very similar aspects of materiality. As Parkinson (2010: 17) recently put it: 'one researcher's bric-a-brac is another researcher's state sponsored voyage'.

My own discussion of the way texts and material culture can be used to establish some basic parameters concerning the politico-economic organisation of ProBA Cyprus has been presented in some detail (Knapp 2008: 324–341). I argued that the people who lived in urban centres such as Enkomi, *Ayios Dhimitrios*, *Paleotaverna*, Kition or Maroni engaged in similar ritual or ceremonial practices, in which they used very similar material goods: cylinder seals and seal iconography; standardised female figurines in both domestic and mortuary contexts; representations of oxhide ingots on seals, bronze stands, pottery and other media; miniature ingots; Base-ring bull rhyta; sets of both local and imported pottery vessels likely used for feasting activities. Bronze statuettes such as the 'Ingot God', the 'Horned God' and the Bomford figurine (Knapp 1986a: 9–14; and see above, Figures 108–109, 122) stand out as insignia of authority, or at the very least as markers of élite identity. The rich and extensive mortuary deposits (with objects crafted in gold, silver, bronze, glass, ivory and faience, amongst others) seen in Tomb 11 at *Ayios Dhimitrios*, or in the ashlar-built British Tomb 66 at Enkomi (=French Tomb 1322) (discussed above) have never been defined as 'royal' in the literature of ProBA Cyprus. Yet it is hard to see the distinction between these deposits and those of the so-called 'royal tombs' at Iron Age Salamis, beyond the monumentality of the latter (most recently, Blackwell 2010).

Along with Webb (1999: 307), I would suggest that most if not all of these material factors must have served as powerful, symbolic media reflecting élite identities as well as a centralised authority. Élite activities were also focused on constructing monuments, securing resources and displaying exotica, investing time, expense and resources into mortuary deposits, producing a range of goods and raw materials (oxhide ingots, bronze statuettes, stands and cauldrons) that were consumed internally and exchanged externally, and developing and maintaining all these symbols of power.

Peltenburg argues that seals without sealings are not unequivocal signs for a centralised administration. He maintains (Peltenburg n.d.) that without independent supportive evidence (surely the documentary evidence from *Alašiya* provides some support?), other material indicators such as bull rhyta, female terracotta images, repeated depictions of deities, common imagery on prestige goods, ashlar masonry and monumental complexes are too precarious a basis to reflect the existence of a sovereign state controlling all of Cyprus. Although he agrees such levels of materiality may equate to an élite status, a shared social identity and social complexity, Peltenburg does not feel these items speak clearly to sociopolitical organisation.

In this compelling new study, Peltenburg has attempted to engage carefully with a wide range of material and documentary evidence relevant to ProBA Cyprus and the Levant. In so doing, however, he takes a minimalist view, whilst my own view may be regarded as maximalist: thus we arrive at an impasse. Unlike my own position, however, Peltenburg's reconstruction of devolved authority largely overcomes what has become a polarised debate between hierarchy and heterarchy, centralised versus regionally based power structures, and the disjuncture between text and material culture, as well as what actually constitutes an 'early state' society. All we can say at this stage with any conviction is that however extensive or circumscribed the authority of the 'king' of *Alašiya* may have been, full engagement with the documentary evidence suggests that interpretations based solely on the material record – of regional, heterarchically organised polities – no longer provide an adequate view of the sociopolitical organisation of ProBA Cyprus.

THE END OF THE BRONZE AGE: COMPLEXITY AND COLLAPSE

> Thus, mass invasions of migrants sweeping in by sea from outside the region (particularly the Aegean) in a very short period of time are held to account like a *deus ex machina* for a whole package of changes (including destructions of sites, the appearance of new types of pottery, new architectural configurations, new patterns of industrial and religious activity) which go to make up what may be regarded as the 'Sea People phenomenon' in the east Mediterranean.... (Sherratt 1998: 292–293)

Many of the major states and polities of the Late Bronze Age – from Greece in the west, through Mesopotamia and Anatolia in the east and north, to Egypt in the south – declined or collapsed within a few decades either side of 1200 BC (see various papers in Gitin et al. 1998; Oren 2000). After this 'collapse' of some of the more dynamic politico-economic regimes of the previous 300–400 years (Liverani 1987), there followed a period, the early Iron Age (ca. 1200/1100–1000/900 BC), during which smaller, regional polities emerged (e.g. Haggis 1993; Sherratt 1998; Iacovou 2002; Gilboa 2006–2007). Amongst the possible causes (or results) of the Late Bronze Age collapse are the following: migrations, predations and destructions by external forces (the Sea Peoples); political struggles and inequalities between centres and peripheries; climatic change and/or natural disasters; internal disruptions or system collapse (e.g. Barako 2000; Killebrew 2005: 33–42; Kaniewski et al. 2010; Yasur-Landau 2010: 171–193). As yet, however, there is no coherent, overarching explanatory scheme that can account for all the changes in different areas, some of which occurred at different times within the late 13th and early 12th centuries BC. Perhaps we should never expect to find a single explanation for such a complex series of phenomena in so many different – even if contiguous – lands.

The 'great historical inscription' of Ramesses III (Kitchen 1983: 39–40; Ockinga in Knapp 1996a: 48) reports that Egypt and its pharaoh confronted and defeated a major, two-pronged attack by the Sea Peoples, one coming by land and the other by sea. If we are to believe this document, these battles resulted in the demise and defeat of a motley crew of warriors, mariners, pirates and brigands, along with their ships, wagons and families. The ships associated with the Sea Peoples are depicted only once in any detail, on the outer walls of Ramesses III's Medinet Habu temple (Wachsmann 2000: 105–106, fig. 6.1). From the sparse narrative and the single (if intricate) depiction at Medinet Habu, the Sea Peoples' phenomenon has generated an extensive scholarly literature, much of it contradictory, on the archaeology and history of the eastern Mediterranean at the end of the Late Bronze Age (Sherratt 1998: 292–293; Silberman 1998). But cause and event are difficult to separate in this case, and the Sea Peoples themselves – whoever they were and whatever their origins – were not just a cause but also a symptom of the widespread collapse of city-states and kingdoms throughout the Aegean, eastern Mediterranean and Near East.

In the most general terms, many scholars would accept that the Sea Peoples (the *Peleset*, *Tjeker*, *Shekelesh*, *Denyen* and *Weshesh*) swept through various regions of the Aegean, Cyprus, Anatolia and the Levant. According to the Medinet Habu inscription, they 'devastated' the kingdoms and states of Hatti and Arzawa (in Anatolia), Qodi (Kadesh in Syria), *Alašiya* (Cyprus) and Carchemish (whose king was in charge of Hittite affairs in Syria, including those at Ugarit – Liverani 1995: 49). Other documents, both earlier and later, also mention some of these groups: for example, the *Šikala* (Tjeker) 'who live on ships' (from Ugarit, RS 43.129 – Dietrich and Loretz 1978; Lehmann 1979; Singer 1999: 721–722); the *Sherden*, *Eqwesh*, *Shekelesh*, *Teresh* and *Lukka* (Egypt, Year 5 of Merneptah, Kitchen 1982: 2–12, 19–22); the *Sherden* and *Weshesh* (Papyrus Harris I 76.7–9); the *Lukka* (EA 38 – Bryce 1992) and several others (Sandars 1978: 105–115; Cifola 1994: 2–15; Barako 2000: 525–526; Yasur-Landau 2010: 171–186). Thus certain elements of the Sea Peoples were known from documentary evidence as early as the 14th century BC, and they are known to have persisted as late as the 11th century BC. Some elements within these group(s) would have formed part of 'the enemy' whose ships and land battles were discussed in some Akkadian documents exchanged between Ugarit and *Alašiya* (Cyprus) towards the end of the 13th century BC (RS 20.18, RSL 1, RS 20.238 – Beckman, in Knapp 1996b: 27; Cifola 1994: 11).

Documentary evidence presents various problems of interpretation, and the Egyptian texts often are filled with hyperbole: they were designed for rhetorical effect rather than reasoned argument, and were often motivated by political concerns. The 'great historical inscription' of Ramesses III in particular is '…anything but a sober, fact-filled record' (Redford 2000: 7). Lesko (1980: 86) even suggested that Ramesses lifted the entire Sea Peoples' episode from Merneptah's mortuary temple and made it his own (see also Muhly 1984: 55). Cifola (1988: 303) regards Ramesses' inscription as a '…narrative condensation of a continuous long-lasting process', where a series of skirmishes between the Egyptians and Sea Peoples have been condensed into two, non-historical battles for propagandistic ends. Liverani (1990: 121) also maintained that

Ramesses' text refers to several minor episodes '…joined together in order to artfully build up a "battle" that as such never took place', but rather was a 'propagandistic celebration' required by pharaonic tradition. Not all scholars are so sceptical: O'Connor (2000: 94–95), for example, believes that by taking account of the conceptual complexity of the reliefs and the compositional intricacy of the narrative, allowing for a fusion of ideology and reality, we might arrive at 'a revealing picture of the actual historical situation'.

All such views beg the questions: just how pervasive were the 'Sea Peoples' movements? Can we regard them at any point collectively, as a unified force? Even if these diverse bands of pirates, marauders and migrants never came together with a unified purpose, nor brought about directly the collapse of the politico-economic and ideological system(s) that linked together so many Bronze Age states and kingdoms in the Aegean and eastern Mediterranean, in the end they suffered the same fate. Most Late Bronze Age polities in the region – Hittites and other Near Eastern states, the Aegean and Levantine city-states, even the citadel of Troy – gradually disintegrated, as did the always-vulnerable interaction sphere(s) that had sustained them. Whereas external factors such as the Sea Peoples surely played a part, so too did internal troubles – social, political, economic – in the different areas.

The ambiguity of the evidence, textual and archaeological, makes it difficult to sort out what was cause, and what was result. On land and at sea, brigandage and piracy accelerated the collapse of international trade. Once ports and harbours throughout the eastern Mediterranean were devastated, however, there was no place left for traders or pirates to conduct their business. Thus what the Egyptian monuments record is the end of a long and indefinable chain reaction, behind which lay a series of 'ethnic' intermixings and demographic movements. Alongside the collapse of towns, city-states and kingdoms, and the demise of the highly specialised production and trade networks in which they were involved, a flurry of 'migrations' took place in the 12th–11th centuries BC: Aramaeans in Syria-Palestine, 'neo-Hittites' in northern Syria, Israelites in the southern Levant, and at least some Aegean people on Cyprus. The new, quite distinctive material culture found in coastal or near-coastal sites of the southern Levant is widely seen, as least by Israeli scholars, as marking the arrival and settlement of the Philistines (e.g. Bunimovitz 1998; Dothan and Zukerman 2004: 28; Ben-Shlomo et al. 2008: 226–227; Yasur-Landau 2010), and perhaps other groups of Sea Peoples farther north (e.g. *Šikala* at Dor, *Sherden* at Akko – Gilboa 2005: 48–52; Yasur-Landau 2010: 170–171).

Here we confront two dilemmas: (1) the difficulty of isolating 'ethnic' groups in the material record (in general, Emberling 1997; Jones 1997; on the 'Sea Peoples' Sandars 1978: 164–170; on Cyprus specifically Knapp 2001), and (2) the quandary that arises from trying to compare or juxtapose data sets that are in large part incomparable or contradictory. Diplomatic and literary evidence in particular, written or composed for specific, often propagandistic purposes by literate rulers or social élites in largely illiterate societies should not be taken as historical fact, nor should it be equated directly with archaeological strata, sequences or site destructions. The tyranny of 'historical contexts' so frequently imposed on archaeology in the eastern Mediterranean (Bunimovitz 1995: 328), is well exemplified in the case that has been made for a 'Philistine' presence on Cyprus: Muhly (1984: 55) has charged scholars of holding the archaeological evidence hostage to '…an often naïve interpretation of a literary text that, at best, is of questionable historical value'. This tyranny is also well exemplified where a presumed historical event, in this case the Aegean 'colonisation' of Cyprus (Karageorghis and Demas 1985: 269–276), is used to explain a stratigraphic sequence and classify an archaeological assemblage (Kling 1987: 103–105).

Attempts to link either specific historical episodes or grand narratives to the archaeological record of Cyprus have proved to be highly contentious. Muhly (1984: 49), for example, was adamant: '…it is no longer possible, I would argue, to find support for any theory that attempts to identify Philistines or any other group of the Sea Peoples in the archaeological record as known from Cyprus at the end of the Late Bronze Age'. Muhly's reaction was directed against those who believe that similarities between Cypriot and Philistine pottery point to the common origin of Aegean settlers on Cyprus and in the southern Levant (e.g. Dothan 1983; Mazar 1985). Such views continue to hold sway (e.g. Stager 1995; Bunimovitz and Yasur-Landau 1996; Bunimovitz 1998), with variations. Killebrew (2005: 231; 2006–07), for example, suggests that the Philistine migration originated in Cyprus or in regions surrounding it (i.e. Cilicia). Sherratt (1998: 301–307), another prominent critic of the Philistine phenomenon, suggests that Late Helladic IIIC:1b pottery ('Philistine' pottery in Israel) was produced and distributed throughout the eastern Mediterranean region by a loosely based confederation of maritime merchants based on or near Cyprus (similarly Bauer 1998). She maintains that the earliest Philistine pottery in Israel should be regarded as '…a functionally determined selection of the Cypriote White Painted Wheelmade III repertoire' (Sherratt 2003: 45; 1998: 298).

In his critique of Sherratt, Barako (2000; 2003; also Killebrew 2006–2007), argues that it is not only the 'Philistine' pottery (i.e. the Late Helladic IIIC:1b or derivative wares) which points to the arrival in the southern Levant by sea – from the Aegean, perhaps via Cyprus – of a new ethnic group (the Philistines). He also lists other material goods and practices entirely foreign to local (Canaanite) cultural traditions: Aegean-style loomweights and figurines (and cooking pots), pebbled hearths and hearth rooms, incised scapulae, the high percentage of pig in faunal assemblages. The scapulae and seated 'Ashdoda' figurines, however, are most likely Cypriot, not Aegean products (Sherratt 1998: 302, n. 17; Russell 2009). Yasur-Landau (2010: 227–281) expands the argument based on material and domestic practices in great detail, focusing on cooking and storage wares, pottery and textile production, and the organisation of domestic space. Here, such debates cannot be resolved; they can only be highlighted to the extent they relate to Cyprus.

On Cyprus itself, a centralised politico-economic system that also embraced competitive traders may have saved the island from the most severe effects of the widespread collapse amongst closely interlinked polities in the surrounding regions. That is, some Cypriot merchants would have operated within a more open economy that existed alongside centrally controlled, élite trade. Sherratt's (1998: 301–302) view is less compromising: the 'urban coastal moguls' of ProBA 3 Cyprus ran an 'aggressively open economy' that undermined the élite-dominated, centralised politico-economic system (similarly, Manning and DeMita 1997). Because several main centres of ProBA Cyprus – including Enkomi, Kalavasos *Ayios Dhimitrios*, Maroni *Vournes*, Morphou *Toumba tou Skourou* and Alassa *Paleotaverna* – were destroyed or abandoned after 1200 BC, it would seem that the wider eastern Mediterranean collapse indeed had an impact on Cyprus. Destructions and abandonments in the coastal centres also affected inland settlements: ceremonial centres, as well as agricultural and mining or pottery-producing villages were disrupted and most of them were also abandoned (e.g. Myrtou *Pigadhes*, Athienou *Bamboulari tis Koukounninas*, Apliki *Karamallos*).

The large coastal towns that survived destructions or abandonments – Enkomi, Palaipaphos, Kition – seem to have become new centres of authority, displacing smaller administrative or ceremonial centres and managing new Cypriot contacts emerging overseas, from the Levant to the central Mediterranean (Knapp 1990b). Moreover, there are signs of cultural continuity – during the 12th and into the 11th centuries BC – in everything from pottery styles and techniques, architecture and town plans, tomb use and religious practices, to metalworking technologies and industrial intensification (Sherratt 1994b; 1998: 293–294; Rupp 1989; Coldstream 1989). Cyprus thus seems to have made tactical as well as commercial adjustments not just to collapse but also to the coming Age of Iron; its economy remained integral to connectivity within the Mediterranean. By 1125/1100 Cal BC, however, the typical settlement patterns and political organisation of the ProBA had come to an end, as new socio-economic structures dictated the establishment of new population and power centres on early Iron Age Cyprus. These new political configurations, much debated by interested scholars, heralded the rise of the island's early historical kingdoms, whether during the 11th, or the 9th–8th centuries BC (Snodgrass 1988; Rupp 1998; Petit 2001; Iacovou 2002; 2006b – see further below, *Mobility, Migrations and Aegeans on Cyprus*).

Migration, Hybridisation and the Aegean 'Colonisation' of Cyprus

However one interprets the complex series of site destructions that took place between about 1200–1100 BC and the demographic displacements that accompanied them, it is clear that the cooperative international relations that had linked various parts of the Mediterranean during the past 300–400 years had come to an end. Nonetheless, the breakdown of the strongly centralised Late Bronze Age economies of the eastern Mediterranean seems to have been offset by a burst of activity that had repercussions far beyond that area (Rowlands 1984: 150–152; Knapp 1990b; Sherratt 1992; 1998: 301–302).

In attempting to understand the migrations that accompanied the breakdown of international relations, it is useful to consider how the boundaries of different groups might be identified in material terms, how such material representations may have been transformed through time into something entirely new, and how a new sense of social identity may have emerged in different social or politico-economic contexts (Sherratt 1992). In such ways, we may be able to capitalise on the diverse and multiple entanglements that characterise the material culture of 13th–12th century BC Cyprus. If Cyprus became the focal point of one or more migrations by groups from the Aegean, the Levant or Anatolia during the 12th–11th centuries BC, then it stands to reason that these incoming peoples would have introduced not just social and 'ethnic' but also material diversity into different regions, towns and villages on the island. On the one hand, then, we may expect that the arrival of new immigrants resulted in new socioeconomic, if not political and ideological links between distant areas; on the other hand, the materiality of these processes – migration, resettlement, negotiation, hybridisation – would have obscured any clear picture of discrete ethnic groups, of 'us' versus 'them' (Bernardini 2005: 46–47).

Over the past century, archaeological opinion, explicitly or implicitly, has overwhelmingly favoured the notion of a 'Mycenaean' (Aegean) colonisation of Cyprus at some point during the 12th and/or 11th centuries BC. This 'colonisation' is regarded to be the result of one or more episodes of migration assumed to be on a major scale (e.g. Coldstream 1994; Karageorghis 1994; 2000a). Maier (1986: 314–316, fig. 1) long ago argued that this 'historical reconstruction' closely followed a scheme first laid down by Gjerstad in 1926, and adopted with little modification – beyond suggesting more 'waves' of migration – throughout the following 60 years by several prominent Cypriot archaeologists: Sjöqvist, Furumark, Desborough, Catling, Dikaios, Åström and Karageorghis. Most scholars, moreover, see an overwhelming 'Greek' influence as the main contributing factor to the Iron Age culture(s) of Cyprus (e.g. Snodgrass 1988; Coldstream 1989; Karageorghis 2000b; Iacovou 1999a; 2003; 2006a). The differences in opinion arise in assessing the size and impact of such a migration, and the extent to which new peoples may have impacted on sociocultural developments in the succeeding periods (e.g. Iacovou 2006b; 2008; Voskos and Knapp 2008).

Other archaeologists have questioned the level of Aegean influence on developments in Cyprus during ProBA 3, that is, between about 1300–1125/1100 Cal BC (e.g. Kling 1989b; Sherratt 1998; 1999; 2001; Steel 1998;

2001; Antoniadou 2004, 2005). Still others dispute when or to what extent Greek-speaking peoples or their political institutions become pre-eminent on Cyprus (Steel 1993; Rupp 1987; 1998; Petit 2001) (see further below). Both Baurain (1984: 355) and Vanschoonwinkel (1991: 454), for example, suggested that the island was colonised by groups from Anatolia (Trojans and perhaps the *Lukka* or 'Sea Peoples') alongside immigrants from the Aegean. Negbi (1992; 2005) felt that both Aegean and Levantine ('Phoenician') ethnic groups migrated to the island during the 12th century BC (ProBA 3). Finally, covering most of the possible options, Sandars (1978: 153–155) postulated that refugees from Ugarit, if not from Anatolia (*Lukka*, Carians, Mycenaeans from Miletos), formed part of the demographic mix on 12th century BC Cyprus, whilst Åström (1985; 1998) suggested an amalgamation of Minoan, Mycenaean, Syro-Palestinian and Anatolian ethnic elements.

Here I suggest another alternative: because a wide range of material evidence shows ambiguous mixtures of native Cypriot, Aegean and Levantine, even Egyptian form, style, motifs and manufacturing techniques, this evidence should be understood and analysed in terms of hybridisation practices. Elsewhere I have presented detailed discussion of many of the relevant objects, materials and practices (Knapp 2008: 252–280); here I summarise only the main points by presenting a sample of the material.

Reduced to its baldest terms, the debate revolves around two opposing positions:

(1) *The colonisation argument* (term coined by Leriou 2002a), which sees two or even three successive waves of Aegean immigrants coming to Cyprus, the first (12th century BC) causing several site destructions or abandonments, the second (11th century BC) less devastating but more permanent, when new pottery styles and mortuary practices, fortifications, architectural elements and metal goods, items of personal adornment, and a transformed settlement pattern become prominent in the archaeological record (Catling 1975: 207–213; Karageorghis 1994, 2002a: 71–113; Åström 1998; Iacovou 1999a; 2003).

(2) *The politico-economic argument*, wherein the manifold changes in Cypriot society during the 12th–11th centuries BC are seen to be the result of new, smaller scale, entrepreneurial patterns of Mediterranean maritime interaction, whose origins lay in the wealthy Cypriot towns of the 13th century BC (ProBA 2) (Sherratt 1992; 1994a; 1998; 2001). The protagonists are seen as 'economic mercenaries' who rose from being intermediaries in a patron/client relationship with various city-states in the eastern Mediterranean to become independent entrepreneurs, economic competitors of those same city-states (Artzy 1997; 1998; 2003).

The material basis for the colonisation argument (12th–11th centuries BC) has always revolved around the Mycenaean pottery found on Cyprus: its origins, development and the transition to local forms of production, the last of which became predominant during the 12th century BC (ProBA 3). Late Helladic I–IIA wares had been imported to Cyprus as early as the late 16th century BC. These imports grew steadily during the 15th–early 14th centuries BC, and in the following two centuries they increased significantly (LH IIIA2, LH IIIB) (Catling 1975: 199–200; Cadogan 1993; Steel 2004b: 70). Although the amount of Mycenaean pottery that came into Cyprus during these centuries is substantial, at least compared to that found in the surrounding regions, Steel (1998; 2004b: 74–75) cautions that such finds must be seen in relation to the total pottery corpus. Mycenaean wares found at Kalavasos *Ayios Dhimitrios*, for example, amount to less than 1% of the pottery recovered in the excavations (Steel 1998: 286 and n. 5; South and Todd 1997: 72–75), and similar patterns prevail throughout the island.

There is a long-standing tension between Cypriot archaeologists who see pottery as evidence of trade and those who see it as an ethnic or cultural marker of large-scale migrations or small-scale movements of individual potters, merchants or refugees (Sherratt 1999: 164–168). The former viewpoint (pottery as trade) tends to hold sway today but the latter (pottery as people) still prevails wherever the local production of previously imported wares can be demonstrated: this is precisely the case for the Aegean-style pottery found in Cyprus and the Levant during the 13th and 12th centuries BC.

Beyond pottery, Aegean 'colonists' are thought to have introduced several other facets of material culture to Cyprus during the 12th century BC. Karageorghis (2001c; 2002a: 71–113), for example, argues that the use of the central hearth – as known from Mycenaean *megara* – at sites such as Maa, Enkomi, Alassa and Hala Sultan Tekke on Cyprus is only explicable if Mycenaeans had settled the island by 1200 BC. Karageorghis has also suggested an Aegean origin for 12th century BC changes in architecture (ashlar masonry, Cyclopean walls, the 'dog-leg' gate), coroplastic art, metallurgy (weaponry, fibulae), clay utensils (clay loomweights, torches) and household items (clay or limestone baths and bathtubs). With a rising tide of criticism, and the knowledge that Cypriot culture flourished unhindered at this time, Karageorghis would no longer maintain that these features are tantamount to a complete Hellenisation of the island; rather Cypriot culture is seen to have developed on Aegean models whilst maintaining local traditions. As we shall see, however, most of the objects, features, technologies or styles in question have very complex biographies, and thus should not be linked solely to the Aegean world.

HYBRIDISATION PRACTICES

Archaeologists working on Cyprus have long agreed that some level of 'cultural assimilation' or 'fusion' between different social groups occurred during the 13th–12th centuries BC (e.g. Gjerstad 1926: 328; Sjöqvist 1940: 97). Catling (1980: 23) in particular felt that the material culture of the 12th century

BC – town planning, monumental architecture, burial customs, metalwork and especially glyptic – revealed a fusion of Cypriot, Aegean and Levantine elements, something so distinctive that '…we must admit the emergence of something entirely new as the result of the amalgamation' (also Catling 1986: 99).

Elsewhere, archaeologists have adopted concepts such as transculturation, creolisation or hybridisation in order to understand better various material and social issues related to migration or colonisation (e.g. van Dommelen 1998; Webster 2001; Dietler and López-Ruiz 2009). Hybridisation practices involve the people, the objects, the materials and the actual interactions that occur in any contact situation. In such contacts, a wide range of objects, ideas and activities may undergo various degrees of mixture or change; in so doing they become recombined into new material and social practices. As a result the original meanings of these materials and practices often become transformed, infused with new meanings based on the 'in-betweeness' and reinterpretation of local materials, products and ideas. In attempting to understand more fully prehistoric (or historical) cases of migration or colonisation, it is useful to focus on local traditions and context, on the ways that hybridisation practices may be expressed in different objects and materials, and on how such social and material mixings led to entirely new forms and meanings of the objects involved. To illustrate some of these points, I cite a few examples from several different classes of ProBA 2–3 Cypriot material culture. In each and every class, however, the evidence is much more extensive, and has been presented in detail elsewhere (Knapp 2008: 264–280; 2012).

The evidence of pottery shapes, styles and decoration forms the mainstay of all arguments supporting an Aegean colonisation of Cyprus. Whilst many vessel shapes continued in use from the 13th into the 12th century BC, that is, from ProBA 2 to ProBA 3 (Kling 1989b), some of the new wheelmade pottery wares imitated earlier handmade forms. For example, at Enkomi, carinated cups in Wheelmade Plain ware were made in imitation of canonical Base-ring II forms (Courtois 1971: 254–255; Steel 2004a: 194). More important for considering hybridisation practices are some motifs of foreign derivation seen on conventional Cypriot shapes. From Kourion, for example, come some low hemispherical bowls with raised wishbone handles, decorated with panels of geometric design common in the Aegean (Furumark 1944: 239). This type of bowl had a long tradition on Cyprus and was found, along with many others of similar type, in Tomb 89 at Kourion (*Bamboula*) (Murray et al. 1900: 74–75, fig. 129 [bottom centre]; Kling 1989a: 139). From Enkomi come several bell kraters and krater fragments – originally an Aegean shape – decorated with bird and/or fish motifs of Levantine, Aegean or Cypriot design (Dikaios 1969–1971: 286–287, 852, nos. 277–288, pl. 81: 26–36; Kling 1989a: 124–125). From Kition comes an amphoroid krater, decorated with motifs from both the Levant (butterfly ornament, fish in vertical row) and the Aegean (the bird, a specific type of fish) (Karageorghis et al. 1981: 8, no. 23, pls. VI: 23; XIII). There

Figure 133. Kouklia Tomb KA T1: strainer jug
decorated with Aegean- or Levantine style bird
and Cypriot-style bull. Kouklia Museum, Cyprus.
Courtesy of the Kouklia Museum, and the
Director, Department of Antiquities, Cyprus.

are forerunners of this vessel, very similar in shape and size, from the Middle
Bronze Age Levant (Yannai 2006: 98–102). Despite the array of influences seen
on this krater, the end product is decidedly Cypriot.

On various locally made White Painted Wheelmade III (=LH IIIC: 1b)
wares, potters used Aegean-based wavy line decoration (Dikaios 1969–1971:
853–855; Iacovou 1988: 11). Some vessels contain decoration that combines
local and foreign motifs: for example, a strainer jug from Kouklia with Aegean-
or Levantine-style birds and Cypriot 'Pastoral' Style bulls (Kling 1988: pl. 37)
(Figure 133). Strainer jugs are usually thought to be Aegean in origin, yet
they are rare in Mycenaean pottery outside of the Dodecanese and combine
features of the Levantine wine set (strainer and jug) in one vessel. The decoration of this particular vessel, from Tomb KA T1 at Kouklia, may blend earlier Aegean traditions (birds found on examples from Rhodes and the Greek
mainland) with the predominant ware of 12th century BC Cyprus (Kling
1988: 272). Other strainer jugs from Alassa *Pano Mandilares* (Hadjisavvas 1991:
173–177, figs. 17.1–2, 17.4–5), found in both mortuary and settlement contexts,
are decorated with a range of Aegean-style motifs (spirals, net patterns, geometric designs).

In fact, a wide range of ProBA 3 pottery wares and decorative features
combine local Cypriot elements with those seen on Aegean or Levantine
wares (Kling 1989a: 171–173; 2000: 282–286). Sherratt (1998: 298) noted that
the increasing use of Aegean pottery shapes and decorative motifs on 12th
century BC Cyprus '…gives the impression of selective eclecticism mixed
with a healthy dose of local improvisation'. It should also be noted that the
people involved in this particular contact situation recombined a mixture of
diverse elements in pottery manufacture and decoration – material markers
of the new, hybridised social practices that occurred during the transitional

period that lasted throughout the 12th century BC. During this time, new typological and decorative elements continuously penetrated the Cypriot pottery repertoire, thus offering a glimpse of the material practices of potters embracing more than one current cultural tradition. In terms of context, these objects were found most often in mortuary deposits, but at Enkomi they also appeared frequently in industrial and domestic contexts, and at least occasionally in ceremonial contexts (Knapp 2012: 34–38). Thus they should not be seen as exotic products accessible only to a few members of society; rather they were reflections of the everyday circumstances of ProBA 3 Cypriot society.

Ivory provides some striking cases of hybridisation practices, and shows the use of local Cypriot, Aegean and Levantine elements. The ivory used in the eastern Mediterranean was either local or imported from Egypt and Africa; the style and iconography of the finished products, however, are still widely debated (Rehak and Younger 1998: 230–231). Many of the ivory objects and pieces of ivory found on Cyprus fuse Aegean and Levantine styles with local elements. For example, a rhyton from Athienou *Bamboulari tis Koukounninas* contains four bands of decoration (similar to Aegean rhyta) depicting stylised, bird-like human heads (Mycenaean iconography), antithetically placed birds (Levantine element), two horned animals (goats or gazelles?), vertically placed fish (paralleled at Ras Shamra in Syria but also known from the Aegean), and stylised plants (Dothan and Ben-Tor 1983: 123–125 and fig. 56). Although the local inspiration for this object seems clear, it encapsulates diverse elements of Aegean and Levantine iconography and design transformed into a uniquely new, hybridised Cypriot product. The rhyton was recovered from a series of pits to the east of the main building complex at Athienou, in context with several other luxury or exotic goods. Whilst the chronological placement and function of these pits remains problematic, the main structure at Athienou arguably served a ceremonial function during the 13th century BC (Åström 1987), but more specifically industrial purposes during the 12th century BC (Webb 1999: 25–29, 285).

Two ivory *pyxis* lids found at Kouklia *Evreti* – in Well TE III 165 and Pit KD 137 – were decorated in a mixed style showing both Levantine and Aegean influences (Maier and Karageorghis 1984: 70, 77, figs. 59–60). Their find-spots are not domestic but rather formed part of the sumptuous mortuary deposit in *Evreti*'s Tomb 8 (Catling 1968: 165). An ivory mirror handle from *Evreti* Tomb 8 (Maier and Karageorghis 1984: 68, 74–75, figs. 55, 58) (Figure 134), and another handle from Tomb 17 at Enkomi (Murray et al. 1900: 31, pl. II, no. 872a) (Figure 135) depict armed warriors in Aegean-style kilts striking a resting lion (*Evreti*) and a griffin (Enkomi). As Feldman (2006: 73–81) has shown, the theme of warriors slaying real or mythical animals has a long tradition in Near Eastern art. Still another ivory mirror handle from Swedish Tomb 19 at Enkomi (Gjerstad et al. 1934, vol. I: 565 no. 91, pls. 92.2, 152.7) was made in the

Figure 134. Kouklia *Evreti* Tomb 8, ivory mirror handle depicting a warrior clad in Aegean-style kilt striking a lion. Cyprus Museum, Inventory no. K.T.E. T.8/34. Courtesy of the Cyprus Museum, Nicosia.

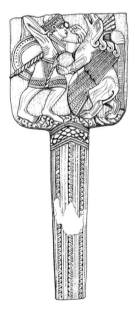

Figure 135. Enkomi Tomb 17, ivory mirror handle decorated with warrior in Aegean-style kilt stabbing griffin. British Museum, London, Inventory 1897,0401.872 AN105792. © The Trustees of the British Museum.

form of a nude woman grasping her breasts, a thematic element seen in both west Asian and Egyptian art (Kantor 1947: 89–90). This handle shows Aegean inspiration in technical and typological terms, but may have been the product of a Levantine school of carving.

Finally, the well-known and widely illustrated ivory box from British Tomb 58 at Enkomi (already discussed above, and see Figure 118) (Murray et al. 1900: 12–15, fig. 19, 31, pl. I; Karageorghis 2002a: 100, fig. 205) portrays a hunting scene with chariot that is of Near Eastern derivation, whilst all the animals are shown in the 'flying gallop' style, an Aegean motif. The bull and a small scene depicting a hunter killing a lion are comparable to details on a gold bowl and plate from Ugarit. This unique ivory box is decorated in a mixture of styles characteristic of hybridised artisanal and social practices on 12th century BC Cyprus. Like the other ivory objects treated here, it offers incontrovertible evidence for the ways that hybridisation practices gave new forms and meanings to materiality.

Although all of these ivory pieces reveal, to varying degrees, a thoroughly mixed style with clear Aegean, Levantine and Egyptian influences, ivory carving was a flourishing local industry on Cyprus throughout the ProBA 2–3 periods. There is evidence for workshops at Kition (Karageorghis 1985b: 336–337), Kouklia *Evreti* (Maier 1969: 40–41; Maier and Karageorghis 1984: 68–70; Maier and von Wartburg 1985: 148), Hala Sultan Tekke (Åström 1992; Fischer 2011), and perhaps Enkomi (Dikaios 1969–1971: 100). Although the examples discussed here derive exclusively from mortuary or ceremonial contexts (Knapp 2012: 40–41), most of the ivories Antoniadou (2007: 494) documented from the 13th–12th centuries BC (ProBA 2–3) were found in domestic contexts. Overall, then, ivories may have had a privileged but not restricted usage, and were not regarded as prestigious objects in the same way that precious metals were.

The hybridised Aegean and Levantine design and decorative elements so obvious on the ivories, as well as their evident local manufacture, are also apparent in metalwork (Catling 1964: 209; Karageorghis and Papasavvas 2001: 345, 347). This is especially true for the intricately crafted four-sided bronze stands (Catling 1964: 203–211; 1984; Papasavvas 2001), and the rod- or cast-tripod stands (Catling 1964: 192–203). Local production for these stands was first indicated by the discovery at Enkomi (Courtois and Webb 1980) and Hala Sultan Tekke (Karageorghis 1989) of two moulds used in producing wax models for some of the figures that decorate them. Papasavvas's (2001) more recent research has demonstrated conclusively that, in terms of their technology, typology and design, most known four-sided bronze stands are Cypriot in origin (also Catling 1984: 88). These stands portray ingot bearers and lyre players, antithetic sphinxes, chariot scenes, and bulls fighting with lions and griffins – all motifs that engage and mix Aegean, Levantine and Cypriot elements (e.g. Karageorghis 1979; 2002a: 98–99 figs. 198–204; discussed further in Knapp 2008: 274).

Two well-known, 12th century BC bronze anthropomorphic figurines from Enkomi – the 'Horned God' and 'Ingot God' – show a similar fusion of Aegean and Levantine elements, again indicative of hybridisation practices (discussed further in Knapp 2008: 221–224). In a new study of the Ingot God, Papasavvas (2011) observes that the 'greaves' (actually a second layer of metal wrapped round the bottom of the figurine), the shield and the miniature ingot were cast onto an existing figurine and thus transformed into an entirely new object. Given the elaborate mix of stylistic and iconographic elements seen on these figurines, they should probably both be regarded as Cypriot in origin and design, perhaps all the more likely since the Ingot God, at least, is made of pure copper (G. Papasavvas, pers. comm., April 2010).

In all these exquisite pieces of metalwork, and especially in the tripods and four-sided stands, we see uniquely Cypriot artefacts bearing the stylistic and iconographic imprint of the Aegean and the Levant, the end product of hybridisation practices. Although many metal objects of the ProBA 2–3 periods, including the bronze stands, weapons and armour, come from mortuary deposits (Knapp 2012: 38–40), the Horned and Ingot Gods are associated with ceremonial contexts, if not feasting activities. At least some of the hybridised metal objects found within and beyond these contexts, not just at Enkomi but also at other sites throughout the island, may have been in use over a long period of time, from the 13th if not the 14th century BC (Muhly 1980: 156–161; Knapp 1986a: 86–87). The fluidity of meanings attached to them, and the ways they were used in this period of intercultural mixings, must have been significantly different.

Much of the iconography used on both 'Elaborate' and 'Derivative' style cylinder seals was foreign in derivation but associated with local ideological and political constructs (Webb 1999: 276; 2002d: 117–126). The very concept of such seals is foreign in origin, and many of them bear Levantine, Near Eastern or Aegean elements (Pini 1979; 1980; Keswani 1989: 69–70). For example, a haematite cylinder seal from the French excavations at Enkomi portrays a standing male figure wearing an Aegean-style kilt and holding two lions by their ears, in Levantine fashion (Karageorghis 2002a: 50, fig. 99) (Figure 136). From Hala Sultan Tekke comes another, recarved, haematite seal depicting a kneeling hero (Cypro-Aegean and Syrian elements) facing a winged griffin (Levantine element) placed opposite a central tree-like motif; Cypro-Minoan signs appear beyond and above the main scene (Porada 1976: 99–101, figs. 75, 78; Smith 2003: 298–299, fig. 6b). Thus we see Levantine and Aegean elements combined with Cypro-Minoan signs in a distinctively Cypriot fashion, resulting in a unique hybridised product.

More specifically Aegean motifs – bulls, lions, aquatic birds, a 'Minoan Genius', flounced dress and breechcloth – were used on 11 ProBA 2–3 Cypriot

Figure 136. Enkomi haematite cylinder seal, depicting a male figure clad in Aegean style, and holding two lions by their ears, in Levantine fashion. Cyprus Museum, French mission 1934, trial trench 2. Courtesy of the Cyprus Museum, Nicosia.

conoid and lenticular seals from Enkomi, Kourion and Maroni (Graziadio 2004: figs. 1–11). These decorative motifs had been assimilated into the Cypriot répertoire over a period of some three centuries, a time during which the island's material culture became assimilated with a whole series of symbolic referents seen on earlier seals and other luxury goods (Graziadio 2004: 224–226). Fuller discussion of hybridised Aegean, Levantine and Cypriot elements found on several ProBA 2–3 cylinder seals is presented elsewhere (Knapp 2008: 274–277).

Whilst approximately 1,000 cylinder and stamp seals have been found on Cyprus, fewer than 400 have a recorded context (Webb 2002d: 114). Many of the best-known cylinder seals lack secure provenance; and even when the provenance known, that information must be treated with caution as these seals were in use (and sometimes reworked) over a long period of time. Thus they would have moved in and out of various contexts, having different usages and meanings. More than 60% of all provenanced, imported cylinder seals were recovered at Enkomi, and more than 50% come from settlement, mortuary or surface deposits (Courtois and Webb 1987: 25, n. 1; Webb 2002d: 114–117, tables 1, 2). Most seals from non-mortuary contexts were lost or discarded during the 12th century BC. Given such statistics and the limitations they imply, we can only say that hybridised cylinder seals appear mainly in mortuary or settlement contexts (Knapp 2012: 43). At least a few examples of locally made, 13th century BC seals come from domestic and industrial, less so from ceremonial contexts at Myrtou *Pigadhes*, Athienou, *Ayios Dhimitrios*, Maroni, Kourion *Bamboula* and Kition (Webb 1999: 247; 2002d: 114–115, nn. 23, 24, with further refs.). In Webb's (2002d: 128) view, seals may have been used as much for personal ornaments as for official purposes.

Several faience objects found on Cyprus (discussed above) depict everything from lion and bull hunts to heraldic designs, and form part of an interregional artistic *koiné* that is by its nature hybridised. Examples of such faience vessels include a hole-mouth bowl from Kition Tomb 9 (lower) with what appears to be a duck's neck spout; a blossom bowl from the same burial whose sharp relief work recalls both Egyptian and Levantine metal prototypes (Peltenburg (1974: 109, 115, fig. 1a); and a blue-glazed *pyxis* from Kition Tomb 9 (upper burial), with a shape common in the Levant but rare in Egypt. A handleless juglet from the upper burial in Kition Tomb 9 recalls the ovoid shape of Cypriot Base-ring juglets; its greenish-white glazing seems more Levantine than Egyptian in technique (Peltenburg 1974: 135). Finally, from the area just outside Tombs 4 and 5 at Kition came the well-known conical faience rhyton, Aegean in shape, Levantine (and Hittite) in decoration, and produced in what is thought to be an Egyptian technical fashion (Peltenburg 1974: 116–136, pl. XCIV). Whilst the combination of Egyptian technique and Levantine elements makes it difficult to pinpoint its origin, most likely it was produced either along the Syrian coast or in southern Cyprus (Peltenburg 1974: 134). Finally, several tripod plates found in tomb deposits from British (Tomb 66) and Cypriot (Tomb 7) excavations at Enkomi bear designs that are strongly Egyptianising (bulls in a marsh-scape, horned animals) (Murray et al. 1900: 35, fig. 63: 1045; Dikaios 1969–1971: 355, no. 2, pls. 199: 22, 200: 17); this style was either of local inspiration or else an Egyptian product intended for export to Cyprus (Peltenburg 1986b: 159).

Beyond these examples, all from mortuary contexts, several faience vessels or fragments – bowls, a few jars or goblets, a single example of an animal-headed rhyton – have been recovered from ProBA 2–3 settlement or industrial contexts at Kition, Enkomi, Maa *Palaeokastro* and Myrtou *Pigadhes* (Antoniadou 2004: 153–155). The contexts of faience vessels seem to change over time: during the 13th century BC (ProBA 2), they occur mainly in industrial and domestic contexts, whilst during the 12th century BC (ProBA 3) they appear in industrial, ceremonial, domestic and working contexts (Antoniadou 2007: 491–492). The earlier deposition of faience objects in industrial or domestic contexts may suggest that foreign symbols were selected for use as items of self-representation (Antoniadou 2007: 490). By the 12th century BC, however, the unrestricted distribution of faience vessels suggests that they served many different people's everyday needs.

Taking a broader view, Antoniadou (2007: 497) noted that there was a decrease in the number and variety of both imports and hybridised objects in mortuary and settlement contexts at Enkomi during the late 13th–early 12th centuries BC. In such a situation, we can no longer regard Mycenaean pottery, metal weapons and figurines, ivory or faience personal goods and vessels as prestigious imports or exclusively élite products. Some locally produced objects, of course, may represent what Sherratt (1998: 295–296, 298) defined as value-added, 'import substitution' products, typically found in 'sub-élite' contexts and often associated with feasting or drinking activities. Thus those who lived on Cyprus during this transitional era (ProBA 2–3) recontextualised, transformed or created anew all sorts of hybridised objects, adapting them to their own needs and adopting them as a way to represent themselves.

Several items presented as 'cultic' in nature – the statuettes of the Horned and Ingot gods, triton shells, bull's head rhyta and bull figurines, horns of consecration and the double axe symbol (Steel 2004a: 204–206) – reveal an eclecticism that is best regarded as Cypriot in origin. They are typical of this transitional era and stand as representative examples of hybridised material and social practices (discussed more fully in Knapp 2008: 277–280). Triton shells (*Charonia sequenzae*) found in ProBA 3 ceremonial contexts at Kition (Reese 1985) and Hala Sultan Tekke (Åström and Reese 1990: 5–6) were reportedly fashioned into musical instruments. Even if, as Åström and Reese (1990: 8–12) argue, they were used in 'liminal' religious contexts in the Late Bronze Age Aegean, this offers no proof that such practices were transmitted to Cyprus during the 12th century BC: it seems more straightforward to see such reworked shells as hybridised objects, here used for social or festive occasions.

Similarly, bull representations of various types are seen as material markers of a bull cult or deity typically associated with the Aegean (e.g. Webb 1999: 179; Hadjisavvas 2001: 209–210; discussed more fully in Steel 2004a: 203–205). From cattle skulls and horns to bronze and terracotta bull figurines, to bull's head rhyta and horns of consecration, it is certainly possible that such bull representations were somehow related to sacrificial or sanctification practices (see Rehak 1995: 450–454 on rhyta in the Aegean). Objects or architectural elements depicting the double axe or horns of consecration, however, had reached Cyprus already during the 14th–13th centuries BC, long before any Aegean colonists are thought to have arrived on the island. Moreover, Steel (2004a: 203–204) has shown that bull's horns had been depicted or represented on Cyprus since at least the PreBA (e.g. on the Vounous bowl and Kotchati model), so there is no need to resort to Aegean prototypes in the search for their origins. Bull representations or symbolism are found widely throughout the Aegean, eastern Mediterranean and Anatolia; in Neolithic Anatolia, at least, such symbolism recently has been equated with maleness and phallocentrism (Hodder and Meskell 2011). On ProBA Cyprus, if they are indeed cultic in nature, they may have been used more intensively in the context of all the social and economic disruptions accompanying the end of the Late Bronze Age in these regions.

Several other material features have been linked either to the Aegean world or else to the movements of the Sea Peoples: architectural elements, bathtubs, loomweights and clay torches, the iconography of ship representations, and more (e.g. Karageorghis 1998b; 2000b). Typically these reveal a mixture of Cypriot, Levantine and Aegean elements, and are much more likely to reflect an amalgam of ideas and influences from all these areas rather than proof for an origin from one any single one. Steel (2004a: 200–210) has discussed other 'ritual' objects, metal hoards and crafts linked to a 12th-century-BC Aegean colonisation of Cyprus, although at least some of them – for example, the ivory box and mirror handles from Enkomi and Kouklia – reveal an iconography more closely associated with Near Eastern royal ideologies (Keswani 2004: 127). Above all, however, it must be recalled that there is good evidence for cultural continuity on Cyprus between the 13th–12th centuries BC (ProBA 3 period), a time during which one of the most salient characteristics of social practices is the '…external referencing and hybridisation of Aegean and Near Eastern iconography and equipment' (Steel 2004a: 204).

Even during the subsequent, Late Cypriot IIIB period (early Iron Age), when major cultural and material discontinuities become apparent in the archaeological record, there is an equally compelling array of evidence pointing to hybridisation practices. For example, the most characteristic pottery style of this period, Proto-White Painted, is an entirely standardised Cypriot product embracing Aegean, Levantine and local pottery traditions (Iacovou 1991: 204; see also Cook 1988; Sherratt 1992: 329–338). Also fully within this eclectic, Proto-White Painted pottery tradition are some zoomorphic vessels in the form of dogs, birds, bulls and horses, as well as two striking, bicephalous human-animal hybrids (Courtois 1971: 287–308, figs. 119–127) (Figure 137). Karageorghis (1993: 53, 60) feels that some of their iconographic features are derivative of the Aegean; even if they are, these vessels appear in Late Cypriot IIIB contexts in new, larger-scale, wheelmade and more abstract forms than those of their earlier counterparts (Webb 1999: 216–219). The 'goddess with upraised arms' (see above, Figure 122), a new genre of female figurine, may have been introduced at this time from Crete, along with models of shrines (Courtois 1971: 326–356; Hägg 1991). Most examples, however, are modelled on (Mycenaean-type) *psi* figurines, some of which appeared in earlier (ProBA 2–3) contexts at Kition (Karageorghis 1985b: 98, 103, 105, pls. CIX, CX); Webb (1999: 213–214), however, concludes that they did not become common until the end of the 12th century BC. At the very least we may suggest that several aspects of coroplastic art resulted from the hybridisation practices so common during this period of transition from the Bronze to the Iron Age.

Distinctive new mortuary practices of the LC IIIB period also draw upon both Aegean and Levantine traditions and materials: for example, infant burials in Levantine-type storage jars within the earliest, 11th century BC levels at Salamis (Calvet 1980); interments with new status symbols including gold jewellery, bronze vessels, imported Levantine unguent vessels and Canaanite amphorae (Rupp 1985; 1989; Coldstream 1989); isolated (extra-mural) cemeteries with both cremations and inhumations frequently placed in ('Mycenaean type') chamber tombs with a long and narrow *dromos*. These new mortuary patterns reveal that, by the 11th–10th centuries BC, people of Aegean, Phoenician or native Cypriot origin living on Cyprus had shared, hybridised

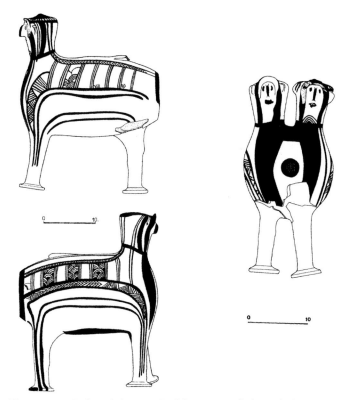

Figure 137. Enkomi (Ingot God 'sanctuary') bicephalous animal-human hybrid. After Courtois 1971: figs. 124, 126; Steel 2004a: 212, fig. 7.9. Courtesy of Louise Steel.

social practices: in Iacovou's (2005: 130–131) words: '…the foreigners were no longer foreigners'.

Finally, and with a view to some of the issues to be raised in the following section, let us consider Tomb 40 at Episkopi *Kaloriziki* and its occupant, reputedly an 'Achaean prince'. This burial contained a suite of bronze vessels and tripods, a bronze-lined shield and reputedly a golden sceptre crowned by a globe and two falcons, decorated in the cloisonné technique and inlaid with blue and white enamel (Coldstream 1989: 332–333; Karageorghis 2002a: 135, fig. 292). Tomb 40 is a rectangular shaft tomb with no dromos, fully in accord with Late Bronze Age Cypriot traditions (Christou 1994b: 183–184). Although some problems with the dating and provenance of the sceptre have been raised (Goring 1995), stylistically it shows similarities with some Aegean sceptres: it was originally interpreted as Mycenaean in origin (McFadden 1954: 134). More likely, this golden sceptre was an indigenous Cypriot product with strong Egyptianising traits (e.g. the falcons – Korou 1994: 204–206). Whether Tomb 40 was the final resting place of an Achaean prince or, more likely, a member of the Cypriot élite, his sceptre forms yet another material witness to the hybridised mortuary practices of Cyprus.

Figure 138. Palaipaphos *Skales* Tomb 49: bronze *obelos* with Cypriot syllabic inscription. Cyprus Museum, *Skales* Tomb 49, no. 16. Courtesy of the Cyprus Museum, Nicosia.

MOBILITY, MIGRATIONS AND AEGEANS ON CYPRUS

By the Cypro-Archaic period (ca. 750–475 BC), we know that Cyprus had become a largely Greek-speaking island (Sherratt 1992: 326; Reyes 1994: 11–13; Iacovou 2005: 127). Whilst 'history' informs us that this fundamental change *did* take place, it does not tell us *how* or *when* it happened, nor has archaeology yet provided decisive evidence. Migrations, however, are a central fact of social life, and memories of them can generate ideas and stories about origins and identities. Through hybridisation practices, the identities of migrants and the people with whom they settle typically become transformed, not least in learning to share a common language. As Iacovou (2005: 132) thus notes: 'It is not ethnicity, therefore, that produces a shared language; it is a shared language that may gradually create or contribute towards an ethnic bond'.

The key question that arises, then, is whether Greek-speaking people were present, and more importantly instrumental in the changes that took place during the 12th and especially the 11th centuries BC. The single, most commonly cited object used to argue for a Greek migration to – or Greek colonisation of – Cyprus during Late Cypriot IIIB is an *obelos*, a barbeque 'spit' (Figure 138). Found in Tomb 49 at Palaipaphos *Skales* (Karageorghis 1983: 59–76; 2002a: 125–127, fig. 263; Iacovou 1999a: 11–12), this object was inscribed with the earliest attested Greek personal name on Cyprus, *Opheltas* (Masson and Masson 1983). On the one hand, the discovery of this object has led to claims that Greek-speaking people were not just present but politically and socially pre-eminent on Cyprus by this time (Snodgrass 1988: 12; less emphatically, Iacovou 1999a: 6–7). On the other hand Sherratt (2003b: 226) points out that this *obelos* is '…a thoroughly Cypriot artefact', and that Opheltas was '…a member of a Greek-speaking community whose culture generally is indistinguishable from that of other contemporary Cypriots, who is using a peculiarly Cypriot form of writing in a thoroughly Cypriot, or rather non-Greek manner'. Of equal interest is that a Greek name was inscribed on this object both in the 'common' Cypriot syllabary and in an even more localised variant used in the Paphos region (Palaima 2005: 36; Egetmeyer 2009: 81–82). Thus we have another clear case of hybridisation practices, namely in the mixing of language (Greek) and the script (Cypriot) used to render it.

More important for our concerns here, however, is Iacovou's (2006b: 324) observation:

> The introduction of a new language was not accompanied by a clearly visible Mycenaean-Greek migrant package. In fact, were it not for the Greek language, the material record left on its own could not defend the migration of Greek speakers to Cyprus at the end of the second millennium BC.

In fact, the material record of 12th–11th century BC Cyprus offers some compelling evidence for a movement of people that, however limited its impact at the time, would become of lasting historical significance for the island of Cyprus (Voskos and Knapp 2008). Anthony (1990: 899) notes that migration occurs most commonly when negative (push) factors at home (in this case, the 'collapse' of Mycenaean palatial systems) are offset by positive (pull) features in the target area (in this case, the stability of Cyprus's socio-economic system). Moreover, those who undertake long-distance migrations are often people whose previous labours had become unsustainable, for example specialised producers or craftspeople. This might help to explain in part what happened to all the specialists – makers of perfumed oils, wines, wool, and the like, as recorded in the Linear B tablets – after the collapse of the Late Bronze Aegean palatial systems (Voskos and Knapp 2008: 678).

Throughout the ProBA 3 period (ca. 1300–1125/1100 Cal BC), documentary and archaeological evidence alike records various patterns of human mobility in the eastern Mediterranean. Any intrusive groups that arrived on Cyprus during this time ultimately will have had an impact on the inhabitants' materiality, memory and identity (Janes 2010). Sherratt (1992: 330) points out that the 11th century BC was '…a time of political and social upheaval during which new political configurations may have begun to emerge – in all probability ones which foreshadowed, however abortively, the eventual rise of the early historical kingdoms on the island'. So, the question then becomes: were the city-kingdoms so well established on the island by the beginning of the Cypro-Archaic 1 period (ca. 750–600 BC) the direct result of social and politico-economic transformations that took place during the 11th century BC? Or were they new social and political formations that emerged from a combination of internal and external factors that took place during the 10th–8th centuries BC? And who were the architects of these developments: displaced Aegean peoples? Phoenicians? 'Eteocypriotes'?

Before we can attempt to answer such questions, we must consider briefly the concept of 'ethnicity' (Knapp 2008: 35–47). Archaeologists, ancient historians and philologists working in the context of early Iron Age Cyprus have quite different views of ethnicity. Various scholars have sought to demonstrate the presence or even the dominance of Aegean, Phoenician or 'Eteocypriote' ethnic groups on the island at this time (discussed by Iacovou 2005; 2006a; see also Egetmeyer 2009). It is widely believed that at least some Phoenicians had settled on the island, in particular at Kition, by the mid-9th century BC (Karageorghis 1976; 2005; Gjerstad 1979: 232–233). It is unlikely, however, that any Phoenician polity held direct political or economic control over any part of Cyprus at this time, even if some of Kition's leaders in the 9th or earlier 8th century BC might have taken the title *mlk* ('king') to assert their control in the face of increasing Phoenician contacts (Smith 2008b: 265).

In any case, Reyes (1994: 11–21) suggests that, by the Cypro-Archaic I period (ca. 750–600 BC), only two ethnic groups inhabited the island: Cypriotes (including former migrants from Greece) and Phoenicians. Egetmeyer (2009: 88–90) insists that, at least at Amathus, the Eteocypriote people and their language continued to exist into the 4th century BC. In the eastern Mediterranean, perhaps more than in any other cultural area, archaeologists still assume that ethnic groups can be identified in the material record, through artistic styles and/or symbolic representations. The material symbols of ethnicity, however, are typically scarce, or difficult to isolate in prehistoric contexts. Such difficulties are compounded when, as in the present case, archaeologists are trying to identify two or three distinctive ethnic groups within a material repertoire that, by the Cypro-Geometric (CG) period (ca. 1050–750 BC), is characterised by its island-wide homogeneity, albeit permeated with a mixture of distinctive elements.

To take one example: the tombs uncovered at (late) LC IIIB *Skales*, like those from other cemeteries around Palaipaphos dated to the following CG I period (*Plakes, Hasan, Lakkos tou Skarnou, Xerolimni/Xylinos*), are relatively uniform in type (chamber tombs) and in their mortuary equipment (summarised in Leriou 2002b: 175). In such a situation, how could anyone establish ethnic boundaries between those who were buried in these tombs? Iacovou (2005: 129) has criticised those who attempt to see an ethnic mosaic in the necropolis at *Skales*, arguing that the early CG mortuary deposits here, and elsewhere at Lapithos, Kythrea, Kition, Amathus and Kourion were '…the well-cared for burial plots of securely established, culturally homogeneous and quite prosperous communities'. Moreover, as I have attempted to show here, many material features of early Iron Age Cyprus – mortuary practices and grave goods, human and zoomorphic representations, Proto-White Painted pottery, sceptres and maceheads, the use of a Cypriot syllabary for writing Greek – demonstrate the hybridisation of Cypriot, Levantine and Aegean elements, and cannot be taken as final proof for any specific ethnic origin.

Those who seek to distinguish a prominent Aegean ethnic element in early Iron Age Cyprus reflect to some extent what Rowlands (1994: 136) termed the 'deceit of historical writing'. The deceit is that past material culture takes on a spontaneous and common sense existence that serves, in the eyes of those chained to documentary or epigraphic evidence, to demonstrate that a specific ethnic group has always existed in one place. Such an approach inevitably obscures smaller-scale changes that must have accompanied the complex social and politico-economic transformations inherent in a period of instability, collapse and human mobility. The identities of migrants, as well as those of the local people in the land where they settle, typically are transformed through social processes such as hybridisation; the resulting mixture exacerbates any attempt to disentangle ethnic origins.

Taking all these issues into account, it may be suggested that at some point during the 11th century BC, some migrants from the Aegean became established on Cyprus. This cannot have been a large-scale migration of people who established dominance over the Cypriotes, as the material culture tells a very different story, one punctuated by the mixing and 'in-betweeness' so characteristic of hybridisation practices. Indeed, those Aegean peoples who came to Cyprus:

> …were more in the nature of economic and cultural migrants moving from the periphery to the core, from the Provinces to Versailles; … for them acculturation and integration to the cosmopolitan society of Cyprus … was a desired and desirable process, and there is every reason to believe from the archaeological record that – assuming they were there at all – this is what they achieved. (Sherratt 1992: 325)

And so, beyond insisting that it was a relatively small-scale or low-key migration, we cannot define or explain this situation any more clearly. Whatever the social or ethnic background of the people involved, their identity came to be altered as much as the material that represented it. In time, after negotiation and reinterpretation amongst all those who were living on the island, a new identity emerged, one that had meaning for all early Iron Age Cypriots. Some of these people were speakers of Greek, and ultimately their entanglement with local Cypriotes led to the 'pan-Cyprian *koiné* culture' of the 11th–10th centuries BC (Iacovou 1999b: 150).

On the basis of present evidence, or rather the lack of definitive settlement evidence, it would seem that the emergence of several territorial kingdoms was the result of an extended process throughout Cyprus's early Iron Age. This process could plausibly be understood from either of the contrasting positions, that is, development in the late 11th century BC (Iacovou 1999a; 2002: 82–85; Steel 1993), or during the late 9th–mid-8th centuries BC (Rupp 1985; 1987; 1998; Petit 2001; discussed further in Knapp 2008: 290–297). Smith (2008b: 278–279) feels that earlier studies have paid insufficient attention to the impact made by Phoenician attempts to control parts of Cyprus during the 9th–early 8th centuries BC and that the most dramatic changes occurred during the 8th century BC, in direct response to Neo-Assyrian political aspirations to its Mediterranean periphery.

What remains entirely unlikely in any of these scenarios is that the Iron Age city kingdoms developed solely as the result of an Aegean migration to the island during or just after the ProBA 3 period. Those who still support the notion of a large-scale Aegean migration to, or colonisation of, Cyprus subscribe to what Dietler (1998: 295–296) termed the 'Hellenization perspective', used to explain the absorption or emulation of Greek/Aegean culture by other, indigenous societies. The meetings and mixings of different cultures – native Cypriot, Aegean, Phoenician – on Cyprus during the early Iron Age was no blanket emulation of Aegean culture, and most scholars writing on the topic today do not present their arguments in such terms. Sherratt, Rupp, Petit, Smith and Iacovou have all presented coherent if not compelling discussions related to the 'colonial encounter' that occurred on Cyprus during the early Iron Age. Scholars such as Negbi (1998; 2005), Baurain (1989) and Cook (1988) have made cases for Levantine or Near Eastern influences on Cyprus, but their 'Orientalist' positions are no less an impediment than the Hellenisation perspective to a better understanding of the relations between incoming migrants and well-established islanders.

None of these scholars has attempted to engage the data that do exist with the concept of hybridisation, and nor have they reached any consensus on the complex issues involved. Furthermore, nobody has given adequate attention to the ways that factors related to distance, mobility, object diasporas and politico-economic power all were entangled in the ways that 'others' impacted on Cypriot society during the ProBA 3 period. Only the recent studies by Janes (2008; 2010) and Blackwell (2010) – engaging the extensive mortuary record with issues of social identity – take account of the materiality of social and cultural interactions on the island during this period of upheaval, transition and change (but cf. Satraki 2010).

OVERVIEW: PROTOHISTORIC BRONZE AGE

During the ProBA, particularly during the centuries between ca. 1450–1150 Cal BC, archaeological data demonstrate Cyprus's deepening involvement in systems of metallurgical production and consumption, within and beyond the island. The agricultural regime was more steadfast, reliant on a constant suite of plants and animals as well as their secondary products. In terms of trade and exchange, there is a clear and sharp increase in Cyprus's connectivity with many regions in the eastern and central Mediterranean, and presumably in the types of mobility (ships, merchants, social exchanges) that made it possible.

With respect to the mortuary record, the economic and ideological bases of earlier mortuary practices seem to have been sundered during the ProBA: collective burials and any secondary treatment of human remains diminished, or at times fell into disuse as the social identity and community standing of new social groups displaced those of earlier ones. As social divisions between different groups widened during the ProBA, some élites in the main town centres sought to perpetuate their identity by constructing ancestral tombs on or beneath streets, residences and workshops. Manning's (1998b: 48–53) spatial analysis of ancestral burial plots at Maroni *Vournes*, for example, suggests the emergence of a new élite group promoting its identity and asserting its authority over those of other social groups. Moreover, in Tomb 11 at *Ayios Dhimitrios* (South 1997: 161; 2000: 348), the array of sumptuous grave goods – gold, silver and glass jewellery, ivory and other precious items – must have emphasised the social status of the women interred there. The imagery seen on some Mycenaean kraters (Steel 1994b; 2002) also signalled élite women's identities, even if it was associated with chariots and chariotry.

The coroplastic art of the period is rich in figurines and other gendered representations; a deeper understanding of their role and relevance – who made them and who used them, and how they were used – provides crucial insights into gendered practices, if not directly into sociopolitical organisation. Until we have a better understanding of their contextual associations, it is difficult to say whom, or what these figurines represent: sexual objects or divine images, cultic practitioners, musicians and dancers, celebrants in some rite of passage, individual people involved in various aspects of daily life. Some of the better-known metal examples – the Ingot and Horned 'gods', the Bomford figurine – likely symbolise social if not political authority and thus point to a dominant, élite identity on ProBA Cyprus (Knapp 1986a; 1988). The individuals and imagery represented on the ProBA 2–3 figurines both reflected and shaped gender ideologies, practices and performances within society.

Innovations in pottery production reflect new social practices, not least a changing diet, differing methods of food preparation and consumption, and more frequent public and ceremonial events or mortuary practices that involved feasting and consuming alcoholic beverages (Crewe 2007a: 229–230; Steel 2010: 109). Imported Mycenaean wares used in feasting and drinking activities were to some extent restricted to élites and thus conveyed complex social messages. These developments in pottery production, distribution and consumption thus parallel some of the other, more dramatic changes seen in the material record of ProBA Cyprus, not least the emergence of the new, mainly coastal town centres and the monumental structures that arose within them. The 'public-inclusive' and 'private-exclusive' ceremonies conducted within these structures (Fisher 2009: 190–195) involved a radically different suite of material components, adopted and adapted by élites as new, unequal power relations came to the fore, and eventually became institutionalised.

In order to exploit Cyprus's copper ore-bodies at the scale that is evident during the ProBA, an increasingly complex level of organisation was required in both the production and distribution spheres. Specialised technological skills, the coordination of time and labour, and social realignments enabled producers, distributors and consumers to interact, whether cooperatively or competitively. All the organisational requirements involved in establishing the Cypriot copper industry promoted the development of a more stratified social order and the growth of power differentials. By controlling access to copper ores, and ultimately by managing the output of dependent smiths or artisans, Cypriot élites consolidated their power base and may have excluded other sectors of society from certain metal goods that symbolised élite membership. Until the late 13th or early 12th century BC (ProBA 3), however, these élites seldom used copper or bronze for display or mortuary deposition, instead replying on exotic items imported from the Aegean, the Levant and Egypt (Keswani 2004: 136–139).

Centralised control over Cypriot copper resources and long-distance exchange, access to luxury goods and desirable imports, and the capacity to maintain neutrality in a turbulent geopolitical climate (Knapp 2008: 24, 327–329) made the island a wealthy, socially stratified polity dominated by a political élite responsive to external demand for its most valuable resource, copper. Whether or not the trade in copper or the production and exchange of bronze objects formed the main focus of ProBA trade, archaeometallurgical practice involved miners, producers and distributors in networks of mobility along which ideas, skills, technologies and people moved, exposing local artisans and traders throughout the Mediterranean to wider regional polities and politico-economic practices (Russell 2011).

The general constellation of ProBA sites as well as the amount and variety of both imported and local goods found in them, suggests that a maritime location, the attraction of overseas markets, and the existence of competing social groups or political alliances were key factors in the location of these sites. Densely populated coastal towns – Enkomi, Kition, Hala Sultan Tekke, Maroni – relied on raw materials, especially copper, and agricultural or manufactured goods from inland centres or production sites to underpin their involvement in interregional and long-distance exchange. Diverse quantitative and contextual analyses of Cypriot and Mycenaean pottery found in the contemporary Levant led Bell (2005: 366, 368) to conclude that Enkomi was a major gateway for Aegean wares travelling to Ugarit and elsewhere in the Levant. All these port towns, i.e. those directly on the sea, were deeply involved in international trade (Lagarce and Lagarce, in Courtois et al. 1986: 59–199; Åström 1996; Manning and DeMita 1997; Smith 2009: 9–10). Oxhide ingots and other products were exported throughout the Mediterranean, as long-distance exchange became vital to the Cypriot economy. Cuneiform letters sent from *Alašiya* (Cyprus) to Egypt and Ugarit reveal that the ruler of Cyprus regulated copper production and trade (Knapp 1996b: 21–24; Yon 2007).

Although difficult to determine unequivocally, politico-economic control, and thus the implementation of foreign trade on Cyprus, seems to have been centred initially at Enkomi during ProBA 1 (Crewe 2007b: 155–157), but subsequently embraced other major coastal or even inland emporia, including Kalavasos *Ayios Dhimitrios*, Maroni *Tsaroukkas*, Alassa *Paleotaverna* (and Episkopi), Hala Sultan Tekke *Vyzakia* and possibly Kition (Knapp 2008: 360–362). Although the material record of ProBA Cyprus reveals no transparent indicators of the palatial or imperial organisations that characterised neighbouring Egyptian, Levantine and Aegean polities (Muhly 1985b: 34), the combined and coherent material and documentary records of ProBA Cyprus leaves little doubt that sociopolitical and economic power were centralised in a royal personage, if not necessarily a specific place. Unlike Peltenburg (n.d.), who suggests that politico-economic power on ProBA Cyprus was shared through devolved authority amongst kin-based households, I see that power vested in a singular institution, but whether an absolute 'king' or a *primus inter pares* remains uncertain.

Taking a longer-term look at settlement patterning, monumentality and 'urban' development (Negbi 1986; 2005) on ProBA Cyprus, we may note, first, that monumental constructions form only one of the many material markers of élite ideology and identity in the archaeological record of the ProBA 1 period (ca. 1700–1450 Cal BC). Differential burial practices, new techniques of pottery manufacture, prestige goods and imports, Cypro-Minoan writing and seals, copper oxhide ingots and centralised storage facilities (Knapp 1996a: 76–77, tables 1–2), along with monumentality (the Enkomi fortress), all point to intensified production, consumption and distribution, the expansion of settlement, the emergence of social inequalities and the centralisation of politico-economic power.

During the ProBA 2 period (ca. 1450–1300 Cal BC, LC IIA–IIC early), we can see the development of a distinctive, three- to four-tiered settlement hierarchy characterised by site size, location and function (Keswani 1993; Knapp 1997: 53–63). The people who lived in urban centres such as Enkomi, Kition, Kalavasos *Ayios Dhimitrios*, Kouklia *Palaipaphos*, Maroni *Vournes* and Alassa *Paleotaverna* shared a very similar material culture: they used widely recognised insignia of group identity (e.g. cylinder seals, depictions of oxhide ingots on various media, gendered representations in figurines), and they erected somewhat standardised monumental buildings. Similarities in both local and imported pottery vessels ('sets' of which were likely used in feasting activities – Steel 2002; 2004c), and in the style and content of seal iconography, must have served as powerful, symbolic media for expressing centralised control and élite identity.

Webb (1999: 307) noted that a coherent iconographic system reflecting a centralised authority was in use throughout the ProBA, and was most evident in ritual or ceremonial practices (e.g. using standardised, female terracotta images in both households and burials; placing Base-ring bull rhyta in mortuary deposits). At the same time, these urban dwellers invested a great deal of time and labour in monumental constructions. Élite activities, however, were not focused exclusively on constructing elaborate buildings but also on procuring resources and exotica, investing more and more energy and material goods into mortuary deposits, developing and maintaining diverse symbols of power, and producing a range of goods and raw materials – bronze statuettes, stands and cauldrons, and copper oxhide ingots – for internal consumption and external exchange. By the end of the ProBA 2 period, élite activities seem to have become increasingly exclusive, as access to monumental structures became more restricted: at Myrtou *Pigadhes*, *Palaipaphos* and Kition, for example, entryways were closed off or hidden, and open courtyards were walled off and segregated.

During the ProBA 3 period (ca. 1300–1125/1100 Cal BC), several of the 'urban' monumental structures were destroyed (e.g. those at Kition, Kouklia *Palaipaphos*, Enkomi, Myrtou *Pigadhes*, Maroni *Vournes*, *Ayios Dhimitrios*, Alassa *Paleotaverna*), and some town centres were abandoned (*Ayios Dhimitrios*, *Paleotaverna*, Hala Sultan Tekke *Vyzakia*, Morphou *Toumba tou Skourou*, Maa *Palaeokastro*, Pyla *Kokkinokremos*, Myrtou *Pigadhes*, Athienou). These destructions and abandonments surely reflect a breakdown in political and economic order on Cyprus; they must be seen in the context of the collapse of eastern Mediterranean palatial systems, and the demise of the iconographic *koiné* (Feldman 2006) that symbolised their connectivity. Despite these disruptions, there is clear continuity in Cypriot material culture, at least throughout the 13th–12th centuries BC (Iacovou 2008; Voskos and Knapp 2008); the major disruption came during the 11th century BC (LC IIIB), the beginning of the early Iron Age.

Economic and industrial activities actually intensified during the 13th–12th centuries BC, as is evident from the mass production of wheelmade pottery, the intensified manufacture of finished metalwork, and the growing manufacture and use of iron tools and weapons (Sherratt 1998: 297–300). At least three major urban centres, at Enkomi, Kition and Kouklia *Palaipaphos*, survived the unsettled circumstances around 1200 BC, and Webb (1999: 292) maintains that the scale and complexity of the monumental structures at Kition ('Temple' 1) and *Palaipaphos* ('Sanctuary' I) during ProBA 3 point to a strongly centralised authority. The monarchs and merchants associated with these enduring town sites must have overseen various aspects of newly emerging Cypriot contacts overseas, everywhere from the Levant to the central Mediterranean (Knapp 1990b; Sherratt 2003: 42–51).

From a postcolonial perspective, one that engages with migration as an interactive process, it is no longer possible to accept the notion of a 'Mycenaean colonisation' of Cyprus. During the late 13th–11th centuries BC, some Aegean peoples came to Cyprus but underwent intensive social transformations in the hybridisation processes that followed. These Aegean settlers became well integrated into Cypriot society, if we are to judge by all the continuities seen in Cypriot material and social practices. It is also no longer viable to argue that local Cypriotes passively adopted a superior Mycenaean culture or that the local inhabitants were absorbed into displaced Aegean power structures. Aegean and Levantine migrants, if not others, integrated with the local inhabitants, developing new social and material practices and taking on a new identity that was far more than the sum of its individual parts.

By the transition to the early Iron Age, the collapse of the international, élite-driven trading system(s) of the Late Bronze Age, and the ensuing loss of certain overseas markets, finally made an impact on Cyprus, both in social and economic terms. Whilst trade with Cilicia and the Levant continued on some indeterminate level (Sherratt 1999; Gilboa 2005), commercial interactions with the Aegean and the central Mediterranean actually increased and diversified. Direct contacts with Sardinia, at least, ensured a continuing outlet for Cypriot copper in the context of the coming age of iron (Knapp 1990b; elaborated by Kassianidou 2001). The loss of state control over trade (Sherratt 1998) may have diminished the capacity of Cypriot élites to display exotica as a means of enhancing their status, but there is nothing in the archaeological record to indicate that Aegean, Phoenician or any other colonists capitalised on this situation. Nonetheless, new élite groups clearly emerged on Cyprus during the early Iron Age, including Phoenician elements in towns such as Kition, local Cypriotes in Amathus, and a mixture of native Cypriote and intrusive Aegean elements elsewhere, if not everywhere on the island. The last, of course, were speakers of Greek, and ultimately their cooperation and entanglement with local Cypriotes led to what Sherratt (1992: 337–338; cf. Karageorghis 1994) termed the 'Greek-Cypriot ethnogenesis' on the island.

Throughout the 12th century BC, there are signs of continuity in both local material culture (e.g. pottery styles, architecture and town plans, mortuary practices and tomb construction, metalworking technologies) and in social practices, albeit in the context of a social transformation that had far-reaching and long-lasting results. The economy of Cyprus was still integrally connected to those of the wider Mediterranean world, even if on a different and almost certainly reduced level. By the end of the ProBA 3 period, however, around 1125–1100 Cal BC, the settlement patterns and centralised political organisation typical of that period are no longer evident in the material record. Most aspects of material culture changed rather dramatically, and the new power centres that emerged on early Iron Age Cyprus had distinctive sociopolitical and economic structures. Someday they would converge – whether during the 11th or the 9th–8th centuries BC – into the island's early historical kingdoms.

My own view on the formation of the territorial kingdoms of the early Iron Age is that we cannot see them as 'a close re-enactment of [Cyprus's] Late Bronze Age politico-economic tradition' (Iacovou 2002: 85), nor can we equate them with the re-emergence of a hierarchical, state-level of organisation (Rupp 1998: 216–218). As I have emphasised throughout this book, the socio-economic, ideological and geopolitical formations that developed and often persisted for long periods of time on the island were always distinctively different from their Aegean, or Levantine, or Anatolian counterparts. Thus we cannot assume or directly relate the polities, communities and peoples of any one period to those of subsequent or previous periods. Instead we must evaluate such developments *sui generis*, engaging with all the material and social factors that were entangled in formulating, maintaining or changing the identities of these islanders over time. The economic, ideological and power relations that characterised encounters between indigenous Cypriotes and others – whether from the Aegean, Anatolia or the Levant – throughout the millennium between about 1800–800 BC, remain issues of ongoing archaeological discussion and analysis.

CHAPTER 8

CONCLUSIONS: INSULARITY, CONNECTIVITY AND IDENTITY ON PREHISTORIC AND PROTOHISTORIC CYPRUS

In the Mediterranean, purposive voyaging already characterised island life during pre-Neolithic times (Ammerman 2010; Knapp 2010); indeed it is possible that people travelled by sea to Crete as early as the Middle Palaeolithic (Strasser et al. 2010; 2011). Current evidence from several Mediterranean islands indicates that seasonal exploitation occurred no later than the 11th millennium Cal BC on Sardinia, and shortly thereafter on Cyprus and some Aegean islands (Sondaar et al. 1995; Simmons 1999; Sampson 2006; 2008; Knapp 2010: 82–100; Ammerman et al. 2011). The physical diversity and biotic store of the Mediterranean's larger islands – Sardinia, Cyprus, Corsica, Crete – ultimately made it possible for people with a sedentary lifestyle to thrive on these islands much earlier than they could on smaller, often less propitious and less fertile islands and island groups, such as the Cyclades (Broodbank 2000; 2009: 684–686).

On Cyprus, by the Late Epipalaeolithic (11,000–9000 Cal BC), seafaring fisher-foragers made brief seasonal visits to Cyprus in order to exploit diverse faunal and marine resources – pygmy hippos and elephants, shellfish, marine invertebrates and avifauna. They came at a time when climatic and other, related, environmental factors perhaps forced them to become more mobile; as a result, the social dynamics of these groups were transformed. Some of those who came on these earliest known, seasonal visits to coastal sites (Akrotiri *Aetokremnos*, perhaps to Nissi Beach and the shores of the Akamas peninsula) must have decided to explore the island and determine its suitability for other kinds of resource exploitation, perhaps even for permanent settlement. On present evidence, these sites seem to be locales where mobile foragers stayed for some period of time, after which they would have returned to other temporary homes somewhere along the shores of the eastern Mediterranean.

Some very early inland sites in the northern and eastern Troodos foothills (*Asprokremmos*, *Palaeokamina*, *Kelaïdhoni*), in the uplands of the western Troodos (Vretsia *Roudias*) and along the south coast (Ayios Tychonas *Klimonas*), probably form the background to the island's subsequent permanent settlement.

Whatever the origin(s) of these early visitors to Cyprus, they came at a time of unprecedented demand upon dwindling subsistence resources, rising sea level and a consequent need to adapt to new social, economic and environmental circumstances. All this new and still-growing evidence for seafaring, foraging and early farming on Cyprus suggests that some people, at least, perceived the risks of insular living as being more advantageous than remaining where they were.

The earliest, permanent settlers came to Cyprus – most likely from the Levant, but perhaps also from Anatolia – with their own cultivated or domesticated plants and cereals, and herded or wild animals. Based on current faunal and radiocarbon evidence, the pig, goat, sheep and cattle from *Shillourokambos* appear to be earlier than domesticates known from the Levant, and as early as those known from Anatolia. Even if new evidence alters that picture, the fact remains that these are the earliest known animals to be introduced successfully by humans to a Mediterranean island. Not only does this suggest that the people who settled Cyprus had some special relationship with these animals, it also demonstrates that they had mastered seafaring skills. Moreover, it now seems apparent that a coastal, foraging way of life continued to flourish on the island for at least another 2,000–3,000 years (Nissi Beach). Thus Cyprus has emerged as a key island context for studying seafaring, mobile foragers and fishers, migration and sedentism, early farmers, and all the associated social transformations.

A lengthy process of 'Neolithisation' followed (McCartney 2010), as the new inhabitants of Cyprus became increasingly reliant on an agricultural lifestyle, establishing dwellings, wells, storage bins and animal pens associated with a sedentary way of life. Both the floral and faunal records indicate that these new immigrants knew the available natural resources on Cyprus well enough to fulfil their subsistence needs (Colledge and Conolly 2007: 68). With their domesticated flocks, they consolidated the mixed farming economy throughout Cyprus but with specific adaptations to an insular situation (e.g. continued reliance on deer hunting). Such insularity, however, need not mean social, cultural or economic isolation. For their own reasons, Cyprus's new settlers may have chosen to isolate themselves, identifying themselves in specific material and mental ways. Or, if we view the sea as a 'highway' rather than a barrier to interaction with the nearby mainlands, we can think of a two-way exchange of ideas through stimulus if not demic diffusion, and we can consider how choices made in technological practices or symbolic values led to new, more active ways of establishing an insular identity (McCartney 2011; see also McCartney et al. 2010: 134).

During the Late Aceramic Neolithic (LAN), Cyprus was never sealed off from the cultures surrounding it. Some degree of isolation, however, seems evident, and we must consider whether this resulted from geographic factors (insularity) or rather represents an intentional decision related to an island identity. The degree and nature of insularity on Cyprus was relative: the people of the LAN period not only adapted reasonably well to any constraints that may have confronted them in their island habitat, but also continued to be involved at least in low-level exchanges with the Levant.

Maritime mobility and the exploitation of coastal or marine resources notwithstanding, the materiality of LAN Cyprus points to the emergence and development of an insular identity (or, more likely, identities). During this long period, people found multiple and diverse means of subsistence – agricultural, pastoral, hunting, fishing – to support themselves. They produced an array of objects and engaged in practices that served to distinguish them from others, within and beyond the island. Even if the communities of LAN had only limited contacts with the outside world, their architecture, mortuary practices and material culture – engraved pebbles, stone and clay figurines, intricately carved stone vessels – indicate that some people were on the move, social readjustments were being made, and goods and ideas were continually being exchanged. As McCartney (in Clarke 2007a: 90) concludes: 'By placing Cyprus in its coastal context we restore it to its contingent history of social interaction and to an active participation within the interactions spheres of the eastern Mediterranean'.

The Aceramic Neolithic overall (ca. 9000/8500–ca. 5200 Cal BC) was a time when a uniquely Cypriot culture crystallised, one that increasingly became separate from those of the mainland after an extensive period of local development. The permanent settlement of Cyprus may have been triggered in part by climatic and environmental stress, but it also involved social factors related to mobility, insularity and symbolic resources or values associated with everything from arrowheads to animal–human relations (Peltenburg 2004a: 4–6; 2004b: xvi; Jones 2008; 2009; Watkins 2008: 164–165). In the end, however, people successfully settled the island not only because of their adaptability but also because they intended to do so.

It is widely perceived that Cyprus had very limited contacts with the outside world during the following Ceramic Neolithic (CN) period (ca. 5000–4000 Cal BC), and further that this isolation constrained social development within the island. Clarke (2003) has reassessed such assumptions by examining regional variation in pottery assemblages throughout Cyprus. She concluded that although ceramic diversity might reflect distinctive regional identities (also Steel 2004a: 68), the broad material culture homogeneity also indicates flexible social boundaries, pointing to a specific identity shared amongst the islanders, and reflecting to some extent Horden and Purcell's (2000: 507) observation on the Iron Age–Medieval Mediterranean, namely '…the differences which resemble are continually striking'.

In Peltenburg's (2003b) view, at least some people's notion of their identities was bound up with CN buildings, as memorials (or genealogies) for their ancestors and as symbols of renewal and continuity. My own view is that island identities are like all others: fluid, situational and dependent upon what people wish to express about themselves, or how they wish to distinguish themselves from others. Island identities are typically linked to a specific place (or 'sense of place' – Feld and Basso 1996) that may be defined as the community. Whilst communities may be as fluid and situational as the identities linked to them, island communities tend to take on a strong sense of common, or shared identity, certainly with respect to their relations – positive or negative, close or distant – with the outside world. In such situations, and Ceramic Neolithic Cyprus seems an obvious case, insularity itself becomes a form of social identity (Broodbank 2000: 33), an intentional strategy that limited overseas contacts and may have created a cultural island in the process.

During the Early–Middle Chalcolithic (ca. 4000/3900–2700 Cal BC), distinctive material and mortuary practices – food storage, feasting, representational art, complex building arrangements, the production and consumption of picrolite and some metals, and elaborate burials with sumptuous grave goods – all point to a social transformation and the likely emergence of individual identities. This transformation and identity formation, however, seem to have developed in a highly insular context. The few foreign artefacts or 'exotic' materials (chlorite, faience) that exist in the archaeological record are insufficient to indicate that Cyprus's isolation from the surrounding world was receding. Indeed, one of the defining characteristics of both the Ceramic Neolithic and Early–Middle Chalcolithic Cyprus is an apparent lack of connectivity with the otherwise closely linked cultures of the contemporary eastern Mediterranean. The extremely limited amount of foreign material present in Chalcolithic contexts (and presumably minimal social contacts) suggests an ongoing, perhaps intentional strategy to maintain a unique, separate insular identity. With little indication of resource stress or competition, and with good evidence for an abundant food supply (adequate for feasting in the views of many) even as population increased, there would have been little need to adapt or change, less so to adopt innovations from outside (Clarke 2007a: 128–129). As a result, right up to the final phases of its earlier prehistory, Cyprus seems to have remained in a state of what Peltenburg (2004c: 84) termed a 'dynamic of stability'.

Duringthe Late Chalcolithic (ca. 2700–2500/2400 Cal BC), several economic and social changes, including the development of foreign contacts, become apparent in a wide range of materials. Of particular significance are metallurgical practices (the exploitation if not production of copper), new pottery fabrics, more varied use of chipped stone and the exploitation of new sources, and changing fashions of personal ornamentation (faience disk beads, dentalium necklaces, new disc bead necklaces). For nearly 4,000 years, from the end of the Early Aceramic Neolithic (ca. 7000/6800 Cal BC) onward, Cyprus seems to have had quite restricted contacts with other peoples and cultures in the eastern Mediterranean. Although there are no direct imports (except perhaps faience beads), by the Late Chalcolithic we find raw materials, artefact classes, design elements and material practices that suggest connections with, or at least inspiration from, Anatolia and the eastern Aegean. Peltenburg (2007a: 154) suggests that these practices represent a selection and adaptation of certain material traits by Cypriotes and for Cypriotes in an insular context. One way or another, the evident long-term isolation of Cyprus was coming to an end, as at least some of its people became involved in new, social and material encounters with various overseas polities.

By the mid-3rd millennium Cal BC, it is widely agreed that some people from the island of Cyprus were in contact with others from Anatolia and the Aegean, if not from the southern Levant. Webb and Frankel (2007; 2011) see these social and material encounters in terms of a 'focal migration' or 'colonisation' (they don't distinguish between the two) stemming from Anatolia. They believe that the communities of Prehistoric Bronze Age (PreBA) 1 Cyprus (ca. 2400–2000 Cal BC) were divided into (1) Anatolian migrants or colonists and (2) indigenous Cypriotes. If two distinct social groups dwelt on Cyprus at this time, we should aim to assess and understand them in terms of their co-presence, and we should also consider the social and material connections that developed between them in terms of how they sought to identify themselves, or to assert their social positions. It is clear that many of the material factors of everyday life – food production, feasting and ritual, mortuary practices – are new to Cyprus, but we need to view all these changes as the outcome of ambivalent interactions between two different groups of people. These interactions I have defined as hybridisation practices, through which indigenous Cypriotes and newcomers revamped their material culture and renegotiated their identities.

Several novel features that characterise the PreBA material record hint at the presence of certain individuals or groups of higher social status. Perhaps the most obvious indicators of this élite social group are the elaborate mortuary practices (especially at Vasilia in the Philia phase) and prestigious burial goods associated with them (at *Vounous*, Lapithos and Karmi in EC I–MC II). We also see the personal use of metal products such as copper hair-rings and copper (and gold/silver/copper) spiral earrings (Philia), calcite vessels (Philia), and the emergence of new, long-distance trading relationships (imported pottery and metal daggers, faience objects, dentalium beads). Throughout the PreBA, agricultural practices intensified, as did (to some degree) involvement in exchange systems within and beyond the island. Alongside the acquisition and display of prestigious metal goods, these developments not only marked a change in the way people identified themselves, but also must have prompted some structural changes in Cypriot society. Taking advantage of a prestige-goods system that developed in response to external demand, and the intensification of metallurgical production that resulted in specialised metal goods, an emerging élite group or some élite individual(s) were able to assume a focal position in PreBA society.

By the early 2nd millennium BC (PreBA 2), these groups or individuals had accumulated new levels of power and wealth. The contextual associations of the plank figurines link them to this emerging, high-status group; people may have used these representations not just to emphasise their individual position in society, but also to proclaim their distinctive identity. At the same time, some individuals or groups had established full control over the production and distribution of copper within and beyond the island, a position they maintained for well over 1,000 years.

By the mid-2nd millennium BC, during the ProBA 1 period (ca. 1700–1450 Cal BC), prominent new coastal towns emerged, virtually all of which show a variety of imports from the surrounding polities in Egypt, the eastern Mediterranean and the Aegean. The social as well as the economic dynamics of these coastal ports ensured the availability of both imports (e.g. pottery, ivory, tin, gold) and domestic products (e.g. pottery, textiles, copper). Imports were received intentionally and opportunistically, both as commodities and as gifts. Locally produced craft products and oxhide ingots were exported throughout the eastern Mediterranean and the Aegean, and long-distance exchange increasingly became a key component of the Cypriot economy.

During the ProBA 1–2 periods (ca. 1700–1300 Cal BC), several burgeoning towns on Cyprus made a major investment in materials and human energy to construct monumental buildings, while Cypriot élites directed further expenditure into creating coherent insignia of their identity and authority. Documentary evidence in the form of letters sent from *Alašiya* (Cyprus) to Ugarit and Egypt demonstrate royal regulation of, and control over, the production and trade in copper (Knapp 1996b: 21–24; Yon 2007). The labour invested in monumental architecture promoted cooperation in food production, ceremonial activities and boundary maintenance, factors that might be defined as 'corporate' strategies (Feinman 1995). This may well be the time that the 'community' emerged on Cyprus as a distinctive conceptual if not necessarily spatial unit (Knapp 2003). The social forces that produce this kind of change are generated within a 'matrix of interaction' (Peterson and Drennan 2005: 5) between people, households, communities and polities. The ideology that evolved and revolved around all these practices was expressed materially through a diverse array of symbols, statuettes and other artefacts that served to establish and express an élite identity within the island (Knapp 1986b; 1988). These élites, together with their overseers and labourers, maintained some level of control over the production and distribution of copper throughout the 1st millennium BC, at least until the Roman era. By then, however, Roman imperial control over the economy – not just the export of copper, grain and timber from the island's main harbour at Salamis but also the social organisation of production (Given and Knapp 2003: 303–305) – had become total, and resulted in very different material markers of identity.

FINAL THOUGHTS ON INSULARITY, CONNECTIVITY AND SOCIAL IDENTITY

Within the ancient Mediterranean, and not least on Cyprus, the interrelationship amongst insularity, connectivity and identity must have impacted deeply, and daily, on people's lives. The ideas, practices and material culture of islanders in general, together with the constraints and opportunities presented by environmental or biological factors, reverberate in the ways that people deal with insularity (Broodbank 2000: 363) and how they establish and refine their habitat. The exploitation of insular and seaborne resources, the concepts of distance and the exotic, as well as maritime interactions and exchanges ('connectivity'), all limit the force and impact of what we term insularity. The social practices and individual needs of those who live on islands may serve to motivate economic development, propel political change and/or transform insular social structures. Any such vectors of contact between and amongst islanders also serve other functions, such as acquiring or transferring subsistence goods, basic commodities, raw materials or luxury items.

Connectivity and maritime exchanges thus may condition the mobility (or insularity) of island groups, the level and intensity of contact between different groups, and the physical and social nature of diverse islandscapes. Connectivity involves mobility, modes of travel and communication, and social exchanges – all mechanisms that motivated or modified island identities, and in turn drove the migrants, mariners and merchants that brought together people and 'things' from different islands and mainlands. In terms of their encounters with the outside world, island communities often develop a strong sense of their common identity. Such a tendency is reinforced during voyages to distant lands or other islands, when insular identities and differences take on special currency (Parker Pearson 2004: 129; Constantakopoulou 2005).

On islands large or small, and throughout any island group, insularity can be felt to some degree. The physical aspects of insularity, however, have to be seen in the context of social and spatial factors that operate differently in each place. Insularity thus is not a fixed geographic condition or environmental variable that can provide a monolithic explanation of biological evolution, much less of cultural diversity or social practices. Rather it is a facet of island living that often modifies political, social or economic developments in unique and unpredictable ways. As I have suggested at least for the Ceramic Neolithic if not the Early–Middle Chalcolithic on Cyprus, insularity may also function as a form of social identity, a cultural strategy employed by islanders to resist external interference (Broodbank 2000: 33). While insularity offers special opportunities and provides certain benefits, at the same time it demands risks and poses special restraints. What is important is the way that different people confront and manipulate insularity, in their own distinctive ways, in different times and places.

In and of itself, identity is a contentious issue, succinctly summed up by Brubaker and Cooper (2000: 1): '"Identity" ... tends to mean too much (when understood in a strong sense), too little (when understood in a weak sense), or nothing at all (because of its sheer ambiguity)'. How we then go about linking materiality to identity involves an even more complex process, likened by Friedman (1992: 853) to '...an elaborate and deadly serious game of mirrors', mirrors that must be situated in space even as they move through time. Many of the distinctive symbols and actions through which people identify and distinguish themselves from others are material symbols and representations of actions. The better we understand how certain material characteristics are shared or differentiated amongst various people, the closer we shall come to unravelling the multiple threads of identity.

In terms of ancient Cypriot identities, I have tried to emphasise throughout this volume the role that 'things' may play in restructuring old or formulating new identities, and how material culture plays a crucial, structuring role in social organisation and human life. Careful analyses of these structured material remains on prehistoric and protohistoric Cyprus – from chipped stone tools and circular huts to gold-alloy earrings and monumental architecture – offer important insights into human movements, intentions and memories. On the island of Cyprus, where archaeology has long been embedded in a culture-historical approach, the study of identity, insularity, mobility and connectivity (from casual seafaring to interregional exchange systems) has received all too little attention. As I hope to have demonstrated, however, such concepts are crucial for any attempt to interpret and understand the rich and diverse material and documentary records of Cyprus.

APPENDIX

A NEW RADIOCARBON CHRONOLOGY FOR PREHISTORIC AND PROTOHISTORIC CYPRUS, CA. 11,000–1050 CAL BC

STURT W. MANNING

INTRODUCTION

This Appendix analyses a large database of virtually all published radiocarbon dates from specific archaeological contexts on Cyprus, from the Late Epipalaeolithic to the end of the Protohistoric Bronze Age (see Sub-Appendix 1, below). Employing a Bayesian analytical framework that combines archaeological information with radiocarbon data, a single dating model has been created. The outputs of this model provide for the first time a consistent and comprehensive chronological framework for all of Cypriot pre- and protohistory. They also highlight the vagaries and history of existing scholarship, which is such that some periods are relatively well dated, others much less so. The chronology presented is the best available in late 2011 – it also forms a guide to where future attention is especially needed. For further details, outputs and some updates through September 2012, see the Supporting Online Materials (SOM) at www.cambridge.org/9780521723473.

The study of Cypriot chronology has formed part of syntheses of Cypriot prehistory from its inception (e.g. Knapp et al. 1994: 379–390; Steele 2004a: 11–18; Clarke 2007a: 9–29). The intention here is not to review previous work, nor to enter into critiques and discussions of existing scholarly positions. Moreover, although there have been many studies addressing the chronology of one or more aspects of Cypriot prehistory, there are in fact very few that have sought to consider the overall prehistoric period, from the earliest currently attested human presence through the end of the Bronze Age. This is the main new and different aim of this study. A coherent and rigorous approximate timeframe is essential for the sophisticated study and discussion of Cypriot prehistory (as for all archaeology and history – with the study of Whittle et al. 2011 offering a new aspiration benchmark). Time structures archaeological analysis and interpretation. The ability to resolve shorter-term events versus longer-term processes, and to consider the agents, identities, social networks and contexts, decisions, values and environmental background of the past all depend on robust and refined chronological resolution (Whittle and Bayliss 2007). For much of Cypriot prehistory and protohistory, this has been only loosely defined; in this study, we highlight areas where more work is necessary.

In previous work on Cyprus, there has been no consistent chronological methodology applied across the prehistoric and protohistoric past. Whereas since the advent of calibrated radiocarbon dating, chronological assessments of earlier prehistoric periods are based on some form of interpretation of available radiocarbon evidence, most studies addressing later prehistory have primarily sought to employ material cultural linkages with the historically dated cultures of Egypt and the Near East to establish dates – sometimes noting contrasts or apparent conflicts with the radiocarbon evidence (e.g. Merrillees 2002). This split in archaeological chronologies is a well-known state of affairs throughout the east Mediterranean; we have radiocarbon dating down to about 3000–2000 BC, and then archaeological cum art-historical chronology afterwards, where possible. The potential value of analysing material culture linkages is self-evident, including for chronology. However, there are also many potentially complicating factors, especially where small numbers of items or indicators, or the unique find, are involved; some past assessments based on a few transfers, or on one particular interpretative framework for them, are possibly suspect. The divide between a radiocarbon-based chronology for the mid-second millennium BC Aegean versus the traditional chronology assembled from one interpretation of the scarce material and stylistic linkages with Egypt and the Near East is the best-known example of an apparent conflict (e.g. Manning 1999; Manning et al. 2006; Warburton 2009; Manning and Kromer 2011).

Now that the extensive study of Bronk Ramsey et al. (2010) has shown that carefully and appropriately analysed radiocarbon dates from Egypt offer a chronology entirely consistent with the historical chronology of Egypt, it is clear that the route to a consistent, robust and potentially high-resolution chronology for the pre- and proto-historical archaeological record of the east Mediterranean is primarily via radiocarbon (assuming and/or requiring the use of sets of good quality data from appropriate samples and contexts, with suitable analysis – Bayliss et al. 2011). Such a firmly based radiocarbon chronology finally ends the so-called temporal fault-line identified by Renfrew (e.g. 1973: 103–106) between the later prehistoric east Mediterranean (dated via linkages to Egyptian chronology) and the rest of Europe (dated by radiocarbon). Such a radiocarbon-based record can then be supplemented and interpreted in light of material culture and stylistic linkages, but such data do not offer a framework when in conflict with good quality radiocarbon evidence.

This study offers a coherent radiocarbon-based chronological framework for all of prehistoric and protohistoric Cyprus. The key analytical tool employed is Bayesian chronological modelling, employing the OxCal software (Bronk Ramsey 2001; 2008; 2009a; 2009b; Bronk Ramsey et al. 2001). OxCal 4.1.7 was used for this study, and is hereafter referred to as either OxCal or OxCal 4.1.7. Archaeologically oriented introductions and discussions of using Bayesian chronological modelling can be found in Bayliss (2007; 2009) and Bayliss et al. (2007; 2011). The current (to mid-2011) northern hemisphere standard radiocarbon calibration curve, IntCal09 (Reimer et al. 2009), is employed for all analyses (with five calendar year curve resolution, with cubic modelling 'on' as default in OxCal), and is hereafter referred to as IntCal09. Considering very fine-scale issues such as possible small regional radiocarbon offsets as may apply in the eastern Mediterranean (Manning et al. 2010b), versus the standard calibration curve, has not been undertaken in this study; such possible issues would make no substantive difference to the findings reported below.

METHODOLOGY

In ideal circumstances, a large-scale radiocarbon study would employ only data for which good controls exist regarding both archaeological and laboratory quality. To be practical, however, here we had to employ as much of the available evidence as possible. These data come from many different excavations (and field methods), and from different radiocarbon laboratories using different technologies, and from work over several decades against constantly improving techniques and instruments. Thus the data are not at all comparable and future work can seek to improve and refine the dating by developing more rigorous protocols and standards. For example, it is noticeable that some data sets run several decades ago exhibit a greater percentage of outlying tendencies than others, especially more recently run data. The Glasgow University (GU) data are a good example: 18 dates in the database of which 8 (or 44.4%) are identified as likely outliers by the final model (Model 8) in this study. In general terms, we have attempted to use as much of the available radiocarbon data (published or cited) from pre- and protohistoric Cyprus, retrieved in 2011: this includes some obviously suspect data and a few instances where we lack full or proper information. The only criteria or screening applied in the initial data collection were as follows:

1. Radiocarbon dates had to come from what were stated to be relatively specific pre- or protohistoric archaeological contexts on Cyprus (i.e. as defined by the associated archaeological assemblage, and not with the date supplying the apparent association that was otherwise unknown). A conventional (5,568-year half-life) radiocarbon age and measurement error had to be available. Thus dates from sites not given any specific archaeological placement were not included.

2. In the case of Akrotiri *Aetokremnos*, only dates on charcoal samples (also Ammerman et al. 2007) or very recent dates on suid bone (Vigne et al. 2009) were considered. The dates on pygmy hippo bones were not considered because (i) subsequent unpublished work by this author and the Oxford Radiocarbon Laboratory that attempted to date a set of such material kindly provided by Alan Simmons found that none of the bones analysed were suitable for safe radiocarbon dating (most produced effectively 0 to in a few cases tiny [ca. ≤0.4 mg] collagen yields; Vigne et al., 2009: 16136, noted a similar problem on pig bones from the site and discussed their attempted strategy to overcome). We suspect this problem applies to much of the bone material from *Aetokremnos*, some of which appeared to be cremated; thus post-death burning – as fuel or whatever – could be the source of some radiocarbon dates on bone previously published. Dates on pygmy hippo bones were also not considered because (ii) they have a large range and would not offer a practical dating set if included in the analyses.

3. In the case of Parekklisha *Shillourokambos*, we have only used the Secteur 1 dates published by Guilaine et al. (2011: 579–581, excluding the three 'datations non acceptables'). We have not used other dates previously published by Guilaine and Briois (2006) that were *not* included in the final publication (Guilaine et al. 2011).

4. In the case of Kritou Marottou *Ais Giorkis*, it is evident that three dates (Beta-213416, 213418, 220597) are not on Neolithic material/contexts but are much more recent, and thus are not included here; we used instead the data in Simmons (2010).

Any other radiocarbon date not in Sub-Appendix 1 is missing because it was not found in the literature review undertaken. In all, 351 radiocarbon dates were available for the initial analysis. These data are shown by broad archaeological period groupings with their 1σ or 68.2% calibrated calendar age ranges in Figure A1. Note that four sets of short-lived samples on materials from the same contexts have been combined – as a weighted average – in the figure; these are the R_Combine samples in Model 1 as listed in the SOM: Apliki basket samples, Apliki cereal samples, a set of short-lived data from Maroni *Tsaroukkas* Building 1 and a set of short-lived data from Maroni *Tsaroukkas* Building 2.

Several observations may be made immediately:

1. While most data offer a general pattern, a few are clearly aberrant, for one reason or another (whether due to incorrect archaeological association, problematic sample where the measured radiocarbon does not date the original archaeological context, or laboratory problems, etc.): see Figure A2.

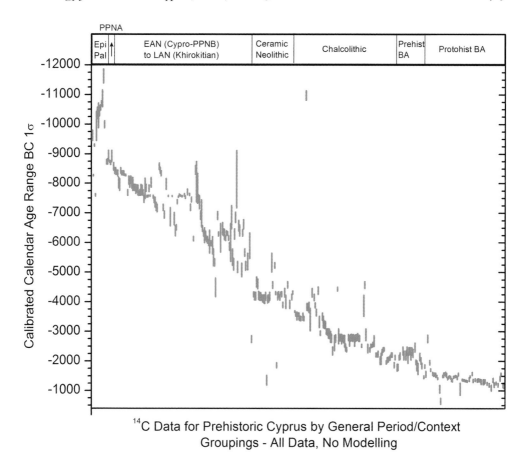

^{14}C Data for Prehistoric Cyprus by General Period/Context
Groupings - All Data, No Modelling

Figure A1. Plot showing all radiocarbon samples in Sub-Appendix 1 with their overall 68.2% probability calibrated calendar age ranges (from IntCal09 using OxCal 4.1.7), excepting those dates on short-lived samples from the same context (four groups with 17 dates) that have been plotted as the calibrated range of the weighted average (see text). These calibrated ranges are, for each date, considered separately and with no Bayesian modelling or other consideration. The main archaeological period groups from which the samples are stated to come are indicated at the top.

2. Most radiocarbon data involved are from charcoal samples. Such samples set a *terminus post quem* date range, with the length of the 'post' depending on how many tree-rings (years of growth) lie either between the tree-rings dated in the charcoal sample (what the radiocarbon date is estimating) and the bark of the relevant tree or branch when cut for use by humans, or between these and when the tree died and the further interval until the wood was collected for use. This is what is often termed the 'old-wood effect' in archaeology (Schiffer 1986; Bowman 1990: 51). In the absence of species identification and specific study of the samples (ring counting where possible), and checking for the presence of bark, it is impossible to assess the relevant 'post' factor. Most occurrences of lower elevation tree species on Cyprus – likely proximate to most

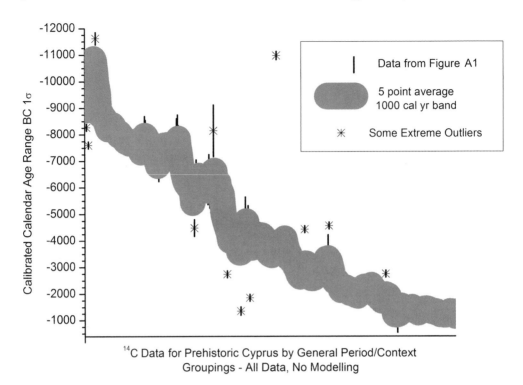

¹⁴C Data for Prehistoric Cyprus by General Period/Context
Groupings - All Data, No Modelling

Figure A2. As Figure A1 but with a 1,000-calendar-year-wide band passed through a
moving five-point average of the calibrated data. This dating band incorporates all, most
or some of over 96% of the data in Figure A1. Just 13 data are entirely distinct from
this dating band and might be suggested to be potential extreme outliers (indicated
in plot) – that is, the samples are not appropriate age estimates for their stated
archaeological context, for diverse reasons. The choice of band width and the like is
entirely arbitrary. It seeks to identify subjectively a small number of the worst outliers in
order that subsequent modelling analyses can run successfully.

of the archaeological sites involved in this study (e.g. lower ranges of
Pinus brutia) – are usually not very long-lived. This assertion is based on
three observations by the author: (a) trees suitable for dendrochronology
found today in the coastal to 400 m elevation range are almost all within
the 1–200 years old range, with most at the younger end of this range,
and with only a few, carefully sought individual examples at the upper
range; (b) wood used in traditional buildings in the coastal to 400 m elevation range examined on Cyprus usually falls in the range of ≤50 years
old and almost all within a 50±50 years range; and (c) examination of
wood samples from several archaeological sites on Cyprus has so far not
yielded any examples beyond a 50±50 years range. It is possible some
species not suitable for dendrochronology, such as olive, may include old
trees, but this is likely relevant only for a small number of samples. Thus
we may assume that on average there is some small tendency towards
slightly older age estimates where the data come from charcoal, but this

is likely of the order on an average basis of 0–100(+) years and is not a consideration included in the dating models (but is approximately considered in the subsequent discussion – see further in SOM Table S2). In one case, radiocarbon dates were obtained on a dendrochronological sequence from wood from a roof at the Late Bronze Age site of Apliki *Karamallos* (Manning and Kuniholm 2007); it is possible to model these dates in terms of the known tree-ring spacing to yield a more precise date ('dendro-wiggle-matching': Bronk Ramsey et al. 2001; Galimberti et al. 2004; Bayliss 2007). Dates on shorter-lived materials – from bones to twigs to sub-annual samples such as grain – should, when they derive from secure archaeological contexts with good associations, yield ages close to the actual date for those contexts. Such samples are of course to be preferred. A future more sophisticated study could look to separate out samples on long- and short-lived materials, and especially should try to acquire more shorter-lived samples from specific targeted periods of interest. Dates on marine shell involve an ocean-derived reservoir age making them appear older than they are. In two cases (two dates from shell from Nissi Beach, GrA-36019 and OxA-X-2232–27, and a date from shell from Akrotiri *Vounarouthkia ton Lamion East* – Site 23, UCLA-307), we removed an approximate rule of thumb 'standard' marine reservoir correction of 400 ^{14}C years from the quoted ages of the samples. This is just rough – were there more samples from important contexts, a more detailed study of the likely relevant marine reservoir age would be appropriate (for the east Mediterranean, see at present e.g. Siani et al. 2000; Reimer and McCormac 2002; Boaretto et al. 2010).

3. Late Epipalaeolithic: there is considerable variation in the age ranges for samples from the one site represented (Akrotiri *Aetokremnos*), even after screening out the pygmy hippo bones. With regard to the four dates published on suid bones, Vigne et al. (2009: 16136) argue to reject the two dates on charred and unburnt apatite (AA-79921 and AA-79920 respectively) – which appear to be outliers and too recent in Figure A2 (two lefthand-most outlier datapoints); they also argue that the bone used for AA-79922 may have suffered from 'limited isotopic exchange with soil waters because of the fact that it was only partially calcined'; it too may be suspect. Vigne et al. (2009) thus prefer the one date on degraded collagen (AA-79923) with AA-79922 the next best possibility; Model 1 onwards employs these two data. Whether the remaining range in the set represents several or repeated human activities at the site over one–two millennia, or is due to other factors, is unknown.

4. Cypro-PPNA (or Initial Aceramic Neolithic): the six available data all come from a small area at Ayia Varvara *Asprokremmos* and form a tight cluster; it is likely when additional sites (e.g. Ayios Tychonas *Klimonas*) and radiocarbon dates are available for this period that the range will become at least a little

larger (on the new dates from Ayios Tychonas *Klimonas*, see the SOM, Table S5, Figures S3 and S4, and Postscript). This cultural-technological phase is new in Cyprus and its place both chronologically and archaeologically should become better known with future work.

5. Early Aceramic Neolithic (EAN, or 'Cypro-PPNB'): recent archaeological interest in the earliest prehistory of Cyprus makes this a well-dated period, and there are a number of relatively tightly clustered data in the late 9th to mid-8th millennia Cal BC.

6. Late Aceramic Neolithic (LAN) (i.e. post-'Cypro-PPNB', Khirokitia Culture): this is a less well-defined phase despite representing some additional 1,500 years of the Aceramic Neolithic on Cyprus. Some data range widely, suggesting issues of quality (whether in terms of archaeological placement/associations, or of the dating of samples). Some dates have large measurement errors, stemming from older laboratory technologies.

7. Ceramic Neolithic (CN): there are less data for this period, and despite a clear main trend of better data, there is quite a bit of evident noise. Around 20% of the data seems rather older than the main trend and around 10% seems aberrant and much younger. Some issues of quality control may be pertinent. Several of these dates represent laboratory output now several decades old; thus both precision and quality are less than would be expected today.

8. Chalcolithic: this overall period presents a good body of published data. There is some noise but a good set of data lies between the 4th to mid-3rd millennia Cal BC, covering Early to Late Chalcolithic contexts.

9. Prehistoric Bronze Age (PreBA, i.e. Philia, Early–Middle Cypriot): there is a surprising scarcity of data, and this period only has any real information thanks to the dates from the recent high-quality excavations at Marki *Alonia*. (Note: also spelled as Margi in some figures and the SOM.) See SOM item 13: Postscript regarding Chalcolithic to MC Cyprus for a note regarding an update and revision concerning the Marki *Alonia* analysis.

10. Protohistoric Bronze Age (ProBA, i.e. Middle Cypriot [MC] III and Late Cypriot [LC]): there is no evidence directly relevant to the late MC or to the start of the LC periods (i.e. the few samples from archaeological contexts of this period are long-lived charcoal samples and so set *terminus post quem* ranges with an unknown 'post' factor). Efforts should be made to remedy this gap in information with sets of dates on shorter/short-lived samples from late MC contexts and from LC IA and IB contexts. For the later part of the period, there is a fairly clear pattern of data with just a handful of dates offering apparent noise. The latest dates included in this study are LC IIIA samples from Alassa *Paleotaverna* (but see the SOM, Tables S5 and S6, for very recent data from Hala Sultan Tekke).

Even though one should try to include as much of the data available as possible in any analyses, it is evident that some of the dates must be outliers irrelevant to the stated archaeological contexts. In a simple and arbitrary screening, Figure A2 identifies some likely extreme outlier cases as those data lying outside a 1,000-year calendar band around a moving five-point average of the calibrated data. Two of these data (Beta-40380, Ly-4785) have large measurement errors and so might be considered (but the large measurement error devalues their worth). The remaining 11 extreme looking outliers should probably be regarded as irrelevant (data listed below in discussion of Model 1).

The radiocarbon data were then put into a dating model for Bayesian analysis with the OxCal software (note that OxCal terms are capitalised hereafter, e.g. Sequence, Phase, Boundary). This model is shown in schematic terms in Figure A3A and B, and the resultant chronological placements of the main archaeological phases and groupings are shown in Figure A4 (below). Within an overall Sequence, the data were separated into Phases containing each of the main archaeological phase horizons: Late Epipalaeolithic, Cypro–PPNA, Early Aceramic Neolithic (EAN) to end of Late Aceramic Neolithic (LAN), Ceramic Neolithic (CN), Early–Middle Chalcolithic (it was not practical to divide into separate Early and Middle Chalcolithic in this study), Late Chalcolithic, Prehistoric Bronze Age (PreBA, i.e. Early Cypriot [EC]–MC II) and ProBA (i.e. MC III–LC). Where necessary, the data for each site within each of these overall Phases were placed into separate site sub-Phases, and then, where a stratigraphic sequence was present for a site (i.e. a known chronological order among samples), and appeared to be useful, a Sequence was created for the site. (Note: several sites with sequences were nonetheless left in one overall site phase for the dating models, as it did not appear that anything significant was to be gained from creating such a sequence, given either the variability of the data from the site, and/or the poor quality/large errors on the data, and/or dates mainly on charcoal – examples are Kalavasos *Tenta*, Khirokitia *Vouni*, Ayios Epiktitos *Vrysi*, Kandou *Kofovounos*). In practical terms, trials where such elaboration was included created more apparent outlying data and in fact made it difficult to get an early model (revised Model 1 or revised Models 2A and 2B) to run successfully at all; hence this step was not done in this study. Sets of dates on short-lived sample matter from the same context were combined into a weighted average (using OxCal's R_Combine function). In this model, the data within each of the phase elements are assumed to be uniformly distributed. This is a reasonable approximation at a fairly coarse level and in cases where we are not trying to date any specific events (such as a particular moment in time like a construction or destruction event at a given site). As discussed by Bayliss et al. (2011: 58–59): '…it is rare for a model based on a uniform distribution to be *importantly wrong*'. The periods of time before, between and after the dating groupings are quantified as Boundaries in OxCal, and questions may also

Prehistoric Cyprus MODEL 1
Late Epipalaeolithic - Akrotiri Aetokremnos charcoal + recently measured suid bone
Cypro-PPNA - Ayia Varvara Asprokremnos
Early Aceramic Neolithic (EAN) (=Cypro-PPNB) to End Later Aceramic Neolithic (LAN)
Shillourokambos
  Shillourokambos Early Phase A
  Shillourokambos Early Phase B + C
  Shillourokambos Middle
  Shillourokambos Late
Mylouthkia 1
  Mylouthkia 1 Phase A
  Mylouthkia 1 Phase B

  Akanthou - Tatlisu, Ciflik Duzu

  Nissi Beach - Marine Shell Dates -400yrs delta R approx. adjustment

  Akrotiri Vounarouthkia ton Lamion East - Site 23 - Marine Shell -400yrs delta R approx. adjustment

  Ais Yiorkis

  Kissonerga Mosphilia Cypro-PPNB

  Kalavasos Tenta

  Dhali Agridhi

  Khirokitia Vouni

  Cape Andreas Kastros

  Kholetria Ortos

  Kalavasos Vasiliko
Cypriot Ceramic Neolithic
Dhali Agridhi

Paralimni Nissia

Ayios Epiktitos Vrysi

Kandou Kofovounos

Sotira Teppes

Philia Drakos A

Kalavasos Pamboules

Kalavasos Kokkinoyia

Pigi Ayios Andronikos

Early-Middle Chalcolithic
Mylouthkia
  Kissonerga Mylouthkia Period 2
  Kissonerga Mylouthkia Period 3
Kalavasos Ayios

Kalavasos Tenta
Kalavasos Tenta
Kissonerga Mosphilia
  Period 2
  Period 3A
  Period 3B
  Period 3 or 4
Lemba Lakkous
  Period 1
  Period 2
Politiko Kokkinorotsos - Late Middle Chal. - between Mosphilia MChal. and LChal.
  Politiko Kokkinorotsos
Late Chalcolithic
  Kissonerga Mosphilia Period 4

Figure A3A. The first part of the OxCal dating model for Model 1 is shown in schematic terms (OxCal Plot Parameters function); the continuing second part is shown in Figure A3B. Within the overall Sequence Prehistoric Cyprus Model 1, the main Phase groupings (Late Epipalaeolithic, Initial Ceramic Neolithic [=Cypro-PPNA], EAN [=Cypro-PPNB] to End of LAN, etc., etc.) are shown and then, where necessary, sub-Phases for each site within these main phases (e.g. *Shillourokambos*, *Mylouthkia 1*, etc.), and then, where there is a stratigraphic sequence (i.e. a known chronological order) for a site, a Sequence is shown for the data from the site (e.g. *Shillourokambos* Early Phase A, then Early Phase B+C, then Middle, then Late). See the text for discussion on this point – not all such possible stratigraphic sequences were attempted. In this model, the data within each phase are assumed to be uniformly distributed; this is clearly not always the case or entirely appropriate but works well for an approximate overall analysis. The periods of time before, between and after the dating groupings are quantified as Boundaries in OxCal, and questions may also be asked, for example, about the periods of time within groups or between events and so on.

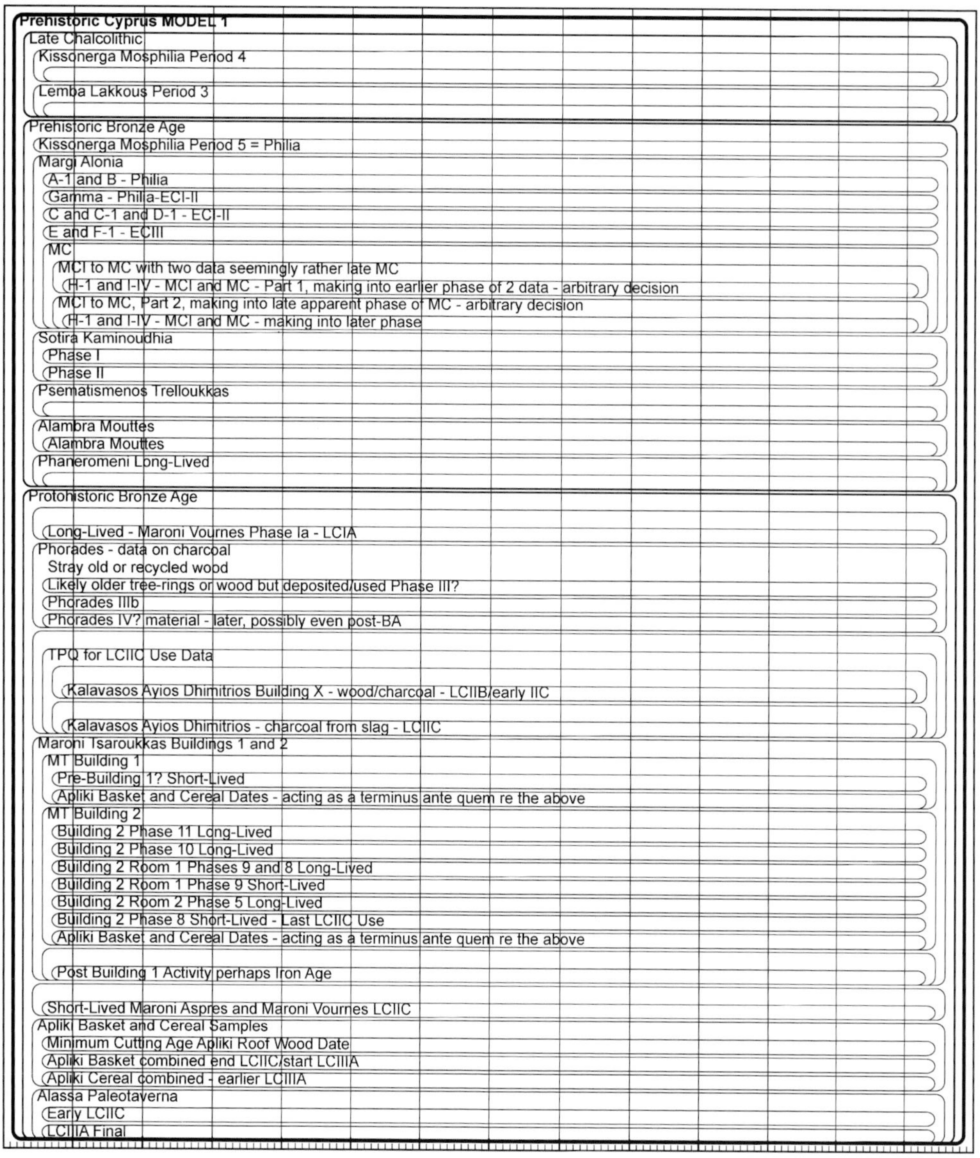

Figure A3B. Second part of the OxCal dating model for Model 1 shown in schematic terms (OxCal Plot Parameters function), continuing from the first part shown in Figure A3A. See Figure A3A caption for description.

be asked, for example, about the periods of time within groups or between events and so on. The Boundaries for the Start (a date range from or after) and End (a date range before or to) of Phases or site Sequences (whether for a stratigraphic Phase within a site Sequence like Lemba *Lakkous* Period 3, or for a whole site Phase or Sequence like *Shillourokambos*, or for an archaeological period grouping like EAN) are the key quantified outcomes from the analyses. All Phases and Sequences are delimited by Boundaries in the model (for the model in detail and with the run file code, see the SOM, Table S1), although not every one of these is given a name.

The OxCal Run File for Model 1 (see below) is listed in full in the SOM (Table S1), and the non-modelled calibrated calendar date ranges for most of the data in Model 1 are listed there in Tables S2 and S4. The quality and reliability of the Models were assessed via the OxCal Agreement Index values for the series (Amodel and Acomb), and for each individual date (A). A satisfactory value in each case is approximately ≥60 (see caption to Figure A5, below). However, when running a very large model (as here) and with data from a variety of materials, methods and laboratories over several decades of work, it is to be anticipated that some screening and progressive rerunning of the model will be required to obtain such satisfactory values. Such screening of large datasets should remove most outlier data, whether samples wrongly placed archaeologically, old or reused materials, problematic measurements at a laboratory, contaminated samples, and so on. Specific outlier analysis as described by Bronk Ramsey (2009b) was not employed, as it proved impossible to run a model of this size successfully with such an outlier model (the general model of Bronk Ramsey 2009b was attempted both on the Oxford server and a dedicated machine without success).

The strategy employed to remove outlying data and to test the reliability of the models was to start with a model including just about as much data as possible but which would run (Model 1), with typical values of Amodel 2.5 and Aoverall 4.3. This was run several times. The next step was to try to move towards a model with at least 'reasonable' poor agreement values and what seemed a path eventually to a ≥60 model: two small sets of data were identified which seemed across various runs of Model 1 (and a few slight variations of Model 1) to comprise major or key outlying data. In all, these represent ≤6% of the data in Model 1. The exact data chosen and the number of them was a totally arbitrary choice. Model 2A represents a more subjective exclusion of some of these key outlying data, whereas Model 2B more simply results from the removal of all data – usually with an individual agreement value below 30 – across several runs of Model 1. Then, since either Model 2A or Model 2B did offer, as hoped, rather better agreement values, and starting from Model 2A (since this excluded slightly less data), the strategy was to remove just a few of the worst apparent outlying data to make Model 3, and to repeat, and so on, until a model was achieved which produced Amodel and Aoverall values ≥60. In the present analysis, this was Model 8. We can examine the findings for each of Models 1 to 8 (see Table A1 below, pp. 519–520) and observe where there is stability of results and where there is some change through progressive models as one or more key and apparently outlying data are excluded. No one model is regarded as correct or the best – rather the pattern of results from the various models offers a good basis for chronology building.

OXCAL MODELS: DESCRIPTIONS

The models employed were as follows:

Model 1

See Figure A4. All data in Sub-Appendix 1 except (i) *Shillourokambos* data in Guilaine and Briois (2006) but *not* in the final publication (Guilaine et al. 2011). Note that these data are listed and noted in the Run File (see Table S1 in the SOM) but are excluded from the analysis because of (i) the // annotation at the start of the relevant lines of code (all other exclusions are denoted by the // annotation); (ii) three obviously post-Neolithic dates from *Ais Giorkis* (Beta-213416, Beta-213418, and Beta-220597), and (iii) the dates identified as extreme-looking outliers in Figure A2, except two with very large measurement errors which I have treated as having mitigating circumstances for Model 1 (which seeks to include as much data as possible). The 11 data excluded are: AA-79921 and A-79920 (Late Epipalaeolithic), P-2549 (EAN), GU-521, OxA-6276 and OxA-20926 (CN), BM-1835R and BM-2280 (Early–Middle Chalcolithic), GU-2966 (Late Chalcolithic), P-2980 (PreBA, based on Hurst and Lawn 1984: 214) and OxA-9972 (ProBA). This leaves 327 'data' included (note: R_Combine elements, of which there are four in the Model, count as 1 datum each in this count – the number of individual radiocarbon dates employed is 340). The OxCal Run File for this model is listed in Table S1 in the SOM. Model 1 ran successfully but offers poor overall OxCal agreement values of (typically) Amodel 2.5 and Aoverall of 4.3: this is because there are several individual dates with very low agreement values (note: every run of such a model produces slightly different outcomes; typical values based on several runs are stated in this study). To assist readers interested in specific sites or dates, the *non*-modelled (or raw) 68.2% probability and 95.4% probability calibrated date ranges for all the data included in Model 1 (i.e. all but the extreme outliers noted above and as identified in Figure A2) are listed in Tables S2 and S4 in the SOM.

Model 2A

As Model 1 but excluding 19 of the apparent outlying data in Model 1 on one assessment: Beta-213413 and P-2781 (EAN), Birm-182, Birm-337 (CN), GU-3397, OxA-2964, GU-2967, AA-10496, BM-2526 and GU-2426 (Early–Middle Chalcolithic), BM-2529, GU-2157 and BM-1353 (Late Chalcolithic), OZB-162, Wk-166434 and OZA-334 (PreBA), and OxA-14951, OxA-8353 and OxA-8350 (ProBA). The choice of 19 data (or less than 6% of the data set) was entirely arbitrary and to an extent subjective (for example some data

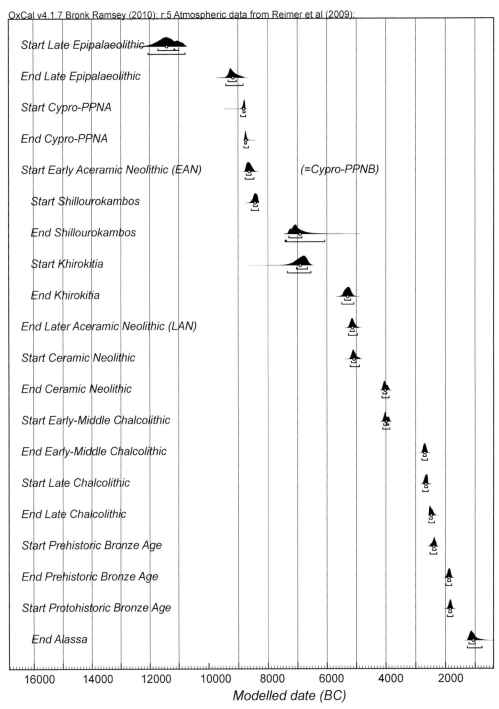

OxCal v4.1.7 Bronk Ramsey (2010); r:5 Atmospheric data from Reimer et al (2009);

Start Late Epipalaeolithic

End Late Epipalaeolithic

Start Cypro-PPNA

End Cypro-PPNA

Start Early Aceramic Neolithic (EAN)   (=Cypro-PPNB)

Start Shillourokambos

End Shillourokambos

Start Khirokitia

End Khirokitia

End Later Aceramic Neolithic (LAN)

Start Ceramic Neolithic

End Ceramic Neolithic

Start Early-Middle Chalcolithic

End Early-Middle Chalcolithic

Start Late Chalcolithic

End Late Chalcolithic

Start Prehistoric Bronze Age

End Prehistoric Bronze Age

Start Protohistoric Bronze Age

End Alassa

16000   14000   12000   10000   8000   6000   4000   2000

Modelled date (BC)

Figure A4. Model 1 with calculated Start and End Boundaries for the main periods and for two selected main site horizons (*Shillourokambos* and Khirokitia) as in Table A1. The small circles indicate the mean (μ) of each distribution (see Table A1). The upper and lower lines under each distribution indicate, respectively, the modelled 68.2% and 95.4% probability ranges. In all, the model calculates a total chronological span of 10,377–11,101 calendar years at 68.2% probability or 10,103–11,486 years at 95.4% probability, with a μ±σ = 10,799±363 years.

appeared more clearly as outliers in one model run and not in another, some data consistently appeared as apparent outliers). It could have been a few less, or a couple more. Some slightly different model formulations were also considered, but these data came up several times as apparent outliers. There remain 309 'data' included (321 individual dates). The OxCal agreement values improve compared to Model 1, but remain relatively poor with typical values of Amodel 20.5, Aoverall 29.1.

Model 2B

As Model 1 but excluding 21 data regularly yielding individual agreement values less than 30 in runs of Model 1: Birm-182, Birm-337, OxA-6175, LTL-1053A, P-2780 (CN), GU-3397, OxA-2964, Gu-2967, AA-10496, BM-2526, GU-2426, BM-2278 (Early–Middle Chalcolithic), GU-2157, BM-1353 (Late Chalcolithic), GU-2167, OZB-161, OZB-162, Wk-166434, OZA-334 (PreBA), OxA-9932 and OxA-8353 (ProBA). Fourteen of these exclusions are common with Model 2A; 308 data remain included (and 319 individual dates). The OxCal agreement values improve compared to Model 1, but remain relatively poor with typical values of Amodel 32.7, Aoverall 46.4. It is evident that the exclusions of some or most of the outlying data identified in Models 2A and 2B allows the overall model to begin to head in the direction of achieving a more satisfactory level of overall agreement. The analysis continued from Model 2A since it excluded less data (and all of the data excluded in Model 2B are progressively excluded in Models 3–8).

Model 3

As Model 2A but with the three worst apparent outlying data excluded: OxA-6175 (CN), P-2780 and BM-2278 (Early–Middle Chalcolithic). There remain 306 data (318 dates) included; Amodel 24.6, Aoverall 33.8.

Model 4

As Model 3 but with the three worst apparent outlying data excluded: GX-2847A and LTL-1053A (CN) and OxA-9932 (ProBA). There remain 303 data (315 dates) included; Amodel 35.8, Aoverall 47.9.

Model 5

As Model 4 but with the three worst apparent outlying data excluded: GU-2167, OZB-161 and OZA-336 (PreBA). There remain 300 data (312 dates) included; Amodel 41.9, Aoverall 54.9. This model excludes three data from the PreBA, two of which (GU-2167 and OZB-161) were, until their exclusion, pushing up the early end of this phase. Their removal sees a sudden 100 calendar years lowering of the calculated Boundary for the Prehistoric Bronze Age Start (see Table A1 below, p. 519). More high-quality data are needed to resolve whether this exclusion (as in Models 5–8) is correct, or whether there should be an early element within the initial PreBA phase (as suggested in Models 1–4). See SOM item 13: Postscript regarding Chalcolithic to MC Cyprus.

Model 6

As Model 5 but with the two worst apparent outlying data excluded: Ly-4785 (LAN) and Beta-82995 (PreBA). There remain 298 data (310 dates) included: Amodel 50.8 and Aoverall 67.9. The Aoverall value is now satisfactory. This model excludes the earliest of the Khirokitia data, Ly-4785 on bone from the Nouveau F work, and this exclusion sees the Boundary for the start of the Khirokitia Phase drop over 70 calendar years compared to Models 1–5. It is unlikely one date should be so important unless from a critically earlier archaeological context; furthermore, this date has a huge quoted measurement error of ±650 radiocarbon years and thus offers little real worth in any discussion. More data are needed to confirm whether there is any earlier element at Khirokitia, whereas the pattern of the other Khirokitia data would suggest this date is likely an older outlier (its mean value is 920 radiocarbon years older than the next oldest date from the site of Khirokitia).

Model 7

As Model 6 but with the two worst apparent outlying data excluded: DRI-3442 (EAN) and OxA-2960 (Late Chalcolithic). There remain 296 data (308 dates) included: Amodel 50.1, Averal 66.6. Again the Aoverall value is satisfactory. Otherwise Model 7 is very similar to Model 6.

Model 8

As Model 6 but removing all data (n = 6) with individual agreements <50: Lyon-931, DRI-3443 (EAN), St-419 (Ceramic Neolithic), BM-1543 (Early–Middle Chalcolithic), OxA-2960 and GU-2158 (Late Chalcolithic). There remain 292 data (304 dates) included: Amodel 62.6 and Aoverall 80.3. Both Agreement index values for the model are now satisfactory and more than 89% of the data in Model 1 remain included.

Model 8_TPQ/TAQ

As Model 8 for the Prehistoric and Protohistoric Bronze Ages (data 94, dates 106), but with a key addition. There is little relevant radiocarbon evidence available that bears on the date of the close of the PreBA (i.e. MC II) or on the date for the start of the ProBA (i.e. MC III–LC I). The three dates from LC I contexts are on long-lived charcoal samples and merely set *terminus post quem* ranges, whilst the few data from late PreBA (i.e. MC) contexts also largely set *terminus post quem* ranges. As a result, when looking at Table A1, the Boundaries calculated for the End of the PreBA (MC II) and the Start of the ProBA (MC III–LC I) are too early in view of other information – namely both archaeological linkages with Egypt and the Near Eastern worlds (see below) and radiocarbon dated chronologies (e.g. in the Aegean), which may be regarded as relevant via archaeological linkages (i.e. dates for the Late Minoan IA and Late Helladic I periods in the Aegean which are approximately contemporary with the earlier part of LC I: see Manning 1999; 2001; 2007; Manning et al. 2002; 2006; Lindblom and Manning 2011). To remedy this situation, this model introduces two additional pieces of prior information and tries to define a slightly different point: the transition from MC III to LC IA. First, it is assumed that at least some of the later MC III period (earlier phase of White Painted Pendent Line Style) must be after 1700 Cal BC (i.e. 1700 Cal BC is made into the *terminus post quem* for a Boundary End of MC III). This assumption is based on several good archaeological linkages for MC III material around and after this point (Merrillees 2002). Second, it is assumed that the LC IA period must begin before the start of the New Kingdom in Egypt, since it is more or less universally agreed that material from the first part of the LC I period occurs in pre-New Kingdom contexts in Egypt and the Levant (see Merrillees 1992b; 2002; 2009b). The date for the start of the New Kingdom (accession of Ahmose) is taken as the mid-point of the estimate for the accession of Ahmose (1559 BC) from the study of Bronk Ramsey et al. (2010) – this date is only nine years older than the standard date from assessments of the historical evidence (e.g. von Beckerath 1997). Model 8_TPQ/TAQ offers a much better estimate for the transition date to the start of the Late Bronze Age (Late Cypriot IA) – Amodel 75.1 and Aoverall 69.4: see Figure A13, below.

CYPRIOT CHRONOLOGY

Late Epipalaeolithic

See Figure A5 and Table A1 (below, p. 519). The available data on charcoal samples or recent suid bone are quite variable and the period is not well defined. At present, our data also all come from just one site (additional data are anticipated, e.g. from the Roudias site – see main text). Removing apparent outlying data, the period lies within limits of/from ca. 11400±337–9170±149 Cal BC. It is unclear if this approximately 1,500 calendar year range represents indications of regular or periodic human activities at Akrotiri *Aetokremnos* over a long period, or whether there is a lot of noise in these data. If one rules out the four

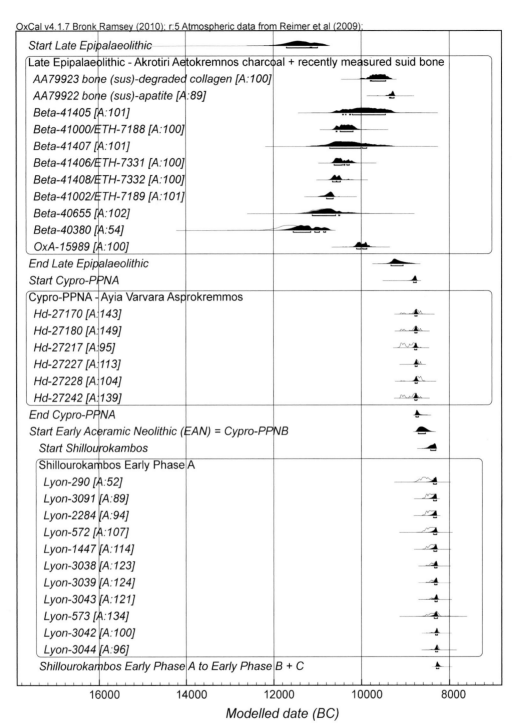

OxCal v4.1.7 Bronk Ramsey (2010); r:5 Atmospheric data from Reimer et al (2009);

Start Late Epipalaeolithic

Late Epipalaeolithic - Akrotiri Aetokremnos charcoal + recently measured suid bone

AA79923 bone (sus)-degraded collagen [A:100]

AA79922 bone (sus)-apatite [A:89]

Beta-41405 [A:101]

Beta-41000/ETH-7188 [A:100]

Beta-41407 [A:101]

Beta-41406/ETH-7331 [A:100]

Beta-41408/ETH-7332 [A:100]

Beta-41002/ETH-7189 [A:101]

Beta-40655 [A:102]

Beta-40380 [A:54]

OxA-15989 [A:100]

End Late Epipalaeolithic

Start Cypro-PPNA

Cypro-PPNA - Ayia Varvara Asprokremmos

Hd-27170 [A:143]

Hd-27180 [A:149]

Hd-27217 [A:95]

Hd-27227 [A:113]

Hd-27228 [A:104]

Hd-27242 [A:139]

End Cypro-PPNA

Start Early Aceramic Neolithic (EAN) = Cypro-PPNB

Start Shillourokambos

Shillourokambos Early Phase A

Lyon-290 [A:52]

Lyon-3091 [A:89]

Lyon-2284 [A:94]

Lyon-572 [A:107]

Lyon-1447 [A:114]

Lyon-3038 [A:123]

Lyon-3039 [A:124]

Lyon-3043 [A:121]

Lyon-573 [A:134]

Lyon-3042 [A:100]

Lyon-3044 [A:96]

Shillourokambos Early Phase A to Early Phase B + C

16000   14000   12000   10000   8000

Modelled date (BC)

Figure A5. Modelled dating evidence and chronology from Model 8 for Cyprus from the Late Epipalaeolithic through *Shillourokambos* Early Phase A (= EAN 1, or Cypro-PPNB 1). The solid histograms show the modelled ranges; the hollow histograms show the original, non-modelled data. The lines under the probability distributions indicate the modelled 68.2% probability ranges. The A values in the square brackets are a calculation of the overlap of the original non-modelled calibrated distribution for each date versus the distribution after the Bayesian modelling. If the overlap falls below 60%, it is approximately equivalent to a combination of normal distributions failing a Chi-squared test at the 95% confidence level.

Beta data (41405, 47407, 40655, 40380) that have very large measurement errors, then the remaining data lie in the 11th through the earlier 10th millennium Cal BC. This may be a more realistic date range. Revised Start and End Boundaries *within* which the Akrotiri phase lies on this basis are (using the mean [μ] and standard deviation [σ] as in Table A1): 10900±253–9155±153 Cal BC. In round terms (century-scale) and allowing for some old-wood effect on the data from charcoal samples (about 50±50 years), we might suggest approximate dates within ca. 11000–9100/9000 Cal BC. We cannot tell from the current evidence if there is a 'gap' between the apparent Late Epipalaeolithic presence and the Cypro-PPNA (Initial Aceramic Neolithic) on Cyprus. The available radiocarbon data indicate that there is a gap of 247–538 calendar years at 68.2% probability, or a minimum of seven to a maximum of 602 years at 95.4% probability, μ±σ = 367±153 years (employing Model 8). But we also have to assume that the Cypro-PPNA in reality occupies a longer time period than indicated by the one very tight set of data from Ayia Varvara *Asprokremmos* (Manning et al. 2010a), perhaps indicated by the new dates from Ayios Tychonas *Klimonas* (see SOM: Figure S4 and discussion there). Some of these dates are likely later, filling in the period towards the earliest Early Aceramic Neolithic (EAN, or 'Cypro-PPNB'), but some may also be earlier, filling in at least some of the present gap to *Aetokremnos* – at present, we just do not know. For an update and additional data, see SOM Postscript to Figure S4.

Initial Aceramic Neolithic (Cypro-PPNA)

See Figure A5 and Table A1 (below, p. 519). At present, the six available dates for this period are known just from charcoal and from one group of contexts at one site, Ayia Varvara *Asprokremmos* (but see the SOM, Table S5, Figures S3, S4, for radiocarbon data from Ayios Tychonas *Klimonas*). This tight group (representing at present just some 0–90 calendar years at 68.2% probability or 0–220 years at 95.4% probability or μ±σ = 76±72 years in Model 8) undoubtedly does not represent the entire chronological range of the Initial Aceramic Neolithic on Cyprus. The Boundary for the Start of the Early Aceramic Neolithic ('Cypro-PPNB') is probably a little too early, as the tight range of the current Cypro-PPNA data leaves apparent space, some of which may yet be filled by later Cypro-PPNA dates (see SOM Figure S4c–d). Similarly, some of the present gap to the end of the Late Epipalaeolithic range may eventually become part of the Cypro-PPNA with further work. As a best guesstimate, and allowing a little for possible old-wood effects on dates from charcoal, we might place Cypro-PPNA as likely within a period from about 8900–8350 Cal BC, give or take about 100 years (see SOM Figure S4d). Whether there is then a gap to the advent of the EAN, or whether there will be an as yet to be recognised late Cypro-PPNA or transitional Cypro-PPNA/Early Aceramic Neolithic phase, is unknown. For an update and additional data, see SOM Postscript to Figure S4.

Early Aceramic Neolithic (EAN, or 'Cypro-PPNB')

See Figures A5 and A6, and Table A1 (below, p. 519). The date for the start of this period is unclear. The current earliest evidence from *Shillourokambos* lies from or after about 8400/8350 Cal BC (allowing for some old-wood effect). Allowing also for the new Ayios Tychonas *Klimonas* dates (see SOM Figure S4), it is likely that the EAN (Cypro-PPNB) begins around or after about 8350 Cal BC. What lies in the 300+ years between this and the Initial Aceramic Neolithic (Cypro-PPNA) attested at Ayia Varvara *Asprokremnos* is not clear but the new radiocarbon dates from Ayios Tychonas *Klimonas* – taken at face value – indicate that the Initial Aceramic Neolithic (Cypro-PPNA) extends down to around 8350 Cal BC. As perhaps demonstrated by these new dates from *Klimonas* (see SOM Figure S4c–d – but cf. SOM Figure S4 Postscript), the Start Boundary for the EAN in the models in Table A1 is perhaps too early, as it is filling part of the present gap in the data (before *Klimonas*). Some of this time might well turn out to be late Cypro-PPNA or transitional Cypro-PPNA to EAN with future work. As a guesstimate, I place the start of the EAN at 8350 Cal BC (see SOM Figure S4d) and assume late Cypro-PPNA and/or a transitional Cypro-PPNA to EAN lies before this. Where to end the EAN is also less than clear-cut. If the overall extent of occupation dated at *Shillourokambos* (1100–1590 calendar years at 68.2% probability and 979–2382 years at 95.4% probability, $\mu\pm\sigma$ = 1496±387 years from Model 8) is regarded as roughly denoting the period, then it ends about 6900/6800 Cal BC. It is clear that other EAN sites had long overall periods of occupation (not necessarily continuous of course) on the basis of the available radiocarbon dates. For example, from Model 8 *Ais Giorkis* has evidence of an overall duration from dates available of 642–918 calendar years at 68.2% probability and 606–1300 years at 95.4% probability with $\mu\pm\sigma$ = 867±197 years; Kalavasos *Tenta* has an apparent duration (exaggerated, however, by the large measurement errors on the data) of 2495–3094 calendar years at 68.2% probability and 2140–3451 years at 95.4% probability with $\mu\pm\sigma$ = 2803±315 years. This is, however, excluding P-2549 (see above on Model 1 and Figure A2). If this date, much later than any other from the site, were to be regarded as indicating a very late temporary encampment at the site (Clarke 2007a: 16), then the final occupation could reach even later.

Late Aceramic Neolithic (LAN, or Khirokitia Phase)

See Figure A7 and Table A1 (below, p. 519). The dates for the range of occupation at Khirokitia lie within limits of ca. 6900/6800–5300/5200 Cal BC. The apparent duration of the site Phase dated in Model 8 is 1299–1774 calendar years at 68.2% probability and 1124–2114 years at 95.4% probability with $\mu\pm\sigma$ = 1588±254 years. If we allow a little for an old-wood effect, a best estimate of ca. 6800–5200 Cal BC seems reasonable. The excavator of Khirokitia regards

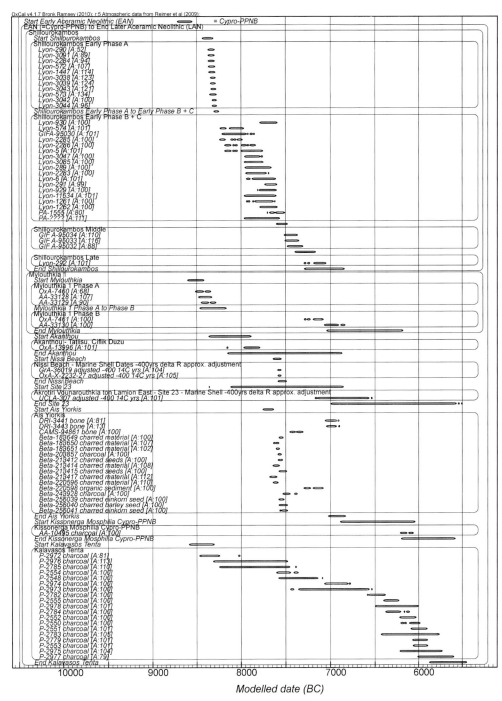

Figure A6. The modeled 68.2% ranges from Model 8 for dates and Boundaries from the Start of EAN (Cypro-PPNB) through a number of sites ending with the data set from Kalavasos *Tenta* (and a point in the LAN). There is a reasonable population of data across this interval due to recent research activity. The modelled Start and End Boundaries for Kalavasos *Tenta* are (μ±σ from Model 8) 8387±178 Cal BC and 5584±231 Cal BC; for Kritou Marottou *Ais Giorkis* they are 7721±75 Cal BC and 6854±163 Cal BC.

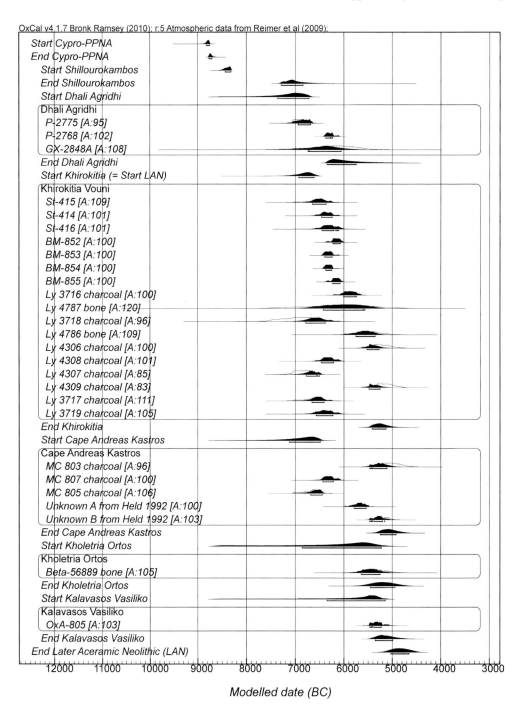

Figure A7. Modelled dating evidence and chronology from Model 8 for Cyprus during the LAN period. The solid histograms show the modelled ranges; the hollow histograms show the original, non-modelled data. The lines under the probability distributions indicate the modelled 68.2% probability ranges. The A values in the square brackets indicate the individual agreement values for each date (modelled versus non-modelled ranges) – a value ≥60% is satisfactory at about the 95% confidence level.

a few of the latest dates as perhaps misleading (see also Clarke 2007a: 16), but their general similarity to other LAN dates suggests not. The lower limit for the dates from Kalavasos *Tenta* lies around 5584±231 Cal BC (excluding, by Model 8, both P-2781 and especially P-2549 which lie later); thus this site continues well into the later part of the LAN after a start in the late 9th millennium Cal BC contemporary with early *Shillourokambos*. The weakness for the *Tenta* data today is that they have large measurement errors derived from dating technology of several decades ago (thus more reliance is placed on the dates from *Shillourokambos*). A renewed program of investigation at Kalavasos *Tenta* aimed at recovering organic samples from its long stratigraphic sequence for a high-resolution radiocarbon programme is an obvious priority for future work.

One of the most problematic areas in the chronology of prehistoric Cyprus is when to place the end of the LAN, and when to start the Ceramic Neolithic (CN), which also raises the question of what happens in between. In Model 1 the End Boundary for the LAN is placed at 5129±77 Cal BC. Yet with the removal as apparent outliers of four of the rather few early CN data by Model 8 (contrast Models 1 and 2A versus Models 2B-8 in Table A1), the date becomes 4833±176 Cal BC. The dates calculated for the Start of the CN accordingly also change from 5079±78 Cal BC in Model 1 to 4524±109 BC in Model 8. Some 500 years of the CN does or does not exist depending on whether to include some or none of four dates found to be likely outliers in Models 2B-8. Of these data, two indicate late 6th millennium Cal BC dates (OxA-6175 from Kandou *Kofovounos* and GX-2847A from Dhali *Agridhi* – the latter with a large measurement error), while Birm-182 is earlier 5th millennium Cal BC and Birm-337 is earlier to mid-5th millennium Cal BC (both from Ayios Epiktitos *Vrysi*). Thus a date before 5000 BC relies on just two data otherwise outlying from the rest of the CN. And a date in the earlier 5th millennium relies on a total of two data. This is clearly unsatisfactory. Khirokitia ends by around 5200 Cal BC. In Model 8 (with OxA-6175 and GX-2847A excluded), some data from a few other sites could potentially continue into the next 100–200 years: with downwards limits around or before ($\mu\pm\sigma$) 5191±249 Cal BC for Kholetria *Ortos*, or 5128±184 Cal BC for Kalavasos *Vasiliko*, or 5052±166 Cal BC for Cape Andreas *Kastros* (these sites ended in the 53rd–52nd centuries BC in Model 1 with the 'early' CN dates still included). Even allowing for a bit of old-wood effect, there is nothing to take us beyond about 5000 BC (and some of the most recent LAN dates from both Cape Andreas *Kastros* and Khirokitia have been questioned by their excavator: see Clarke 2007a: 16); these sites could easily end by or before ca. 5200 BC (as in Model 1). Thus I end the LAN period at 5200/5000 Cal BC. Whether the CN began then, or only after an interval, is entirely unclear from the data to hand. I use the date 5000 BC to begin the CN, but the first 500 years remain more or less undocumented at present. It is self-evident that more high-quality data are needed to clarify this time period.

Ceramic Neolithic (CN)

See Figure A8 and Table A1 (below, p. 519). The majority of the radiocarbon
data for this period fall or can be modelled nicely in the later 5th millennium
Cal BC. Just a few data (considering only those which survived into Model 1),
excluded as outlying in Models 2B and 3–8, indicate an earlier 5th millennium
Cal BC date or later 6th millennium Cal BC date: GX-2847A on bone from
Dhali *Agridhi*, Birm-182 and Birm-337 on charcoal from Ayios Epiktitos *Vrysi*,
and OxA-6175 on charcoal from Kandou *Kofovounos*. The data from the latter
two sites stand out as old versus the rest of the dates from their sites, and seem
to form an unreliable basis to assume a real date range. Thus what is happening
in the earlier 5th millennium Cal BC on Cyprus is somewhat unclear. P-2769
on bone from Dhali *Agridhi* lies in the mid-5th millennium Cal BC (Model 1
places it 4707–4492 Cal BC at 68.2% probability and Model 8 at 4486–4343
Cal BC at 68.2% probability, with $\mu\pm\sigma$ respectively of 4596±108 Cal BC and
4421±77 Cal BC); in material culture terms this may represent an earlier phase
of the period compared to *Vrysi* (Clarke 2007a: 18). This perhaps gives us
something to support a date from about 4600/4400 BC. If we assume that
there is no 'gap', and that the LAN ends no later than about 5200–5000 Cal
BC, then the CN should start about 5000 Cal BC – but we lack much positive
evidence for at least 400 years. There is an obvious vagueness to our chronology here on the scale of several centuries. It is possible on current evidence
that we lack secure evidence for occupation on Cyprus from ca. 5200/5000
Cal BC to around 4600/4400 Cal BC. More high-quality data are needed. An
end date for the CN around 4100/4000 Cal BC seems appropriate from the
data to hand, especially if any small old-wood effect is allowed for in quite a
number of the dates.

Early to Middle Chalcolithic

See Figure A9 and Table A1 (below, p. 519). Conveniently the data indicate a
start around, to a century after, 4000 Cal BC, more or less following on from
the end of the CN. There is no longer a case for a gap of several centuries
(e.g. 600 years) in the archaeological record as previously thought possible
(discussed in Steel 2004a: 83). The end limit for the Middle Chalcolithic lies
around 2700 Cal BC. This lower boundary is especially set by the recent data
from Politiko *Kokkinorotsos*. This site is placed as late Middle Chalcolithic, filling a gap between the Middle Chalcolithic as observed at Kissonerga *Mosphilia*,
but lying before the advent of the Late Chalcolithic (following Webb et al.
2009; Frankel 2010). Since these data are on shorter/short-lived sample material, this end boundary should be relatively close to the real transition, and so
a more or less directly applicable date. A division between Early and Middle
Chalcolithic is problematic on current evidence (Clarke 2007a: 20–22). Where

OxCal v4.1.7 Bronk Ramsey (2010); r:5 Atmospheric data from Reimer et al (2009):

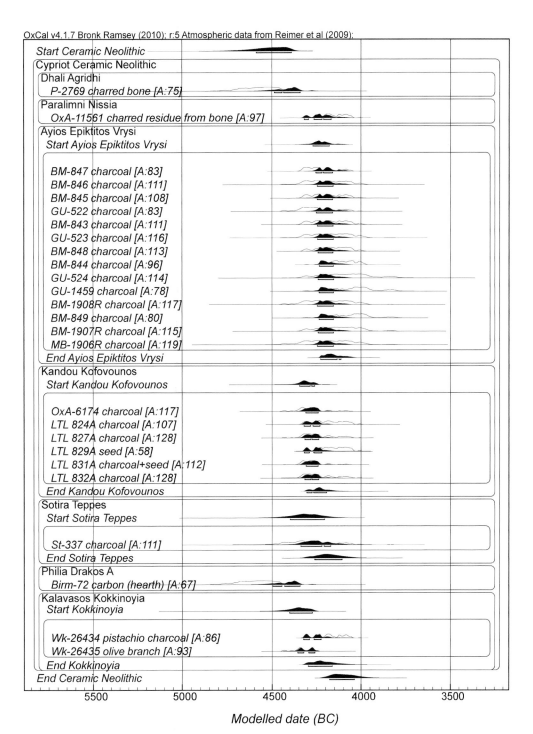

Modelled date (BC)

Figure A8. Modelled dating evidence and chronology from Model 8 for Cyprus for the CN period. The solid histograms show the modelled ranges; the hollow histograms show the original, non-modelled data. The lines under the probability distributions indicate the modelled 68.2% probability ranges. The A values in the square brackets indicate the individual agreement values for each date (modelled versus non-modelled ranges) – a value ≥60% is satisfactory at about the 95% confidence level. Note: selected elements plotted, some titles and boundaries, and sites whose data have been excluded in analysis between Models 1 and 8 are left out to save space here. The modelled Start and End Boundaries for Ayios Epiktitos *Vrysi* are (μ±σ from Model 8 as shown) 4222±52 Cal BC and 4152±52 Cal BC.

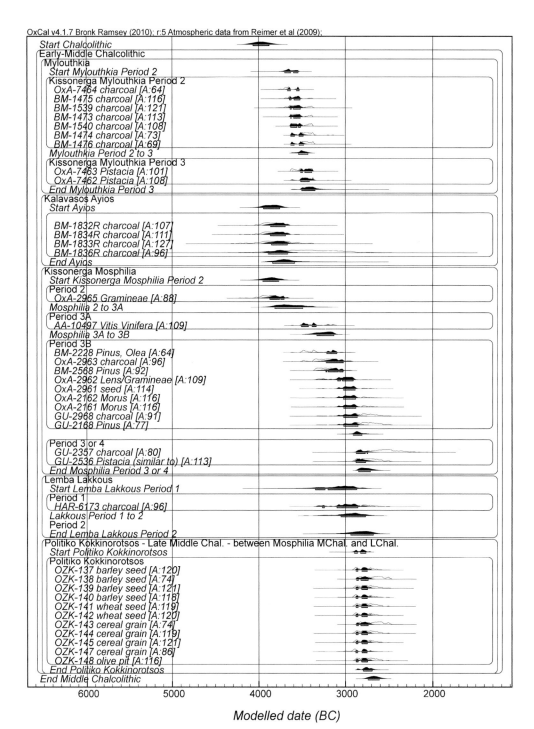

OxCal v4.1.7 Bronk Ramsey (2010); r:5 Atmospheric data from Reimer et al (2009);

Start Chalcolithic
Early-Middle Chalcolithic
Mylouthkia
    Start Mylouthkia Period 2
    Kissonerga Mylouthkia Period 2
        OxA-7464 charcoal [A:64]
        BM-1475 charcoal [A:116]
        BM-1539 charcoal [A:121]
        BM-1473 charcoal [A:113]
        BM-1540 charcoal [A:108]
        BM-1474 charcoal [A:73]
        BM-1476 charcoal [A:69]
    Mylouthkia Period 2 to 3
    Kissonerga Mylouthkia Period 3
        OxA-7463 Pistacia [A:101]
        OxA-7462 Pistacia [A:108]
        End Mylouthkia Period 3
Kalavasos Ayios
    Start Ayios

        BM-1832R charcoal [A:107]
        BM-1834R charcoal [A:111]
        BM-1833R charcoal [A:127]
        BM-1836R charcoal [A:96]
    End Ayios
Kissonerga Mosphilia
    Start Kissonerga Mosphilia Period 2
Period 2
    OxA-2965 Gramineae [A:88]
Mosphilia 2 to 3A
Period 3A
    AA-10497 Vitis Vinifera [A:109]
Mosphilia 3A to 3B
Period 3B
    BM-2228 Pinus, Olea [A:64]
    OxA-2963 charcoal [A:96]
    BM-2568 Pinus [A:92]
    OxA-2962 Lens/Gramineae [A:109]
    OxA-2961 seed [A:114]
    OxA-2162 Morus [A:116]
    OxA-2161 Morus [A:116]
    GU-2968 charcoal [A:91]
    GU-2168 Pinus [A:77]

Period 3 or 4
    GU-2357 charcoal [A:80]
    GU-2536 Pistacia (similar to) [A:113]
    End Mosphilia Period 3 or 4
Lemba Lakkous
    Start Lemba Lakkous Period 1
Period 1
    HAR-6173 charcoal [A:96]
Lakkous Period 1 to 2
Period 2
    End Lemba Lakkous Period 2
Politiko Kokkinorotsos - Late Middle Chal. - between Mosphilia MChal. and LChal.
    Start Politiko Kokkinorotsos
Politiko Kokkinorotsos
    OZK-137 barley seed [A:120]
    OZK-138 barley seed [A:74]
    OZK-139 barley seed [A:121]
    OZK-140 barley seed [A:118]
    OZK-141 wheat seed [A:119]
    OZK-142 wheat seed [A:120]
    OZK-143 cereal grain [A:74]
    OZK-144 cereal grain [A:119]
    OZK-145 cereal grain [A:121]
    OZK-147 cereal grain [A:86]
    OZK-148 olive pit [A:116]
    End Politiko Kokkinorotsos
End Middle Chalcolithic

6000   5000   4000   3000   2000

Modelled date (BC)

Figure A9. Modelled dating evidence and chronology from Model 8 for Cyprus for the Early to Middle Chalcolithic periods. The solid histograms show the modelled ranges; the hollow histograms show the original, non-modelled data. The lines under the probability distributions indicate the modelled 68.2% probability ranges. The A values in the square brackets indicate the individual agreement values for each date (modelled versus non-modelled ranges) – a value ≥60% is satisfactory at about the 95% confidence level. The modelled Start and End Boundaries for Kissonerga *Mylouthkia* Period 2 are (μ±σ from Model 8 as shown) 3641±62 Cal BC and 3499±54 Cal BC. The modelled Start and End Boundaries for Politiko *Kokkinorotsos* are (μ±σ from Model 8 as shown) 2823±53 Cal BC and 2754±55 Cal BC.

there is a stratigraphic sequence, as at Kissonerga *Mosphilia*, we have very little apparently reliable Early Chalcolithic radiocarbon data for the Early phase. At Lemba *Lakkous* only two Period 1 dates survive beyond Model 1 (and one of these is lost for Model 8) and they suggest a much later transition (2899±105 Cal BC in Model 1) than the other sites. The end limit (mean ±σ) in Model 8 for Kalavasos *Ayious* is 3654±154 Cal BC; for Kissonerga *Mylouthkia* (after Period 3) it is 3390±113 Cal BC, and for *Mylouthkia* after Period 2 (i.e. Period 2 to 3 transition) it is 3499±54 Cal BC; for the transition between Kissonerga *Mosphilia* Period 2 and 3A it is 3627±160 Cal BC. An estimate somewhere between ca. 3600–3400 Cal BC for the transition between Early and Middle Chalcolithic might be reasonable for most of our evidence; this is also consistent with the existing conventional date of ca. 3500 Cal BC (perhaps a reasonable, best-number estimate). Better definition is needed from additional data.

Late Chalcolithic

See Figure A10 and Table A1 (below, p. 519). There are relatively few data. Those we have indicate a start ca. 2650/2600 Cal BC and an end ca. 2500 Cal BC to perhaps 2450 or even 2400 Cal BC, if allowance is made for any old-wood effect. There is a small gap back to where the Middle Chalcolithic data end. In view of the relative scarcity of Late Chalcolithic data, it seems more likely that the 'gap' should be filled by the Late Chalcolithic and hopefully further data in the future will address this point: so for an approximate chronology, we start the period from ca. 2700 Cal BC.

Prehistoric Bronze Age (PreBA)

See Figures A10 and A13, and Table A1 (below, p. 519). The modelled start limit for the period changes by around a century between Models 1–4 versus Models 5–8. As noted above, Model 5 onwards exclude three data from the PreBA and notably two data (GU-2167 and OZB-161) which otherwise would push back the early part of this phase. We need additional high-quality data to resolve whether this exclusion (as in Models 5–8) is correct, or whether there should be an earlier element within the initial PreBA phase (as suggested in Models 1–4). The present 'gap' in time between the end of the Late Chalcolithic and the start of the PreBA is problematic as neither is well dated, although there seems more room for movement especially at the start of the latter (i.e. Philia and Early Cypriot [EC] I). The Start Boundary (i.e. a date range from or after) for Marki *Alonia* and thus for the initial phase represented in that site's radiocarbon dates (A-1 and B – Philia) is 2299–2251 Cal BC at 68.2% probability in Model 1 and 2236–2251 Cal BC in Model 8 (μ±σ respectively of 2271±31 Cal BC and 2208±35 Cal BC). There is a single earlier Philia date from Kissonerga *Mosphilia* Period 5 (GU-2167), but this is an outlier even in Model 1. Thus our available

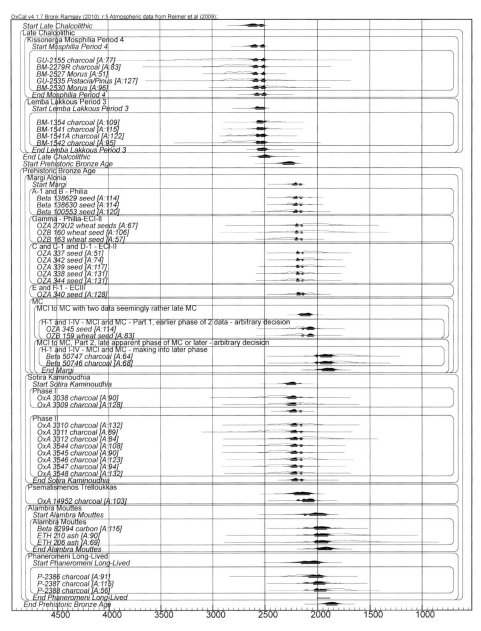

OxCal v4.1.7 Bronk Ramsey (2010); r:5 Atmospheric data from Reimer et al (2009);

Start Late Chalcolithic
Late Chalcolithic
Kissonerga Mosphilia Period 4
  Start Mosphilia Period 4

    GU-2155 charcoal [A:77]
    BM-2279R charcoal [A:83]
    BM-2527 Morus [A:51]
    GU-2535 Pistacia/Pinus [A:127]
    BM-2530 Morus [A:96]
  End Mosphilia Period 4
Lemba Lakkous Period 3
  Start Lemba Lakkous Period 3

    BM-1354 charcoal [A:109]
    BM-1541 charcoal [A:115]
    BM-1541A charcoal [A:122]
    BM-1542 charcoal [A:95]
  End Lemba Lakkous Period 3
End Late Chalcolithic
Start Prehistoric Bronze Age
Prehistoric Bronze Age
Margi Alonia
  Start Margi
  A-1 and B - Philia
    Beta 138629 seed [A:114]
    Beta 138630 seed [A:114]
    Beta 100553 seed [A:120]
  Gamma - Philia-ECI-II
    OZA 279U2 wheat seeds [A:67]
    OZB 160 wheat seed [A:106]
    OZB 163 wheat seed [A:57]
  C and C-1 and D-1 - ECI-II
    OZA 337 seed [A:51]
    OZA 342 seed [A:74]
    OZA 339 seed [A:117]
    OZA 338 seed [A:131]
    OZA 344 seed [A:131]
  E and F-1 - ECIII
    OZA 340 seed [A:128]
  MC
    MCI to MC with two data seemingly rather late MC
    H-1 and I-IV - MCI and MC - Part 1, earlier phase of 2 data - arbitrary decision
      OZA 345 seed [A:114]
      OZB 159 wheat seed [A:83]
    MCI to MC, Part 2, late apparent phase of MC or later - arbitrary decision
    H-1 and I-IV - MCI and MC - making into later phase
      Beta 50747 charcoal [A:64]
      Beta 50746 charcoal [A:68]
    End Margi
Sotira Kaminoudhia
  Start Sotira Kaminoudhia
  Phase I
    OxA 3038 charcoal [A:90]
    OxA 3309 charcoal [A:128]

  Phase II
    OxA 3310 charcoal [A:132]
    OxA 3311 charcoal [A:89]
    OxA 3312 charcoal [A:84]
    OxA 3544 charcoal [A:108]
    OxA 3545 charcoal [A:90]
    OxA 3546 charcoal [A:123]
    OxA 3547 charcoal [A:94]
    OxA 3548 charcoal [A:132]
  End Sotira Kaminoudhia
Psematismenos Trelloukkas
    OxA 14952 charcoal [A:103]
Alambra Mouttes
  Start Alambra Mouttes
  Alambra Mouttes
    Beta 82994 carbon [A:116]
    ETH 210 ash [A:90]
    ETH 206 ash [A:69]
  End Alambra Mouttes
Phaneromeni Long-Lived
  Start Phaneromeni Long-Lived

    P-2386 charcoal [A:91]
    P-2387 charcoal [A:115]
    P-2388 charcoal [A:56]
  End Phaneromeni Long-Lived
End Prehistoric Bronze Age

4500   4000   3500   3000   2500   2000   1500   1000

Modelled date (BC)

Figure A10. Modelled dating evidence and chronology from Model 8 for Cyprus during the Late Chalcolithic period through the PreBA (Philia, EC–MC II). The solid histograms show the modelled ranges; the hollow histograms show the original, non-modelled data. The lines under the probability distributions indicate the modelled 68.2% probability ranges. The A values in the square brackets indicate the individual agreement values for each date (modelled versus non-modelled ranges) – a value ≥60% is satisfactory at about the 95% confidence level. Note: selected elements plotted, some titles and boundaries, and sites whose data have been excluded in analysis between Models 1 and 8, are left out to save space here. The modelled Start and End Boundaries for Sotira *Kaminoudhia* are (μ±σ – from Model 8 as shown) 2248±48 Cal BC and 2199±44 Cal BC (but, as all are charcoal samples, one might consider a 50±50-year-old wood allowance – if so, these would become: 2198±69 Cal BC and 2149±67 Cal BC). For Marki *Alonia* the dates (mainly on short-lived samples and so relevant as they stand) are 2208±35 Cal BC and 1909±59 Cal BC. The Start and End Boundary dates on the same basis from Alambra *Mouttes* are 2036±89 Cal BC and 1934±62 Cal BC; however, as all the data are from carbon or ash, we might assume a TPQ factor and adjust by something like 50±50 years and thus suggest upper and lower limits (dates from or after, and then before or to) of ca. 1986±102 Cal BC and 1884±84 Cal BC. Regarding Marki and the MC, see SOM 13. Postscript regarding Chalcolithic to MC Cyprus.

evidence does not support a range before about 2300 BC (and perhaps not even this early). It might be that Late Chalcolithic and the initial PreBA meet in the 24th century BC – but it is possible that earlier Philia/initial EC will be found at some point and push this back towards around 2400 Cal BC; thus we use the date of 2400/2350 Cal BC as the best estimate. The end of the PreBA is not well defined either with the data to hand: hence Model 8_TPQ/TAQ (recalling that this model, however, is defining the transition between Middle Cypriot [MC] III and the start of Late Cypriot [LC] IA). This suggests a date within a 68.2% range of 1705–1686 Cal BC and at 95.4% between 1705–1669 Cal BC. Allowing that our later MC data come from charcoal samples and so set *terminus post quem* ranges, and also allowing for some old-wood effect, a date for the end of the period from about the mean of the calculated boundary (1691 Cal BC) to about 1650 Cal BC seems plausible (and consistent with the independent Aegean radiocarbon chronology and its dates for Late Minoan [LM] IA and Late Helladic [LH] I – with an approximate association of LH I and LM IA with LC IA known from several material exchanges: see discussion above). The date for the close of the PreBA as used in this book (i.e. MC II) is earlier. Following the logic of Merrillees (2002), MC II should end somewhere after 1750 Cal BC (his estimate), down to no later than ca. 1700 Cal BC. We use the earlier number as it seems more consistent with the available radiocarbon dates we do have for the end of this period.

Protohistoric Bronze Age (ProBA)

See Figures A11–A14 and Table A1 (below, p. 519). A start date (for LC I) is placed from Model 8_TPQ/TAQ, taking the mean ±σ at about 1679±14 Cal BC. Given the discussion on the end of the preceding period, this is treated as 1680/1650 Cal BC. The date for the start of the ProBA (MC III onwards) used in this book is earlier and here the estimate of ca. 1750 BC (no later than 1700 BC) is used as in the previous paragraph, following Merrillees (2002). The limit for a point late in LC IIIA is placed around or before about 1050 Cal BC plus or minus about 150 years in all models; allowing a little for old-wood effect, 1050 Cal BC perhaps represents a suitable round number for the latest estimate for the end of LC IIIA, although the period might well have ended nearer 1100 Cal BC. A reasonable amount of evidence relates to the dating of the LC IIC period (using Model 8 and quoting the mean ±σ). The *terminus post quem* for the long-lived wood from Kalavasos *Ayios Dhimitrios* lies at 1391±22 Cal BC. The various earlier, long-lived samples from Maroni *Tsaroukkas* lie in the 15th to mid-14th centuries Cal BC, with the group from Building 2, Room 1, Phases 9 and 8 placed in Model 8 (μ±σ) between 1343–1341±25/26 Cal BC. The latter might offer a fairly close *terminus post quem* range for the main LC IIC occupation in the building. The last extant tree-ring in the Apliki *Karamallos* roof wood lies at 1323±28 Cal BC. In Model 8

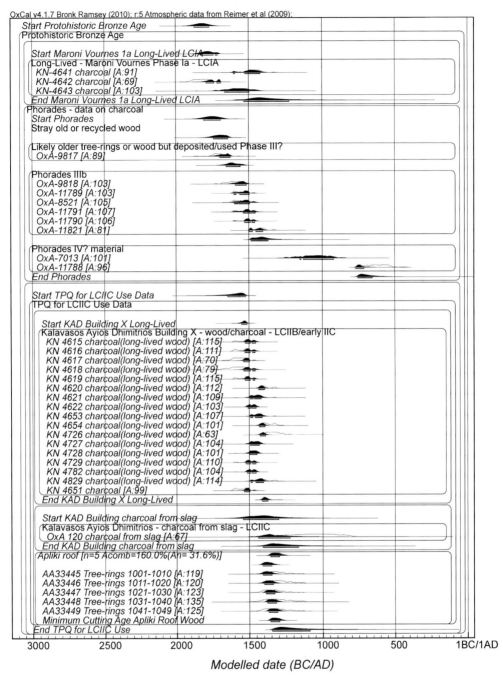

Figure A11. Modelled dating evidence and chronology from Model 8 for Cyprus during the earlier ProBA (pre-LC IIC). The solid histograms show the modelled ranges; the hollow histograms show the original, non-modelled data. The lines under the probability distributions indicate the modelled 68.2% probability ranges. The A values in the square brackets indicate the individual agreement values for each date (modelled versus non-modelled ranges) – a value ≥60% is satisfactory at about the 95% confidence level. Note: selected elements plotted, some titles and boundaries, and sites whose data have been excluded in analysis between Models 1 and 8, are left out to save space or are not labelled.

the transition (i.e. the Boundary) between the long-lived samples from Maroni *Tsaroukkas* Building 2 Room 1, Phases 9 and 8, to the short-lived sample from the same locus of Phase 9 lies at 1351–1292 Cal BC ($\mu\pm\sigma$ of 1324$\pm$27 Cal BC). This all suggests that LC IIC begins no later than around 1325 BC (and perhaps even a little earlier, ca. 1340 BC). The end of Maroni *Tsaroukkas* Buildings 1 and 2 in late LC IIC lie respectively 1220$\pm$33 Cal BC and 1222$\pm$31 Cal BC, consistent with an end of the phase around the traditional date of about 1200 BC (compare Manning et al. 2001; Manning 2006–2007). The limit for the end of the Apliki evidence (after the roof wood, basket samples and cereal samples) is 1127$\pm$104 Cal BC. The end of LC IIIA lies between here and the estimate from Alassa at 1050 Cal BC. Finally, it should be noted that some additional ProBA radiocarbon data from Hala Sultan Teke, provided by Peter Fischer, are listed in the SOM, Table S6 and Figure S5.

The approximate summary chronology resolved is set out in Table A2 (below, p. 521).

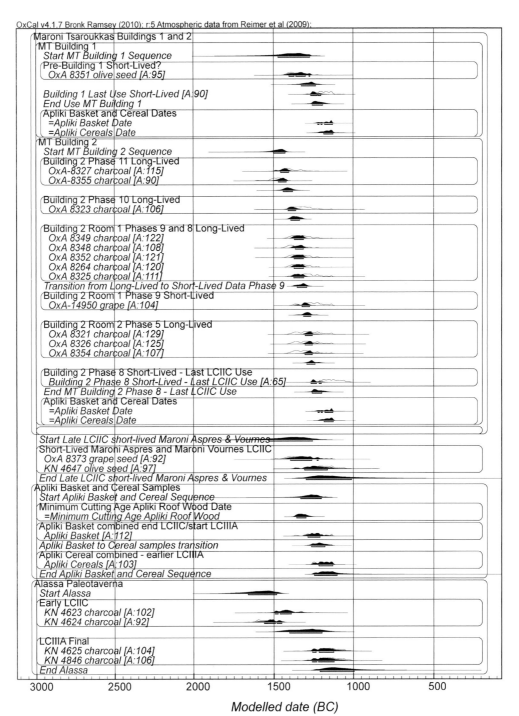

OxCal v4.1.7 Bronk Ramsey (2010); r:5 Atmospheric data from Reimer et al (2009);

Maroni Tsaroukkas Buildings 1 and 2

MT Building 1
  Start MT Building 1 Sequence
  Pre-Building 1 Short-Lived?
    OxA 8351 olive seed [A:95]

  Building 1 Last Use Short-Lived [A:90]
  End Use MT Building 1
  Apliki Basket and Cereal Dates
    =Apliki Basket Date
    =Apliki Cereals Date
MT Building 2
  Start MT Building 2 Sequence
  Building 2 Phase 11 Long-Lived
    OxA-8327 charcoal [A:115]
    OxA-8355 charcoal [A:90]

  Building 2 Phase 10 Long-Lived
    OxA 8323 charcoal [A:106]

  Building 2 Room 1 Phases 9 and 8 Long-Lived
    OxA 8349 charcoal [A:122]
    OxA 8348 charcoal [A:108]
    OxA 8352 charcoal [A:121]
    OxA 8264 charcoal [A:120]
    OxA 8325 charcoal [A:111]
  Transition from Long-Lived to Short-Lived Data Phase 9
  Building 2 Room 1 Phase 9 Short-Lived
    OxA-14950 grape [A:104]

  Building 2 Room 2 Phase 5 Long-Lived
    OxA 8321 charcoal [A:129]
    OxA 8326 charcoal [A:125]
    OxA 8354 charcoal [A:107]

  Building 2 Phase 8 Short-Lived - Last LCIIC Use
    Building 2 Phase 8 Short-Lived - Last LCIIC Use [A:65]
  End MT Building 2 Phase 8 - Last LCIIC Use
  Apliki Basket and Cereal Dates
    =Apliki Basket Date
    =Apliki Cereals Date

Start Late LCIIC short-lived Maroni Aspres & Vournes
Short-Lived Maroni Aspres and Maroni Vournes LCIIC
  OxA 8373 grape seed [A:92]
  KN 4647 olive seed [A:97]
End Late LCIIC short-lived Maroni Aspres & Vournes
Apliki Basket and Cereal Samples
  Start Apliki Basket and Cereal Sequence
Minimum Cutting Age Apliki Roof Wood Date
  =Minimum Cutting Age Apliki Roof Wood
Apliki Basket combined end LCIIC/start LCIIIA
  Apliki Basket [A:112]
Apliki Basket to Cereal samples transition
Apliki Cereal combined - earlier LCIIIA
  Apliki Cereals [A:103]
  End Apliki Basket and Cereal Sequence
Alassa Paleotaverna
  Start Alassa
Early LCIIC
  KN 4623 charcoal [A:102]
  KN 4624 charcoal [A:92]

LCIIIA Final
  KN 4625 charcoal [A:104]
  KN 4846 charcoal [A:106]
  End Alassa

| 3000 | 2500 | 2000 | 1500 | 1000 | 500 |

Modelled date (BC)

Figure A12. Modelled dating evidence and chronology from Model 8 for Cyprus during the later ProBA – LC IIC to IIIA. The solid histograms show the modelled ranges; the hollow histograms show the original, non-modelled data. The lines under the probability distributions indicate the modelled 68.2% probability ranges. The A values in the square brackets indicate the individual agreement values for each date (modelled versus non-modelled ranges) – a value ≥60% is satisfactory at about the 95% confidence level. Note: selected elements plotted, some titles and boundaries, and sites whose data have been excluded in analysis between Models 1 and 8, are left out to save space. The Apliki Basket and Cereal samples appear twice in the Maroni *Tsaroukkas* analyses, as they are each employed as a *terminus ante quem* for the last use of Maroni *Tsaroukkas* Buildings 1 and 2 (see Manning et al. 2001; Manning 2006–2007).

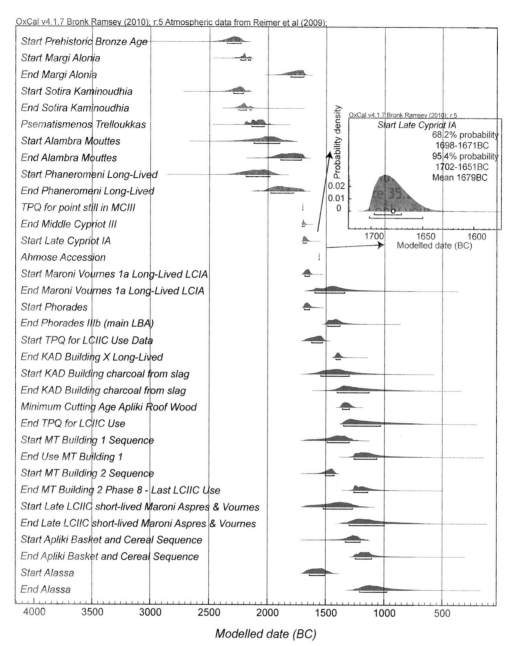

Figure A13. Model 8_TPQ/TAQ, which calculates (in contrast to previous models) the dates for the End of MC III period and the Start of LC IA period through the addition of the *terminus post quem* and the *terminus ante quem* assumptions discussed in the text for MC III and LC IA. The resultant modelled calendar date range of the End of MC III and the Start of LCIA are shown. The inset graph shows this Start Boundary for the LC IA period in more detail.

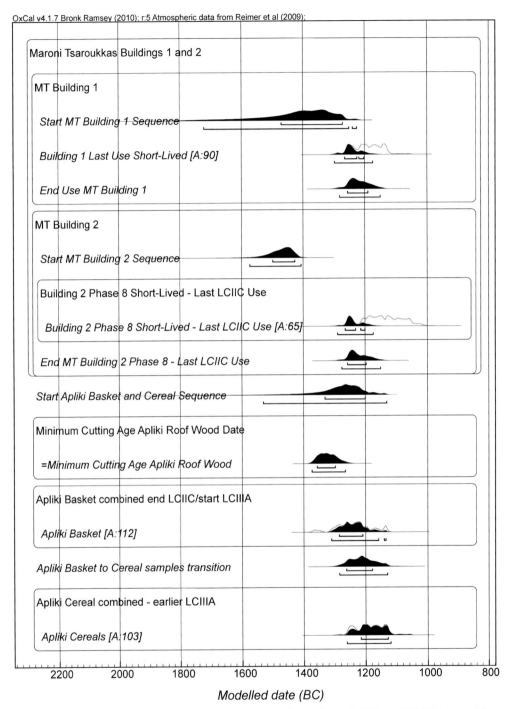

Figure A14. Details selected from Figure A12 to show the LC IIC to LC IIIA transition data and analysis from Maroni and Apliki.

TABLE A1A. *See joint table caption below*

Modelled Date Ranges BC within which the following occur (beginning and ending constraints) μ±σ unless stated otherwise

Model	Amodel	Aoverall	Late Epipal Start	Late Epipal End	Cypro-PPNA Start	Cypro-PPNA End	EAN (overall) Start	Shillourkm Start	Shillourkm End = ca. EAN End	Khirokitia site = LAN Start	Khirokitia site End	LAN (overall) End	Data Used
1	2.5	4.3	11416±345	9170±149	8804±49	8728±37	8620±77	8427±66	6912±358	6902±213	5293±104	5128±75	327
1		*68.2% ranges*	*11710–10990*	*9331–9055*	*8821–8756*	*8768–8708*	*8719–8559*	*8478–8345*	*7289–6845*	*7030–6657*	*5400–5188*	*5212–5068*	
2A	20.5	29.1	11425±342	9170±149	8804±49	8728±37	8616±78	8427±66	6914±355	6904±212	5302±99	5153±75	309
2B	32.7	46.4	11391±332	9170±148	8803±49	8728±37	8621±77	8428±66	6907±380	6901±213	5235±149	4824±163	308
3	24.6	33.8	11397±330	9170±149	8804±49	8728±37	8618±77	8428±66	6904±378	6898±211	5239±146	4848±167	306
4	35.8	47.9	11423±345	9169±148	8804±49	8728±38	8617±78	8428±66	6904±380	6900±212	5236±149	4820±180	303
5	41.9	54.9	11424±346	9170±149	8804±49	8728±38	8617±78	8429±66	6896±380	6897±209	5237±148	4824±179	300
6	50.8	67.9	11447±348	9168±149	8804±49	8728±37	8617±78	8429±66	6900±382	6826±179	5233±148	4820±179	298
7	50.1	66.6	11412±343	9170±148	8804±49	8728±37	8617±77	8428±66	6900±380	6827±179	5234±148	4824±179	296
8	62.6	80.3	11402±337	9170±149	8804±49	8728±38	8614±80	8400±64	6904±378	6828±181	5234±148	4833±176	292
8		*68.2% ranges*	*11694–10991*	*9332–9057*	*8821–8756*	*8768–8708*	*8717–8552*	*8436–8316*	*7289–6843*	*6936–6617*	*5414–5126*	*5030–4655*	

TABLE A1B.

Model	Amodel	Aoverall	Modelled Date Ranges BC within Which the following occur (beginning and ending constraints) μ±σ unless otherwise stated											
			Ceram Neo Start	Ceram Neo End	Early Chalco Start	Middle Chalco End	Late Chalco Start	Late Chalco End	PreBA Start	PreBA End	ProtoHist BA Start	Alassa End	Data Used
1	2.5	4.3	5078±78	4024±64	3998±66	2696±49	2655±49	2476±53	2394±58	1880±49	1844±47	1061±131	327
1		68.2% ranges	5166–5021	4106–3971	4081–3906	2750–2648	2691–2596	2547–2443	2438–2319	1927–1827	1889–1793	1209–999	
2A	20.5	29.1	5100±76	3987±68	3953±72	2701±49	2656±48	2504±54	2401±66	1885±52	1846±49	1061±131	309
2B	32.7	46.4	4557±111	4064±73	3957±84	2708±46	2669±45	2504±54	2406±67	1860±54	1816±50	1061±130	308
3	24.6	33.8	4570±112	4044±74	3946±82	2710±52	2662±50	2502±54	2401±65	1884±52	1845±49	1056±133	306
4	35.8	47.9	4500±100	4082±74	3968±87	2710±51	2661±50	2504±53	2408±65	1860±53	1815±50	1061±130	303
5	41.9	54.9	4503±99	4080±72	3968±86	2712±51	2666±50	2481±67	2301±66	1886±64	1831±56	1067±127	300
6	50.8	67.9	4503±102	4081±73	3968±87	2713±51	2667±50	2479±69	2284±59	1877±59	1826±53	1061±131	298
7	50.1	66.6	4504±101	4081±73	3986±86	2696±56	2640±55	2483±65	2286±59	1874±56	1825±52	1058±132	296
8	62.6	80.3	4524±109	4094±70	3971±88	2671±62	2603±58	2482±59	2287±59	1874±55	1825±51	1059±132	292
8		68.2% ranges	4588–4392	4178–4039	4064–3880	2739–2612	2658–2513	2554–2448	2327–2221	1922–1816	1871–1771	1209–997	
8_TPQ/										End MC III	Start LC IA		
TAQ	75.1	69.4								1691±10	1679±14		94
		68.2% ranges								1705–1686	1698–1671		
		95.4% ranges								1705–1669	1702–1651		

The start Boundaries (boundary before, i.e. *terminus post quem*) and end Boundaries (boundary after, i.e. a *terminus ante quem*) for the main macro-archaeological phases for the data listed in Appendix 1 (and as shown in schematic form in Figures A3A and A3B) are given from a succession of OxCal models with IntCal09: see text for summaries of each model and discussion of dates included and excluded. For the initial Model 1 and final Model 8, the most likely 68.2% modelled calendar age ranges are given (in italics). For all models the mean (μ) of the modeled distribution is given plus or minus the Standard Deviation (±σ). The start and end Boundaries for two key sites are also given: *Shillourokambos* (representing more or less the EAN, or Cypro-PPNB period) and Khirokitia (representing the LAN). Typical results shown; each run of such a model produces slightly different outcomes.

TABLE A2.

Archaeological Periods	Start after or by Cal BC	End before or by Cal BC
Late Epipalaeolithic (Akrotiri Phase)	11000	(9100–) 9000
Cypro-PPNA	(9000–) 8900	8600 (–8500)
Early Aceramic Neolithic (EAN) (or Cypro-PPNB)	(8500–) 8400	(6900–) 6800
Late Aceramic Neolithic (LAN) (or Khirokitia Phase)	6800	5200 (–5000?)
Ceramic Neolithic	(?5000–) 4600	4100/4000
Early Chalcolithic	4000/3900	3600/3400
Middle Chalcolithic	3600/3400	2700
Late Chalcolithic	2700/2600	2500/2400
Prehistoric Bronze Age (Philia phase-MC II)	2400	1690/1650
Protohistoric Bronze Age	1680/1650	1100/1050
Middle Cypriot (MC) III	1750 (1700)	1680/1650
Late Cypriot (LC) I (A-B)	1680/1650	≈1450 (no 14C)
Late Cypriot IIC	1340/1325	1200

Summary chronology for Cyprus based on the models analysed in this study and the commentary in the text above. Dates are rounded to nearest 100 years down to 2400 Cal BC and nearest 10 years thereafter. The dates for the start of MC III are based on a minimum date of ca. 1700 Cal BC (after Merrillees 2002) and follow his estimate of a likely start date of about 1750 BC (Merrillees 1992; 2002). The dates for the end of the Initial Aceramic Neolithic (Cypro-PPNA) and for the start of the Early Aceramic Neolithic (Cypro-PPNB) stated above come from SOM Figure 4c–d, *revising* the Model 1–8 outcomes for the very early period in light of the Ayios Tychonas *Klimonas* radiocarbon dates (only published after this Appendix was finalised and Models 1–8 were run). The original dates (from Models 1–8) without the *Klimonas* evidence were: End of Initial Aceramic Neolithic/Cypro-PPNA 8600 (–8500) Cal BC and Start of EAN/Cypro-PPNB (8500–) 8400 Cal BC. Since the *Klimonas* finds are not EAN, and if some of the site's older radiocarbon dates on bone or teeth are representative ages and not too recent, then these new data seem to indicate that the Initial Aceramic Neolithic/Cypro-PPNA continued into the period ca. 8600–8350 Cal BC, with the EAN following. See SOM Figure S4 Postscript for additional data and disscussion.

Sub-Appendix 1: Radiocarbon dates from Cyprus employed in this study (for non-modelled calibrated ranges for most of these dates, see Tables S2 and S4 in the SOM) (for references cited, see References to main text)

Period/Site Name	ID	Material (where known)	Date (14C years) BP	Error 1SD	Period/Phase	References
Late Epipalaeolithic						
Aetokremnos	AA79920	bone (sus)-apatite	8588	50		Vigne et al. 2009: 16136, table 1
	AA79921	bone (sus)-apatite	9055	52		ditto
	AA79922	bone (sus)-apatite	9842	54		
	AA79923	bone (sus)-degraded collagen	10045	69		
	Beta 41405	charcoal	10190	230	2A	Simmons 1999: 196–97, table 8–1
	Beta 41000/ETH–7188	charcoal	10420	85	2A	ditto
	Beta 41407	charcoal	10480	300	2A	
	Beta 41406/ETH–7331	charcoal	10485	80	2A	
	Beta 41408/ETH–7332	charcoal	10575	80	2A	
	Beta 41002/ETH–7189	charcoal	10770	90	2A (lower)	
	Beta 40655	charcoal	10840	270	2A (lower)	
	Beta 40380	charcoal	11720	240	2A	
	OxA–15989	charcoal	10185	50	2	Simmons and Mandel 2007: 479
Cypro-PPNA						
Asprokremnos	Hd–27170/ETH 35142	charcoal	9465	46		Manning et al. 2010a: 700, table 1
	Hd–27180/ETH–35155	charcoal	9477	43		ditto
	Hd–27217/ETH–35157	charcoal	9525	49		
	Hd–27227/ETH–35183	charcoal	9452	25		
	Hd–27228/ETH 35170	charcoal	9432	49		
	Hd–27242/ETH–35158	charcoal	9497	46		
Early Aceramic Neolithic						
Mylouthkia 1 (A)	OxA–7460	barley	9315	60	Period 1A	Peltenburg et al. 2003: 83, table 11.1
	AA–33128	grain	9235	70	1A	ditto
	AA–33129	grain	9110	70	1A	

Site	Lab code	Material	BP	±	Phase	Reference
Mylouthkia (1B)	OxA-7461	pistacia	8185	55	1B	Peltenburg et al. 2003: 83, table 11.1
	AA-33130	Lolium sp.	8025	65	1B	ditto
Shillourkambos Early/A	Lyon 290		9310	80		Guilaine et al. 2011: 579–580
	Lyon 3091		9225	45		ditto
	Lyon 2284		9220	50		
	Lyon 572		9205	75		
	Lyon 1447		9180	55		
	Lyon 3038		9145	45		
	Lyon 3039		9140	45		
	Lyon 3043		9115	50		
	Lyon 573		9110	90		
	Lyon 3042		9090	45		
	Lyon 3044		9080	50		
	Lyon 931		8860	90		
Akanthou (Tatlisu)	OxA-13996	seeds	8820	38		Higham et al. 2007: S34
Nissi Beach	GrA-36019	shell (Patella)	8940	40		Ammerman et al. 2008: 14, fig. 6
	OxA-X-2232–27	shell (Patella)	8522	39		ditto
Shillourkambos Early/B+C	Lyon 2285		8940	50		Guilaine et al. 2011: 580–581
	Lyon 574		8930	75		ditto
	GifA 95030		8870	90		
	Lyon 2286		8845	45		
	Lyon 5		8825	100		
	Lyon 3047		8800	45		
	Lyon 3085		8800	50		
	Lyon 289		8760	80		
	Lyon 2283		8760	60		
	Lyon 11634		8740	125		
	Lyon 1261		8735	75		
	Lyon 6		8725	100		
	Lyon 929		8700	70		
	Lyon 930		8670	80		
	Lyon 1262		8670	80		
	Lyon 291		8655	65		

(continued)

SUB-APPENDIX 1. (continued)

Period/Site Name	ID	Material (where known)	Date (14C years) BP	Error 1SD	Period/Phase	References
	PA (????)		8620	200		NB: ID not known/stated – no. 29, p. 580
	PA 1555		8435	120		
Shillourokambos Middle	GIF A-95034		8390	70		Guilaine et al. 2011: 581
	GIF A-95033		8340	100		ditto
	GIF A-95032		8230	90		
Shillourokambos Late	Lyon-292		8125	70		Guilaine et al. 2011: 581
Ais Yorkis	DRI 3441	bone (bos)	7867	106		Simmons 2003b: 3, table 1
	DRI 3442	bones (sus)	7540	169		ditto
	DRI 3443	bone (dama)	7658	105		
	CAMS 94861	bone (bos)	8290	35		Simmons 2010 (in press), table 1
	Beta-183649	charred material	8480	40		ditto
	Beta-183650	charred material	8600	40		
	Beta-183651	charred material	8540	40		
	Beta-203857	charcoal	8530	40		
	Beta-213412	charred seeds	8510	50		
	Beta-213413	charred	6840	40		
	Beta-213414	charred material	8590	50		
	Beta-213415	charred seeds	8450	60		
	Beta-213417	charred material	8720	60		
	Beta-220596	charred material	8620	40		
	Beta-220598	organic sediment	8190	60		
	Beta-243928	charcoal	8390	50		
	Beta-256039	charred einkorn seed	8470	50		
	Beta-256040	charred barley seed	8440	60		
	Beta-256041	charred einkorn seed	8430	50		
Kissonerga *Mosphilia*	AA-10495	charcoal	7255	60	Period 1a	Peltenburg et al. 1998: 12, table 2.3
Kalavasos *Tenta*	P-2972	charcoal	9240	130	Period 5	Todd 2001: 100, table 1
	P-2976	charcoal	8870	500	Period 3/later	ditto

Lab no.	Material	BP	±	Period	Reference
P-2785	charcoal	8720	400	Period 5/4	
P-2554	charcoal	8480	110	Period 2	
P-2548	charcoal	8350	200	Period 3/later	
P-2974	charcoal	8020	90	Period 2	
P-2973	charcoal	8010	360	Period 2	
P-2782	charcoal	7600	100	Period 4/3	
P-2555	charcoal	7430	90	Period 4	
P-2978	charcoal	7400	260	Period 4	
P-278	charcoal	7380	100	Period 4/3	
P-2552	charcoal	7250	100	Period 3	
P-2550	charcoal	7180	90	Period 3/later	
P-2551	charcoal	7140	90	Period 3/later	
P-2783	charcoal	7130	410	Period 4	
P-2779	charcoal	7120	90	Period 4	
P-2553	charcoal	7110	90	Period 3	
P-2975	charcoal	6970	310	Period ?	
P-2977	charcoal	6580	290	Period 2	
P-2781	charcoal	6300	80	Period 4/3	
P-2549	charcoal	5630	260	Period 5/4	
UCLA-307	marine shell (~400 14c yrs)	7950	250		Peltenburg et al. 2001a: 40, fig. 3

Akrotiri Vounarouthkia ton Lamion East – Site 23
Late Aceramic Neolithic

Lab no.	BP	±	Reference
Dhali Agridhi			
P-2775	7990	80	*Radiocarbon* 23 (1981): 228–229
P-2768	7400	60	ditto
GX 2847A	??	??	
GX-2848A	7290	465	
Khirokitia Vouni			
St-415	7655	160	Todd 1987: 175, table 5
St-414	7515	125	Todd 1987: 175, table 5
St-416	7445	160	ditto
BM-852	7294	78	
BM-853	7451	81	
BM-854	7442	61	

(continued)

SUB-APPENDIX 1. (*continued*)

Period/Site Name	ID	Material (where known)	Date (14C years) BP	Error 1SD	Period/Phase	References
	BM-855		7308	74		
	Ly 3716	charcoal	7000	150	Niveau C	Le Brun 1989a:17
	Ly 4787	bone	7070	610	Niveau C	Le Brun 1994: 27–28
	Ly 3718	charcoal	7930	320	Niveau C	Le Brun 1989a:17
	Ly 4786	bone	6590	260	Niveau D	Le Brun 1994: 27–28
	Ly 4306	charcoal	6310	170	Niveau F	Le Brun 1989a:17
	Ly 4308	charcoal	7470	140	Niveau F	ditto
	Ly 4307	charcoal	7930	130	Niveau F	
	Ly 4785	bone	8850	650	Niveau F	Le Brun 1994: 27–28
	Ly 4309	charcoal	6230	160	Niveau G	Le Brun 1989a:17
	Ly 3717	charcoal	7700	150	Niv. III/west	ditto
	Ly 3719	charcoal	7540	180	Niv. III/west	
Cape Andreas *Kastros*	MC 803	charcoal	6140	200	Niveau V	Le Brun 1981:71, table 36
	MC 807	charcoal	7450	120	Niveau V	ditto
	MC 805	charcoal	7775	125	Niveau VI	
	Unknown A		6760	140		Held 1992b: 166
	Unknown B		6275	105		ditto
Kholetria *Ortos*	Beta-56889	bone	6450	230		Clarke 2007: 17, fig. 2.2
Kalavasos *Vasiliko*	OxA-805	6330	6330	100		Todd 2004: 106
Ceramic Neolithic						
Pigi *Ayios Andronikos*	OxA-20926	animal bone	4127	31	early	Ammerman et al. 2009: 27
Ayios Epiktitos *Vrysi*	BM-847	charcoal	5389	53	early	Clarke 2007: 18, fig. 2.3
	BM-846	charcoal	5372	92	early	ditto
	BM-845	charcoal	5360	57	early–middle	
	Birm-182	charcoal	5825	145	middle	
	Birm-337	charcoal	5740	140	middle	
	GU-522	charcoal	5420	80	middle	
	BM-843	charcoal	5355	67	middle	
	GU-523	charcoal	5340	95	middle	
	BM-848	charcoal	5330	57	middle	
	BM-844	charcoal	5275	47	middle	
	GU-524	charcoal	5255	120	middle	

Site	Lab code	Material	BP	±	Phase/Period	Reference
	GU-1459	charcoal	5210	85	middle	
	BM-1908R	charcoal	5360	110	middle	
	GU-521	charcoal	3105	130	middle	
	BM-849	charcoal	5224	78	middle–late	
	BM-1907R	charcoal	5290	100	late	
	MB-1906R	charcoal	5360	120	late	
Dhali *Agridhi*	GX-2847A	charred bone	6415	310		Clarke 2007: 18, fig. 2.3
	P-2769	charred bone	5700	100		Lehavy 1989: 216, table 6; Clarke
Kandou *Kofovounos*	OxA-6175	charcoal	6270	60	Phase I	Mantzourani 2009: 241, fig. 1
	OxA-6174	charcoal	5445	60	Phase III	ditto
	OxA-6276	bone	3540	55	Phase III	
	LTL 824A	charcoal	5358	60	Phase IV	
	LTL 827A	charcoal	5406	60	Phase IV	
	LTL 829A	seed	5322	40	Phase III	
	LTL 831A	charcoal, seed	5429	50	Phase III	
	LTL 832A	charcoal	5407	60	Phase III	
	LTL 1053A	charcoal	5135	60	Phase IV	
Sotira *Teppes*	St-337	charcoal	5460	110	Phase 1	Clarke 2007: 18, fig. 2.3
	St-350	charcoal	5150	130	?	ditto
Philia *Drakos A*	Birm-72	carbon (hearth)	5720	100	Phase 3	Clarke 2007: 18, fig. 2.3
Kalavasos *Pamboules*	St-419	charcoal	5140	110		Clarke 2007: 18, fig. 2.3
Kalavasos *Kokkinoyia*	Wk-26434	pistachio charcoal	5349	30		Clarke, pers. comm. 12/09
	Wk-26435	olive branch	5488	43		Clarke, pers. comm. 12/09
Paralimni *Nissia*	OxA-11561	burned bone	5345	40		Flourentzos 2008: 95–96

Early–Middle Chalcolithic

Site	Lab code	Material	BP	±	Period	Reference
Kissonerga *Mylouthkia*	OxA-7464	charcoal	4885	45	Period 2	Peltenburg et al. 2003: 259, table 24.2
	BM-1475	charcoal	4815	60	Period 2	ditto
	BM-1539	charcoal	4790	80	Period 2	
	BM-1473	charcoal	4765	55	Period 2	
	BM-1540	charcoal	4740	50	Period 2	
	BM-1474	charcoal	4665	50	Period 2	
	BM-1476	charcoal	4650	50	Period 2	

(continued)

SUB–APPENDIX 1. (*continued*)

Period/Site Name	ID	Material (where known)	Date (14C years) BP	Error 1SD	Period/Phase	References
Kissonerga *Mylouthkia*	OxA-7463	*Pistacia*	4710	50	Period 3	Peltenburg et al. 2003: 259, table 24.2
	OxA-7462	*Pistacia*	4650	50	Period 3	ditto
Kalavasos *Ayious*	BM-1835R	charcoal	11,020	130	??	Todd and Croft 2004: 219, table 4
	BM-1832R	charcoal	5040	110		ditto
	BM-1834R	charcoal	5030	120	early phase	
	BM-1833R	charcoal	5000	170	early phase	
	BM-1836R	charcoal	4700	310	early phase	
Kalavasos *Tenta*	P-2780	carbon	5460	110		Clarke 2007: 21, fig. 2.4
Kissonerga *Mosphilia*	GU-3397	charcoal	5320	90	Period 2	Peltenburg et al. 1998: 12, table 2.3
	OxA-2965	Gramineae	5100	80	Period 2	ditto
	OxA-2964	charcoal	4860	80	Period 2	
	GU-2967	charcoal	5540	110	Period 3A	
	AA-10497	*Vitis Vinifera*	4605	55	3A	
	AA-10496	*Lens*	4285	60	3A?	
	GU-2357	charcoal	4020	110	3A/4	
	BM-2526	*Pinus*	4690	70	Period 3B	
	BM-2228	*Pinus, Olea*	4600	60	3B	
	OxA-2963	charcoal	4520	80	3B	
	BM-2568	*Pinus*	4490	50	3B	
	OxA-2962	*Lens*/Gramineae	4370	70	3B	
	OxA-2961	seed	4310	75	3B	
	OxA-2162	*Morus*	4300	80	3B	
	OxA-2161	*Morus*	4290	80	3B	
	GU-2968	charcoal	4240	100	3B	
	GU-2168	*Pinus*	4210	105	3B	
	GU-2426	*Morus*	3880	100	3B	
	GU-2536	*Pistacia* (similar to)	4170	80	Period 3/4	
Lemba *Lakkous*	BM-1543	charcoal	5000	260	Period 1	Peltenburg et al. 1985: 16, table 2
	BM-2280	charcoal	5710	100	Period 1	ditto
	HAR-6173	charcoal	4280	100	Period 1	
	BM-2278	charcoal	3930	100	Period 2	

Site / Sample	Lab code	Material	Date BP	±	Period	Reference
Politiko *Kokkinorotsos*	OZK-137	barley seed	4210	60		Webb et al. 2009: 192, table 1
	OZK-138	barley seed	4090	60		Webb et al. 2009: 200, fig. 11
	OZK-139	barley seed	4190	70		ditto
	OZK-140	barley seed	4220	60		
	OZK-141	wheat seed	4180	70		
	OZK-142	wheat seed	4210	60		
	OZK-143	cereal grain	4090	60		
	OZK-144	cereal grain	4180	70		
	OZK-145	cereal grain	4200	60		
	OZK-147	cereal grain	4260	60		
	OZK-148	olive pit	4170	60		
	WK-18983	charcoal	4151	38		
Late Chalcolithic						
Lemba *Lakkous*	BM-1353	charcoal	3890	50	Period 3	Peltenburg et al. 1985: 16, table 2
	BM-1354	charcoal	3970	45	Period 3	ditto
	BM-1541	charcoal	4000	45	Period 3	
	BM-1541A	charcoal	4050	50	Period 3	
	BM-1542	charcoal	4090	90	Period 3	
Kissonerga *Mosphilia*	GU-2966	*Pistacia*	5620	60	Period 4	Peltenburg et al. 1998: 13, table 2.3
	GU-2155	charcoal	4250	170	4	ditto
	GU-2158	*Pinus*	4220	75	4	
	OxA-2960	Gramineae	4220	70	4	
	BM-2279R	charcoal	4180	130	4	
	BM-2529	*Morus*	4160	50	4	
	BM-2527	*Morus*	4130	50	4	
	GU-2535	*Pistacia/Pinus*	4070	130	4	
	BM-2530	*Morus*	3960	80	4	
	GU-2157	*Morus*	3900	50	4	
Prehistoric Bronze Age						
Kalavasos–Panayia Church	P-2980	charcoal	4330	80	I–IV (MC)	Hurst and Lawn 1984: 214
Marki *Alonia*	Beta 50747	charcoal	3460	90	I–IV (MC)	Frankel and Webb 2006a: 37, table 3.3
	Beta 50746	charcoal	3480	80	E (EC III)	ditto
	OZA 334	seed	3550	50		

(continued)

SUB–APPENDIX 1. (*continued*)

Period/Site Name	ID	Material (where known)	Date (14C years) BP	Error 1SD	Period/Phase	References
	Wk 16043 4	seed	3597	39	C-1 (EC I–II)	
	OZA 279U	2 wheat seeds	3645	95	γ(Philia–EC I–II)	
	OZA 336	seed	3650	50	D-1 (EC I–II)	
	OZA 337	seed	3670	50	D-1 (EC I–II)	
	OZB 160	wheat seed	3675	118	γ(Philia–EC I–II)	
	OZA 342	seed	3700	40	D-1 (EC I–II)	
	OZA 339	seed	3720	50	D-1 (EC I–II)	
	OZA 345	seed	3730	50	H-1 (MC I)	
	OZA 340	seed	3740	40	F-1 (EC III)	
	OZB 159	wheat seed	3764	50	H-1 (MC I)	
	OZA 338	seed	3770	50	C (EC I–II)	
	OZA 344	seed	3770	50	C-1 (EC I–II)	
	Beta 138629	seed	3780	30	A-1 (Philia)	
	Beta 138630	seed	3780	30	A-1 (Philia)	
	Beta 100553	seed	3810	50	B (Philia)	
	OZB 163	wheat seed	3834	42	γ(Philia–EC I–II)	
	OZB 161	wheat seed	3888	42	γ(Philia–EC I–II)	
	OZB 162	wheat seed	3892	39	γ(Philia–EC I–II)	
Sotira *Kaminoudhia*	OxA 3038	charcoal	3890	90	Phase I	Swiny et al. 2003: 503–504
	OxA 3309	charcoal	3780	90	Phase I	
	OxA 3310	charcoal	3780	90	Phase II	
	OxA 3311	charcoal	3890	100	II	
	OxA 3312	charcoal	3690	100	II	
	OxA 3544	charcoal	3840	75	II	
	OxA 3545	charcoal	3860	75	II	
	OxA 3546	charcoal	3760	75	II	
	OxA 3547	charcoal	3860	80	II	Swiny et al. 2003: 505
	OxA 3548	charcoal	3800	75	II	

Site	Lab no.	BP	±	Material	Period	Reference
Alambra *Mouttes*	Beta 82995	3970	90	carbon		Coleman et al. 1996: 339, table 29
	Beta 82994	3610	60	carbon		ditto
	ETH 210	3500	120	ash		
	ETH 206	3440	140	ash		
Kissonerga *Mosphilia*	GU-2167	3990	50	*Morus*	Period 5 (Philia)	Peltenburg et al. 1998: 14, table 2.3
Psematismenos	OxA 14952	3709	35	charcoal		Manning and Sewell 2006: 68
Trelloukkas						
Episkopi *Phaneromeni*	P-2386	3720	70	charcoal		Fishman et al. 1977: 189
	P-2387	3620	60	charcoal		ditto
	P-2388	3520	70	charcoal		
Protohistoric Bronze Age						
Alassa *Paleotaverna*	KN 4623	3139	48	charcoal	early LC IIC	Manning et al. 2001:330–331, table 2, fig. 2
	KN 4624	3267	38	charcoal	early LC IIC	ditto
	KN 4625	2942	36	charcoal	LC IIIA final	
	KN 4846	2942	43	charcoal	LC IIIA final	
Kalavasos *Ayios Dhimitrios*	KN 4615	3243	31	charcoal (long-lived wood)	LC IIB/early IIC	Manning et al. 2001:330–331, table 2, fig. 2
	KN 4616	3252	33	charcoal (long-lived wood)	LC IIB/early IIC	ditto
	KN 4617	3294	33	charcoal (long-lived wood)	LC IIB/early IIC	
	KN 4618	3295	55	charcoal (long-lived wood)	LC IIB/early IIC	
	KN 4619	3249	26	charcoal (long-lived wood)	LC IIB/early IIC	
	KN 4620	3121	30	charcoal (long-lived wood)	LC IIB/early IIC	
	KN 4621	3172	43	charcoal (long-lived wood)	LC IIB/early IIC	
	KN 4622	3224	22	charcoal (long-lived wood)	LC IIB/early IIC	
	KN 4653	3162	37	charcoal (long-lived wood)	LC IIB/early IIC	
	KN 4654	3102	35	charcoal (long-lived wood)	LC IIB/early IIC	
	KN 4726	3064	38	charcoal (long-lived wood)	LC IIB/early IIC	
	KN 4727	3187	37	charcoal (long-lived wood)	LC IIB/early IIC	
	KN 4728	3206	25	charcoal (long-lived wood)	LC IIB/early IIC	
	KN 4729	3236	26	charcoal (long-lived wood)	LC IIB/early IIC	
	KN 4782	3227	23	charcoal (long-lived wood)	LC IIB/early IIC	

(continued)

SUB-APPENDIX 1. (continued)

Period/Site Name	ID	Material (where known)	Date (14C years) BP	Error 1SD	Period/Phase	References
	KN 4829	charcoal (long-lived wood)	3144	44	LC IIB/early IIC	Archaeometry 26 (1984) 18
	OxA 120	charcoal from slag	2860	150	LC IIC	(Weniger letter to SWM 29/11/95)
	KN 4651	charcoal	3269	26		
Apliki Karamallos	AA 33440	wood	2990	55	LC IIC/early IIIA	Manning and Kumiholm 2007: 334, table 53
	AA 33441	wood	2960	60	LC IIC/early IIIA	ditto
	AA 33442	wood	3015	55	LC IIC/early IIIA	
	AA 33443	wood	3050	55	LC IIC/early IIIA	
	AA 33444	wood	2955	55	LC IIC/early IIIA	
	AA 33445	charcoal (tree-ring)	3075	50	LC IIC	
	AA 33446	charcoal (tree-ring)	3050	55	LC IIC	
	AA 33447	charcoal (tree-ring)	3080	50	LC IIC	
	AA 33448	charcoal (tree-ring)	3065	70	LC IIC	
	AA 33449	charcoal (tree-ring)	3070	55	LC IIC	
	AA 33450	grain	2990	45	LC IIC/IIIA	
	AA 33451	grain	2960	45	LC IIC/IIIA	
	AA 33452	grain	2930	60	LC IIC/IIIA	
	AA 33452A	grain	2945	50	LC IIC/IIIA	
	AA 33453	grain	2960	50	LC IIC/IIIA	
	AA 33454	grain	2955	65	LC IIC/IIIA	
Maroni Aspres	OxA 8373	grape seed	3085	60	LC IIC	Manning et al. 2001:330–331, table 2, fig. 2
Maroni Vournes	KN 4647	olive seed	2969	44	LC IIC late	Manning et al. 2001:330–331, table 2, fig. 2
	KN 4642	charcoal	3494	38		(Weniger letter to SWM 29/11/95)
	Kn 4643	charcoal	3284	76		(Weniger letter to SWM 29/11/95)
Maroni Tsaroukkas B.1	OxA 8351	olive seed	3085	40	LC IIC early–mid	Manning et al. 2001:330–331, table 2, fig. 2, 334, fig. 5
	OxA 8372	charcoal	2890	60	LC IIC late	ditto
	OxA 8265	olive seed	2960	35	LC IIC late	
	OxA 8266	olive seed	2985	35	LC IIC late	
	OxA 8267	olive seed	2940	35	LC IIC late	
Maroni Tsaroukkas B.2	OxA 8353	charcoal	3310	40	LC I/IIA–B	
	OxA 8355	charcoal	3215	35	LC I/IIA–B	
	OxA 8327	charcoal	3130	45	LC I/IIA–B	

	Lab code	Material	BP	±	Phase	Reference
	OxA 8323	charcoal	3055	45	LC I/IIA–B	
	OxA 8349	charcoal	3060	40	LC IIC early	
	OxA 8348	charcoal	3090	40	LC IIC early	
	OxA 8352	charcoal	3065	40	LC IIC late	
	OxA 8324	olive seed	2930	40	LC IIC late	
	OxA 8321	charcoal	3020	45	LC IIC late	
	OxA 8326	charcoal	3025	40	LC IIC late	
	OxA 8354	charcoal	3040	40	collapse	
	OxA 8350	*prunus* seed	3080	40	post-use	
	OxA 8264	charcoal	3060	35	post-use	
	OxA 8325	charcoal	3030	40	post-use	
	OxA 8322	olive seed	2935	45	post-use	
	OxA-14950	grape seed	3005	34		unpublished
	OxA-14951	olive seed	3073	33		unpublished
Politiko *Phorades*	OxA 9972	charcoal	4160	90		Knapp and Kassianidou 2008: 139, fig. 6
	OxA 9932	charcoal	3585	60		ditto
	OxA 9817	charcoal	3402	34		
	OxA 9818	charcoal	3315	36		
	OxA-11789	charcoal	3266	28		
	OxA-8521	charcoal	3265	40		
	OxA-11791	charcoal	3247	33		
	OxA-11790	charcoal	3239	27		
	OxA-11821	charcoal	3134	33		
	OxA-7013	charcoal	2865	75		
	OxA-11788	charcoal	2483	25		

REFERENCES

Åström, P.

1964   Remains of ancient cloth from Cyprus. *Opuscula Atheniensia* 5: 111–114.

1966   *Excavations at Kalopsidha and Ayios Iakovos in Cyprus*. Studies in Mediterranean Archaeology 2. Lund, Sweden: P. Åström's Förlag.

1971   *Who's Who in Cypriote Archaeology*. Studies in Mediterranean Archaeology 23. Göteborg, Sweden: P. Åström's Förlag.

1972   The Swedish Cyprus Expedition IV: 1C. *The Late Cypriote Bronze Age. Architecture and Pottery*. Lund: Swedish Cyprus Expedition.

1979   A faience sceptre with a cartouche of Horemheb. In V. Karageorghis (ed.), *Studies Presented in Memory of Porphyrios Dikaios*, 46–48. Nicosia: Lion's Club.

1982   The bronzes of Hala Sultan Tekke. In J.D. Muhly, R. Maddin and V. Karageorghis (eds), *Early Metallurgy in Cyprus, 4000–500 BC*, 177–183. Nicosia: Pierides Foundation.

1985   An ashlar building at Hala Sultan Tekke. In V. Karageorghis (ed.), *Acts of the Second International Cyprological Congress*, 181–183. Nicosia: Society of Cypriot Studies.

1986   Hala Sultan Tekke – an international harbour town of the Late Cypriote Bronze Age. *Opuscula Atheniensia* 16: 7–17.

1987   Votive deposits in the Late Cypriote Bronze Age. In T. Linders and G.C. Nordquist (eds), *Gifts to the Gods*. Acta Universitatis Upsaliensis, Boreas 15: 177–199. Uppsala, Sweden: Uppsala University Press.

1988   A Cypriot cult scene. *Journal of Prehistoric Religion* 2: 5–11.

1989   *Katydhata. A Bronze Age Site in Cyprus*. Studies in Mediterranean Archaeology 86. Göteborg, Sweden: P. Åström's Förlag.

1992   Ivories from Hala Sultan Tekke. In J.L. Fitton (ed.), *Ivory in Greece and the Eastern Mediterranean, from the Bronze Age to the Hellenistic Period*. British Museum Occasional Paper 85: 101–104. London: British Museum Publications.

1996   Hala Sultan Tekke – a Late Cypriote harbour town. In P. Åström and E. Herscher (eds), *Late Bronze Age Settlements in Cyprus: Function and Relationship*. Studies in Mediterranean Archaeology and Literature, Pocket-book 126: 9–14. Jonsered, Sweden: P. Åström's Förlag.

1998   Continuity or discontinuity: indigenous and foreign elements in Cyprus around 1200 BCE. In S. Gitin, A. Mazar and E. Stern (eds), *Mediterranean Peoples in Transition: Thirteenth to Tenth Centuries BCE*, 80–86. Jerusalem: Israel Exploration Society.

2001a   (ed.) *The Chronology of Base-ring Ware and Bichrome Wheel-made Ware*. Konferenser 54. Stockholm: Kungl.

Vitterhets Historie och Antikvitets Akademien.

2001b Bichrome hand-made ware and Bichrome wheel-made ware on Cyprus. In P. Åström (ed.), *The Chronology of Base-ring Ware and Bichrome Wheel-made Ware*. Konferenser 54: 131–142. Stockholm: Kungl. Vitterhets Historie och Antikvitets Akademien.

Åström, P. (with collaborators)

1989 *Hala Sultan Tekke 9: Trenches 1972–1987*. Studies in Mediterranean Archaeology 45(9). Göteborg, Sweden: P. Åström's Förlag.

2001 *Hala Sultan Tekke 11: Trial Trenches at Dromolaxia-Vyzakia Adjacent to Areas 6 and 8*. Studies in Mediterranean Archaeology 45(11). Jonsered, Sweden: P. Åström's Förlag.

Åström, P., and D.S. Reese

1990 Triton shells in east Mediterranean cults. *Journal of Prehistoric Religion* 3–4: 5–14.

Åström, P., and G.R.H. Wright

1962 Two Bronze Age tombs at Dhenia in Cyprus. *Opuscula Atheniensia* 4: 225–276.

A Campo, A.L.

1994 *Anthropomorphic Representations in Prehistoric Cyprus: A Formal and Symbolic Analysis of Figurines, c. 3500–1800 BC*. Studies in Mediterranean Archaeology and Literature, Pocket-book 109. Jonsered, Sweden: P. Åström's Förlag.

Abbo, S., S. Lev-Yadun and A. Gopher

2010 Yield stability: an agronomic perspective on the origin of Near Eastern agriculture. *Vegetation History and Archaeobotany* 19: 143–150.

Adams, R., and D. Simmons

1996 Archaeobotanical remains. In D. Frankel and J.M. Webb, *Marki Alonia: An Early and Middle Bronze Age Town in Cyprus. Excavations 1990–1994*. Studies in Mediterranean Archaeology 123(1): 223–226. Jonsered, Sweden: P. Åström's Förlag.

Adovasio, J.M., G.F. Fry, J.D. Gunn and R.F. Maslowski

1975 Prehistoric and historic settlement patterns in western Cyprus (with a discussion of Cypriot Neolithic stone tool technology). *World Archaeology* 6: 339–364.

1978 Prehistoric and historic settlement patterns in western Cyprus: an overview. *Report of the Department of Antiquities, Cyprus*: 39–57.

Akkermans, P.M.M.G., and G.M. Schwartz

2003 *The Archaeology of Syria: From Complex Hunter-Gatherers to Early Urban Societies (ca. 16,000–300 BC)*. Cambridge: Cambridge University Press.

Albarella, U., K. Dobney and P. Rowley-Conwy

2006 The domestication of the pig (*Sus scrofa*): new challenges and approaches. In M.A. Zeder, E. Emshwiller, B.D. Smith and D.G. Bradley (eds), *Documenting Domestication: New Genetic and Archaeological Paradigms*, 209–227. Berkeley: University of California Press.

Alberti, G.

2005 The earliest contacts between southeastern Sicily and Cyprus in the Late Bronze Age. In R. Laffineur and E. Greco (eds), *Emporia: Aegeans in the Central and Eastern Mediterranean*. Aegaeum 25(1): 343–351. Liège, Belgium, Austin: Université de Liège, University of Texas at Austin.

2008 There is something Cypriot in the air. Some thoughts on the problem of the Base Ring pottery and other Cyprus-related items from (local) Middle Bronze Age contexts in Sicily. In A.P. McCarthy (ed.), *Island Dialogues: Cyprus in the Mediterranean Network*. University of Edinburgh Archaeology Occasional Paper 21: 130–153. Edinburgh: Dept of Archaeology. (online publication: http://www.shc.ed.ac.uk/archaeology/publications/occ_papers.htm/)

Alberti, M.E., and N. Parise

2005 Towards a unification of mass-units between the Aegean and the Levant. In R. Laffineur and E. Greco (eds), *Emporia: Aegeans in the Central and Eastern Mediterranean*. Aegaeum 25(1): 381–391. Liège, Belgium, Austin: Université de Liège, University of Texas at Austin.

Alcock, S.E.

1993 *Graecia Capta: The Landscapes of Roman Greece*. Cambridge: Cambridge University Press.

Alcover, J.A.

2008 The first Mallorcans: prehistoric colonization in the western Mediterranean. *Journal of World Prehistory* 21: 19–84.

Almagro-Gorbea, M., and F. Fontes

1997 The introduction of wheel-made pottery in the Iberian peninsula: Mycenaeans or pre-Orientalizing contacts? *Oxford Journal of Archaeology* 16: 345–361.

Aloupi, E., V. Perdikatsis and A. Lekka

2001   Assessment of the White Slip classification scheme based on physico-chemical aspects of the technique. In V. Karageorghis (ed.), *The White Slip Ware of Late Bronze Age Cyprus*. Österreichische Akademie der Wissenschaften, Denkschriften der Gesamtakademie, Band 20. Contributions to the Chronology of the Eastern Mediterranean 2: 15–26. Vienna: Österreichische Akademie der Wissenschaften.

Al-Radi, S.M.S.

1983   *Phlamoudhi-Vounari: A Sanctuary Site in Cyprus*. Studies in Mediterranean Archaeology 65. Göteborg, Sweden: P. Åström's Förlag.

Ames, K., and H. Maschner (eds)

1998   *People of the Northwest Coast: Their Archaeology and Prehisory*. London: Thames and Hudson.

Ammerman, A.J.

2010   The first argonauts: towards the study of the earliest seafaring in the Mediterranean. In A. Anderson, J.H. Barrett and K.V. Boyle (eds), *The Global Origins and Development of Seafaring*, 81–92. Cambridge: McDonald Institute for Archaeological Research.

Ammerman, A.J., and J.S. Noller

2005   New light on Aetokremnos. *World Archaeology* 37: 533–543.

Ammerman, A., and D. Sorabji

2005   Pigi *Agios Andronikos*: a new Neolithic site at Stroumpi (Pafos). *Report of the Department of Antiquities, Cyprus*: 31–40.

Ammerman, A.J., P. Flourentzos, C. McCartney, J. Noller and D. Sorabji

2006   Two new early sites on Cyprus. *Report of the Department of Antiquities, Cyprus*: 1–22.

Ammerman, A.J., P. Flourentzos, R. Gabrielli, C. McCartney, J.S. Noller, D. Peloso and D. Sorabji

2007   More on the new early sites on Cyprus. *Report of the Department of Antiquities, Cyprus*: 1–26.

Ammerman, A.J., P. Flourentzos, R. Gabrielli, T. Higham, C. McCartney and T. Turnbull

2008   Third report on early sites on Cyprus. *Report of the Department of Antiquities, Cyprus*: 1–32.

Ammerman, A., P. Flourentzos and J.S. Noller

2009   Excavations at the site of Pigi *Agios Andronikos* in Stroumpi (Pafos). *Report of the Department of Antiquities, Cyprus*: 17–38.

Ammerman, A.J., D. Howitt-Marshall, J. Benjamin, and T. Turnbull

2011   Underwater investigations at the early sites of Aspros and Nissi Beach on Cyprus. In J. Benjamin, C. Bonsall, C. Pickard and A. Fischer (eds), *Submerged Prehistory*, 263–271. Oxford: Oxbow.

Anderson, A.

2004   Islands of ambivalence. In S.M. Fitzpatrick (ed.), *Voyages of Discovery: The Archaeology of Islands*, 251–273. New York: Praeger.

Anderson, A., J. Barrett and K. Boyle (eds)

2010   *The Global Origins and Development of Seafaring*. Cambridge: McDonald Institute for Archaeological Research.

Anderson, B.

1991   *Imagined Communities: Reflections on the Origin and Spread of Nationalism*. 2nd edition. London: Verso.

Angel, J.L.

1953   The human remains from Khirokitia. Appendix II, in P. Dikaios, *Khirokitia*. Monograph, Department of Antiquities, Government of Cyprus 1: 416–430. Oxford: Oxford University Press.

1966   Porotic hyperostosis, anemias, malarias, and marshes in the prehistoric eastern Mediterranean. *Science* 153/3737: 760–763.

Anthony, D.W.

1990   Migration in archaeology: the baby and the bathwater. *American Anthropologist* 92: 895–914.

Antoniadou, S.

2004   The Impact of Trade on the Society of Cyprus during the Late Bronze Age: Settlements, Artefacts and Social Change. Unpublished PhD thesis, Department of Archaeology, University of Edinburgh.

2005   The impact of trade on Late Cypriot society: a contextual study of imports from Enkomi. In J. Clarke (ed.), *Archaeological Perspectives on the Transmission and Transformation of Culture in the Eastern Mediterranean*. Levant Supplementary Series 2: 66–77. Oxford: Oxbow.

2007   Common materials, different meanings: changes in Late Cypriot society. In S. Antoniadou and A. Pace (eds), *Mediterranean Crossroads*, 483–508. Athens, Oxford: Pierides Foundation, Oxbow.

Aravantinos, V.L.

1991   Agricultural production and subsistence economy in Cyprus during the Late

Cypriot II period. In V. Karageorghis (ed.), *Proceedings of an International Symposium: The Civilizations of the Aegean and Their Diffusion in Cyprus and the Eastern Mediterranean, 2000–600 BC*, 57–65. Larnaca: Pierides Foundation.

Arensberg, C.M.

1954   The community study method. *American Journal of Sociology* 60: 109–127.

Arimura, M.

2007   The lithic industry of early PPNB layers at Tell Ain el-Kerkh, northwestern Syria. In L. Astruc, D. Binder and F. Briois (eds), *Systèmes techniques et communautés du Néolithique précéramique au Proche-Orient*, 137–152. Antibes: Éditions APDCA.

Arnold, D.E.

1985   *Ceramic Theory and Cultural Process*. Cambridge: Cambridge University Press.

Artzy, M.

1985   Supply and demand: a study of second millennium Cypriote pottery in the Levant. In A.B. Knapp and T. Stech (eds), *Prehistoric Production and Exchange: The Aegean and East Mediterranean*. UCLA Institute of Archaeology Monograph 25: 93–99. Los Angeles: UCLA Institute of Archaeology.

1997   Nomads of the sea. In S. Swiny, R. Hohlfelder and H.W. Swiny (eds), *Res Maritimae: Cyprus and the Eastern Mediterranean from Prehistory through Late Antiquity*. Cyprus American Archaeological Research Institute Monograph 1: 1–16. Atlanta, Georgia: Scholars Press.

1998   Routes, trade, boats and 'nomads of the sea'. In S. Gitin, A. Mazar and E. Stern (eds), *Mediterranean Peoples in Transition: Thirteenth to Tenth Centuries BCE*, 439–448. Jerusalem: Israel Exploration Society.

2002   The Aegean, Cyprus, the Levant and Bichrome Ware: eastern Mediterranean Middle Bronze Age koine? In E.D. Oren and S. Ahituv (eds), *Aharon Kempinski Memorial Volume: Studies in Archaeology and Related Disciplines*. Ben Gurion University, Beer-Sheva 15: 1–20. Beersheva: Ben-Gurion University of Negev Press.

2003   Mariners and their boats at the end of the Late Bronze Age and the beginning of the Iron Age in the eastern Mediterranean. *Tel Aviv* 30: 232–246.

Artzy, M., I. Perlman and F. Asaro

1981   Cypriote pottery imports at Ras Shamra. *Israel Exploration Journal* 31: 37–47.

Ashmore, W.

2003   Decisions and dispositions: socializing spatial archaeology. *American Anthropologist* 104: 1172–1183.

Astruc, L.

1994   L'outillage en pierre non-taillée et les petits objets. In A. Le Brun, *Fouilles récent a Khirokitia (Chypre). 1988–1991*, 215–289. Paris: ADPF.

2004   *L'Outillage Lithique Taillé de Khirokitia*. CRA Monographies 25. Paris: CNRS Editions.

Aupert, P., and M.-C. Hellman (eds)

1984   *Amathonte I. Testimonia I. Auteurs anciens, monnayage, voyageurs, fouilles, origine, géographie*. Recherche sur les Civilisations, Memoire 33. Paris: ADPF.

Aurenche, O., P. Galet, E. Régagnon-Caroline and J. Évin

2001   Proto-Neolithic and Neolithic cultures in the Middle East – the birth of agriculture, livestock raising, and ceramics: a calibrated 14C chronology 12,500–5500 BC. In J. Bruins, I. Carmi and E. Boaretto (eds), *Near East: Chronology, Archaeology and Environment*. Radiocarbon 43(3): 1191–1202.

Averett, E.W.

2002–2004   Drumming for the divine: a female tympanon player from Cyprus. *Muse* 36–38: 14–28.

Badre, L.

2003   Handmade Burnished Ware and contemporary imported pottery from Tell Kazel. In N.C. Stampolidis and V. Karageorghis (eds), *Ploes... Sea Routes...: Interconnections in the Mediterranean, 16th–6th c. BC*, 83–99. Athens: University of Crete, Leventis Foundation.

Bailey, D.W.

1994   Reading prehistoric figurines as individuals. *World Archaeology* 25: 321–331.

Bailey, G.

2004   World prehistory from the margins: The role of coastlines in human evolution. *Journal of Interdisciplinary Studies in History and Archaeology* 1(1): 39–50.

Bailey, G., and N. Milner

2002   Coastal hunter-gatherers and social evolution: marginal or central? *Before Farming* 3–4(1): 129–150.

Bailey, G.N., and J. Parkington (eds)
1988 *The Archaeology of Prehistoric Coastlines.* Cambridge: Cambridge University Press.

Baird, D.J.
1985 Survey in Peyia village territory, Paphos, 1983. *Report of the Department of Antiquities, Cyprus*: 340–349.
1987 (in E.J. Peltenburg) Survey in the Stavros tis Psokas 1985. *Report of the Department of Antiquities, Cyprus*: 15–16.
2005 The history of settlement and social landscapes in the Early Holocene in the Çatalhöyük area. In I. Hodder (ed.), *Çatalhöyük Perspectives: Themes from the 1995–1999 Seasons*, 55–74. Cambridge: McDonald Institute for Archaeological Research, British Institute of Archaeology at Ankara.

Balthazar, J.W.
1990 *Copper and Bronze Working in Early through Middle Bronze Age Cyprus.* Studies in Mediterranean Archaeology and Literature, Pocket-book 84. Göteborg, Sweden: P. Åström's Förlag.

Barako, T.J.
2000 The Philistine settlement as mercantile phenomenon? *American Journal of Archaeology* 104: 510–530.
2003 The changing perception of the Sea Peoples phenomenon: migration, invasion or cultural diffusion? In N.C. Stampolidis and V. Karageorghis (eds), *Ploes… Sea Routes…: Interconnections in the Mediterranean, 16th–6th c. BC*, 163–172. Athens: University of Crete, Leventis Foundation.

Barber, E.J.W.
1991 *Prehistoric Textiles.* Princeton: Princeton University Press.

Barkai, R., and A. Gopher
1999 The last Neolithic flint industry: a study of the technology, typology and social implications of the lithic assemblage from Nahal Zehora I, a Wadi Raba (Pottery Neolithic) site in the Menashe Hills, Israel. *Journal of the Israel Prehistoric Society* 29: 41–122.

Barker, G.
2005 Agriculture, pastoralism, and Mediterranean landscapes in prehistory. In E. Blake and A.B. Knapp (eds), *The Archaeology of Mediterranean Prehistory*, 46–76. Oxford: Blackwell.

Barlow, J.A.
1985 Middle Cypriote settlement evidence: a perspective on the chronological foundations. *Report of the Department of Antiquities, Cyprus*: 47–54.

Barlow, J., D. Bolger and B. Kling (eds)
1991 *Cypriot Ceramics: Reading the Prehistoric Record.* University Museum Monograph 74. Philadelphia: University Museum, University of Pennsylvania.

Barrett, J.C.
1991 Towards an archaeology of ritual. In P. Garwood, D. Jennings, R. Skeates and J. Toms (eds), *Sacred and Profane.* Oxford University Committee for Archaeology Monograph 32: 1–9. Oxford: Oxbow.

Bar-Yosef, O.
2001 The world around Cyprus: from Epipaleolithic foragers to the collapse of the PPNB civilization. In S. Swiny (ed.), *The Earliest Prehistory of Cyprus: From Colonization to Exploitation.* Cyprus American Archaeological Research Institute Monograph 2: 129–151. Boston: American Schools of Oriental Research.
2003 Away from home: prehistoric colonizations, exchanges and diffusions in the Mediterranean basin. In B. Vandermeersch (ed.), *Échanges et diffusion dans la préhistoire méditerranéenne: actes du 121e Congrés national des sociétés historiques et scientifiques, section pré- et protohistoire, Nice 1996*, 71–81. Paris: Éditions de Comité des travaux historiques et scientifiques.
2007 The emergence of social complexity in the Neolithic of the Near East. In D.R. Edwards and C.T. McCollough (eds), *The Archaeology of Difference: Gender, Ethnicity, Class and the 'Other' in Antiquity. Studies in Honor of Eric M. Meyers.* Annual of the American Schools of Oriental Research 60/61: 19–39. Boston: American Schools of Oriental Research.

Bar-Yosef, O., and A. Belfer-Cohen
1989 The Levantine PPNB interaction sphere. In I. Hershkovitz (ed.), *People and Culture in Change.* British Archaeological Reports, International Series 508: 59–72. Oxford: British Archaeological Reports.

Baruch, U., and S. Bottema
1991 Palynological evidence for climatic changes in the Levant ca. 17,000–9,000 B.P. In O. Bar-Yosef and F.R. Valla (eds), *The Natufian Culture in the Levant.*

International Monographs in Prehistory, Archaeological Series 1: 11–20. Ann Arbor: International Monographs in Prehistory.

Baudou, E., and R. Engelmark

1983 The Tremithios Valley Project: a preliminary report for 1981–1982. *Report of the Department of Antiquities, Cyprus*: 1–8.

Baudou, E., R. Engelmark, K. Niklasson and B. Wennberg

1985 The Tremithios Valley Project. In T. Papadopoulos and S.A. Hadjistyllis (eds), *Acts of the Second International Congress of Cypriot Studies (Nicosia, 20–25 April 1982)*, 369–371. Nicosia: Society of Cypriot Studies.

Bauer, A.

1998 Cities of the sea: maritime trade and the origin of Philistine settlement in the Early Iron Age southern Levant. *Oxford Journal of Archaeology* 17: 149–168.

Baurain, C.

1984 *Chypre et la Mediterranée Orientale au Bronze Récent: Synthese Historique*. Études Chypriotes 4. Paris: E. de Boccard.

1989 Passé légendaire, archéologie et réalité historique: l'hellénisation de Chypre. *Annales: Économies, Sociétés, Civilisations* 44: 463–477.

Baxivani, E.

1997 From settlement to cemetery burial: Cyprus and Crete in the Early Bronze Age. In D. Christou (ed.), *Cyprus and the Aegean in Antiquity: From the Prehistoric Period to the 7th Century A.D.*, 57–69. Nicosia: Department of Antiquities, Cyprus.

Bayliss, A.

2007 Bayesian buildings: an introduction for the numerically challenged. *Vernacular Architecture* 38: 75–86.

2009 Rolling out revolution: using radiocarbon dating in archaeology. *Radiocarbon* 51: 123–147.

Bayliss, A., C. Bronk Ramsey, J. van der Plicht and A. Whittle

2007 Bradshaw and Bayes: towards a timetable for the Neolithic. *Cambridge Journal of Archaeology* 17: 1–28.

Bayliss, A., J. van der Plicht, C. Bronk Ramsey, G. McCormac, F. Healy and A. Whittle

2011 Towards generational time-scales: the quantitative interpretation of archaeological chronologies. In A. Whittle, F. Healy

and A. Bayliss, *Gathering Time: Dating the Early Neolithic Enclosures of Southern Britain and Ireland:* 17–59. Oxford: Oxbow.

Bear, L.M.

1963 *The Mineral Resources and Mining Industry of Cyprus*. Geological Survey of Cyprus, Bulletin 1. Nicosia: Geological Survey Dept, Ministry of Science and Industry.

Bednarik, R.G.

2003 Seafaring in the Pleistocene. *Cambridge Archaeological Journal* 13: 41–66.

Begemann, F., S. Schmitt-Strecker, E. Pernicka and F. Lo Schiavo

2001 Chemical composition and lead isotopy of copper and bronze from Nuragic Sardinia. *European Journal of Archaeology* 4: 43–85.

Begg, P.

1991 *Late Cypriot Terracotta Figurines: A Study in Context*. Studies in Mediterranean Archaeology and Literature, Pocket-book 101. Jonsered, Sweden: P. Åström's Förlag.

Beile-Bohn, M., C. Gerber, M. Morsch and K. Schmidt

1998 Neolithische Forschungen in Obermesopotamien. Gürcütepe and Göbekli Tepe. *Istanbuler Mitteilungen* 48: 5–78.

Belgiorno, M.R.

1984 Le statuette antropomorfe cipriote dell'Eta del Bronzo. I parte-gli idoli del Bronzo Antico III–Bronzo Medio I. *Studi Micenei ed Egeo-Anatolici* 25: 9–63.

1999 Preliminary report on Pyrgos excavations 1996, 1997. *Report of the Department of Antiquities, Cyprus*: 71–86.

2000 Project 'Pyrame' 1988–1999: archaeological, metallurgical and historical evidence at Pyrgos (Limassol). *Report of the Department of Antiquities, Cyprus*: 1–17.

2002 Rescue-excavated tombs of the Early and Middle Bronze Age from Pyrgos (Limassol). *Report of the Department of Antiquities, Cyprus*: 1–33.

2004 *Pyrgos-Mavroraki: Advanced Technology in Bronze Age Cyprus*. Nicosia: Theopress Ltd.

Bell, C.

2005 Wheels within wheels? A view of Mycenaean trade from the Levantine emporia. In R. Laffineur and E. Greco (eds), *Emporia: Aegeans in the Central and Eastern Mediterranean*. Aegaeum 25(1): 363–370. Liège, Belgium, Austin:

Université de Liège, University of Texas at Austin.

Ben-Shlomo, D., I. Shai, A. Zukerman and A.M. Maeir

2008   Cooking identities: Aegean-style cooking jugs and cultural interaction in Iron Age Philistia and neighboring regions. *American Journal of Archaeology* 112: 225–246.

Ben-Shlomo, D., A.C. Hill and Y. Garfinkel

2009   Feasting between the revolutions: evidence from Chalcolithic Tel Tsaf, Israel. *Journal of Mediterranean Archaeology* 22: 129–150.

Bender, B.

1998   *Stonehenge: Making Space*. Oxford: Berg.

Bender, B., S. Hamilton and C. Tilley

1997   Leskernick: stone worlds; alternative narrative; nested landscapes. *Proceedings of the Prehistoric Society* 63: 147–178.

Benson, J.L.

1972   *Bamboula at Kourion: The Necropolis and the Finds*. University Museum Monograph 12. Philadelphia: University of Pennsylvania Press.

Berdan, F.

1983   The reconstruction of ancient economies: perspectives from archaeology and ethnohistory. In S. Ortiz (ed.), *Economic Anthropology: Topics and Theories*. Monographs in Economic Anthropology 1: 83–95. Lanham, Maryland: University Press of America.

Bergoffen, C.

1991   Overland trade in Northern Sinai: the evidence of the Late Cypriot pottery. *Bulletin of the American Schools of Oriental Research* 284: 59–76.

2001a   The Proto White Slip and White Slip I pottery from Tell el-Ajjul. In V. Karageorghis (ed.), *The White Slip Ware of Late Bronze Age Cyprus*. Österreichische Akademie der Wissenschaften, Denkschriften der Gesamtakademie 20. Contributions to the Chronology of the Eastern Mediterranen 2: 145–155. Vienna: Österreichische Akademie der Wissenschaften.

2001b   The Base-ring pottery from Tell el-'Ajjul. In P. Åström (ed.), *The Chronology of Base-ring Ware and Bichrome Wheel-made Ware*. Konferenser 54: 31–50. Stockholm: Kungl. Vitterhets Historie och Antikvitets Akademien.

2005   *The Cypriote Bronze Age Pottery from Sir Leonard Woolley's Excavations at Alalakh (Tell Atchana)*. Contributions to the Chronology of the Eastern Mediterranean 5. Vienna: Österreichischen Akademie der Wissenschaften.

2007   Reflections on two 'lustrous' Base Ring I kraters from Alalakh. In I. Hein (ed.), *The Lustrous Wares of Late Bronze Age Cyprus and the Eastern Mediterranean*. Contributions to the Chronology of the Eastern Mediterranean 13: 25–36. Vienna: Österreichische Akademie der Wissenschaften.

2009   Plank figurines as cradleboards. *Medelhavsmuseet. Focus on the Mediterranean* 5: 63–75.

Bernardini, W.

2005   Reconsidering spatial and temporal aspects of prehistoric cultural identity. *American Antiquity* 70: 31–54.

Betancourt, P.P.

1998   Middle Minoan objects in the Near East. In E.H. Cline and D. Harris-Cline (eds), *The Aegean and the Orient in the Second Millennium: Proceedings of the 50th Anniversary Symposium, Cincinnati, 18–20 April 1997*. Aegaeum 18: 5–12. Liège, Belgium: Université de Liège.

Bhabha, H.K.

1994   *The Location of Culture*. London: Routledge.

Bietak, M.

2003   Science versus archaeology: problems and consequences of high Aegean chronology. In M. Bietak (ed.), *The Synchronisation of Civilsations in the Eastern Mediterranean in the Second Millennium BC II*. Denkschriften der Gesamtakademie 29. Contributions to the Chronology of the Eastern Mediterranean 4: 23–33. Vienna: Österreichischen Akademie der Wissenschaften.

Bietti Sestieri, A.M.

1988   The Mycenaean Connection and its impact on the central Mediterranean societies. *Dialoghi di Archaeologia* 6: 23–51.

Binford, L.

2000   Review of A. H. Simmons, *Faunal Extinction in an Island Society: Pygmy Hippopotamus Hunters of Cyprus* (Boston: Kluwer, 1999), in American Antiquity 65: 771.

Bintliff, J.L., and W. van Zeist (eds)

1982   *Palaeoclimates, Palaeo-environments and Human Communities in the Eastern*

Mediterranean Region in Later Prehistory.
British Archaeological Reports, Inter-
national Series 133: 1, 2. Oxford: British
Archaeological Reports.

Blackwell, N.G.
2010   Mortuary variability at Salamis (Cyprus):
relationships between and within the
royal necropolis and the Cellarka cemetery. *Journal of Mediterranean Archaeology*
23: 143–167.

Boaretto, E., H.K. Mienis and D. Sivan
2010   Reservoir age based on pre-bomb shells
from the intertidal zone along the coast
of Israel. *Nuclear Instruments and Methods
in Physics Research* B 268: 966–968.

Boekschoten, G., and P. Sondaar
1972   On the fossil mammals of Cyprus.
*Proceedings of the Koninklijke Nederlanse
Akademie van Wetenschappen, Series B* 75:
306–338.

Boivin, N., and D.Q. Fuller
2009   Shell middens, ships and seeds: exploring coastal subsistence, maritime trade
and the dispersal of domesticates in and
around the ancient Arabian Peninsula.
Journal of World Prehistory 22: 113–180.

Bolger, D.L.
1985   Erimi-Pamboula: A Study of the Site in
Light of Recent Evidence. Unpublished
PhD dissertation, Department of Classics,
University of Cincinnati, Ohio.

1987   Is there a western Cyprus? A Chalcolithic
viewpoint. In D.W. Rupp (ed.),
Western Cyprus: Connections. Studies in
Mediterranean Archaeology 77: 69–81.
Göteborg, Sweden: P. Åström's Förlag.

1988   *Erimi-Pamboula: A Chalcolithic Settlement
in Cyprus.* British Archaeological Reports,
International Series 443. Oxford: British
Archaeological Reports.

1991   The evolution of the Chalcolithic painted
style. *Bulletin of the American Schools of
Oriental Research* 282–283: 81–93.

1992   The archaeology of fertility and birth: a
ritual deposit from Chalcolithic Cyprus.
Journal of Anthropological Research 48:
145–164.

1993   The feminine mystique: gender and society in prehistoric Cypriot studies. *Report
of the Department of Antiquities, Cyprus*:
29–42.

1994   Engendering Cypriot archaeology: wom-
en's roles and statuses before the Bronze
Age. *Opuscula Atheniensia* 20: 9–17.

1996   Figurines, fertility, and the emergence of
complex society in prehistoric Cyprus.
Current Anthropology 37: 365–372.

2002   Gender and mortuary ritual in
Chalcolithic Cyprus. In D. Bolger and
N. Serwint (eds), *Engendering Aphrodite:
Women and Society in Ancient Cyprus.*
ASOR Archaeological Reports 7.
Cyprus American Archaeological
Research Institute Monograph 3: 67–86.
Boston: American Schools of Oriental
Research.

2003   *Gender in Ancient Cyprus: Narratives of
Social Change on a Mediterranean Island.*
Walnut Creek, California: Altamira Press.

2007   Cultural interaction in 3rd millennium BC Cyprus: evidence of ceramics. In S. Antoniadou and A. Pace (eds),
Mediterranean Crossroads, 162–186. Athens,
Oxford: Pierides Foundation, Oxbow.

2009   Beyond male/female: recent approaches
to gender in Cypriot prehistory. In K.
Kopaka (ed.), *Fylo: Engendering Prehistoric
'Stratigraphies' in the Aegean and the
Mediterraenan.* Aegaeum 30: 41–48. Liège,
Belgium, Austin: Université de Liège,
University of Texas at Austin.

2010   Gender and social complexity in prehistoric and protohistoric Cyprus. In
D. Bolger and L. Maguire (eds), *The
Development of Pre-State Communities in
the Ancient Near East. Studies in Honour
of Edgar Peltenburg.* BANEA Publication
Series 2: 156–165. Oxford: Oxbow.

Bolger, D., and N. Serwent (eds)
2002   *Engendering Aphrodite: Women and Society
in Ancient Cyprus.* ASOR Archaeological
Reports 7. Cyprus American Archaeological Research Institute Monograph
3. Boston: American Schools of Oriental
Research.

Bolger, D., C. McCartney and E. Peltenburg
2004   Regional interaction in the prehistoric
west: Lemba Archaeological Project
Western Cyprus Survey. In M. Iacovou
(ed.), *Archaeological Field Survey in Cyprus.
Past History, Future Potentials.* British
School at Athens, Studies 11: 105–123.
London: British School at Athens.

Bombardieri, L.
2009   The MBA–LBA I period in the Kourion
region: new evidence from Erimi *Laonin
tou Porakou* (Lemesos, Cyprus). *Antiguo
Oriente* 7: 281–300.

2010a Surveying the Kourion land: Kouris valley survey and preliminary excavations at Erimi *Laonin tou Porakou* (2007–2008 seasons). In A.M. Jasink and L. Bombardieri (eds), *Researches in Cypriote History and Archaeology. Proceedings of the Meeting held in Florence April 29–30th 2009*, 33–52. Florence: Firenze University Press.

2010b Excavations at Erimi-*Laonin tou Porakou*: 2009 Preliminary Report. *Report of the Department of Antiquities, Cyprus*: 139–168.

Bombardieri, L., O. Menozzi, D. Fossataro and A.M. Jasink

2009a Preliminary excavations at Erimi *Laonin tou Porakou*. *Report of the Department of Antiquities, Cyprus*: 131–162.

Bombardieri, L., D. Fossataro, O. Menozzi and A.M. Jasink

2009b The Kouris Valley Survey Project: 2008 preliminary report. *Report of the Department of Antiquities, Cyprus*: 117–129.

Bordreuil, P., and F. Malbran-Labat

1995 L'Archives de la maison d'Ourtenou. *Académie des Inscriptions et Belles-Lettres: Comptes-Rendus des Séances*: 443–449.

Boserup, E.

1965 *The Conditions of Agricultural Growth: The Economics of Agrarian Change under Population Pressure*. Chicago: Aldine.

Bottema, S.

1995 The Younger Dryas in the eastern Mediterranean. *Quaternary Science Reviews* 14: 883–891.

Bourriau, J.

1987 Kom Rabi'a (Memphis). *Bulletin de Liaison du Groupe Internationale d'Étude de la Céramique Égyptienne* 12: 10–11. Institut Français d'Archéologie Orientale du Caire.

n.d. Aegean pottery from stratified contexts at Memphis, Kom Rabia. Unpublished ms. in possession of author.

Boutin, A., A.B. Knapp, I. Banks, M. Given and M. Horowitz

2003 Settlement and cemetery in and around Katydhata village: from prehistory to the Roman era. *Report of the Department of Antiquities, Cyprus*: 335–349.

Bover, P., and J.A. Alcover

2003 Understanding Late Quaternary extinctions: the case of *Myotragus balearicus* (Bate 1909). *Journal of Biogeography* 30: 771–781.

Bowman, S.

1990 *Radiocarbon Dating*. London: British Museum.

Boyd, B.

1995 Houses and hearths, pits and burials: Natufian mortuary practices at Mallaha (Eynan), upper Jordan valley. In S. Campbell and A. Green (eds), *The Archaeology of Death in the Ancient Near East*. Oxbow Monograph 51: 17–23. Oxford: Oxbow.

2001 The Natufian burials from el-Wad, Mount Carmel: beyond issues of social differentiation. *Journal of the Israel Prehistoric Society* 31: 185–200.

2002 Ways of eating/ways of being in the later Epipalaeolithic (Natufian) Levant. In Y. Hamilakis, M. Pluciennik and S. Tarlow (eds), *Thinking through the Body: Archaeologies of Corporeality*, 137–152. New York: Kluwer Academic/Plenum.

2005 Transforming food practices in the Epipalaeolithic and Pre-Pottery Neolithic Levant. In J. Clarke (ed.), *Archaeological Perspectives on the Transmission and Transformation of Culture in the Eastern Mediterranean*. Levant Supplementary Series 2: 106–112. Oxford: Oxbow.

Braudel, F.

1972 *The Mediterranean and the Mediterranean World in the Age of Philip II* 1. New York: Harper and Row.

Briois, F.

2003 Nature et évolution des industries lithiques de Shillourokambos. In J. Guilaine and A. Le Brun (eds), *Le Néolithique de Chypre*. Bulletin de Correspondance Hellénique, Supplément 43: 121–133. Athens: École Française de'Athènes.

Briois, F., B. Gratuze and J. Guilaine

1997 Obsidiennes du site Néolithique Précéramique de Shillourokambos (Chypre). *Paléorient* 23(1): 95–112.

Briois, F., C. Petit-Aupert and P.-Y. Péchoux

2005 *Histoire des Campagnes d'Amathonte* 1. *L'occupation du sol au Néolithique*. Études Chypriotes 16. Athens: École Française d'Athènes.

Bromage, T., W. Kirks, H. Erdjument-Bromage, M. Huck, O. Kulmer, R. Öner, O. Sandrock and F. Schrenk

2002 A life history and climate change solution to the evolution and extinction of insular dwarfs: a Cypriot experience. In W.H. Waldren and J.A. Ensenyat (eds),

World Islands in Prehistory. V Deia International Conference of Prehistory. British Archaeological Reports, International Series 1095: 420–427. Oxford: Archaeopress.

Bronk Ramsey, C.

2001 Development of the radiocarbon calibration program OxCal. *Radiocarbon* 43: 355–363.

2008 Deposition models for chronological records. *Quaternary Science Reviews* 27: 42–60.

2009a Bayesian analysis of radiocarbon dates. *Radiocarbon* 51: 337–360.

2009b Dealing with outliers and offsets in radiocarbon dating. *Radiocarbon* 51: 1023–1045.

Bronk Ramsey, C., J. van der Plicht and B. Weninger

2001 'Wiggle matching' radiocarbon dates. *Radiocarbon* 43: 381–389.

Bronk Ramsey, C., S.W. Manning and M. Galimberti

2004 Dating the volcanic eruption at Thera. *Radiocarbon* 46: 325–344.

Bronk Ramsey, C., C.E. Buck, S.W. Manning, P. Reimer and H. van der Plicht

2006 Developments for radiocarbon calibration for archaeology. *Antiquity* 80/310: 783–798.

Bronk Ramsey, C., M.W. Dee, J.M. Rowland, T.F.G. Higham, S.A. Harris, F.A. Brock, A. Quiles, E. Wild, E.S. Marcus and A.J. Shortland

2010 Radiocarbon-based chronology for Dynastic Egypt. *Science* 328: 1554–1557.

Broodbank, C.

2000 *An Island Archaeology of the Early Cyclades.* Cambridge: Cambridge University Press.

2006 The origins and early development of Mediterranean maritime activity. *Journal of Mediterranean Archaeology* 19: 199–230.

2009 The Mediterranean and its hinterland. In B. Cunliffe, C. Gosden and R. Joyce (eds), *The Oxford Handbook of Archaeology*, 677–722. Oxford: Oxford University Press.

2010 'Ships a-sail from over the rim of the sea': voyaging, sailing and the making of Mediterranean societies c. 3500–800 BC. In A. Anderson, J. Barrett and K. Boyle (eds), *The Global Origins and Development of Seafaring*, 249–264. Cambridge: McDonald Institute for Archaeological Research.

Brooks, N.

2006 Cultural responses to aridity in the Middle Holocene and increased social compexity. *Quaternary International* 151: 29–49.

Brown, M.

2009 Pyla Kokkinokremos survey and soundings. *Bulletin of the Council for British Research in the Levant* 4: 67–68.

Brown, W.

2010 *Walled States, Waning Sovereignty.* Cambridge, Massachusetts: Zone Books, MIT Press.

Brubaker, R., and F. Cooper

2000 Beyond 'identity'. *Theory and Society* 29: 1–47.

Brumfiel, E.M.

1996 Figurines and the Aztec state: testing the effectiveness of ideological domination. In R.P. Wright (ed.), *Gender and Archaeology*, 143–166. Philadelphia: University of Pennsylvania Press.

Bryce, T.R.

1992 Lukka revisited. *Journal of Near Eastern Studies* 51: 121–130.

Buchholz, H.-G.

1973 Tamassos, Zypern, 1970–1972. *Archaologisches Anzeiger* (1973:3): 295–388.

1979 Bronzen Schafthorhaxte aus Tamassos und Ungebung. In V. Karageorghis (ed.), *Studies Presented in Memory of Porphyrios Dikaios*, 76–88. Nicosia: Lions Club.

Buchholz, H.-G., and V. Karageorghis

1973 *Prehistoric Greece and Cyprus.* London: Phaidon Press.

Buchholz, H.-G., and K. Untiedt

1996 *Tamassos. Ein Antikes Königreich auf Zypern.* Studies in Mediterranean Archaeology and Literature, Pocket-book 136. Jonsered, Sweden: P. Åström's Förlag.

Budd, P., A.M. Pollard, B. Scaife and R.G. Thomas

1995 Oxhide ingots, recycling and the Mediterranean metals trade. *Journal of Mediterranean Archaeology* 8: 1–32.

Budin, S.L.

2002 Creating a goddess of sex. In D. Bolger and N. Serwint (eds), *Engendering Aphrodite: Women and Society in Ancient Cyprus.* ASOR Archaeological Reports 7. Cyprus American Archaeological Research Institute Monograph 3: 315–324. Boston: American Schools of Oriental Research.

2003   *The Origins of Aphrodite.* Bethesda, Maryland: CDL Press.

2011   *Images of Woman and Child from the Bronze Age. Reconsidering Fertility, Maternity, and Gender in the Ancient World.* Cambridge: Cambridge University Press.

Bunimovitz, S.

1995   On the edge of empires – Late Bronze Age (1500–1200 BCE). In T.E. Levy (ed.), *The Archaeology of Society in the Holy Land*, 320–331. Leicester, England: Leicester University Press.

1998   Sea Peoples in Cyprus and Israel: a comparative study of immigration processes. In S. Gitin, A. Mazar and E. Stern (eds), *Mediterranean Peoples in Transition: Thirteenth to Tenth Centuries BCE*, 103–113. Jerusalem: Israel Exploration Society.

Bunimovitz, S., and R. Barkai

1996   Ancient bones and modern myths: ninth millennium BC hippopotamus hunters at Akrotiri *Aetokremnos*, Cyprus? *Journal of Mediterranean Archaeology* 9: 85–96.

Bunimovitz, S., and A. Yasur-Landau

1996   Philistine and Israelite pottery: a comparative approach to the question of pots and people. *Tel Aviv* 23: 88–101.

Burns, B.E.

2010   *Mycenaean Greece, Mediterranean Commerce, and the Formation of Identity.* Cambridge: Cambridge University Press.

Butzer, K.W.

1975   Patterns of environmental change in the Near East during late Pleistocene and early Holocene times. In F. Wendorf and A.E. Marks (eds), *Problems in Prehistory: North Africa and the Levant*, 389–410. Dallas, Texas: Southern Methodist University Press.

2005   Environmental history in the Mediterranean world: cross-disciplinary investigation of cause-and-effect for degradation and soil erosion. *Journal of Archaeological Science* 32(12): 1773–1800.

Butzer, K.W., and S.E. Harris

2007   Geoarchaeological approaches to the environmental history of Cyprus: explication and critical evaluation. *Journal of Archaeological Science* 34: 1932–1952.

Cadogan, G.

1987   Maroni III. *Report of the Department of Antiquities, Cyprus*: 81–84.

1989   Maroni and the monuments. In E.J. Peltenburg (ed.), *Early Society in Cyprus*, 43–51. Edinburgh: Edinburgh University Press.

1993   Cyprus, Mycenaean pottery, trade and colonisation. In C. Zerner, P. Zerner and J. Winder (eds), *Proceedings of the International Conference Wace and Blegen: Pottery as Evidence for Trade in the Aegean Bronze Age 1939–1989*, 91–99. Amsterdam: Gieben.

1996   Maroni: change in Late Bronze Age Cyprus. In P. Åström and E. Herscher (eds), *Late Bronze Age Settlement in Cyprus: Function and Relationship.* Studies in Mediterranean Archaeology, Pocket-book 126: 15–22. Jonsered, Sweden: P. Åström's Förlag.

Cadogan, G., E. Herscher, P. Russell and S.W. Manning

2001   Maroni-*Vournes*: a long White Slip sequence and its chronology. In V. Karageorghis (ed.), *The White Slip Ware of Late Bronze Age Cyprus.* Österreichische Akademie der Wissenschaften, Denkschriften der Gesamtakademie, Band 20. Contributions to the Chronology of the Eastern Mediterranean 2: 75–88. Vienna: Österreichische Akademie der Wissenschaften.

Calvet, Y.

1980   Sur certains rites funéraires à Salamine de Chypre. In M. Yon (ed.), *Salamine de Chypre. Histoire et archéologie: état des recherches.* Colloques internationaux du Centre national de la recherche scientifique 578: 115–120. Paris: Éditions du Centre national de la recherche scientifique.

Caneva, I.

1999   Early farmers on the Cilician coast: Yumuktepe in the seventh millennium BC. In M. Özdoğan and N. Başgelen (eds), *Neolithic in Turkey: The Cradle of Civilization. New Discoveries*, 105–111. Istanbul: Arkeoloji ve Sanat Yayinlari.

Canuto, M.A., and J. Yaeger (eds)

2000   *Archaeology of Communities: A New World Perspective.* London: Routledge.

Caraher, W., R.S. Moore, J.S. Noller and D. Pettegrew

2005   The Pyla-*Koutopetria* Archaeological Project: first preliminary report (2003–2004 seasons). *Report of the Department of Antiquities, Cyprus*: 245–267.

Casana, J., and T. Wilkinson
2005   Settlement and landscapes in the Amuq region. In K.A. Yener (ed.), *The Amuq Valley Regional Projects*, Volume 1. *Surveys in the Plain of Antioch and Orontes Delta, Turkey, 1995–2002*. Oriental Institute Publications 131: 25–65. Chicago: Oriental Institute, University of Chicago.

Casson, S.
1938   *Ancient Cyprus*. London: Methuen.

Catling, H.W.
1957   The Bronze Age pottery. In J. Du Plat Taylor, *Myrtou-Pighades: A Late Bronze Age Sanctuary in Cyprus*, 26–59. Oxford: Ashmolean Museum.
1962   Patterns of settlement in Bronze Age Cyprus. *Opuscula Atheniensia* 4: 129–169.
1964   *Cypriot Bronzework in the Mycenaean World*. Oxford: Oxford University Press.
1968   Kouklia: Evreti tomb 8. *Bulletin de Correspondance Héllenique* 92: 162–169.
1971a   Cyprus in the Early Bronze Age. In I.E.S. Edwards, C.J. Gadd and N.G.L. Hammond (eds), *Cambridge Ancient History* I: 2, 808–823. Cambridge: Cambridge University Press.
1971b   A Cypriot bronze statuette in the Bomford Collection. In C.F.A. Schaeffer (ed.), *Alasia* I. *Mission Archéologique d'Alasia* 4: 15–32. Paris: Klincksieck.
1973   Cyprus in the Middle Bronze Age. In I.E.S. Edwards, C.J. Gadd and N.G.L. Hammond (eds), *Cambridge Ancient History* II: 1, 165–175. Cambridge: Cambridge University Press.
1975   Cyprus in the Late Bronze Age. In I.E.S. Edwards, C.J. Gadd, N.G.L. Hammond and E. Sollberger (eds), *Cambridge Ancient History* II: 2, 188–216. Cambridge: Cambridge University Press.
1976   The Phlamoudhi survey again. *Report of the Department of Antiquities, Cyprus*: 29–34.
1979   Reflections upon the interpretation of the archaeological evidence for the history of Cyprus. In V. Karageorghis (ed.), *Studies Presented in Memory of Porphyrios Dikaios*, 194–205. Nicosia: Lion's Club.
1980   *Cyprus and the West 1600–1050 B.C.* Ian Sanders Memorial Lecture, Sheffield, England, 19 November, 1980. Sheffield, England: Department of Prehistory and Archaeology, University of Sheffield.
1984   Workshop and heirloom: prehistoric bronze stands in the east Mediterranean. *Report of the Department of Antiquities, Cyprus*: 69–91.
1986   Cypriote bronzework: east or west? In V. Karageorghis (ed.), *Acts of the International Archaeological Symposium: Cyprus Between the Orient and the Occident*, 91–103. Nicosia: Department of Antiquities.
1991   Bronze Age trade in the Mediterranean: a view. In N.H. Gale (ed.), *Bronze Age Trade in the Mediterranean*. Studies in Mediterranean Archaeology 90: 1–13. Göteborg, Sweden: P. Åström's Förlag.

Catling, H.W., and J.A. MacGillivray
1983   An Early Cypriot II vase from the palace at Knossos. *Annual of the British School at Athens* 78: 1–8.

Caubet, A.
1974   Une terre cuite chalcolithique Chypriote au Louvre. *Report of the Department of Antiquities, Cyprus*: 35–37.

Cauvin, J.
1968   *Les outillages néolithiques de Byblos et du littoral libanais*. Fouilles de Byblos 4. Paris: Librairie d'Amérique et d'Orient, Adrien Maisonnneuve.
1991   L'obsidenne au Levant préhistorique: provenance et fonction. *Cahiers de l'Euphrate* 5–6: 163–190.

Cauvin, J. (trans. T. Watkins)
2000   *The Birth of the Gods and the Origins of Agriculture*. Cambridge: Cambridge University Press.

Cauvin, M.C., and J. Cauvin
1993   La sequence néolithique PPNB au Levant nord. *Paléorient* 19(1): 23–28.

Chelidonio, G.
2001   Manufatti litici su ciottolo da Milos (isole Cicladi) (nota preliminare). *Pegaso* 1: 116–144.

Cherry, J.F.
1981   Pattern and process in the earliest colonisation of the Mediterranean islands. *Proceedings of the Prehistoric Society* 47: 41–68.
1990   The first colonization of the Mediterranean islands: a review of recent research. *Journal of Mediterranean Archaeology* 3: 145–221.
1992   Palaeolithic Sardinians? Some questions of evidence and method. In R.H. Tykot and T.K. Andrews (eds), *Sardinia*

in the Mediterranean: A Footprint in the Sea. Monographs in Mediterranean Archaeology 3: 28–39. Sheffield, England: Sheffield Academic Press.

2004 Mediterranean island prehistory: what's different and what's new? In S.M. Fitzpatrick (ed.), *Voyages of Discovery: The Archaeology of Islands,* 233–248. New York: Praeger.

2009 Sorting out Crete's prepalatial off-island interactions. In W.A. Parkinson and M.L. Galaty (eds), *Archaic State Interaction: The Eastern Mediterranean in the Bronze Age,* 107–140. Santa Fe, New Mexico: SAR Press.

Cherry, J.F., J.L. Davis and E. Mantzourani

1991 *Landscape Archaeology as Long-Term History: Northern Keos in the Cycladic Islands from Earliest Settlement to Modern Times.* Monumenta Archaeologica 16. Los Angeles: UCLA Institute of Archaeology.

Chesson, M.

1999 Libraries of the dead. *Journal of Anthropological Archaeology* 18(2): 137–164.

2001 Embodied memories of place and people: death and society in an early urban community. In M. Chesson (ed.), *Social Memory, Identity, and Death: Anthropological Perspectives on Mortuary Rituals.* American Anthropological Association, Archaeological Paper 10: 100–113. Arlington, Virginia: American Anthropological Association.

Chilardi, S., D.W. Frayer, P. Gioia, R. Macchiarelli and M. Mussi

1996 Fontana Nuova di Ragusa (Sicily, Italy): southernmost Aurignacian site in Europe. *Antiquity* 70(269): 553–563.

Christodoulou, D.

1959 *The Evolution of the Rural Land Use Pattern in Cyprus.* World Land Use Survey, Monograph 2. Cornwall, England: Geographical Publications.

Christou, D.

1989 The Chalcolithic cemetery at Souskiou-Vathyrkakas. In E.J. Peltenburg (ed.), *Early Society in Cyprus,* 82–94. Edinburgh: Edinburgh University Press.

1994a Chronique des fouilles et découvertes archéologiques à Chypre en 1993. *Bulletin de Correspondance Hellénique* 118: 647–693.

1994b Kourion in the 11th century BC. In V. Karageorghis (ed.), *Cyprus in the 11th Century BC,* 177–188. Nicosia: Leventis Foundation and University of Cyprus.

Cifola, B.

1994 The role of the Sea Peoples and the end of the Late Bronze Age: a reassessment of textual and archaeological evidence. *Orientis Antiqui Miscellanea* 1: 1–23.

Clarke, J.T.

2001 Style and society in Ceramic Neolithic Cyprus. *Levant* 33: 65–80.

2003 Insularity and identity in prehistoric Cyprus. In J. Guilaine and A. Le Brun (eds), *Le Néolithique de Chypre.* Bulletin de Correspondance Hellénique, Supplément 43: 203–218. Athens: École Française d'Athènes.

2004 Excavations at Kalavasos *Kokkinoyia* and Kalavasos *Pamboules* 2002–3. *Report of the Department of Antiquities, Cyprus:* 51–71.

2005 (ed.) *Archaeological Perspectives on the Transmission and Transformation of Culture in the Eastern Mediterranean.* Levant Supplementary Series 2. Oxford: Council for British Research in the Levant and Oxbow.

2007a (with C. McCartney and A. Wasse) *On the Margins of Southwest Asia: Cyprus during the 6th to 4th Millennia BC.* Oxford: Oxbow.

2007b Site diversity in Cyprus in the late 5th millennium Cal BC: evidence from Kalavasos *Kokkinoyia. Levant* 39: 13–26.

2009 Excavations at Kalavasos-*Kokkinoyia,* 2004 to 2007. *Report of the Department of Antiquities, Cyprus:* 39–57.

2010 Contextualising Neolithic Cyprus: preliminary investigations into connections between Cyprus and the Near East in the later Neolithic. In D. Bolger and L. Maguire (eds), *The Development of Pre-state Communities in the Ancient Near East: Studies in Honour of Edgar Peltenburg.* BANEA Publication Series 2: 197–206. Oxford: Oxbow.

Clarke, J.T., P. Croft and C. McCartney

2007 The 1940s excavaions at Kalavasos *Kokkinoyia* and Kalavasos *Pamboules. Report of the Department of Antiquities, Cyprus:* 45–86.

Cline, E.H.

1994 *Sailing the Wine-Dark Sea: International Trade and the Late Bronze Age Aegean.* British Archaeological Reports, International Series 591. Oxford: Archeopress.

1999   Coals to Newcastle, wall brackets to Tiryns: irrationality, gift exchange, and distance value. In P. Betancourt, V. Karageorghis, R. Laffineur and W.D. Niemeier (eds), *Meletemata: Studies in Aegean Archaeology Presented to Malcolm H. Wiener as He Enters His 65th Year*. Aegaeum 20(1): 119–123. Liège, Belgium, Austin: Université de Liège, University of Texas at Austin.

2010   (ed.) *The Oxford Handbook of the Bronze Age Aegean*. Oxford: Oxford University Press.

Cline, E.H., and D. Harris-Cline (eds)

1998   *The Aegean and the Orient in the Second Millennium: Proceedings of the 50th Anniversary Symposium, Cincinnati 18–20 April 1997*. Aegaeum 18. Liège, Belgium: Université de Liège.

Cobham, C.D.

1908   *Excerpta Cypria: Materials for a History of Cyprus*. Oxford: Oxford University Press.

Cohen, C., J. Maran and M. Vetters

2010   An ivory rod with a cuneiform inscription, most probably Ugaritic, from a Final Palatial workshop in the lower citadel of Tiryns. *Archäologischer Anzeiger* (2010: 2): 1–22.

Coldstream, J.N.

1989   Status symbols in Cyprus in the eleventh century BC. In E.J. Peltenburg (ed.), *Early Society in Cyprus*, 325–335. Edinburgh: Edinburgh University Press.

1994   What sort of Aegean migration? In V. Karageorghis (ed.), *Cyprus in the 11th Century BC*, 143–147. Nicosia: Leventis Foundation.

Coleman, J.E.

1992   Greece, the Aegean and Cyprus. In Robert W. Ehrich (ed.), *Chronologies in Old World Archaeology*. 3rd edition. Volume I: 247–288; Volume II: 203–229. Chicago: University of Chicago Press.

Coleman, J.E., J.A. Barlow, M. Mogelonsky and K.W. Scharr

1996   *Alambra: A Middle Bronze Age Site in Cyprus. Investigations by Cornell University, 1975–1978*. Studies in Mediterranean Archaeology 118. Jonsered, Sweden: P. Åström's Förlag.

Colledge, S.

2003   The charred plant remains in three of the pits. In E.J. Peltenburg (ed.), *The Colonisation and Settlement of Cyprus: Investigations at Kissonerga Mylouthkia, 1976–1996*. Studies in Mediterranean Archaeology 70(4): 239–243. Sävedalen, Sweden: P. Åström's Förlag.

2004   Reappraisal of the archaeobotanical evidence for the emergence and dispersal of the 'founder crops'. In E.J. Peltenburg and A. Wasse (eds), *Neolithic Revolution: New Perspectives on Southwest Asia in Light of Recent Discoveries on Cyprus*. Levant Supplementary Series 1: 49–60. Oxford: Oxbow.

Colledge, S., and J. Conolly

2007   A review and synthesis of the evidence for the origins of farming on Cyprus and Crete. In S. Colledge and J. Conolly (eds), *The Origins and Spread of Domestic Plants in Southwest Asia and Europe*, 53–74. Walnut Creek, California: Left Coast Press.

Colledge, S., J. Conolly and S. Shennan

2004   Archaeobotanical evidence for the spread of farming in the eastern Mediterranean. *Current Anthropology* 45: S35–S58.

Collombier, A.M.

1988   Harbour or harbours of Kition on southeastern coastal Cyprus. In A. Raban (ed.), *Archaeology of Coastal Changes*. British Archaeological Reports, International Series 404: 35–46. Oxford: British Archaeological Reports.

Conkey, M.W., and J.M. Gero

1997   Program to practice: gender and feminism in archaeology. *Annual Review of Anthropology* 26: 411–437. Palo Alto, California: Annual Reviews Inc.

Conolly, J., S. Colledge, K. Dobney, J.-D. Vigne, J. Peters, B. Stopp, K. Manning and S. Shennan

2011   Meta-analysis of zooarchaeological data from SW Asia and SE Europe provides insight into the origins and spread of animal husbandry. *Journal of Archaeological Science* 38: 538–545.

Constantakopoulou, C.

2005   Proud to be an islander: island identity in multi-polis islands in the Classical and Hellenistic Aegean. *Mediterranean Historical Review* 20: 1–34.

Constantinou, G.

1982   Geological features and ancient exploitation of the cupriferous sulphide orebodies of Cyprus. In J.D. Muhly, R. Maddin and V. Karageorghis (eds), *Early Metallurgy in Cyprus, 4000–500 BC*, 13–24. Nicosia: Pierides Foundation.

1992 Ancient copper mining in Cyprus. In A. Marangou and K. Psillides (eds), *Cyprus, Copper and the Sea*, 43–74. Nicosia: Government of Cyprus.

Cook, V.

1988 Cyprus and the outside world during the transition from the Bronze Age to the Iron Age. *Opuscula Atheniensia* 17: 13–32.

Coqueugniot, E.

2003 Unité et diversité des industries lithiques tallées au Proche-Orient (Levant et Anatolie méridionale) du IXe au VIIe millénaire av. J.C. In J. Guilaine and A. Le Brun (eds), *Le Néolithique de Chypre*. Bulletin de Correspondance Hellénique, Supplément 43: 373–388. Athens: École Français D'Athènes.

2004 Les industries lithiques du Néolithique ancien entre Moyen Euphrate et Jezireh orientale – Réflexions sur deux voies évolutives. In O. Aurenche, M. Le Miere and P. Sanlaville (eds), *From the River to the Seas: The Palaeolithic and the Neolithic on the Euphrates and in the Northern Levant, Studies in Honour of Lorraine Copeland*. British Archaeological Reports, International Series 1263: 295–308. Oxford: Archaeopress.

Costa, L., J.-D. Vigne, N. Cocherens, N. Desse-Berset, C. Heinz, F. de Lanfarnchi, J. Magdeleine, M.-P. Ruas, S. Thiébault and C. Tozzi

2003 Early settlement on Tyrrhenian islands (8th millennium cal. BC): Mesolithic adaption to local resources in Corsica and northern Sardinia. In L. Larsson, H. Kindgren, K. Knutsson, D. Loeffler and A. Åkerlund (eds), *Mesolithic on the Move: Papers Presented at the Sixth International Conference on the Mesolithic in Europe, Stockholm 2000*, 3–10. Oxford: Oxbow.

Counts, D.B.

2008 Master of the lion: representation and hybridity in Cypriote sanctuaries. *American Journal of Archaeology* 112: 3–27.

Courtois, J.-C.

1971 Le sanctuaire du dieu au lingot d'Enkomi-Alasia. In C.F.A. Schaeffer (ed.), *Alasia* I. Mission Archéologique d'Alasia 4: 151–362. Paris: Klincksieck.

1982 L'activité métallurgique et les bronzes d'Enkomi au Bronze Récent (1650–1000

avant J.C.). In J.D. Muhly, R. Maddin and V. Karageorghis (eds), *Early Metallurgy in Cyprus, 4000–500 BC*, 155–176. Nicosia: Pierides Foundation.

1983 Le tresor de poids de Kalavasos-*Ayios Dhimitrios* 1982. *Report of the Department of Antiquities, Cyprus*: 117–130.

1984 *Alasia* III. *Les Objets des Niveaux stratifiés d'Enkomi. Fouilles C.F.A. Schaeffer 1947–1970*. Éditions Recherches sur les Civilisations, Memoire 32. Paris: EDPF.

1986 A propos des apports orientaux dans la civilisation du Bronze Récent à Chypre. In V. Karageorghis (ed.), *Acts of the International Archaeological Symposium: Cyprus between the Orient and Occident*, 69–87. Nicosia: Department of Antiquities.

Courtois, J.-C., J. Lagarce and E. Lagarce

1986 *Enkomi et le Bronze Récent à Chypre*. Nicosia: Leventis Foundation.

Courtois, J.-C., and J.M. Webb

1980 A steatite relief mould from Enkomi. *Report of the Department of Antiquities, Cyprus*: 151–158.

1987 *Les Cylindres-Sceaux d'Enkomi (Fouilles Françaises 1957–1970)*. Nicosia: Mission Archéologique Française d'Alasia, Zavallis Press.

Courtois, L.

1970 Note préliminaire sur l'origine des différentes fabriques de la poterie du Chypriote récent. *Report of the Department of Antiquities, Cyprus*: 81–85.

1977 Céramique et métallurgie anciennes: le bol à lait de Chypre. *Bulletin de l'Académie et de la Société Lorraines des Sciences* 16(1): 9–17.

Crewe, L.

1998 *Spindle Whorls: A Study of Form, Function and Decoration in Prehistoric Bronze Age Cyprus*. Studies in Mediterranean Archaeology and Literature, Pocket-book 149. Jonsered, Sweden: P. Åström's Förlag.

2004 Social Complexity and Ceramic Technology on Late Bronze Age Cyprus: The New Evidence from Enkomi. Unpublished PhD thesis: Department of Archaeology, University of Edinburgh.

2007a Sophistication in simplicity: the first production of wheelmade pottery on

Late Bronze Age Cyprus. *Journal of Mediterranean Archaeology* 20: 209–238.

2007b *Early Enkomi. Regionalism, Trade and Society at the Beginning of the Late Bronze Age on Cyprus.* British Archaeological Reports, International Series 1706. Oxford: Archaeopress.

2010a Third season of excavation at Kissonerga *Skalia* Bronze Age settlement. *Bulletin of the Council for British Research in the Levant* 5: 69–71.

2010b Rethinking Kalopsidha: from specialisation to state marginalisation. In D. Bolger and L.C. Maguire (eds), *The Development of Pre-State Communities in the Ancient Near East.* BANEA Publication Series 2: 63–71. Oxford: Oxbow.

Crewe, L., C. Lorentz, E. Peltenburg and S. Spanou

2005 Treatments of the dead: preliminary report of investigations at Souskiou *Laona* Chalcolithic cemetery, 2001–2004. *Report of the Department of Antiquities, Cyprus*: 41–67.

Crewe, L., E. Peltenburg and S. Spanou

2002 Contexts for cruciforms: figurines of prehistoric Cyprus. *Antiquity* 76/291: 21–22.

Crielaard, J.P., V. Stissi and G.J. van Wijngaarden (eds)

1999 *The Complex Past of Pottery: Production, Circulation and Consumption of Mycenaean and Greek Pottery (sixteenth to early fifth centuries BC).* Amsterdam: J.C. Gieben.

Croft, P.

1985 The mammalian faunal remains: summary and conclusions. In E.J. Peltenburg, *Lemba Archaeological Project* I: *Excavations at Lemba Lakkous, 1976–1983.* Studies in Mediterranean Archaeology 70(1): 295–296. Göteborg, Sweden: P. Åström's Förlag.

1988 Animal remains from Maa *Palaeokastro*. In V. Karageorghis and M. Demas, *Excavations at Maa-Palaeokastro 1979–1986*, 449–457. Nicosia: Department of Antiquities, Cyprus.

1989 Animal bones. In A.K. South, *Vasilikos Valley Project 3. Kalavasos-Ayios Dhimitrios* 2. Studies in Mediterranean Archaeology 71(3): 70–72. Göteborg, Sweden: P. Åström's Förlag.

1991 Man and beast in Chalcolithic Cyprus. *Bulletin of the American Schools of Oriental Research* 282–283: 63–79.

1996 Animal remains. In D. Frankel and J. Webb, *Marki Alonia: An Early and Middle Bronze Age Town in Cyprus. Excavations 1990–1994.* Studies in Mediterranean Archaeology 123(1): 217–220. Jonsered, Sweden: P. Åström's Förlag.

2002 Game management in early prehistoric Cyprus. *Zeitschrift der Jagdwissenschaft* 48 (supplement): 172–179.

2003a Water-holes and cowboys – animal remains from the Paphian Neolithic. In J. Guilaine and A. Le Brun (eds), *Le Néolithique de Chypre.* Bulletin de Correspondance Hellénique, Supplément 43: 269–278. Athens: École Française d'Athènes.

2003b The animal remains. In Swiny et al. (eds), *Sotira Kamminoudhia: An Early Bronze Age Site in Cyprus.* American Schools of Oriental Research, Archaeological Reports 8. Cyprus American Archaeological Research Institute Monograph 4:439–447. Boston: American Schools of Oriental Research.

2003c The animal bones [Chalcolithic]. In E.J. Peltenburg (ed.), *The Colonisation and Settlement of Cyprus: Investigations at Kissonerga* Mylouthkia, *1976–1996.* Studies in Mediterranean Archaeology 70(4): 225–237. Sävedalen, Sweden: P. Åström's Förlag.

2003d The animal bones [EAN]. In E.J. Peltenburg (ed.), *The Colonisation and Settlement of Cyprus: Investigations at Kissonerga* Mylouthkia, *1976–1996.* Studies in Mediterranean Archaeology 70(4): 49–58. Sävedalen, Sweden: P. Åström's Förlag.

2005 Mammalian fauna. In I. Todd, *Excavations at Kalavasos-Tenta.* Vasilikos Valley Project 7. Studies in Mediterranean Archaeology 71(7): 342–367. Sävedalen, Sweden: P. Åström's Förlag.

2006 Animal bones. In D. Frankel and J.M. Webb, *Marki Alonia: An Early and Middle Bronze Age Settlement in Cyprus. Excavations 1995–2000.* Studies in Mediterranean Archaeology 123(2): 263–281. Sävedalen, Sweden: P. Åström's Förlag.

2010 Herds lost in time: animal remains from the 1969–1970 excavation seasons at the Ceramic Neolithic site of Philia-Drakos Site A, Cyprus. In D. Bolger and L. Maguire (eds), *The Development of*

Pre-State Communities in the Ancient Near East. Studies in Honour of Edgar Peltenburg. BANEA Publication Series 2: 131–137. Oxford: Oxbow.

Crowley, J.L.

1989 *The Aegean and the East: An Investigation into the Transference of Artistic Motifs between the Aegean, Egypt, and the Near East in the Bronze Age.* Studies in Mediterranean Archaeology and Literature, Pocket-book 51. Jonsered, Sweden: P. Åström's Förlag.

Crubézy, E., J.-D. Vigne, J. Guilaine, T. Giraud, P. Gerard and F. Briois

2003 Aux origines des sepultures collectives: la structure 23 de *Shillourokambos* (Chypre, 7500 BC). In J. Guilaine and A. Le Brun (eds), *Le Néolithique de Chypre.* Bulletin de Correspondance Hellénique, Supplément 43: 295–311. Athens: École Française d'Athènes.

Cucchi, T., J.-D. Vigne, J.-C. Auffray, P. Croft and E. Peltenburg

2002 Introduction involontaire de la souris domestique (*Mus musculus domesticus*) à Chypre dès le Néolithique précéramique ancien (fin IXe et VIIIe millénaires av. J.C.). *Comptes rendus Palévol* 1(4): 235–241.

Cucchi, T., A. Orth, J.-C. Auffray, S. Renaud, L. Fabre, J. Catalan, E. Hadjisterkotis, F. Bonhomme and J.-D. Vigne

2006 A new endemic species of the subgenus Mus (Rodentia, Mammalia) on the island of Cyprus. *Zootaxa* 1241: 1–35.

Cusick, J.G.

1998 Historiography of acculturation: an evaluation of concepts and their application in archaeology. In J.G. Cusick (ed.), *Studies in Culture Contact: Interaction, Culture Change and Archaeology.* Center for Archaeological Investigations, Occasional Paper 25: 126–145. Carbondale: Southern Illinois University Press.

D'Agata, A.L.

2000 Interactions between Aegean groups and local communities in Sicily in the Bronze Age: the evidence from pottery. *Studi Micenei e Egeo-Anatolici* 42: 61–83.

2005 Cult activity on Crete and Cyprus at the end of the Late Bronze Age and the beginning of the Early Iron Age. In V. Karageorghis, H. Matthäus and S. Rogge (eds), *Cyprus: Religion and Society from the Late Bronze Age to the End of the Archaic Period,* 1–17. Möhnesee-Wamel, Germany: Biblipolis.

D'Altroy, T.N., and T.K. Earle

1985 Staple finance, wealth finance, and storage in the Inka political economy. *Current Anthropology* 25: 187–206.

D'Arcy, P.

1997 The people of the sea. In D. Denoon (ed.), *The Cambridge History of the Pacific Islanders,* 74–77. Cambridge: Cambridge University Press.

Dabney, M.

2007 Marketing Mycenaean pottery in the Levant. In P.P. Betancourt, M.C. Nelson and E.H. Williams (eds), *Krinoi kai Limenai: Studies in Honor of Joseph and Maria Shaw,* 191–197. Philadelphia: INSTAP Academic Press.

Daniel, J.F.

1938 Excavations at Kourion. The Late Bronze Age settlement – provisional report. *American Journal of Archaeology* 42: 261–275.

Davaras, C., and P.P. Betancourt

2004 *Hagia Photia Cemetery* I: *The Tomb Groups and Architecture.* Institute for Aegean Prehistory, Prehistory Monograph 14. Philadelphia: Institute for Aegean Prehistory Academic Press.

David, B., and J. Thomas

2008 *Handbook of Landscape Archaeology.* Walnut Creek, California: Left Coast Press.

Davies, P.

1997 Mortuary practice in Prehistoric Bronze Age Cyprus: problems and potential. *Report of the Department of Antiquities, Cyprus:* 11–26.

Davis, S.J.M.

1985 Tiny elephants and giant mice. *New Scientist* 1437 (3 January): 25–27.

1989 Some more animal remains from the aceramic Neolithic of Cyprus. In A. Le Brun, *Fouilles récent a Khirokitia (Chypre) – 1983– 1986.* Recherches sur les Civilisation, Memoire 81: 189–221. Paris: ADPF.

2003 The zooarchaeology of Khirokitia (Neolithic Cyprus), including a view from the mainland. In J. Guilaine and A. Le Brun (eds), *Le Néolithique de Chypre.* Bulletin de Correspondance Hellénique, Supplément 43: 253–268. Athens: École Française d'Athènes.

De Contenson, H.

1992 *Préhistoire de Ras Shamra. Les sondages stratigraphiques de 1955 à 1976.* Ras

Shamra-Ougarit 8.1: Texte. Paris: Éditions Recherche sur les Civilisations.

de Jesus, P.S.

1980   *The Development of Prehistoric Mining and Metallurgy in Anatolia.* British Archaeological Reports, International Series 74. Oxford: British Archaeological Reports.

DeMarrais, E., L.J. Castillo and T.K. Earle

1996   Ideology, materialization, and power strategies. *Current Anthropology* 37: 15–31.

Deshayes, J.

1963   *La Nécropole de Ktima.* Institut Français d'Archéologie de Beyrouth. Bibliothèque de Historique 75. Mission Jean Bérard 1953–1955. Paris: P. Geuthner.

Desse, J., and N. Desse-Bersot

1994   Stratégies de pêche au 8e millénaire: les poissons de Cap Andreas-*Kastros.* In A. Le Brun, *Fouilles récent a Khirokitia (Chypre) 1988–1991,* 335–360. Paris: ADPF.

Devillers, B.

2004   Holocene morphogenesis and land use in eastern *Mesaoria* (Cyprus), preliminary results. In E. Fouach (ed.), *Dynamiques environnementales et histoire en milieux méditerranéens,* 361–369. Paris: Elsevier.

Diaz-Andreu, M.

1995   Archaeology and nationalism in Spain. In P.L. Kohl and C. Fawcett (eds), *Nationalism, Politics, and the Practice of Archaeology,* 39–56. Cambridge: Cambridge University Press.

Dietler, M.

1998   Consumption, agency, and cultural entanglement: theoretical implications of a Mediterranean colonial encounter. In J.G. Cusick (ed.), *Studies in Culture Contact: Interaction, Culture Change, and Archaeology.* Center for Archaeological Investigations, Occasional Paper 25: 288–315. Carbondale: Southern Illinois University Press.

Dietler, M., and C. López-Ruiz (eds)

2009   *Colonial Encounters in Ancient Iberia: Phoenician, Greeks, and Indigenous Relations.* Chicago: University of Chicago Press.

Dietrich, M., and O. Loretz

1978   Der 'Seefahrende Volk' von *Sikila* (RS 34.129). *Ugarit-Forschungen* 10: 53–56.

Dikaios, P.

1935   Some Neolithic sites on Cyprus. *Report of the Department of Antiquities, Cyprus:* 11–13.

1936   The excavations at Erimi, 1933–1935. Final report. *Report of the Department of Antiquities, Cyprus:* 1–81.

1940   *The Excavations at Vounous-Bellapais in Cyprus, 1931–2.* Archaeologia 88: 1–174. Oxford: Society of Antiquaries of London.

1946   Early Copper Age discoveries in Cyprus, 3rd millennium B.C. copper mining. *Illustrated London News* (2 March 1946): 244–245.

1953   *Khirokitia.* Monograph of the Department of Antiquities, Government of Cyprus, No. 1. Oxford: Oxford University Press.

1960   A conspectus of architecture in ancient Cyprus. *Kypriakai Spoudai* 24: 3–30.

1961   *Sotira.* Philadelphia: University Museum, University of Pennsylvania.

1962   The Stone Age. In P. Dikaios and J.R. Stewart, *Swedish Cyprus Expedition* IV.1A: 1–204. Lund: Swedish Cyprus Expedition.

1969–71   *Enkomi. Excavations 1948–1958.* 3 Volumes. Mainz-am-Rhein, Germany: Philip von Zabern.

Domurad, M.

1986   The Populations of Ancient Cyprus. Unpublished PhD dissertation, University of Cincinnati, Cincinnati, Ohio.

1989   Whence the first Cypriots? In E.J. Peltenburg (ed.), *Early Society in Cyprus,* 66–70. Edinburgh: Edinburgh University Press.

Dothan, T.

1983   Some aspects of the appearance of the Sea Peoples and Philistines in Canaan. In S. Deger-Jalkotzy (ed.), *Griechenland, die Ägäis und die Levante wahrend der Dark Ages vom 12. bis zum 9. Jahrhundert v. Chr.* Sitzungberichte der Österreichische Akademie der Wissenschaften 418. Mykenische Forschung 10: 99–117. Vienna: Österreichische Akademie der Wissenschaften.

1993   Mediterranean archaeology. *Biblical Archaeologist* 56: 132–134.

Dothan, T., and A. Ben-Tor

1983   *Excavations at Athienou, Cyprus.* Qedem 16. Jerusalem: Institute of Archaeology, Hebrew University.

Dothan, T., and A. Zukerman

2004   A preliminary study of the Mycenaean IIIC:1 pottery assemblages from Tel Miqne-Ekron and Ashdod. *Bulletin of the American Schools of Oriental Research* 333: 1–54.

Dousougli, A.

1999   Palaeolithic Leukas. In G.N. Bailey, E. Adam, E. Panagopoulou, C. Perlès and

K. Zachos, *The Palaeolithic Archaeology of Greece and Adjacent Areas*. British School at Athens 3: 288–292. London: British School at Athens.

Ducos, P.
2000 The introduction of animals by man in Cyprus: an alternative to the Noah's ark model. In M. Mashkour, A.M. Choyke, H. Buitenhuis and F. Poplin (eds), *Archaeozoology of the Near East IVA. Proceedings of the Fourth International Symposium on the Archaeozoology of Southwestern Asia and Adjacent Areas*. ARC Publicatie 32: 74–82. Groningen, The Netherlands: Centrum voor Archeologische Research and Consultancy.

Dunand, M.
1973 *Fouilles de Byblos* 5. Paris: Maisonneuve.

Dunn-Vaturi, A.-E.
2003 *Vounous, C.F.A. Shaeffer's Excavations in 1933. Tombs 49–79*. Studies in Mediterranean Archaeology 130. Jonsered, Sweden: P. Åström's Förlag.

Du Plat Taylor, J.
1952 A Late Bronze Age settlement at Apliki, Cyprus. *Antiquaries Journal* 32: 133–167.
1957 *Myrtou-Pighades: A Late Bronze Age Sanctuary in Cyprus*. Oxford: Ashmolean Museum.

Edwards, P.C.
1989 Problems of recognizing earliest sedentism: the Natufian example. *Journal of Mediterranean Archaeology* 2: 5–48.

Efstratiou, N.
1985 *Ayios Petros: A Neolithic Site in the Northern Sporades*. British Archaeological Reports, International Series 241. Oxford: British Archaeological Reports.

Efstratiou, N., C. McCartney, P. Karkanas and D. Kyriakou
2010 An upland early site in the Troodos mountains. *Report of the Department of Antiquities, Cyprus*. (in press)
1995 *Heterarchy and the Analysis of Complex Societies*. American Anthropological Association, Archaeological Paper 6. Arlington, Virginia: American Anthropological Association.

Egetmeyer, M.
2009 The recent debate on Eteocypriote people and language. *Pasiphae* 3: 69–90.

Ehrenreich, R.M., C.L. Crumley and J.E. Levy (eds)
1995 *Heterarchy and the Analysis of Complex Societies*. American Anthropological Association, Archaeological Paper 6. Arlington, Virginia: American Anthropological Association.

Eirikh-Rose, A.
2004 Geometric patterns on pebbles: early identity symbols. In E.J. Peltenburg and A. Wasse (eds), *Neolithic Revolution: New Perspectives on Southwest Asia in Light of Recent Discoveries on Cyprus*. Levant Supplementary Series 1: 163–173. Oxford: Oxbow.

Eleftheriou, A.
2003 *About Thalassaemia*. Nicosia: Thalassaemia International Federation.

Elliot, C.
1983 Kissonerga-*Mylouthkia*: an outline of the ground stone industry. *Levant* 15: 11–37.

Ember, C.R.
1983 The relative decline in women's contribution to agriculture with intensification. *American Anthropologist* 85: 285–304.

Emberling, G.
1997 Ethnicity in complex societies: archaeological perspectives. *Journal of Archaeological Research* 5: 295–344.

Erdogu, B.
2003 Visualizing Neolithic landscapes: the early settled communities in western Anatolia and eastern Aegean islands. *European Journal of Archaeology* 6: 7–23.

Ervynck, A., K. Dobney, H. Hongo and R. Meadow
2001 Born free? New evidence for the status of *Sus scrofa* at Neolithic Cayönü Tepesi (southeastern Anatolia, Turkey). *Paléorient* 27(2): 47–74.

Evans, J.D.
1977 Island archaeology in the Mediterranean: problems and opportunities. *World Archaeology* 9: 12–26.

Evershed, R.P., S. Payne, A.G. Sherrat, M.S. Copley, J. Coolidge, D. Urem-Kotsu, K. Kotsakis, M. Özdoğan, A.E. Özdoğan, O. Nieuwenhuyse, P.M.M.G. Akkermans, D. Bailey, R.-R. Andeescu, S. Campbell, S. Farid, I. Hodder, N. Yalman, M. Özbaşaran, E. Biçakci, Y. Garfinkel, T. Levy and M.M. Burton
2008 Earliest date for milk use in the Near East and southeastern Europe linked to cattle herding. *Nature* 455: 528–531.

Falconer, S.E., P.L. Fall, T.W. Davis, M. Horowitz and J. Hunt
2005 Initial archaeological investigations at Politiko-*Troullia*, 2004. *Report of the Department of Antiquities, Cyprus*: 69–85.

Falconer, S.E., P.L. Fall, J. Hunt and M.C. Metzter
2010   Agrarian settlement at Politiko Troullia, 2008. *Report of the Department of Antiquities, Cyprus*: 183–198.

Fall, P.L., S.E. Falconer, M. Horowitz, J. Hunt, M.C. Metzger and D. Ryter
2008   Bronze Age settlement and landscape of Politiko *Troullia*, 2005–2007. *Report of the Department of Antiquities, Cyprus*: 183–208.

Fasnacht, W., and N. Künzler Wagner
2001   Stone casting moulds from Marki-*Alonia*. *Report of the Department of Antiquities, Cyprus*: 38–41.

Feinman, G.M.
1995   The emergence of inequality: a focus on strategies and processes. In T.D. Price and G.M. Feinman (eds), *Foundations of Social Inequality*, 255–280. New York: Plenum Press.

Feinman, G.M., and J. Neitzel
1984   Too many types – an overview of sedentary prestate societies in the Americas. *Advances in Archaeological Method and Theory* 7: 39–102.

Feld, S., and K.H. Basso (eds)
1996   *Senses of Place*. Santa Fe, New Mexico: School of American Research Press.

Feldman, M.H.
2002   Luxurious forms: redefining a Mediterranean 'International Style', 1400–1200 B.C.E. *Art Bulletin* 84: 6–29.

2006   *Diplomacy by Design: Luxury Arts and an 'International Style' in the Ancient Near East, 1400–1200 BC*. Chicago: University of Chicago Press.

2010   Object agency? Spatial perspective, social relations, and the Stele of Hammurabi. In S.R. Steadman and J.C. Ross (eds), *Agency and Identity in the Ancient Near East: New Paths Forward*, 193–200. London: Equinox.

Feldman, M.H., and C. Sauvage
2010   Objects of prestige? Chariots in the Late Bronze Age eastern Mediterranean and Near East. *Ägypten und Levante* 20: 67–181.

Ferrarese Ceruti, M.L.
1997   I vani c, p, q, del complesso nuragico di Antigori. In A. Antona and F. Lo Schiavo (eds), *Archeologia della Sardegna Preistorica e Protostorica*, 437–443. Nuoro, Sardinia, Italy: Poliedro.

Ferrarese Ceruti, M.L., and R. Assorgia
1982   Il complesso nuragico di Antigori (Sarroch, Cagliari). In L. Vagnetti (ed.), *Magna Grecia e Mondo Miceneo. Nuovi Documenti*, 167–176. Taranto, Sicily, Italy: Istituto per la Storia e l'Archeologia della Magna Grecia.

Finlayson, B.
2004   Island colonization, insularity or mainstream? In E.J. Peltenburg and A. Wasse (eds), *Neolithic Revolution: New Perspectives on Southwest Asia in Light of Recent Discoveries on Cyprus*. Levant Supplementary Series 1: 15–22. Oxford: Oxbow.

Fischer, P.M.
1986   *Prehistoric Cypriot Skulls, A Medico-Anthropological, Archaeological and Micro-Analytical Investigation*. Studies in Mediterranean Archaeology 75. Göteborg, Sweden: P. Åström's Förlag.

2011   The new Swedish Cyprus Expedition 2010: excavations at Dromolaxia *Vizatzia/Hala Sultan Tekke*. *Opuscula* 4: 69–98.

Fisher, K.D.
2006   Messages in stone: constructing sociopolitical inequality in Late Bronze Age Cyprus. In E.C. Robertson, J.W. Seibert, D.C. Fernandez and M.U. Zender (eds), *Space and Spatial Analysis in Archaeology*, 123–132. Calgary, Canada: University of Calgary Press, University of New Mexico Press.

2007   Building Power: Architecture, Interaction, and Sociopolitical Relations in Late Bronze Age Cyprus. Unpublished PhD Thesis, Department of Anthropology, University of Toronto, Canada.

2009   Elite place-making and social interaction in the Late Cypriot Bronze Age. *Journal of Mediterranean Archaeology* 22: 183–210.

Fishman, B., H. Forbes and B. Lawn
1977   University of Pennsylvania radiocarbon dates XIX. *Radiocarbon* 19: 188–228.

Fitzpatrick, S.M. (ed.)
2004   *Voyages of Discovery: The Archaeology of Islands*. New York: Praeger.

Flannery, K.V.
1972   The origins of the village as a settlement type in Mesoamerica and the Near East. In P.J. Ucko, R. Tringham and G.W. Dimbleby (eds), *Man, Settlement and Urbanism*, 23–53. London: Duckworth.

Fleming, D.E.
2002   Schloen's patrimonial pyramid: explaining Bronze Age society. *Bulletin of the*

American Schools of Oriental Research 328: 73–80.

Flemming, N.C.

1998 Archaeological evidence for vertical movement on the continental shelf during the Palaeolithic, Neolithic and Bronze Age periods. In I. Stewart and C. Vita-Finzi (eds), *Coastal Tectonics*. Geological Society of London, Special Publications 146: 129–146. London: Geological Society.

Flourentzos, P.

1989 A group of tombs of Middle Bronze Age date from Linou. In P. Åström, *Katydhata. A Bronze Age Site in Cyprus*. Studies in Mediterranean Archaeology 86: 61–70. Göteborg, Sweden: P. Åström's Förlag.

1997 Excavations at the Neolithic site of Paralimni. A preliminary report. *Report of the Department of Antiquities, Cyprus*: 1–10.

2003 Paralimni *Nissia*: a unique Neolithic settlement in Cyprus. In J. Guilaine and A. Le Brun (eds), *Le Néolithique de Chypre*. Bulletin de Correspondance Hellénique, Supplément 43: 73–83. Athens: École Française d'Athènes.

2008 *The Neolithic Settlement of Paralimni*. Nicosia: Department of Antiquities, Cyprus.

Fortin, M.

1983 Recherches sur l'architecture militaire de l'Age du Bronze à Chypre. *Echos du Monde Classique* 27 (n.s. 2): 206–219.

Fox, W.A.

1987 The Neolithic occupation of western Cyprus. In D.W. Rupp (ed.), *Western Cyprus: Connections*. Studies in Mediterranean Archaeology 77: 19–42. Göteborg, Sweden: P. Åström's Förlag.

Frame, S.

2002 Island neolithics: animal exploitation in the Aceramic Neolithic of Cyprus. In W.H. Waldren and J.A. Ensenyat (eds), *World Islands in Prehistory. V Deia International Conference of Prehistory*. British Archaeological Reports, International Series 1095: 233–238. Oxford: Archaeopress.

Frankel, D.

1974 *Middle Cypriot White Painted Pottery: An Analytical Study of the Decoration*. Studies in Mediterranean Archaeology 42. Göteborg, Sweden: P. Åström's Förlag.

1988 Pottery production in prehistoric Bronze Age Cyprus: assessing the problem. *Journal of Mediterranean Archaeology* 1(2): 27–55.

1997 Cypriot figurines and the origins of patriarchy. *Current Anthropology* 38: 84–86.

2000 Migration and ethnicity in prehistoric Cyprus: technology as *habitus*. *European Journal of Archaeology* 3: 167–187.

2002 Social stratification, gender and ethnicity in third millennium Cyprus. In D. Bolger and N. Serwint (eds), *Engendering Aphrodite: Women and Society in Ancient Cyprus*. Cyprus American Archaeological Research Institute Monograph 3: 171–179. Boston: American Schools of Oriental Research.

2005 Becoming Bronze Age. Acculturation and enculturation in third millennium BC Cyprus. In J. Clarke (ed.), *Archaeological Perspectives on the Transmission and Transformation of Culture in the Eastern Mediterranean*. Levant Supplementary Series 2: 18–24. Oxford: Oxbow.

2009 What do we mean by 'regionalism'? In I. Hein (ed.), *The Formation of Cyprus in the 2nd Millennium BC. Studies in Regionalism during the Middle and Late Bronze Ages*. Österreichische Akademie der Wissenschaften, Denkschriften der Gesamtakademie 52. Contributions to the Chronology of the Eastern Mediterranean 20: 15–25. Vienna: Österreichische Akademie der Wissenschaften.

2010 A different Chalcolithic: a central Cypriot scene. In D. Bolger and L.C. Maguire (eds), *The Development of Pre-State Communities in the Ancient Near East: Studies in Honour of Edgar Peltenburg*. BANEA Publication Series 2: 38–45. Oxford: Oxbow.

Frankel, D., and A. Tamvaki

1973 Cypriote shrine models and decorated tombs. *Australian Journal of Biblical Archaeology* 2(2): 39–44.

Frankel, D., and J.M. Webb

1996 *Marki Alonia: An Early and Middle Bronze Age Town in Cyprus. Excavations 1990–1994*. Studies in Mediterranean Archaeology 123.1. Jonsered, Sweden: P. Åström's Förlag.

1998 Three faces of identity. Ethnicity, community and status in the Cypriot Bronze Age. *Mediterranean Archaeology* 11: 1–12.

2000 Excavations at Marki Alonia, 1999–2000. *Report of the Department of Antiquities, Cyprus*: 65–94.

2001 Population, households, and ceramic consumption in a prehistoric Cypriot village. *Journal of Field Archaeology* 28: 115–129.

2004 An Early Bronze Age shell pendant from Cyprus. *Bulletin of the American Schools of Oriental Research* 336: 1–9.

2006a *Marki Alonia: An Early and Middle Bronze Age Settlement in Cyprus. Excavations 1995–2000.* Studies in Mediterranean Archaeology 123.2. Sävedalen, Sweden: P. Åström's Förlag.

2006b Neighbours: negotiating space in a prehistoric village. *Antiquity* 80/308: 287–302.

2007 *The Bronze Age Cemeteries at Deneia in Cyprus.* Studies in Mediterranean Archaeology 135. Sävedalen, Sweden: P. Åström's Förlag.

Frankel, D., J.M. Webb and C. Eslick

1996 Anatolia and Cyprus in the third millennium BCE. A speculative model of interaction. In G. Bunnens (ed.), *Cultural Interaction in the Ancient Near East.* Abr Nahrain Supplement 5: 37–50. Louvain, Belgium: Peeters.

Friedman, J.

1992 The past in the future: history and the politics of identity. *American Anthropologist* 94: 837–859.

Frumkin, A., G. Kadan, Y. Yenzel and Y. Eyal

2001 Radiocarbon chronology of the Holocene Dead Sea: attempting a regional correlaton. *Radiocarbon* 43(3): 1179–1189.

Fuller, D.Q., R.B. Allaby and C. Stevens

2010 Domestication as innovation: the entanglement of techniques, technology and chance in the domestication of cereal crops. *World Archaeology* 42: 13–28.

Furumark, A.

1944 The Mycenaean IIIC pottery and its relation to Cypriot fabrics. *Opuscula Archaeologica* 3: 194–265.

1965 The excavations at Sinda: some historical results. *Opuscula Atheniensia* 6: 99–116.

Furumark, A., and C. Adelman (with P. Åström, N.-G. Gejwall and H. Hemming von der Osten)

2003 *Swedish Excavations at Sinda, Cyprus: Excavations Conducted by Arne Furumark, 1947–1948.* Skrifter Utgivna av Svenska Institutet i Athen 50. Stockholm: Svenska Institutet i Athen.

Galanidou, N., and C. Perlès (eds)

2003 *The Greek Mesolithic: Problems and Perspectives.* British School at Athens, Studies 10. London: British School at Athens.

Galaty, M.L., and W.A. Parkinson (eds)

2007 *Rethinking Mycenaean Palaces* II. Cotsen Institute of Archaeology, UCLA,

Monograph 60. Los Angeles: Cotsen Institute of Archaeology, UCLA.

Gale, N.H.

1989 Archaeometallurgical studies of Late Bronze Age copper oxhide ingots from the Mediterranean region. In A. Hauptmann, E. Pernicka and G.A. Wagner (eds), *Old World Archaeometallurgy.* Der Anschnitt 7: 247–268. Bochum, Germany: Deutsches Bergbau-Museums.

1991a Metals and metallurgy in the Chalcolithic period. *Bulletin of the American Schools of Oriental Research* 282–283: 37–62.

1991b Copper oxhide ingots and their relation to the Bronze Age metals trade. In N.H. Gale (ed.), *Bronze Age Trade in the Mediterranean.* Studies in Mediterranean Archaeology 90: 197–239. Göteborg, Sweden: P. Åström's Förlag.

1999 Lead isotope characterization of the ore deposits of Cyprus and Sardinia and its application to the discovery of sources of copper for Late Bronze Age oxhide ingots. In S.M.M. Young, A.M. Pollard, P. Budd and R.A. Ixer (eds), *Metals in Antiquity.* British Archaeological Reports, International Series 792: 110–121. Oxford: Archaeopress.

2005 Die Kupferbarren von Uluburun. Teil 2: Bleisotopenanalysen von Bohrkernen aus den Barren. In Ü. Yalçin, C. Pulak and R. Slotter (eds), *Das Schiff von Uluburun: Welthandel vor 3000 Jahren,* 141–148. Bochum, Germany: Deutsches Bergbau-Museum.

2009 A response to the paper of A.M. Pollard: What a long, strange trip it's been: lead isotopes and archaeology. In A.J. Shortland, I.C. Freestone and T. Rehren (eds), *From Mine to Microscope: Advances in the Study of Ancient Technology,* 191–196. Oxford: Oxbow.

Gale, N.H., and Z. Stos-Gale

1989 Some aspects of Cypriote metallurgy in the Middle and Late Bronze Age. In R. Laffineur (ed.), *Transition: Le Monde Égéen du Bronze Moyen et Bronze Récent.* Aegaeum 3: 251–256. Liège, Belgium: Université de Liège.

2002 Archaeometallurgical research in the Aegean. In M. Bartelheim, E. Pernicka and R. Krause (eds), *The Beginnings of Metallurgy in the Old World,* 277–302. Rahden, Germany: Verlag Marie Leidorf.

2005 Zur Herkunft der Kupferbarren aus dem Schiffswrack von Uluburun und der spätbronzezeitliche Metallhandel im Mittelmeerraum. In Ü. Yalçin, C. Pulak and R. Slotter (eds), *Das Schiff von Uluburun: Welthandel vor 3000 Jahren*, 117–131. Bochum, Germany: Deutsches Bergbau-Museum.

2012 The role of the Apliki mine region in the post ≈1400 BC copper production and trade networks in Cyprus and in the wider Mediterranean. In V. Kassianidou and G. Papasavvas (eds), *Eastern Mediterranean Metallurgy and Metalwork in the Second Millennium BC*, 68–80. Oxford: Oxbow.

Gale, N.H., Z.A. Stos-Gale and W. Fasnacht
1996 Copper and copper working at Alambra. In J.E. Coleman, J.A. Barlow, M.K. Mogelonsky and K.W. Scharr, *Alambra: A Middle Bronze Age Site in Cyprus. Investigations by Cornell University, 1974–1984*. Studies In Mediterranean Archaeology 118: 359–426. Jonsered, Sweden: P. Åström's Forlag.

Galili, E., V. Eshed, A. Gopher and I. Hershkovitz
2005 Burial practices at the submerged Pre-Pottery Neolithic C site of Atlit-Yam, northern coast of Israel. *Bulletin of the American Schools of Oriental Research* 339: 1–19.

Galili, E., and Y. Nir
1993 The submerged Pre-Pottery Neolithic water well of Atlit-Yam, northern Israel, and its palaeoenvironmental implications. *The Holocene* 3: 265–270.

Galili, E., B. Rosen, A. Gopher and L. Kolska Horwitz
2002 The emergence and dispersion of the eastern Mediterranean Fishing Village: evidence from submerged Neolithic settlements off the Carmel coast, Israel. *Journal of Mediterranean Archaeology* 15: 167–198.

Galili, E., B. Rosen, A. Gopher and L. Kolska Horowitz
2004 The emergence of the Mediterranean Fishing Village in the Levant and the anomaly of Neolithic Cyprus. In E.J. Peltenburg and A. Wasse (eds), *Neolithic Revolution: New Perspectives on Southwest Asia in Light of Recent Discoveries on Cyprus*. Levant Supplementary Series 1: 91–101. Oxford: Oxbow.

Galimberti, M., C. Bronk Ramsey and S.W. Manning
2004 Wiggle-match dating of tree-ring sequences. *Radiocarbon* 46: 917–924.

Gamble, G.
2003 *Timewalkers: The Prehistory of Global Colonization*. Stroud, England: Sutton Publishing.

Garfinkel, Y.
1993 The Yarmukian culture in Israel. *Paléorient* 19(1): 115–134.

Garrard, A.
1999 Charting the emergence of cereal and pulse domestication in south-west Asia. *Environmental Archaeology* 4: 57–76.

Garrod, D.
1957 The Natufian culture: the life and economy of a Mesolithic people in the Near East. *Proceedings of the Prehistoric Society* 43: 211–227.

Gass, I.G.
1968 Is the Troodos massif of Cyprus a fragment of Mesozoic ocean floor? *Nature* 220: 39–42.

Georgiou, G.
2007 The Topography of Human Settlement in Cyprus in the Early and Middle Bronze Ages. Unpublished PhD dissertation, University of Cyprus, Nicosia. (in Greek)

2009 The dynamism of central Cyprus during Middle Cypriot III: funerary evidence from Nicosia *Agia Paraskevi*. In I. Hein (ed.), *The Formation of Cyprus in the Second Millennium BC: Studies in Regionalism during the Middle and Late Bronze Ages*. Österreichische Akademie Der Wissenschaften, Denkschriften Der Gesamtakademie 52. Contributions to the Chronology of the Eastern Mediterranean 20: 65–78. Vienna: Österreichische Akademie Der Wissenschaften.

Geraga, M., S. Tsaila-Monopolis, C. Ioakim, G. Papatheodorou and G. Ferentinos
2005 Short-term climate changes in the southern Aegean Sea over the last 48,000 years. *Palaeogeography, Palaeoclimatology, Palaeoecology* 220: 311–332.

Giardino, C.
1992 Nuragic Sardinia and the Mediterranean: metallurgy and maritime traffic. In R.H. Tykot and T.K. Andrews (eds), *Sardinia in the Mediterranean: A Footprint in the Sea*. Monographs in Mediterranean Archaeology 3: 304–316. Sheffield, England: Sheffield Academic Press.

Giardino, C., G.E. Gigante and S. Ridolfe

2003   Archeometallurgical studies. Appendix 8.1, in S. Swiny, G. Rapp and E. Herscher (eds), *Sotira Kaminoudhia: An Early Bronze Age Site in Cyprus*. Cyprus American Archaeological Research Institute Monograph 4: 385–396. Boston: American Schools of Oriental Research.

Gifford, J.A.

1985   Paleogeography of ancient harbour sites of the Larnaca lowlands, southeastern Cyprus. In A. Raban (ed.), *Harbour Archaeology*. British Archaeological Reports, International Series 257: 45–48. Oxford: British Archaeological Reports.

Gilboa, A.

2005   Sea Peoples and Phoenicians along the southern Phoenician coast – a reconciliation: an interpretation of Sikila (SKL) material culture. *Bulletin of the American Schools of Oriental Research* 337: 47–78.

2006–2007 Fragmenting the Sea Peoples, with an emphasis on Cyprus, Syria and Egypt: a Tel Dor perspective. *Scripta Mediterranea* 27–28: 209–244.

Gilman, P.A.

1987   Architecture as artifact: pit structures and pueblos in the American southwest. *American Antiquity* 52: 538–564.

Gitin, S., A. Mazar and E. Stern (eds)

1998   *Mediterranean Peoples in Transition: Thirteenth to Early Tenth Centuries BCE*. Jerusalem: Israel Exploration Society.

Gittlen, B.M.

1975   Cypriote White Slip pottery in its Palestinian stratigraphic context. In N. Robertson (ed.), *The Archaeology of Cyprus: Recent Developments*, 111–120. Park Ridge, New Jersey: Noyes Press.

1981   The cultural and chronological implications of the Cypro-Palestinian trade during the Late Bronze Age. *Bulletin of the American Schools of Oriental Research* 241: 49–59.

Given, M.

1998   Inventing the Eteocypriots: imperialist archaeology and the manipulation of ethnic identity. *Journal of Mediterranean Archaeology* 11: 3–29.

2002   Maps, fields, and boundary cairns: demarcation and resistance in colonial Cyprus. *International Journal of Historical Archaeology* 6: 1–22.

Given, M., V. Kassianidou, A.B. Knapp and J. Noller

2002   Troodos Archaeological and Environmental Survey Project, Cyprus: report on the 2001 season. *Levant* 34: 25–38.

Given, M., and A.B. Knapp

2003   *The Sydney Cyprus Survey Project: Social Approaches to Regional Archaeological Survey*. Monumenta Archaeologica 21. Los Angeles: Cotsen Institute of Archaeology, UCLA.

Given, M., A.B. Knapp, L. Sollars, J. Noller and V. Kassianidou

n.d.   *Landscape and Interaction: The Troodos Archaeological and Environmental Survey Project, Cyprus*. Oxford: Oxbow; Council for British Research in the Levant.

Gjerstad, E.

1926   *Studies on Prehistoric Cyprus*. Uppsala, Sweden: Uppsala Universitets Arsskrift.

1979   The Phoenician colonization and expansion in Cyprus. *Report of the Department of Antiquities, Cyprus*: 230–254.

Gjerstad, E., J. Lindos, E. Sjöqvist and A. Westholm

1934   *Swedish Cyprus Expedition* I, II: *Finds and Results of the Excavations in Cyprus 1927–1931*. Stockholm: Swedish Cyprus Expedition.

Gkiasta, M.

2010   Social identities, materiality and connectivity in Early Bronze Age Crete. In P. van Dommelen and A.B. Knapp (eds), *Material Connections in the Ancient Mediterranean: Mobility, Materiality and Mediterranean Identities*, 85–105. London: Routledge.

Goldman, H.

1956   *Excavations at Gözlu Küle* II. Princeton: Princeton University Press.

Goldstein, L.

1981   One-dimensional archaeology and multidimensional people: spatial organisation and mortuary analysis. In R. Chapman, I. Kinnes and K. Randsborg (eds), *The Archaeology of Death*, 95–105. Cambridge: Cambridge University Press.

Gomez, B.

1987   The alluvial terraces and fills of the Lower Vasilikos Valley, in the vicinity of Kalavasos, Cyprus. *Transactions of the Institute of British Geographers* 12: 345–359.

Gomez, B., M.D. Gascock, M.J. Blackman and I.A. Todd

1995 Neutron Activation Analysis of obsidian from Kalavasos-*Tenta*. *Journal of Field Archaeology* 22: 503–508.

González-Ruibal, A., A. Hernando and G. Politis

2011 Ontology of the self and material culture: arrow-making among the Awá hunter–gatherers (Brazil). *Journal of Anthropological Archaeology* 30: 1–16.

Gopher, A.

1994 *Arrowheads of the Neolithic Levant.* ASOR Dissertation Series 10. Winona Lake, Indiana: American Schools of Oriental Research/Eisenbrauns.

Goren, Y., S. Bunimovitz, I. Finkelstein and N. Na'aman

2003 The location of *Alashiya*: new evidence from petrographic investigation of Alashiyan tablets from el-Amarna and Ugarit. *American Journal of Archaeology* 107: 233–255.

Goren, Y., I. Finkelstein and N. Na'aman

2004 *Inscribed in Clay: Provenance Study of the Amarna Tablets and Other Ancient Near Eastern Texts.* Sonia and Marco Nader Institute of Archaeology, Monograph Series 23. Tel Aviv: Institute of Archaeology, Tel Aviv University.

Goring, E.

1988 *A Mischievous Pastime: Digging in Cyprus in the Nineteenth Century.* Edinburgh: National Museums of Scotland.

1989 Death in everyday life: aspects of burial practice in the Late Bronze Age. In E.J. Peltenburg (ed.), *Early Society in Cyprus*, 95–105. Edinburgh: Edinburgh University Press.

1995 The Kourion sceptre: some facts and factoids. In C. Morris (ed.), *Klados: Essays in Honour of J.N. Coldstream.* Bulletin of the Institute of Classical Studies, University College London. Supplement 63: 103–110. London: Institute of Classical Studies.

Goring-Morris, A.N.

2005 Life, death and the emergence of differential status in the Near Eastern Neolithic: evidence from Kfar HaHoresh, Lower Galilee, Israel. In J. Clarke (ed.), *Archaeological Perspectives on the Transmission and Transformation of Culture in the Eastern Mediterranean.* Levant Supplementary Series 2: 89–105. Oxford: Oxbow.

Goring-Morris, A.N., and A. Belfer-Cohen

1997 The articulation of cultural processes and late Quaternary environmental changes in Cisjordan. *Paléorient* 23(2): 71–93.

Gosden, C., and C. Pavlides

1994 Are islands insular? Landscape vs seascape in the case of the Arawe islands, Papua New Guinea. *Archaeology in Oceania* 29: 162–171.

Grace, V.

1940 A Cypriote tomb and Minoan evidence for its date. *American Journal of Archaeology* 44: 10–52.

Grayson, D.K.

2000 Review of A.H. Simmons, *Faunal Extinction in an Island Society: Pygmy Hippopotamus Hunters of Cyprus* (Boston: Kluwer, 1999), in *Geoarchaeology* 15: 379–381.

Graziadio, G.

1997 Le presenze Cipriote in Italia nel quadro del commercio Mediterraneo dei secoli xiv e xiii a.c. *Studi Classici e Orientali* 46: 681–719.

2004 Le influenze egee si sigilli conoidi Ciprioti ed i problemi cronologici connessi. In S. Bruni, T. Caruso and M. Massa (eds), *Archaeologica Pisana: Scritti per Orlands Pancrazzi*, 220–228. Pisa, Italy: Giardini Editori e Stampatori.

Greenfield, H.J.

2010 The Secondary Products Revolution: the past, the present and the future. *World Archaeology* 42: 29–54.

Grigson, C.

1995 Plough and pasture in the early economy of the southern Levant. In T.E. Levy (ed.), *The Archaeology of Society in the Holy Land*, 245–268. Leicester, England: Leicester University Press.

Grima, R.

2001 An iconography of insularity: a cosmological interpretation of some images and spaces in the Late Neolithic temples of Malta. *Papers from the Institute of Archaeology* 12: 48–65.

Guilaine, J.

2003a Parekklisha *Shillourokambos*: périodisation et aménagements domestiques. In J. Guilaine and A. Le Brun (eds), *Le Néolithique de Chypre.* Bulletin de Correspondance Hellénique, Supplément 43: 3–14. Athens: École Française d'Athènes.

2003b   Objets 'symboliques' et parures de
         Parekklisha *Shillourokambos*. In J. Guilaine
         and A. Le Brun (eds), *Le Néolithique de
         Chypre*. Bulletin de Correspondance
         Hellénique, Supplément 43: 329–340.
         Athens: École Française d'Athènes.

Guilaine, J., and F. Briois
2001   Parekklisha *Shillourokambos*: an early
         Neolithic site on Cyprus. In S. Swiny
         (ed.), *The Earliest Prehistory of Cyprus:
         From Colonization to Exploitation*.
         Cyprus American Archaeological
         Research Institute Monograph 2: 37–53.
         Boston: American Schools of Oriental
         Research.
2006   *Shillourokambos* and the Neolithization
         of Cyprus: some reflections. *Eurasian
         Prehistory* 4(1–2): 159–175.

Guilaine, J., and A. Le Brun (eds)
2003   *Le Néolithique de Chypre*. Bulletin de
         Correspondance Hellénique, Supplément
         43. Athens: École Française d'Athènes.

Guilaine, J., and P.L. van Berg (eds)
2006   *La Néolithisation. The Neolithisation
         Process*. British Archaeological Reports,
         International Series 1520. Oxford:
         Archaeopress.

Guilaine, J., P. Devéze, J. Coularou and F. Briois
1999   Tête sculptée en pierre dans le Néolithique
         Pré-céramique de Shillourokampos
         (Parekklisia, Chypre). *Report of the
         Department of Antiquities, Cyprus*: 1–12.

Guilaine, J., F. Briois, J.-D. Vigne and I. Carrère
2000   Découverte d'un Néolithique pré-
         céramique ancien chypriote (fin 9e,
         début 8e millénaires cal. BC), apparenté
         au PPNB ancien/moyen du Levant nord.
         *Comptes Rendus des Séances de l'Académie
         des Sciences, Paris, Sciences de la Terre et de
         Planétes* 330: 75–82.

Guilaine, J., F. Briois and J.-D. Vigne (eds)
2011   *Shillourokambos. Un établissement néolithique
         pré-céramique à Chypre*. Paris: Éditions
         Errances.

Gunneweg, J., F. Asaro, H.V. Michel, and I.
         Perlman
1992   On the origin of a Mycenaean IIIA char-
         iot krater and other related Mycenaean
         pottery from tomb 387 at Laish/Dan.
         Eretz-Israel 23: 54–63.

Gupta, A., and J. Ferguson (eds)
1997   *Culture, Power, Place*. Durham, North
         Carolina: Duke University Press.

Hadjicosti, M.
1991   The Late Bronze Age Tomb 2 from
         Mathiatis (new perspectives for the
         Mathiatis region). *Report of the Department
         of Antiquities, Cyprus*: 75–91.

Hadjisavvas, S.
1989   A Late Cypriot community at Alassa.
         In E.J. Peltenburg (ed.), *Early Society in
         Cyprus*, 32–42. Edinburgh: Edinburgh
         University Press.
1991   LCIIC to LCIIIA without intruders: the
         case of Alassa. In J. Barlow, D. Bolger and
         B. Kling (eds), *Cypriot Ceramics: Reading
         the Prehistoric Record*. University Museum
         Monograph 74: 173–180. Philadelphia:
         University of Pennsylvania, University
         Museum Monographs.
1992   *Olive Oil Processing in Cyprus. From the
         Bronze Age to the Byzantine Period*. Studies
         in Mediterranean Archaeology 99.
         Jonsered, Sweden: P. Åström's Förlag.
1996   Alassa: a regional center of Alashiya? In P.
         Åström and E. Herscher (eds), *Late Bronze
         Age Settlements in Cyprus: Function and
         Relationship*. Studies in Mediterranean
         Archaeology and Literature, Pocket-book
         126: 23–38. Jonsered, Sweden: P. Åström's
         Förlag.
2001   Crete and Cyprus: religion and script.
         The case of Alassa. In A. Kyriatsoulis (ed.),
         *Kreta und Zypern: Religion und Schrift. Von
         der Frühgeschichte biz zum Ende der archai-
         schen Zeit*, 205–231. Altenburg, Germany:
         DZA Verlag für Kultur und Wissenschaft.
2003   Ashlar buildings. In S. Hadjisavvas
         (ed.), *From Ishtar to Aphrodite: 3200 Years
         of Cypriot Hellenism. Treasures from the
         Museums of Cyprus*, 31–34. New York:
         Onassis Public Benefit Foundation.
2006   Aspects of Late Bronze Age trade as seen
         from Alassa *Pano Mandilares*. In E. Czerny,
         I. Hein, H. Hunger, D. Melman and A.
         Schwab (eds), *Timelines. Studies in Honour
         of Manfred Bietak*, Volume 2. Orientalia
         Lovaniensia Analecta 149(2): 449–453.
         Leuven, Belgium: Uitgeverij Peeters en
         Departement Oosterse Studies.
2009   Aspects of regionalism in Late Cypriot
         architecture. In I. Hein (ed.), *The Formation
         of Cyprus in the 2nd Millennium BC. Studies
         in Regionalism during the Middle and Late
         Bronze Ages*. Österreichische Akademie
         Der Wissenschaften, Denkschriften Der

Gesamtakademie 52: 127–133. Vienna: Österreichische Akademie Der Wissenschaften.

Hadjisavvas, S. (published by P. Flourentzos)

2007   *Annual Report of the Department of Antiquities for the Year 2000.* Nicosia: Republic of Cyprus.

Hadjisavvas, S., and I. Hadjisavva

1997   Aegean Influence at Alassa. In D. Christou (ed.), *Cyprus and the Aegean in Antiquity*, 143–148. Nicosia: Department of Antiquities, Cyprus.

Hadjisavvas, S., and V. Karageorghis (eds)

2000   *The Problem of Unpublished Excavations. Proceedings of a Conference Organised by the Department of Antiquities and the A.G. Leventis Foundation, Nicosia 25–26 November 1999.* Nicosia: Department of Antiquities Cyprus, Leventis Foundation.

Hadjisterkotis, E., and D. Reese

2008   Considerations on the potential use of cliffs and caves by the extinct endemic late Pleistocene hippopotami and elephants of Cyprus. *European Journal of Wildlife Research* 54: 122–133.

Hägg, R.

1991   Sacred horns and *naiskoi*. Remarks on Aegean religious sybmolism in Cyprus. In V. Karageorghis (ed.), *The Civilizations of the Aegean and Their Diffusion in Cyprus and the Eastern Mediterranean, 2000–600 BC*, 79–83. Larnaca: Pierides Foundation.

Haggis, D.C.

1993   Intensive survey, traditional settlement patterns, and Dark Age Crete: the case of Early Iron Age Kavousi. *Journal of Mediterranean Archaeology* 6: 131–174.

Haldane, C.

1990   Shipwrecked plant remains. *Biblical Archaeologist* 53(1): 55–60.

1993   Direct evidence for organic cargoes in the Late Bronze Age. *World Archaeology* 24: 348–360.

Hall, J.M.

1997   *Ethnic Identity in Greek Antiquity.* Cambridge: Cambridge University Press.

Halstead, P.

1977   A preliminary report on the faunal remains from Late Bronze Age Kouklia, Paphos. *Report of the Department of Antiquities, Cyprus*: 261–275.

1981   From determinism to uncertainty: social storage and the rise of the Minoan palace. In A. Sheridan and G. Bailey (eds), *Economic Archaeology*. British Archaeological Reports, International Series 96: 97–117. Oxford: British Archaeological Reports.

1987   Traditional and ancient rural economy in Mediterranean Europe: plus ça change? *Journal of Hellenic Studies* 107: 77–87.

Halstead, P., and J. O'Shea

1982   A friend in need is a friend indeed: social storage and the origins of social ranking. In C. Renfrew and S. Shennan (eds), *Ranking, Resource and Exchange*, 92–99. Cambridge: Cambridge University Press.

1989   (eds) *Bad Year Economics.* Cambridge: Cambridge University Press.

Hamilakis, Y.

2003   Legacies of Mediterranean prehistory. Unpublished paper in possession of author.

Hamilakis, Y., M. Pluciennik and S. Tarlow (eds)

2002   *Thinking through the Body: Archaeologies of Corporeality.* New York: Kluwer Academic/Plenum.

Hamilton, N.

1994   A fresh look at the 'seated gentleman' in the Pierides Foundation Museum, Republic of Cyprus. *Cambridge Archaeological Journal* 4: 302–312.

2000   Ungendering archaeology: concepts of sex and gender in figurine studies in prehistory. In M. Donald and L. Hurcombe (eds), *Representations of Gender from Prehistory to the Present*, 17–30. London: Macmillan.

Hamilton, S., and R. Whitehouse

2006   Three senses of dwelling: beginning to socialise the Neolithic ditched villages of the Tavoliere, southeast Italy. *Journal of Iberian Archaeology* 8: 159–184.

Hansen, J.

1988   Agriculture in the prehistoric Aegean: data versus speculation. *American Journal of Archaeology* 92: 39–52.

1991   Palaeoethnobotany in Cyprus: recent research. In J. Renfrew (ed.), *New Light on Early Farming: Recent Developments in Palaeoethnobotany*, 225–236. Edinburgh: Edinburgh University Press.

2001   Aceramic Neolithic plant remains in Cyprus: clues to their origins? In S. Swiny (ed.), *The Earliest Prehistory of Cyprus: From Colonization to Exploitation.* Cyprus

American Archaeological Research Institute Monograph 2: 119–128. Boston: American Schools of Oriental Research.

2003   The botanical remains. In S. Swiny, G. Rapp and E. Herscher (eds), *Sotira Kamminoudhia: An Early Bronze Age Site in Cyprus*. American Schools of Oriental Research, Archaeological Reports 8. Cyprus American Archaeological Research Institute, Monograph Series 4: 449–453. Boston: American Schools of Oriental Research.

Harper, N.
2008   Short skulls, long skulls, and thalassemia: J. Lawrence Angel and the development of Cypriot anthropology. *Near Eastern Archaeology* 71: 111–119.

Harper, N., and S.C. Fox
2008   Recent research in Cypriot bioarchaeology. *Bioarchaeology of the Near East* 2: 1–38.

Harter-Lailheugue, S., F. Le Mort, J.-D. Vigne, J. Guilaine, A. Le Brun and F. Bouchet
2005   Premières données parasitologiques sur les populations humaines pré-céramiques chypriotes (VIIIe et VIIe millénaires av. J.C.). *Paléorient* 31: 43–54.

Hatcher, H.
2002   White Slip wares from Bronze Age Cyprus and the Levant. In G. Muskett, A. Koltsida and M. Georgiadis (eds), *SOMA 2001: Symposium on Mediterranean Archaeology*. British Archaeological Reports: International Series 1040: 161–168. Oxford: Archeopress.

Hauptmann, A., R. Maddin and M. Prange
2002   On the structure and composition of copper and tin ingots excavated from the shipwreck of Uluburun. *Bulletin of the American Schools of Oriental Research* 328: 1–30.

Hein, A., and V. Kilikoglou
2007   Modeling of thermal behavior of ancient metallurgical ceramics. *Journal of the American Ceramic Society* 90: 878–884.

Hein, A., V. Kilikoglou and V. Kassianidou
2007   Chemical and mineralogical examination of metallurgical ceramics from a Late Bronze Age copper smelting site in Cyprus. *Journal of Archaeological Science* 34: 141–154.

Hein, I. (ed.)
2009   *The Formation of Cyprus in the 2nd Millennium BC. Studies in Regionalism during the Middle and Late Bronze Ages*. Österreichische Akademie Der Wissenschaften, Denkschriften Der Gesamtakademie 52. Vienna: Österreichische Akademie Der Wissenschaften.

Helbaek, H.
1962   Late Cypriot vegetable diet at Apliki. *Opuscula Atheniensia* 4: 171–186.

1966   What farming produced at Cypriote Kalopsidha. In P. Åström, *Excavations at Kalopsidha and Ayios Iakovos in Cyprus*. Studies in Mediterranean Archaeology 2: 115–126. Lund, Sweden: P. Åström's Förlag.

Held, S.O.
1988   Sotira *Kaminoudhia* survey: preliminary report of the 1983 and 1984 seasons. *Report of the Department of Antiquities, Cyprus*: 53–62.

1989a   Early Prehistoric Island Archaeology in Cyprus: Configurations of Formative Culture Growth from the Pleistocene/ Holocene Boundary to the mid-3rd Millennium BC. Unpublished PhD thesis, Institute of Archaeology, University College London.

1989b   Colonization cycles on Cyprus I: the biogeographic and paleontological foundations of Early Prehistoric settlement. *Report of the Department of Antiquities, Cyprus*: 7–28.

1990   Back to what future? New directions for Cypriot Early Prehistoric research in the 1990s. *Report of the Department of Antiquities, Cyprus*: 1–43.

1992a   Colonization and extinction on Early Prehistoric Cyprus. In P. Åström (ed.), *Acta Cypria* 2. Studies in Mediterranean Archaeology and Literature, Pocket-book 117: 104–164. Jonsered, Sweden: P. Åström's Förlag.

1992b   *Pleistocene Fauna and Holocene Humans: A Gazetteer of Paleontological and Early Archaeological Sites on Cyprus*. Studies in Mediterranean Archeology 92. Jonsered, Sweden: P. Åström's Förlag.

1993   Insularity as a modifier of cultural change: the case of prehistoric Cyprus. *Bulletin of the American Schools of Oriental Research* 292: 25–33.

Helms, M.W.
1988   *Ulysses' Sail: An Ethnographic Odyssey of Power, Knowledge, and Geographical Distance*. Princeton: Princeton University Press.

Hennessy, J.B.

1964   *Stephania: A Middle and Late Bronze Age Cemetery in Cyprus.* London: Bernard Quaritch Ltd.

Hennessy, J.B., K. Eriksson and I. Kehrberg

1988   *Ayia Paraskevi and Vasilia: Excavations by the Late J.R. Stewart.* Studies in Mediterranean Archaeology 82. Göteborg, Sweden: P. Åström's Förlag.

Hermansen, B.D.

2004   Supra-regional concepts from a local perspective. *Neo-Lithics* 1/04: 34–37.

Hermary, A.

1999   Amathus before the 8th century BC. In M. Iacovou and D. Michaelides (eds), *Cyprus: The Historicity of the Geometric Horizon*, 55–67. Nicosia: Archaeological Research Unit, University of Cyprus; Bank of Cyprus Cultural Foundation, Ministry of Education and Culture.

Herscher, E.

1978   The Bronze Age Cemetery at Lapithos, *Vrysi tou Barba*, Cyprus: Results of the University of Pennsylvania Museum Excavation, 1931. Unpublished PhD dissertation, University of Pennsylvania, Philadelphia.

1991   Beyond regionalism: toward an island-wide Early and Middle Cypriot sequence. In J. Barlow, D. Bolger and B. Kling (eds), *Cypriot Ceramics: Reading the Prehistoric Record.* University Museum Monograph 74: 45–50. Philadelphia: University of Pennsylvania, University Museum Monographs.

1995   Archaeology in Cyprus. *American Journal of Archaeology* 99: 257–294.

1997   Representational relief on Early and Middle Cypriot pottery. In V. Karageorghis, R. Laffineur and F. Vandenabeele (eds), *Four Thousand Years of Images on Cypriote Pottery. Proceedings of the Third International Conference of Cypriote Studies*, 25–36. Nicosia, Brussels, Liège, Belgium: Leventis Foundation, University of Cyprus; Vrije Universiteit Brussels; Université de Liège.

Herscher, E., and S. Swiny

1992   Picking up the pieces: two plundered Bronze Age cemeteries. In G.C. Ioannides (ed.), *Studies in Honour of Vassos Karageorghis*, 69–83. Nicosia: Society of Cypriot Studies, Leventis Foundation.

Higham, T.F.G., C. Bronk Ramsey, F. Brock, D. Baker and P. Ditchfield

2007   Radiocarbon dates from the Oxford AMS system: *Archaeometry* Datelist 32. *Archaeometry* 49: S1–S60.

Hirschfeld, N.

1996   Cypriots in the Mycenaean Aegean. In E. De Miro, L Godart and A. Sacconi (eds), *Atti e Memorie del Secondo Congresso Internazionale di Micenologia, Roma-Napoli, 14–20 Ottobre 1991.* 2 volumes. Incunabula Graeca 98(1): 289–297. Rome: Gruppo Editoriale Internazionale.

Hitchcock, L.

2000   Engendering ambiguity in Minoan Crete: it's a drag to be a king. In M. Donald and L. Hurcombe (eds), *Representations of Gender from Prehistory to the Present*, 69–86. London: Macmillan.

Hjelmqvist, H.

1979   Some economic plants and weeds from the Bronze Age of Cyprus. In U. Öbrink (ed.), *Hala Sultan Tekke 5.* Studies in Mediterranean Archaeology 45(5): 110–133. Göteborg, Sweden: P. Åström's Förlag.

Hodder, I.A.

1990   *The Domestication of Europe: Structure and Contingency in Neolithic Societies.* Oxford: Blackwell.

2006   *Catalhöyük: The Leopard's Tale. Revealing the Mysteries of Turkey's Ancient 'Town'.* London: Thames and Hudson.

Hodder, I., and L. Meskell

2011   A 'curious and sometimes a trifle macabre artistry': some aspects of symbolism in Neolithic Turkey. *Current Anthropology* 52: 235–263.

Holmboe, J.

1914   *Studies on the Vegetation of Cyprus.* Bergens Museums Skrifter. Ny Raekke 1, No. 2. Bergen, Norway: Griegs.

Hongo, H., and R.H. Meadow

2000   Faunal remains from Prepottery Neolithic levels at Çayönü, southeastern Turkey: a preliminary report focusing on pigs (*Sus* sp.). In M. Mashkour, A.M. Choyke, H. Buitenhuis and F. Poplin (eds), *Archaeozoology of the Near East IVA. Proceedings of the Fourth International Symposium on the Archaeozoology of Southwestern Asia and Adjacent Areas.* ARC Publicatie 32: 121–140. Groningen, The Netherlands: Centrum voor Archeologische Research and Consultancy.

Hood, S.

1978 Discrepancies in 14C dating as illustrated from the Egyptian New and Middle Kingdoms and from the Aegean Bronze Age and Neolithic. *Archaeometry* 20: 197–199.

Horden, P., and N. Purcell

2000 *The Corrupting Sea: A Study of Mediterranean History*. Oxford: Blackwell.

Horowitz, M.

2008 Phlamoudi *Vounari*: a multi-function site in Cyprus. In J.S. Smith (ed.), *Views from Phlamoudhi, Cyprus*. Annual of the American Schools of Oriental Research 63: 69–85. Boston: American Schools of Oriental Research.

Horwitz, L.K., E. Tchernov and H. Hongo

2004 The domestic status of the early Neolithic fauna of Cyprus. In E.J. Peltenburg and A. Wasse (eds), *Neolithic Revolution: New Perspectives on Southwest Asia in Light of Recent Discoveries on Cyprus*. Levant Supplementary Series 1: 35–48. Oxford: Oxbow.

Hosler, D.

1995 Sound, color and meaning in the metallurgy of ancient Mexico. *World Archaeology* 27: 100–115.

Houby-Nielsen, S., and K. Slej (eds)

2005 *The Swedish Cyprus Expedition on Tour: Medelhavsmuseet Visits Bucharest*. Stockholm: Medelhavmuseet.

Hours, F., and L. Copeland

1983 Les rapports entre l'Anatolie et la Syrie du Nord a l'époque des premières communautes villageoises de bergers et de paysans (7.600–5.000 BC). In P.E.L. Smith and P. Mortensen (eds), *The Hilly Flanks and Beyond*. Studies in Ancient Oriental Civilization 36: 75–90. Chicago: Oriental Institute.

Hsü, K.J.

1972 When the Mediterranean dried up. *Scientific American* 227: 27–36.

Hulin, L.C.

1989 The identification of Cypriot cult figures through cross-cultural comparison: some problems. In E.J. Peltenburg (ed.), *Early Society in Cyprus*, 127–139. Edinburgh: Edinburgh University Press.

Hult, G.

1992 *Nitovikla Reconsidered*. Medelhavsmuseet Memoir 8. Stockholm: Medelhavsmuseet.

Hurst, B.J., and B. Lawn

1984 University of Pennsylvania radiocarbon dates XXII. *Radiocarbon* 26: 212–240.

Iacovou, M.

1988 *The Pictorial Pottery of Eleventh Century BC Cyprus*. Studies in Mediterranean Archaeology 79. Göteborg, Sweden: P. Åström's Förlag.

1994 The topography of eleventh century BC Cyprus. In V. Karageorghis (ed.), *Cyprus in the 11th Century BC*, 149–165. Nicosia: Leventis Foundation and University of Cyprus.

1991 Proto-White Painted pottery: a classification of the ware. Cypriot sequence. In J. Barlow, D. Bolger and B. Kling (eds), *Cypriot Ceramics: Reading the Prehistoric Record*. University Museum Monograph 74: 199–205. Philadelphia: University of Pennsylvania, University Museum Monographs.

1999a The Greek exodus to Cyprus: the antiquity of Hellenism. *Mediterranean Historical Review* 14(2): 1–28.

1999b Excerpta Cypria Geometrica: materials for a history of Geometric Cyprus. In M. Iacovou and D Michaelides (eds), *Cyprus: The Historicity of the Geometric Horizon*, 141–166. Nicosia: Archaeological Research Unit, University of Cyprus; Bank of Cyprus Cultural Foundation, Ministry of Education and Culture.

2002 From ten to naught: formation, consolidation and abolition of Cyprus' Iron Age polities. *Cahier du Centre d'Études Chypriotes* 32: 73–87.

2003 The Late Bronze Age origins of Cypriot Hellenism and the establishment of the Iron Age kingdoms. In S. Hadjisavvas (ed.), *From Ishtar to Aphrodite: 3200 Years of Cypriot Hellenism. Treasures from the Museums of Cyprus*, 79–85. New York: Onassis Public Benefit Foundation.

2004 (ed.) *Archaeological Field Survey in Cyprus: Past History, Future Potentials*. British School at Athens, Studies 11. London: British School at Athens.

2005 Cyprus at the dawn of the first millennium BCE: cultural homogenisation versus the tyranny of ethnic identification.

In J. Clarke (ed.), *Archaeological Perspectives on the Transmission and Transformation of Culture in the Eastern Mediterranean*. Levant Supplementary Series 2: 125–134. Oxford: Oxbow; Council for British Research in the Levant.

2006a 'Greeks', 'Phoenicians' and 'Eteocypriots': ethnic identities in the Cypriote kingdoms. In J. Chrysostomides and C. Dendrinos (eds), *'Sweet Land…': Lectures on the History and Culture of Cyprus*, 27–59. Camberley, England: Porphyrogenitus.

2006b From the Mycenaean *qa-si-re-u* to the Cypriote *pa-si-le-wo-se*: the basileus in the kingdoms of Cyprus. In S. Deger-Jalotzy and I.S. Lemos (eds), *Ancient Greece: From the Mycenaean Palaces to the Age of Homer*. Edinburgh Leventis Studies 3: 315–335. Edinburgh: Edinburgh University Press.

2007 Site size estimates and the diversity factor in Late Cypriot settlement histories. *Bulletin of the American Schools of Oriental Research* 348: 1–23.

2008 Cultural and political configurations in Iron Age Cyprus: the sequel to a protohistoric episode. *American Journal of Archaeology* 112: 625–657.

Ionas, I.
1985 The altar at Myrtou-*Pigadhes*: a re-examination of its reconstruction. *Report of the Department of Antiquities, Cyprus*: 137–142.

Irwin, G.
1992 *The Prehistoric Exploration and Colonisation of the Pacific*. Cambridge: Cambridge University Press.

Isbell, W.H.
2000 What we should be studying: the 'imagined community' and the 'natural community'. In M.A. Canuto and J. Yaeger (eds), *Archaeology of Communities: A New World Perspective*, 243–266. London: Routledge.

Jacobs, A.
2009 Considering ceramic variability on Late Bronze Age Cyprus. A case study: the plain vessels of Alassa *Pano Mandilares*. In I. Hein (ed.), *The Formation of Cyprus in the 2nd Millennium BC. Studies in Regionalism during the Middle and Late Bronze Ages*. Österreichische Akademie Der Wissenschaften, Denkschriften Der Gesamtakademie 52: 91–105. Vienna: Österreichische Akademie Der Wissenschaften.

Jacobs, J.M.
1996 *Edge of Empire: Postcolonialism and the City*. London: Routledge.

Jameson, M.H., C.N. Runnels and T.H. Van Andel
1994 *A Greek Countryside: The Southern Argolid from Prehistory to the Present Day*. Palo Alto, California: Stanford University Press.

Janes, S.
2010 Negotiating island interactions: Cyprus, the Aegean and the Levant in the Late Bronze to Early Iron Ages. In P. van Dommelen and A.B. Knapp (eds), *Material Connections in the Ancient Mediterranean: Mobility, Materiality and Mediterranean Identities*, 127–146. London: Routledge.

Johnson, G.A.
1977 Aspects of regional analysis in archaeology. *Annual Review of Anthropology* 6: 479–508.

Johnson, P.
1982 The Middle Cypriote pottery found in Palestine. *Opuscula Atheniensia* 14: 49–72.

Johnston, R.
1998 Approaches to the perception of landscape: philosophy, theory, methodology. *Archaeological Dialogues* 5: 54–68.

Jones, A., and G. MacGregor
2002 Introduction: wonderful things – colour studies in archaeology from Munsell to materiality. In A. Jones and G. MacGregor (eds), *Colouring the Past: The Significance of Colour in Archaeological Research*, 1–21. London: Berg.

Jones, D.K., L.F.H. Merton, M.E.D Poore and D.R. Harris
1958 *Report on Pasture Research, Survey and Development in Cyprus*. Nicosia: Republic of Cyprus.

Jones, M., R.G. Allaby and T.A. Brown
1998 Wheat domestication. *Science* 279: 302–303.

Jones, P.L.
2008 *Moving Heaven and Earth: Landscape, Death and Memory in the Aceramic Neolithic of Cyprus*. British Archaeological Reports, International Series 1795. Oxford: Archaeopress.

2009 Considering living-beings in the Aceramic Neolithic of Cyprus. *Journal of Mediterranean Archaeology* 22: 75–99.

Jones, R.E.
1986   *Greek and Cypriot Pottery: A Review of Scientific Studies.* British School at Athens, Fitch Laboratory, Occasional Paper 1. Athens: British School at Athens.

Jones, R.E., and P. Day
1987   Aegean-type pottery on Sardinia: identification of imports and local imitations by chemical analysis. In M.S. Balmuth (ed.), *Nuragic Sardinia and the Mycenaean World.* Studies in Sardinian Archaeology 3. British Archaeological Reports International Series 387: 257–269. Oxford: British Archaeological Reports.

Jones, R.E., S.T. Levi and M. Bettelli
2005   Mycenaean pottery in the central Mediterranean: imports, imitations and derivatives. In R. Laffineur and E. Greco (eds), *Emporia: Aegeans in the Central and Eastern Mediterranean.* Aegaeum 25(2): 539–545. Liège, Belgium, Austin: Université de Liège, University of Texas at Austin.

Jones, S.
1997   *The Archaeology of Ethnicity: Reconstructing Identities in the Past and the Present.* London: Routledge.

Joyce, R.A.
2008   *Ancient Bodies, Ancient Lives: Sex, Gender, and Archaeology.* London: Thames and Hudson.

Kaniewski, D., E. Paulissen, E. Van Campo, H. Weiss, T. Otto, J. Bretschneider and K. Van Lerberghe
2010   Late second–early first millennium BC abrupt climate changes in coastal Syria and their possible significance for the history of the Eastern Mediterranean. *Quaternary Research* 74: 207–215.

Kantor, H.J.
1947   *The Aegean and the Orient in the Second Millennium B.C.* Archaeological Institute of America: Monograph 1. Bloomington, Indiana: Archaeological Institute of America.

Kaplan, M.
1980   *The Origin and Distribution of Tell Yahudiyeh Ware.* Studies in Mediterranean Archaeology 62. Göteborg, Sweden : P. Åström's Förlag.

Karageorghis, J.
1977   *La Grande Déesse de Chypre et son Culte.* Lyon: Collection de la Maison de l'Orient.

2005   *Kypris: The Aphrodite of Cyprus. Ancient Sources and Archaeological Evidence.* Nicosia: Leventis Foundation.

Karageorghis, J., and V. Karageorghis
2002   The great goddess of Cyprus or the genesis of Aphrodite in Cyprus. In S. Parpola and R.M. Whiting (eds), *Sex and Gender in the Ancient Near East,* 263–282. Winona Lake, Indiana: Eisenbrauns.

Karageorghis, V.
1958   Finds from Early Cypriot cemeteries. *Report of the Department of Antiquities, Cyprus 1940–48*: 115–152.

1965a   Fouilles des tombes du Chypriote Récent à Akhera. *Noveaux Documents pour l'Étude du Bronze Récent à Chypre.* Études Chypriotes 3: 71–156. Paris: E. De Boccard.

1965b   Une nécropole du Chypriote Récent à Pendayia. *Noveaux Documents pour l'Étude du Bronze Récent à Chypre.* Études Chypriotes 3: 2–70. Paris: E. De Boccard.

1965c   A Late Cypriot tomb at Tamassos. *Report of the Department of Antiquities, Cyprus*: 11–29.

1969   *Salamis in Cyprus. Homeric, Hellenistic and Roman.* London: Thames and Hudson.

1970   Two religious documents of the Early Cypriote Bronze Age. *Report of the Department of Antiquities, Cyprus*: 10–13.

1976   *View from the Bronze Age: Mycenaean and Phoenician Discoveries at Kition.* New York: E.P. Dutton.

1977   A Cypro-Mycenaean IIIC:1 amphora from Kition. In K. Kinzl (ed.), *Greece and the Eastern Mediterranean in Ancient History and Prehistory: Studies Presented to F. Schachermeyr on the Occasion of his Eightieth Birthday,* 192–198. Berlin: De Gruyter.

1979   Kypriaka IV: a 12th century bronze stand from Cyprus. *Report of the Department of Antiquities, Cyprus*: 203–208.

1982   *Cyprus. From the Stone Age to the Romans.* London: Thames and Hudson.

1983   *Palaepaphos-Skales: An Iron Age Cemetery in Cyprus.* Alt-Paphos 3. Konstanz, Germany: Universitätsverlag.

1985a   (ed.) *Archaeology in Cyprus 1960–1985.* Nicosia: Leventis Foundation.

1985b   *Excavations at Kition* V(2). The Pre-Phoenician Levels. Nicosia: Department of Antiquities, Cyprus.

1986   (ed.) *Acts of the International Archaeological Symposium: Cyprus between the Orient and the Occident.* Nicosia: Department of Antiquities.

1987   *The Archaeology of Cyprus: The Ninety Years after Myres.* Thirteenth J.L. Myres Memorial Lecture. London: Leopard's Head Press.

1989   A Late Bronze Age mould from Hala Sultan Tekke. *Bulletin de Correspondance Hellènique* 113: 439–446.

1991   *The Coroplastic Art of Ancient Cyprus* I: *Chalcolithic–Late Cypriote I.* Nicosia: Leventis Foundation.

1993   *The Coroplastic Art of Ancient Cyprus* II: *Late Cypriote II–Cypro-Geometric III.* Nicosia: Leventis Foundation.

1994   The prehistory of an ethnogenesis. In V. Karageorghis (ed.), *Cyprus in the 11th Century B.C.,* 1–10. Nicosia: Leventis Foundation.

1994–1995 Archaeology in Cyprus: the last sixty years. *Modern Greek Studies Yearbook* 10–11: 849–895.

1995   Cyprus and the western Mediterranean: some new evidence for interrelations. In J.B. Carter and S.P. Morris (eds), *The Ages of Homer: A Tribute to Emily Townsend Vermeule,* 93–97. Austin: University of Texas Press.

1998a   Mycenaean defensive outposts in the Aegean and Cyprus: some comparisons. In E.H. Cline and D. Harris-Cline (eds), *The Aegean and the Orient in the Second Millennium.* Aegaeum 18: 127–136. Liège, Belgium: Université de Liège.

1998b   Hearths and bathtubs in Cyprus: a 'Sea Peoples' innovation? In S. Gitin, A. Mazar and E. Stern (eds), *Mediterranean Peoples in Transition: Thirteenth to Early Tenth Centuries BCE,* 276–282. Jerusalem: Israel Exploration Society.

1999a   *Excavating at Salamis in Cyprus 1952–1974.* Athens: Leventis Foundation.

1999b   (ed.) *Ancient Cypriote Art in the Severis Collection.* Athens: Costakis and Leto Severis Foundation.

2000a   Some aspects of Cyprus at the end of the Late Bronze Age. *Scienze dell'antichità* 10: 599–626.

2000b   Cultural innovations in Cyprus relating to the Sea Peoples. In E.D. Oren (ed.), *The Sea Peoples and Their World: A Reassessment.* University Museum Monograph 108, University Museum Symposium Series 11: 255–279.

Philadelphia: University Museum, University of Pennsylvania.

2001a   Two anthropomorphic vases of the Early Cypriote Bronze Age. *Report of the Department of Antiquities, Cyprus*: 45–48.

2001b   (ed.) *The White Slip Ware of Late Bronze Age Cyprus.* Österreichische Akademie der Wissenschaften, Denkschriften der Gesamtakademie, Band 20. Contributions to the Chronology of the Eastern Mediterranean 2. Vienna: Österreichische Akademie der Wissenschaften.

2001c   The hellenisation of Cyprus and Crete: some similarities and differences. In A. Kyriatsoulis (ed.), *Kreta und Zypern: Religion und Schrift. Von der Frühgeschichte biz zum Ende der archaischen Zeit,* 265–277. Altenburg, Germany: DZA Verlag für Kultur und Wissenschaft.

2002a   *Early Cyprus: Crossroads of the Mediterranean.* Los Angeles: Getty Museum.

2002b   Cypriote antiquities repatriated. *Report of the Department of Antiquities, Cyprus*: 67–82.

2003   The cult of Astarte on Cyprus. In W.G. Dever and S. Gitin (eds), *Symbiosis, Symbolism, and the Power of the Past: Canaan, Ancient Israel, and Their Neighbors, from the Late Bronze Age through Roman Palaestina,* 215–221. Winona Lake, Indiana: Eisenbrauns.

2005   *Excavations at Kition* VI. *The Phoenician and Later Levels.* Nicosia: Department of Antiquities, Cyprus.

2006   *Aspects of Everyday Life in Ancient Cyprus: Iconic Representations.* Nicosia: Leventis Foundation.

2008   Notes on a Late Cypriote amphoroid crater of Pastoral Style from Byblos. *Bulletin d'Archéologie et d'Architecture Libanaises* 12: 171–181.

Karageorghis, V., and M. Demas

1984   *Pyla-Kokkinokremos: A Late 13th Century B.C. Fortified Settlement in Cyprus.* Nicosia: Department of Antiquities, Cyprus.

1985   *Excavations at Kition* V. *The Pre-Phoenician Levels.* Nicosia: Department of Antiquities, Cyprus.

1988   *Excavations at Maa-Palaeokastro 1979–1986.* Nicosia: Department of Antiquities, Cyprus.

Karageorghis, V., and G. Papasavvas

2001   A bronze ingot-bearer from Cyprus. *Oxford Journal of Archaeology* 20: 339–354.

Karageorghis, V., and L. Vagnetti

1981   A Chalcolithic terracotta figurine in the Pierides Foundation Museum, Cyprus. In J. Reade (ed.), *Chalcolithic Cyprus and Western Asia*. British Museum Occasional Publication 26: 52–55. London: British Museum.

Karageorghis, V., J.N. Coldstream, P.M. Bikai, A.W. Johnston, M. Robertson and L. Jehasse

1981   *Excavations at Kition* IV. *The Non-Cypriote Pottery*. Nicosia: Department of Antiquities, Cyprus.

Karageorghis, V., E. Vassilika and P. Wilson

1999   *The Art of Ancient Cyprus in the Fitzwilliam Museum, Cambridge*. Nicosia: Leventis Foundation.

Karageorghis, V., with S. Houby-Nielsen, K. Slej, M.-L. Windblah, S. Nordin Fischer and O. Kaneberg

2003   *The Cyprus Collections in the Medelhavsmuseet*. Nicosia, Stockholm: Leventis Foundation; Medelhavsmuseet.

Karkanas, P.

2006   Late Neolithic household activities in marginal areas: the micromorphological evidence from the Kouveleiki caves, Peloponnese, Greece. *Journal of Archaeological Science* 33(11): 1628–1641.

Kassianidou, V.

2001   Cypriot copper to Sardinia: yet another case of bringing coals to Newcastle. In L. Bonfante and V. Karageorghis (eds), *Italy and Cyprus in Antiquity, 1500–450 BC*, 97–119. Nicosia: Leventis Foundation.

2004   Recording Cyprus's mining history through archaeological survey. In M. Iacovou (ed.), *Archaeological Field Survey in Cyprus. Past History, Future Potentials*. British School at Athens, Studies 11: 95–104. London: British School at Athens.

2008   The formative years of the Cypriot copper industry. In I. Tzachili (ed.), *Aegean Metallurgy in the Bronze Age*, 249–267. Rethymnon, Crete: Ta Pragmata.

2009   Oxhide ingots in Cyprus. In F. Lo Schiavo, J.D. Muhly, R. Maddin and A. Giumlia Mair (eds), *Oxhide Ingots in the Central Mediterranean*, 41–81. Rome: Leventis Foundation, INSTAP and Consiglio Nazionale delle Ricerche.

2012   Metallurgy and metalwork in Enkomi: the early phases. In V. Kassianidou and G. Papasavvas (eds), *Eastern Mediterranean Metallurgy and Metalwork in the Second Millennium BC*, 92–104. Oxford: Oxbow.

Kassianidou, V., and A.B. Knapp

2005   Archaeometallurgy in the Mediterranean: the social context of mining, technology and trade. In E. Blake and A.B. Knapp (eds), *The Archaeology of Mediterranean Prehistory*, 215–251. Oxford: Blackwell.

Keegan, W.F., and J.M. Diamond

1987   Colonization of islands by humans: a biogeographical perspective. In M.B. Schiffer (ed.), *Advances in Archaeological Method and Theory* 10: 49–92. San Diego, California: Academic Press.

Kemp, B.J., and R.S. Merrillees

1980   *Minoan Pottery in Second Millennium Egypt*. Mainz am Rhein, Germany: Phillip von Zabern.

Keswani, P.S.

1989   Dimensions of social hierarchy in Late Bronze Age Cyprus: an analysis of the mortuary data from Enkomi. *Journal of Mediterranean Archaeology* 2: 49–86.

1991   A preliminary investigation of systems of ceramic production and distribution in Cyprus during the Late Bronze Age. In J. Barlow, D. Bolger and B. Kling (eds), *Cypriot Ceramics: Reading the Prehistoric Record*. University Museum Monograph 74: 97–118. Philadelphia: University Museum, University of Pennsylvania.

1992   Gas chromatography analyses of pithoi from Kalavasos *Ayios Dhimitrios*: a preliminary report. In A. South, 'Kalavasos Ayios Dhimitrios 1991'. *Report of the Department of Antiquities, Cyprus*: 141–145.

1993   Models of local exchange in Late Bronze Age Cyprus. *Bulletin of the American Schools of Oriental Research* 292: 73–83.

1994   The social context of animal husbandry in early agricultural societies: ethnographic insights and an archaeological example from Cyprus. *Journal of Anthropological Archaeology* 13: 255–277.

1996   Hierarchies, heterarchies, and urbanization processes: the view from Bronze Age Cyprus. *Journal of Mediterranean Archaeology* 9: 211–249.

2004   *Mortuary Ritual and Society in Bronze Age Cyprus*. Monographs in Mediterranean Archaeology 9. London: Equinox.

2005 Death, prestige, and copper in Bronze Age Cyprus. *American Journal of Archaeology* 109: 341–401.

2009 Exploring regional variation in Late Cypriot II–III pithoi: perspectives from Alassa and Kalavasos. In I. Hein (ed.), *The Formation of Cyprus in the 2nd Millennium BC. Studies in Regionalism during the Middle and Late Bronze Ages*. Österreichische Akademie Der Wissenschaften, Denkschriften Der Gesamtakademie 52: 107–125. Vienna: Österreichische Akademie Der Wissenschaften.

Keswani, P.S., and A.B. Knapp

2003 Bronze Age boundaries and social exchange in northwest Cyprus. *Oxford Journal of Archaeology* 22: 213–223.

Kilian, K.

1983 Ausgrabungen in Tiryns: Bericht zu den Grabungen. *Archäologischer Anzeiger* (1983:3): 277–328.

1988 Ausgrabungen in Tiryns 1982/83: Bericht zu den Grabungen. *Archäeologische Anzeiger* (1988:1): 105–151.

Kilian, K., C. Podzuweit and H.-J. Weisshaar

1981 Ausgrabungen in Tiryns 1978, 1979. *Archäeologische Anzeiger* (1981:2): 149–256.

Killebrew, A.

2005 *Biblical Peoples and Ethnicity: An Archaeological Study of Egyptians, Canaanites, Philistine, and Early Israel 1300–1100 BCE*. Atlanta, Georgia: Society of Biblical Literature.

2006–2007 The Philistines in context: the transmission and appropriation of Mycenaean-style culture in the east Aegean, southeastern coastal Anatolia, and the Levant. *Scripta Mediterranea* 27–28: 245–266.

King, R., L. Proudfoot and B. Smith

1997 *The Mediterranean: Environment and Society*. London: Arnold.

Kirch, P.V.

1986 (ed.) *Island Societies: Archaeological Approaches to Evolution and Transformation*. Cambridge: Cambridge University Press.

Kitchen, K.A.

1982 *Ramesside Inscriptions. Historical and Biographical*. Volume 4. Oxford: Blackwell.

1983 *Ramesside Inscriptions. Historical and Biographical*. Volume 5. Oxford: Blackwell.

Klein Hofmeijer, G., and P.Y. Sondaar

1992 Pleistocene humans in the island environment of Sardinia. In R.H. Tykot and T.K. Andrews (eds), *Sardinia in the Mediterranean: A Footprint in the Sea*. Monographs in Mediterranean Archaeology 3: 49–56. Sheffield, England: Sheffield Academic Press.

Kling, B.

1987 Pottery classification and relative chronology of the LCIIC–LCIIIA periods. In D.W. Rupp (ed.), *Western Cyprus: Connections*. Studies in Mediterranean Archaeology 77: 97–113. Göteborg, Sweden: P. Åström's Förlag.

1988 The strainer jug from Kouklia Tomb KA1: a stylistic hybrid. *Report of the Department of Antiquities, Cyprus*: 271–274.

1989a *Mycenaean IIIC:1b and Related Pottery in Cyprus*. Studies in Mediterranean Archaeology 87. Göteborg, Sweden: P. Åström's Förlag.

1989b Local Cypriot features in the ceramics of the Late Cypriot IIIA period. In E.J. Peltenburg (ed.), *Early Society in Cyprus*, 153–159. Edinburgh: Edinburgh University Press.

2000 Mycenaean IIIC:1b and related pottery in Cyprus: comments on the current state of research. In Eliezer D. Oren (ed.), *The Sea Peoples and Their World: A Reassessment*. University Museum Monograph 108, University Museum Symposium Series 11: 281–295. Philadelphia: University Museum, University of Pennsylvania.

Kling, B., and J.D. Muhly

2007 *Joan du Plat Taylor's Excavations at the Late Bronze Age Mining Settlement at Apliki Karamallos, Cyprus*. Studies in Mediterranean Archaeology 134(1). Sävedalen, Sweden: P. Åström's Förlag.

Klinge, J., and P. Fall

2010 Archaeobotanical inference of Bronze Age land use and land cover in the eastern Mediterranean. *Journal of Archaeological Science* 37: 2622–2629.

Knapp, A.B.

1980 KBo I 26: Alashiya and Hatti. *Journal of Cuneiform Studies* 32: 43–47.

1986a *Copper Production and Divine Protection: Archaeology, Ideology and Social Complexity on Bronze Age Cyprus*. Studies in Mediterranean Archaeology and Literature, Pocket-book 42. Göteborg, Sweden: P. Åström's Förlag.

1986b Production, exchange and socio-political complexity on Bronze Age Cyprus. *Oxford Journal of Archaeology* 5: 35–60.

1988 Ideology, archaeology and polity. *Man* 23: 133–163.

1990a Production, location and integration in Bronze Age Cyprus. *Current Anthropology* 31: 147–176.

1990b Entrepreneurship, ethnicity, exchange: Mediterranean inter-island relations in the Late Bronze Age. *Annual of the British School at Athens* 85: 115–153.

1991 Spice, drugs, grain and grog: organic goods in Bronze Age eastern Mediterranean trade. In N.H. Gale (ed.), *Bronze Age Trade in the Mediterranean*. Studies in Mediterranean Archaeology 90: 21–68. Göteborg, Sweden : P. Åström's Förlag.

1992 Independence and imperialism: politico-economic structures in the Bronze Age Levant. In A.B. Knapp (ed.), *Annales, Archaeology and Ethnohistory*, 83–98. Cambridge: Cambridge University Press.

1993a Social complexity: incipience, emergence and development on prehistoric Cyprus. *Bulletin of the American Schools of Oriental Research* 292: 85–106.

1993b Thalassocracies in Bronze Age eastern Mediterranean trade: making and breaking a myth. *World Archaeology* 24: 332–347.

1994 Emergence, development and decline on Bronze Age Cyprus. In C. Mathers and S. Stoddart (eds), *Development and Decline in the Mediterranean Bronze Age*. Sheffield Archaeological Monograph 8: 271–304. Sheffield, England: John Collis Publications.

1996a The Bronze Age economy of Cyprus: ritual, ideology and the sacred landscape. In V. Karageorghis and D. Michaelides (eds), *The Development of the Cypriot Economy*, 71–106. Nicosia: University of Cyprus; Bank of Cyprus.

1996b (ed.) *Near Eastern and Aegean Texts from the Third to the First Millennia BC*. Sources for the History of Cyprus 2, P.W. Wallace and A.G. Orphanides (eds). Altamont, New York: Greece and Cyprus Research Center.

1997 *The Archaeology of Late Bronze Age Cypriot Society: The Study of Settlement, Survey and Landscape*. Glasgow, Scotland: University of Glasgow, Department of Archaeology, Occasional Paper 4.

1998a Who's come a long way, baby? Gendering society, gendering archae-ology. *Archaeological Dialogues* 5: 91–106, 115–125.

1998b Mediterranean Bronze Age trade: distance, power and place. In E.H. Cline and D. Harris-Cline (eds), *The Aegean and the Orient in the Second Millennium*. Aegaeum 18: 260–280. Liège, Belgium: Université de Liège.

1999a Ideational and industrial landscape on prehistoric Cyprus. In W. Ashmore and A.B. Knapp (eds), *Archaeologies of Landscapes: Contemporary Perspectives*, 229–252. Oxford: Blackwell.

1999b The archaeology of mining: fieldwork perspectives from the Sydney Cyprus Survey Project. In S.M.M. Young, A.M. Pollard, P. Budd and R.A. Ixer (eds), *Metals in Antiquity*. British Archaeological Reports, International Series 792: 98–109. Oxford: Archaeopress.

2000 Archaeology, science-based archaeology and the Mediterranean Bronze Age metals trade. *European Journal of Archaeology* 3: 31–56.

2001 Archaeology and ethnicity: a dangerous liaison. *Archaeologia Cypria* 4: 29–46.

2003 The archaeology of community on Bronze Age Cyprus: Politiko *Phorades* in context. *American Journal of Archaeology* 107: 559–580.

2006 Orientalisation and prehistoric Cyprus: the social life of Oriental goods. In Corinna Riva and Nicholas Vella (eds), *Debating Orientalisation: Multi-disciplinary Approaches to Change in the Ancient Mediterranean*. Monographs in Mediterranean Archaeology 10: 48–65. London: Equinox Press.

2008 *Identity, Insularity and Connectivity: Prehistoric and Protohistoric Cyprus*. Oxford: Oxford University Press.

2009a Representations: female figurines and social identity on protohistoric Cyprus. *Medelhavsmuseet. Focus on the Mediterranean* 5: 137–144.

2009b Monumental architecture, identity and memory. *Proceedings of the Symposium: Bronze Age Architectural Traditions in the East Mediterranean. Diffusion and Diversity (Gasteig, Munich, 7–8 May 2008)*, 47–59. Weilheim, Germany: Verein zur Förderung der Aufarbeitung der Hellenischen Geschichte.

2010 Cyprus's earliest prehistory: seafarers, foragers and settlers. *Journal of World Prehistory* 23: 79–120.

2011 Sounds of silence: music and musical practice in Late Bronze–Iron Age Cyprus. In W. Heimpel and G. Szabo (eds), *Strings and Threads: A Celebration of the Work of Anne D. Kilmer*, 121–132. Winona Lake, Indiana: Eisenbrauns.

2012 Matter of fact: transcultural contacts in the Late Bronze Age eastern Mediterranean. In J. Maran and P. Stockhammer (eds), *Materiality and Social Practice: Transformative Capacities of Intercultural Encounters*, 32–50. Oxford: Oxbow.

Knapp, A.B. (with S.O. Held and S.W. Manning)
1994 Problems and prospects in Cypriote prehistory. *Journal of World Prehistory* 8: 377–452.

Knapp, A.B., and S. Antoniadou
1998 Archaeology, politics and the cultural heritage of Cyprus. In L. Meskell (ed.), *Archaeology under Fire: Nationalism, Politics and Heritage in the Eastern Mediterranean and Middle East*, 13–43. London: Routledge.

Knapp, A.B., and W. Ashmore
1999 Archaeological landscapes: constructed, conceptualised, ideational. In W. Ashmore and A.B. Knapp (eds), *Archaeologies of Landscape: Contemporary Perspectives*, 1–30. Oxford: Blackwell.

Knapp, A.B., and J.F. Cherry
1994 *Provenience Studies and Bronze Age Cyprus: Production, Exchange, and Politico-Economic Change*. Monographs in World Archaeology 21. Madison, Wisconsin: Prehistory Press.

Knapp, A.B., and V. Kassianidou
2008 The archaeology of Late Bronze Age copper production: Politiko *Phorades* on Cyprus. In Ü. Yalçin (ed.), *Anatolian Metal IV: Frühe Rohstoffgewinnung in Anatolien und seinen Nachbarländern*. Die Anschnitt, Beiheft 21. Veröffentlichungen aus dem Deutschen Bergbau-Museum 157: 135–147. Bochum, Germany: Deutsches Bergbau-Museum.

Knapp, A.B., V. Kassianidou and M. Donnelly
2001 The excavations at Politiko *Phorades*, Cyprus: 1996–2000. *Near Eastern Archaeology* 64(4): 202–208.

Knapp, A.B., V. Kassianidou, P. Duffy, M. Donnelly and J. Noller

n.d. *The Excavations at Politiko Phorades (1996–2000): The Archaeology and Archaeometallurgy of a Bronze Age Smelting Site*. Philadelphia: INSTAP Academic Press.

Knapp, A.B., and L.M. Meskell
1997 Bodies of evidence on prehistoric Cyprus. *Cambridge Archaeological Journal* 7: 183–204.

Knapp, A.B., and P. van Dommelen
2008 Past practices: rethinking individuals and agents in archaeology. *Cambridge Archaeological Journal* 18: 15–34.

Knappett, C.
1999 Assessing a polity in Protopalatial Crete: the Malia-Lasithi state. *American Journal of Archaeology* 103: 615–639.

Knappett, C., and V. Kilikoglou
2007 Provenancing Red Lustrous Wheelmade Ware: scales of analysis and floating fabrics. In I. Hein (ed.), *The Lustrous Wares of Late Bronze Age Cyprus and the Eastern Mediterranean*. Contributions to the Chronology of the Eastern Mediterranean 13: 115–140. Vienna: Österreichische Akademie der Wissenschaften.

Kolb, C.
1985 Demographic estimates in archaeology: contributions from ethnoarchaeology on Mesoamerican peasants. *Current Anthropology* 26: 581–600.

Kolotourou, K.
2005 Music and cult: the significance of percussion and the Cypriote connection. In V. Karageorghis, H. Matthäus and S. Rogge (eds), *Cyprus: Religion and Society from the Late Bronze Age to the End of the Archaic Period*, 183–204. Möhnesee-Wamel, Germany: Bibliopolis.

Korou, N.
2004 Sceptres and maces in Cyprus before, during and immediately after the 11th century. In V. Karageorghis (ed.), *Cyprus in the 11th Century BC*, 203–227. Nicosia: Leventis Foundation; University of Cyprus.

Kostoula, M., and J. Maran
2012 A group of animal-headed faience vessels from Tiryns. In M. Gruber, S. Ahituv, G. Lehmann and Z. Talshir (eds.), *All the Wisdom of the East. Studies in Near Eastern Archaeology and History in Honor of Eliezer D. Oren*. Orbis Biblicus et Orientalis 255: 193–234. Fribourg and

Gottingen: Fribourg Academic Press and Vandenhoeck & Ruprecht.

Kouka, O.

2009   Cross-cultural links and elite-identities: the eastern Aegean/western Anatolia and Cyprus from the early third through the early second millennium BC. In V. Karageorghis and O. Kouka (eds), *Cypus and the East Aegean: Intercultural Contacts from 3000 to 500 BC*, 31–47. Nicosia: Leventis Foundation.

Kourtessi-Phillipaki, G.

1999   The Lower and Middle Palaeolithic in the Ionian islands: new finds. In G.N. Bailey, E. Adam, E. Panagopoulou, C. Perlès and K. Zachos, *The Palaeolithic Archaeology of Greece and Adjacent Areas*. British School at Athens 3: 282–287. London: British School at Athens.

Kromholz, S.F.

1982   *The Bronze Age Necropolis at Ayia Paraskevi (Nicosia): Unpublished Tombs in the Cyprus Museum*. Studies in Mediterranean Archaeology and Literature, Pocket-book 17. Göteborg, Sweden: P. Åström's Förlag.

Kuhn, S.L., M.C. Stiner and E. Güleç

1999   Initial Upper Palaeolithic in south-central Turkey and its regional context: a preliminary report. *Antiquity* 73/281: 505–517.

Kuijt, I.

2000a   People and space in early agricultural villages: exploring daily lives, community size, and architecture in the Late Pre-Pottery Neolithic. *Journal of Anthropological Archaeology* 19: 75–102.

2000b   Keeping the peace: ritual, skull caching, and community integration in the Levantine Neolithic. In I. Kuijt (ed.), *Life in Neolithic Farming Communities: Social Organization, Identity, and Differentiation*, 137–162. Boston: Kluwer Academic/Plenum.

2004   Cyprus as a regional Neolithic entity: do researchers need to revisit the concept of the Levantine PPNB Interaction Sphere? *Neo-Lithics* 1/04: 8–9.

Kuijt, I., and N. Goring-Morris

2002   Foraging, farming, and social complexity in the Pre-Pottery Neolithic of the southern Levant: a review and synthesis. *Journal of World Prehistory* 16: 361–440.

Kuijt, I., and M. Chesson

2005   Lumps of clay and pieces of stone: ambiguity, bodies, and identity as portrayed in Neolithic figurines. In S. Pollock and R. Bernbeck (eds), *Archaeologies of the Middle East: Critical Perspectives*, 153–183. Oxford: Blackwell.

Kuijt, I., and N. Goodale

2009   Daily practice and the organization of space at the dawn of agriculture: a case study from the Near East. *Antiquity* 74: 403–422.

Laffineur, R., and E. Greco (eds)

2005   *Emporia: Aegeans in the Central and Eastern Mediterranean*. Aegaeum 25. Liège, Belgium, Austin: Université de Liège, University of Texas at Austin Program in Aegean Scripts and Prehistory.

Lagarce, J., and E. Lagarce

1985   *Alasia IV. Deux Tombes du Chypriote Récent d'Enkomi*. Tombes 1851 et 1907. Mission Archéologique d'Alasia 7. Recherches sur les Civilisations, Memoire 51. Paris: ADPF.

1986   Les découvertes d'Enkomi et leur place dans la culture internationale du bronze récent. In J.-C. Courtois, J. Lagarce and E. Lagarce, *Enkomi et le Bronze Récent en Chypre*, 59–199. Nicosia: Leventis Foundation.

Lambeck, K., and J. Chappell

2001   Sea level change through the last glacial cycle. *Science* 292: 679–686.

Lambeck, K., and A. Purcell

2005   Sea-level change in the Mediterranean Sea since the LGM: model predictions for tectonically stable areas. *Quaternary Science Reviews* 24: 1969–1988.

Laskaris, N., A. Sampson, F. Mavridis and I. Liritzis

2011   Late Pleistocene/Early Holocene seafaring in the Aegean: new obsidian hydration dates with the SIMS-SS method. *Journal of Archaeological Science* 38(9): 2475–2479.

Le Brun, A.

1981   *Un Site Néolithique Précéramique en Chypre: Cap Andreas Kastros*. Recherche sur les Grandes Civilisations, Mémoire 5 (Études Néolithiques). Paris: ADPF.

1984   *Fouilles récent à Khirokitia (Chypre) – 1977– 1981*. Recherches sur les Civilisation, Memoire 41 (Études Néolithiques). Paris: ADPF.

1985   Cap Andreas-*Kastros* et Khirokitia. In V. Karageorghis (ed.), *Archaeology in Cyprus 1960–1985*, 73–80. Nicosia: Leventis Foundation.

1989a *Fouilles récent à Khirokitia (Chypre) – 1983–1986*. Recherches sur les Civilisation, Memoire 81 (Études Néolithiques). Paris: ADPF.

1989b Le traitement des morts et les representations des vivants à Khirokitia. In E.J. Peltenburg (ed.), *Early Society in Cyprus*, 71–81. Edinburgh: Edinburgh University Press.

1993 Recherches sur le Néolithique précéramique de Chypre: les fouilles du Cap Andreas-Kastros et de Khirokitia. In M. Yon (ed.), *Kinyras: L'archéologie française à Chypre. Table Ronde, Lyon, 5–6 novembre 1991*. Maison de l'Orient, Travaux 22: 55–80. Lyon: Maison de l'Orient.

1994 *Fouilles récent à Khirokitia (Chypre). 1988–1991*. Études Néolithiques. Paris: ADPF.

1996 L'économie de Chypre au Néolithique. In V. Karageorghis and D. Michaelides (eds), *The Development of the Cypriot Economy*, 1–15. Nicosia: University of Cyprus; Bank of Cyprus.

1997 *Khirokitia: A Neolithic Site*. Bank of Cyprus, Cultural Foundation Guide Book. Nicosia: Bank of Cyprus, Cultural Foundation.

2001 At the other end of the sequence: the Cypriot Aceramic Neolithic as seen from Khirokitia. In S. Swiny (ed.), *The Earliest Prehistory of Cyprus: From Colonization to Exploitation*. Cyprus American Archaeological Research Institute Monograph 2: 109–118. Boston: American Schools of Oriental Research.

2002 Neolithic society in Cyprus: a tentative analysis. In D. Bolger and N. Serwint (eds), *Engendering Aphrodite: Women and Society in Ancient Cyprus*. Cyprus American Archaeological Research Institute Monograph 3: 23–31. Boston: American Schools of Oriental Research.

2004 Brèves remarques sur une longue histoire. *Neo-Lithics* 1/04: 10–11.

2005 Like a bull in a china shop: identity and ideology in Neolithic Cyprus. In J. Clarke (ed.), *Archaeological Perspectives on the Transmission and Transformation of Culture in the Eastern Mediterranean*. Levant Supplementary Series 2: 113–117. Oxford: Oxbow.

Le Brun, A., S. Cluzan, S.J.M. Davis, J. Hansen and J. Renault-Miskovsky

1987 Le Neolithique préceramique de Chypre. *L'Anthropologie* (Paris) 91(1): 283–316.

Le Brun, A., and O. Daune-Le Brun

2003 Deux aspects du Néolithique pré-céramique récent de Chypre: Khirolitia et Cap Andreas-Kastros. In J. Guilaine and A. Le Brun (eds), *Le Néolithique de Chypre*. Bulletin de Correspondance Hellénique, Supplément 43: 45–59. Athens: École Française d'Athénes.

2009 Khirokitia (Chypre): la taille et les pulsations de l'établisssement néolithique pré-céramiques, nouvelles données. *Paléorient* 35(2): 69–78.

Le Mort, F.

2000 The Neolithic subadult skeletons from Khirokitia (Cyprus): taphonomy and infant mortality. *Anthropologie: International Journal of the Science of Man* 38: 63–70.

2003 Les restes humains de Khirokitia: particularités et interprétations. In J. Guilaine and A. Le Brun (eds), *Le Néolithique de Chypre*. Bulletin de Correspondance Hellénique, Supplément 43: 313–325. Athens: École Française d'Athénes.

2007 Artificial cranial deformation in the Aceramic Neolithic Near East: evidence from Cyprus. In M. Faerman, L. Kokska Horwitz, T. Kahana and U. Ziberman (eds), *Faces from the Past: Diachronic Patterns in the Biology of Human Populations from the Eastern Mediterranean*. British Archaeological Reports: International Series 1603: 151–158. Oxford: Archeopress.

2008 Infant burials in Pre-Pottery Neolithic Cyprus: evidence from Khirokitia. In K. Bacvarov (ed.), *Babies Reborn: Infant/Child Burials in Pre- and Protohistory*. British Archaeological Reports, International Series 1832: 23–32. Oxford: Archaeopress.

Legge, T.

1996 The beginning of caprine domestication in southwest Asia. In D.R. Harris (ed.), *The Origins and Spread of Agriculture and Pastoralism in Eurasia*, 238–262. Washington, DC: Smithsonian Institution.

Legrand-Pineau, A.

2007 *Fabrication et utilisation de l'outillage en matières osseuses du Néolithique de Chypre. Khirokitia et Cap Andreas-Kastros*. British

Archaeological Reports, International Series 1678. Oxford: Archaeopress.

2009   Bridging the gap: bone tools as markers of continuity between Aceramic (Khirokitia Culture) and Ceramic Neolithic (Sotira Culture) in Cyprus (7th–5th millennia Cal BC). *Paléorient* 35(2): 113–123.

Lehavy, Y.

1974   Excavations at Neolithic Dhali-*Agridi*, Part 1. Excavation report. In L.E. Stager, A. Walker and G.E. Wright (eds), *The American Expedition to Idalion, Cyprus. First Preliminary Report: Seasons of 1971 and 1972*. Bulletin of the American Schools of Oriental Research, Supplement 18: 95–102. Cambridge, Massachusetts: American Schools of Oriental Research.

1989   Dhali-*Agridhi*: the Neolithic by the river. In L.E. Stager and A. Walker (eds), *American Expedition to Idalion, Cyprus 1973–1980*. Oriental Institute Communications 24: 203–243. Chicago: Oriental Institute, University of Chicago.

Lehmann, G.A.

1979   Die *sikalaju* – ein neues Zeugnis zu den Seevölker-Heerfahrten im späten 13 Jh. v. Chr. (RS 34.129). *Ugarit-Forschungen* 11: 481–494.

Leighton, R.

1999   *Sicily before History: An Archaeological Survey from the Palaeolithic to the Iron Age.* London: Duckworth.

Leonard, A., Jr.

1981   Considerations of morphological variation in the Mycenaean pottery from the southeastern Mediterranean. *Bulletin of the American Schools of Oriental Research* 241: 87–101.

2004   The Larnaca Hinterland Project. In J. Balensi, J.-Y. Monchambert and S. Müller-Celku (eds), *La Céramique Mycénienne de l'Égée au Levant*. Travaux de la Maison de l'Orient 41: 87–96. Lyon: Travaux de la Maison de l'Orient.

Leriou, A.

2002a   Constructing an archaeological narrative: the hellenization of Cyprus. *Stanford Archaeological Journal* 1: 1–32. (online publication)

2002b   The Mycenaean colonisation of Cyprus under the magnifying glass: emblematic indica versus defining criteria at Palaepaphos. In G. Muskett, A. Koltsida and M. Georgiadis (eds), *SOMA 2001:*

Symposium on Mediterranean Archaeology. British Archaeological Reports: International Series 1040: 169–177. Oxford: Archeopress.

Lesko, L.H.

1980   The wars of Ramesses III. *Serapis* 6: 83–86.

Levi, S.T.

2004   Produzioni artigianali: la ceramica. Circolazione dei produtti e organizzazione della manufattura. In D. Cocchi Genick (ed.), *L'Età del Bronzo Recente in Italia. Atti del Congresso Nazionale di Lido di Camaiore, 26–29 Ottobre 2000*, 233–242. Viareggio, Italy: Mauro Baroni.

Lindblom, M., and S.W. Manning

2011   The chronology of the Lerna shaft graves. In W. Gauß, M. Lindblom, R.A.K. Smith and J.C. Wright (eds), *Our Cups Are Full: Pottery and Society in the Aegean Bronze Age. Papers Presented to Jeremy B. Rutter on the Occasion of his 65th Birthday*. British Archaeological Reports, International Series 2227: 140–153. Oxford: Archaeopress.

Liverani, M.

1987   The collapse of the Near Eastern regional system at the end of the Bronze Age: the case of Syria. In M. Rowlands, M.T. Larsen and K. Kristiansen (eds), *Centre and Periphery in the Ancient World*, 66–73. Cambridge: Cambridge University Press.

1990   *Prestige and Interest: International Relations in the Near East ca. 1600–1100 BC.* Padua, Italy: Sargon Press.

1995   Le royaume d'Ougarit. In M. Yon, M. Szyncer and P. Bordreuil (eds), *Le pays d'Ougarit autour de 1200 av. J.-C.: histoire et archéologie*. Ras Shamra-Ougarit 11: 47–54. Paris: Éditions Recherche sur les Civilisations.

Loney, H.

2000   Society and technological control: a critical review of models of technological change in ceramic studies. *American Antiquity* 65: 646–668.

2007   Prehistoric Italian pottery production: motor memory, motor development and technological transfer. *Journal of Mediterranean Archaeology* 20: 183–207.

Lorentz, K.

2003   Minding the Body: The Growing Body in Cyprus from the Aceramic Neolithic to the Late Bronze Age. Unpublished PhD dissertation, Cambridge University, Cambridge.

2006 Headshaping at Marki and its socio-cultural significance. In D. Frankel and J. Webb, *Marki Alonia: An Early and Middle Bronze Age Settlement in Cyprus. Excavations 1995–2000*. Studies in Mediterranean Archaeology 123(2): 297–303. Sävedalen, Sweden: P. Åström's Förlag.

2009 Modifying the body: headshaping in Cyprus. *Medelhavsmuseet. Focus on the Mediterranean* 4: 21–27.

Lo Schiavo, F.

1985 *Nuraghic Sardinia in its Mediterranean Setting*. Edinburgh University, Department of Archaeology, Occasional Paper 12. Edinburgh: University of Edinburgh, Department of Archaeology.

1990 Copper oxhide and plano-convex ingots in Sardinia. In F. Lo Schiavo, R. Maddin, J. Merkel, J.D. Muhly and T. Stech, *Metallographic and Statistical Analyses of Copper Ingots from Sardinia*. Ministero per i Beni Culturali e Ambientali, Soprintendenza ai Beni Archaeologici per le Province de Sassari e Nuoro, Quaderni 17: 15–40. Torchietto, Italy: Ozieri.

1998 Sardinian oxhide ingots 1998. In T. Rehren, A. Hauptmann and J.D. Muhly (eds), *Metallurgica Antiqua: In Honour of Hans-Gert Bachmann and Robert Maddin*. Der Anschnitt, Beiheft 8: 99–112. Bochum, Germany: Deutsches Bergbaumuseum.

2001 Late Cypriot bronzework and bronze-workers in Sardinia, Italy and elsewhere in the west. In L. Bonfante and V. Karageorghis (eds), *Italy and Cyprus in Antiquity, 1500–450 BC*, 131–152. Nicosia: Leventis Foundation.

2003 Sardinia between east and west: interconnections in the Mediterranean. In N.C. Stampolidis and V. Karageorghis (eds), *Ploes… Sea Route…: Interconnections in the Mediterranean, 16th–6th c. BC*, 15–34. Athens: University of Crete, Leventis Foundation.

2005a Oxhide ingots, Cyprus and Sardinia. In F. Lo Schiavo, A. Giumla-Mair, U. Sanna and R. Valera (eds), *Archaeometallurgy in Sardinia: From the Origin to the Early Iron Age*. Monographies Instrumentum 30: 305–331. Montagnac, France: Editions Monique Mergoil.

2005b Early documents on Nuragic metal-lurgy. In F. Lo Schiavo, A. Giumla-Mair, U. Sanna and R. Valera (eds), *Archaeometallurgy in Sardinia: From the Origin to the Early Iron Age*. Monographies Instrumentum 30: 289–296. Montagnac, France: Editions Monique Mergoil.

2008 Oxhide ingots in the central Mediterranean: recent perspectives. In I. Tzachili (ed.), *Aegean Metallurgy in the Bronze Age*, 227–245. Rethymnon, Crete: Ta Pragmata.

Lo Schiavo, F., E. MacNamara and L. Vagnetti

1985 Late Cypriote imports to Italy and their influence on local bronzework. *Papers of the British School at Rome* 53: 1–71.

Lo Schiavo, F., R.M. Albanese Procelli and A. Giumlia Mair

2009 Oxhide ingots in Sicily. In F. Lo Schiavo, J.D. Muhly, R. Maddin and A. Giumlia Mair (eds), *Oxhide Ingots in the Central Mediterranean*, 135–221. Nicosia, Rome: Leventis Foundation, Istituto di Studi sulle Civiltà dell'Egeo e del Vicino Oriente, Consiglio Nazionale delle Ricerche.

Lo Schiavo, F., J.D. Muhly, R. Maddin and A. Guimlia Mair (eds)

2009 *Oxhide Ingots in the Central Mediterranean*. Nicosia, Rome: Leventis Foundation Istituto di Studi sulle Civiltà dell'Egeo e del Vicino Oriente Consiglio Nazionale delle Ricerche.

Low, S.M.

2000 *On the Plaza: The Politics of Public Space and Culture*. Austin: University of Texas Press.

Lubsen-Admiraal, S.M.

1994 Bronze Age plank figurines in the Zintilis Collection in Amsterdam. In F. Vandenabeele and R. Laffineur (eds), *Cypriot Stone Sculpture. Proceedings of the Second International Conference of Cypriote Studies, Brussels-Liège-Amsterdam (May 1993)*, 23–25. Nicosia, Brussels, Liège, Belgium: Leventis Foundation; Free University Brussels; Université de Liège.

2003 *Corpus of Cypriot Antiquities 25. Ancient Cypriot Art in the T.N. Zintilis Collection*. Studies in Mediterranean Archaeology 20: 25. Sävedalen, Sweden: P. Åström's Förlag.

Lunt, D.A.

1995 Lemba-*Lakkous* and Kissonerga-*Mosphilia*: evidence from the dentition in Chalcolithic Cyprus. In S. Campbell and A. Green (eds), *The Archaeology of Death in the Ancient Near East*. Oxbow Monograph 51: 55–61. Oxford: Oxbow.

McCartney, C.J.

1998   Preliminary report on the chipped stone assemblage from the Aceramic Neolithic site of Ayia Varvara *Asprokremnos*, Cyprus. *Levant* 30: 85–90.

1999   Opposed platform core technology and the Cypriot Aceramic Neolithic. *Neo-Lithics* 1/1999: 7–10.

2000   Prehistoric occurrences in the Ranti State Forest: a preliminary report of the Ranti Forest Project. *Report of the Department of Antiquities, Cyprus*: 33–46.

2002   Women's knives. In D. Bolger and N. Serwint (eds), *Engendering Aphrodite: Women and Society in Ancient Cyprus.* ASOR Archaeological Reports 7. Cyprus American Archaeological Research Institute Monograph 3: 237–249. Boston: American Schools of Oriental Research.

2003   The *Mylouthkia* and *Tenta* chipped stone industries and their interpretation within a redefined Cypriot Aceramic Neolithic. In J. Guilaine and A. Le Brun (eds), *Le Néolithique de Chypre*. Bulletin de Correspondance Héllenique, Supplément 43: 135–146. Athens: École Française d'Athènes.

2004   Cypriot Neolithic chipped stone industries and the progress of regionalization. In E. Peltenburg and A. Wasse (eds), *Neolithic Revolution. New Perspectives on Southwest Asia in Light of Recent Discoveries on Cyprus*. Levant Supplementary Series 1: 103–122. Oxford: Oxbow.

2005   Preliminary report on the re-survey of three early Neolithic sites in Cyprus. *Report of the Department of Antiquities, Cyprus*: 1–21.

2007   Assemblage diversity in the Early Middle Cypriot Aceramic Neolithic. In L. Astruc, D. Binder and F. Briois (eds), *Systèmes techniques et communautés du Néolithique précéramique au Proche-Orient: Technical Systems and Near Eastern PPN Communities*, 215–228. Antibes, France: Éditions APDCA.

2010   Outside the corridor: the Neolithisation of Cyprus. In D. Bolger and L. Maguire (eds), *The Development of Pre-state Communities in the Ancient Near East:*

Studies in Honour of Edgar Peltenburg. BANEA Publication Series 2: 187–196. Oxford: Oxbow.

2011   The lithic assemblage of Ayia Varvara *Asprokremnos*: a new perspective on the Early Neolithic of Cyprus. In E. Healey, S. Campbell and O. Maeda (eds), *The State of the Stone: Terminologies, Continuities and Contexts in Near Eastern Lithics*. Studies in Early Near Eastern Production, Subsistence, and Environment 13: 185–196. Berlin: Ex Oriente.

McCartney, C., and B. Gratuze

2003   The chipped stone. In E.J. Peltenburg and Project Members, *Lemba Archaeological Projects, Cyprus* 3: 1. *The Colonisation and Settlement of Cyprus: Investigations at Kissonerga-Mylouthkia, 1976–1996.* Studies in Mediterranean Archaeology 70(4): 11–34. Sävedalen, Sweden: P. Åström's Förlag.

McCartney, C., and I. Todd

2005   Tenta chipped stone report. In I. Todd (ed.), *Excavations at Kalavasos-Tenta 2. Vasilikos Valley Project* 7. Studies in Mediterranean Archaeology 71(7): 177–264. Sävedalen, Sweden: P. Åström's Förlag.

McCartney, C., S.W. Manning, D. Sewell and S.T. Stewart

2006   Elaborating Early Neolithic Cyprus (EENC). *Report of the Department of Antiquities, Cyprus*: 39–62.

2007   The EENC 2006 field season: excavations at Agia Varvara *Asprokremnos* and survey of the local early Holocene landscape. *Report of the Department of Antiquities, Cyprus:* 27–44.

McCartney, C., S.W. Manning, S. Rosendahl and S.T. Stewart

2008   Elaborating Early Neolithic Cyprus (EENC) preliminary report on the 2007 field season: excavations and regional field survey at Agia Varvara-*Asprokremnos*. *Report of the Department of Antiquities, Cyprus*: 67–86.

McCartney, C., P. Croft, S.W. Manning and S. Rosendahl

2009   Preliminary report on the 2008 EENC excavations at Agia Varvara *Asprokremnos* and regional field survey. *Report of the Department of Antiquities, Cyprus*: 1–16.

McCartney, C.J., S.W. Manning, D. Sewell and S.T. Stewart

2010   Reconsidering Early Holocene Cyprus within the eastern Mediterranean landscape. In B. Finlayson and G. Warren (eds), *Landscapes in Transition*, 131–145. London: Council for British Research in the Levant.

MacConnell, B.E.

1989   Mediterranean archaeology and modern nationalism: a preface. *Revue des Archaeologues et Historiens d'Art de Louvain* 22: 107–113.

McCorriston, J., and F. Hole

1991   The ecology of seasonal stress and the origins of agriculture in the Near East. *American Anthropologist* 93: 46–69.

McFadden, G.H.

1946   A tomb of the necropolis of Ayios Ermoyenis at Kourion. *American Journal of Archaeology* 50: 449–489.

1954   A Late Cypriot III tomb from Kourion *Kaloriziki*. *American Journal of Archaeology* 58: 131–142.

McGeough, K.M.

2007   *Exchange Relationships at Ugarit*. Ancient Near Eastern Studies, Supplement 26. Leuven: Peeters.

McKechnie, R.

2002   Islands of indifference. In W.H. Waldren and J.A. Ensenyat (eds), *World Islands in Prehistory. V Deia International Conference of Prehistory*. British Archaeological Reports, International Series 1095: 127–134. Oxford: Archaeopress.

MacLachlan, B.

2002   The ungendering of Aphrodite. In D. Bolger and N. Serwint (eds), *Engendering Aphrodite: Women and Society in Ancient Cyprus*. Cyprus American Archaeological Research Institute Monograph 3: 365–378. Boston: American Schools of Oriental Research.

MacLaurin, L.

1985   Shape and fabric in Cypriote red polished pottery. In T. Papadopoullou and S.A. Hadjistellis (eds), *Acts of the Second International Cyprological Congress (Nicosia, 20–25 April 1982)*, 73–107. Nicosia: Leventis Foundation.

Macnamara, E.

2002   Some bronze typologies in Sardinia and Italy from 1200 to 700 BC: their origin and development. In O. Paoletti and L.T. Perna (eds), *Etruria e Sardinia Centro-Settentrionale tra l'Età del Bronzo Finale e l'Arcaismo: Atti del XXI Convegno di Studi Etruschi ed Italici, Sassari, Alghero, Oristano, Torralba, 13–17 Ottobre 1998*, 151–174. Pisa, Italy: Istituti Editoriali e Poligrafici Internazionali.

McNeill, J.R.

1992   *The Mountains of the Mediterranean World*. Cambridge: Cambridge University Press.

McNiven, I., and R. Feldman

2003   Ritually oriented seascapes: hunting magic and dugong bone mounds in Torres Strait, NE Australia. *Cambridge Archaeological Journal* 13: 169–194.

Maddin, R., J.D. Muhly and T. Stech Wheeler

1983   Metal working. In T. Dothan and A. Ben-Tor, *Excavations at Athienou, Cyprus, 1971–1972*. Qedem 16: 132–138. Jerusalem: Institute of Archaeology, Hebrew University.

Maguire, L.C.

1991   The classification of Middle Bronze Age painted pottery: wares, style … workshops? In J. Barlow, D. Bolger and B. Kling (eds), *Cypriot Ceramics: Reading the Prehistoric Record*. University Museum Monograph 74: 59–66. Philadelphia: University Museum, University of Pennsylvania.

2009   *The Cypriot Pottery and Its Circulation in the Levant*. Tell el-Dab'a 21. Österreichische Akademie der Wissenschaften, Denkschriften der Gesamtakademie 51. Vienna: Österreichische Akademie der Wissenschaften.

Maher, L.A., E.B. Banning and Michael Chazan

2011   Oasis or mirage? Assessing the role of abrupt climate change in the prehistory of the southern Levant. *Cambridge Archaeological Journal* 21: 1–29.

Maier, F.-G.

1969   Excavations at Kouklia (Palaepaphos), 1968. *Report of the Department of Antiquities, Cyprus*: 33–42.

1986   Kinyras and Agapenor. In V. Karageorghis (ed.), *Acts of the International Archaeological Symposium: Cyprus between the Orient and the Occident*, 311–320. Nicosia: Department of Antiquities, Cyprus.

1987   *Paphos in the History of Cyprus*. Third annual lecture on the History and

Archaeology of Cyprus. Nicosia: Bank of Cyprus Cultural Foundation.

Maier, F.-G., and V. Karageorghis
1984 *Paphos: History and Archaeology*. Nicosia: Leventis Foundation.

Maier, F.-G., and M.-L. von Wartburg
1985 Reconstructing history from the earth, c. 2800 B.C.–1600 A.D.: excavating at Palaepaphos, 1966–1984. In V. Karageorghis (ed.), *Archaeology in Cyprus 1960–1985*, 142–172. Nicosia: Leventis Foundation.

Malbran-Labat, F.
1999 Nouvelles données épigraphiques sur Chypre et Ougarit. *Report of the Department of Antiquities, Cyprus*: 121–123.

Mandel, R.D., and A.H. Simmons
1997 Geoarchaeology of the Akrotiri *Aetokremnos* rockshelter, southern Cyprus. *Geoarchaeology* 12: 567–605.

Manning, S.W.
1993 Prestige, distinction and competition: the anatomy of socio-economic complexity in 4th–2nd millennium B.C.E. Cyprus. *Bulletin of the American Schools of Oriental Research* 292: 35–58.

1998a Tsaroukkas, Mycenaeans and Trade Project: preliminary report on the 1996–97 seasons. *Report of the Department of Antiquities, Cyprus*: 39–54.

1998b Changing pasts and socio-political cognition in Late Bronze Age Cyprus. *World Archaeology* 30: 39–58.

1999 *A Test of Time: The Volcano of Thera and the Chronology and History of the Aegean and East Mediterranean in the Mid-Second Millennium BC*. Oxford: Oxbow.

2001 The chronology and foreign connections of the Late Cypriot I period: times they are a-changin'. In P. Åström (ed.), *The Chronology of Base-ring Ware and Bichrome Wheel-made Ware*. Konferenser 54: 69–94. Stockholm: Kungl. Vitterhets Historie och Antikvitets Akademien.

2006–2007 Why radiocarbon dating 1200 BCE is difficult: a sidelight on dating the end of the Late Bronze Age and the contrarian contribution. *Scripta Mediterranea* 27: 53–80.

2010 Chronology and terminology. In E.H. Cline (ed.), *The Oxford Handbook of the Bronze Age Aegean*, 11–28. Oxford: Oxford University Press.

Manning, S.W., and F.A. DeMita, Jr.
1997 Cyprus, the Aegean and Maroni *Tsaroukkas*. In D. Christou (ed.), *Cyprus and the Aegean in Antiquity*, 103–142. Nicosia: Department of Antiquities, Cyprus.

Manning, S.W., and S.J. Monks
1998 Late Cypriot tombs at Maroni *Tsarroukkas*, Cyprus. *Annual of the British School at Athens* 93: 297–351.

Manning, S.W., and S. Swiny
1994 Sotira *Kaminoudhia* and the chronology of the Early Bronze Age in Cyprus. *Oxford Journal of Archaeology* 13: 149–172.

Manning, S.W., B. Weniger, A.K. South, B. Kling, P.I. Kuniholm, J.D. Muhly, S. Hadjisavvas, D.A. Sewell and G. Cadogan
2001 Absolute age range of the Late Cypriot IIC period on Cyprus. *Antiquity* 75: 328–340.

Manning, S.W., D. Sewell and E. Herscher
2002 Late Cypriot IA maritime trade in action: underwater survey at Maroni *Tsarroukkas* and the contemporary east Mediterranean trading system. *Annual of the British School at Athens* 97: 97–162.

Manning, S.W., and L. Hulin
2005 Maritime commerce and geographies of mobility in the Late Bronze Age of the eastern Mediterranean: problematizations. In E. Blake and A.B. Knapp (eds), *The Archaeology of Mediterranean Prehistory*, 275–307. Oxford: Blackwell.

Manning, S.W., and D. Sewell
2006 Psematismenos *Trelloukkas* Project, Cyprus. *Council for British Research in the Levant, Bulletin* 1: 66–68.

Manning, S.W., C. Bronk Ramsey, W. Kutschera, T. Higham, B. Kromer, P. Steier and E. Wild
2006 Chronology for the Aegean Late Bronze Age. *Science* 312: 565–569.

Manning, S.W., and P.I. Kuniholm
2007 Absolute dating at Apliki *Karamalos*. In B. Kling and J.D. Muhly (eds), *Joan du Plat Taylor's Excavations at the Late Bronze Age Mining Settlement at Apliki Karamalos, Cyprus*. Studies in Mediterranean Archaeology 134(1): 325–335. Sävedalen, Sweden: P. Åström's Förlag.

Manning, S.W., and C.B. Ramsey
2007 Clarifying the 'high' v. 'low' Aegean/Cypriot chronology for the mid-second

millennium BC: assessing the evidence, interpretive frameworks, and current state of the debate. In M. Bietak and E. Czerny (eds), *The Synchronisation of Civilsations in the Eastern Mediterranean in the Second Millennium BC* III. Denkschriften der Gesamtakademie 37. Contributions to the Chronology of the Eastern Mediterranean 9: 101–137. Vienna: Österreichischen Akademie der Wissenschaften.

Manning, S.W., C. McCartney, B. Kromer and S.T. Stewart

2010a The earlier Neolithic in Cyprus: recognition and dating of Pre-Pottery Neolithic A occupation. *Antiquity* 84/325: 693–706.

Manning, S.W., B. Kromer, C. Bronk Ramsey, C.L. Pearson, S. Talamo, N. Trano and J.D. Watkins

2010b 14C record and wiggle-match placement for the Anatolian (Gordion area) juniper tree-ring chronology ~1729 to 751 Cal BC. *Radiocarbon* 52: 1571–1597.

Manning, S.W., and B. Kromer

2011 Radiocarbon dating archaeological samples in the eastern Mediterranean 1730–1480 BC: further exploring the atmospheric radiocarbon calibration record and the archaeological implications. *Archaeometry* 53: 413–439.

Manning, S.W., B. Kromer, M. Dee, M. Friedrich, T. Higham and C. Bronk Ramsey

n.d. Radiocarbon calibration in the mid-to-later 14th century BC and radiocarbon dating Tell el-Amarna, Egypt. In C. Bronk Ramsey and A.J. Shortland (eds), *Radiocarbon and the Chronologies of Egypt*. Oxford: Oxbow. (in press)

Mantzourani, E.

1994a Έκθεση Αποτελεσμάτων της Ανασκαφής στη θέση Καντού-*Κουφόβουνος*. *Report of the Department of Antquities, Cyprus*: 1–29.

1994b Το ανθρωπομόρφο ειδώλιο από το νεολιθικό Καντού-*Κουφόβουνος*. *Report of the Department of Antiquities, Cyprus*: 31–38.

1997 Ταφικές πρακτικές στους νησιώτικους οικισμούς του Ελλάδα και την Κύπρο στα Νεολιθικά χρόνια: συκριτική θεώρηση. In D. Christou (ed.), *Cyprus and the Aegean in Antiquity: From the Prehistoric Period to the 7th Century AD*, 21–32. Nicosia: Department of Antiquities.

2001 Η κόσμηση κατά νεολιθική εποχή στην Κύπρο: η περίπτωση του Καντού-Κουφόβοθνου. *Archaeologia Cypria* 4: 47–70.

2003a Kandou *Kourphovounos*: a Late Neolithic site in the Limassol district. In J. Guilaine and A. Le Brun (eds), *Le Néolithique de Chypre*. Bulletin de Correspondance Héllenique, Supplément 43: 85–98. Athens: École Française d'Athènes.

2003b Architectural and social organization of space in Late Neolithic Cyprus: the north–south divide revisited. *Mediterranean Archaeology and Archaeometry* 3(2): 35–52.

2009 Η Ανασκαφή του Νεολιθικού Οικισμού Καντού-Κουφόβουνος στην Κύπρο. Nicosia: Department of Antiquities, Cyprus.

Mantzourani, E., and D. Catapoti

2004 Histories carved in stone: ground stone tool production and consumption in the Limassol district during the Late Neolithic. *Report of the Department of Antiquities, Cyprus*: 1–17.

Mantzourani, E., and I. Liritizis

2006 Chemical analysis of pottery samples from Late Neolithic Kantou *Kouphovounos* and Sotira *Teppes*. *Report of the Department of Antiquities, Cyprus*: 63–76.

Maran, J.

2004 The spreading of objects and ideas in the Late Bronze Age eastern Mediterranean: two case examples from the Argolid of the 13th and 12th centuries B.C. *Bulletin of the American Schools of Oriental Research* 336: 11–30.

2006 Coming to terms with the past: ideology and power in Late Helladic IIIC. In S. Deger-Jalkotzy and I.S. Lemos (eds), *Ancient Greece: From the Mycenaean Palaces to the Age of Homer*. Edinburgh Leventis Studies 3: 123–150. Oxford: Oxbow.

2008 Forschungen in der Unterburg von Tiryns 2000–2003. *Archäologischer Anzeiger* (2008: 1) 35–111.

2009 The crisis years? Reflections on signs of instability in the last decades of the Mycenaean palaces. *Scienze dell'antichità* 15: 241–262.

Marazzi, M., S. Tusa and L. Vagnetti (eds)

1986 *Traffici Micenei nel Mediterraneo: Problemi Storici e Documentazione Archeologica (Atti del Convegno di Palermo, 11–12 May & 2–3 Dec. 1985)*. Magna Graecia 3. Taranto, Sicily: Istituto per la Storia e l'Arch. della Magno Grecia.

Marcus, E.

2002a Early seafaring and maritime activity in the southern Levant from prehistory through the third millennium BCE. In E.C.M. van den Brink and T.E. Levy (eds), *Egypt and the Levant: Interrelations from the 4th through the Early 3rd Millennium BC*, 403–417. London: Leicester University Press.

2002b The southern Levant and maritime trade during the Middle Bronze IIA period. In E.D. Oren and S. Ahituv (eds), *Aharon Kempinski Memorial Volume: Studies in Archaeology and Related Disciplines*. Beer-Sheva 15: 241–263. Beersheva, Israel: Ben-Gurion University of Negev Press.

Markoe, G.

1985 *Phoenician Bronze and Silver Bowls from Cyprus and the Mediterranean*. University of California Classical Studies 26. Berkeley: University of California Press.

Mart, Y., and W.B.F. Ryan

2002 The complex tectonic regime of the Cyprus Arc: a short review. *Israel Journal of Earth Science* 51: 117–134.

Martin, P.S.

1984 Prehistoric overkill: the global model. In P.S. Martin and R.G. Klein (eds), *Quaternary Extinctions*, 354–403. Tucson: University of Arizona Press.

Martín de la Cruz, J.C.

1988 Mykenische keramik aus bronzezeitlichen Siedlungsschichten von Montaro am Guadalquivir. *Madrider Mitteilungen* 29: 77–92.

Martlew, H.

2004 Minoan and Mycenaean technology as revealed through organic residue analysis. In J.D. Bourriau and J. Phillips (eds), *Invention and Innovation: The Social Context of Technological Change 2. Egypt, the Aegean and the Near East, 1650–1150 BC*, 121–148. Oxford: Oxbow.

Masseti, M.

2006 Domestic fauna and anthropochorous fauna. *Human Evolution* 21: 85–93.

Masson, E.

1976 À la recherche des vestiges proche-orientaux à Chypre, fin du bronze moyen et début du bronze récent. *Archäologischer Anzierger* (1976:2): 139–165.

Masson, E., and O. Masson

1983 Les objets inscrits de Palaepaphos-*Skales*. In V. Karageorghis, *Palaepaphos-Skales: An Iron Age Cemetery in Cyprus*. Alt-Paphos 3: 411–415. Konstanz, Germany: Universitätsverlag.

Mazar, A.

1985 The emergence of the Philistine material culture. *Israel Exploration Journal* 35: 95–107.

Meiggs, R.

1982 *Trees and Timber in the Mediterranean World*. Oxford: Clarendon Press.

Meikle, R.D.

1977 *The Flora of Cyprus* 1. London: Bentham-Mixon Trust.

1985 *The Flora of Cyprus* 2. London: Bentham-Mixon Trust.

Mellaart, J.

1975 *The Neolithic of the Near East*. New York: Scribner.

Mellink, M.J.

1986 The Early Bronze Age in west Anatolia: Aegean and Asiatic correlations. In G. Cadogan (ed.), *The End of the Early Bronze Age in the Aegean*. Cincinnati Classical Studies n.s. 6: 139–152. Leiden, The Netherlands: Brill.

1991 Anatolian contacts with Chalcolithic Cyprus. *Bulletin of the American Schools of Oriental Research* 282–283: 167–175.

1993 The Anatolian south coast in the Early Bronze Age: the Cilician perspective. In M. Frangipane, H. Hauptmann, M. Liverani, P. Matthiae and M. Mellink (eds), *Between the Rivers and Over the Mountains. Archaeologica Anatolica et Mesopotamica, Alba Palmieri Dedicata*, 495–508. Rome: Universita di Roma 'La Sapienza'.

Merrillees, R.S.

1962 Opium trade in the Bronze Age Levant. *Antiquity* 36: 287–292.

1965 Reflections on the Late Bronze Age in Cyprus. *Opuscula Atheniensia* 6: 139–148.

1968 *The Cypriote Bronze Age Pottery found in Egypt*. Studies in Mediterranean Archaeology 18. Lund, Sweden: P. Åström's Förlag.

1969 Opium again in antiquity. *Levant* 11: 167–171.

1971 The early history of Late Cypriote I. *Levant* 3: 56–79.

1973 Settlement, sanctuary and cemetery in Bronze Age Cyprus. *Australian Studies in Archaeology* 1: 44–57.

1977 The absolute chronology of the Bronze Age in Cyprus. *Report of the Department of Antiquities, Cyprus*: 33–50.

1978 *Introduction to the Bronze Age Archaeology of Cyprus.* Studies in Mediterranean Archaeology, Pocket-book 9. Göteborg, Sweden: P. Åström's Förlag.

1980 Representations of the human form in prehistoric Cyprus. *Opuscula Atheniensia* 13: 171–184.

1982 Archaeological Symposium: Early Metallurgy in Cyprus, 4000–500 BC: historical summary. In J.D. Muhly, R. Maddin and V. Karageorghis (eds), *Early Metallurgy in Cyprus, 4000–500 BC*, 373–376. Nicosia: Pierides Foundation.

1984 Ambelikou-*Aletri*: a preliminary report. *Report of the Department of Antiquities, Cyprus*: 1–13.

1988 Mother and child: a Late Cypriot variation on an eternal theme. *Mediterranean Archaeology* 1: 42–56.

1992a The government of Cyprus in the Late Bronze Age. In P. Åström (ed.), *Acta Cypria* 3. Studies in Mediterranean Archaeology and Literature, Pocket-book 120: 310–329. Jonsered, Sweden: P. Åström's Förlag.

1992b The absolute chronology of the Bronze Age in Cyprus: a revision. *Bulletin of the American Schools of Oriental Research* 288: 47–52.

2002 The relative and absolute chronology of the Cypriote White Painted Pendent Line Style. *Bulletin of American Schools of Oriental Research* 326: 1–9.

2007 The ethnic implications of Tell el-Yahudiyeh ware for the history of the Middle to Late Bronze Age in Cyprus. *Cahier du Centre d'Études Chypriotes* 337: 87–96.

2009a The stone vases of the Philia culture from Vasilia: Cypriot, Egyptian or other? In D. Michaelides, V. Kassianidou and R. Merrillees (eds), *Egypt and Cyprus in Antiquity*, 23–28. Oxford: Oxbow.

2009b Chronological conundrums: Cypriot and Levantine imports from Thera. In D.A. Warburton (ed.), *Time's Up! Dating the Minoan Eruption of Santorini.* Monographs of the Danish Institute at Athens 10: 247–251. Athens: Danish Institute at Athens.

2011 *Alashiya*: a scientific quest for its location In P.P. Betancourt and S.C. Ferrence (eds), *Metallurgy: Understanding How, Learning Why. Studies in Honor of James D. Muhly*, 255–264. Philadelphia: Institute for Aegean Prehistory Press.

Merrillees, R.S. (and J. Evans)

1989 Highs and lows in the Holy Land: opium in Biblical times. In A. Ben-Tor, J. Greenfield and A. Malamat (eds), *Yigael Yadin Memorial Volume.* Eretz Israel 20: 148*–154*. Jerusalem: Hebrew University, Israel Exploration Society.

Meskell, L.

1998a (ed.) *Archaeology Under Fire: Archaeology and Politics in the Eastern Mediterranean.* London: Routledge.

1998b Twin peaks: the archaeologies of Çatalhöyük. In Lucy Goodison and C. Morris (eds), *Ancient Goddesses*, 46–62. London: British Museum Press.

2001 Archaeologies of identity. In I. Hodder (ed.), *Archaeological Theory Today*, 187–213. Cambridge: Polity Press.

2002a *Private Life in New Kingdom Egypt.* Princeton: Princeton University Press.

2002b The intersections of identity and politics in archaeology. *Annual Review of Anthropology* 31: 279–301.

Michailidou, A.

2009 *Weight and Value in Pre-Coinage Societies 2: Sidelights on Measurement from the Aegean and the Orient.* Meletemata 61. Paris, Athens: Diffusion de Boccard.

Mielke, D.P.

2007 Red Lustrous Wheelmade Ware from Hittite contexts. In I. Hein (ed.), *The Lustrous Wares of Late Bronze Age Cyprus and the Eastern Mediterranean.* Contributions to the Chronology of the Eastern Mediterranean 13: 155–168. Vienna: Österreichische Akademie der Wissenschaften.

Miksicek, C.H.

1988 A preliminary test of flotation for recovery of charred plant remains from Maa-*Palaeokastro*. In V. Karageorghis and M. Demas, *Excavations at Maa-Palaeokastro 1979–1986*, 467–470. Nicosia: Department of Antiquities, Cyprus.

Milevski, I.

2011   *Early Bronze Age Goods Exchange in the Southern Levant: A Marxist Perspective.* London: Equinox.

Militello, P.

2004   Commercianti, architetti ed artigiani: riflessioni sulla presenza micenea nell'area Iblea. In V. La Rosa (ed.), *Le Presenze Micenee nel Territorio Siricusano. I Simposio Siricusano di Preistoria Siciliana in Memoria di Paolo Orsi. Siracusa, 15–16 Dicembre 2003,* 295–336. Padua, Italy: Bottega d'Erasmo.

Mills, B.J.

2004   Identity, feasting, and the archaeology of the greater Southwest. In B.J. Mills (ed.), *Identity, Feasting, and the Archaeology of the Greater Southwest,* 1–23. Boulder: University Press of Colorado.

Milner, N.

2005   Can seasonality studies be used to identify sedentism in the past? In D. Bailey, A. Whittle and V. Cummings (eds), *(Un) settling the Neolithic,* 32–37. Oxford: Oxbow.

Mina, M.

2008   *Anthropomorphic Figurines from the Neolithic and Early Bronze Age Aegean: Gender Dynamics and Implications for the Understanding of Early Aegean Prehistory.* British Archaeological Reports: International Series 1894. Oxford: Archeopress.

Mitford, T.B., and J.H. Iliffe

1951   Excavations at Kouklia (Old Paphos) Cyprus, 1950. *Antiquaries Journal* 31: 51–66.

Mithen, S.

2003   *After the Ice: A Global Human History, 20,000–5000 BC.* London: Weidenfeld and Nicolson.

Mogelonsky, M.K.

1991   A typological system for Early and Middle Cypriot anthropomorphic terracotta figurines. *Report of the Department of Antiquities, Cyprus:* 19–36.

Monroe, C.M.

2002   Review of J.D. Schloen, *The House of the Father as Fact and Symbol: Patrimonialism in Ugarit and the Ancient Near East* (Winona Lake, Indiana: Eisenbrauns, 2001). In *Journal of the American Oriental Society* 122: 904–907.

2009   *Scales of Fate: Trade, Tradition, and Transformation in the Eastern Mediterranean.*

Alter Orient und Altes Testament 357. Münster, Germany: Ugarit-Verlag.

Moore, A.M.T., and G.C. Hillman

1992   The Pleistocene to Holocene transition and human economy in southwest Asia: the impact of the Younger Dryas. *American Antiquity* 57: 482–494.

Moores, E.M., P.T. Robinson, J.G. Malpas and C. Xenophontos

1984   A model for the origin of the Troodos massif, Cyprus, and other mideast ophiolites. *Geology* 12: 500–503.

Moran, W.L.

1992   *The Amarna Letters.* Baltimore: Johns Hopkins University Press.

Morhange, C., J.P. Goiran, M. Bourcier, P. Carbonel, J. Le Campion, J.M. Rouchy and M. Yon

2000   Recent Holocene paleo-environmental evolution and coastline changes of Kition, Larnaca, Cyprus, Mediterranean Sea. *Marine Geology* 170: 205–230.

Morris, C.

2009   Configuring the individual: bodies of figurines in Minoan Crete. In A.L. D'Agata and A. Van de Moortel (eds), *Archaeologies of Cult: Essays on Ritual and Cult in Crete in Honor of Geraldine C. Gesell.* Hesperia Supplement 42: 179–187. Princeton, New Jersey: American School of Classical Studies in Athens.

Morris, D.

1985   *The Art of Ancient Cyprus.* Oxford: Phaidon Press.

Morrison, I.A., and T.F. Watkins

1974   Kataliondas-*Kourvellos*: a survey of an aceramic Neolithic site and its environs in Cyprus. *Palestine Exploration Quarterly* 106: 67–75.

Mountjoy, P.A.

1993   *Mycenaean Pottery: An Introduction.* Oxford: Oxford University Committee on Archaeology.

Muhly, J.D.

1980   Bronze figurines and Near Eastern metalwork. Review of O. Negbi, *Canaanite Gods in Metal* (Tel Aviv: Institute of Archaeology, Tel Aviv University, 1976). In *Israel Exploration Journal* 30: 148–161.

1984   The role of the Sea Peoples in Cyprus during the LCIII period. In V. Karageorghis and J.D. Muhly (eds), *Cyprus at the Close of the Late Bronze Age*, 39–55. Nicosia: Leventis Foundation.

1985a   Sources of tin and the beginnings of bronze metallurgy. *American Journal of Archaeology* 89: 275–291.

1985b   The Late Bronze Age in Cyprus: a 25 year retrospect. In V. Karageorghis (ed.), *Archaeology in Cyprus 1960–1985*, 20–46. Nicosia: Leventis Foundation.

1989   The organisation of the copper industry in Late Bronze Age Cyprus. In E.J. Peltenburg (ed.), *Early Society in Cyprus*, 298–314. Edinburgh: Edinburgh University Press.

1991a   Copper in Cyprus: the earliest phase. In J.-P. Mohen and C. Eluere (eds), *Découverte du Métal*. Amis du Musée des Antiquites Nationales, Millénaires, Dossier 2: 357–374. Paris: Picard.

1991b   The development of copper metallurgy in Late Bronze Age Cyprus. In N.H. Gale (ed.), *Bronze Age Trade in the Mediterranean*. Studies in Mediterranean Archaeology 90: 180–196. Göteborg, Sweden: P. Åström's Förlag.

1995   Lead isotope analysis and the archaeologist. *Journal of Mediterranean Archaeology* 8: 54–58.

1996   The significance of metals in the Late Bronze Age economy of Cyprus. In V. Karageorghis and D. Michaelides (eds), *The Development of the Cypriot Economy*, 45–60. Nicosia: University of Cyprus; Bank of Cyprus.

2002   Early metallurgy in Greece and Cyprus. In Ü. Yalçin (ed.), *Anatolian Metal* II. Der Anschnitt, Beiheft 15: 77–82. Bochum, Germany: Deutsches Bergbau-Museum.

2003   Trade in metals in the Late Bronze Age and Iron Age. In N.C. Stampolidis and V. Karageorghis (eds), *Ploes… Sea Routes…: Interconnections in the Mediterranean, 16th–6th c. BC*, 141–150. Athens: University of Crete, Leventis Foundation.

Muhly, J.D., R. Maddin and V. Karageorghis (eds)

1982   *Early Metallurgy in Cyprus, 4000–500 B.C.* Nicosia: Pierides Foundation.

Muhly, J.D., R. Maddin and T. Stech

1988   Cyprus, Crete and Sardinia: copper oxhide ingots and the metals trade. *Report of the Department of Antiquities, Cyprus*: 281–298.

Murray, A.S., A.H. Smith and H.B. Walters

1900   *Excavations in Cyprus*. London: British Museum.

Murray, M.A.

2003   The plant remains. In E.J. Peltenburg (ed.), *The Colonisation and Settlement of Cyprus: Investigations at Kissonerga Mylouthkia, 1976–1996*. Studies in Mediterranean Archaeology 70(4): 59–71. Sävedalen, Sweden: P. Åström's Förlag.

Mussi, M., and R.T. Melis

2002   Santa Maria is Acquas e le problematiche del Paleolitico superiore in Sardegna. *Origini. Preistoria e Protostoria delle Civiltà Antiche* 24: 67–94.

Myres, J.L.

1914   *Handbook of the Cesnola Collection of Antiquities from Cyprus*. New York: Metropolitan Museum of Art.

Myres, J.L., and M. Ohnefalsch-Richter

1899   *A Catalogue of the Cyprus Museum, with a Chronicle of Excavations Undertaken since the British Occupation and Introductory Notes on Cypriot Archaeology*. Oxford: Clarendon Press.

Nakou, G.

1995   The cutting edge: a new look at early Aegean metallurgy. *Journal of Mediterranean Archaeology* 8: 1–32.

Nanoglou, S.

2006   Regional perspectives on the Neolithic anthropomorphic imagery of northern Greece. *Journal of Mediterranean Archaeology* 19: 155–176.

Narroll, R.

1962   Floor area and settlement population. *American Antiquity* 27: 587–589.

Negbi, O.

1986   The climax of urban development in Bronze Age Cyprus. *Report of the Department of Antiquities, Cyprus*: 97–121.

1998   Reflections on the ethnicity of Cyprus in the eleventh century BC. In S. Gitin, A. Mazar and E. Stern (eds), *Mediterranean Peoples in Transition: Thirteenth to Tenth Centuries BCE*, 87–93. Jerusalem: Israel Exploration Society.

2005   Urbanism on Late Bronze Age Cyprus: LC II in retrospect. *Bulletin of the American Schools of Oriental Research* 337: 1–45.

Nesbitt, M.

2002   When and where did domesticated cereals first occur in southwest Asia? In R.T.J.

Cappers and S. Bottema (eds), *The Dawn of Farming in the Near East*. Studies in Early Near Eastern Production, Subsistence, and Environment 6: 113–132. Berlin: Ex Oriente.

Nicolaou, I., and K. Nicolaou

1989   *Kazaphani: A Middle/Late Cypriot Tomb at Kazaphani-Ayios Andronikos: T.2 A,B.* Nicosia: Department of Antiquities, Cyprus.

Nicolaou, K.

1967   The distribution of settlements in Stone Age Cyprus. *Kypriakai Spoudhai* 31: 37–52.

1976   *The Historical Topography of Kition*. Studies in Mediterranean Archaeology 43. Göteborg, Sweden: P. Åström's Förlag.

Niklasson, K.

1991   *Early Prehistoric Burials in Cyprus*. Studies in Mediterranean Archaeology 96. Jonsered, Sweden: P. Åström's Förlag.

Niklasson-Sönnerby, K.

1987   Late Cypriote III shaft graves: burial customs of the last phase of the Bronze Age. In R. Laffineur (ed.), *Thanatos:Les Coutumes Funéraires en Égée à l'Age du Bronze*. Aegaeum 1: 219–225. Liège, Belgium: Université de Liège.

Noller, J.S., Z. Zomeni and I. Panayides

2005   Report on the preliminary assessment of tsunami hazard in Cyprus. *Reports of the Geological Survey of Cyprus*: 1–26.

Noy, T.

1994   Gilgal. In E. Stern (ed.), *New Encyclopedia of Archaeological Excavations in the Holy Land*, 517–518. Jerusalem: Carta.

O'Connor, D.

2000   The Sea Peoples and the Egyptian sources. In E.D. Oren (ed.), *The Sea Peoples and Their World: A Reassessment*. University Museum Monograph 108. University Museum Symposium Series 11: 85–102. Philadelphia: University Museum, University of Pennsylvania.

Oren, E.D. (ed.)

2000   *The Sea Peoples and Their World: A Reassessment*. University Museum Monograph 108, University Museum Symposium Series 11. Philadelphia: University Museum, University of Pennsylvania.

Orphanides, A.G.

1988   A classification of the Bronze Age terracotta anthropomorphic figurines

from Cyprus. *Report of the Department of Antiquities, Cyprus*: 187–201.

Osaki, D., and J. Harris (eds)

1990   *Cyprus Before the Bronze Age: Art of the Chalcolithic Period*. Malibu, California: Getty Museum.

Overbeck, J.C., and S. Swiny

1972   *Two Cypriot Bronze Age Sites at Kafkallia (Dhali)*. Studies in Mediterranean Archaeology 33. Göteborg, Sweden: P. Åström's Förlag.

Özdoğan, M.

2004   Cyprus: a regional component of the Levantine PPN. *Neo-Lithics* 1/04: 11–12.

Pacci, M.

1986   Presenze Micenee a Cipro. In M. Marazzi, S. Tusa and L. Vagnetti (eds), *Traffici Micenei nel Mediterraneo*, 335–342. Taranto, Italy: Istituto per la Storia e l'Archeologia della Magna Grecia.

Palaima, T.

2005   *The Triple Invention of Writing in Cyprus and Written Sources for Cypriote History*. A.G. Leventis Annual Lecture, 2004. Nicosia: Leventis Foundation.

Palma de Cesnola, A.

1882   *Salaminia: The History, Treasures, & Antiquities of Salamis in the Island of Cyprus*. London: Trübner and Co.

Palma de Cesnola, L.

1877   *Cyprus: Its Ancient Cities, Tombs, and Temples*. London: John Murray.

Pálsson, G.

1988   Hunter-gatherers of the sea. In T. Ingold, D. Riches and J. Woodburn (eds), *Hunters and Gatherers: History, Evolution and Social Change*, 63–81. Oxford: Berg.

Papaconstantinou, D.

2005   Constructing identities in the Neolithic eastern Mediterranean: cultural difference and the role of architecture. In J. Clarke (ed.), *Archaeological Perspectives on the Transmission and Transformation of Culture in the Eastern Mediterranean*, 12–17. Oxford: Oxbow.

2006   *Identifying Domestic Space in the Neolithic Eastern Mediterranean: Method and Theory in Spatial Studies*. British Archaeological Reports, International Series 1480. Oxford: Archaeopress.

2010   Abandonment processes and closure ceremonies in prehistoric Cyprus: in search of ritual. In D. Bolger and L. Maguire (eds),

The Development of Pre-state Communities in the Ancient Near East: Studies in Honour of Edgar Peltenburg. BANEA Publication Series 2: 29–37. Oxford: Oxbow.

Papadakis, Y.

1998 Greek Cypriot narratives of history and collective identity: nationalism as a contested process. *American Ethnologist* 25: 149–165.

2005 *Echoes from the Dead Zone: Across the Cyprus Divide*. London: I.B. Tauris.

Papadopoulos, T. (ed.)

1997 *A History of Cyprus*. 2 volumes. Nicosia: Archbishop Makarios III Foundation. (in Greek)

Papagianni, D.

1997 Late Neolithic flint technologies in Cyprus. *Lithics* 17–18: 70–81.

Papasavvas, G.

2001 *Bronze Stands from Cyprus and Crete*. Nicosia: Leventis Foundation. (in Greek, with English summary)

2011 From smiting into smithing: the transformation of a Cypriot god. In P.P. Betancourt and S.C. Ferrence (eds), *Metallurgy: Understanding How, Learning Why. Studies in Honor of James D. Muhly*, 59–66. Philadelphia: Institute for Aegean Prehistory Press.

Papastergiadis, N.

2005 Hybridity and ambivalence: places and flows in contemporary art and culture. *Theory, Culture and Society* 22: 39–64.

Pareschi, M.T., E. Boschi and M. Favalli

2007 Holocene tsunamis from Mount Etna and the fate of Israeli Neolithic communities. *Geophysical Research Letters* 34(L16317): 1–6.

Parker Pearson, M.

2004 Island prehistories: a view of Orkney from South Uist. In J.F. Cherry, C. Scarre and S. Shennan (eds), *Explaining Social Change: Studies in Honour of Colin Renfrew*, 127–140. Cambridge: McDonald Institute for Archaeological Research.

Parker Pearson, M., and C. Richards

1994 Ordering the world: perceptions of architecture, space and time. In M. Parker Pearson and C. Richards (eds), *Architecture and Order: Approaches to Social Space*, 1–37. London: Routledge.

Parkinson, W.A.

2010 Beyond the peer: social interaction and political evolution in the Bronze Age

Aegean. In D.J. Pullen (ed.), *Political Economies of the Aegean Bronze Age*, 11–35. Oxford: Oxbow.

Parras, Z.

2006 Looking for immigrants at Kissonerga *Mosphilia* in the Late Chalcolithic: a dental non-metric perspective of Chalcolithic and Early Bronze Age southwest Cyprus. In A.P. McCarthy (ed.), *Island Dialogues: Cyprus in the Mediterranean Network*. University of Edinburgh Archaeology Occasional Paper 21: 63–74. Edinburgh: University of Edinburgh. (online publication: http://www.shca.ed.ac.uk/archaeology/publications/occ_papers.htm/)

Pearlman, D.A.

1993 The Kholetria *Ortos* head. In L.W. Sorensen and D.W. Rupp (eds), *The Land of the Paphian Aphrodite* 2. Studies in Mediterranean Archaeology 104(2): 201–203. Göteborg, Sweden: P. Åström's Förlag.

Pecorella, P.E.

1973 Mycenaean pottery from Ayia Irini. In V. Karageorghis (ed.), *Acts of the International Archaeological Symposium: The Mycenaeans in the Eastern Mediterranean*, 19–24. Nicosia: Department of Antiquities, Cyprus.

1977 *Le Tombe dell'Età del Bronzo Tardo della Necropoli a Mare di Ayia Irini 'Paleokastro'*. Biblioteca di Antichità Cipriote 4. Rome: Consiglio nazionale delle ricerche, Istituto per gli studi micenei ed egeo-anatolici.

Peltenburg, E.J.

1974 The glazed vases (including a polychrome rhyton). Appendix I. In V. Karageorghis, *Excavations at Kition* I. *The Tombs*, 105–144. Nicosia: Department of Antiquities, Cyprus.

1977 Chalcolithic figurine from Lemba, Cyprus. *Antiquity* 51: 140–143.

1978 The Sotira Culture: regional diversity and cultural unity in Late Neolithic Cyprus. *Levant* 10: 55–74.

1979a Troulli reconsidered. In V. Karageorghis (ed.), *Studies Presented in Memory of Porphyrios Dikaios*, 21–45. Nicosia: Lions Club.

1979b The prehistory of west Cyprus: Ktima lowlands investigations 1976–1978. *Report of the Department of Antiquities, Cyprus*: 69–99.

1982a *Recent Developments in the Later Prehistory of Cyprus*. Studies in Mediterranean

Archaeology and Literature, Pocket-book 16. Göteborg, Sweden: P. Åström's Förlag.

1982b   *Vrysi: A Subterranean Settlement in Cyprus.* Warminster, England: Aris and Phillips.

1982c   Early copperwork in Cyprus and the exploitation of picrolite: evidence from the Lemba Archaeological Project. In J.D. Muhly, R. Maddin and V. Karageorghis (eds), *Early Metallurgy in Cyprus, 4000–500 BC,* 41–62. Nicosia: Pierides Foundation.

1985a   Pattern and purpose in the prehistoric Cypriot village of Ayios Epiktitos Vrysi. In Y. de Siké (ed.), *Chypre: La Vie Quotidienne,* 46–64. Paris: Musée de l'Homme.

1985b   Settlement aspects of the later prehistory of Cyprus: Ayios Epiktitos-*Vrysi* and Lemba. In V. Karageorghis (ed.), *Archaeology in Cyprus, 1960–1985,* 92–114. Nicosia: Zavallis Press.

1986a   Excavations at Kissonerga-*Mosphilia* 1985. *Report of the Department of Antiquities, Cyprus:* 28–39.

1986b   Ramesside Egypt and Cyprus. In V. Karageorghis (ed.), *Cyprus between the Orient and the Occident,* 149–179. Nicosia: Department of Antiquities, Cyprus.

1989a   (ed.) *Early Society in Cyprus.* Edinburgh: Edinburgh University Press.

1989b   The beginnings of religion in Cyprus. In E.J. Peltenburg (ed.), *Early Society in Cyprus,* 108–126. Edinburgh: Edinburgh University Press.

1991a   Kissonerga-*Mosphilia*: a major Chalcolithic site in Cyprus. *Bulletin of the American Schools of Oriental Research* 282–283: 17–35.

1991b   Local exchange in prehistoric Cyprus: an initial assessment of picrolite. *Bulletin of the American Schools of Oriental Research* 282–283: 107–126.

1991c   *Lemba Archaeological Project* II:2. *A Ceremonial Area at Kissonerga.* Studies in Mediterranean Archaeology 70: 3. Göteborg, Sweden: P. Åström's Förlag.

1992   Birth pendants in life and death: evidence from Kissonerga grave 563. In G.C. Ioannides (ed.), *Studies in Honour of Vassos Karageorghis,* 27–36. Nicosia: Leventis Foundation.

1993   Settlement discontinuity and resistance to complexity in Cyprus, ca. 4500–2500 B.C. *Bulletin of the American Schools of Oriental Research* 292: 9–23.

1994   Constructing authority: the Vounous enclosure model. *Opuscula Atheniensia* 20: 157–62.

1995   Kissonerga in Cyprus and the appearance of faience in the east Mediterranean. In S. Bourke and J.-P. Descoeudres (eds), *Trade, Contact, and the Movement of People in the Eastern Mediterranean.* Mediterranean Archaeology, Supplement 3: 31–41. Sydney: Department of Archaeology, University of Sydney.

1996   From isolation to state formation in Cyprus, c. 3500–1500 B.C. In V. Karageorghis and D. Michaelides (eds), *The Development of the Cypriot Economy,* 17–44. Nicosia: University of Cyprus; Bank of Cyprus.

1997   The Chalcolithic period c. 3800–2300 BC. In T. Papadopoulos (ed.), *A History of Cyprus* I, 117–170. Nicosia: Archbishop Makarios III Foundation. (in Greek)

2002   East Mediterranean faience: changing patterns of production and exchange at the end of the 2nd millenniuim BC. In E.A. Braun-Holzinger and H. Matthäus (eds), *Die nahöstlichen Kulturen und Griechenland an der Wende zom 2 zum 1 Jahrtausend v. Chr.,* 75–107. Möhnesee, Germany: Bibliopolis.

2003a   Identifying settlement of the Xth–IXth millennium BP in Cyprus from the contents of the Kissonerga-*Mylouthkia* wells. In J. Guilaine and A. Le Brun (eds), *Le Néolithique de Chypre.* Bulletin de Correspondance Hellénique, Supplément 43: 15–33. Athens: École Française d'Athènes.

2003b   Incorporated house, memory and identity in prehistoric Cyprus: inferences from Ayios Epiktitos-*Vrysi.* In J. Guilaine and A. Le Brun (eds), *Le Néolithique de Chypre.* Bulletin de Correspondance Hellénique, Supplément 43: 99–118. Athens: École Française d'Athènes.

2004a   Cyprus: a regional component of the Levantine PPN. *Neo-Lithics* 1/04: 3–7.

2004b   Introduction: a revised Cypriot prehistory and some implications for the study of the Neolithic. In E. Peltenburg and A. Wasse (eds), *Neolithic Revolution. New Perspectives on Southwest Asia in Light of Recent Discoveries on Cyprus.* Levant Supplementary Series 1: xi–xx. Oxford: Oxbow.

2004c Social space in early sedentary communities of southwest Asia and Cyprus. In E. Peltenburg and A. Wasse (eds), *Neolithic Revolution. New Perspectives on Southwest Asia in Light of Recent Discoveries on Cyprus*. Levant Supplementary Series 1: 71–89. Oxford: Oxbow.

2006 (Co-ordinator) *The Chalcolithic Cemetery at Souskiou-Vathyrkakas, Cyprus. Investigations of Four Missions, from 1950 to 1997*. Nicosia: Department of Antiquities, Cyprus.

2007a East Mediterranean interactions in the 3rd millennium BC. In S. Antoniadou and A. Pace (eds), *Mediterranean Crossroads*, 141–161. Athens, Oxford: Pierides Foundation; Oxbow.

2007b Hathor, faience and copper on Late Bronze Age Cyprus. *Cahier du Centre d'Études Chypriotes* 337: 375–394.

2008 Nitovikla and Tell el-Burak: Cypriot mid-second millennium B.C. forts in a Levantine context. *Report of the Department of Antiquities, Cyprus*: 145–157.

2011a Cypriot Chalcolithic metalwork. In P.P. Betancourt and S.C. Ferrence (eds), *Metallurgy: Understanding How, Learning Why. Studies in Honor of James D. Muhly*, 3–10. Philadelphia: Institute for Aegean Prehistory Press.

2011b The prehistoric centre of Souskiou in southwest Cyprus. In A. Demetriou (ed.), *Proceedings of the IV International Cyprological Congress, Lefkosia 29 April–3 May 2008*, 681–689. Nicosia: Society of Cypriot Studies.

n.d. Text meets material culture in Late Bronze Age Cyprus. In A. Georgiou (ed.), *Cyprus: An island Culture. Society and Social Relations from the Bronze Age to the Venetian Period*. Oxford: Oxbow. (in press)

Peltenburg, E.J., and E. Goring

1991 Terracotta figurines and ritual at Kissonerga-*Mosphilia*. In F. Vandenaeele and R. Laffineur (eds), *Cypriote Terracottas: Proceedings of the First International Conference of Cypriote Studies*, 17–26. Brussels, Liège, Belgium: Leventis Foundation; Free University Brussels; Université de Liège.

Peltenburg, E.J., and Project Members

1985 *Lemba Archaeological Project* I. *Excavations 1976–1983*. Studies in Mediterranean Archaeology 70(1). Göteborg, Sweden: P. Åström's Förlag.

1998 *Lemba Archaeological Project II.1A. Excavations at Kissonerga-Mosphilia 1979–1992*. Studies in Mediterranean Archaeology 70: 2. Jonsered, Sweden: P. Åström's Förlag.

2003 *Lemba Archaeological Projects, Cyprus III:1. The Colonisation and Settlement of Cyprus: Investigations at Kissonerga-Mylouthkia, 1976–1996*. Studies in Mediterranean Archaeology 70(4). Sävedalen, Sweden: P. Åström's Förlag.

Peltenburg, E.J., S. Colledge, P. Croft, A. Jackson, C. McCartney and M.A. Murray

2001a Neolithic dispersals from the Levantine corridor: a Mediterranean perspective. *Levant* 33: 35–64.

Peltenburg, E., P. Croft, A. Jackson, C. McCartney and M.A. Murray

2001b Well-established colonists: Mylouthkia I and the Cypro-Pre-Pottery Neolithic B. In S. Swiny (ed.), *The Earliest Prehistory of Cyprus: From Colonization to Exploitation*. Cyprus American Archaeological Research Institute Monograph 2: 61–93. Boston: American Schools of Oriental Research.

Peltenburg, E., and A. Wasse (eds)

2004 *Neolithic Revolution. New Perspectives on Southwest Asia in Light of Recent Discoveries on Cyprus*. Levant Supplementary Series 1. Oxford: Oxbow.

Peltenburg, E., D. Bolger, M. Kincey, A. McCarthy, C. McCartney and D. Sewell

2006 Investigations at Souskiou-*Laona* settlement, Dhiarizos valley, 2005. *Report of the Department of Antiquities, Cyprus*: 77–105.

Peregrine, P.

1991 Some political aspects of craft specialization. *World Archaeology* 23: 1–11.

Perlès, C.

1987 *Les industries lithiques taillées de Franchthi (Argolide, Grèce)* 1: *Présentation générale et industries paléolithiques*. Excavations at Franchthi Cave, Greece 3. Bloomington: Indiana University Press.

1992 Systems of exchange and organization of production in Neolithic Greece. *Journal of Mediterranean Archaeology* 5: 115–164.

2001 *The Early Neolithic in Greece*. Cambridge: Cambridge University Press.

Peters, J., D. Helmer, A. von den Driesch and M. Saña Segui

1999   Early animal husbandry in the northern Levant. *Paléorient* 25(2): 27–47.

Peters, J., A. von den Driesch and D. Helmer
2005   The upper Euphrates-Tigris basin: cradle of agropastoralism. In J.-D. Vigne, J. Peters and D. Helmer (eds), *The First Steps of Animal Domestication*, 96–124. Oxford: Oxbow.

Peterson, C.E., and R.D. Drennan
2005   Communities, settlements, sites, and surveys: regional-scale analysis of prehistoric human interaction. *American Antiquity* 70: 5–30.

Petit, T.
2001   The first palace of Amathus and the Cypriot poleogenesis. In I. Nielsen (ed.), *The Royal Palace Institution in the First Millennium BC. Regional Development and Cultural Interchange between East and West*. Monographs of the Danish Institute at Athens 4: 53–75. Athens: Danish Institute at Athens.

Petit Marie, N.
2004   Climatic crises and man in the Mediterranean basin: the last 20,000 years. In *Human Records of Recent Geological Evolution in the Mediterranean Basin – Historical and Archeological Evidence*. CIESM Workshop Monographs 24: 17–24. Monaco: CIESM.

Philip, G.
1991   Cypriot bronzework in the Levantine world: conservatism, innovation and social change. *Journal of Mediterranean Archaeology* 4: 59–107.

1995   Warrior burials in the ancient Near Eastern Bronze Age: the evidence from Mesopotamia, western Iran and Syria-Palestine. In S. Campbell and A. Green (eds), *The Archaeology of Death in the Ancient Near East*. Oxbow Monograph 51: 140–154. Oxford: Oxbow.

Philip, G., P.W. Clogg, D. Dungworth and S. Stos
2003   Copper metallurgy in the Jordan Valley from the third to the first millennia BC: chemical, metallographic and lead isotope analysis of artefacts from Pella. *Levant* 35: 71–100.

Phillips, J.
2008   *Aegyptiaca on the Island of Crete in their Chronological Context: A Critical Review*. Contributions to the Chronology of the Eastern Mediterranean. 2 Volumes. Vienna: Österreichisches Akademie der Wissenschaften.

Pickles, S., and E.J. Peltenburg
1998   Metallurgy, society and the Bronze/Iron transition in the east Mediterranean and the Near East. *Report of the Department of Antiquities, Cyprus*: 67–100.

Pieridou, A.
1967   Pieces of cloth from the Early and Middle Cypriote periods. *Report of the Department of Antiquities, Cyprus*: 25–29.

Pilides, D.
1996   Storage jars as evidence of the economy of Cyprus in the Late Bronze Age. In V. Karageorghis and D. Michaelides (eds), *The Development of the Cypriot Economy*, 107–126. Nicosia: University of Cyprus; Bank of Cyprus.

Pinhasi, R., and M. Pluciennik
2004   A regional biological approach to the spread of farming in Europe, Anatolia, the Levant, southeastern Europe, and the Mediterranean. *Current Anthropology* 45(S4): S59–S82.

Pini, I.
1979   Cypro-Aegean cylinder seals: on the definition and origin of the class. In V. Karageorghis (ed.), *The Relations between Cyprus and Crete, ca. 2000–500 BC*, 121–127. Nicosia: Department of Antiquities, Cyprus.

1980   Kypro-ägäische Rollseigel. Ein beitrag zur definition und zum Ursprung der Gruppe. *Jahrbuch des deutschen Archäologischen Instituts* 95: 77–108.

2010   *Aegean and Cypro-Aegean Non-Sphragistic Decorated Gold Finger Rings of the Bronze Age*. Aegaeum 31. Liège, Belgium, Austin: Université de Liège, University of Texas at Austin.

Pirazzoli, P.A.
2005   A review of possible eustatic, isostatic and tectonic contributions in eight late-Holocene relative sea-level histories from the Mediterranean area. *Quaternary Science Reviews* 24: 1989–2001.

Pollard, M.
2009   What a long, strange trip it's been: lead isotopes and archaeology. In A.J. Shortland, I.C. Freestone and T. Rehren (eds), *From Mine to Microscope: Advances in the Study of Ancient Technology*, 181–189. Oxford: Oxbow.

Poole, A.J., and A.H.F. Robertson
1998   Pleistocene fanglomerate deposition related to uplift of the Troodos Ophiolite,

Cyprus. In A.H.F. Robertson, K.C. Emeis, C. Richter and A. Camerlenghi (eds), *Proceedings of the Ocean Drilling Program – Scientific Results* 160: 545–566.

Porada, E.

1976   Three cylinder seals from Tombs 1 and 2 of Hala Sultan Tekke. In P. Åström, D.M. Bailey and V. Karageorghis (eds), *Hala Sultan Tekke* 1. Studies in Mediterranean Archaeology 45(1): 98–103. Göteborg, Sweden: P. Åström's Förlag.

Portugali, Y., and A.B. Knapp

1985   Cyprus and the Aegean: a spatial analysis of interaction in the 17th–14th centuries B.C. In A.B. Knapp and T. Stech (eds), *Prehistoric Production and Exchange, The Aegean and the eastern Mediterranean.* UCLA Institute of Archaeology, Monograph 25: 44–78. Los Angeles: UCLA Institute of Archaeology.

Pulak, Ç.

1997   The Uluburun shipwreck. In S. Swiny, R. Hohlfelder and Helena W. Swiny (eds), *Res Maritimae: Cyprus and the Eastern Mediterranean from Prehistory through the Roman Period.* Cyprus American Archaeological Research Institute Monograph 1: 233–262. Atlanta, Georgia: ASOR/Scholars Press.

2000   The copper and tin ingots from the Late Bronze Age shipwreck at Uluburun. In Ü. Yalçin (ed.), *Anatolian Metal* I. Der Anschnitt, Beiheft 13: 137–157. Bochum, Germany: Deutsches Bergbau-Museum.

2001   The cargo of the Uluburun shipwreck and evidence for trade with the Aegean and beyond. In L. Bonfante and V. Karageorghis (eds), *Italy and Cyprus in Antiquity, 1500–450 BC*, 13–60. Nicosia: Leventis Foundation.

2008   The Uluburun shipwreck and Late Bronze Age trade. In J. Aruz, K. Benzel and J.M. Evans (eds), *Beyond Babylon: Art, Trade, and Diplomacy in the Second Millennium BC*, 289–310. New York: Metropolitan Museum of Art, Yale University Press.

2009   The Uluburun tin ingots and the shipment of tin by sea in the Late Bronze Age Mediterranean. *Tübaar* 12: 189–207.

Rahmstorf, L.

2005   Ethnicity and changes in weaving technology in Cyprus and the eastern Mediterranean in the 12th century BC. In V. Karageorghis, H. Matthäus and S. Rogge (eds), *Cyprus: Religion and Society from the Late Bronze Age to the End of the Archaic Period*, 143–169. Möhnesee-Wamel, Germany: Bibliopolis.

Rainbird, P.

2004   *The Archaeology of Micronesia.* Cambridge: Cambridge University Press.

2007   *The Archaeology of Islands.* Cambridge: Cambridge University Press.

Ramis, D., J.A. Alcover, J. Coll and M. Trias

2002   The chronology of the first settlement of the Balearic Islands. *Journal of Mediterranean Archaeology* 15: 3–24.

Raptou, E.

2002   Nouveaux témoignages sur Palaepaphos à l'époque géométrique, d'après les fouilles de Kouklia-*Plakes. Cahier du Centre d'Études Chypriotes* 32: 115–133.

Rautenschlein, M.

1987   Geology and Geochemistry of Akaki Volcanics, Cyprus. Unpublished PhD dissertation, Rurh-Universität, Bochum, Germany.

Redding, R.W.

2005   Breaking the mold: a consideration of variation in the evolution of animal domestication. In J.-D. Vigne, J. Peters and D. Helmer (eds), *The First Steps of Animal Domestication*, 41–48. Oxford: Oxbow.

Redfield, R.

1955   *The Little Community: Viewpoints for the Study of a Human Whole.* Chicago: University of Chicago Press.

Redford, D.B.

2000   Egypt and western Asia in the late New Kingdom: an overview. In E.D. Oren (ed.), *The Sea Peoples and Their World: A Reassessment.* University Museum Monograph 108. University Museum Symposium Series 11: 1–20. Philadelphia: University Museum, University of Pennsylvania.

Reese, D.S.

1985   Shells, ostrich eggshells and other exotic faunal remains from Kition. In V. Karageorghis and M. Demas, *Excavations at Kition* V(2): 340–415. Nicosia: Department of Antiquities, Cyprus.

1995   *The Pleistocene Vertebrate Sites and Fauna of Cyprus.* Geological Survey Department, Republic of Cyprus, Bulletin 9. Nicosia: Geological Survey Department.

1996a   Animal bones and shells. Appendix 8. In J.E. Coleman, J.A. Barlow, M. Mogelonsky and K.W. Scharr, *Alambra: A Middle Bronze Age Site in Cyprus. Investigations by Cornell University, 1975–1978.* Studies in Mediterranean Archaeology 118: 477–514. Jonsered, Sweden: P. Åström's Förlag.

1996b Cypriot hippo hunters no myth. *Journal of Mediterranean Archaeology* 9: 107–112.

2006–2007 Organic imports from Late Bronze Age Cyprus (with special reference to Hala Sultan Tekke). *Opuscula Atheniensia* 31–32: 191–209.

Rehak, P.

1995 The use and destruction of Minoan stone bull's head rhyta. In R. Laffineur and W.-D. Neimeier (eds), *Politeia: Society and State in the Aegean Bronze Age.* Aegaeum 12: 435–459. Liège, Belgium, Austin, Texas: Histoire de l'art et archéologie de la Grèce antique; Program in Aegean Scripts and Prehistory.

1996 Aegean breechcloths, kilts, and the Keftiu paintings. *American Journal of Archaeology* 100: 35–51.

1999 The Mycenaean 'warrior goddess' revisited. In R. Laffineur (ed.), *Polemos: Le contexte guerrier en Égée à l'âge du Bronze.* 2 Volumes. Aegaeum 19(1): 227–239. Liège, Belgium, Austin: Université de Liège, University of Texas at Austin.

2002 Imag(in)ing a women's world in Bronze Age Greece: the frescoes from Xeste 3 at Akrotiri, Thera. In N.S. Rabinowitz and L. Auanger (eds), *Among Women: From the Homosocial to the Homoerotic in the Ancient World,* 34–59. Austin: University of Texas Press.

Rehak, P., and J.G. Younger

1998 International styles in ivory carving in the Late Bronze Age. In E.H. Cline and D. Harris-Cline (eds), *The Aegean and the Orient in the Second Millennium: Proceedings of the 50th Anniversary Symposium, Cincinnati, 18–20 April 1997.* Aegaeum 18: 229–256. Liège, Belgium, Austin: Université de Liège, University of Texas at Austin.

Reimer, P.J., and F.G. McCormac

2002 Marine radiocarbon reservoir corrections for the Mediterranean and Aegean Sea. *Radiocarbon* 44: 159–166.

Reimer, P.J., M.G.L. Baillie, E. Bard, A. Bayliss, J.W. Beck, C.J.H. Bertrand, P.G. Blackwell, C.E. Buch, G.S. Burr, K.B. Cutler, P.E. Damon, R.L. Edwards, R.G. Fairbanks, M. Friedrich, T.P. Guilderson, A.G. Hogg, K.A. Hughen, B. Kromer, G. McCormac, S. Manning, C.B. Ramsey, R.W. Reimer, S. Remmele, J.R. Southon, M. Suiver, S. Talamo, F.W. Taylor, J. van der Plicht and C.E. Weyhenmeyer

2004 IntCal04 terrestrial radiocarbon age calibration, 0–26 cal kyr BP. *Radiocarbon* 46: 1029–1058.

Reimer, P.J., M.G.L. Baillie, E. Bard, A. Bayliss, J.W. Beck, P.G. Blackwell, C. Bronk Ramsey, C.E. Buck, G.S. Burr, R.L. Edwards, M. Friedrich, P.M. Grootes, T.P. Guilderson, I. Hajdas, T.J. Heaton, A.G. Hogg, K.A. Hughen, K.F. Kaiser, B. Kromer, F.G. McCormac, S.W. Manning, R.W. Reimer, D.A. Richards, J.R. Southon, S. Talamo, C.S.M. Turney, J. van der Plicht and C.E. Weyhenmeyer

2009 IntCal09 and Marine09 radiocarbon age calibration curves, 0–50,000 years cal BP. *Radiocarbon* 51: 1111–1150.

Reitler, R.

1963 Neolithische Statuetten aus Cypern. *Jahrbuch für Praehistorische und Ethnographische Kunst* 20: 22–27.

Renault-Miskovsky, J.

1989 Étude paléobotanique, paléoclimatique et palethnographique du site néolithique de Khirokitia à Chypre: rapport de la palynologie. In A. Le Brun, *Fouilles récent à Khirokitia (Chypre) – 1983–1986.* Recherches sur les Civilisation, Memoire 81: 251–276. Paris: ADPF.

Renfrew, C.

1973 *Before Civilization: The Radiocarbon Revolution and Prehistoric Europe.* London: Jonathan Cape.

2004 Islands out of time? Towards an analytical framework. In S.M. Fitzpatrick (ed.), *Voyages of Discovery: The Archaeology of Islands,* 275–294. New York: Praeger.

Renfrew, C., and A. Aspinall

1990 Aegean obsidian and Franchthi Cave. In C. Perlès, *Les industries lithiques taillées de Franchthi (Argolide, Grece) 2: Les industries du Mésolithique et du Néolithique Initial.* Excavations at Franchthi Cave, Greece 5: 257–270. Bloomington: Indiana University Press.

Reyes, A.T.

1994 *Archaic Cyprus: A Study of the Textual and Archaeological Evidence.* Oxford: Clarendon Press.

Ribeiro, E.

2002 Altering the body: representations of pre-pubescent gender groups on Early and Middle Cypriot 'scenic compositions'. In D. Bolger and N. Serwint (eds), *Engendering Aphrodite: Women and Society in Ancient Cyprus*. Cyprus American Archaeological Research Institute Monograph 3: 197–209. Boston: American Schools of Oriental Research.

Rice, P.M.

1981 Evolution of specialized pottery production: a trial model. *Current Anthropology* 22: 219–240.

Richards, C.

1996 Henges and water: towards an elemental understanding of monumentality and landscape in Late Neolithic Britain. *Journal of Material Culture* 1: 313–336.

Robb, J.

2001 Island identities: ritual, travel and the creation of difference in Neolithic Malta. *European Journal of Archaeology* 4: 175–202.

Roberts, N.

1998 *The Holocene: An Environmental History.* 2nd edition. Oxford: Blackwell.

Robertson, A.H.F.

2000 Tectonic evolution of Cyprus in its easternmost Mediterranean setting. In I. Panayides, C. Xenophontos and J. Malpas (eds), *Proceedings of the Third International Conference on the Geology of the Eastern Mediterranean, Nicosia*, 11–44. Nicosia: Cyprus Geological Survey.

Robertson, A.H.F., S.E. Eaton, E.J. Follows and A.S. Payne

1995 Depositional processes and basin analysis of Messinian evaporites in Cyprus. *Terra Nova* 7: 233–253.

Robertson, A.H.F., and N.H. Woodcock

1980 Tectonic setting of the Troodos massif in the east Mediterranean. In A. Panayiotou (ed.), *Ophiolites: Proceedings, International Ophiolite Symposium, Cyprus 1979*, 36–49. Nicosia: Geological Survey Department.

Robinson, S.A., S. Black, B.W. Sellwood and P.J. Valdes

2006 A review of palaeoclimates and palaeoenvironments in the Levant and Eastern Mediterranean from 25,000 to 5000 years BP: setting the environmental background for the evolution of human civilization. *Quaternary Science Reviews* 25:1517–1541.

Rodden, J.

1981 The development of the Three Age System: archaeology's first paradigm. In G. Daniel (ed.), *Towards a History of Archaeology*, 51–68. London: Thames and Hudson.

Rollefson, G.

2004 Cultural genealogies: Cyprus and its relationship to the PPN mainland. *Neo-Lithics* 1/04: 12–13.

Ronen, A.

1995 Core, periphery and ideology in Aceramic Cyprus. *Quartär* 45/46: 177–206.

Rosen, A.M.

2007 *Civilizing Climate: The Social Impact of Climate Change in the Ancient Near East.* Walnut Creek, California: Altamira Press.

Rosenberg, M., M. Nesbitt, R.W. Redding and B. Peasnall

1998 Hallan Çemi, pig husbandry, and post-Pleistocene adaptations along the Taurus-Zagros arc (Turkey). *Paléorient* 24(1): 25–41.

Rossignol-Strick, M.

1995 Sea–land correlation of pollen records in the Eastern Mediterranean for the glacial–interglacial transition: biostratigraphy versus radiometric time-scale. *Quaternary Science Reviews* 14: 893–915.

1999 The Holocene climatic optimum and pollen records of sapropel 1 in the Eastern Mediterranean, 9000–6000 BP. *Quaternary Science Reviews* 18: 515–530.

Routledge, B., and K. McGeough

2009 Just what collapsed? A network perspective on 'palatial 'and 'private' trade at Ugarit. In C. Bachhuber and R.G. Roberts (eds), *Forces of Transformation: The End of the Bronze Age in the Mediterranean.* Themes from the Ancient Near East, BANEA Publication Series 1: 22–29. Oxford: Oxbow.

Roux, V.

2003 A dynamic systems framework for studying technological change: application to the emergence of the potter's wheel in the Southern Levant. *Journal of Archaeological Method and Theory* 10: 1–30.

Roux, V., and P. de Miroschedji

2009 Revisiting the history of the potter's wheel in the southern Levant. *Levant* 41: 155–173.

Rowlands, M.J.

1984 Conceptualising the European Bronze and Iron Ages. In J. Bintliff (ed.), *European*

Social Evolution, 147–156. Bradford, England: Bradford University Press.

1994   The politics of identity in archaeology. In G.C. Bond and A. Gilliam (eds), *Social Construction of the Past: Representation as Power*. One World Archaeology 24: 129–143. London: Routledge.

Runnels, C.

2009   Mesolithic sites and surveys in Greece: a case study from the southern Argolid. *Journal of Mediterranean Archaeology* 22: 57–73.

Runnels, C.N., and T.H. van Andel

1988   Trade and the origins of agriculture in the eastern Mediterranean. *Journal of Mediterranean Archaeology* 1: 83–109.

Runnels, C., E. Panagopoulou, P. Murray, G. Tsartsidou, S. Allen, K. Mullen and E. Tourloukis

2005   A Mesolithic landscape in Greece: testing a site-location model in the Argolid at Kandia. *Journal of Mediterranean Archaeology* 18: 259–285.

Rupp, D.W.

1985   Prologomena to a study of stratification and social organization in Iron Age Cyprus. In M. Thompson, M.T. Garcia and F.J. Kense (eds), *Status, Structure and Stratification: Current Archaeological Reconstructions*, 119–132. Calgary: Archaeological Association, University of Calgary.

1987   Vive le Roi: the emergence of the state in Iron Age Cyprus. In D.W. Rupp (ed.), *Western Cyprus: Connections*. Studies in Mediterranean Archaeology 77: 147–168. Göteborg, Sweden: P. Åström's Förlag.

1988   The Royal Tombs at Salamis, Cyprus: ideological messages of power and authority. *Journal of Mediterranean Archaeology* 1: 111–139.

1989   Puttin' on the Ritz: manifestations of high status in Iron Age Cyprus. In E.J. Peltenburg (ed.), *Early Society in Cyprus*, 336–362. Edinburgh: Edinburgh University Press.

1998   The seven kings of the Land of Ia', a district on *Ia-ad-na-na*: Achaean blue-bloods, Cypriot parvenus, or both? In K.J. Hartswick and M. Sturgeon (eds), *Stefanoß: Studies in Honor of Brunilde Sismondo Ridgway*, 209–222. Philadelphia: University Museum, University of Pennsylvania.

Rupp, D.W., J.T. Clarke, C. D'Annibale and S. Stewart

1992   The Canadian Palaipaphos Survey Project: 1991 field season. *Report of the Department of Antiquities, Cyprus*: 285–317.

Rupp, D.W., and C. D'Annibale

1995   Preliminary report of the 1994/95 field season of the Western Cyprus Project at Prastio-*Ayios Savvas tis Karonis* Monastery. *Report of the Department of Antiquities, Cyprus*: 33–48.

Russell, A.

2009   Deconstructing Ashdoda: migration, hybridisation, and the Philistine identity. *Babesch* 84: 1–15.

2010   Foreign materials, islander mobility and elite identity in Late Bronze Age Sardinia. In P. van Dommelen and A.B. Knapp (eds), *Material Connections in the Ancient Mediterranean: Mobility, Materiality and Identity*, 106–126. London: Routledge.

2011   In the Middle of the Corrupting Sea: Cultural Encounters in Sicily and Sardinia between 1450–900 BC. Unpublished PhD thesis, Department of Archaeology, University of Glasgow.

Rutter, J.B.

2006   Ceramic imports of the Neopalatial and later Bronze Age eras. In J.W. Shaw and M.C. Shaw (eds), *Kommos: An Excavation on the South Coast of Crete by the University of Toronto under the Auspices of the American School of Classical Studies in Athens. Kommos V: The Monumental Minoan Buildings at Kommos*, 646–688, 712–715. Princeton: Princeton University Press.

Sader, H., and J. Kamlah

2010   Tell el-Burak: a new Middle Bronze Age site from Lebanon. *Near Eastern Archaeology* 73: 130–141.

Şahoğlu, V.

2005   The Anatolian Trade Network and the Izmir region during the Early Bronze Age. *Oxford Journal of Archaeology* 24: 339–361.

Salles, J.F.

1995   Rituel mortuaire et rituel social à Ras Shamra/Ougarit. In S. Campbell and A. Green (eds), *The Archaeology of Death in the Ancient Near East*. Oxbow Monograph 51: 171–184. Oxford: Oxbow.

Sampson, A.

1998   The Neolithic and Mesolithic occupation of the cave of Cyclope, Youra

Alonessos, Greece. *Annual of the British School at Athens* 93: 1–22.

2006   *The Cave of the Cyclops: Mesolithic and Neolithic Networks in the Northern Aegean, Greece 1: Intra-Site Analyses, Local Industries, and Regional Site Distribution.* Institute for Aegean Prehistory, Prehistory Monographs 21. Philadelphia: Institute for Aegean Prehistory Academic Press.

2008   The Mesolithic settlement and cemetery of Maroulas on Kythnos. In N. Brodie, J. Doole, G. Gavalas and C. Renfrew (eds), *Horizon: A Colloquium on the Prehistory of the Cyclades,* 13–17. Cambridge: McDonald Institute for Archaeological Research.

Sampson, A., J. Koslowski, M. Kaszanowska and B. Giannouli

2002   The Mesolithic settlement at Maroulas, Kythnos. *Mediterranean Archaeology and Archaeometry* 2: 45–67.

Samuelson, A.-G.

1993   *Bronze Age White Painted I Ware in Cyprus: A Reinvestigation.* Studies in Mediterranean Archaeology and Literature, Pocket-book 121. Jonsered, Sweden: P. Åström's Förlag.

Sandars, N.K.

1978   *The Sea Peoples: Warriors of the Ancient Mediterranean 1250–1150 BC.* London: Thames and Hudson.

Sanlaville, P.

1997   Les changements dans l'environnement au Moyen-Orient de 20,000 BP à 6,000 BP. *Paléorient* 23(2): 249–262.

Satraki, A.

2010   Από τον *Kosmassos στο Νικοκρέοντα: Η πολιτειακή οργάνωση της αρχαίας Κύπρου από την Ύστερη Χαλκοκρατία μέχρι το τέλος της Κυπροκλασικής περιόδου. Unpublished PhD dissertation, University of Cyprus, Nicosia.

Scarre, C. (ed.)

2005   *The Human Past: World Prehistory and the Development of Human Societies.* London: Thames and Hudson.

Schaeffer, C.F.A.

1936   *Missions en Chypre, 1932–1935.* Paris: Geuthner.

1952   *Enkomi-Alasia I. Nouvelles Missions en Chypre 1946–1950.* Paris: Klincksieck.

1969   Chars de culte de Chypre. *Syria* 46: 267–276.

1971   *Alasia* I. Mission Archeologique d'Alasia 4. Paris: Klincksieck.

1984   *Alasia* III. *Les Objets des Niveaux Stratifies d'Enkomi (Fouilles C.F.A. Schaeffer 1947–1970).* Editions Recherches sur les Civilisations, Memoire 32. Paris: Editions Recherches sur les Civilisations.

Schaub, R.T., and W.E. Rast

1989   *Bab edh-Dhra: Excavations in the Cemetery. Directed by Paul Lapp (1965–1967).* Reports of the Expedition to the Dead Sea Plain, Jordan, Volume 1. Winona Lake, Indiana: Eisenbrauns.

Schiffer, M.B.

1986   Radiocarbon dating and the 'old wood' problem: the case of the Hohokam chronology. *Journal of Archaeological Science* 13: 13–30.

Schloen, J.D.

2001   *The House of the Father as Fact and Symbol: Patrimonialism in Ugarit and the Ancient Near East.* Studies in the Archaeology and History of the Levant 2. Winona Lake, Indiana: Eisenbrauns.

Schmandt-Besserat, D.

1992   *Before Writing 1: From Counting to Cuneiform.* Austin: University of Texas Press.

1994   Tokens: a prehistoric archive system. In P. Ferioli, E. Fiandra, G. Giacomo Fissore and M. Frangipane (eds), *Archives Before Writing. Proceedings of the International Colloquium Oriolo Romano, October 23–25, 1991,* 13–28. Rome: Centro Internazionale di Richerche Archeologiche, Antropologiche e Storiche.

Schon, R.

2009   Think locally, act globally: Mycenaean elites and the Late Bronze Age world system. In W.A. Parkinson and M.L. Galaty (eds), *Archaic State Interaction: The Eastern Mediterranean in the Bronze Age,* 213–236. Santa Fe, New Mexico: School for Advanced Research Press.

Schüle, W.

1993   Mammals, vegetation and the initial human settlement of the Mediterranean islands: a palaeoecological approach. *Journal of Biogeography* 20: 399–412.

Schwartz, J.H.

1973   The palaeozoology of Cyprus: a preliminary report on recently analysed sites. *World Archaeology* 5: 215–220.

Scott, B.

1981   The Eurasian-Arabian and African continental margin from Iran to Greece. *Journal of the Geological Society* 138: 719–733.

Şevketoğlu, M.

2000   *Archaeological Field Survey of the Neolithic and Chalcolithic Settlement Sites in Kyrenia District, North Cyprus. Systematic Surface Collection and the Interpretation of Artefact Scatters.* British Archaeological Reports, International Series 834. Oxford: Archeopress.

2002   Akanthou-*Arkosyko* (Tatlisu-*Çiftlikdüzü*): the Anatolian connections in the 9th millennium BC. In W.H. Waldren and J.A. Ensenyat (eds), *World Islands in Prehistory. V Deia International Conference of Prehistory.* British Archaeological Reports, International Series 1095: 98–106. Oxford: Archaeopress.

2006   Cypro-Anatolian relations in the 9th millennium BC: Akanthou/Tatlisu rescue excavation. *Anadolu/Anatolia* 30: 119–136.

2008   Early settlements and precurement of raw materials – new evidence based on research at Akanthou-*Arkosykos* (Tatlisu-*Çiftlikdüzü*), northern Cyprus. *Tübaar* 11: 63–73.

Shackleton, J.C., T.H. van Andel and C.N. Runnels

1984   Coastal paleogeography of the central and western Mediterranean during the last 125,000 years and its archaeological implications. *Journal of Field Archaeology* 11: 307–314.

Shaw, J.W.

1998   Kommos in southern Crete: an Aegean barometer for east–west connections. In V. Karageorghis and N.C. Stampolidis (eds), *Proceedings of the International Symposium: Eastern Mediterranean, Cyprus-Dodecanese-Crete 16th–6th Centuries B.C.,* 13–27. Athens: University of Crete and Leventis Foundation.

Shennan, S.J.

1986   Central Europe in the third millennium B.C.: an evolutionary trajectory for the beginning of the European Bronze Age. *Journal of Anthropological Archaeology* 5: 115–146.

Sherratt, A.G.

1981   Plough and pastoralism: aspects of the Secondary Products Revolution. In I. Hodder, G. Issac and N. Hammond (eds), *Pattern of the Past: Studies in Honour of David Clarke,* 261–305. Cambridge: Cambridge University Press.

1983   The secondary exploitation of animals in the Old World. *World Archaeology* 15: 90–104.

2007   Diverse origins: regional contributions to the genesis of farming. In S. Colledge and J. Conolly (eds), *The Origins and Spread of Domestic Plants in Southwest Asia and Europe,* 1–20. Walnut Creek, California: Left Coast Press.

Sherratt, A.G., and E.S. Sherratt

1991   From luxuries to commodities: the nature of Mediterranean Bronze Age trading systems. In N.H. Gale (ed.), *Bronze Age Trade in the Mediterranean.* Studies in Mediterranean Archaeology 90: 351–386. Göteborg, Sweden: P. Åström's Förlag.

Sherratt, S.

1991   Cypriot pottery of Aegean type in LCII–III: problems of classification, chronology and interpretation. In J. Barlow, D. Bolger, and B. Kling (eds), *Cypriot Ceramics: Reading the Prehistoric Record.* University Museum Monograph 74: 185–198. Philadelphia: University Museum, University of Pennsylvania.

1992   Immigration and archaeology: some indirect reflections. In P. Åström (ed.), *Acta Cypria* 2. Studies in Mediterranean Archaeology and Literature, Pocket-book 117: 316–347. Jonsered, Sweden: P. Åström's Förlag.

1994a Patterns of contact between the Aegean and Cyprus in the 13th and 12th centuries B.C. *Archaeologia Cypria* 3: 35–46.

1994b Commerce, iron and ideology: metallurgical innovation in 12th–11th century Cyprus. In V. Karageorghis (ed.), *Proceedings of the International Symposium: Cyprus in the 11th Century BC,* 59–106. Nicosia: Leventis Foundation.

1998   'Sea Peoples' and the economic structure of the late second millennium in the eastern Mediterranean. In S. Gitin, A. Mazar and E. Stern (eds), *Mediterranean Peoples in Transition: Thirteenth to Tenth Centuries BCE,* 292–313. Jerusalem: Israel Exploration Society.

1999   *E pur si muove*: pots, markets and values in the second millennium Mediterranean. In J.P. Crielaard, V. Stissi and G.J. van Wijngaarden (eds), *The Complex Past of Pottery: Production, Circulation and Consumption of Mycenaean and Greek*

Pottery (sixteenth to early fifth centuries BC), 163–211. Amsterdam: Gieben.

2001 Potemkin palaces and route-based economies. In S. Voutsaki and J. Killen (eds), *Economy and Politics in the Mycenaean Palace States*. Cambridge Philological Society, Supplementary Volume 27: 214–238. Cambridge: Cambridge Philological Society.

2003 The Mediterranean economy: 'globalization' at the end of the second millennium BCE. In W.G. Dever and S. Gitin (eds), *Symbiosis, Symbolism, and the Power of the Past: Canaan, Ancient Israel, and Their Neighbors, from the Late Bronze Age through Roman Palaestina*, 37–62. Winona Lake, Indiana: Eisenbrauns.

Siani, G., M. Paterne, M. Arnold, E. Bard, B. Metivier, N. Tisnerat and F. Bassinot

2000 Radiocarbon reservoir ages in the Mediterranean Sea and Black Sea. *Radiocarbon* 42: 271–280.

Silberman, N.A.

1995 Promised lands and chosen people: the politics and poetics of archaeological narrative. In P.L. Kohl and C. Fawcett (eds), *Nationalism, Politics, and the Practise of Archaeology*, 249–262. Cambridge: Cambridge University Press.

1998 The Sea Peoples, the Victorians and us: modern social ideology and changing archaeological interpretations of the Late Bronze Age collapse. In S. Gitin, A. Mazar and E. Stern (eds), *Mediterranean Peoples in Transition: Thirteenth to Tenth Centuries BCE*, 268–275. Jerusalem: Israel Exploration Society.

Simmons, A.H.

1996a Whose myth? Archaeological data, interpretations, and implications for the human association with extinct Pleistocene fauna at Akrotiri *Aetokremnos*, Cyprus. *Journal of Mediterranean Archaeology* 9: 97–105.

1996b Preliminary report on multidisciplinary investigations at Neolithic Kholetria *Ortos*, Paphos district. *Report of the Department of Antiquities, Cyprus*: 29–44.

1998 Of tiny hippos, large cows and early colonists in Cyprus. *Journal of Mediterranean Archaeology* 11: 232–241.

1999 (and Associates) *Faunal Extinction in an Island Society: Pygmy Hippopotamus Hunters*

of Cyprus. Boston: Kluwer Academic/ Plenum.

2003a Villages without walls, cows without corrals. In J. Guilaine and A. Le Brun (eds), *Le Néolithique de Chypre*. Bulletin de Correspondance Héllénique, Supplément 43: 61–70. Athens: École Française de' Athènes.

2003b Preliminary report of the 2002 excavations at *Ais Giorkis*, an aceramic Neolithic site in western Cyprus. *Report of the Department of Antiquities, Cyprus*: 1–10.

2004a Bitter hippos of Cyprus: the island's first occupants and last endemic animals – setting the stage for colonization. In E.J. Peltenburg and A. Wasse (eds), *Neolithic Revolution: New Perspectives on Southwest Asia in Light of Recent Discoveries on Cyprus*. Levant Supplementary Series 1: 1–14. Oxford: Oxbow.

2004b The Mediterranean PPNB interaction sphere? *Neo-Lithics* 1/04: 16–19.

2005 *Ais Giorkis*, an upland Aceramic Neolithic site in western Cyprus: progress report of the 2003 excavations. *Report of the Department of Antiquities, Cyprus*: 23–30.

2008 American researchers and the earliest Cypriots. *Near Eastern Archaeology* 71(1–2): 21–29.

2009 Until the cows come home: cattle and Early Neolithic Cyprus. *Before Farming* 2009/1 (article 5): 1–10.

2010 *Ais Giorkis*, an upland Early Aceramic Neolithic site in western Cyprus: progress report of the 1997–2009 investigations. *Report of the Department of Antiquities, Cyprus*: 27–52.

Simmons, A., and R. Mandel

2007 Not such a new light: a response to Ammerman and Noller. *World Archaeology* 39: 475–482.

Singer, I.

1999 A Political History of Ugarit. In W.G.E. Watson and N. Wyatt (eds), *Handbook of Ugaritic Studies*. Handbuch der Orientalistik, Abteilung 1, Der Nahe und Mittlere Osten, Band 39: 603–733. Leiden, The Netherlands: Brill.

Sjöqvist, E.

1940 *Problems of the Late Cypriote Bronze Age*. Stockholm: Swedish Cyprus Expedition.

Skeates, R.

2005 Museum archaeology and the Mediterranean cultural heritage. In E. Blake and A.B. Knapp (eds), *The Archaeology of Mediterranean Prehistory*, 303–320. Oxford: Blackwell.

2009 Trade and interaction. In B. Cunliffe, C. Gosden and R. Joyce (eds), *The Oxford Handbook of Archaeology*, 555–578. Oxford: Oxford University Press.

Smith, B.D.

2007 Niche construction and the behavioral context of plant and animal domestication. *Evolutionary Anthropology* 16: 189–199.

Smith, J.S.

1994 Seals for Sealing in the Late Cypriot Period. Unpublished PhD dissertation, Bryn Mawr College, Bryn Mawr, Pennsylvania.

2002a Changes in the workplace: women and textile production on Late Bronze Age Cyprus. In D. Bolger and N. Serwint (eds), *Engendering Aphrodite: Women and Society in Ancient Cyprus*. Cyprus American Archaeological Research Institute Monograph 3: 281–312. Boston: American Schools of Oriental Research.

2002b Problems and prospects in the study of script and seal use on Cyprus in the Bronze and Iron Ages. In J.S. Smith (ed.), *Script and Seal Use on Cyprus in the Bronze and Iron Ages*. AIA Colloquia and Conference Papers 4: 1–47. Boston: Archaeological Institute of America.

2003 International style in Mediterranean Late Bronze Age seals. In N.C. Stampolidis and V. Karageorghis (eds), *Ploes… Sea Routes…: Interconnections in the Mediterranean, 16th–6th c. BC*, 291–304. Athens: University of Crete, Leventis Foundation.

2008a (ed.) *Views from Phlamoudhi, Cyprus*. Annual of the American Schools of Oriental Research 63. Boston: American Schools of Oriental Research.

2008b Cyprus, the Phoenicians and Kition. In C. Sagona (ed.), *Beyond the Homeland: Markers in Phoenician Chronology*. Ancient Near Eastern Studies 28: 261–303. Leuven, Belgium: Peeters.

2009 *Art and Society in Cyprus from the Bronze Age into the Iron Age*. Cambridge: Cambridge University Press.

Smith, T.R.

1987 *Mycenaean Trade and Interaction in the West Central Mediterranean*. British Archaeological Reports, International Series 371. Oxford: British Archaeological Reports.

Smith, W.S.

1965 *Interconnections in the Ancient Near East : A Study of the Relationships between the Arts of Egypt, the Aegean, and Western Asia*. New Haven: Yale University Press.

Snape, S.R.

2000 Imported pottery at Zawiyet Umm el-Rakham: preliminary report. *Bulletin de Liaison du Groupe International d'Étude de la Céramique Egyptienne* 21: 17–22.

2003 Zawiyet Umm el-Rakham and Egyptian foreign trade in the 13th century BC. In N.C. Stampolidis and V. Karageorghis (eds), *Ploes… Sea Routes…: Interconnections in the Mediterranean, 16th–6th c. BC*, 63–70. Athens: University of Crete, Leventis Foundation.

Sneddon, A.C.

2002 *The Cemeteries at Marki: Using a Looted Landscape to Investigate Prehistoric Bronze Age Cyprus*. British Archaeological Reports: International Series 1028. Oxford: Archeopress.

Snodgrass, A.M.

1988 *Cyprus and Early Greek History*. Bank of Cyprus, Cultural Foundation, 4th Annual Lecture. Nicosia: Bank of Cyprus Cultural Foundation.

1991 Bronze Age exchange: a minimalist position. In N. Gale (ed.), *Bronze Age Trade in the Mediterranean*. Studies in Mediterranean Archaeology 90: 15–20. Göteborg, Sweden: P. Åström's Förlag.

Sondaar, P.Y., F. Martini, A. Ulzega and G. Klein Hofmeijer

1991 L'homme pléistocène en Sardaigne. *L'anthropologie* (Paris) 95: 181–200.

Sondaar, P.Y., R. Elburg, G. Klein Hofmeijer, F. Martini, M. Sanges, A. Spaan and H. de Visser

1995 The human colonisation of Sardinia: a late Pleistocene human fossil from Corbeddu cave. *Comptes Rendus de l'Academie des Sciences* 320 (IIa): 145–150.

Sondaar, P.Y., and S.A.E. van der Geer

2000 Mesolithic environment and animal exploitation on Cyprus and Sardinia/ Corsica. In M. Mashkour, A. M. Choyke,

H. Buitenhuis and F. Poplin (eds), *Archaeozoology of the Near East* IVA. *Proceedings of the Fourth International Symposium on the Archaeozoology of Southwestern Asia and Adjacent Areas*. ARC Publicatie 32: 67–73. Groningen, The Netherlands: Centrum voor Archeologische Research and Consultancy.

Sordinas, A.

2003 The 'Sidarian': maritime Mesolithic non-geometric microliths in western Greece. In N. Galanidou and C. Perlès (eds), *The Greek Mesolithic: Problems and Perspectives*. British School at Athens, Studies 10: 89–97. London: British School at Athens.

Sørensen, A.H.

2006 The Cypriot connection: aspects of Cretan contacts with Cyprus during the MB–LBI periods. In A. McCarthy (ed.), *Island Dialogues: Cyprus in the Mediterranean Network*. University of Edinburgh Archaeology, Occasional Paper 21: 154–172. (online publication: http://www.shca.ed.ac.uk/archaeology/publications/occ_papers.htm/)

Sørensen, L.W., and D.W. Rupp (eds)

1993 *The Land of the Paphian Aphrodite* 2. Studies in Mediterranean Archaeology 104(2). Göteborg, Sweden: P. Åström's Förlag.

South, A.K.

1988 Kalavasos-*Ayios Dhimitrios* 1987: an important ceramic group from Building X. *Report of the Department of Antiquities, Cyprus*: 223–228.

1989 From copper to kingship: aspects of Bronze Age society viewed from the Vasilikos Valley. In E.J. Peltenburg (ed.), *Early Society in Cyprus*, 315–324. Edinburgh: Edinburgh University Press.

1992 Kalavasos-*Ayios Dhimitrios* 1991. *Report of the Department of Antiquities, Cyprus*: 133–146.

1996 Kalavasos-*Ayios Dhimitrios* and the organisation of Late Bronze Age Cyprus. In P. Åström and E. Herscher (eds), *Late Bronze Age Settlement in Cyprus: Function and Relationship*. Studies in Mediterranean Archaeology and Literature, Pocket-book 126: 39–49. Jonsered, Sweden: P. Åström's Förlag.

1997 Kalavasos-*Ayios Dhimitrios* 1992–1996. *Report of the Department of Antiquities, Cyprus*: 151–175.

2000 Late Bronze Age burials at Kalavasos *Ayios Dhimitrios*. In G.C. Ioannides and S.A. Hadjistellis (eds), *Acts of the Third International Congress of Cypriot Studies*, 345–364. Nicosia: Society of Cypriot Studies.

South-Todd, A.

2002 Late Bronze Age settlement patterns in southern Cyprus: the first kingdoms? *Cahier du Centre d'Études Chypriotes* 32: 59–72.

South, A.K., P. Russell and P.S. Keswani

1989 *Vasilikos Valley Project* 3: *Kalavasos-Ayios Dhimitrios* II *(Ceramics, Objects, Tombs, Specialist Studies)*. Studies in Mediterranean Archaeology 71(3). Göteborg, Sweden : P. Åström's Förlag.

South, A.K., and L. Steel

2001 The White Slip sequence at Kalavasos. In V. Karageorghis (ed.), *The White Slip Ware of Late Bronze Age Cyprus*. Österreichische Akademie der Wissenschaften, Denkschriften der Gesamtakademie, Band 20. Contributions to the Chronology of the Eastern Mediterranean 2: 65–74. Vienna: Österreichische Akademie der Wissenschaften.

South, A.K., and I.A. Todd

1985 In quest of the Cypriote copper traders: excavations at Ayios Dhimitrios. *Archaeology* 38(5): 40–47.

1997 The Vasilikos Valley and the Aegean from the Neolithic to the Bronze Age. In D. Christou (ed.), *Cyprus and the Aegean in Antiquity*, 71–77. Nicosia: Department of Antiquities, Cyprus.

Spigelman, M.

2006 Investigating the faunal record from Bronze Age Cyprus: diversification and intensification. In A. McCarthy (ed.), *Island Dialogues: Cyprus in the Mediterranean Network*. University of Edinburgh Archaeology, Occasional Paper 21: 119–129. (online publication: http://www.shca.ed.ac.uk/archaeology/publications/occ_papers.htm/)

Stager, L.

1995 The impact of the Sea Peoples in Canaan (1185–1050 BCE). In T.E. Levy (ed.), *The Archaeology of Society in the Holy Land*, 332–348. Leicester, England: Leicester University Press.

Stager, L.E., A. Walker and G.E. Wright (eds)

1974 *The American Expedition to Idalion, Cyprus. First Preliminary Report: Seasons of 1971 and*

1972. Bulletin of the American Schools of Oriental Research, Supplementary Volume 18. Cambridge, Massachusetts: American Schools of Oriental Research.

Stager, L.E., and A. Walker (eds)

1989   *American Expedition to Idalion, Cyprus 1974–1980.* Oriental Institute Communications 24. Chicago: Oriental Institute, University of Chicago.

Stanley Price, N.P.

1977a   Khirokitia and the initial settlement of Cyprus. *Levant* 9: 66–89.

1977b   Colonisation and continuity in the early prehistory of Cyprus. *World Archaeology* 9: 27–41.

1979a   *Early Prehistoric Settlement in Cyprus: A Review and Gazetteer of Sites, c. 6500–3000 BC.* British Archaeological Reports, International Series 65. Oxford: British Archaeological Reports.

1979b   On terminology and models in Cypriote prehistory. In V. Karageorghis (ed.), *Studies Presented in Memory of Porphyrios Dikaios*, 1–11. Nicosia: Lions Club.

1979c   The structure of settlement at Sotira in Cyprus. *Levant* 11: 46–83.

Stanley Price, N.P., and D. Christou

1973   Excavations at Khirokitia, 1972. *Report of the Department of Antiquities, Cyprus:* 1–33.

Stanley Price, N.P., and D. Frankel

n.d.   The palaeozoology of Cyprus: some comments on a recent article by J.H. Schwartz. Unpublished paper (1974) in possession of author.

Staubwasser, M., and H. Weiss

2006   Holocene climate and cultural evolution in late prehistoric–early historic West Asia. *Quaternary Research* 66: 372–387.

Stech, T.

1982   Urban metallurgy in Late Bronze Age Cyprus. In J.D. Muhly, R. Maddin and V. Karageorghis (eds), *Early Metallurgy in Cyprus, 4000–500 BC*, 105–115. Nicosia: Pierides Foundation.

1985   Copper and society in Late Bronze Age Cyprus. In A.B. Knapp and T. Stech (eds), *Prehistoric Production and Exchange: The Aegean and East Mediterranean*. UCLA Institute of Archaeology, Monograph 25: 100–105. Los Angeles: UCLA Institute of Archaeology.

Steel, L.

1993   The establishment of the city kingdoms in Iron Age Cyprus: an archaeological commentary. *Report of the Department of Antiquities, Cyprus:* 147–156.

1994a   Pottery production on Cyprus in the eleventh century BC. In V. Karageorghis (ed.), *Cyprus in the 11th Century BC*, 39–46. Nicosia: Leventis Foundation.

1994b   Representations of a shrine on a Mycenaean chariot krater from Kalavasos-*Ayios Dhimitrios,* Cyprus. *Annual of the British School at Athens* 89: 201–211.

1995   Differential burial practices in Cyprus at the beginning of the Iron Age. In S. Campbell and A. Green (eds), *The Archaeology of Death in the Ancient Near East.* Oxbow Monograph 51: 199–204. Oxford: Oxbow.

1998   The social impact of Mycenaean imported pottery on Cyprus. *Annual of the British School at Athens* 93: 285–296.

1999   Wine, kraters and chariots: the Mycenaean pictorial style reconsidered. In P. Betancourt, V. Karageorghis, R. Laffineur and W.D. Niemeier (eds), *Meletemata: Studies in Aegean Archaeology Presented to Malcolm H. Wiener as He Enters His 65th Year.* Aegaeum 20: 803–811. Liège, Belgium, Austin: Université de Liège, University of Texas at Austin.

2001   The British Museum and the invention of the Cypriot Late Bronze Age. In V. Tatton-Brown (ed.), *Cyprus in the Nineteenth Century BC: Fact, Fancy and Fiction*, 160–167. Oxford: Oxbow.

2002   Wine, women and song: drinking ritual in Cyprus in the Late Bronze Age and Early Iron Age. In D. Bolger and N. Serwint (eds), *Engendering Aphrodite: Women and Society in Ancient Cyprus.* ASOR Archaeological Reports 7. Cyprus American Archaeological Research Institute Monograph 3: 105–119. Boston: American Schools of Oriental Research.

2003–2004   Archaeology in Cyprus, 1997–2002. *Archaeological Reports* 50: 93–111.

2004a   *Cyprus before History: From the Earliest Settlers to the End of the Bronze Age.* London: Duckworth.

2004b   A reappraisal of the distribution, context and function of Mycenaean pottery in Cyprus. In J. Balensi, J.-Y. Monchambert and S. Müller-Celku (eds), *La Ceramique Mycénienne de l'Égée au Levant.* Travaux de la Maison de l'Orient 41: 69–85.

Lyon, France: Travaux de la Maison de l'Orient.

2004c A goodly feast … a cup of mellow wine: feasting in Bronze Age Cyprus. In J.C. Wright (ed.), *Mycenaean Feasting.* Hesperia Supplement 73(2): 161–180. Princeton: American School of Classical Studies in Athens.

2008 Creation and expression of identity in Cyprus at the end of the Late Bronze Age. In C. Gallou, M. Georgiadis and G.W. Muskett (eds), *DIOSKOUROI: Studies Presented to W.G. Cavanagh and C.B. Mee on the Anniversary of their 30-year Joint Contribution to Aegean Achaeology.* British Archaeological Reports, International Series 1889: 154–175. Oxford: Archeopress.

2010 Late Cypriot ceramic production: heterarchy or hierarchy? In D. Bolger and L. Maguire (eds), *The Development of Pre-State Communities in the Ancient Near East. Studies in Honour of Edgar Peltenburg.* BANEA Publication Series 2: 106–116. Oxford: Oxbow.

Steel, L., and S. Janes

2005 Survey at Aredhiou *Vouppes*, Cyprus. *Report of the Department of Antiquities, Cyprus*: 231–244.

Steel, L., and C. McCartney

2008 Survey at Arediou *Vouppes* (*Lithosouros*), a Late Bronze Age agricultural settlement on Cyprus: a preliminary analysis of the material culture assemblages. *Bulletin of the American Schools of Oriental Research* 351: 9–37.

Steel, L., and S. Thomas

2008 Excavations at Aredhiou *Vouppes* (*Lithosouros*): an interim report on excavations 2005–2006. *Report of the Department of Antiquities, Cyprus*: 227–249.

Stein, G.

1992 Archaeological survey at Sürük Mevkii: a Ceramic Neolithic site in the Euphrates River Valley, southeast Turkey. *Anatolica* 18: 19–32.

2001 Understanding ancient state societies in the Old World. In G. Feinman and T.D. Price (eds), *Archaeology at the Millennium: A Sourcebook*, 353–379. Dordrecht: Kluwer Academic/Plenum.

Steward, J.H.

1950 *Area Research: Theory and Practice.* Social Science Research Council, Bulletin 63.

Washington DC: Social Science Research Council.

Stewart, E., and J.R. Stewart

1950 *Vounous 1937–1938.* Skrifter Utgivna av Svenska Institutet i Rom 14. Lund: Svenska Institutet i Rom.

Stewart, I., and C. Morhange

2009 Coastal geomorphology and sea-level change. In J. Woodward (ed.), *The Physical Geography of the Mediterranean*, 385–413. Oxford: Oxford University Press.

Stewart, J.R.

1957 The Melbourne Cyprus Expedition, 1955. *University of Melbourne Gazette* 13(1): 1–3.

1962 The Early Cypriote Bronze Age. In P. Dikaios and J.R. Stewart, *Swedish Cyprus Expedition* IV.1A: 205–401. Lund, Sweden: Swedish Cyprus Expedition.

1963 The tomb of the seafarer at Karmi in Cyprus. *Opuscula Atheniensia* 4: 197–204.

1974 *Tell el 'Ajjul: The Middle Bronze Age Remains.* Studies in Mediterranean Archaeology 38. Göteborg, Sweden: P. Åström's Förlag.

1992 *Corpus of Cypriote Artefacts of the Early Bronze Age*, Part 2. Studies in Mediterranean Archaeology III:2. Göteborg, Sweden: P. Åström's Förlag.

Stewart, S.T.

2004 Hill and vale: understanding prehistoric lithic use on Cyprus. In E.J. Peltenburg and A. Wasse (eds), *Neolithic Revolution: New Perspectives on Southwest Asia in Light of Recent Discoveries on Cyprus.* Levant Supplementary Series 1: 123–132. Oxford: Oxbow.

Stewart, S.T., and D.W. Rupp

2004 Tools and toys or traces of trade: the problem of the enigmatic incised objects from Cyprus and the Levant. In E.J. Peltenburg and A. Wasse (eds), *Neolithic Revolution: New Perspectives on Southwest Asia in Light of Recent Discoveries on Cyprus.* Levant Supplementary Series 1: 145–162. Oxford: Oxbow.

Stockhammer, P.

2007 Kontinuität und Wandel: Die Keramik der Nachpalastzeit aus der Unterstadt von Tiryns. Unpublished PhD dissertation, Ruprecht-Karls Universität, Heidelberg, Germany.

2011 Conceptualizing cultural hybridization in archaeology. In P.W. Stockhammer (ed.), *Conceptualizing Cultural Hybridization:*

A Transdisciplinary Approach, 43–58. Dordrecht: Springer.

Stockton, E.

1968   Pre-Neolithic remains at Kyrenia, Cyprus. *Report of the Department of Antiquities, Cyprus*: 16–19.

Stordeur, D.

2003a De la Vallée de l'Euphrate à Chypre? À la recherche d'indices de relations au néolithique. In J. Guilaine and A. Le Brun (eds), *Le Néolithique de Chypre*. Bulletin de Correspondance Hellénique, Supplément 43: 353–371. Athens: École Française d'Athènes.

2003b Symboles et imaginaire des premières cultures Néolithiques du Proche-Orient (Haute et Moyenne vallée de l'Euphrate). In J. Guilaine (ed.), *Art et symbols du Néolithique à la Protohistoire*, 15–36. Paris: Éditions Errance.

2004   New insights and concepts: two themes of the Neolithic in Syria and south-east Anatolia. *Neo-Lithics* 1/04: 49–51.

Stos-Gale, Z.A.

2001   Minoan foreign relations and copper metallurgy in Protopalatial and Neopalatial Crete. In A. Shortland (ed.), *The Social Context of Technological Change in Egypt and the Near East, 1650–1550 BC*, 195–210. Oxford: Oxbow.

Stos-Gale, Z.A., and N.H. Gale

2010   Bronze Age metal artefacts found on Cyprus – metal from Anatolia and the western Mediterranean. *Trabajos de Prehistoria* 67: 389–403.

Stos-Gale, Z.A., G. Maliotis, N.H. Gale and N. Annetts

1997   Lead isotope characteristics of the Cyprus copper ore deposits applied to provenance studies of copper oxhide ingots. *Archaeometry* 39: 83–123.

Stos-Gale, Z.A., N.H. Gale and D. Evely

2000   An interpretation of the metal finds, using lead isotope and chemical analytical procedures. In E. Hallager and B.P. Hallager (eds), *The Greek–Swedish Excavations at the Agia Aikaterini Square, Kastelli, Khania. 1970–1987* II: *The Late Minoan IIIC Settlement*, 206–214. Stockholm: P. Åström's Förlag.

Strasser, T.F.

1996   Archaeological myths and the overkill hypothesis in Cypriot prehistory. *Journal of Mediterranean Archaeology* 9: 113–116.

Strasser, T.F., E. Panagopoulou, C.N. Runnels, P.M. Murray, N. Thompson, P. Karkanas, F.T. McCoy and K.W. Wegmann

2010   Stone Age seafaring in the Mediterranean: evidence from the Plakias region for Lower Palaeolithic and Mesolithic habitation of Crete. *Hesperia* 79: 145–190.

Strasser, T.F., C.N. Runnels, K.W. Wegmann, E. Panagopoulou, F.T.McCoy, C.DiGregorio, P. Karkanas and N. Thomspon

2011   Dating Palaeolithic sites in southwestern Crete, Greece. *Journal of Quaternary Science* 26: 553–560.

Stutz, A.J., N.D. Munro and G. Bar-Oz

2009   Increasing the resolution of the Broad Spectrum Revolution in the southern Levantine Epipaleolithic (19–12 ka). *Journal of Human Evolution* 56: 294–306.

Sürenhagen, D.

2001   Die Bezeichnung Zyperns (Alasija) zum hethitischen Reich und seinen nordyrien Vassalen während der 2. Hälfte des 2. Jahrtausends v. Chr. In A. Kyriatsoulis (ed.), *Kreta und Zypern: Religion und Schrift. Von der Frühgeschichte biz zum Ende der archaischen Zeit*, 249–263. Altenburg, Germany: DZA Verlag für Kultur und Wissenschaft.

Swantek, L.A.

2006   'There's no Jewelry without a State of Society'. The Cultural Biography of Picrolite in Prehistoric Cyprus. Unpublished M.A. thesis, Department of Classics, State University of New York at Albany.

Swiny, H.W., and S. Swiny

1983   An anthropomorphic figurine from the Sotira area. *Report of the Department of Antiquities, Cyprus*: 56–59.

Swiny, S.

1980   Bronze Age gaming stones from Cyprus. *Report of the Department of Antiquities, Cyprus*: 54–78.

1981   Bronze Age settlement patterns in southwest Cyprus. *Levant* 13: 51–87.

1982   Correlations between the compositon and function of Bronze Age metal types in Cyprus. In R. Maddin, J.D. Muhly and V. Karageorghis (eds), *Early Metallurgy in Cyprus, 4000–500 BC*, 69–80. Nicosia: Pierides Foundation.

1986a *The Kent State University Expedition to Episkopi Phaneromeni*. Studies in Mediterranean Archaeology 74(2). Göteborg, Sweden: P. Åström's Förlag.

1986b The Philia Culture and its foreign relations. In V. Karageorghis (ed.), *Acts of the International Archaeological Symposium: Cyprus between the Orient and the Occident*, 29–44. Nicosia: Department of Antiquities.

1988 The Pleistocene fauna of Cyprus and recent discoveries on the Akrotiri Peninsula. *Report of the Department of Antiquities, Cyprus*: 1–14.

1989 From round house to duplex: a reassessment of prehistoric Cypriot Bronze Age society. In E.J. Peltenburg (ed.), *Early Society in Cyprus*, 14–31. Edinburgh: Edinburgh University Press.

1997 The Early Bronze Age. In T. Papadopoulos (ed.), *A History of Cyprus* 1: 171–212. Nicosia: Archbishop Makarios III Foundation. (in Greek)

2001 (ed.) *The Earliest Prehistory of Cyprus: From Colonization to Exploitation.* Cyprus American Archaeological Research Institute Monograph 2. Boston: American Schools of Oriental Research.

2008 Of cows, copper, corners, and cult: the emergence of the Cypriot Bronze Age. *Near Eastern Archaeology* 71 (1–2): 41–51.

Swiny, S., and C. Mavromatis

2000 Land behind Kourion: results of the 1997 Sotira Archaeological Project Survey. *Report of the Department of Antiquities, Cyprus*: 433–452.

Swiny, S., G. Rapp and E. Herscher (eds)

2003 *Sotira Kamminoudhia: An Early Bronze Age Site in Cyprus.* American Schools of Oriental Research, Archaeological Reports 8. Cyprus American Archaeological Research Institute Monograph 4. Boston: American Schools of Oriental Research.

Symeonoglou, S.

1972 Archaeological survey in the area of Phlamoudhi, Cyprus. *Report of the Department of Antiquities, Cyprus*: 187–198.

Taçon, P.S.C.

1999 Identifying ancient sacred landscapes in Australia: from physical to social. In W. Ashmore and A.B. Knapp (eds), *Archaeologies of Landscape: Contemporary Perspectives*, 33–57. Oxford: Blackwell.

Talalay, L.

2000 Archaeological Ms.conceptions: contemplating gender and the Greek Neolithic. In M. Donald and L. Hurcombe (eds),

Representations of Gender from Prehistory to the Present, 3–16. London: Macmillan.

2004 Heady business: skulls, heads, and decapitation in Neolithic Anatolia and Greece. *Journal of Mediterranean Archaeology* 17: 139–163.

2005 The Gendered Sea: iconography, gender and Mediterranean prehistory. In E. Blake and A.B. Knapp (eds), *The Archaeology of Mediterranean Prehistory*, 130–155. Oxford: Blackwell.

Talalay, L., and T. Cullen

2002 Sexual ambiguity in plank figurines from Bronze Age Cyprus. In D. Bolger and N. Serwint (eds), *Engendering Aphrodite: Women and Society in Ancient Cyprus.* ASOR Archaeological Reports 7. Cyprus American Archaeological Research Institute, Monograph 3: 181–195. Boston: American Schools of Oriental Research.

Tanasi, D.

2005 Mycenaean pottery imports and local imitations: Sicily vs. southern Italy. In R. Laffineur and E. Greco (eds), *Emporia: Aegeans in the Central and Eastern Mediterranean.* Aegaeum 25(2): 561–569. Liège, Belgium, Austin: Université de Liège, University of Texas at Austin.

2009 Sicily at the end of the Bronze Age: 'catching the echo'. In C. Bachhuber and R.G. Roberts (eds), *Forces of Transformation: The End of the Bronze Age in the Mediterranean: Themes from the Ancient Near East.* BANEA Publication Series 1: 51–58. Oxford: Oxbow.

Tartaron, T.F.

2010 Between and beyond: political economy in the non-palatial Mycenaean worlds. In D.J. Pullen (ed.), *Political Economies of the Aegean Bronze Age*, 161–183. Oxford: Oxbow.

Terrell, J.

1986 *Prehistory in the Pacific Islands.* Cambridge: Cambridge University Press.

1999 Comment on Paul Rainbird, 'Islands out of time: towards a critique of island archaeology'. *Journal of Mediterranean Archaeology* 12: 240–245.

2010 Language and material culture on the Sepik coast of Papua New Guinea: using social network analysis to simulate, graph, identify, and analyze social and cultural boundaries between communities. *Journal of Island and Coastal Archaeology* 5: 3–32.

Terrell, J., T.L. Hunt and C. Gosden
1997   The dimensions of social life in the Pacific: human diversity and the myth of the primitive isolate. *Current Anthropology* 38: 155–195.

Thiébault, S.
2003   Les paysages végétaux de Chypre au néolithique: premières données anthracologiques. In J. Guilaine and A. Le Brun (eds), *Le Néolithique de Chypre.* Bulletin de Correspondance Héllenique, Supplément 43: 221–230. Athens: École Française de'Athènes.

Thomas, J.
1987   Relations of production and social change in the Neolithic of north-west Europe. *Man* 22: 405–430.
2002   Archaeology's humanism and the materiality of the body. In Y. Hamilakis, M. Pluciennik and S. Tarlow (eds), *Thinking Through the Body: Archaeologies of Corporeality*, 29–45. New York: Kluwer Academic/Plenum.
2004   The Great Dark Book: archaeology, experience, and interpretation. In J. Bintliff (ed.), *A Companion to Archaeology*, 21–36. Oxford: Blackwell.

Thomas, N.
1991   *Entangled Objects: Exchange, Material Culture, and Colonialism in the Pacific.* Cambridge, Massachusetts: Harvard University Press.

Thomas, S.
2003   Imports at Zawiyet Unn al-Rakham. In Z. Hawass (ed.), *Egyptology at the Dawn of the Twenty-first Century. Proceedings of the Eighth International Congress of Egyptologists Cairo 2000* 1: *Archaeology*, 522–529. New York, Cairo: American University in Cairo Press.

Tilley, C.
1994   *A Phenomenology of Landscape.* Oxford: Berg.

Todd, I.A.
1981   Current research in the Vasilikos Valley. In J. Reade (ed.), *Chalcolithic Cyprus and Western Asia.* British Museum Occasional Paper 26: 57–68. London: British Museum Press.
1985   The Vasilikos Valley and the Neolithic/Chalcolithic periods in Cyprus. In T. Papadopoulou and S. Hadjistylli (eds), *Praktika tou Deuterou Diethnous Kyprologikou Synedriou*, 5–12. Nicosia: Leventis Foundation.

1986   (ed.) *The Bronze Age Cemetery in Kalavasos Village.* Vasilikos Valley Project 1. Studies in Mediterranean Archaeology 71(1). Göteborg, Sweden: P. Åström's Förlag.
1987   *Excavations at Kalavasos-Tenta* I. *Vasilikos Valley Project* 6. Studies in Mediterranean Archaeology 71(6). Göteborg, Sweden: P. Åström's Förlag.
1988   The Middle Bronze Age in the Kalavasos area. *Report of the Department of Antiquities, Cyprus*: 133–140.
1998   *Kalavasos-Tenta.* Bank of Cyprus, Cultural Foundation Guide Book. Nicosia: Bank of Cyprus, Cultural Foundation.
2000   Excavations at Sanidha, a Late Bronze Age ceramic manufacturing centre. In G.C. Ioannides and S.A. Hadjistellis (eds), *Acts of the Third International Congress of Cypriot Studies*, 301–325. Nicosia: Society of Cypriot Studies.
2001   Kalavasos *Tenta* revisited. In S. Swiny (ed.), *The Earliest Prehistory of Cyprus: From Colonization to Exploitation.* Cyprus American Archaeological Research Institute Monograph 2: 95–107. Boston: American Schools of Oriental Research.
2003   Kalavasos-*Tenta*: a reappraisal. In J. Guilaine and A. Le Brun (eds), *Le Néolithique de Chypre.* Bulletin de Correspondance Hellénique, Supplément 43: 35–44. Athens: École Française de'Athènes.
2004   *The Field Survey of the Vasilikos Valley.* Volume 1. Vasilikos Valley Project 9. Studies in Mediterranean Archaeology 71(9). Sävedalen, Sweden: P. Åström's Förlag.
2005   *Excavations at Kalavasos-Tenta.* Vasilikos Valley Project 7. Studies in Mediterranean Archaeology 71(7). Sävedalen, Sweden: P. Åström's Förlag.

Todd, I.A., and P. Croft (eds)
2004   *Excavations at Kalavasos-Ayious.* Vasilikos Valley Project 8. Studies in Mediterranean Archaeology 71(8). Sävedalen, Sweden: P. Åström's Förlag.

Todd, I.A., and D. Pilides
2001   The archaeology of White Slip production. In V. Karageorghis (ed.), *The White Slip Ware of Late Bronze Age Cyprus.* Österreichische Akademie der Wissenschaften, Denkschriften der Gesamtakademie, Band 20. Contributions to the Chronology of the Eastern Mediterranean 2: 27–41. Vienna: Verlag

der Österreichische Akademie der Wissenschaften.

Tomasello, F.

2004 L'architettura 'micenea' nel Siracusano. To-ko-do-mo a-pe-o o de-me-o-te? In V. La Rosa (ed.), *Le Presenze Micenee nel Territorio Siricusano. I Simposio Siricusano di Preistoria Siciliana in Memoria di Paolo Orsi. Siracusa, 15–16 Dicembre 2003*, 187–215. Padua, Italy: Bottega d'Erasmo.

Tomka, S., and M. Stevenson

1993 Understanding abandonment processes. In C. Cameron and S.A. Tomka (eds), *Abandonment of Settelements and Regions: Ethnoarcaheological and Archaeological Approaches*, 191–195. Cambridge: Cambridge University Press.

Tomkins, P.

2009 Domesticity by default. Ritual, ritualization and cave-use in the Neolithic Aegean. *Oxford Journal of Archaeology* 28: 125–53.

Tomlinson, J.E., J.B. Rutter and S.M.A. Hoffman

2010 Mycenaean and Cypriot Late Bronze Age ceramic imports to Kommos: an investigation by Neutron Activation Analysis. *Hesperia* 79: 191–231.

Toumazou, M.K.

1987 Aspects of Burial Practices in Early Prehistoric Cypriote Sites, c.7000–2500/2300 B.C. Unpublished Ph.D dissertation, Bryn Mawr College, Bryn Mawr, Pennsylvania.

Trantalidou, C.

2003 Faunal remains from the earliest strata of the Cave of Cyclops. In N. Galanidou and C. Perlès (eds), *The Greek Mesolithic: Problems and Perspectives*. British School at Athens, Studies 10: 143–172. London: British School at Athens.

Trigger, B.G.

1990 Monumental architecture: a thermodynamic explanation of symbolic behaviour. *World Archaeology* 22: 119–131.

Tsuneki, A., M. Arimura, O. Maeda, K. Tanno and T. Anezaki

2006 The Early PPNB in the north Levant: a new prespective from Tell Ain el-Kerkh, northwest Syria. *Paléorient* 32(1): 47–71.

Tuan, Y.

1977 *Space and Place: The Perspective of Experience.* Minneapolis: University of Minnesota Press.

Twiss, K.C.

2008 Transformations in an early agricultural society: feasting in the southern Levantine Pre-Pottery Neolithic. *Journal of Anthropological Archaeology* 27: 418–442.

Tylecote, R.F.

1982 The Late Bronze Age: copper and bronze metallurgy at Enkomi and Kition. In J.D. Muhly, R. Maddin and V. Karageorghis (eds), *Early Metallurgy in Cyprus, 4000–500 BC*, 81–103. Nicosia: Pierides Foundation.

Urban, G.

1996 *Metaphysical Community.* Austin: University of Texas Press.

Vagnetti, L.

1974 Preliminary remarks on Cypriote Chalcolithic figurines. *Report of the Department of Antiquities, Cyprus*: 24–34.

1980 Figurines and minor objects from a Chalcolithic cemetery at Souskiou-Vathyrkakas. *Studi Micenei ed Egeo-Anatolici* 21: 17–72.

2001 Some observations on Late Cypriot pottery from the central Mediterranean. In L. Bonfante and V. Karageorghis (eds), *Italy and Cyprus in Antiquity, 1500–450 BC*, 77–96. Nicosia: Leventis Foundation.

van Andel, T.H.

1989 Late Quaternary sea-level changes and archaeology. *Antiquity* 63/241: 733–745.

van de Mieroop, M.

1999 *The Ancient Mesopotamian City.* Oxford: Clarendon Press.

van Dommelen, P.

1997 Colonial constructs: colonialism and archaeology in the Mediterranean. *World Archaeology* 28: 305–323.

1998 *On Colonial Grounds: A Comparative Study of Colonialism and Rural Settlement in First Millennium BC West Central Sardinia.* Leiden University Archaeological Studies. Leiden, The Netherlands: Faculty of Archaeology, Leiden University.

2005 Colonial interactions and hybrid practices: Phoenician and Carthaginian settlement in the ancient Mediterranean. In G.J. Stein (ed.), *The Archaeology of Colonial Encounters*, 109–141. Sante Fe, New Mexico: School of American Research Press.

2006 Colonial matters: material culture and postcolonial theory in colonial situations. In C. Tilley, W. Keane, S. Kuechler, M.

Rowlands and P. Spyer (eds), *Handbook of Material Culture*, 104–124. London: Sage.

van Dommelen, P., and A.B. Knapp (eds)

2010   *Material Connections in the Ancient Mediterranean: Mobility, Materiality and Mediterranean Identities*. London: Routledge.

Vandenabeele, F., and R. Laffineur (eds)

1991   *Cypriote Terracottas. Proceedings of the First International Conference of Cypriote Studies (Brussels-Liège- Amsterdam, 29 May–1 June 1989)*. Nicosia, Brussels, Liège, Belgium: Leventis Foundation; Free University Brussels; Université de Liège.

Vanschoonwinkel, J.

1991   *L'Égée et la Méditerranée Orientale à la fin du deuxième millénaire. Témoignages archéologiques et sources écrites*. Archaeologia Transatlantica 9. Louvain-la-Neuve, Belgium: Université Catholique du Louvain.

Vassiliou, E., and E. Stylianou

2004   Dropping in on Late Bronze Age Erimi. Erimi *Pitharka*, preliminary excavation report. *Report of the Department of Antiquities, Cyprus*: 181–200.

Vaughan, S.

1991   Late Cypriot Base Ring ware: studies in raw materials and technology. In A. Middleton and I. Freestone (eds), *Recent Developments in Ceramic Petrology*. British Museum Occasional Paper 81: 337–368. London: British Museum.

1994   Base Ring Ware: a regional study in Cyprus. In A.B. Knapp and J.F. Cherry, *Provenience Studies and Bronze Age Cyprus: Production, Exchange, and Politico-Economic Change*. Monographs in World Archaeology 21: 86–92. Madison, Wisconsin: Prehistory Press.

Vayda, A.P., and R. Rappaport

1963   Island cultures. In F.R. Fosberg (ed.), *Man's Place in the Island Ecosystem: A Symposium*, 133–144. Honolulu, Hawaii: Bishop Museum Press.

Vercoutter, J.

1956   *L'Égypte et le monde égéen préhellénique*. Bibliothèque des Études 22. Cairo: Institut Français d'archéologie orientale.

Vermeule, E., and F.Z. Wolsky

1990   *Toumba tou Skourou: A Bronze Age Potter's Quarter on Morphou Bay in Cyprus*.

Cambridge, Massachusetts: Harvard University Press.

Vianello, A.

2005   *Late Bronze Age Mycenaean and Italic Products in the West Mediterranean: A Social and Economic Analysis*. British Archaeological Reports, International Series 1439. Oxford: Archeopress.

Vigne, J.-D.

1987   L'extinction holocène du fonds de peuplement mammalien indigène des îles de Méditerranée occidentale. *Mémoires de la Société Géologique de France* 150 (n.s.): 167–177.

1993   Domestication et appropriation par la chasse: histoire d'un choix socio-cultural depuis le Néolithique. L'exemple des cerfs (Cervus). In J. Desse and F. Audoin-Rouzeau (eds), *Exploitation des animaux sauvages à travers le temps*, 201–220. Juan Les Pins, France: Éditions de APDCA.

1996   Did man provoke extinctions of endemic large mammals on the Mediterranean islands? The view from Corsica. *Journal of Mediterranean Archaeology* 9: 117–120.

2001   Large mammals of early Aceramic Neolithic Cyprus: preliminary results from Parekklisha *Shillourokambos*. In S. Swiny (ed.), *The Earliest Prehistory of Cyprus: From Colonization to Exploitation*. Cyprus American Archaeological Research Institute Monograph 2: 55–60. Boston: American Schools of Oriental Research.

Vigne, J.-D., and N. Desse-Berset

1995   The exploitation of animal resources in Mediterranean islands during the Pre-Neolithic: the example of Corsica. In A. Fisher (ed.), *Man and Sea in the Mesolithic*. Oxbow Monograph 53: 309–318. Oxford: Oxbow.

Vigne, J.-D., and H. Buitenhuis (with S. Davis)

1999   Les premiers pas de la domestication animale à l'ouest de l'Euphrate: Chypre et l'Anatolie centrale. *Paléorient* 25(2): 49–62.

Vigne, J.-D., I. Carrère, J.-F. Saliège, A. Person, H. Bocherens, J. Guilaine and J.F. Briois

2000   Predomestic cattle, sheep, goat and pig during the late 9th and the 8th millennium Cal BC on Cyprus: preliminary results of Shillourokambos (Parekklisha, Limassol). In M. Mashkour, A.M.

Choyke, H. Buitenhuis and F. Poplin (eds), *Archaeozoology of the Near East IVA. Proceedings of the Fourth International Symposium on the Archaeozoology of Southwestern Asia and Adjacent Areas.* ARC Publicatie 32: 83–106. Groningen, The Netherlands: Centrum voor Archeologische Research and Consultancy.

Vigne, J.-D., I. Carrère and J. Guilaine
2003 Unstable status of early domestic ungulates in the Near East: the example of Shillourokambos (Cyprus, IXth–VIIIth millennia cal. BC). In J. Guilaine and A. Le Brun (eds), *Le Néolithique de Chypre.* Bulletin de Correspondance Hellénique, Supplément 43: 239–251. Athens: École Française de'Athènes.

Vigne, J.-D., J. Guilaine, K. Debue, L. Haye and P. Gérard
2004 Early taming of the cat in Cyprus. *Science* 304(9 April 2004): 259.

Vigne, J.-D., and T. Cucchi
2005 Premières navigations au Proche-Orient: les informations indirectes de Chypre. *Paléorient* 31(1): 186–194.

Vigne, J.-D., J. Peters and D. Helmer
2005 New archaeozoological approaches to trace the first steps of animal domestication. In J.-D. Vigne, J. Peters and D. Helmer (eds), *The First Steps of Animal Domestication,* 1–16. Oxford: Oxbow.

Vigne, J.-D., and D. Helmer
2007 Was milk a 'secondary product' in the Old World Neolithisation process? Its role in the domestication of cattle, sheep and goats. *Anthropozoologica* 42: 9–40.

Vigne, J.-D., A. Zazzo, J.-F. Saliège, F. Poplin, J. Guilaine and A. Simmons
2009 Pre-Neolithic wild boar management and introduction to Cyprus more than 11,400 years ago. *Proceedings of the National Academy of Sciences* 106(38): 16135–16138 (22 September 2009).

Vigne, J.-D., F. Briois, A. Zazzo, I. Carrère, J. Daujat and J. Guilaine
2011a A new early Pre-Pottery Neolithic site in Cyprus: Ayios Tychonas-*Klimonas* (ca. 8700 cal. BC). *Neo-Lithics* 1/11: 3–18.

Vigne, J.-D., I. Carrère, F. Briois and J. Guilaine
2011b The early process of mammal domestication in the Near East: new evidence from the pre-Neolithic and Pre-Pottery Neolithic in Cyprus. *Current Anthropology* 52(Supplement 4): S255–S271.

Villamil, L.P.
2008 Creating, transforming, rejecting, and reinterpreting Ancient Maya urban landscapes: insights from Lagartera and Margarita. In N. Yoffee (ed.), *Identity, Memory, and Landscape in Archaeological Research,* 183–214. Tucson: University of Arizona Press.

Vita-Finzi, C.
1969 *The Mediterranean Valleys: Geological Changes in Historical Times.* Cambridge: Cambridge University Press.
1973 Paleolithic finds from Cyprus? *Proceedings of the Prehistoric Society* 39: 453–454.

Vives-Ferrándiz, J.
2008 Negotiating colonial encounters: hybrid practices and consumption in eastern Iberia (8th–6th centuries BC). *Journal of Mediterranean Archaeology* 21: 241–272.

von Beckerath, J.
1997 *Chronologie des Pharaonischen Ägypten. Die Zeitbestimmung der Ägyptischen Geschichte von der Vorzeit bis 332 v. Chr.* Mainz, Germany: Philipp von Zabern.

Voskos, I., and A.B. Knapp
2008 Cyprus at the end of the Late Bronze Age: crisis and colonization, or continuity and hybridization? *American Journal of Archaeology* 112: 659–684.

Voss, B.L.
2008 Sexuality studies in archaeology. *Annual Review of Anthropology* 37: 317–336.

Wachsmann, S.
2000 To the sea of the Philistines. In E.D. Oren (ed.), *The Sea Peoples and Their World: A Reassessment.* University Museum Monograph 108. University Museum Symposium Series 11: 103–143. Philadelphia: University Museum, University of Pennsylvania.

Waines, J.G., and N.P. Stanley Price
1975–1977 Plant remains from Khirokitia in Cyprus. *Paléorient* 3(3): 281–284.

Walker, M.J.
1975 Early Neolithic skeletons from Philia-*Drakos,* Site A (Cyprus). *Australian Journal of Biblical Archaeology* 2(3): 77–92.

Warburton, D.A. (ed.)
2009 *Time's Up! Dating the Minoan Eruption of Santorini.* Monographs of the Danish Institute at Athens 10. Athens: Danish Institute at Athens.

Ward, C.A.

2010 Seafaring in the Bronze Age Aegean: evidence and speculation. In D.J. Pullen (ed.), *Political Economies of the Aegean Bronze Age*, 149–160. Oxford: Oxbow.

Wasse, A.

2007 Climate, economy and change: Cyprus and the Levant during the Late Pleistocene–mid Holocene. In J. Clarke, *On the Margins of Southwest Asia: Cyprus during the 6th to 4th Millennia BC*, 43–63. Oxford: Oxbow.

Watkins, T.F.

1970 Philia-*Drakos* Site A: pottery, stratigraphy, chronology. *Report of the Department of Antiquities, Cyprus*: 1–9.

1971 Philia-*Drakos* (Mission britannique). In V. Karageorghis, Chronique des fouilles et découvertes archéologiques à Chypre en 1970. *Bulletin de Correspondance Hellénique* 95: 371–374.

1972 Cypriote Neolithic chronology and the pottery from Philia *Drakos* A. In V. Karageorghis and A. Christodoulou (eds), *Acts of the First International Cyprological Congress*, 167–174. Nicosia: Department of Antiquities.

1973 Some problems of the Neolithic and Chalcolithic period in Cyprus. *Report of the Department of Antiquities, Cyprus*: 34–61.

1979 Kataliondas-*Kourvellos*: the analysis of the surface collected data. In V. Karageorghis (ed.), *Studies Presented in Memory of Porphyrios Dikaios*, 12–20. Nicosia: Lions Club.

1981 The Chalcolithic period in Cyprus: the background to current research. In J. Reade (ed.), *Chalcolithic Cyprus and Western Asia*. British Museum Occasional Publication 26: 9–20. London: British Museum.

2004 Putting the colonization of Cyprus into context. In E.J. Peltenburg and A. Wasse (eds), *Neolithic Revolution: New Perspectives on Southwest Asia in Light of Recent Discoveries on Cyprus*. Levant Supplementary Series 1: 23–34. Oxford: Oxbow.

2005 From foragers to complex societies in southwest Asia. In C. Scarre (ed.), *The Human Past*, 200–233. London: Thames and Hudson.

2008 Supra-regional networks in the Neolithic of southwest Asia. *Journal of World Prehistory* 21: 139–171.

Watrous, L.V.

1985 Late Bronze Age Kommos: imported pottery as evidence for foreign contact. *Scripta Mediterranea* 6: 7–10.

1992 *Kommos* III: *The Late Bronze Age Pottery*. Princeton: Princeton University Press.

Watson, J.P.N., and N.P. Stanley Price

1977 The verebrate fauna from the 1972 sounding at Khirokitia. *Report of the Department of Antiquities, Cyprus*: 232–263.

Wattenmaker, P.

1998 *Household and State in Upper Mesopotamia: Specialized Economy and the Social Uses of Goods in an Early Complex Society*. Washington DC: Smithsonian Institution Press.

Webb, J.M.

1992 Funerary ideology in Bronze Age Cyprus – towards the recognition and analysis of Cypriote ritual data. In G.K. Ioannides (ed.), *Studies in Honour of Vassos Karageorghis*, 87–99. Nicosia: Society of Cypriot Studies.

1995 Abandonment processes and curate/discard strategies at Marki *Alonia*, Cyprus. *The Artifact* 18: 64–70.

1998 Lithic technology and discard at Marki, Cyprus: consumer behaviour and site formation in the prehistoric Bronze Age. *Antiquity* 72: 796–805.

1999 *Ritual Architecture, Iconography and Practice in the Late Cypriote Bronze Age*. Studies in Mediterranean Archaeology and Literature, Pocket-book 75. Jonsered, Sweden: P. Åström's Förlag.

2001 The sanctuary of the Ingot God at Enkomi: a new reading of its construction, use and abandonment. In P.M. Fischer (ed.), *Contributions to the Archaeology and History of the Bronze and Iron Ages in the Eastern Mediterranean: Studies in Honour of Paul Åström*. Österreichisches Archäologisches Institut: Sonderschriften Band 39: 69–82. Vienna: Österreichisches Archäologisches Institut.

2002a *Exploring the Bronze Age in Cyprus. Australian Perspectives*. The Fifth Museum of Antiquities Maurice Kelly Lecture. Armidale, New South Wales, Australia: University of New England.

2002b Engendering the built environment: household and community in prehistoric Bronze Age Cyprus. In D. Bolger and N. Serwint (eds), *Engendering Aphrodite: Women and Society in Ancient Cyprus*. Cyprus American Archaeological Research Institute Monograph 3: 87–101. Boston: American Schools of Oriental Research.

2002c New evidence for the origins of textile production in Bronze Age Cyprus. *Antiquity* 76/292: 364–371.

2002d Device, image and coercion. The role of glyptic in the political economy of Late Bronze Age Cyprus. In J. Smith (ed.), *Script and Seal Use on Cyprus in the Bronze and Iron Ages*. Archaeological Institute of America, Colloquia and Conference Papers 4: 111–154. Boston: Archaeological Institute of America.

2005 Ideology, iconography and identity: the role of foreign goods and images in the establishment of social hierarchy in Late Bronze Age Cyprus. In J. Clarke (ed.), *Archaeological Perspectives on the Transmission and Transformation of Culture in the Eastern Mediterranean*. Levant Supplementary Series 2: 176–182. Oxford: Council for British Research in the Levant; Oxbow.

2009 Keeping house: our developing understanding of the Early and Middle Cypriot household (1926–2006). *Medelhavsmuseet. Focus on the Mediterranean* 5: 255–267.

2010 The ceramic industry of Deneia: crafting community and place in Middle Bronze Age Cyprus. In D. Bolger and L. Maguire (eds), *The Development of Pre-State Communities in the Ancient Near East. Studies in Honour of Edgar Peltenburg*. BANEA Publication Series 2: 174–182. Oxford: Oxbow.

n.d. Cyprus in the Early Bronze Age. In M.L. Steiner and A.E. Killebrew (eds), *The Oxford Handbook of the Archaeology of the Levant*. Oxford: Oxford University Press. (in press)

Webb, J.M., and D. Frankel

1994 Making an impression: storage and surplus finance in Late Bronze Age Cyprus. *Journal of Mediterranean Archaeology* 7: 5–26.

1999 Characterising the Philia facies. Material culture, chronology and the origin of the Bronze Age in Cyprus. *American Journal of Archaeology* 103: 3–43.

2004 Intensive site survey. Implications for estimating settlement size, population and duration in prehistoric Bronze Age Cyprus. In M. Iacovou (ed.), *Archaeological Field Survey in Cyprus. Past History, Future Potentials*. British School at Athens, Studies 11: 125–137. London: British School at Athens.

2007 Identifying population movements by everyday practice: the case of 3rd millennium Cyprus. In S. Antoniadou and A. Pace (eds), *Mediterranean Crossroads*, 189–216. Athens, Oxford: Pierides Foundation, Oxbow.

2008 Fine ware ceramics, consumption and commensality: mechanisms of horizontal and vertical integration in Early Bronze Age Cyprus. In L.A. Hitchcock, R. Laffineur and J. Crowley (eds), *DAIS. The Aegean Feast*. Aegaeum 29: 287–295. Liège, Belgium, Austin: Université de Liège, University of Texas at Austin.

2009 Exploiting a damaged and diminishing resource: survey, sampling and society at a Bronze Age cemetery complex in Cyprus. *Antiquity* 83/319: 54–68.

2010 Social strategies, ritual and cosmology in Early Bronze Age Cyprus: an investigation of burial data from the north coast. *Levant* 42: 185–209.

2011 Hearth and home as identifiers of community in mid-third millennium Cyprus. In V. Karageorghis and O. Kouka (eds), *On Cooking Pots, Drinking Cups, Loomweights and Ethnicity in Bronze Age Cyprus and Neighbouring Regions*, 29–42. Nicosia: Leventis Foundation.

Webb, J., D. Frankel, Z.A. Stos and N. Gale

2006 Early Bronze Age metals trade in the eastern Mediterranean. New compositional and lead isotope evidence from Cyprus. *Oxford Journal of Archaeology* 25: 261–288.

Webb, J., D. Frankel, P. Croft and C. McCartney

2009a Excavations at Politiko *Kokkinorotsos*. A Chalcolithic hunting station in Cyprus. *Proceedings of the Prehistoric Society* 75: 189–237.

Webb, J.F., D. Frankel, K. Eriksson and J.B. Hennessy

2009b *The Bronze Age Cemeteries at Karmi Paleolana and Lapatsa in Cyprus. Excavations by J.R.B. Stewart.* Studies in Mediterranean Archaeology 136. Göteborg, Sweden: P. Åström's Förlag.

Webster, J.

2001 Creolizing the Roman provinces. *American Journal of Archaeology* 105: 209–225.

Weinberg, S.S.

1983 *Bamboula at Kourion: The Architecture.* University Museum Monograph 42. Philadelphia: University of Pennsylvania Press.

Weiss, E., M.E. Kislev and A. Hartmann

2006 Autonomous cultivation before domestication. *Science* 312: 1608–1610.

Wendorf, F.

1968 Site 117: a Nubian Final Paleolithic graveyard near Jebel Sahaba, Sudan. In F. Wendorf (ed.), *The Prehistory of Nubia* 2: 954–995. Dallas: Fort Burgwin Research Center; Southern Methodist University Press.

Wengrow, D.

2009 The voyages of Europa: ritual and trade in the eastern Mediterranean circa 2300–1850 BC. In W.A. Parkinson and M.L. Galaty (eds), *Archaic State Interaction: The Eastern Mediterranean in the Bronze Age,* 141–160. Santa Fe, New Mexico: School for Advanced Research Press.

Weninger, B., E. Alram-Stern, E. Bauer, L. Clare, U. Danzeglocke, O. Jöris, C. Kubatzki, G. Rollefson, H. Todorova and T. van Andel

2006 Climate forcing due to the 8200 cal yr bp event observed at Early Neolithic sites in the eastern Mediterranean. *Quaternary Research* 66: 401–20.

Whelan, F., and D. Kelletat

2002 Geomorphic evidence and relative and absolute dating results for tsunami events on Cyprus. *Science of Tsunami Hazards* 20(1): 3–16.

White, D.

1986 1985 excavations on Bate's Island, Marsa Matruh. *Journal of the American Research Center in Egypt* 23: 51–84.

1999 Water, wood, dung and eggs: reciprocity in trade along the LBA Mamarican coast. In P.P. Betancourt, V. Karageorghis, R. Laffineur and W.-D. Niemeier (eds), *Meletemata: Studies in Aegean Archaeology Presented to Malcolm H. Weiner as He Enters his 65th Year.* Aegaeum 20(3): 931–935.

Liège, Belgium, Austin: Université de Liège, University of Texas at Austin.

2002 *Marsa Matruh* II: *The Objects. The University of Pennsylvania Museum of Archaeology and Anthropology's Excavations on Bate's Island, Marsa Matruh, Egypt 1985–1989.* Institute for Aegean Prehistory, Prehistory Monographs 2. Philadelphia: Institute for Aegean Prehistory Academic Press.

2003 *Multum in parvo:* Bates's island on the NW coast of Egypt. In N.C. Stampolidis and V. Karageorghis (eds), *Ploes... Sea Routes...: Interconnections in the Mediterranean, 16th–6th c. BC,* 71–82. Athens: University of Crete, Leventis Foundation.

Whittle, A., and A. Bayliss

2007 The times of their lives: from chronological precision to kinds of history and change. *Cambridge Archaeological Journal* 17: 21–28.

Whittle, A., F. Healy and A. Bayliss

2011 *Gathering Time: Dating the Early Neolithic Enclosures of Southern Britain and Ireland.* Oxford: Oxbow.

Wiessner, P.

1983 Style and social information in Kalahari San projectile points. *American Antiquity* 48: 252–276.

Willcox, G.

1999 Agrarian change and the beginnings of cultivation in the Near East: evidence from wild progenitors, experimental cultivation and archaeobotanical data. In C. Gosden and J.C. Hather (eds), *The Prehistory of Food: Appetites for Change.* One World Archaeology 32: 478–500. London: Routledge.

2000 Présence des céréales dans le Néolithique Précéramique de Shillourokambos à Chypre: résultats de la campagne 1999. *Paléorient* 26(1): 129–135.

2002 Geographical variation in major cereal components and evidence for independent domestication events in Western Asia. In R. Cappers and S. Bottema (eds), *The Dawn of Farming in the Near East.* Studies in Near Eastern Production, Subsistence and Environment 6: 133–140. Berlin: Ex Oriente.

2003 The origins of Cypriot farming. In J. Guilaine and A. Le Brun (eds), *Le Néolithique de Chypre.* Bulletin de Correspondance Hellénique, Supplément

43: 231–238. Athens: École Française de'Athènes.

2004 Measuring grain size and identifying Near Eastern cereal domestication: evidence from the Euphrates valley. *Journal of Archaeological Science* 31: 145–150.

2007 The adoption of farming and the beginnings of the Neolithic in the Euphrates Valley. In S. Colledge and J. Conolly (eds), *The Origins and Spread of Domestic Plants in Southwest Asia and Europe*, 21–36. Walnut Creek, California: Left Coast Press.

Willcox, G., S. Fornite and L. Herveux

2008 Early Holocene cultivation before domestication in northern Syria. *Vegetation History and Archaeobotany* 17: 313–325.

Willcox, G., R. Buxo and L. Herveux

2009 Late Pleistocene and early Holocene climate and the beginnings of cultivation in northern Syria. *The Holocene* 19: 151–158.

Wright, G.R.H.

1992 *Ancient Building in Cyprus*. Handbuch der Orientalistik 7. Abteilung, Kunst und Archaeologie. I Band, Der Alte Vordere Orient. 2B/7/1 and 2B/7/2. Leiden, The Netherlands: Brill.

Xenophontos, C.

1991 Picrolite, its nature, provenance, and possible distribution patterns in the Chalcolithic period of Cyprus. *Bulletin of the American Schools of Oriental Research* 282–283: 127–138.

Yaeger, J.

2000 The social construction of communities in the Classic Maya countryside: strategies of affiliation in western Belize. In M.A. Canuto and J. Yaeger (eds), *The Archaeology of Communities: A New World Perspective*, 123–142. London: Routledge.

Yalçin, Ü., C. Pulak and R. Slotta (eds)

2005 *Das Schiff von Uluburun: Welthandel vor 3000 Jahren*. Bochum, Germany: Deutsches Bergbau-Museum.

Yannai, E.

2006 The origin and distribution of the collared rim pithos and krater: a case of conservative pottery production in the ancient Near East from the fourth to the first millennium BCE. In A.M. Maier and P. de Miroschedji (eds), *'I Will Speak the Riddle of Ancient Times': Archaeological and Historical Studies in Honor of Amihai Mazar on the Occasion of his Sixtieth*

Birthday, 89–111. Winona Lake, Indiana: Eisenbrauns.

Yasur-Landau, A.

2010 *The Philistines and Aegean Migration at the End of the Late Bronze Age*. Cambridge: Cambridge University Press.

2011 Deep change in domestic behavioural patterns and theoretical aspects of interregional interactions in the 12th century Levant. In V. Karageorghis and O. Kouka (eds), *On Cooking Pots, Drinking Cups, Loomweights and Ethnicity in Bronze Age Cyprus and Neighbouring Regions*, 245–255. Nicosia: Leventis Foundation.

Yener, K.A.

2000 *The Domestication of Metals: The Rise of Complex Metal Industries in Anatolia*. Culture and History of the Ancient Near East 4. Leiden, The Netherlands: Brill.

Yon, M.

2001 White Slip in the northern Levant. In V. Karageorghis (ed.), *The White Slip Ware of Late Bronze Age Cyprus*. Österreichische Akademie der Wissenschaften, Denkschriften der Gesamtakademie 20: 117–125. Vienna: Österreichische Akademie der Wissenschaften.

2006a *The City of Ugarit at Tell Ras Shamra*. Winona Lake, Indiana: Eisenbrauns.

2006b Palais et royauté à Chypre. In P. Butterlin, M. Leveau, J.-Y. Monchambert, J.L. Montero Fenollós and B. Muller (eds), *Les espaces syro-Mésopotamiens: dimensions de l'expérience humaine au Proche-Orient Ancien*. Subartu 17: 77–86. Turnhout, Belgium: Brepols.

2007 'Au roi d'Alasia, mon père…'. *Cahier du Centre d'Études Chypriotes* 337: 15–39.

Zeder, M.

2006 Archaeological approaches to documenting animal domestication. In M.A. Zeder, E. Emshwiller, B.D. Smith and D.G. Bradley (eds), *Documenting Domestication: New Genetic and Archaeological Paradigms*, 171–180. Berkeley: University of California Press.

2008 Domestication and early agriculture in the Mediterranean basin: origins, diffusion, and impact. *Proceedings of the National Academy of Sciences* 105(33): 11597–11604.

2009   The Neolithic macro-(r)evolution: macro-
        evolutionary theory and the study of
        culture change. *Journal of Archaeological
        Research* 17: 1–63.

Zeder, M.A., and B. Hesse

2000   The initial domestication of goats (*Capra
        hircus*) in the Zagros mountains 10,000
        years ago. *Science* 287: 2254–2257.

Zeder, M.A., E. Emshwiller, B.D. Smith and D.G.
        Bradley (eds)

2006   *Documenting Domestication: New Genetic
        and Archaeological Paradigms.* Berkeley:
        University of California Press.

Zeuner, F.E.

1958   Animal remains from a Late Bronze Age
        sanctuary on Cyprus, and the problems of

        the domestication of fallow deer. *Journal of
        the Palaeontological Society of India* 3: 131–135.

Zohary, D.

1996   The mode of domestication of the foun-
        der crops of southwest Asian agricul-
        ture. In D.R. Harris (ed.), *The Origins
        and Spread of Agriculture and Pastoralism
        in Eurasia*, 142–158. London: University
        College London Press.

Zwicker, U.

1988   Investigations of material from Maa-
        Palaeokastro and copper ores from the
        surrounding area. In V. Karageorghis and
        M. Demas, *Excavations at Maa-Palaeokastro
        1979–1986*, 427–448. Nicosia: Department
        of Antiquities, Cyprus.

INDEX